CONTROVERSIES IN VOTING BEHAVIOR

SECOND EDITION

CONTROVERSIES IN VOTING BEHAVIOR

SECOND EDITION

Richard G. Niemi
University of Rochester

Herbert F. Weisberg
The Ohio State University

A division of Congressional Quarterly Inc.
1414 22nd Street, N.W., Washington, D.C. 20037

Printed in the United States of America

Second Printing

Library of Congress Cataloging in Publication Data

Main entry under title:

Controversies in voting behavior.

Includes bibliographical references and indexes.
1. Elections—Addresses, essays, lectures. 2. Voting—Addresses, essays, lectures. I. Niemi, Richard G. II. Weisberg, Herbert F.
JF1001.C575 1984 324.9 84-9605
ISBN 0-87187-307-9

To Our Wives,
Shirley Niemi
Judy Weisberg

TABLE OF CONTENTS

PREFACE

"New technical developments, new data sources, new theoretical models, and changes in the real voting world all have combined to provide renewed interest and growth in the area of voting behavior." Since 1976, when we made this observation in the first edition, then called *Controversies in American Voting Behavior,* important changes have taken place in each of these dimensions. Perhaps the most salient change is that the comparative study of voting and elections has grown into a major subfield. Consequently, we have widened our scope of coverage in this edition—reflected in our new title—to include some research on voting outside of the United States.

Our purpose, however, remains the same: to enable readers to make sense of a wide array of recent studies on voting and elections. In light of the wealth of new material on the 1978 congressional elections, the effects of economic variables, and voting behavior in other countries, it is especially useful to step back and try to gain an overview of the entire field. With this in mind, we have written entirely new introductory essays and have selected a completely new set of articles. As before, the introductory essays are intended to provide the background necessary for a full appreciation of current work and to do it in such a way as to highlight what the underlying scholarly disputes are and what has been learned in spite of the controversies that remain.

The enormous growth of election research throughout the world means that we can include only a fraction of the relevant studies from both here and abroad. Therefore, we urge the interested reader to consult our suggestions for further readings as well as the list of references at the back of the book.

Of the many areas of continuing and developing controversy on voting behavior, we have chosen six to explore in detail in this edition: election turnout, determinants of the vote, congressional elections, the ideological level of the electorate, the nature of partisanship, and the nature of partisan change. In some areas, controversies have ebbed sufficiently that they no longer merit the same attention as in the first edition. And in other areas, such as the consequences of elections and the impact of the media, the controversies are not yet sufficiently developed to be included.

Finally, we would like to express our appreciation to those who helped us on this edition: to Joanne Daniels, Barbara R. de Boinville, and Mary Ames Booker at CQ Press; to John Aldrich and Russ Dalton for reviewing the manuscript; to Janice Brown, Mary Heinmiller, and David Sweasey for assistance in manuscript preparation; and to Kai Hildebrandt for numerous helpful discussions about the project.

R.G.N.
H.F.W.

June 1984

LIST OF CONTRIBUTORS
with Current Affiliations

Kendall L. Baker, *Bowling Green State University*
Paul Allen Beck, *Florida State University*
Bruce E. Cain, *California Institute of Technology*
Edward G. Carmines, *Indiana University*
Pamela Johnston Conover, *University of North Carolina*
Philip E. Converse, *University of Michigan*
Russell J. Dalton, *Florida State University*
Stanley Feldman, *University of Kentucky*
John A. Ferejohn, *Stanford University*
Morris P. Fiorina, *Harvard University*
Douglas A. Hibbs, Jr., *Harvard University*
Kai Hildebrandt, *University of Windsor*
Ronald Inglehart, *University of Michigan*
Gary C. Jacobson, *University of California, San Diego*
M. Kent Jennings, *University of California, Santa Barbara*
Calvin C. Jones, *National Opinion Research Center*
Samuel Kernell, *University of California, San Diego*
D. Roderick Kiewiet, *California Institute of Technology*
Donald R. Kinder, *University of Michigan*
Lawrence LeDuc, *University of Windsor*
Thomas E. Mann, *American Political Science Association*
Gregory B. Markus, *University of Michigan*
Norman H. Nie, *University of Chicago*
Richard G. Niemi, *University of Rochester*
Helmut Norpoth, *State University of New York at Stony Brook*
Benjamin I. Page, *University of Texas*
Annick Percheron, *Fondation Nationale de Sciences Politique*
John R. Petrocik, *University of California, Los Angeles*
G. Bingham Powell, Jr., *University of Rochester*
Stephen H. Renten, *Florida State University*
Steven J. Rosenstone, *Yale University*
James A. Stimson, *University of Houston*
Nicholas Vasilatos, *Harvard University*
Sidney Verba, *Harvard University*
Herbert F. Weisberg, *Ohio State University*
Raymond E. Wolfinger, *University of California, Berkeley*

INTRODUCTION

1. THE STUDY OF VOTING AND ELECTIONS

According to one textbook image, elections serve several functions in a democracy. Not only do they allow citizens to choose the government, but they also restrain political leaders who must behave in a way that maximizes their chances of reelection. Elections are thus one means of linking public attitudes with governmental policy. In addition, electing a government is a way of legitimizing its authority. Elections provide a peaceful means for political change. And they permit social groups to resolve their conflicting needs peacefully. Along with this view of elections is a corresponding view of voters as choosing intelligently among the candidates. Although no one would argue that all voters are well informed, the view from this perspective is that voters as a whole make careful and informed choices.

An opposite view holds that elections are just "symbolic" in character. According to this position, elections are a secular ritual of democracy, and voting makes citizens consider themselves participants in the nation's governance. Voters feel they have fulfilled their civic duty by voting, even if the chance of a single vote's affecting the election outcome is nearly nil and even if the election outcome is not really going to alter the future of public policy. Correspondingly, according to this view voters do not make intelligent, informed decisions. Few know anything about the candidates, and what they do know is often irrelevant to governance. Consequently, election results are uninterpretable. This view of elections emphasizes that voting does more to make citizens feel good than to alter political outcomes.

The controversy as to the role of voting and elections turns to a considerable extent on the actual effects of elections. Do elections matter? In the United States, do Democratic and Republican administrations pursue different policies? In other nations, is public policy different under left-wing and right-wing governments? To some extent, these are subjective questions. A Marxist would perceive little difference between Democratic and Republican policies in the United States. A monarchist in Europe might regard policies of left-wing and right-wing governments with equal disdain.

Fortunately, whether elections matter is also partly an empirical question. Government policy outputs under Democratic and Republican administrations can be compared, as can those under left-wing and right-wing governments. There is an increasing body of empirical studies that nearly always finds policy differences between governments. Budget allocations to health and education tend to be higher in the United States under Democratic presidents and in Europe under left-wing governments (Bunce, 1980). Unemployment rates tend to be lower when the Democrats/left are in power, while inflation rates tend to be lower when the Republicans/right are in power (Hibbs, 1977). Monetary policies are pursued differently by governments of the left and those of the right (Cowart, 1978a, 1978b). Each of these studies demonstrates that there are policy consequences of elections. Voters do face choices with consequences. Similarly, the thrust of much of the recent work on voters is that they are reasonably well informed. Whether voting for the president or for legislatures, prospectively or retrospectively, on the basis of economics or other issues, voters are far from arbitrary or capricious.

Nor does it always require scholarly studies to reveal the consequences of elections. In 1964, Barry Goldwater ran for president of the United States as a conservative candidate offering "a choice and not an echo," and when he lost in a landslide President Lyndon B. Johnson instituted liberal Great Society programs such as the War on Poverty. In 1980 Ronald Reagan ran on virtually an antigovernment platform, and he turned his large victory margin over President Jimmy Carter into a mandate for conservative action in restraining the growth of government domestic programs. Margaret Thatcher's 1979 victory over James Callaghan in Britain led to the denationalization of some industries that previous Labour governments had nationalized, while François Mitterand's 1981 victory over Valéry Giscard d'Estaing in France led to the nationalization of some industries. These are policy consequences of elections that voters will notice. The recent election of black mayors in several U.S. cities—though not a policy shift as such—suggests another important kind of change, and the extensive voting along racial lines in recent mayoral elections and in 1984 presidential primaries is prima facie evidence of voter awareness of at least this difference in candidates.

A more difficult question is whether there are any policy consequences that make a difference to citizens in the long run. Does it really matter if there is a war on poverty, restrained growth of federal programs, denationalization of industry, or nationalization? Problems seem to remain in any case. This is particularly true of economic problems. We seem to be on a roller coaster, going from severe inflation to harsh unemployment and then back again to inflation. Neither Keynesian nor supply-side economics has been able to strike a proper balance between the two. And economic problems are increasingly international. No one European nation could have solved the problems of high inflation in the late 1970s or high unemployment in the early 1980s without international cooperation (and some would say policy leadership by the United States).

Significantly, the electorate has had a reaction if not an answer to this possibly unanswerable question. There seems to be a trend toward voting on the basis of perceived candidate competence. Carter's defeat in 1980 was less a mandate for Reagan's conservative policies than a rejection of Carter's inability to handle inflation, the American hostages in Teheran, and other such problems (Miller and Wattenberg, 1981). Mrs. Thatcher's reelection in 1983 reflected public satisfaction with her successful victory against Argentina in the Falkland Islands war and simultaneous dismay over Labour's extreme and sometimes incoherent disarmament policy. It may be that there are no solutions that work, but the public knows enough to reject leaders who cannot deliver while keeping those who achieve some success. If policies do not have desired effects, voters still use elections to choose leaders they want to follow or at least to reject ones they do not want to follow.

Whether in terms of policy consequences or leadership choices, elections retain their importance in democracies. They do make a difference, at least in the short run. And voters to some degree make choices on the basis of this difference. At the same time, it must be admitted that we do not yet fully understand voting and elections. Our understanding of these topics has changed a great deal in the past few decades, paralleling changes in our ways of studying them. Yet to our frequent dismay, many of the major questions in the field are not yet settled, despite the considerable attention that has been paid to them. Nevertheless, we are getting closer to answering some of these questions than casual consideration would suggest. In particular, several topics covered in the first edition of this book, published in 1976, are no longer contentious, while we have gained a better understanding of most of the others. But a full discussion of this topic requires some familiarity with the history of the study of voting and elections.

How to Study Voting

The Methodology

In the beginning, the study of voting amounted to a journalistic or historical analysis of party positions, campaigns, and election results. The meaning of an election was ascertained by inspection of the party platforms and speeches. It was assumed that voters were paying attention to what was being said by politicians. Trends were spotted by examining changes in election results over time. It was assumed, again without verification, that these reflected corresponding changes in voter attitudes.

Such analysis remains an important part of election coverage today, with occasional amplifications of the earlier procedures. For example, ever since Theodore H. White wrote *The Making of the President, 1960,* journalists have written books about American presidential elections reporting the intricacies of campaign organizations and events, always assuming that these have had some impact on individual voters. But a comparison of any two books on the same election shows how little consensus there can be on the meaning of campaign events—with the greatest contrast being between White's establishment view in *The Making of the President, 1972* and Dr. Hunter S. Thompson's countercultural view of the same election in *Fear and Loathing on the Campaign Trail, 1972* (based on his articles in the rock-music magazine, *Rolling Stone*). In addition, even if these books do a fine job of describing candidates' strategies, organizations, and personalities, they are confined to looking at elections at the elite level.

Similarly, analysis of trends in election returns is an important part of election-night reporting on television and newspaper coverage the following morning. Reporters focus on the votes gained or lost by each party and on key districts that contain concentrations of important social groups. Unfortunately, scientific analysis shows that this information can be misleading. For example, showing that the Republican vote in a particular district dropped by 10 percent from one election to the next does not necessarily prove that 10 percent of the electorate switched from the Republicans to the Democrats. Instead of attitude conversion, the change might reflect more complex patterns of population replacement (newly eligible voters being less Republican than other voters or people who died since the last election being primarily Republican) or vote mobilization (those who voted Republican in the last election abstaining heavily and previous abstainers voting heavily Democratic). In addition, a net change of 10 percent could actually conceal much greater gross change—such as 40 percent of the Republican voters switching to the Democrats and 30 percent of the Democratic voters switching to the Republicans. Election returns are not adequate for studying electoral change.

The above example does not mean that election returns are entirely useless as sources of political information. Statisticians have devoted much effort to handling problems of the "ecological fallacy" (for example, Goodman 1959), and fascinating historical work has been done using statistical procedures that minimize the problems.[1] But at the very least, care must be exercised when interpreting election returns, since they do not necessarily lend themselves to the types of interpretations that reporters want to give them. The moral is that individual voting can best be understood by directly studying individuals.

The above considerations are increasingly understood by students of politics, including campaign consultants and political reporters as well as political scientists. Understanding voting and elections requires interviewing individual citizens. As a result, nowadays election polls are carefully scrutinized by campaign organizations, journalists, and political researchers. Indeed, most of the analyses in this book are based on such surveys.

Of course, questions can be raised about the validity of survey evidence, too. Why should one accept as correct results based on surveys of perhaps 1,500 voters out of an electorate of millions? A complete answer to that question would require a lengthy statistical explanation, but some brief points can be made. Most important in conducting a survey is the way the sample is selected. Surveys that interview a few "typical" voters or that interview people at a single street corner should not be taken seriously, for there is no reason to believe that the people interviewed are typical of the electorate. By contrast, the best scientific sampling procedures give everyone in the population an equal (or at least a known) probability of being part of the sample. Probability theory can then be used to estimate how close results for the sample are to those for the population of interest. For example, using conventional sampling techniques, a sample of about 1,500 people will give results that are generally (95 percent of the time) within 3 percent of the true result. Thus, a survey finding that 65 percent of the electorate supports a particular party should really be interpreted as meaning that its level of support is (almost certainly) between 62 and 68 percent.

There is inevitable error in attempting to describe a population with just a sample, but such error is generally tolerable. For example, it does not matter for most purposes if a party's support really is 62 percent or 68 percent. The 3 percent error margin could be reduced, but that would probably not be cost-effective, since cutting the error to, say, 1.5 percent would require the expense of 4,500 more interviews. Only when trying to predict a very close election might greater accuracy be necessary, and in such cases the pollsters prefer to admit that the election is "too close to call." Note, by the way, that the size of the sample is what matters for most purposes, not the size of the population. Thus, one would want about 1,500 interviews for a national sample or for a sample of the California electorate.[2]

The Data Base

Political polling has an ancient history, but its ubiquity is a much more recent development. The 1920s saw the first reports of political polls in the media and in political science research. Scientific surveys began to be used just before the outbreak of World War II, such as in the Erie County study of the 1940 election (see Table 1-1). Survey procedures were further refined in the military studies made during the war, especially Stouffer's (1949) *The American Soldier*. Surveys came into their own after the war—especially after the polls improved their sampling procedures as a result of the 1948 debacle in which the pollsters predicted Dewey to win the presidential race.

The longest academic series of American national election surveys is that by the University of Michigan's Institute for Social Research.[3] Since 1948, its Survey Research Center and subsequently its Center for Political Studies have undertaken large-scale surveys of every presidential election and most congressional elections. In presidential years, its personnel have interviewed the same people before and after the election. The Michigan surveys are now administered by the National Election Studies under a grant from the National Science Foundation, with researchers from universities across the country having the opportunity to participate in preparing questions for the surveys and in analyzing the results. (About half the studies in this book rely on the Michigan surveys.) Since they ask citizens hundreds of questions about the parties, the candidates, and the issues, the Michigan surveys are of greater interest than media polls, which are so often used only to predict who is going to win the election and by how much.[4]

While there has been continuity in the NES/CPS/SRC election studies over the years, there have also been significant new developments. In a real sense, the preparation of each survey is marked by the conflicting demands for continuity and change. Asking the same questions in each election is very useful for tracking trends over time, as we can see by examining a pair of books that summarize the results from 1952 to 1976 (Miller et al., 1980; Converse et al., 1980). Yet researchers also want to add questions that relate to new issues and to new theories of understanding voting. Since the time constraints on the interviews mean that to ask a new question researchers must drop an old one, questions are changed less often than some might prefer.[5]

One important recent change in the election studies has to do with congressional voting. While the 1958 survey was a major study of congressional voting, including interviews with congressional candidates as well as with voters, subsequent off-year studies were more minor. By 1978 congressional scholars were doubting many of the findings from the 1958 study and were developing new theories of congressional voting. The 1978 study became a major study of voting for Congress, and it resulted in a vast explosion of work on the topic, as shown in the section of this book on congressional elections. It would be useful if future studies were able to expand coverage in a similar fashion for senatorial and gubernatorial elections.

Another important development has been the use of "panel studies" in which the same respondents are interviewed repeatedly. The early Columbia University voting studies (1940 and 1948) were panel studies, but the panel approach fell out of favor when those studies found little change over the course of the election year. The Michigan 1956-1958-1960 election study was a panel design, and analysis of the data showed how useful the panel approach is. Panel designs not only are better indicators of the true amount of attitude change, but they also can be used to test dynamic theories of voting (see chapter 7). In the usual cross-section survey, for example, one cannot tell whether people vote for the candidate to whom they are closer on the issues or whether people report they are closer on the issues to the candidate for whom they are planning to vote. Panel data provide better opportunities for differentiating true issue voting from rationalization and other psychological processes (see chapter 5). The Michigan election studies used the panel approach again in 1972, 1974, and 1976, allowing Markus and Converse to examine differences from the panel study of the 1950s (chapter 18) and to study the dynamics of voting (chapter 7). The 1980 Michigan study included a panel component with waves in January—February, June—July, and September—October, along with telephone interviews conducted after the election to determine how the respondents actually voted (Markus, 1982). Panel data are not entirely definitive, as we shall see in the different interpretations of the 1972 and 1976 elections by Page and Jones on the one hand and Markus and Converse on the other (chapters 6 and 7), but they are very useful in furthering our understanding of the dynamics of attitude change and voting.

A third development of importance has been an increasing emphasis on economics in political survey questions and analysis. New questions in the Michigan surveys, for example, examine respondents' perceptions of a trade-off between inflation and unemployment. Economic variables are crucial to many new theories of voting, from Kramer's (1971) understanding of voting in congressional elections to Fiorina's (1981b) emphasis on retrospective voting, wherein the citizens decide how satisfied they are with the past performance of the parties, especially the government's handling of the economy. The result has been very much a marrying of political and economic concerns in a study of the political economy of elections.

Another development in election studies is an increasing use of sophisticated analysis methods. In part, this has been a borrowing of techniques from econometrics, such as the simultaneous equations approach used by Page and Jones in chapter 6, but it also includes greater use of factor analysis and many other sophisticated techniques. What is surprising is that this is not necessarily leading to greater consensus on the leading controversies in the field. Instead, as we will see when we contrast two of the most sophisticated models of voting and when we discuss economic analysis (chapter 5), the more sophisticated techniques frequently require arbitrary decisions and untestable assumptions. As a result, the debates become more advanced without leading to an incontestable conclusion.

The final development of importance in surveys about elections is that they are now important in predicting and understanding elections in other countries as well as in the United States. Parties conduct their own polls on numerous matters; in countries where the election date is not fixed, prime ministers now consult these polls before deciding on the timing of the election. The media poll extensively during the campaigns, so much so that there are daily reports of new polls in countries that have short election campaigns.

Academic polling is also of increasing importance in many countries. Some of the early cross-national research represented attempts to replicate the Michigan surveys in other countries, often by collaboration between some of the original Michigan researchers and investigators from the country in question. These early studies frequently found that the concepts and questions developed in the American surveys were not applicable in other countries, as will be brought out in the discussion of party identification (chapter 21). As a result, the more recent election studies have been typified by native researchers developing new questions and concepts based on their understanding of their countries. In some cases parallel developments have taken place across countries, as in frequent cross-national use of panel studies (see chapter 23 and Niemi and Westholm, 1984).

The first edition of this book focused exclusively on American studies, but it is now clear that an understanding of how individuals vote requires a broader terrain. The United States is interesting to study as a two-party system with a president elected separately from the legislature, but other countries provide opportunities to examine voting in multiparty and parliamentary systems. Unfortunately, it would require a book many times the size of this one to include reports on all topics for all countries that have been studied, so it has been necessary for us to select only one or two articles on each topic to give an indication of comparative work in that area. Still, at best we are providing only an introduction to comparative electoral research.

For reference purposes, Table 1-1 lists the major American election studies, along with the chief reports of them. In the further readings sections we list major English-language books about elections studies in other countries. While these studies were originally conducted by principal investigators for their own analysis, most are now available in major social science data archives for secondary analysis by the broader social science community.[6]

How to Understand Voting

The Theory

There are countless ways of understanding voting. The 1940 Columbia study initially employed a consumer preference model. The researchers assumed that each party presented a product to the public and that people considered these competing products throughout the advertising campaign, carefully considering each alternative, and then stepped into the booth on election day to record their final choices. The problem with this model was that most people knew how they would vote even before the national conventions were held. President Franklin D. Roosevelt was running for a third term in office, and, by 1940, people knew whether they were going to vote for or against him without listening attentively to the whole campaign. The consumer preference model of voting was of little use in that election and has never since been seriously suggested in its simplest form.

The Columbia researchers instead explained the 1940 election with a sociological model. They found that a person's socioeconomic status (education, income, and class), religion, and place of residence (rural or urban) were strongly related to the person's vote. They combined these into an "index of political predisposition" (IPP). For example, Protestants from rural areas and with high

Table 1-1 Major Electoral Behavior Surveys and Major Reports on Them

Year	*Study*	*Report*
1940	Columbia University, Bureau of Applied Social Research, sample of Erie County, Ohio	P. Lazarsfeld, B. Berelson, and H. Gaudet, *The People's Choice,* Duell, Sloan & Pearce, 1944.
1944	National Opinion Research Center, national sample	
1948	Columbia University, Bureau of Applied Social Research, sample of Elmira, N.Y.	B. Berelson, P. Lazarsfeld, and W. McPhee, *Voting,* University of Chicago Press, 1954.
1948	University of Michigan SRC, national sample	A. Campbell and R. Kahn, *The People Elect a President,* SRC, University of Michigan, 1952.
1950	Columbia University, Bureau of Applied Social Research, four state samples	W. McPhee and W. Glaser, *Public Opinion and the Congressional Elections,* Free Press, 1962.
1952	University of Michigan SRC, national sample	A. Campbell, G. Gurin, and W. Miller, *The Voter Decides,* Row, Peterson, 1954. *See also* 1956 listing.
1954	University of Michigan SRC, pre-election national sample	A. Campbell and H. Cooper, *Group Differences in Attitudes and Votes,* SRC, University of Michigan, 1956.
1956	University of Michigan SRC, national sample	A. Campbell, P. Converse, W. Miller, and D. Stokes, *The American Voter,* Wiley, 1960.
1958	University of Michigan SRC, national sample, representation study	D. Stokes and W. Miller, "Party Government and the Saliency of Congress," POQ,[1] Winter 1962. W. Miller and D. Stokes, "Constituency Influence in Congress," *APSR,*[2] March 1963. A. Campbell, "Surge and Decline," POQ, Fall 1960.
1960	University of Michigan SRC, national sample	P. Converse, A. Campbell, W. Miller, and D. Stokes, "Stability and Change in 1960: A Reinstating Election," *APSR,* June 1961. *See also* A. Campbell, P. Converse, W. Miller, and D. Stokes, *Elections and the Political Order,* Wiley, 1966.
1956-58-60	University of Michigan SRC, national sample, panel study	P. Converse, "The Nature of Belief Systems in Mass Publics," in D. Apter, *Ideology and Discontent,* Free Press, 1964.

1961	University of North Carolina, sample of South	D. Matthews and J. Prothro, *Negroes and the New Southern Politics,* Harcourt, 1966.
1962	University of Michigan SRC, national sample	
1964	University of Michigan SRC, national sample	P. Converse, A. Clausen, and W. Miller, "Electoral Myth and Reality: The 1964 Election," *APSR,* June 1965.
1966	University of Michigan SRC, national sample	
1967	NORC, University of Chicago, national sample	S. Verba and N. Nie, *Participation in America,* Harper & Row, 1972.
1968	University of Michigan SRC, national sample	P. Converse, W. Miller, J. Rusk, and A. Wolfe, "Continuity and Change in American Politics: Parties and Issues in the 1968 Election," *APSR,* December 1969.
1968	Opinion Research Corp., national sample	B. Page and R. Brody, "Policy Voting and the Electoral Process," *APSR,* September 1972.
1968	University of North Carolina, thirteen state samples	D. Kovenock, J. Prothro and Associates, *Explaining the Vote,* Institute for Research in Social Science, University of North Carolina, 1973.
1970	University of Michigan CPS, national sample	
1972	University of Michigan CPS, national sample	A. Miller, W. Miller, A. Raine, and T. Brown, "A Majority Party in Disarray," *APSR,* September 1976.
1972	Syracuse University, Onondaga County, N.Y.	T. Patterson and R. McClure, *The Unseeing Eye,* Putnam, 1976.
1974	University of Michigan CPS, national sample	
1976	University of Michigan CPS, national sample	A. Miller, "Partisanship Reinstated," *BJPS,*[3] April 1978.
1972-74-76	University of Michigan CPS, national sample, panel study	P. Converse and G. Markus, "Plus ca Change. . . : The New CPS Election Study Panel," *APSR,* March 1979.
1976	CBS/New York Times, national samples	
1976	Syracuse University, Erie County, Pennsylvania and Los Angeles	T. Patterson, *The Mass Media Election,* Praeger, 1980.
1978	University of Michigan NES, national sample	L. Maisel and J. Cooper, eds., *Congressional Elections,* Sage, 1981.

Table 1-1 continued.

Year	*Study*	*Report*
1978	CBS/New York Times, national and congressional candidate sample	G. Bishop and K. Frankovic, "Ideological Consensus and Constraint among Party Leaders and Followers in the 1978 Election," *Micropolitics,* No. 2, 1981.
1980	University of Michigan NES, national sample, panel study	W. Miller and J. M. Shanks, "Policy Directions and Presidential Leadership," *BJPS,* July 1982. G. Markus, Political Attitudes During an Election Year: A Report on the 1980 Panel Study," *APSR,* September 1982.
1980	CBS/New York Times, national samples	
1982	University of Michigan NES, national sample	

Note: All the above studies involve postelection interviews, except for the 1954 preelection study, the 1961 study of the South, and the 1967 study of participation. Most also involve one or more preelection interviews.
[1] *Public Opinion Quarterly*
[2] *American Political Science Review*
[3] *British Journal of Political Science*

socioeconomic status were most likely to vote Republican. The social group factors accounted for most of the differences in voting. Yet this model doesn't try to explain *why* more Protestants voted Republican than did Catholics. It doesn't consider the political aspects of an election. And it is not useful in explaining change across elections, since different parties are elected in different years even if these social characteristics don't change much. Moreover, it doesn't always work. In 1948, the Michigan researchers replicated the IPP on their national sample. They found that 61 percent voted according to the IPP prediction, while 50 percent accuracy could have been obtained by flipping a coin. Thus, the sociological model may have been useful in 1940 for Erie County, but it didn't hold up nationally in 1948. The 1948 Columbia survey was also based on a sociological model, with emphasis on the group context of voting and the community context of voting and with more emphasis on issues, but the time had come for a sharp break with the sociological model.

The Michigan Survey Research Center analyzed the 1952 election using a social-psychological model. Group characteristics of the vote received less attention, with major emphasis instead on three psychological aspects—the person's attachment to a party, the person's orientation toward the issues, and the person's orientation toward the candidates. People predisposed toward the Democratic party, the Democratic issue positions, and the Democratic candidates were particularly likely to vote Democratic. Parties, candidates, and issues—finally the political variables were explicitly incorporated into the voting model.

A theory as to how these variables interrelate in their effects on the vote came in the landmark Michigan report on the 1952 and 1956 elections, *The American Voter.* A person's identification with a party became the core of the model. It in turn affected the persons's attitudes toward candidates and issues. The authors describe this in terms of a "funnel of causality." The phenomenon to be explained—voting—is at the tip of the funnel. But it depends on many factors that occur earlier. The funnel's axis is time. Events follow one another, converging in a series of causal chains and moving from the mouth to the stem of the funnel. Thus a multitude of causes narrow into the voting act. At the mouth of the funnel are sociological background characteristics (ethnicity, race, region, religion, and the like), social status characteristics (education, occupation, class), and parental characteristics (class, partisanship). All affect the person's choice of party identification, the next item in the funnel. Party identification in turn influences the person's evaluation of the candidates and the issues, which takes us further into the funnel. The next part of the funnel includes incidents from the campaign itself, as these events are reported by the media. Even closer to the tip are conversations the voter has with family and friends about the election. Then comes the vote itself. Each of the prior factors affects the vote, though the Michigan group has concentrated on party, candidates, and issues, rather than on the very early social characteristics or the communications network near the tip of the funnel.

This remains the basic Michigan model, with a more explicit division today between what are termed long-term and short-term factors. Party identification is an important long-term factor affecting the vote. Issues and especially candidates are short-term factors specific to the election. Using this approach the Michigan group has reported on each presidential election since 1956, but the reports are article-length rather than book-length. This social-psychological model of the vote has affected virtually all later research, serving as the prime paradigm of the vote decision. The Michigan group has also extended its work by studying elections in numerous other countries, research that is reflected in several chapters of this book. Finally, the researchers have now studied parental influence directly in much greater detail (Jennings and Niemi, 1974, 1981; Jennings, Allerbeck, and Rosenmayer, 1979).

Yet there are additional ways in which the vote can be understood. One is to emphasize more the social-historical context of the vote. Elections can be analyzed within the framework of social movements and elite theories. A given election occurs at a particular moment of time, but it is the result of a set of historical forces that shape the voting. From this point of view, the emphasis on individuals' reasons for voting misses an important aspect of the electoral process. For example, to understand the voting of the American South it is necessary to understand the social structure, class, and racial situation of the past century. The solid Democratic South resulted from post-Civil War tensions. The Wallace movement of the 1960s can be traced back to class and race conflicts in the South of the end of the last century. Similarly, while the black vote can be studied in terms of issue voting, it might be more appropriate to understand it in terms of the social cleavages and group consciousness that led to its rapid mobilization.

This political sociology model of voting underlies the work of several writers, though it cannot be identified with a particular school or study as easily as can be the sociological and social-psychological approaches. It is most obvious in studies of particular groups—such as in studies of black voting, ethnic voting, southern voting—and in studies that adopt a historical approach.

The other model of voting that has become popular is a rational voter model. According to this model, voters decide whether or not to vote and for which candidate to vote on some rational basis—usually on the basis of which action gives them greater expected benefits. They vote only if they perceive greater gains from voting than the cost (mainly in time) of voting. In the usual formulation, they vote for the candidate closest to them on the issues. A major contribution of this approach is that it provides a more explicit, precise theoretical basis for voting decisions and for their analysis than do other approaches. If voters are rational in this sense, then we can expect certain types of behavior in specified circumstances. In addition, this model lends itself more than others to predictions of the effects of changes in external conditions. But because the model is so much more precise (that is, more mathematical), and because it is newer, it has not yet been developed very far. Some of the propositions from it are very nearly tautological. Increasingly, however, it is being realized that survey research provides a mechanism for testing some of the conclusions of the rational voter model. If people with particular attitudes do not behave as predicted, then the assumptions of the theory might have to be revised. If their behavior is correctly predicted, then we can extend the theory further. Substantively, the major contribution of the rational voter approach has been to emphasize the role of issues, which sometimes were submerged in other approaches.

The articles reprinted in this book reflect a variety of theories about voting. They are largely based on the social-psychological approach, modifying and adapting the Michigan model of the 1950s to accommodate later elections and new interpretations of voting. At the same time, many of the pieces are strongly influenced by the rational-voter perspective, most explicitly Fiorina's account of a rational voter theory of party identification (chapter 22).

The Controversies

One might expect that the combination of sophisticated methodology, high-quality data, and effective theories would yield a commonly accepted understanding of voting and elections. This has not been the case. Instead, as we anticipated when we wrote in 1976, there has been an expansion in the number of diverse views. But we do not see this as a lack of progress, since in every instance the nature of the controversy has changed over the intervening years and the original controversy has to some degree been resolved.

The primary change in the nature of the arguments has been that in every case the controversy has now expanded to include cross-cultural and cross-time dimensions. Thus, for example, we no longer simply ask whether voters choose on the basis of party identification or issues. Instead, we ask in what circumstances each is important, knowing that each is sometimes the dominant explanation. We also ask what kinds of issues are important—both in a generic sense (whether retrospective or prospective views predominate) and in the specific sense of which issues are crucial. And we ask whether the same kinds of issues (for example, economic issues, the environment, women's issues, and so on) are significant throughout the set of countries with elections. Thus we have made some progress in our understanding of voters and elections, but considerable controversy remains.

The first half of the book is organized around themes relating to the understanding of election results. We begin with the nature of participation in a democracy, focusing especially on the question of voter turnout. We then turn to the matter of what determines the way in which people vote. This section treats the question of issues generally, but it also deals at some length with the recently raised question of the effects of economic variables. Next we treat the topic of congressional elections in the United States, where the question of economic factors enters once again. Even here, however, some of the analysis has been extended to legislative elections in other countries, and we take due cognizance of it.

Although, as noted, the time element increasingly enters into all analyses of voting, long-term determinants of the vote and electoral change are dealt with most directly in the second half of the book. Initially we consider the extent to which voters think ideologically. Recent studies have shown convincingly that voters often use ideological terms, but the question remains about their understanding of those terms. Then we treat multiple questions surrounding party identification. Here more than any other place, the question is raised as to whether the concept—originally conceived in the United States—extends well to voting in other countries. But even in the United States doubts have been raised about the meaning of the concept, specifically about whether there is only one dimension of partisanship. Finally, we take up the nature of contemporary partisan change. Perhaps surprisingly, this question can be treated at a global level. Though specific partisan fluctuations are unique to each country, at least the directions of change and the underlying conflicts may be quite similar across many countries.

The various topics represented in these sections are among the most important themes about voting and elections, and the readings we have selected are among the best available. Naturally, however, we could not reprint all the top-quality research of recent years. Nonetheless, having worked his or her way through the material included here, the reader will have a rather substantial grasp of the continuing controversies that are bound to exist in so dynamic a field.

NOTES

1. The ecological problem refers to the invalidity of inferring individual attitudes or behavior from data on aggregate units. (Robinson, 1950) For example, a higher Democratic vote in election districts with more Catholics does not prove that Catholics vote more Democratic. It could be that non-Catholics are more likely to vote Democratic in districts with a high proportion of Catholics.
2. Sampling error can still be a problem for almost any sample size if small subsets of the population are compared. A national sample of 1,500 in the United States would contain only about 150 blacks, and an estimate of their responses would be subject to

more than three percent error. Oversampling of selected groups is sometimes used to overcome this problem. There are, of course, other sources of errors in surveys, such as the exact wording of questions.
3. Since the mid-1930s George Gallup has conducted public opinion polls that often contain questions on politics and elections. They are reported in a multivolume book, *The Gallup Poll.*
4. Many of the current media polls are of very fine quality and have begun to be used for much broader purposes. See Table 1-1.
5. A small scale research-and-development pilot study in 1979 led to a significant number of new questions in the 1980 survey. See Chapter 25 for an example of the resulting new questions and the analysis they permit.
6. Two major consortia are the Inter-University Consortium for Political and Social Research (ICPSR) at the University of Michigan and the Social Science Research Council (SSRC) Data Archive at the University of Essex. Most countries with elections also maintain their own archives.

FURTHER READINGS

The Role of Elections

Murray Edelman, *The Symbolic Uses of Politics* (Urbana: University of Illinois Press, 1964). Elections serve primarily a symbolic function.

Anthony King, "What Do Elections Decide?" in *Democracy at the Polls: A Comparative Study of Competitive Elections,* ed. David Butler, Howard R. Penniman, and Austin Ranney (Washington: American Enterprise Institute, 1981). Review of the effects of elections on public policy formation.

Benjamin Ginsberg, *The Consequences of Consent: Elections, Citizen Control, and Popular Acquiescence* (Reading, Mass.: Addison-Wesley, 1982). The significance of elections for the establishment of popular influence and governmental authority.

Benjamin I. Page and Robert Y. Shapiro, "Effects of Public Opinion on Policy," *American Political Science Review* (1983) 77:175-90. Relates survey results of public opinion to governmental policy changes.

Summary Statements of the Michigan SRC/CPS Theory of Voting

Angus Campbell, Philip E. Converse, Warren E. Miller, and Donald E. Stokes, *The American Voter* (New York: Wiley, 1960), chap 2 (not in abridged version). Statement of the "funnel of causality" analogy.

Philip E. Converse, "Public Opinion and Voting Behavior," in *The Handbook of Political Science,* vol. 4, ed. Fred I. Greenstein and Nelson W. Polsby (Reading, Mass.: Addison Wesley, 1975). Reactions to work that challenges *The American Voter* interpretations.

Books Reflecting a "Rational" Spatial Model Approach

Anthony Downs, *An Economic Theory of Democracy* (New York: Harper and Row, 1957). Formal statement of turnout and vote choice as rational behavior.

Morris P. Fiorina, *Retrospective Voting in American National Elections* (New Haven: Yale University Press, 1981). Elections as referenda on past governmental performance.

James M. Enelow and Melvin J. Hinich, *An Introduction to the Spatial Theory of Voting* (Cambridge: Cambridge University Press, 1984). Mathematical treatment of elections over multidimensional issue spaces.

Books Studying Voting Across a Series of U.S. Elections

Norman H. Nie, Sidney Verba, and John P. Petrocik, *The Changing American Voter,* rev. ed. (Cambridge: Harvard University Press, 1979). Revisionist look at the American voter.

Philip E. Converse, Jean D. Dotson, Wendy J. Hoag, and William H. McGee, *American Social Attitudes Data Sourcebook* (Cambridge: Harvard University Press, 1980). Compilation of responses to questions on social attitudes in SRC/CPS surveys.

Warren E. Miller, Arthur H. Miller, and Edward J. Schneider, *American National Election Studies Sourcebook,* 1952-1978 (Cambridge: Harvard University Press, 1980). Compilation of responses and crosstabs to SRC/CPS political questions.

Paul R. Abramson, *Political Attitudes in America* (San Francisco: Freeman, 1983). Continuity and change from 1950s to 1980s in party loyalties, political efficacy, political trust, and other political variables.

Paul R. Abramson, John H. Aldrich, and David W. Rohde, *Change and Continuity in the 1980 Elections,* rev. ed. (Washington, D.C.: CQ Press, 1983).

William H. Flanigan and Nancy H. Zingale, *Political Behavior of the American Electorate,* 5th ed. (Boston: Allyn & Bacon, 1983).

Herbert Asher, *Presidential Elections and American Politics,* 3rd ed. (Homewood, Ill.: Dorsey, 1984).

English Language Books on Voting Behavior in Other Countries

Alan Arian, *The Choosing People: Voting Behavior in Israel* (Cleveland: Case Western Reserve University, 1973).

Don Aitkin, *Stability and Change in Australian Politics* (Canberra: Australian National University Press, 1977).

American Enterprise Institute series, *(Country) at the Polls,* various years.

Kendall Baker, Russell J. Dalton, and Kai Hildebrandt, *Germany Transformed* (Cambridge: Harvard University Press, 1981). Development of voter attitudes toward parties and politics in post-war Germany.

David Butler and Donald Stokes, *Political Change in Britain* (New York: St. Martin's Press, 1969; 2d ed., 1974). Approach and conclusions often parallel *The American Voter.*

Harold D. Clarke, Lawrence LeDuc, Jane Jenson, and Jon H. Pammett, *Political Choice in Canada* (Toronto: McGraw-Hill Ryerson, 1979).

Harold D. Clarke, Jane Jenson, Lawrence LeDuc, and Jon H. Pammett, *The Absent Mandate: The Politics of Discontent in Canada* (Toronto: Gage, 1984). Examines forces of change in Canadian politics in the 1970s and 1980s.

Max Kaase and Klaus von Beyme, eds., *Elections and Parties: Socio-Political Change and Participation in the West German Federal Election of 1976* (London: Sage, 1978).

Arend Lijphart, *The Politics of Accommodation: Pluralism and Democracy in the Netherlands* (Berkeley: University of California Press, 1968).

Bo Särlvik and Ivor Crewe, *Decade of Dealignment* (Cambridge: Cambridge University Press, 1983). Declining role of parties in Britain in the 1970s.

Henry Valen and Daniel Katz, *Political Parties in Norway* (Oslo: Universitetsforlaget, 1964).

Kenneth D. Wald, *Crosses on the Ballot: Patterns of British Voter Alignment Since 1885* (Princeton: Princeton University Press, 1983). Explores relationships between social divisions and the vote, especially for the period 1885-1910.

Books on Voting Behavior Across Several Different Countries

Seymour Lipset and Stein Rokkan, eds., *Party Systems and Voter Alignments* (New York: Free Press, 1967). Discussion of voting cleavages in several countries; set in a theoretical perspective.

Richard Rose, ed., *Electoral Behavior: A Comparative Handbook* (New York: Free Press, 1974).

Ian Budge, Ivor Crewe, and Dennis Farlie, eds., *Party Identification and Beyond* (London: Wiley, 1976). Questions utility of party identification in European countries.

Hans Daalder and Peter Mair, eds., *Western European Party Systems* (Beverly Hills: Sage, 1983). Parties, turnout, and voting behavior in Europe.

Russell J. Dalton, Scott C. Flanagan, and Paul Allen Beck, eds., *Electoral Change in Advanced Industrial Societies: Realignment or Dealignment* (Princeton: Princeton University Press, 1984). Examines forces of change common to political systems of Western democracies in the past decade.

DETERMINANTS OF ELECTION OUTCOMES

I ELECTION TURNOUT

II DETERMINANTS OF THE VOTE

III CONGRESSIONAL ELECTIONS

ELECTION TURNOUT

2. WHAT DETERMINES TURNOUT?

We are accustomed to hearing that turnout in the United States is unusually low compared to that in other democratic nations. What is less well known is that present-day turnout is also much less than that of nineteenth-century America. Given these somewhat embarrassing facts, political scientists have devoted a good deal of attention to the question of what determines voter turnout.

Answers are legion. From a theoretical perspective, one answer has been given in terms of costs and benefits. Anthony Downs (1957) began this tradition when he suggested that the costs of voting (including transportation, of course, but also the cost of gathering information and making a decision) might outweigh the benefits derived from it. Tullock (1967) formalized this in a rather convincing way when he observed that the probability of any one person's altering the outcome with his or her vote was almost nil in a large electorate. Therefore, the "expected" benefit (the benefit derived from voting times the probability of affecting the outcome) was near zero, and even a small cost of voting was likely to outweigh this expected gain. In their specification of the "calculus of voting," Riker and Ordeshook (1968) modified this computation to try to account for the fact that millions of people vote despite the apparent irrationality. They suggested that there were benefits from voting that went beyond altering the outcome—for example, preserving the democratic system. They denoted these benefits by the term "citizen duty."

According to this theoretical perspective, nonvoting could be due either to high costs of voting or to low benefits from voting. Indeed, much of the controversy swirling around the determinants of turnout revolves around those two possibilities: is nonvoting largely due to institutional changes that have increased the cost of voting, or is nonvoting due to weakened party organizations and diminished party competition that have depressed the benefits of voting? Adherents of each viewpoint make use of both historical and contemporary data from the United States and many other countries. This makes a useful opening into the study of controversies in voting behavior, because it exemplifies the attempt in recent years to expand our understanding of voting behavior in terms of both time and space.[1]

Nonvoting as a Result of Institutional Changes

In 1965 Burnham published "The Changing Shape of the American Political Universe," in which he called attention to the major changes in

American voting habits that occurred in the late nineteenth and early twentieth centuries. Burnham reported that after 1896 there was a decline in voting turnout, an increase in split-ticket voting, a growing gap between turnout in off-years and in presidential elections ("drop-off"), an increasing tendency to vote only for the highest offices on the ballot ("roll-off"), and greater partisan vote swing between elections. An institutional explanation of these changes (in contrast to Burnham's own explanation that will be presented in the second half of this chapter) has been offered by Rusk and Converse. They observed that major changes were also occurring at this time in the mechanics of conducting elections and that the trends Burnham reported could be explained almost entirely by these reforms. Consider, for example, split-ticket voting. Prior to 1890, voting was done by "party strips." These were ballots printed by each party, listing only its own candidates, and made distinctive enough to be easily recognized. Not surprisingly, the use of such ballots made split-ticket voting difficult (Rusk, 1970). Thus the introduction of the official and secret ("Australian") ballot very directly accounts for one of the changes cited by Burnham.

More to the point here, the absence of any registration requirement and the lack of a secret ballot made fraudulent turnout more likely. Such practices as "voting the graveyard" and "repeated voting" were more easily accomplished when all that was required was a personal declaration that one was an eligible voter. Similarly, fraud was more tempting when party managers could be sure that the fraudulent votes were cast for the right party. The reforms were intended to cut such fraud, so it would be surprising if the imposition of stricter controls on who voted and the use of a secret ballot had not resulted in many fewer votes being cast. At the same time these reforms made it more costly even for those eligible, cutting turnout further. In fact, the sharp declines in turnout that accompanied these reforms are prima facie evidence of such effects (Converse, 1972; Rusk, 1974). Moreover, the apparent magnitude of the fraud suggests just how great a decline could have resulted from these factors alone (Converse, 1972, pp. 282-294; see also Kousser, 1974, pp. 45-47). Turnout also declined in areas not covered by strong registration requirements, especially rural areas. But the secret ballot alone would have had some effect, and the reformist fervor in the cities was likely to have had some spillover effects (Converse, 1974).[2] In short, a legal-institutional theory can account for most of if not all the changes in late nineteenth-century voting habits.[3]

Most of the work cited so far refers strictly to the nonsouthern areas of the country, since the South is regarded as a special case. However, evidence from the South even more strongly supports a legal-institutional theory. Of course, the poll tax and literacy tests were instituted to disenfranchise blacks. Southern turnout decreased sharply in the 1892-1904 period and can be traced rather directly to the imposition of restrictive laws (Kousser, 1974, Rusk and Stucker, 1978). Kousser points out, however, that the secret ballot was also an effective exclusionary device, especially when used explicitly for that purpose. For example, "voters in one Virginia congressional district in 1894 confronted a ballot printed in the German Fraktur script" (p. 52). Moreover, poor and illiterate whites were frequently excluded along with blacks— often, it appears, as a conscious effort to restrict the electorate to those who could be counted on to vote Democratic (Kousser, chap. 2).

A different though equally important type of institutional change occurred in the twentieth century when women were given the vote throughout Europe and in the United States. The sharp decline in U.S. turnout in 1920, just after adoption of the Nineteenth Amendment, and the gradual increase throughout the 1920s and 1930s are precisely what one might expect: a new, inexperienced electorate votes relatively little at first but gradually catches up to the established electorate as older, nonvoting generations are replaced by newer cohorts. But we do not have to rely on circumstantial evidence. A number of European countries and one American state—Illinois—tabulated the turnout separately for men and women. In every case, turnout of women was lower than that of men, ranging as high as 24 percent in Iceland and even higher in Illinois (Tingsten, 1937, chap. 1; Kleppner, 1982a, p. 627). Similarly, among Mexican women, able to vote for president for the first time in 1958, about 50 percent went to the polls compared to about 84 percent of Mexican men.[4] Thus, while the intent of female enfranchisement was very different from that of the late nineteenth-century reforms, the effect was the same—an immediate and relatively long-lasting decline in turnout (relative to the number of eligible voters). One can only presume that earlier extensions of the franchise had quite similar depressing effects.

As strong as the evidence for the legal-institutional theory is, analysis of late nineteenth- and early twentieth-century changes is hindered by their complexity and by the frequent absence of direct, reliable data. Thus it is important that contemporary evidence also supports the theory. Initial support is found in what happened to Dutch turnout in the last decade. Turnout was at the 95 percent level (for elections to the Second Chamber) in the 1950s and 1960s. After compulsory voting was abolished in 1971, turnout dropped to 79 percent. While it has since climbed upward, it has remained below the 90 percent level, thus indicating at least a small, lasting effect of this institutional change (van der Eijk and Niemöller, 1983, p. 11).[5]

Broader evidence of the effects of legal-institutional factors is found in a study by G. Bingham Powell, reprinted here as chapter 3. Powell finds three institutional factors to be important. Two of them—the impact of compulsory voting laws and the indirect effects of proportional representation—are quite different from those noted above, while the third—the type of registration system in force—is more familiar. Thus, Powell's study lends substantial support to the legal-institutional theory as well as extending the range of institutional features that can be said to influence turnout levels. In addition, Powell's work is interesting inasmuch as it is truly comparative—a study of an entire *set* of countries. Also, unlike most work on voting, it is based on aggregate data rather than on survey research.

Other contemporary work also indicates that legal factors play a role in determining turnout levels. One frequently cited though very small effect involves lowering the voting age. The U.S. national voting age was dropped from 21 to 18 in 1971. Wolfinger and Rosenstone (1980, p. 58) estimate that about a 1.2 percent decline in American turnout from 1968 to 1972 can be attributed to this change. In Denmark, a slightly larger decline was observed after the voting age was lowered in 1978 (Svensson, cited by Dittrich and Johansen, 1983, p. 102). By contrast, instituting provisions for absentee voting increases turnout. This evidently happened in Belgium when such a provision was introduced in 1971, even though turnout prior to that had already been about 90 percent (Fraeys, cited by Dittrich and Johansen, 1983, p. 106).[6]

Another factor that may account for some of the turnout variation is the election calendar. In European nations it is not difficult to build interest in an election because typically there is at most one election per year. In the United States, by contrast, interest in a particular election may be harder to generate because of a large number of elections in any given year (national elections, sometimes separate state elections, state primaries, sometimes separate presidential primaries, plus possibly state runoff elections, and then local elections and perhaps separate elections on tax issues). As Boyd (1981) argues, by focusing on the low turnout rate for a particular type of election in the United States, we may be overlooking the high voting frequency across a wide variety of elections.[7] Boyd also points out that many states have shifted from two-year governorships elected at the time of the presidential election to four-year governorships chosen during the congressional election year. Separating statewide elections from presidential elections may reduce turnout in the latter, especially in states where political machines are more concerned with getting their voters out to help them guarantee control of the state government and its patronage jobs than with the more remote national offices.

Also very important are the effects of restrictive registration laws. Theoretically this should not be surprising, since having to register as a separate act from voting—often in person rather than by mail or phone and a month or more in advance of election day—considerably raises the cost of voting. On the empirical side, higher turnout in Europe (where the government takes responsibility for maintaining an accurate list of eligible voters) than in the United States is often cited as supportive evidence, although other institutional differences make this comparison difficult.

Within the United States, the best evidence is provided by Rosenstone and Wolfinger, whose work we reprint as chapter 4. On the basis of massive Bureau of the Census surveys, which allowed them to estimate the effects of a variety of registration laws while controlling for education and age, they conclude that restrictive laws lowered turnout by nine percentage points. Moreover, existing laws vary only slightly—for example, early versus late closing dates for registration and the presence or absence of Saturday and evening registration. European-type registration systems would make an even greater difference in turnout.

Evidence from a wide range of places and times thus supports a legal-institutional explanation for varying levels of voter turnout. Since so many of the factors discussed seem to depress turnout, it should be mentioned that in most instances this was not the intent. Extensions of the franchise, of course, were intended to expand participation. Most other laws, such as registration requirements, originally were and still are intended to make the system fair and equitable. But by increasing the costs of voting, they have helped cut turnout. Of course, it is possible for institutional changes to increase turnout, as for example among blacks in the United States in the 1960s. Yet whatever the intended effects, changes in the legal-institutional setting appear to have a substantial impact on turnout.

Nonvoting as a Result of Party Competition and Organization

A competing theory of turnout begins with the supposition that laws do not operate in a vacuum. Specifically, levels of turnout depend heavily on the degree of party competition and associated levels of political party organization and activity. Theoretically, these factors operate primarily by affecting the benefits of voting. If party competition is intense and close, the benefit from one party's winning and the likelihood of one's vote making a difference in the outcome both rise. Costs may also be affected. The psychic costs of gathering information and of making a decision about whom to vote for may both be lower if who wins is an important matter.

The first argument that would be made by those stressing party factors as an explanation of low turnout is that the effects described in the previous section for the extension of the franchise are not all that large. For example, the evidence surrounding the enfranchisement of women is not as convincing as implied above. While it is true that postenfranchisement turnout among females was lower in every case than among males, the differences were often quite small (Tingsten, 1937). In Finland and New Zealand, for example, the initial difference was only about 8 percent. In Austria the gap was only about 4 percent, with over 80 percent of the women going to the polls. Moreover, if previous disenfranchisement were all that was involved, one would expect a declining male-female difference across successive elections as young cohorts of women who had not been previously disenfranchised replaced the older generations and as older women were gradually persuaded to vote. Yet the evidence for this is mixed. In several countries the difference actually increased slightly in the years after enfranchisement, and in others the decline was quite small (Kleppner, 1982a, based on data in Tingsten, 1937).

The behavior of other new electorates also suggests that the newly eligible do not necessarily shy away from the polls. In the early history of the United States, the variety of laws and the even greater variety in the degree of enforcement make it difficult to determine precise turnout rates. Yet the rapid increases in overall turnout after the democratizing reforms in the 1820s make it likely that new voters went to the polls at relatively high rates. Turnout among adult white males rose from about 35 percent in 1824 to nearly 60 percent four years later and to 80 percent by 1940 (Chambers and Davis, 1978, p. 177). In twentieth-century new electorates, not only has turnout been quite high overall (for example, 77 percent in 1977 in Spain after 40 years without free elections—Linz, 1980, p. 119), but also older adults, long used to being disenfranchised, went to the polls in large numbers immediately after enfranchisement (Niemi, Stanley, and Evans, 1984, p. 381-82). These results, even more than the data on new female voters, suggest a much more rapid mobilization than is possible under the generational replacement and socialization-learning models implicitly assumed by the legal-institutional theory.

The varying turnout levels of the newly enfranchised imply that something more is going on than simply changes in the legal setting. That "something" is likely to be the degree of party competition and organization. For the 1820s, 1830s, and 1840s, this is suggested by Chambers and Davis's detailed analysis.

They find, for example, a correlation of .58 between competition and turnout (p. 185), a correlation that is remarkably robust across individual states. But they conclude that the level of party organization was equally if not more important in promoting voter turnout (see also Kleppner, 1982b, pp. 28-33). Extraordinary levels of party activity—greater than almost anything seen in the twentieth century—combined with this intense competition to bring about the rapid and long-maintained mobilization of the nineteenth-century electorate.

Kleppner's (1982a) analysis of female enfranchisement substantiates this conclusion by contrasting competition levels in the nineteenth century with those characteristic of the early twentieth century, when women were being given the vote. Turnout undeniably dropped after 1896. Yet Kleppner concludes that "neither female enfranchisement by itself, nor even in additive combination with a continuation of the pre-1920 secular trend, adequately explains the observed turnout levels of the 1920s" (1982a, p. 642). Rather, "politics generally lacked its earlier intensity and strong voter stimulus. If these conditions failed to arouse female interest in electoral politics, that should not be puzzling: those same conditions had an analogous effect on male voters as well" (p. 643).

The apparent effects of ballot reform and registration requirements during the 1890s can also be explained by an organization-competition theory. This was first recognized by Burnham (1965) in the article referred to earlier. Since then it has been discussed in a series of works by Burnham (1970, 1971, 1974, 1980, 1981) and has been strengthened in work by Jensen (1971) and especially by Kleppner and Baker (1979, 1980).

Burnham's thesis involves an interpretation of voting patterns and of elite behavior in 1896 and during the ensuing decades. Following the depression of 1893, the Democratic party turned in 1896 from Grover Cleveland to the populist William Jennings Bryan. A political realignment followed, one that lined up Democratic strength in the South and West and in poor rural areas against Republican strength in the East, in cities, and among business elites. This shift made the Republicans the dominant party throughout the first decades of this century, in contrast to the even party balance in the last decades of the previous one. The sharp decline in competition between the parties, judicial decisions favorable to leading capitalists, and reforms that resulted in the loss of functions performed by political parties (primarily federal control of ballots and the spread of the direct primary system) led both to a decline in the strength of party organizations and to a lessening of the incentive to vote (Burnham, 1965, 1970, pp. 74-76). In effect, Burnham contended that the leaders of the Industrial Revolution stole the electoral system away from the people without doing away with the procedures and traditions of a democratic system. With the importance of their decisions greatly reduced, voters gradually became alienated and regarded their participation as relatively meaningless. Weakened party organizations could do little to overcome the declining partisan feelings. Given these changes, turnout would have declined and the regularity of party voting would have decreased even in the absence of reforms such as the introduction of personal registration systems.[8]

In his recent analysis, Burnham (1980) emphasizes the class basis for the American party system. He finds that turnout differences between the classes are much greater in the United States than in Europe, where socialist parties can mobilize the working-class vote. He then describes the American party system that came into being by the end of World War I as a system that "rested on two non-competitive party hegemonies and upon a huge mass of non-voters. This implies, of course, that an American electorate had come into being: that is, one heavily skewed toward the middle classes *in the absence of an organizable socialist mass movement capable of mobilizing lower-class voters*" (1980, pp. 57-58, emphasis in original). This class-based interpretation of nonvoting in the United States leads Burnham to conclude that increased turnout would require developing political structures "for the representation of interests which are now feebly or not at all represented in electoral politics. This could not be accomplished without fundamental changes in political consciousness and equally fundamental challenges to things which upper- and upper-middle class Americans believe to be sacrosanct" (p. 68).

The party organization—party competition theory does not rest only on verbal interpretations, however. While it may be impossible to test the theory directly, at least the alternative—the legal-institutional theory—can be subjected to rigorous analysis. In a systematic study modeling the possible effects of the legal-institutional theory in several different ways, Kleppner and Baker (1980) conclude that registration requirements had some negative impact on turnout, but that their effects were not consistent and were often not very strong. For example, "even where their effects should have been clearest, in states that abruptly implemented them around the turn of the century, 40.0 percent of the [before and after] trials produced results anomalous to the theory's predictions" (Kleppner and Baker, 1980, p. 220). In a regression analysis, party competition was by far the chief explanatory variable; registration and residency requirements were very weak predictors of turnout (p. 214). Burnham had earlier concluded the same. Registration variables had some effect, but they could explain considerably less than half the observed declines (1974, p. 1012).

There remains the corruption aspect of the legal-institutional theory. By its nature, this argument is much more difficult to evaluate. Corrupt practitioners are hardly likely to leave a clearly traceable record, and one must be very careful in interpreting verbal, even if contemporary, descriptions of the phenomenon. Thus, there is always room for some doubt, but historians who have examined the question most thoroughly are convinced that fraud is unlikely to explain the very high turnout in the nineteenth century, and that the elimination of that fraud is unlikely to explain the sharp declines after 1896 (Kleppner and Baker, 1979, pp. 38-46; Jensen, 1971, pp. 34-43; and especially Allen and Allen, 1981). Moreover, to the extent that fraud existed and was eliminated by the introduction of personal registration and the Australian ballot, it can hardly explain the declines in turnout after 1900 (Kleppner and Baker, 1979, p. 45).

Historical evidence, thus, lends considerable support to a theory based on changes in party organization and party competition. So too does contemporary evidence. Powell, in the analysis reprinted here, includes "party system" information as well as the legal-institutional factors noted earlier. He finds that the existence of strong linkages between parties and social classes and religions is a strong predictor of voting turnout. This is true even when controlling for the legal setting. This result supports the conclusion that it is the way in which parties are organized that makes a difference. As in nineteenth-century America, turnout is enhanced where parties reach out to specific groups, especially those who are otherwise less likely to vote.

Contemporary evidence on party competition is less clear. Powell cites examples of several European countries in which the degree of competition over time has been related to turnout levels, but he also points out that evidence is sparse because of the difficulty of measuring competition in multiparty systems. In Britain, however, Denver and Hands (1974) found that closeness of elections is quite strongly related to turnout even with other constituency factors (for example, percent nonmanual workers, minor party vote) controlled. Interestingly, they point out that the explanation may not be that voters are aware of the closeness of elections but rather that parties more vigorously contest these elections.

In the United States, with predominantly two-party contests, analysis of state-level variations in turnout (Kelley, Ayres, and Bowen, 1967; Kim, Petrocik, and Enokson, 1975) indicate that competition levels are indeed important. And the "solid South" of the first half of the twentieth century is noteworthy for its low levels of turnout. Institutional explanations are naturally important for this region, but it is significant that in spite of the strong increases in turnout outside the South during the New Deal era, turnout remained low until the South became competitive at the presidential level in 1952.[9]

Survey work in the United States and elsewhere has also pointed to party-related factors as sources of rising and declining turnout. Budge and Farlie (1976), for example, found that party identification was the most consistent and strongest predictor of turnout across seven countries on three continents. In the United States, Abramson and Aldrich (1982) found that "between two-thirds and seven-tenths of the decline in presidential turnout" between 1960 and 1980 can be explained "largely from the combined impact of two attitudinal trends, the weakening of party identification and declining beliefs about government responsiveness" (1982, p. 502). A similar behavioral explanation was given by Ferejohn and Fiorina (1979), who argued that the decline results from decreasing concern with the electoral outcome.[10]

Thus both historical changes in turnout levels and contemporary cross-sectional variations can be explained by the nature of party systems—their degree of organization and level of competitiveness. As the party system has changed, Americans may perceive less difference between the parties and therefore expect less benefit from voting. And decreasing political competitiveness makes citizens feel that their votes do not matter, again cutting expected benefits from voting.

Conclusion

Even on purely statistical grounds, it is difficult to assess precisely the contribution of various structural and behavioral explanations of fluctuations in turnout. This is especially true for times past, since existing data are aggregate rather than individual-level and are of questionable accuracy. Yet we think that the collection of studies reviewed and reprinted here makes it an inescapable conclusion that both legal-institutional and party-related factors play a role in determining the level of turnout. Rosenstone and Wolfinger's work for the contemporary U.S. population and Powell's work on a broader scale make it clear that registration systems and other legal features help or hinder turnout. The work of Kleppner and Burnham for the late nineteenth and early twentieth centuries shows the same. Yet nowhere do legal factors account for all the changes or all the variance in turnout levels. Party organizations, competitiveness of the parties, and strength of party identification contribute to turnout levels as much as or perhaps even more than does the institutional setting.

From an American perspective, this "middling" conclusion is of great importance. If voting is to be increased, changes are necessary, first of all, in registration and voting procedures. Easing registration requirements would help, but still other changes—such as voting on Sunday, keeping the polls open for the same "real" time (for example, 8:00 A.M. to 11:00 P.M. in the East but 5:00 A.M. to 8:00 P.M. in the West) to prevent winner projections prior to the close of polls in the West, and so on—are necessary. But that will not be enough to achieve turnout levels of 85-90 percent. Such turnout levels will only be achieved if parties are also strengthened and if party competition exists throughout most of the country. Reformers who weaken parties in the name of giving power to the people and legislators who dampen competition through use of the power of office (see chapter 11) and through bipartisan gerrymandering must take some responsibility for low levels of turnout. We have adopted many reforms over the years without prior consideration of their impact on turnout levels. Before turnout continues to fall to levels that make a mockery of "government by the people," it soon may be necessary to consider reforms explicitly designed to boost turnout.

NOTES

1. Turnout, of course, is just one of many modes of political participation, but that does not mean that the determinants are the same. Verba and Nie (1972) and Verba, Nie, and Kim (1978) show that other modes of participation (campaign activity, cooperative activities, and citizen-initiated contacts with officials) have different causal processes. Similarly, Barnes, Kasse, et al. (1979) stress that unconventional participation through protest differs in its determinants from more conventional participation.
2. Rusk (1970) and Converse (1972, pp. 281, 293-95) also show how the reforms affected drop-off, roll-off, and partisan swing.
3. Cox and Kousser (1981) point out that Converse was wrong in thinking that fraud only inflated turnout. But they lend some support to the legal-institutional theory anyway by showing that most of the fraud prior to 1890 was inflationary while most after 1890 was deflationary.
4. Computed by the editors based on the Almond-Verba (1963) five-nation study.
5. Simultaneously, the proportion of invalid ballots (including blank ballots) fell from 2-3 percent to less than 1 percent, suggesting that part of the higher turnout with compulsory voting is not very meaningful. For a discussion of blank and invalid votes as protest votes, see Rosenthal and Sen (1973).
6. Dittrich and Johansen also note that there was no such drop in the Netherlands in 1972, but this change occurred during a period in which turnout was on an upward trend.
7. Given the differences between American elections, it is important to check how much the electorates differ across elections. The major studies to date contrast presidential

and off-year electorates. Wolfinger, Rosenstone, and McIntosh (1981) find virtually no sizable differences between the demographic composition of the midterm electorate and the presidential year electorate. As they conclude, "the most prominent feature of a midterm election is its lower turnout. Once this is taken into account, conclusions about the demographic correlates of turnout in presidential elections are also germane to midterm years" (p. 255). Earlier, Arseneau and Wolfinger (1973) showed that congressional voters do not differ significantly from presidential voters on political (chiefly partisan) characteristics either. These results contrast with Campbell's (1960) hypothesis that the surge in turnout in presidential elections resulted in a greater number of marginal, less partisan voters than in the off-year declines.

8. In most of his recent papers (for example, 1974) Burnham also incorporates the religious-ethnic interpretations of mid- to late nineteenth-century politics forwarded by Kleppner (1970) and Jensen (1971). See also Kleppner, 1981. The decline of the highly personal, intense religious-ethnic politics and the rising importance of economic factors are seen as part of the reason for declining party competition.
9. Closeness of election outcomes is a key component in Riker and Ordeshook's (1968) "calculus of voting" and has been studied in a number of articles using both aggregate and survey data. For references, see Thompson, 1982. The results are inconclusive, but we question whether the tests are based on adequate measures of closeness (and other variables in the equation).
10. Alienation over poor candidate selection and indifference between candidates has also been suggested as the explanation (Brody and Page, 1973; Hinich, 1978). However, Weisberg and Grofman's (1981) systematic analysis of 1976 data indicate that both these factors have little bearing on abstention.

FURTHER READINGS

Survey Studies of Turnout

Richard A. Brody, "The Puzzle of Political Participation in America," in *The New American Political System,* ed. Anthony King (Washington, D.C.: American Enterprise Institute, 1978). Discusses the question of declining turnout in the face of increasing education.

Raymond E. Wolfinger and Steven R. Rosenstone, *Who Votes?* (New Haven: Yale University Press, 1980). Relationship of education, age, sex, laws, and other variables to turnout.

Paul A. Abramson and John H. Aldrich, "The Decline of Participation in America," *American Political Science Review* (1982) 76:502-21. Accounts for turnout declines by weakening party identification and declining beliefs about governmental responsiveness.

Aggregate Studies of Turnout

Herbert Tingsten, *Political Behavior* (London: King, 1937). Turnout data from the early twentieth century.

Walter Dean Burnham, "The Changing Shape of the American Political Universe," *American Political Science Review* (1965) 59:7-28. First raised important questions about nineteenth-century voting behavior.

Jerrold G. Rusk, "The Effect of the Australian Ballot Reform on Split Ticket Voting," *American Political Science Review* (1970) 64:1220-38. The secret ballot encouraged split-ticket voting.

Ivor Crewe, "Electoral Participation," in *Democracy at the Polls,* ed. David Butler, Howard R. Penniman, and Austin Ranney (Washington, D.C.: American Enterprise Institute, 1981). Cross-national survey of eligibility, frequency of elections, and turnout rates, and explanations of turnout variations.

Karl Dittrich and Lars Nørby Johansen, "Voting Turnout in Europe, 1945-1978: Myths and Realities," in *Western European Party Systems,* ed. Hans Daalder and Peter Mair (London: Sage, 1983). Turnout in Europe related to party system characteristics.

Empirical Studies of Political Participation

Sidney Verba and Norman H. Nie, *Participation in America* (New York: Harper & Row, 1972). Analysis of modes of participation, and effects of participation in a national sample.

Lester W. Milbrath and M. L. Goel, *Political Participation,* 2d ed. (Chicago: Rand McNally, 1977). Summary of voluminous literature on participation.

Sidney Verba, Norman H. Nie, and Jae-on Kim, *Participation and Political Equality: A Seven-Nation Comparison* (Cambridge: Cambridge University Press, 1978). Modes, correlates, and effects of participation in seven distinct settings.

Samuel H. Barnes, Max Kaase et al. *Political Action* (Beverly Hills: Sage, 1979). Five-nation study of participation, emphasizing unconventional participation.

Richard Rose, ed., *Electoral Participation: A Comparative Analysis* (Beverly Hills: Sage, 1980). Comparative studies of voting.

Rationality of Voting

William H. Riker and Peter C. Ordeshook, "A Theory of the Calculus of Voting," *American Political Science Review* (1968) 62:25-42. Importance of perceptions of how close the vote in an election will be.

George J. Stigler, "Economic Competition and Political Competition," *Public Choice* (1972) 13:91-106. Voting can always make a difference.

John A. Ferejohn and Morris P. Fiorina, "The Paradox of Not Voting: A Decision Theoretic Analysis," *American Political Science Review* (1974) 67:525-36. Voting in order to not regret not voting.

3. VOTING TURNOUT IN THIRTY DEMOCRACIES: PARTISAN, LEGAL, AND SOCIO-ECONOMIC INFLUENCES

G. Bingham Powell, Jr.

Voting occupies a central place in democratic politics and in contemporary political science. Increasingly sophisticated studies have analyzed the sources of partisan support and political participation, especially voting, among different individuals and groups within nations (e.g., Campbell, et al., 1960, 1966; Verba, Nie, and Kim, 1971; Rose, 1974; Pomper, 1975; Nie, Verba and Petrocik, 1976; Milbrath and Goel, 1977; Verba, Nie, and Kim, 1978). Who chooses to stay home and who goes to the polls can often determine who wins an election, and voting is a major instrument by which leaders are compelled to be attentive to citizens (Eulau and Prewitt, 1973; Verba and Nie, 1972). Moreover, voting turnout is a critical indication of the involvement of citizens in the national political life of a society (Deutsch, 1961).

Yet, there have been few, if any, attempts to compare and explain the large and rather stable differences in voting turnout across the full range of democratic nations. Average turnout levels in recent decades ranged from 60 percent or less in nations such as India, Lebanon, Switzerland, and the United States, to around 90 percent in Italy, the Netherlands, and Austria.

Voting Turnout in Democracies

A brief survey of the political systems of the world in the early 1960s suggests that some 30 nations of over one million in population have met for a substantial period of time the criteria of competitive, mass party politics and relative freedom of communication and organization that roughly constitute contemporary standards of democracy. Although democratic regimes were overthrown or temporarily suspended in some of these nations, their experience while working democracies remains a useful source of material for comparative analysis. Table 3-1 lists these countries in alphabetical order, and indicates the years during which national elections took place from 1960 to the

---

Author's Note: I should like to thank Peter H. Lemieux, Lynda W. Powell, Seymour Martin Lipset, and Richard Rose for helpful comments and suggestions at various stages of this analysis.

Table 3-1 Voting Participation in Thirty Democracies, 1960-1978

Nation	*Democratic elections included in study*[1]	*Average turnout as percentage registered* %	*Average turnout as percentage eligible age groups*[3] %
Australia	1961,63,66,69,72,75	95	86
Austria	1962,66,70,71,75	93	89
Belgium	1961,65,68,71,74,77	92	88
Canada	1962,63,65,68,72,74	77	71
Ceylon (S.L.)	1960,60,65,70	80	72
Chile	1964,70	84	71
Costa Rica	1962,66,70,78	81	73
Denmark	1960,64,66,68,71,73,75,77	88	87
Finland	1962,66,70,72,75	83	84
France	1962,67,68,73,78	77	70
Germany (W.)	1961,65,69,72,76	89	84
Greece	1963,64,74,78	81	85
India	1962,67,71,77	58	60
Ireland	1961,65,69,73,77	75	75
Israel	1961,65,69,73,77	81	81
Italy	1963,68,72,76	93	94
Jamaica	1962,67,72	72	61
Japan	1960,63,67,69,72,76	72	71
Lebanon	1960,64,68,72	53	56
Netherlands	1959,63,67//71,72,77	95[2]	90[2]
New Zealand	1960,63,66,69,72,75	88	81
Norway	1961,65,69,73,77	82	82
Philippines	1957,61,65	77	77
Sweden	1960,64,68,70,73,76	88	86
Switzerland	1963,67,71,75	60	53
Turkey	1965,69,73	67	62
United Kingdom	1964,66,70,74,74	75	74
United States	1960,64,68,72,76	n.a.	59
Uruguay	1958,63,68,71	77	71
Venezuela	1958,63,68,73	95	80

[1] Figures are for national legislative elections, unless there is a strong president, nonparliamentary system. Figures for Chile, Philippines, and United States are for presidential elections only; Uruguay, 1971, is presidential. Data were not available for Ceylon (Sri Lanka) 1977, Costa Rica 1974, Jamaica 1976, Philippines 1969, Turkey 1977, Venezuela 1978, and New Zealand 1978.

[2] Averages for the Netherlands are for years in which voting was compulsory.

[3] In the Philippines and pre-1970 Chile the eligibles exclude illiterates. In Ceylon (Sri Lanka) the eligibles exclude the Indian Tamils.

present. While country experts and theorists alike will probably disagree on the inclusion or exclusion of some particular countries as "democracies," there is substantial agreement on most of this universe. (For comparisons, see Dahl, 1971.)

Table 3-1 also presents data on average voting participation. The data include, insofar as possible, all voters who went to the polls, whether they cast valid or invalid ballots. There are two reasons for looking at all votes. First, in some cases casting a blank or spoiled ballot may be a deliberate act that meets our definition of participation in every respect, e.g., a protest at some party being excluded from the ballot. Second, countries vary greatly in how they judge ballots as valid; hence the same actions can result in valid or invalid ballots in different countries. In some countries with compulsory voting the percentage of invalid ballots is relatively high; e.g., it runs around seven percent in Belgium.

The calculation of turnout depends on one's definition of the universe of potential voters. In conducting this research it became gradually clear that different studies were reporting different "electorates" in calculating voting participation. Although the differences in reported absolute numbers of votes were seldom very great, the differences in turnout percentages were often notable, especially in Latin American democracies. In European nations, scholars and journalists invariably offer percent of the registered electorate as their measure of turnout. In discussing the United States, it is always percent of the population of voting age, national registration figures are not available; elsewhere practices vary.

In Table 3-1 the third column shows the average turnout as a percentage of registered voters; the fourth column shows turnout as a percentage of citizens of eligible age, calculated from United Nations census data.[1] We can see that there are some sharp discrepancies between the two figures. Such differences are most pronounced in nations where registration is a citizen's responsibility, rather than an automatic process carried out by the government: Australia, Chile, Costa Rica, France, post-1962 Jamaica, New Zealand, the United States, Uruguay, and Venezuela.[2] These differences, whose effect on turnout itself is discussed at more length below, shape both size and make-up of the registered electorate. In countries such as the USA, where registration is for many citizens more difficult than voting, the registered electorate clearly represents a more interested and involved subset of potential eligibles than in countries with automatic registration. Thus, despite some error in census-based estimates of eligibles, the last column, voting participation as percent of all citizens of enfranchised age, is the most appropriate figure for comparative analysis across the full range of countries. We shall use it throughout.

It is important to note that, in general, turnout from election to election is consistent within nations. For the most part, the averages in Table 3-1 do not conceal precipitous swings. A turnout increase or decrease of five percent is a large shift in most of these nations. Some important exceptions, such as the step level changes in turnout in Costa Rica and the Netherlands caused by changes in penalties for non-voting, and the shift in Jamaica caused by altering registration laws, are discussed below. But normally campaigning seems to result in rather small turnout differences. Of course, the effects of dramatic party contests can occasionally be found. A good example is the "surge" in Indian turnout in 1967, when the opposition parties first united to challenge seriously Congress's dominance: turnout increased from 55 to 61 percent of the registered electorate, a level reached again in the dramatic election which ousted Mrs. Ghandi in 1977.

Scholars noting the relative stability of turnout rates within individual nations frequently characterize a country's turnout as "high" or "low." Comparisons are often made to well-known, but statistically deviant, cases such as the United States or Italy. Table 3-1 suggests more useful comparative benchmarks. Turnout averages 76 percent of the eligible age groups (about 80 percent of the registered electorate), across elections in thirty countries.

We expect the average levels of voting participation in a society to be shaped by a wide variety of factors. These would include the values and skills of its citizens, the issues and problems of the society, the legal and constitutional rules, and the political structures which link the individual voters to collective outcomes. We do not have available comparative data on the citizen's normative beliefs about the importance of participation, although some studies of voting participation within individual countries have demonstrated the importance of such attitudes (see Milbrath and Goel, 1977). However, the broad environmental setting for citizen choice does explain a great deal of the cross-national variation. The two aspects of that environment most immediately proximate to the citizen seem to be the national party system, which presents the voting options, and the incentives or costs created by the legal system.

Factors Shaping Comparative Voting Turnout: The Legal Setting

Penalties for Failure to Vote

In comparing voting participation across the nations, we need to put "first things first" and consider the legal incentives or hindrances acting directly on the individual citizen. In over a quarter of the democracies substantial penalties exist, or did exist during several elections, for individual citizens failing to vote in national elections.[3] As Tingsten (1937) demonstrated quite clearly forty years ago, the imposition of relatively small fines or other penalties can have a major impact on voting turnout. Although this effect is hardly surprising, it is a factor we must take account of before we can assess the impact of other political and social conditions.

In Australia, Belgium, and Venezuela non-voters are in violation of the law and subject to fines and other penalties for failure to vote unless excused by illness. The potential sanctions in Venezuela are particularly harsh. Such penalties have also existed in Costa Rica since 1960 and were in effect in the Netherlands until the 1971 election. Similar penalties and requirements also existed in Chile before its democracy was overthrown, and apparently in Greece before the 1967 military coup, as well as presently. Italy does not have legally designated compulsory voting, but non-voters are stamped as such on their official work and identification papers. It is widely believed, at least, that such non-voters are subject to discrimination in receiving employment and other benefits. (See Galli and Prandi, 1970: 28-32; Zariski, 1972: 75) The potential penalties for not voting are apparently quite substantial.

The impact of these sanctions can be seen in Table 3-2. None of the countries with penalties for non-voting had average turnout levels under 70 percent of the eligible electorate, or under 80 percent of the registered electorate. The average turnout was about 10 percent higher in the countries with penalties for non-voting. The relationship is strong and statistically significant at the 0.01 level. Further, two nations changed their laws on penalties for non-voting: Costa Rica and the Netherlands. The introduction of penalties for non-voting increased turnout in Costa Rica by about 15 percent. Elimination of penalties in the Netherlands led to an initial decrease of 16 percent, although turnout has leveled off at 10 percent below earlier levels. (See also Tingsten, 1937)

We have, therefore, both cross-sectional and longitudinal evidence that penalties for non-voting have a major and significant impact on turnout across the contemporary democracies. We need to recognize, however, that establishing such penalties does not guarantee turnout. The extent of enforcement and magnitude of penalties vary greatly. Moreover, different penalties affect different parts of the population. The aged and unemployed, those in remote villages or those outside the cash economy will often be untouched by various penalties for non-voting and/or even unnoticed by registration officials.

Registration Laws: Application or Automatic Registration

A second way in which the legal setting may affect voting turnout is through variations in registration laws and bureaucratic machinery. In about two-thirds of the democracies, the government assumes the responsibility for voter registration, either through maintaining continually updated lists of registered citizens compiled from census and other official materials, or through periodic and systematic canvasses of all citizens to create or update registration rolls. In other countries it is up to the potential voter to apply to the proper authorities to be entered on the registration lists. In most of the latter countries, there is some legal requirement for citizens to become registered, either in conjunction with compulsory voting, or as a citizenship duty where voting itself is voluntary (New Zealand and Uruguay). Only the United States, France, and post-

Table 3-2 Voting Laws and Turnout of Eligible Age Group[1]

Types of Voting Laws		*Level of Voting Turnout of Eligibles*					
Compulsion penalties	*Automatic registration*	*50-65%*	*66-75%*	*76-85%*	*86-95%*	*Total %*	*(N)*
NO	NO	40%	40%	20%	0	100	(5)
NO	YES	24	29	29	18	100	(17)
YES	NO	0	50	25	25	100	(4)
YES	YES	0	0	25	75	100	(4)

[1] Turnout data from Table 3-1. Countries with penalties for failure to vote are Australia, Belgium, Chile, Costa Rica, Greece, Italy, Netherlands, and Venezuela. Countries in which registration is by application of citizens, rather than automatic, are Australia, Chile, Costa Rica, France, Jamaica, New Zealand, United States, Uruguay, and Venezuela. New Zealand and Uruguay, as well as the compulsory voting countries, provide some penalties for failure to make registration application.

1962 Jamaica rely totally on the initiative of citizens, sometimes encouraged by their political parties, to get on the electoral rolls. (See Herman, 1976, for comparison of registration laws in 22 of the democracies considered here.) Clearly, when citizens must make the double effort to register and to vote, voting becomes a significantly more difficult act, and we would expect turnout to be lower.

Table 3-2 shows that the presence of automatic registration procedures, in contrast to citizen application, facilitates citizen turnout, even within countries having penalties for non-voting. These effects are also confirmed in multivariate analysis,[4] and Spackman (1969) describes vividly the drop in citizen registration in Jamaica in areas where "enumerated" citizens were additionally required to take their enumeration certificate and a photograph to a registration center to be enrolled.

Studies within the United States have demonstrated that in some states the registration laws are much more facilitating than in others, although these differences have probably declined. Kelley, Ayers, and Bowen (1967) found that differences in registration laws were a major factor in explaining turnout differences across cities, as did Kim, Petrocik and Enokson (1975) across states. (Also see Campbell et al., 1960: ch. 11; and Rose, 1978.) Rosenstone and Wolfinger (1978:41) estimate that voting turnout in the 1972 Presidential election might have been about nine percent higher if all states had registration laws as facilitative as those in a few states.

Other effects of the legal arrangements for voting seem much less significant than the various experiments with compulsory voting and the provision of automatic registration of eligible citizens. Different arrangements for absentee voting do not seem associated with major turnout differences, although data are incomplete and these may be important in a few specific cases. Baaklini (1976) suggests that the absence of any provisions for absentee balloting in Lebanon depressed turnout, especially as many citizens lived and worked away from their home villages.

The Legal Environment: Single Member Districts or Multimember Proportional Representation

It has frequently been suggested that voting participation is or would be enhanced by the introduction of multimember legislative districts and proportional representation of parties, as opposed to single member district plurality or majority representation. (For example, see Lakeman, 1974:151-163.) A variety of arguments to this effect has been offered. Among the more plausible are the following: (1) with single member districts, it is likely that some districts will be noncompetitive, giving citizens less incentive to vote; parties, less incentive to campaign there; (2) the single member district system of representation can lead to great distortion between votes given to a party and the legislative representation it receives (see Rae, 1967:74); these distortions may alienate and discourage sympathizers of disadvantaged parties; (3) single member districts may encourage the formation of more diffusely based political parties, whose ability to mobilize easily identifiable demographic groups of supporters, especially social class groups, will be inhibited.

In counter-argument, it can be said that with single member districts the individual representatives may seem closer to constituents, more identifiable as personal linkages to the national centers of power. Observers of such complex PR systems as those in Finland and Switzerland have also suggested that the very complexity of the voters' choice situation may serve to discourage participation by some citizens.

We shall use Blondel (1969) to classify electoral systems as either providing single representatives for most districts (whether through majority, plurality, or preferential mechanisms) or some form of multimember PR arrangement. We find that there is a substantial association between PR and turnout of enfranchised citizens. Turnout averages about 78 percent in the PR systems, but only about 71 percent in the single member district systems. The Pearson correlation between electoral laws and turnout is 0.30, significant at the 0.05 level across the 30 countries. However, controlling for compulsory voting and the registration laws reduces this relationship sharply; a multiple regression with the two voting law variables produces an insignificant Beta of 0.07 for the electoral laws. Thus, while PR is on average associated with higher turnout, much of the association seems to be due to facilitating registration and compulsory voting, which are more frequently present in the PR systems.

Factors Shaping Comparative Voting Turnout: Party Systems

Political parties are the institutions meant to link individual citizen voting choices and aggregate electoral outcomes in the competitive democracies. The political parties set the alternatives offered citizens and their organized activities encourage voting. Studies of voting participation have emphasized the key role of citizens' ties to political parties in explaining different participation levels of individuals and social groups (e.g., Campbell et al., 1960; Verba, Nie and Kim, 1978; and the various party identification studies reviewed by Milbrath and Goel, 1977:53-55). Indeed, in their comparative analyses of participation in seven nations, Verba, Nie and Kim note that "with the exception of the United States, then, we find that (party) institutions are dominant over voting activity; they both mobilize the affiliated and restrict the unaffiliated" (1978:121). Voting is in this respect contrasted with other forms of campaign activity, where both party affiliation and socioeconomic resources shape citizens' activities.

Party Systems and Cleavage Alignments

In explaining the role of parties in shaping voting participation, we expect the relationships between party systems and national cleavage structures to play a major role. In some countries the national parties have developed close and enduring ties to particular demographic groups. In other countries, the different parties have relied upon more diffuse, less differentiated support, as in the United States, or upon varying alliances with local organizations and factions, as in many developing nations.

Theoretically, where strong linkages exist between national parties, or blocs of parties, and demographic groups, voting participation should be encouraged. Alford suggested in his analysis of class voting that "where workers have a party clearly appealing to their interests, their participation and sense of political efficacy is as great as middle-class persons" (1963:302). Thus, where the national parties represent different, meaningful, cleavage groups, the electoral outcomes take on an easily identifiable significance. Where these linkages are relatively stable, they provide cues to even poorly informed and less interested voters as to the interpretation of issue and candidate choices in given elections. That such linkages can be highly durable has been demonstrated by Lipset and Rokkan (1967b), who point out that the efforts of particular Western European parties to organize and mobilize particular demographic groups—workers, farmers, believing Catholics, businessmen—in the period between 1880 and 1920, had continuing effects on voting alignments through the 1960s. Moreover, the presence of strong, continuing expectations about parties and cleavage alignments not only creates easily identifiable choices for citizens, but also makes it easier for parties to seek out supporters and mobilize them at election time. The creation of enduring relationships between parties and organized social and economic groups, such as trade unions and economic and religious organizations, also contributes to linkages.

Therefore we expect that voting participation will increase to the extent that political parties are linked with nationally identifiable cleavage groups. The critical empirical question here is not one of party labels and aspirations, but of the de facto success of the parties in creating these linkages. We are not concerned, then, with the presence of "Socialist" or "Catholic" parties as such, but with differential success achieved by such parties in building linkages to workers, believing Catholics, and so on. Perhaps surprisingly, given the plausibility of the argument and the influence of the work of Alford (1963) and Lipset and Rokkan (1967b), the comparative effects of cleavage alignments on voting turnout have not been previously explored.

A simple and straightforward measure of the strength of the alignment between parties and cleavage groups is the degree to which we can predict individuals' partisan preferences from knowledge of their demographic characteristics. Where our predictive capacity is high, then cleavage group alignments are strong and we expect rather high levels of voting participation. Where knowledge of individuals' cleavage group membership is of little help in predicting their partisanship, then cleavage group alignments are weak, and, ceteris paribus, we expect lower levels of electoral participation.

Reliable construction of measures of *national party-group linkages* requires survey data within each country to link an individual's party preferences to his demographic characteristics. The closest approximation to such data is provided by Rose (1974:17), who offers a table showing the percent of variance in partisanship explained by various demographic characteristics in 15 countries. In fact, the correlation between Rose's measure of variance explained for these 15 countries and their average voting turnout as reported in the last column of Table 3-1 is 0.66. (If we add the percent variance for Japan provided by Flanagan and Richardson—19 percent—it fits perfectly and the correlation is unaltered.) If we exclude the five cases with compulsory voting, the correlation increases somewhat. Even with so few cases, these relationships are significant at the 0.01 level.

Using a cruder set of measures based on published tables of the relationship between occupation and partisanship, and religiosity and partisanship, as shown in Table 3-3, it is possible to extend a measure of party-group linkages to 24 nations. The measures here are based on the work of Alford (1963) and his "index of class voting." Alford's well-known index is the percentage of manual workers voting for "left" parties, minus the percentage of non-manual workers voting for "left" parties. For example, in Sweden in 1964, some 84 percent of workers supported the Communists or the Social Democrats, whereas only 32 percent of these in all other occupations did so—yielding a "class support index" of 52 for that year. In the United States, in contrast, in that same year 78 percent of the manual workers favored the Democrats over the Republicans, while 61 percent of those in other occupations did so—yielding a "class support" index of only 17 for that year.

As described in the footnote to Table 3-3, we have replicated that index in as many nations as possible. Where equivalent original data were available from several sources, or over several elections in the appropriate time period, all the scores were averaged to improve the estimate. In a few countries it was necessary to use alternative measures of the occupation of the head of the household, and religion was not available in all cases. As most data sources did not report class and religion jointly, and hence the interactions could not be estimated, the measure of national party-group linkage, shown in the last column in Table 3-3, is either the class or religious support index, whichever is higher. The Pearson correlation between this group support index and voting turnout (as a percent of citizens of voting age) is 0.58 for the twenty-four countries, significant at the 0.01 level.

As the measure of group support involves dichotomizing both the independent and dependent variables, and the exclusion of the uncertain respondents, there is some element of judgment in coding and creating the indices. There is, however, a very high correlation (0.85 for 14 cases) between the scores reported here and those reported by Lijphart (1971) in his sophisticated effort to extend and replicate the work of Alford. (Also see Inglehart, 1977: chs. 7, 8.) The major differences among the subset of fourteen cases for which Lijphart reports data are in Belgium, where the rise of ethnic parties has decreased the power of religion, and in France, where religion has become somewhat less important in the Fifth Republic than it was in the Fourth. Comparison of Lijphart's scores, based usually on surveys about five years earlier, with the data in Rose and with later data in Inglehart (1977) and Berglund and Lindstrom (1978) suggests that the relative magnitude of these linkages tends to be rather stable over time, at least in modernized systems. At a general level this conclusion is also supported by the time series analyses in Britain by Crewe, Särlvik and Alt (1977), in Scandinavia by Berglund and Lindstrom (1978), and in the United States by Pomper (1975). Although Crewe et al. demonstrate that class voting was declining in Britain from the 1950s to the 1970s, as was turnout, the size of the shifts is such that Britain's comparative rank in both respects does not change greatly. The tendency of demographic party-group alignments to be "frozen" for substantial time periods, so powerfully argued by Lipset and Rokkan (1967b) is quite evident here, even as regards the magnitude of the linkages.[5]

The strong association between the measure of party-group linkage and voting turnout is shown in Table 3-4. Controlling for required voting increases the relationships: the zero-order gamma between group linkage and turnout is

Table 3-3 Social Cleavage and Party Support Alignments in Twenty-Four Democracies

Nation	*Years of survey*	*Major cleavage alignment of party system*	*National party-cleavage group linkage index*[1]
Netherlands	1968	Religion: Relig. Parties v. Other	64
Finland	1966, 72	Occupation: Comm./Socialist v. Other	55
Belgium	1968,71	Religion: Catholic v. Other	50
Austria	1967,69	Religion: OeVP v. Socialist	49
Denmark	1964,71,73	Occupation: SPP/Socialist v. Other	47
Sweden	1964,68,73	Occupation: Comm./Socialist v. Other	46
Switzerland	1972	Religion: Catholic v. Other	45
New Zealand	1966*	Occupation: Labour v. National	42
Italy	1968,71,75	Religion: Christ. Dem. v. Other	40
Norway	1965,73	Occupation: SSP/Labour v. Other	40
United Kingdom	1964-74	Occupation: Labour v. Conservative	38
W. Germany	1967,71	Religion: CDU/CSU v. SPD	36
Israel	1969	Religion: Alignment v. Other	34
France	1967,71,73	Religion: Gaullist/Rep./Cent. v. Other	34
Australia	1967	Occupation: Labour/DLP v. Other	33
Canada	1965,68	Religion: Liberal v. Other	28
Chile	1972*	Income: Allende v. Other	25
Japan	1967	Occupation: Liberal/Dem. Soc. v. Other	24
Ireland	1969	Occupation: Labour v. Other	21
Philippines	1969	Language: Marcos v. Other	20
United States	1960-72	Religion: Republican v. Democratic	20
Jamaica	1967*	Occupation: PNP v. JLP	18
India	1971*	Landholding: JS/Swatranta v. Other	13
Venezuela	1973	Religion: COPEI v. Other	13

* Sub-national sample. Indian sample is national, but of males only.

[1] Index for occupation is percent of manual workers supporting the left parties, minus percent of those in other occupations supporting the left parties. For religion, the index is usually the percent regular church attenders supporting religious parties, minus non-regular attenders supporting such parties; in the U.S., Canada, and Switzerland the religious cleavage contrasts Catholics and Protestants. Support is measured by party preference or intended vote; don't know and independent responses, not reported in many countries, are excluded from percentages. Unlike Alford (1963) and Lijphart (1971), the rural populations are included.

Source: Indices are calculated from published tables in Rose (1974) for the Netherlands, Finland, Belgium, Sweden, Italy, Norway, Germany, Australia, Canada, and Ireland; from tables for Finland, Denmark, Sweden, and Norway in Berglund and Lindstrom (1978); from tables for Belgium, France, and Germany in Inglehart (1977:199, 224). Where equivalent data were available for several years or sources, these were averaged to provide the best estimate. Data for these and other countries for the 1960 to 1978 period were calculated from tables in the following: Austria (Inglehart, 1971; Powell, 1976); Canada (Meisel, 1974); Chile (Prothro and Chappario, 1974); Denmark (Damgaard, 1974; Thomas, 1973); France (Sondages, 1967, 1973); Israel (Arian, 1973); India (Sheth, 1975); Italy (Sani, 1977); Jamaica (Stone, 1973); New Zealand (Mitchell, 1969); Philippines (Averch, Koehler and Denton, 1971); Switzerland (Kerr, 1974); United Kingdom (Crewe, Sarlvik, and Alt, 1977); United States (Pomper, 1975). The Philippine tables were re-estimated for the size of language groups as given by census data. Data for Japan were generously provided by Norman H. Nie and Sidney Verba (also see Watanuki, 1967). Tables for Venezuela were contributed with great kindness by Enrique Baloyra and John Martz; the study is described in Martz and Baloyra (1976). In most countries with strong linkages, one cleavage was clearly more important than the second. In Austria, Israel, and the United States, however, occupation and religion were of about equal strength. In India size of landholding was somewhat stronger than either caste or occupation. In all countries, cutting points were chosen to divide the population into roughly equal size groups where possible.

Table 3-4 Linkages Between Cleavage Groups and Parties and Average Voting Turnout of Eligibles in Twenty-Four Democracies[1]

	National cleavage group-party linkage index	*Average Turnout of Eligible Age Group* 50-65%	66-75%	76-85%	86-95%	*Total %*	*(N)*
Compulsory Voting NO	0-30	43%	43%	14%	0	100	(7)
	31-45	14	29	57	0	100	(7)
	46-70	0	0	25	75	100	(4)
Compulsory Voting YES	0-30	0	50	50	0	100	(2)
	31-45	0	0	0	100	100	(2)
	46-70	0	0	0	100	100	(2)

[1] Average turnout data from Table 3-1. National Cleavage Group-Party Linkage index scores from Table 3-3. Tau-c for 18 nations without compulsory voting penalties is 0.69, significant at the 0.01 level. Tau-c for all 24 nations combined is 0.68, also significant at 0.01. Relationships are also significant using turnout as percent of registered electorate.

0.84 for the twenty-four countries; controlling for required voting, the first-order partial gamma is 0.87.

In short, the examination of the relationship between strength of party-group linkages and voting turnout yields a consistent and robust conclusion: strong linkages between citizens' cleavage group memberships and their party preferences are a powerful predictor of voting turnout across nations. This relationship holds up well using several different statistical measures of linkage, using several alternative subsets of countries and various tests of association, and in multiple regression analysis controlling for registration laws and compulsory voting (Beta = 0.47).

Party Competition

Among students of voting participation, it seems largely agreed that increased levels of party competition should be associated with higher voting turnout. A number of studies across cities and states in the U.S.A. support that conclusion (e.g., Kelley, Ayres and Bowen, 1967; Kim, Petrocik, and Enokson, 1975; and the review by Milbrath and Goel, 1977). Unfortunately, it seems to be difficult to find agreement on the meaning of competitiveness once one moves beyond the simplicity of two-party dominated elections. In the American case, researchers have assumed that where one of the two major parties predominates, interest will be less among both voters and party activists, and turnout lessened. Where a given election outcome seems a foregone conclusion, turnout will decline in that election (see Aldrich, 1976). In a Third World perspective, Huntington has argued that citizen mobilization should be greatest in two-party systems, followed by predominant party situations, with least mobilization in multiparty situations (Huntington, 1968: 428 ff.), an argument somewhat supported by McDonough's findings in India (1971), although the differences are not great.

Huntington notes, however, that multiparty systems in modernized nations may develop strong ties between parties and special constituencies of the sort we have explored above, and these would facilitate mobilization.

In general the problem of theoretical expectations about voting turnout in multiparty systems is compounded by the variety of coalition arrangements, formal and informal, in such systems. In Denmark in the 1960s, for example, the complex system of five substantial parties took on virtually a two-party clarity for voters and activists with the consolidation of pro- and anti-Socialist blocs. The emergence of these apparently sharply contrasted opposing blocs, evenly balanced in voting strength, was associated with a moderate increase in voting turnout, as was the situation of evenly balanced bloc-confrontation in Sweden in the 1970s, and Norway from 1965.

At the other extreme of the complex relationship between multiparty competition and legislative/electoral outcomes, we find Switzerland. The Swiss case is extremely "deviant" in terms of voting turnout. Switzerland is a highly economically developed, small country, with automatic registration and rather strong linkages between parties and cleavage groups along religious lines. Four cantons even have required voting. Most of our theoretical arguments lead us to predict high voting turnout in Switzerland. But in fact it is very low, even before the enfranchisement of inexperienced female voters in the early 1970s. Turnout has been steadily declining, moreover, several percent in each election, since the 1930s. The most likely explanation is offered by Przeworski (1975): the deliberate demobilization of party competition by the major national parties themselves. Since the late 1930s, the four major parties, each linked to a cleavage group, have guaranteed themselves roughly equal place in the shared collective national executive, which has a rotating chairmanship. Unless a new party should suddenly break into the big four, the electoral outcomes at the national level are virtually meaningless. There is not the intense juggling of ministries and party balances which marked the responsiveness of the German and Austrian Grand Coalitions to electoral outcomes. Moreover, most important policy decisions are made at the Cantonal level. There is little incentive for voters to go to the polls, or for the major parties to try to mobilize them. (See Steiner, 1974.)

The Swiss case, and consideration of changes in coalition competitiveness in the Scandinavian nations, support the idea that intensity of competition is associated with increased voting turnout. However, they also suggest the difficulty of finding unambiguous measures of such composition. One attempt to classify party systems by types of competition is that of Sartori (1976:314). Of our democracies he identifies six party systems as "two-party," another six as "predominant,' and another eleven as having some form of multipartyism. We find turnout averages 77 percent in the two-party systems, 79 percent in the multiparty systems, and 72 percent in the predominant systems. The purported advantages of two-party competition in mobilizing support seems to hold up vis-à-vis one-party predominance. But the multiparty systems do not seem disadvantaged, except in the case of Switzerland. Moreover, each type shows substantial variation, relating in part to the cleavage alignment and voting law differences. Moreover, most of the Third World nations in Sartori's analysis are predominant system countries, which weighs down the turnout level of that type of party system. In multivariate analysis, the impact of single-party predominance is insignificant.

Another approach is to look at the apparent connection between elections and legislative/executive outcomes. If a single party dominates the electoral process, or if deliberate inter-party agreements predetermine the electoral outcomes, we might expect the lesser importance of elections to reduce voting participation. In four countries such dominance or pre-election agreements seemed virtually to determine the cabinet and chief executive before the elections: India, where the Congress Party dominated national politics until 1977; Japan, where the Liberal Democrats have dominated national politics throughout the post-war period; Switzerland, where the four large parties have had a predetermined share in the collective executive; and Lebanon, where the constitution guarantees sets to religious subfactions and personalistic "parties" have represented these. Average turnout in these four countries was, respectively, 60, 71, 53 and 56 percent, all well below the general average for the democracies. In these rather extreme cases of limited electoral/executive connections, we seem to see some sharp effects in lowering election participation. However, if we construct a typology for the remaining countries, in which we classify countries in terms of the frequency with which elections lead directly and unambiguously to executive change, we find no simple anticipated differences in turnout levels.[6]

Factors Shaping Comparative Voting Turnout: Social Structure

Economic Development and Social Modernization

Probably the largest body of writing on theories of cross-national participation is the literature on social modernization and political mobilization. (See Lerner, 1958; Deutsch, 1961; Almond and Powell, 1978; Huntington, 1968; Nie, Powell and Prewitt, 1969; and Inkeles and Smith, 1974.) The various approaches suggest that "economic development" has important consequences for mass political activity, as the achievement of higher levels of economic development is associated with major transformations of the social and economic structure of the society. Some analyses emphasize the exposure of individuals to a modern, secular political culture, which stresses the ability of human beings to transform their physical and social environment. Others stress the creation and dispersion of personal social resources, such as information, status, and social awareness. While yet other studies discuss the transformation of group relations within the society, the networks and dependencies which link individuals together in various ways.

Despite the vast body of theory, the only published studies which examine the relationship between economic development and voting turnout across a large set of countries draw on the data in Russett et al (1964). In the original analysis Russett et al., report a strong (Pearson) correlation of 0.47 between economic development and voting participation of citizens in enfranchised age groups for a single election (p. 83). However, the majority of their 90 countries are not democracies; franchises vary sharply; the meaning of the voting act, as well as inducements and penalties for participation, no doubt varies widely. Other studies using these data, with similar conclusions, include Alker (1966) and Tanter (1967).

In Figure 3-1 we show a scattergram of GNP/Capita level and average voting turnout as a percent of the eligible age groups for the thirty democracies. As sanctions for non-voting are quite important, the countries which tend to compel voting through legal penalties are indicated with stars, rather than dots. The best-fit regression lines for turnout with log GNP per Capita—the most commonly used measure of economic development—are shown separately for countries with required and voluntary voting. Both sets show relationships significant at the 0.05 level. The simple Pearson correlation between log GNP/Capita and turnout is 0.35, significant at the 0.05 level. Other measures of modernization, such as literacy level (r = 0.40) and percent employed in non-agricultural occupations (r = 0.36), are similarly related to voting turnout.

A rough but useful indication of the magnitude of the modernization effect is provided by breaking down the countries into two major groups of developing and developed nations as of 1965. The former group includes the twelve nations with 1965 GNP/Capita under $900, the wealthiest of which was Venezuela. The latter includes the eighteen nations with GNP/Capita at $1,000 or more, the poorest of which were Ireland and Italy. The average turnout levels are about 12 percent higher in the developed nations, controlling for legal penalties:

Nations without penalties for non-voting
GNP/Capita $100—$900 Average Turnout 66% (8 nations)
GNP/Capita $901—$3,600 Average Turnout 77% (14 nations)

Nations with penalties for non-voting
GNP/Capita $100—$900 Average Turnout 77% (4 nations)
GNP/Capita $901—$3,600 Average Turnout 90% (4 nations)

All of these results support the expectation that economic development and turnout are associated in the democratic political systems, although they do not resolve theoretical issues regarding the individual level linkages or dynamic relationships involved. We might add, too, that as the poorer countries are more likely to employ compulsory voting to get their citizens to the polls, the effect of compulsory voting laws has been to diminish the depressing effect of low economic development on voting turnout. The most striking example is Venezuela, which has very harsh penalties for unexcused non-voting and high turnout. Baloyra (1977) reports that over 40 percent of the citizens say they would not vote if the penalties were removed. The simple gamma between dichotomized GNP/Capita and turnout was 0.68, and the first-order partial controlling for compulsory voting was 0.77. Similarly, when GNP per capita (log) is entered into a regression analysis with registration laws and compulsory voting, its impact on turnout increases, with the Beta up to a highly significant 0.41.

Multivariate Analysis

Multivariate analysis can show how much of the total variance in voting turnout is explained by environmental characteristics. We can use simultaneous multiple regression to guard against accepting or rejecting associations spuriously. Causal modeling can also be of help in dealing with direct and indirect relationships.

Figure 3-1 Economic Development Level and Voting Turnout

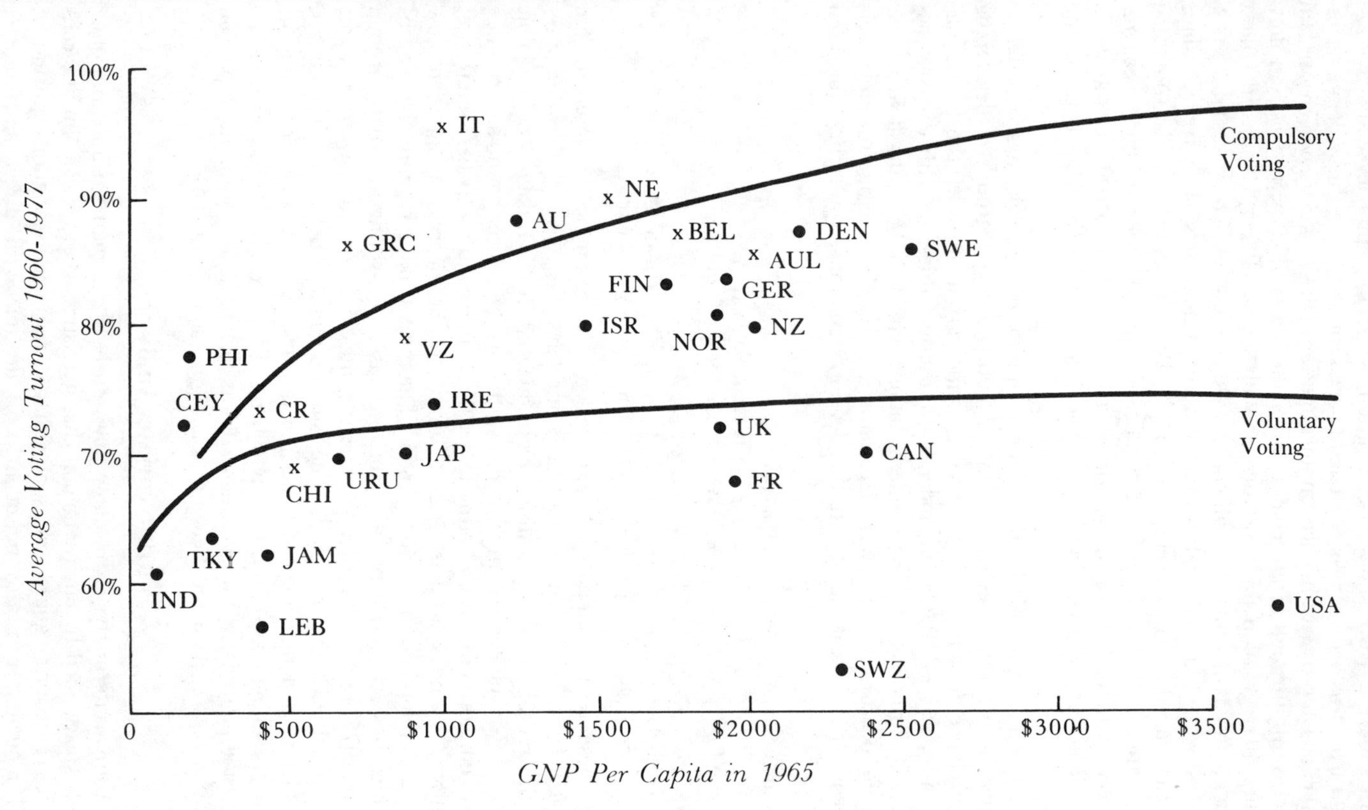

Multiple Regression

We have survey evidence on the linkages between cleavage groups and parties in only twenty-four of our thirty democracies. The missing cases are without exception nations at lower levels of wealth and socio-economic modernization. Our conclusions must, therefore, be drawn with some care.

1. If we enter GNP/Capita (log), Electoral Laws (PR Dummy), Compulsory Voting, and Registration Laws into a multiple regression equation with voting turnout, the Beta for electoral laws is insignificant. The other three variables are each significant at the 0.05 level. Running the equations with and without log Population Size yields the same result. Re-running the equation only with GNP/Capita (log), Compulsory Voting, and Registration Laws finds each of them clearly significant, with the Bs well over twice the standard error (Betas of 0.41, 0.47, and 0.39). The three variables yield a multiple R of 0.67, explaining some 45 percent of the variance in voting turnout for the thirty democracies. These results support our previous conclusions that PR electoral laws have no direct significant effects, while the level of economic development and compulsory voting and registration do.

2. The simple competitiveness dichotomy does establish itself as a powerful and significant variable, along with compulsory voting and registration laws. Although only four nations were classified as noncompetitive, they clearly had turnout below the levels otherwise anticipated. Addition of the competitiveness dummy variable to GNP/Capita, Compulsory Voting, and Registration Laws increases the percent variance explained from 45 percent to 69 percent for the thirty countries. Interestingly enough, the impact of GNP per capita is weakened, although still significant ($\beta = 0.29$).

3. In the smaller set of 24 countries for which we have survey data on the relationship between cleavage groups and parties, first-stage analysis, before considering party factors, basically confirms the above findings. When we introduce the measure of linkage between parties and cleavage groups, the variance explained increases sharply. Party Linkage replaces GNP/Capita in importance; the latter loses all significance. This result strongly suggests that much of the effect of modernization operates through the creation or maintenance of more clear-cut linkages between parties and cleavage groups in the more modernized societies. The secondary literature on party systems in those nations for which we do not have data certainly suggests that linkages between parties and national cleavage groups tends to be weak in the less developed countries. Personalism and patronage dominate party politics in the democracies such as Costa Rica, Uruguay, the Philippines, Lebanon, Greece, and Turkey. (See McDonald, 1972, for some limited survey evidence for Uruguay.)

Introducing the dichotomous competitiveness variable yields four significant variables explaining turnout in the twenty-four countries: Competitiveness (dummy), Party Linkage, Compulsory Voting, and Registration Laws. The Multiple R is 0.85, explaining 73 percent of the variance in voting turnout, and the respective Bs are all twice the size of the standard error, Betas being respectively, 0.52, 0.28, 0.31, and 0.41. (Additional consideration of GNP/Capita, Population Size, and Electoral Laws does not increase the explanatory power or yield additional significant coefficients.)

However, given our theoretical understanding of the working of the party linkages to cleavage groups—that they will make it easier to identify mobilizable supporters, and that elections will be more clearly significant in their effects to citizen group members—it is not clear that we should expect such influences to operate *within* highly non-competitive situations. It is appropriate, then, to recognize the impact of non-competitiveness in its own right—in this rather extreme version where election outcomes are largely predetermined—and to run the multivariate model only on the twenty-one competitive cases, the twenty-four for which survey data is available less Switzerland, India and Japan. If we do so, we find that Party Linkages, Compulsory Voting, and Registration Laws alone explain 74 percent of the variance in turnout, with highly significant Betas of respectively, 0.47, 0.36, and 0.43. It is interesting to see that compulsory voting, although strong and significant, is the least powerful of these three. No other influence is significant when added to this model.

Concluding Comments

We can explain a substantial amount of the variance in average voting turnout across democracies by a few characteristics of the party system and electoral laws. The specific tactics of candidates and the specific issues and alliances of individual elections play a lesser role in shaping voting participation. Linkages between parties and cleavage groups, the presence of successul party competition, automatic registration, and compulsory voting account for nearly 75 percent of the variance in turnout across the twenty-four democracies for which data were available.

The literature on voting participation suggested a number of factors which should affect cross-national turnout differences. Some of these expectations, such as those regarding registration laws and compulsory voting, were confirmed. On the other hand, such frequently cited factors as small population size, proportional representation, and the number of competitive parties did not have any direct effect on turnout after controlling for legal factors. In analyzing the effects of party competition, only the general dichotomy between systems with and without a recent history of elections altering the composition of the executive had a notable impact on turnout. As only four countries qualified as "noncompetitive," this variable retains a somewhat doubtful status. Linkages between parties and cleavage groups, however, had strong and consistent effects in mobilizing voters.

Given the large literature describing the mobilizing role of economic development and social modernization, we expected to find average voting turnout related to measures of modernization in the democracies. So it was, and modernization variables remained significant after controlling for the legal factors. At best we can judge from these data, however, that much of the modernization effect seemed to occur through the shaping of ties between parties and national cleavage groups, rather than through individual level increases in status or information. This conclusion seems consistent with the most recent individual level studies of voting participation in modernizing countries. (See Huntington and Nelson, 1976; and especially, Verba, Nie and Kim, 1978.) Individual resources and status changes may have major impact on non-partisan participation and on the more difficult participatory acts, but the relation of the party system to individuals and social groups is critical for voting.

A full scale causal model has not been presented. The assumptions of causal modeling require an analysis of the sources of registration laws and compulsory voting which is beyond the scope of this study. But the data are consistent with causal effects in which both modernization and, to a lesser extent, proportional representation, act to increase the likelihood of close ties developing between parties and national cleavage groups. The religious and ethnic compositions of the population, as well as historical events, help determine whether these linkages will be primarily based on social class alone, or based on other demographic groups as well. The strength of these linkages, then, together with registration laws and penalties for non-voting, strongly determine the average voting turnout levels in countries with even moderate degrees of party competition. This argument can be summarized in the following sketch [Figure 3-2]:[7]

Figure 3-2

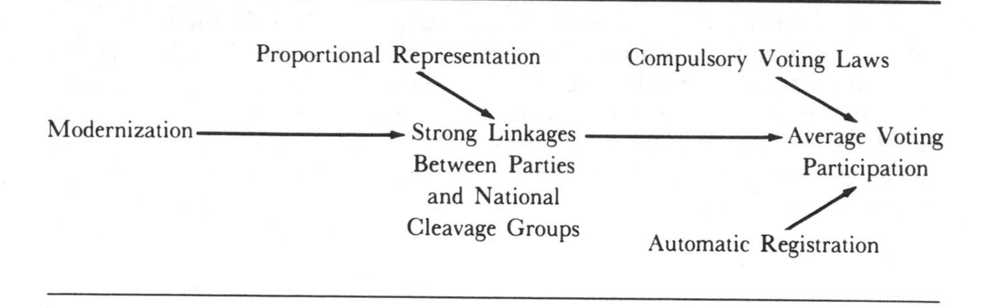

The absence of proportional representation is usually associated (r = 0.9) with British or American culture (or colonial tutelage) at the time of constitution making. The countries with single-member district electoral systems in 1959-1977 are Australia, Canada, Ceylon (Sri Lanka), France, India, Jamaica, New Zealand, Philippines, the United Kingdom and the United States. Cultural assumptions about representation are a major influence upon electoral laws; calculation of political advantage is also present and occasionally overriding.

It is also revealing to replicate all of the analysis in this paper using the turnout of registered voters (Column 3, in Table 3-1), rather than voters as a percent of the enfranchised age groups. We have to delete the United States from such analysis, as reliable national registration figures are not available. For some countries, however, the difference between turnout of registered voters and turnout of enfranchised eligibles is quite substantial. Not surprisingly, we find that the effects of the registration laws themselves are negligible in predicting turnout of those registered. The predictive power of compulsory voting, on the other hand, increases sharply. Penalties for non-voting seem particularly effective in getting those already on the registration rolls to the voting booth. Party variables remain about equally significant in explaining the turnout of registered as of enfranchised voters. The party effects seem quite robust. However, as so few of the democracies were notably non-competitive, we cannot be as confident of competitiveness as of party-group linkages. Modernization plays a similar role in explaining the turnout of registered as of eligible voters: it is significant until the party linkage is introduced, and apparently mediated through it to a large extent.

Whichever version of the dependent variable we use, the effects of modernization seem to have impact on the turnout-enhancing development of party ties to demographic groups. The positive indirect effects on turnout appear even in the more modernized subset of nations where zero-order relationships are negligible. However, there is evidence that the strength of occupational group linkages to parties has declined somewhat in recent years in at least some Western nations, especially in Britain and Denmark. And in many of the European nations religion continues to be the primary orienting cleavage at a time when church attendance is falling. These facts suggest that a post-industrial society may see a decline in the strength of party-group linkages, or a period of uncertainty as realignment occurs and new linkages are developed. One might expect such events to produce lower voting turnout.

The data here indeed emphasize the direct and immediate effects on voting turnout of party ties to identifiable demographic groups. Among several subsets of countries and with several measures of the group basis of party preference, this influence is a major predictor of turnout. Group-based partisanship also has important connections to other aspects of democratic politics, such as the patterns of conflict and the stability of party and voting coalitions. We need to explore further the basis of the party-group linkage relationship, its sensitivity to change, and the extent to which it is founded on citizens' incentives or the mobilizing effectiveness of political parties, or both.

NOTES

1. The population of appropriate age was calculated from the United Nations *Demographic Yearbook 1970* and later editions. The *World Book Atlas* (1977) was used for estimating population size for several elections after 1976. Some interpolation was necessary in many countries and data are clearly more accurate for years close to those of general national censuses. However, average turnout changes from election to election correspond quite systematically to differences in turnout of registered voters in most countries. (In Venezuela the registration roles were expanded from 1958 to 1968.) Raw turnout figures are largely from Mackie and Rose (1974); the *European Journal of Political Research; Keesing's Archives;* and individual country studies listed in the bibliography, especially the excellent AEI "At the Polls" series. The ages of eligibility were derived primarily from Mackie and Rose (1974); United Nations Secretary General's Report, 1968; and Herman (1976).
2. A major exception is Ceylon, with automatic registration and a substantial discrepancy between "eligibles" and the electorate registered. This difference may be due in part to the need to estimate size of the voting age Indian Tamil population (10.6 percent of total population in the 1963 Census) who are disenfranchised in these elections, and for whom age distribution figures were not available. (See Kearney, 1973.) Analysis deleting Ceylon does not materially change any results reported below.
3. Two other countries, Austria and Switzerland, had compulsory voting for citizens residing in several Provinces or Cantons. These made up less than 10 percent of the

total national population, and their inclusion or exclusion does not greatly alter the national averages in the two countries. Hence, they are classified as non-penalty countries. But within each nation, it is true that average turnout is higher in the subunits where penalties exist.

4. The registration law variable in multivariate results reported below is trichotomized: Automatic registration = 3; Required citizen-initiated application = 2; voluntary citizen-initiated application = 1. See the footnote to Table 3-2 for countries in each category. Jamaica, a "3" in 1962 and a "1" in part of 1967 and 1972, is coded "2." The same conclusions follow, with a slightly weaker Beta for registration laws, using a dichotomized "Dummy" variable distinguishing only automatic and voluntary registration.
5. More recently, a sharp drop in the absolute level of linkage between parties and cleavage groups took place in Denmark. The sudden emergence of the Progress Party, general weakening in the strength of the Social Democrats, and decline in the size of the agricultural population, reduced the strength of occupation-party ties from an index figure of over 50 (Berglund and Lindstrom, 1978; Thomas, 1973) to around 40 (Berglund and Lindstrom, 1978; Damgaard, 1974), between the late 1960s and mid-1970s. However, even the latter figure is relatively high in comparative perspective, double that of the U.S.A.
6. The initial competitiveness analysis distinguished four levels of effects on executive control: (1) systems in which during all elections there had been at least one example of direct responsiveness to an election in the decade before; (2) systems in which a responsiveness history was present during only part of the elections averaged; (3) systems in which such effects were discernible in at least a few elections, but of a complex type, as in the Italian cabinet changes; (4) systems in which no responsiveness had been present in the decade before any election averaged into the study. Respectively, the countries so classified were: (1) Australia, Austria, Belgium, Ceylon, Chile, Costa Rica, W. Germany, Jamaica, New Zealand, Philippines, Turkey, U.K., U.S.A.; (2) Canada, Denmark, France, Greece, Ireland, Norway, Uruguay, Venezuela; (3) Finland, Italy, Netherlands, Sweden, Israel; (4) India, Japan, Lebanon, Switzerland. As pointed out in the text, although some over-time differences in the expected direction can be found *within* countries in category (2), only category (4) clearly is distinguished by lower average turnout.
7. We can, of course, offer a partial causal model of the "sketch" [Figure 3-2] in the text, in which it is described by two simultaneous regression equations. In one equation, Voting Participation is the dependent variable, and all other five variables are independent. In this equation, the R for Voting Participation is 0.87, and the only significant Beta's are those for Linkages (0.44), Compulsory Voting (0.32) and Registration Laws (0.36), each with a B over twice the standard error. In the second equation, Linkages is the dependent variable, predicated only by Modernization (GNP/Capita) and Proportional Representation. In this equation the R for Linkages is 0.58, and the Beta's for both GNP/Capita (0.42) and Proportional Representation (0.38) are significant. That is, given the assumptions of causal priority implied, each of the arrows shown in the causal sketch yields a significant coefficient, and no other possible causal connections do so.

4. THE EFFECT OF REGISTRATION LAWS ON VOTER TURNOUT

Steven J. Rosenstone and Raymond E. Wolfinger

Most Americans, in order to vote, must establish their eligibility by registering prior to election day. This requirement makes voting a more difficult act than it otherwise would be. Not only must citizens care enough to go to the polls, but to register they must also make an earlier expenditure of time and energy. Indeed, registration is often more difficult than voting. It may require a longer journey, at a less convenient hour, to complete a more complicated procedure—and at a time when interest in the campaign is far from its peak.

This aspect of the American electoral system is unusual. In most democratic countries the government assumes responsibility for enrolling all citizens on a permanent, nationwide electoral register. This difference is widely considered a major cause of the low rate of voter turnout in the United States.

Previous research provided reasons for accepting the omnibus proposition that the state registration laws in force in 1960 made a difference in turnout that year. Two studies showed that much of the variation in voting levels among cities and states was explained by interstate differences in laws governing the registration of voters (Kelley, Ayres, and Bowen, 1967; Kim, Petrocik, and Enokson, 1975). But little light was shed on *what* provisions had *how much* influence on the voting levels of *what kinds of people.* The sweeping changes in election laws since 1960 further reduced the contemporary relevance of these studies. Perhaps because of these uncertainties, some scholars, publicists, and politicians expressed doubts that registration laws in the 1970s have much to do with the number of Americans who go to the polls (Phillips and Blackman, 1975,

---

Authors' Note: A previous version of this article was delivered at the 1976 Annual Meeting of the American Political Science Association. Comments by Malcolm E. Jewell and Edward R. Tufte aided our revision of that paper. Thomas Reynolds of the Boalt School of Law at Berkeley kindly advised us on legal research and the use of his school's Law Library. The extraordinary problems of processing our data were overcome with the help of Margaret Baker, Frank Many, and Harvey Weinstein of the Berkeley Survey Research Center. Catherine Winter of the Institute of Governmental Studies and Mary Brunn of the Survey Research Center handled various typing and reproduction tasks with great efficiency. Christopher Achen advised us generously on many aspects of the data analysis. Our research was supported by a grant from the Academic Senate Committee on research and by funds made available by the Department of Political Science.

Source: *American Political Science Review* (1978) 72:22-45. Reprinted with permission of the publisher.

p. 14; Tarrance, 1976, pp. 11-12; see also the minority views in Committee on Post Office and Civil Service, *Voter Registration by Postcard,* Senate Document 352, 93rd Congress, 2nd sess.). Others insist that the existing legal situation still "results in disenfranchisement on a massive scale." [1]

This debate underlies continuing attempts, at both state and federal levels, to ease further the burden of registration. President Carter's unsuccessful 1977 proposal for election-day registration was the latest example. In 1976 a bill to establish a scheme for nationwide postcard registration was justified by its congressional sponsors as a remedy for the "obstacle course" produced by existing state laws.[2] Scholars are interested not only in the accuracy of this claim, but in the more fundamental questions raised by the debate. Discerning variations in the impediments to voting posed by alternate registration provisions helps us understand the saliency to individuals of political participation. If apparently trivial differences in the prerequisites to casting a ballot have substantial effects on the probability of voting, what does this tell us about the relative costs and perceived benefits of going to the polls? How do individuals differ in the extent to which registration requirements impede their access to the ballot box? In attempting to answer these questions, we will be concerned not only with the extent to which registration provisions affect turnout, but also with the political consequences of relaxing the registration laws to make voting everywhere as easy as in the most permissive states. The last section of this article compares the actual presidential electorate in 1972 to the larger, hypothetical electorate that would be produced by easier registration.

In estimating the impact of registration laws, one is identifying the degree to which statewide legal provisions influence individuals. Previous researchers did not dispute the desirability of using individual-level data to study the problems. They used aggregate voting and demographic data because the existing academic surveys, with samples ranging from 1500 to 2300 respondents selected from fewer than 40 states, were an inadequate data base. In this study our data come from the Current Population Survey conducted by the Bureau of the Census in November 1972.[3] The sample is nearly 40 times larger than that used by the University of Michigan Center for Political Studies and includes respondents from all 50 states. We will describe our data sources in detail, after a discussion of recent changes in American suffrage laws.

State Suffrage Laws, 1960-73

Each state determines its own registration laws, subject only to certain limitations imposed by the U.S. Constitution, court decisions, and national legislation. Despite these limitations (many of which are quite recent), the states differ widely in the extent to which registration significantly increases the time and energy costs of voting. In some cases registration is relatively easy; some have abolished this prerequisite altogether. In other states registration is relatively onerous.

Our examination of state laws begins in 1960 because that year's election provided the data for the two principal studies of the effect of these laws on voter turnout (Kelley et al., 1967; Kim et al., 1975). For our purposes, 11 different areas of legal regulation are identified.

1. *Poll taxes.* In 1960 some southern states imposed a tax as a condition for registration. A few states made the tax liability cumulative, i.e., before being allowed to register, one had to pay not only the current year's tax, but the tax for all earlier and unpaid years of his eligibility. The Twenty-fourth Amendment to the Constitution prohibited poll taxes in federal elections in 1964. Two years later the Supreme Court abolished the practice altogether.[4]

2. *Literacy tests.* Most common in the South, these ranged from requiring simple literacy to a demand that the applicant interpret a provision of the state or federal constitution. Through inequitable enforcement, this was the principal administrative means of disenfranchising southern blacks. Literacy tests were suspended in much of the South by the Voting Rights Act of 1965. They were abolished everywhere by the Voting Rights Act Amendments (VRAA) of 1970.

3. *Permanent or periodic registration.* In 1960 a number of states required potential voters to re-register at intervals of as little as one year. By 1972, this practice was followed in only two states which required re-registration at ten-year intervals. A few states allowed re-registration at the discretion of local officials. This option has been exercised in a couple of southern states, presumably as a means of reducing black turnout (Reitman and Davidson, 1972, pp. 33-34).

4. *Purging for nonvoting.* Akin to periodic registration is the requirement that people who have not voted within a stated time be dropped from the registration rolls. The period ranges from two to eight years. Some states have no purging provision at all.

5. *Residency requirements.* In the early 1960s, 38 states required at least a year's residence in the state before one could register. The 1970 Voting Rights Act Amendments in effect imposed a maximum 30-day residency requirement for presidential elections. They also permitted new residents to vote in their previous state either in person or by absentee ballot. In March 1972 the Supreme Court, in *Dunn* v. *Blumstein,* struck down Tennessee's one-year requirement.[5] As a result of this decision, residency requirements for other elections were restricted. Although the Court did not impose a new limit, its decision was interpreted as strongly suggesting a maximum residency requirement of 30 days before the election.

6. *Closing date.* This is the last day one can register before the election—the date registration is closed. The 1970 VRAA mandated a closing date of at most 30 days before presidential elections. The Court's decision in *Dunn* v. *Blumstein* said that "30 days appears to be an ample period of time" in other elections. But a year later, the Court permitted Arizona and Georgia to retain their 50-day closing dates.[6] It is easy to confuse closing dates and residency requirements, and the two are, of course, interdependent.

7. *Regular office hours.* Most states require registration offices to remain open Monday through Friday during normal business hours. Other states either impose less stringent schedules or are silent on this subject. Thus offices in some states may be open only a few hours on some days of the week, drastically reducing opportunities for registration.

8. *Evening and Saturday registration.* Recognizing that most people work during the day from Monday to Friday, many states require that registration offices be open after normal working hours, on Saturday, or both.

9. *County, city, or neighborhood offices.* In some states potential voters can register only at the county seat. Elsewhere registration offices are located in each city. Most convenient is neighborhood registration, usually in firehouses, libraries, and the like.

10. *Deputy registrars.* Some states authorize deputizing ordinary citizens to register voters. Deputy registrars go from house to house, set up tables in shopping centers, and so on. Such provisions are often exploited by political parties and interest groups.

11. *Absentee registration.* The 1970 VRAA required all states to permit absentee registration in presidential elections solely on grounds of absence. This is a minimum standard. Some states permit absentee registration for various other reasons, and a few authorize it for anyone. Federal postcard registration would authorize nationwide absentee registration. A major issue in congressional debate has been whether postcards should be mailed to everyone, or whether the individual would have to obtain a postcard to mail in. The latter alternative resembles the system used by five states in 1972.

Previous Research

For a considerable period after the advent of survey research on voting behavior, systematic evidence about the effects of registration laws was scarce and limited. The authors of *The American Voter* reported that legal considerations seemed unrelated to voting levels in the North, but reduced turnout in the South by about nine percent.[7] Rough estimates about the number of people kept from the polls by residency requirements were commonplace. Perhaps the best-known figure was provided by the President's Commission on Registration and Voting Participation, which claimed that eight million Americans had been unable to vote in 1960 because of residency requirements.[8]

The paucity of detailed evidence reflected the considerable difficulties of research. Several aspects of registration can be handled in various ways; thus numerous combinations of legal provisions are possible. The combinations are far from random, however. States with restrictive procedures in one aspect of registration are likely to be more demanding in other respects. Moreover, individuals who vote less, such as uneducated people and southerners, are more likely to be found in states with restrictive laws.

The first scholars to tackle these problems were Stanley Kelley, Jr., and his associates (1967). Acknowledging that registration is an inescapable prerequisite to voting, they set out to explain variations in registration among 104 cities in 1960. By means of multiple regression they estimated the differences in registration related to demographic characteristics and to registration laws, all measured on a city-wide basis.[9] They concluded that "local differences in the turnout for elections are to a large extent related to local differences in rates of registration, and these in turn reflect to a considerable degree local differences in the rules governing, and arrangements for handling, the registering of voters."[10]

One drawback of explaining variance at the aggregate level is an inevitable inflation of the importance of the laws.[11] Cities (and states) are much more similar with respect to demographic than legal variables. The latter often are dichotomous, whereas aggregate demographic differences represent points along a continuum that rarely are very far apart. Since there is not very much state-to-state variation in demographic variables, they cannot explain much of the variance in turnout. This is not the case with legal variables, which do vary dramatically from state to state. As a result, this approach exaggerates the importance of the laws (c.f. Johnston, 1972, pp. 34-35, 129).

We do not consider "explaining variance" as interesting as establishing the extent to which particular provisions increase or decrease turnout. This would be a more satisfactory estimate of the effect that the laws have on turnout. It would also allow one to forecast the consequences of proposed changes in the laws. Moreover, previous studies did not consider possible interaction effects between particular provisions and specific groups in the population. They assumed that whatever the effect of a provision, it fell equally on everybody.[12]

Quite apart from their merits as sources of insight into turnout in 1960, these studies have lost much of their contemporary relevance because of subsequent sweeping changes in state and federal law. Poll taxes and literacy tests have been abolished; periodic registration has vanished except for ten-year re-registration in Arizona and South Carolina; residency requirements are measured in days rather than years; closing dates are closer to election day; and there are minimum national standards for absentee registration. With the present range of interstate variation so drastically reduced, do the remaining differences still have any impact on turnout? [13]

Another major change since the early 1960s is the massive reduction of barriers to black voting in the South. As long as blacks were prevented from registering by intimidation and maladministration of the laws, it was difficult to sort out the extent to which turnout was related to intimidation and to race, education, region, and restrictive laws. By enfranchising millions of southern blacks, the federal Voting Rights Act of 1965 removed one cause of the strong relationships between turnout and race, region, and education.[14] In addition to reducing the importance of race, region, and education as independent variables, the Voting Rights Act may well have reduced the interaction effect of these factors. That is, the Act may have reduced the likelihood that any given provision has a different impact on different people, instead of falling with equal effect on the entire population. Thus the findings that registration laws affect turnout only in the South may be as obsolete as Jim Crow laws.

Data Sources

We used survey data on individual demographic characteristics and turnout in the 1972 general election. This information was gathered in the Current Population Survey conducted by the Bureau of the Census in November 1972. Beginning in 1964, the November Current Population Survey in each even-numbered year has included questions on registration and turnout, as well as the customary demographic and employment data.[15]

Several characteristics of this data collection make it well-suited for our purposes. Most obvious is the sheer size of the sample: 93,339 respondents were interviewed. Weighting to achieve a representative sample of the civilian noninstitutional population yields 136,203 cases for analysis.[16] Other aspects of the sampling procedure are perhaps more important. The sample includes all 50 states and the District of Columbia; only three states have less than 200 actual respondents. In contrast, the Michigan Center for Political Studies 1972 National

Election Study has no respondents from 13 states, including some with the least restrictive registration laws, and 45 or fewer respondents in an additional 13 states.[17] Moreover, the Census survey uses a very large number of sampling units. The 1972 survey was drawn from 461 primary sampling units (PSUs), compared to 74 PSUs in the Michigan sample.[18]

Taken together, these properties of our sample mean that the sampling variability is very small and thus the resulting population estimates are unusually precise. Moreover, geographic categorization of the respondents need not be limited to gross regional divisions. Because there is a relatively large number of respondents from every state, the effects of state laws can be estimated precisely.[19]

We deleted noncitizens from the sample, thus losing 2,444 actual respondents (the weighted N = 3,522). We also excluded from analysis all cases where the respondent did not know whether a vote had been cast, or where this information was not ascertained by the interviewer. This reduced the sample by 2,790 actual respondents, or a weighted N of 4,099. These modifications bring us to 88,105 actual respondents, or a weighted N of 128,582. A fuller description of our sample and comparison with other data sets is presented in Appendix A.

Data on Registration Provisions. Obtaining information about each state's voting laws proved to be more difficult than we had expected. Several publications contain lists of state registration laws for the 1972 general election.[20] Unfortunately, they were all compiled before the Court handed down its ruling in *Dunn* v. *Blumstein*.[21] Thus they do not take account of that decision, nor of the numerous state-level responses to it that changed residency requirements or closing dates for the November election.

We tried to obtain the information by sending a one-page questionnaire to each state's chief election official. They were quick to respond to our inquiry; 41 of them replied within a few weeks, although not always with accurate responses. A check with the statutes themselves indicated that over a third of the returned questionnaires had at least one error. We think this reflected the time that had passed since the 1972 election, changes both in personnel and in state laws, and possible confusion between laws governing presidential and other elections.

We finally gathered the information directly from the Library of the Boalt School of Law on the Berkeley Campus of the University of California. This material for each state includes not only the state code, but all relevant state and federal court decisions, and also state attorney general opinions if federal legislation or court decisions altered the application of state statutes.

Our coding scheme for the state laws is described in Appendix B. Here we discuss some of the ways we reconciled the complexities of real life to the more simplistic world of quantitative analysis. One set of problems along these lines pertains to states that mandated different procedures for different areas, usually on the basis of population. For example, Iowa, Minnesota, Missouri, Ohio, and Wisconsin exempted their less populous counties from registration requirements. Since in each case only a small fraction of the state population was excluded and we could not identify our respondents' counties, we ignored this deviation from the laws governing most of the states' residents.

A second set of problems was encountered with the differences between state laws that required a particular practice, or allowed it, or forbade it. We have no

Table 4-1 State Turnout and Registration Laws, 1972[a]

State	*Turnout*[b]	*Residency Requirement*	*Closing Date— Days Before Election*	*Where to Register*[c]	*Deputy Registrars Allowed*	*Registration Office Open 40 Hours a Week*	*Evening and/or Sat. Registration Required*	*Absentee Regis-tration*[d]	*Years of Non-Voting Before Cut From Rolls*
Utah	69.4	31	11	C		X	X	X	4
South Dakota	68.9	15	15	T	X	X	X	X	4
Minnesota	68.9	30	20	T	X	X	X	X	4
Connecticut	68.6	7	24	P	X		X	X	None
North Dakota	68.2	10	No Registration[e]						
Montana	68.1	30	30	P	X	X		X	2
New Hampshire	65.5	30	9	T				X	None
Massachusetts	65.2	29	28	T	X	X	X	X[f]	None
Washington	65.1	31	31	P	X	X			2.5
Illinois	64.2	30	28	P	X	X	X	U	4
Wyoming	64.1	30	15	T		X		X	2
Idaho	63.8	3	3	P	X	X		U	8
Iowa	63.6	10	10	P	X	X	X	X	4
Rhode Island	63.5	30	30	T	X	X	X	X	5
California	63.0	7	30	P	X	X	X	X	2
Delaware	63.0	17	17	P	X		X		4
West Virginia	62.7	30	29	C		X		X	2.4
Wisconsin	62.5	1	13/20[g]	T	X	X		X	2
Oregon	62.5	1	31	P	X	X		X	None
Vermont	62.3	30	3	T					None
Maine	62.2	30	8[h]	T	X		X	X	None
New Jersey	62.0	30	40	T	X	X	X	X	4
Indiana	61.2	30	29	P	X	X		X	2
Colorado	60.8	29	32	P		X		X	2
Michigan	60.6	30	30	T	X	X	X	X	4
Kansas	59.3	1	20	C	X	X	X	X	2

New York	59.1	30	24	P	X	X		X	2
New Mexico	58.3	30	42	P	X	X		X	2
Ohio	58.1	14	13	C	X	X		X	2
Missouri	57.8	30	28	T	X	X		X	4[h]
Oklahoma	57.2	15	11	P	X	X			2/4[i]
Pennsylvania	56.6	30	31	T	X	X		X	2
Nebraska	56.3	2	11	C	X	X		X	4
Hawaii	54.2	26	26	P	X	X		U	2
Nevada	51.9	30	38	C	X	X	X		2
Florida	51.3	30	31	T	X	X		X	2
Maryland	51.1	30	29	T	X			X	5
Arizona	49.0	30	50	P	X	X		X	2
Alaska	48.9	30	30	P		X		U	4
Kentucky	48.5	30	30	T	X	X			2
Arkansas	47.9	30	20	C		X		X	4
Texas	46.2	61	30	C	X	X		U	3
Virginia	45.9	30	30	T	X				None
Mississippi	45.1	30	30	C		X			None
Louisiana	44.6	30	30	C	X	X	X		4
Tennessee	43.7	50	30	C	X		X	X	4
Alabama	43.6	11	11	C				X	None
North Carolina	43.6	4	29	P		X			4
South Carolina	38.7	30	31	C	X	X			4
Georgia	38.1	30	50	C	X	X		X	3

[a] See Appendix B for sources and coding procedures.

[b] Percentage of *citizens* of voting age who cast a ballot in the presidential election. Source: Census Bureau, "Language Minority, Illiteracy, and Voting Data Used in Making Determinations for the Voting Rights Act Amendments of 1975 (PL 94-73)," *Current Population Reports*, Series P-25, No. 627; and letter from Gilbert R. Felton, Census Bureau, Dec. 29, 1976.

[c] C = county only; T = town or city; P = precinct or neighborhood.

[d] U = universal absentee registration; X = permitted for absence and/or illness.

[e] Closing date was coded "0." Where to register was coded "P." Deputy registrars was coded "allowed." Registration office hours was coded "open 40 hours a week." Evening and/or Saturday registration was coded "required." Absentee registration was coded "universal." Years of non-voting before purging from rolls was coded "none."

[f] Only permitted if absent from county, but residing within the state, and then not by mail.

[g] Respondents living in the central cities of SMSAs under one million persons were coded "20." All other respondents were coded "13."

[h] Some intrastate variation which cannot be specifically coded.

[i] Respondents living in the central cities and suburbs of SMSAs under one million persons were coded "4." All other respondents were coded "2."

way of knowing the extent to which permissive state legislation actually is exploited at the local level. For example, many states authorize the appointment of deputy registrars. This is not the same thing as requiring the deputizing of a set number of registrars to go from door to door or sit at tables in shopping centers and student unions. Lacking knowledge of the extent to which registrars are appointed (not to mention the vigor with which they do their work), we could only distinguish between states that permit deputy registrars and those that do not. On the question of regular hours for registration offices, we classified as "irregular" all states that prescribed any schedule less than regular business hours five days a week. We combined states that required such schedules and those that did not legislate on the issue when our preliminary analysis showed no differences in turnout. States that required evening and/or Saturday office hours were separated from those that did not. (A token Saturday or two was not enough.)

In short, a great deal is often left up to local officials and the initiative of local interest groups and parties.[22] In view of these large areas of discretion, we acknowledge that our data do not necessarily describe the reality of administration and enforcement at the local level.[23] They do describe state-level enactments, which still vary considerably, as Table 4-1 shows. (Other specific coding decisions are described in the footnotes to Table 4-1.)

Estimating the Impact of Registration Laws on Turnout

Two general propositions about the effect of registration requirements on turnout are suggested by the literature on the personal costs of voting: (1) The more time and energy required to vote, the lower the probability that an individual will vote (Downs, 1957, pp. 255-56, 273). (2) The costs of voting affect some people more than others; registration laws have their greatest impact on people with less education (Wolfinger and Rosenstone, 1980).

We think that there are two explanations for the second proposition. First, more than any other personal characteristic, education increases political interest. More exposure to school produces more information about public issues and greater capacity to understand them. Therefore, better-educated people are more likely to be interested enough to overcome the inconveniences of limited office hours and earlier deadlines. Second, the bureaucratic skills acquired in school reduce the difficulty of overcoming these hurdles. In other words, the likelihood that an individual will vote is not merely a behavioral manifestation of certain individual interests. It also reflects the ease with which these individual predilections can be expressed in action. More education produces both a bigger incentive to jump the hurdle and a lower hurdle.

As Table 4-1 shows, states that have restrictive requirements in one aspect of registration are likely to have restrictive provisions in other aspects. Moreover, demographic variables such as race, region, age, and education are correlated both with the registration provisions and with turnout. Better-educated people, northerners, and whites are more likely to vote. They also tend to live in states with more permissive registration laws. To estimate the effect on turnout of a particular registration requirement, the other legal provisions and demographic variables must be held constant. Perhaps the most common technique for doing this is ordinary least squares (OLS) multiple regression. But because our dependent variable (turnout) is dichotomous, our data do not meet the usual OLS assumptions. We used probit analysis rather than multiple regression to estimate the effect of registration laws. (See Appendix C for a comparison of probit and OLS.) Like OLS, probit allows us to estimate the effect of a single independent variable on the dependent variable while holding constant all other independent variables in the equation. In the discussion that follows all estimates have been converted to probabilities.

Because of the tremendous cost of estimating a series of equations using all respondents in our sample, we took a subsample for the probit analysis.[24] We designed this subsample to maximize the variation among registration requirements, thus improving the estimates of their impact on turnout.[25] We ignored the weighting factor and, within each state, randomly selected actual respondents. For most states, we chose about 150 respondents per state.[26] (Alaska, Nevada, and Vermont each had less than 150 respondents, all of whom were selected.) Seven states with unusual combinations of registration provisions were oversampled to increase further the variation in the independent variables. Alabama, Arkansas, Georgia, Idaho, Louisiana, and Utah were oversampled by 50 percent; and all 202 respondents from North Dakota were included. The resulting subsample of

Table 4-2 Equation II Estimates of the Effect of Demographic Variables and Registration Laws on Turnout in 1972[a]

Variable	*Probit Estimate*	*Standard Error*
(Constant)	−2.7001	.2410
Education	.1847	.0120
Education squared	.0120	.0050
Age	.0707	.0045
Age squared	−.0006	.0001
Region	−.1371	.0413
Closing date	−.0073	.0015
Irregular office hours	−.1005	.0438
Open evening and/or Saturday	.1253	.0345
No absentee registration	−.0909	.0403
Hours polls open	.0336	.0159
Gubernatorial election	.0634	.0338

Number of cases = 7,936
Percentage of cases correctly predicted = 71.4
Log of the likelihood function = −4445.63
−2 times the log likelihood ratio = 1154.66
Degrees of freedom = 11

[a] Estimates for the variables deleted from this equation are given in Appendix D.

7,936 actual respondents was used in all subsequent analyses. In no way did we bias our estimates of the effects of the registration laws by using this subsample instead of the full sample. The only statistical "cost" is a slight increase in the standard error for each estimate.[27]

The demographic variables in our equation were education, age, and region. We also included squared terms for education and age to provide a better fit of the nonlinear relationship between these variables and turnout. When these variables are controlled, race does not have an independent effect on turnout.

Four registration provisions had a consequential impact on the probability of voting and were therefore included in the final equation (Equation II): (a) closing date; (b) regular hours for registration offices; (c) offices open evenings and/or Saturdays; and (d) the availability of absentee registration. Two other variables were included in the final equation because they had a small positive correlation with both the statutes and with turnout: the hours the polls were open on election day and a concurrent gubernatorial election in the state.[28] The estimated parameters of our final equation (Equation II) are in Table 4-2.

The effect of the registration provisions on the probability of *individuals* voting is summarized in Table 4-3. The provision with the largest impact is the closing date. Depending on one's probability of otherwise voting, a 30-day closing date decreased the likelihood of voting by 3 to 9 percentage points.[29] A 50-day closing date (in effect in Arizona and Georgia) lowered the probability of voting by about 17 percent for those with a 40 to 60 percent chance of going to the polls.

Variations in some other provisions also affected turnout. Irregular registration office hours (less than 40 hours a week) lowered by 2 to 4 percentage points

Table 4-3 The Effect of Registration Requirements on the Likelihood of an Individual Voting in the 1972 Election[a]

Probability of an Individual Voting (%)	*30-Day Closing Date*	*Irregular Office Hours*	*No Saturday or Evening Registration*	*No Absentee Registration*
20	−6.7	−2.9	−3.8	−2.6
30	−8.1	−3.6	−4.7	−3.2
40	−8.7	−3.9	−5.1	−3.5
50	−8.7	−4.0	−5.5	−3.6
60	−8.2	−3.8	−4.9	−3.4
70	−8.1	−3.4	−3.4	−3.1
80	−5.6	−2.9	−3.4	−2.4
90	−3.3	−1.7	−2.1	−1.5

[a] The effect on turnout of a registration provision depends on the probability that an individual would otherwise vote. The cell entry is the estimated effect of the provision on an individual with the specified probability of voting. For example, a person who was otherwise 40 percent likely to vote was 8.7 percent less likely to do so if he lived in a state with a 30-day closing date. A person who was 90 percent likely to vote was only 3.3 percent less likely to do so as a result of a 30-day closing date. These estimates were derived by using the cumulative normal distribution to evaluate the probit estimates in Table 4-2.

the probability that a person would vote. Offices closed on Saturdays and in the evening decreased by 2 to 6 percent the probability of voting. In states that did not allow any form of absentee registration the chances of voting were 2 to 4 percent lower.

Two contextual variables other than the registration laws had an independent effect on turnout. Longer voting hours increased turnout a bit. Keeping the polls open for 14 hours increased the probability of an individual voting from 1 to 3 percent. A concurrent gubernatorial election raised turnout from 1 to 2 percent. On the other hand, a concurrent senatorial contest had no discernible impact on turnout. This difference between elections for senator and governor reflects the latter office's greater capacity to generate organizational resources for get-out-the-vote drives (Wolfinger and Rosenstone, 1980).

Southerners were somewhat less likely to vote than northerners even when education, age, and the registration laws were controlled. The regional gap varied between 2 and 6 percent. In other words, the continued lower turnout in the South is not fully explained by its demographic characteristics nor by its more restrictive registration laws.

We could find no evidence to suggest that in 1972 this regional gap was due to coercion of blacks in the South. An interaction term for southern blacks was included in the analysis. Interaction terms also were entered for southern blacks with each of the registration provisions. The estimated coefficients for these variables were neither substantively nor statistically significant. Southern blacks were no less likely to vote than one would expect on the basis of their age, education, and region. Voter registration provisions in 1972 did not have an added impact on southern blacks over and above this impact on white southerners with the same age and education.

Registration Law Reform and Nationwide Turnout

The estimates described above measure the impact of registration provisions on the probability of individuals voting in the 1972 general election. The question remains what the effect would be on the level of national turnout if certain changes in the laws were adopted in every state. This cannot be learned directly from the probit estimates alone. For example, if a certain provision had a coefficient of −.10 but affected only 15 percent of the population, changing it would not have as much impact on aggregate turnout as would changing a provision that had a coefficient of −.07 but affected half the population.

To estimate the national electoral consequences of changes in the laws, we reweighted the subsample to be a representative sample of the civilian, citizen, voting-age population, excluding the District of Columbia.[30] Using Equation II, for each respondent we predicted what turnout would be if we assumed that certain registration provisions were enacted into law in every state. In each case, the projected provision was the more permissive alternative already used in some states. In other words, for each provision we assumed that every state had adopted the most permissive alternative in force in at least one state in 1972. From this estimate we subtracted the predicted turnout given the provisions as they actually existed in 1972. Summing across respondents yields an estimate of the projected aggregate change in turnout.[31]

Table 4-4 presents these projected increases in turnout for the country as a whole and for various demographic groups. The entries in each column represent the projected increase in turnout for the indicated group if the provision listed at the head of the column were adopted nationwide. The 1972 data do not allow us to estimate directly the increase in turnout that would result from allowing citizens to register *at the polls* on election day or from abolishing registration altogether. The most liberal reforms whose consequences we can estimate can be simulated by setting the registration provisions to the most permissive value existing in 1972. Therefore the "Total" column shows the total projected increase that would result from nationwide adoption of the following provisions:

a. eliminating the closing date;
b. opening registration offices during the 40 hour work week;
c. opening registration offices in the evening and/or on Saturday;
d. permitting absentee registration for the sick, disabled, and absent.

In short, Table 4-4 permits us to answer the questions about the impact of registration laws most interesting to policy makers: what will be the consequences, for what groups, of specified changes in the registration laws?

If all states adopted the provisions listed above, turnout would increase by approximately 9.1 percentage points.[32] In 1972, with a national potential electorate of about 134 million, this percentage translates into a projection that an additional 12.2 million people would have voted as a result of the indicated changes in the registration laws. We will decompose this aggregate projection in two ways: (1) To describe those changes that would have the greatest effect and those having relatively little impact; (2) to describe the types of people most affected by the changes.

As we said earlier, our findings indicate that relaxing existing provisions in some areas of registration would have no appreciable effect on turnout. In four areas, more permissive provisions would do little to increase voting.

1. *Residency Requirements.* In 1972, only two states had effective residency requirements of more than 31 days. Tennessee law produced a *de facto* 50-day requirement. In Texas, it was 61 days. Moreover, the 1970 VRAA required absentee voting in presidential elections for people who had recently moved. Our check of election codes indicates that every state had adopted such a provision by 1972. The result was that relatively few people were still affected by residency requirements. Our estimates indicate that the probability of voting in the 1972 general election was not affected by existing residency requirements anywhere. Further relaxation of residency requirements would produce no appreciable increase in voting. This represents a substantial shift from conclusions about the effect of residency requirements in 1960, and doubtless reflects the enormous legal changes since then. Present requirements, in combination with provisions for absentee voting by new residents, have made residency requirements relatively unobtrusive.

2. *Deputy Registrars.* With other variables controlled, people in states that authorize deputy registrars are no likelier to vote. Authorizing the appointment of deputy registrars in every state would not have an appreciable effect on turnout.

Table 4-4 Projected Percentage Increase in Turnout by Changing Registration Laws

	Percentage Increase in Turnout if Registration Laws Changed Everywhere to:				
	Elimination of Closing Date	*Regular Office Hours*	*Evening and/or Saturday Registration*	*Some Absentee Registration*	*Total Increase*[a]
National	6.1	.4	2.5	.5	9.1
North	5.6	.2	2.1	.2	7.8
South	7.3	.9	3.6	1.4	12.8
Whites	5.9	.4	2.4	.5	8.9
Blacks	7.2	.5	3.0	.8	11.3
Northern Whites	5.5	.2	2.1	.2	7.7
Northern Blacks	6.5	.3	2.4	.1	9.1
Southern Whites	7.2	.9	3.5	1.3	12.4
Southern Blacks	8.2	.8	3.9	1.8	14.5
Years of Education					
0-4	8.2	.5	3.3	1.0	13.2
5-7	7.9	.6	3.1	.9	12.6
8	6.9	.4	2.8	.6	10.4
9-11	7.0	.4	2.7	.6	10.4
12	6.1	.4	2.6	.5	9.3
1-3 college	5.4	.3	2.1	.4	7.8
4 college	3.8	.3	1.7	.4	5.6
5 or more college	1.9	.1	.9	.1	2.8
Family Income					
Under $2,000	7.1	.6	2.9	1.0	11.4
$2,000-7,499	6.6	.4	2.8	.6	10.1
$7,500-9,999	6.3	.4	2.6	.5	9.6
$10,000-14,999	5.8	.4	2.4	.4	8.7
$15,000-24,999	5.1	.4	2.1	.3	7.4
$25,000 and over	4.3	.3	1.7	.2	6.2
Age					
18-24	7.2	.4	2.9	.5	11.0
25-31	6.7	.4	2.8	.6	10.2
32-36	6.0	.5	2.5	.5	9.1
37-50	5.5	.4	2.2	.5	8.2
51-69	5.3	.4	2.3	.5	8.1
70-78	6.0	.3	2.1	.5	8.7
79 and over	6.8	.3	2.9	.5	10.4

[a] The number in this column is the projected increase in turnout if each of the provisions at the head of the first four columns were adopted in all states. The first four columns do not add up to the figure in the total column because the joint effect of a combination of changes is not equal to the arithmetic sum of the individual effects.

3. *Where to Register.* The location of the registrar's office does not affect the probability that people will vote. Being able to register in one's neighborhood as opposed to going to a municipal or county level office does not increase turnout.

4. *Years Before Purging.* Periodic purging from the registration rolls of those who did not vote in the previous election does not decrease the likelihood that otherwise eligible citizens will go to the polls. Allowing a citizen who fails to vote to remain on the rolls for eight years does not increase voter turnout above what it would be if he were purged from the rolls for failure to vote in a single election.

Changes in four other areas of registration laws would increase turnout, although in only one respect—the closing date—would the change be substantial.

1. *Absentee Registration.* Ten states did not permit civilian absentee registration. This affects the sick and disabled, and people who are away from home because of business, school, or vacations. Allowing civilian absentee registration for these groups will increase national turnout by about half of one percent. Nearly all this increase would be in the South.

Five states had universal civilian absentee registration, permitting anyone to register by mail, not just the absent, disabled, and sick. This plan received considerable attention in 1976 as Congress debated nationwide postcard registration. The House passed a bill for postcard registration, but only after amending it to delete authority for the government to mail the cards to every household. Thus the burden of obtaining the postcard was left on the individual, although presumably civic and political groups could distribute the cards. The House bill was similar to the system used by five states in 1972. Our estimates indicate that in 1972 this type of registration system did *not* result in higher turnout than the more limited absentee registration discussed in the preceding paragraph. Therefore it looks as if this plan would not have much effect. The crucial amendment to the House bill shifted the initiative from the government to the individual. Our data do not permit us to estimate the impact of a scheme that, like the original bill, removed from the individual the burden of initiating registration proceedings.

2. *Irregular Weekday Office Hours.* Although the location of the registrar's office does not affect the level of voter turnout, the hours it remains open does. Residents of states where registration offices are not regularly open during normal business hours are less likely to vote than are people in states where one can register any time during the business week. Allowing registration at any time during the work week would increase national turnout by about 0.4 percentage points. Turnout in the South would increase by 0.9 percent, compared to 0.2 percentage points in the North.

3. *Evening and Saturday Registration.* People living in states where registration offices are required to remain open outside normal business hours are more likely to vote than are residents of states where offices need not be open in the evening or on Saturday. Requiring evening and/or Saturday registration everywhere in the country would raise turnout by 2.5 percent.

This expansion of office hours would be most beneficial to the less educated. Turnout by people with less than five years of school would increase 3.3 percent, compared to 2.8 percent for grammar school graduates, 2.6 percent for high school graduates, and less than 2 percent for those with a college degree. Evening and/or Saturday registration would have more impact in the South. An additional 3.9 percent of southern blacks and 3.5 percent of southern whites would go to the polls. The comparable figures for the North are 2.4 and 2.1 percent.

4. *Closing Date.* Of the legal changes considered here, the one that would have the greatest impact on the level of voter turnout would be elimination of the closing date. An early closing date decreases the probability of voting. If one could register up until election day itself, when media coverage is widest and interest is greatest, turnout would increase by about 6.1 percentage points. This would have meant an additional eight million voters in 1972. If the closing date were a week before the election everywhere in the country, turnout in 1972 would have been 4.5 percent higher.

Because of the earlier closing dates in the South, people living there would be affected more than northerners by such changes. People with less schooling would benefit most if registration were permitted until election day. Turnout would increase by about 6 percentage points for those without a grammar school education, 4.6 percent for high school graduates, and just 2 percent for people with a college degree.

Our projections indicate that if all the changes summarized in Table 4-4 had been instituted throughout the country in 1972, turnout in the presidential election that year would have been 9.1 percent higher. This represents 12.2 million additional voters if the registration laws everywhere had been as lenient as in the most permissive states. (With a seven-day closing date, the total increase in turnout would have been 7.7 percent.)

Variations in the Effect of Registration Laws

We have already seen that the effect of relaxing registration laws would not be felt evenly across the population. One reason, of course, is that the gap between the status quo and uniformly permissive provisions is much greater in some places than in others. In 1972 few states came close to the hypothetical permissive situation assumed in Table 4-4.[33] The laws in the southern states would undergo the biggest change. Therefore making registration easier would have the greatest impact in that part of the country. If all four provisions described in Table 4-4 were enacted, turnout in the South would increase by approximately 12.8 percentage points while turnout in the North would go up by about 7.8 percent. This difference between the regions is caused by two factors. First, as observed in Table 4-1, the southern states presently have more restrictive statutes than the rest of the country. Therefore easing the laws would cause greater changes in the South. Second, since those with fewer years of formal education would benefit most from the changes and since the South has a lower mean level of education than the northern states, a greater percentage of southerners would benefit from the changes.

Within the South, the projected increases in turnout for blacks and whites are relatively similar. Whites would vote 12.4 percent more, while black turnout in the South would go up by 14.5 percentage points. In the North, where the gap between the races in educational attainment is smaller, there is less racial difference in projected turnout. An additional 7.7 percent of northern whites would go to the polls, compared to a gain in turnout of 9.1 percent for the blacks.

The most striking variations in the effects of registration reform would be among people at different levels of education.[34] Liberalizing registration provisions would have by far the greatest impact on the least educated, and relatively little effect on well-educated people. Turnout would increase 10.2 percent among people with less than five years of school, by 10.4 percent among elementary school graduates, 9.3 percent among those with a high school diploma, and only 2.8 percent among people with some postgraduate schooling.

Seeing how the costs of voting affect some people more than others aids our understanding of variations in the importance of politics to individual citizens. Before examining this subject, we can dispose of an alternative explanation for the greater impact of restrictive registration laws on the uneducated: that education is in large measure a surrogate for income and occupation. Better-off people, so the argument might go, have more free time for nonessentials like registering and voting, while the harried low-income worker cannot afford long journeys during business hours. But the impact of the laws diminishes with every increment in education. High school graduates and college dropouts are no more able to take time off from work than the less-educated citizens whose behavior is most affected by the laws. A couple of years of college do not admit one to the leisure class. Moreover, data on time use show that blue-collar workers have slightly *more* free time than executives, professionals, and other white-collar people (Robinson and Converse, 1972, pp. 74-75; see also Wolfinger and Rosenstone 1980, for more discussion of the relationship between free time and turnout).

It is useful to ponder the costs and benefits of voting, and how they are distributed in the population. The appeal of participating in an election increases with education, and the costs of doing so vary inversely with education. It is little wonder, then, that apparently trivial increments in the burden of registering may raise the cost of voting above the threshold of many people. We see that threshold established by two factors: the individual's level of interest in the election, and his ability to manage the procedural steps required to cast a ballot.

Formal education increases one's capacity for understanding and working with complex, abstract, and intangible subjects (that is, subjects like politics). Acquisition of these skills and facts heightens interest in politics. Schooling also imparts experience with bureaucratic relationships and such simple information-seeking skills as looking up a necessary item in a book. Irrespective of one's degree of political interest, this heightened level of understanding and information would also reduce the costs of registering, even in the most restrictive state. In short, education is likely to increase interest in politics and reduce the costs of manifesting that interest by voting.

The more permissive the registration laws, the lower the time, energy, and information costs of voting. This is of greatest benefit to people whose interest is not sufficient to carry them across the higher threshold imposed by more restrictive provisions. The costs imposed by restrictive laws might be trifling to an educated person, and increasingly daunting to those with little schooling.

Thus for someone who is interested in politics, can anticipate the need for registration before the peak excitement of election eve, and can easily locate the registrar's office, registration is a relatively costless act. On the other hand, for someone whose interest is aroused only a few days before the election, has minimal exposure to information, and is less adept at learning things like places and hours of registration, the whole process is a much more difficult hurdle. The barriers imposed by restrictive laws seem to make little difference to the well-educated, but are a fairly formidable impediment to people with less interest and bureaucratic skill. To put it another way, the difference in turnout produced by variations in registration laws is an indication of the varying commitment and capacity to vote of different kinds of people.

The Political Consequences of Registration Law Reform

Liberalizing the registration laws would expand the electorate and would increase disproportionately the turnout of low-income groups. Because of this differential impact, most scholars, journalists, and politicians have assumed that easier registration would markedly change the social class composition of the electorate. The result would be a less interested and knowledgeable voting population and a windfall of votes for the Democratic party.[35] The prevailing view is expressed in conservative columnist James Kilpatrick's comment on President Carter's election-day registration plan: "The thinly disguised ulterior motive [for Carter's proposal], freely if privately conceded on Capitol Hill, is to benefit the Democratic party. This is a political power play, as brazen as any stunt ever pulled in the bad old days of Tammany Hall. . . ." [36] It seems safe to conclude that these fears help explain Republican and southern Democratic opposition to legislative proposals for making registration easier.

To the extent that such assumptions have an empirical base, it consists of findings about the types of people whose turnout would be most affected by liberalized registration provisions. What is overlooked is the elementary (if not obvious) statistical point that the politically significant facts are not rates of change, but whether the expanded electorate resulting from registration law reform would be politically different from the smaller actual electorate.

Using Equation II we have projected what the demographic, partisan, and ideological composition of the electorate would have been in 1972 if the registration provisions assumed in Table 4-4 were instituted nationally. We have compared these projections to the composition of the actual electorate, in order to estimate how the electorate would change as a result of making registration easier.[37] The demographic comparisons, based on our original Census sample, are summarized in Table 4-5. Tables 4-6 and 4-7 compare the two electorates with respect to party identification and attitudes on various issues. They are based on data from the 1972 National Election Study of the Center for Political Studies of the University of Michigan.[38] All three tables lead to the same conclusion: the expanded electorate produced by relaxing registration laws would be remarkably similar to the smaller, actual electorate.

Table 4-5 Composition of the Actual 1972 Electorate and of the Projected Electorate After Relaxation of Registration Laws

	Northern Electorate		*Southern Electorate*		*Total Electorate*	
	Actual	*Projected*	*Actual*	*Projected*	*Actual*	*Projected*
Years of Education						
0-4	1.4%	1.6%	3.9%	4.6%	2.0%	2.4%
5-7	3.7	4.0	6.9	7.8	4.4	4.9
8	9.6	9.9	6.1	6.5	8.8	9.1
9-11	14.5	14.9	14.3	15.0	14.5	14.9
12	38.9	39.0	36.5	36.5	38.4	38.3
1-3 college	16.8	16.4	15.2	14.6	16.4	16.0
4 college	8.4	8.0	10.5	9.5	8.9	8.4
5+ college	6.7	6.2	6.5	5.6	6.7	6.1
	100.0%	100.0%	99.9%	100.1%	100.1%	100.1%
Family income						
Under $2,000	4.2%	4.4%	7.7%	8.1%	5.0%	5.3%
$2,000-7,499	28.9	29.4	35.9	37.0	30.5	31.3
$7,500-9,999	14.5	14.6	13.0	13.2	14.1	14.3
$10,000-14,999	28.7	28.6	23.8	23.2	27.6	27.3
$15,000-24,999	18.0	17.6	15.4	14.5	17.4	16.8
$25,000 and over	5.7	5.5	4.3	3.9	5.4	5.1
	100.0%	100.0%	100.1%	99.9%	100.0%	100.1%
Race						
Whites	92.5%	92.3%	87.2%	86.3%	91.3%	90.8%
Non-whites	7.5	7.7	12.8	13.7	8.7	9.1
	100.0%	100.0%	100.0%	100.0%	100.0%	99.9%
Age						
18-24	14.6%	15.4%	12.5%	13.9%	14.1%	15.0%
25-31	13.9	14.1	15.4	15.7	14.2	14.5
32-36	9.0	8.9	9.5	9.4	9.1	9.1
37-50	25.5	24.9	26.5	25.6	25.7	25.1
51-69	28.1	27.6	27.3	26.6	28.0	27.3
70-78	6.7	6.7	5.7	5.7	6.5	6.4
79 and over	2.3	2.4	3.0	3.1	2.4	2.5
	100.1%	100.0%	99.9%	100.0%	100.0%	99.9%

The largest increases would occur in demographic categories. With more permissive registration laws, the electorate would include slightly larger proportions of groups that traditionally vote less. The change, such as it is, would be greatest in the South. In 1972, people who had not graduated from high school comprised 29.7 percent of the nationwide electorate. Relaxing registration provisions would have increased their share of the electorate by 1.6 percent. In the North, this category would have accounted for an additional 1.2 percent of the voting population. In the South, the increase would be 2.7 percent. *This latter figure is the largest shift in the composition of the electorate that we could find in any descriptive category.* College-educated voters would account for a correspondingly smaller share of the electorate, down from 31.9 to 30.6 percent in the North, from 32.2 to 29.7 percent in the South, and 32 to 30.5 percent in the country as a whole.

Differences in income are generally more important to political choice than are educational cleavages, and here the impact of registration reform would be even smaller. The proportion of the national electorate comprised of people with annual family incomes of less than $10,000 would increase by 1.3 percent. The gain would be 0.8 percent in the North and 1.4 percent in the South.

Projected changes in the racial composition of the electorate would be smaller still. Non-whites would comprise an additional 0.3 percent of the national electorate. The increase would be 0.2 percent in the North and 0.9 percent in the South.

Finally, the proportion of the national electorate comprised of people under the age of 32 would increase from 28.3 percent to 29.5 percent. The increase would be 1.1 percent in the North and 1.7 percent in the South.

In sum, making it easier for people to register, although it would increase turnout, would have a very small impact on the demographic composition of the electorate. Voters in the aggregate would be marginally less educated, poorer, blacker, and younger. These changes would be somewhat greater in the South.

Some people have speculated that, with a bigger share of the electorate young, poor, and uneducated, voters would be substantially less interested in politics (Polsby and Wildavsky, p. 76, pp. 239-41; Key, 1964, p. 590). As one might suspect on the basis of the demographic projections just summarized, changes in this regard would be very modest.[39] Liberalizing registration laws would increase by 0.6 percent the proportion of the electorate who have hardly any interest in the campaign. An additional 0.8 percent of the electorate would be comprised of those who follow politics only now and then or hardly at all. The electorate's level of attentiveness to politics would not be significantly altered by relaxing voter registration laws.

These findings about the minimal changes in the demographic composition of the electorate are inconsistent with the general belief that easier registration laws would be a major boon for Democrats. Our projection, in Table 4-6, confirms doubts about the validity of the conventional wisdom. The partisan composition of the hypothetical expanded electorate would be virtually identical to that of the actual electorate. In 1972, 36.4 percent of those voting were aligned with the Republican party, as outright identifiers or Independents who said they were "closer to" the Republicans.[40] With more liberal registration laws, Republicans would comprise 35.9 percent of the electorate—a wholly insignificant shift. The Democratic windfall would be equally trivial—a gain of 0.3 percent. The comparative popularity of McGovern and Nixon would be identical in the actual and hypothetical electorates.[41]

Although the partisan balance of the electorate would not be affected by registration reform, is it possible that these changes would increase the voting

Table 4-6 Partisan Composition of the Actual and Projected Electorates in 1972

Party Identification	*Actual Electorate*	*Projected Electorate*
Strong Democrat	14.6%	14.7%
Weak Democrat	25.3	25.5
Independent Democrat	11.2	11.2
Independent	12.4	12.6
Independent Republican	10.9	10.9
Weak Republican	14.2	14.0
Strong Republican	11.3	11.0
	99.9%	100.0%
(N)	(1,809)	(2,044)

strength of people with particular attitude configurations? It has been suggested, for example, that this would result in more ballot strength for people who are liberal on economic issues but conservative on social and racial issues. Comparing the actual and hypothetical electorates on a number of issue attitudes measured in the 1972 Michigan study, we found traces of this pattern, but the differences were inconsistent and invariably tiny. Some comparisons of attitude distributions in the actual and projected electorates are presented in Table 4-7. This table reports the *largest* differences we found on issues.

With the electorate expanded through permissive registration, the proportion of voters who say that the federal government should see that everyone has a job and an adequate standard of living would increase by 0.3 percentage points. Support for government-sponsored health insurance would increase by 0.1 percent. The effect of registration reform on voters' support for social welfare issues, in short, would be negligible.

Virtually the same can be said of other issue domains. The expanded electorate would include 0.7 percent more people who think the federal government should shun involvement in school integration, and 0.3 percent more opponents of school busing. The picture is the same on "social issues." Support for the proposition that woman's place is in the home would increase by half a percentage point. Opponents of legalized marijuana would make up an additional 0.6 percent. The proportion of voters who identify themselves as liberals would remain unchanged. In short, the ideological composition of the expanded electorate would be virtually identical to that of the actual electorate in 1972.

Table 4-7 Issue Attitudes of the Actual and Projected Electorates in 1972

	Actual Electorate	*Projected Electorate*
Government should see everyone has a job and good standard of living	30.4%	30.7%
Middle of the road	23.9	23.7
People should get ahead on own	45.7	45.6
	100.0	100.0
Federal government should ensure school integration	44.7%	44.0%
Government should stay out of this issue	55.3	56.0
	100.0	100.0
Legalize marijuana	22.7%	22.3%
Middle of the road	11.3	11.1
Increase penalties for use	66.0	66.6
	100.0	100.0
Women deserve equal role in business and government	50.0%	49.7%
Middle of the road	20.8	20.7
Women's place is in the home	29.2	29.6
	100.0	100.0
Self-described liberals	25.8%	25.8%
Moderates	36.2	36.5
Conservatives	38.0	37.7
	100.0	100.0

Conclusions

We have found that if every state had had registration laws in 1972 as permissive as those in the most permissive states, turnout would have been about nine percentage points higher in the presidential election. Registration provisions have most effect on the least educated.

The political consequences of registration law reform are measured by comparing the actual electorate to the hypothetical electorate estimated by projecting rates of change in turnout. This comparison shows that relaxing registration requirements would produce a voting population very similar to the actual 1972 electorate. The electorate would be expanded with virtually no change in its demographic, partisan, or ideological characteristics. It would be bigger but not different.

How should we assess the significance of our findings about the effect of laws on turnout? Is a nine percent increase in voter turnout disappointingly small, or gratifyingly substantial? Measured against the rhetoric of some champions of voter registration reform, nine percent is fairly small potatoes. But political rhetoric is seldom a good yardstick for policy analysis.

The changes we have considered are within a narrow compass of alternatives. One question that remains is how much national voter turnout would increase if the burden for registration shifted from the individual to the government. What would be the increase in turnout if, as in most democracies, the government took the initiative for registering voters by establishing national voter lists through a door-to-door canvass or by mailing postcards to all citizens? Our data do not allow us to make a precise estimate of the impact of a registration system in which the government bore responsibility for establishing voter eligibility and where virtually all the costs of registering were removed from the individual. Given the results that would be achieved by the relatively minor changes discussed above, we are confident that establishing a European-type registration system would increase voter turnout substantially more than nine percent.

We should note that the registration laws are not the only environmental variables affecting turnout. The modern peak of voter turnout was reached in 1960, when one- and two-year residency requirements, poll taxes, and literacy tests were common; and when millions of southern blacks were disenfranchised through maladministration of the laws. Since then all these barriers have been removed, the nation's educational level has risen substantially, and turnout has fallen. The 18-year-old vote does not explain the drop in turnout. Other aspects of the political environment clearly are at work. This caution, however, should not distract us from the finding of this paper that registration laws have a substantial effect on the number of people who go to the polls on election day.

Appendix A
Samples for the Study of Turnout

Estimates of turnout in sample surveys are always somewhat higher than those based on the total number of ballots cast by the aggregate voting-age population. Since 1948, reported turnout in sample surveys has ranged between 5 percent and 17 percent higher than the aggregate estimates.[42] The 1972 election is no exception, as Table 4-A demonstrates. The commonly cited aggregate turnout figure is 55.4 percent, while reported turnout from our Current Population Survey sample is 66.7 percent, a gap of 11.3 percent. The turnout reported by the Michigan study is 72.8 percent, 17.4 percent above the aggregate estimate.

Observers of this persistent gap between survey reports and "the real figure" sometimes jump to the conclusion that the discrepancy reflects only misreporting by respondents reluctant to admit that they did not do their civic duty. This is only one of a number of contributing factors, however. First, it should be understood that the aggregate percentage *underestimates* turnout. The denominator of the percentage is an estimate of the total number of people of voting age.[43] This includes millions of people who are ineligible to vote: aliens, inmates of prisons and mental institutions, and ex-convicts, who cannot vote in many states.[44] If noncitizens are removed from the denominator of the aggregate computation, the turnout estimate rises from 55.4 to 56.7 percent. The numerator of the aggregate percentage represents the total number of valid counted votes for

Table 4-A Estimates of Voter Turnout in the 1972 General Election

	Estimated Voter Turnout
Proportion of voting age population casting votes for president[a]	55.4%
Proportion of citizens of voting age casting votes for president[b]	56.7
Current Population Survey[c]	66.7
Center for Political Studies National Election Study[d]	72.8

[a] Bureau of the Census, "Projection of the Population of Voting Age for States: November 1974," *Current Population Reports*, Series P-25, No. 526, September 1974, p. 8, Table 3. The number of votes cast is based upon: U.S. Congress, Clerk of the House, *Statistics of the Presidential and Congressional Election, 1972.*

[b] Letter to authors from Gilbert R. Felton, Population Division of the Bureau of the Census, 29 December 1976.

[c] *Current Population Reports*, Series P-20, No. 253, our analysis. (We excluded from the sample noncitizens and cases where the respondent did not know if a vote had been cast. This produced a weighted N of 128,582 cases.)

[d] Variable 0477 (N = 2,283).

a president. This excludes people who cast a spoiled ballot (they think they voted, but their vote is not counted), those who go to the polls but do not vote for president, and people whose votes for miscellaneous write-in candidates are not tallied. The best available estimates indicate that 2 to 3 million people are "uncounted voters."[45]

Survey estimates of turnout are also inflated by sample design. Most surveys do not include some categories of people who are eligible to vote but rather unlikely to do so. Students in dormitories, people living on military reservations in the United States, and inmates of institutions for the elderly are all left out of the Census sample. The institutional population amounted to 5.8 million people in 1970. In addition to such deliberate exclusions, surveys consistently tend to undersample some demographic groups with low turnout rates, and to oversample others which are more likely to vote.[46]

Finally, there is the problem of response error, generally in the form of respondents falsely claiming that a vote was cast. One estimate of overreporting, based on a comparison of 1964 survey responses with the voting records, suggested that response error was about 8 percent.[47] Clearly, some response error exists in our data, although we cannot say just how much. We feel safe assuming that the response error is uncorrelated with the registration statutes. On the basis of the foregoing discussion, however, we caution readers against assuming that overreporting is the sole cause of the discrepancy between our estimated turnout and the aggregate figure.

The additional discrepancy of 6.1 percent between reported turnout in the Census survey and the Michigan Center for Political Studies survey can be attributed to three factors.[48] First, the Census Bureau had a higher interview completion rate. In 1972 the Census completed interviews with 93.7 percent of those selected for its sample, compared to 84.4 percent for the post-election interview in the Michigan study.[49] Respondents whose post-election interviews could not be completed tended to come from groups with lower turnout rates (Campbell et al., 1960, p. 95; Clausen, 1968-69, pp. 592-93). Second, the sample includes the "rooming-house population," a low-turnout group excluded from the Michigan sample. Third, the Census has a few political questions only in the November interview, compared to the heavily political content of the pre- and post-election interviews conducted by the Michigan study. This raises the possibility that some Michigan respondents were politically stimulated by the pre-election interview, a possibility that is precluded in the Census study (Kraut and McConahay, 1973; Yalch, 1976). Needless to say, these three points of difference suggest further advantages of the Census survey for estimating voter turnout.

Appendix B
Description of the Variables and Coding Procedures

Individual Level Data

All individual level data were taken from the November 1972 Bureau of the Census Current Population Survey described above.

Turnout: Did not vote = 0; Voted = 1.

Region: North = 0; South = 1 (Alabama, Arkansas, Florida, Georgia, Louisiana, Mississippi, North Carolina, South Carolina, Tennessee, Texas and Virginia).

Race: Whites = 0; Non-whites = 1.

Education: 0-4 years = 1; 5-7 years = 2; 8 years = 3; 9-11 years = 4; 12 years = 5, 1-3 years of college = 6; 4 years of college = 7; 5 + years of college = 8.

Age: The number coded was the actual age of the respondent. (People over the age of 99 were coded "99" by the Bureau of the Census.)

Registration Provisions

Residency Requirement: The coding was done so that the variable is the *de facto* residency requirement in the state. By this we mean the following: If a state has no residency requirement but the last day new residents can register is 30 days before the election, then the state has a 30-day *de facto* residency requirement. Even though there is no explicit residency requirement, new residents must have been in the state at least 30 days prior to the election in order to register. This state is coded as having a 30-day *de facto* residency requirement, not a zero day requirement. Similarly a state that had a closing date of 30 days but a special provision for new residents to register up to 7 days before the election, was coded as having a 7-day *de facto* residency requirement.

Closing Date: The number coded was the number of days before the election on which a resident could last register to vote.

Where to Register: County office only = 1; Other = 0. Precinct or neighborhood locations below the town level = 1; Other = 9.

Deputy Registrars: Allowed = 0; Not allowed = 1.

Monday through Friday Registration Office Hours: Regular Hours (40 hours a week, every week) = 0; Irregular Hours = 1.

Evening and/or Saturday Registration Hours: Not required = 0; Regularly required = 1.

Absentee Registration by Mail: Permitted for ill, disabled and/or absent from voting unit = 0; None permitted = 1. Universal absentee registration = 1; Other = 0.

Years Before Purging: The number of years of non-voting after which one's name is removed from the registration rolls. Number of years coded = 2-8; No purging = 8. (Our preliminary estimates were made using two variables. The first was coded 2-8 years, with no purging coded 0. A separate dummy variable was included (1 = no purging) to estimate this category. There is no significant loss of information by using the single variable described above.

Other Variables

Hours Polls Open: The number coded was the number of hours the polls are open on election day.

Gubernatorial Election: No concurrent gubernatorial election = 0; Gubernatorial election = 1.

Senatorial Election: Concurrent senatorial election = 0; No senatorial election = 1.

Appendix C
Probit Analysis

In the probit model the conditional probability of voting $p(x)$ is defined as

$$p(x) = F(\beta_0 + \beta_1 + \ldots + \beta_n X_n$$

or, equivalently,

$$F(p(x)) \quad \beta_0 + \beta_1 X + \ldots + \beta_n X_n$$

where $F(\quad)$ represents the value of the cumulative standard normal distribution. Using numerical maximum methods (because the normal equations are non-linear in the parameters) the parameters β_0, $\beta_1 \ldots, \beta_n$, can be estimated.

Figure 4-1 illustrates the differences between the OLS model and the probit model. The OLS model assumes a linear relationship between the parameters and the probability of voting; a unit increase in an independent variable has the same impact on the probability of voting regardless of the values of the other independent variables. For example, consider an OLS equation in which a registration requirement (represented by a dummy variable) has a coefficient of −.13. We would conclude that living under this requirement decreases the probability of voting by 13 percent (—.13 x 1 x 100%). That is, a person who is otherwise 90 percent likely to vote would have a probability of voting of 77 percent as a result of this statute. The effect would be the same for everyone; a probability of voting of 60 percent would be reduced to 47 percent; a 40 percent probability would now be 27 percent; and a person who is otherwise 10 percent likely to vote would have a probability of voting of −.03!

As we have argued, there is reason to believe that the impact of registration statutes on the probability of voting is not constant across all individuals. Rather, the effect varies with the probability that the individual would otherwise vote. A college graduate who is 90 percent likely to vote is much less affected by a

Figure 4-1

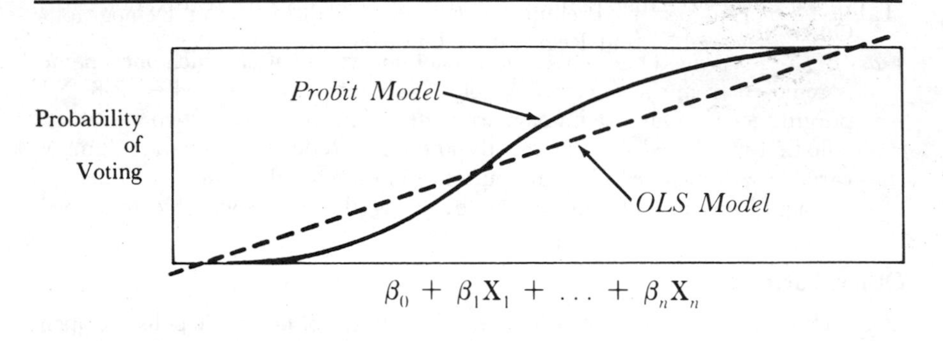

registration statute than a high school dropout who is only 55 percent likely to vote.

The probit model takes this into account. Returning to our previous example, suppose the registration requirement had an estimated probit coefficient of −.13. Among those people who are either 10 percent likely to vote or 90 percent likely to vote, the probability of voting would decrease by approximately 2 percent. Among those who are between 40 and 60 percent likely to vote, the probability of voting would decrease by approximately 5 percent. The variable has the smallest impact on those who are either least likely to vote or nearly certain to vote. It has the greatest impact in the middle of the distribution, on those who are between 40 and 60 percent likely to vote.

As one can see, a probit equation is not as easy to interpret as the familiar OLS equation. Unlike OLS, the probit coefficient does not directly represent an estimate of the amount of change in the dependent variable resulting from a unit increase in the independent variable. Rather, with probit analysis, the coefficient is an estimate of the amount of change on the cumulative standard normal distribution that would result from a change in one unit in the independent variable, with the other variables held constant. This value is then easily converted to a probability.

There are ways to compensate for the linearity of the coefficients in the OLS model. The most common approach is the inclusion of interaction terms which allow the effect of one independent variable to vary with the value of another independent variable. However, two problems still remain.

As suggested by our example and by Figure 4-1, with an OLS equation the predicted probability of voting will not necessarily be confined to the 0-1 interval. That is, with OLS some values of the independent variables may yield estimated probabilities that are less than 0 or greater than 1. The probit estimates are always between 0 and 1.

Second, with OLS the error variance is not constant across all observations. The variance of the residuals will be small for predicted probabilities close to either 0 or 1 while the variance will be much larger for predictions between .4 and .6. As a result, the OLS estimates are inefficient. See Finney (1971); Goldberger (1964, pp. 248-51); Cox (1970, pp. 1-29); Hanushek and Jackson (1977, Chapter 7); and Aldrich and Cnudde (1975).

Appendix D

Table 4-D Equation I—Preliminary Estimates of the Effect of Demographic Variables and Registration Laws on Turnout in 1972

Variable	*Probit Estimate*	*Standard Error*
(Constant)	−2.7646	.2740
Education	.1838	.0451
Education squared	.0121	.0050
Age	.0706	.0045
Age squared	−.0006	.0001
Race	−.0189	.0549
Region	−.1279	.0546
Residency requirement	.0025	.0018
Closing date	−.0089	.0021
No deputy registrars	.0161	.0448
Irregular office hours	−.1540	.0547
Open evening and/or Saturday	.01271	.0398
Years before purging	.0098	.0105
Register only at county seat	−.0165	.0494
Register in neighborhood	.0564	.0484
No absentee registration	−.1054	.0421
Universal absentee registration	−.0891	.0627
Hours polls open	.0357	.0175
Gubernatorial election	.0441	.0369
No Senatorial election	−.0293	.0385

Log of the likelihood function = −4442.82
−2 times the log likelihood ratio = 1160.27
Degrees of freedom = 19
Number of cases = 7936

NOTES

1. Senator Gale McGee, *Congressional Record,* 13 March 1975, p. S6451. For other claims by politicians, see *Voter Registration by Postcard;* and the speeches by Senators McGee, Kennedy, Cranston, Williams, Montoya, and Humphrey on March 13, reported on pp. S6450-54 of the *Congressional Record.* Probably the most active and pervasive interest group working to loosen registration laws is the League of Women Voters. See, for example, *Administrative Obstacles to Voting,* Pub. No. 206 (Washington: League of Women Voters of the United States, 1972). The Yankelovich polling organization suggested that registration laws kept 26 million people from the polls in 1972. This figure is an extrapolation from the survey respondents who told interviewers that they would have voted if they had not had to register. "A Study of the Registration Process in the United States (The Registered and the Non Registered)" by Daniel Yankelovich, Inc. for The Student Vote, Inc., 1973, p. 23.

2. Similar bills were introduced in 1971, 1973, and 1975. All of them foundered on opposition by Republicans and southern Democrats.
3. A description of sampling procedures and other technical matters is in Bureau of the Census, "Voting and Registration in the Election of November 1972," *Current Population Reports, Population Characteristics,* October 1973, Series P-20, No. 253. We obtained the data tape from the Inter-University Consortium for Political Research. Neither the ICPR nor the Census Bureau is responsible for our tabulations and analyses.
4. *Harper* v. *Virginia State Board of Elections,* 383 U.S. 663 (1966).
5. *Dunn* v. *Blumstein,* 405 U.S. 330 (1972).
6. *Marston* v. *Lewis,* 410 U.S. 679 (1973); and *Burns* v. *Fortson,* 410 U.S. 686 (1973).
7. Campbell, Converse, Miller, Stokes (1960, p. 277). The only legal variables studied were residency requirements and literacy tests in the North, and poll taxes and residency in the South (p. 269). Legal variables seemed to have more impact on blacks in the South, but the small number of cases precluded controls for education (pp. 279-80). For a similar conclusion, see Milbrath (1965, p. 47).
8. Report of the President's Commission on Registration and Voting Participation, November 1963, p. 13. Campbell and his associates said that residency requirements "prevented at least 3 percent of our respondents from voting." (1960, p. 90n).
9. Some of the legal variables were assigned numerical values on the basis of the researchers' "guesses" about their impact on registration (Kelley et al., 1967, 366n.).
10. Kelley et al., (1967, pp. 373-74). Another study concluded that registration laws explained a good deal of the variations in turnout among the states in 1960. See Kim et al., 1975.
11. Kelley et al., 1967, recognized that "inter-city analysis is less appropriate for an examination of the effects on registration of individual characteristics such as sex, age, education, and income, which can be better studied by treating the individual as the unit of observation" (p. 362).
12. Another unsatisfactory approach is asking respondents why they were not registered. Answers to this question are in our data set. We tabulated the registration laws in each respondent's state of residence with the reasons offered for failure to register. The result is disillusioning for anyone who believes that human motivation can be discerned by asking people to explain their behavior. We found no relationship between the objective permissiveness of the laws and the proportion of respondents who said they were unregistered because they could not satisfy the residency requirement or had been unable to register. For example, in states where registration offices were required to remain open at night or on Saturday, 15 percent of those who were not registered attributed this condition to their inability to register, compared to 14 percent who gave this excuse where such extended hours were not required.
13. One recent study comparing turnout in the 1960 and 1972 elections is Ashenfelter and Kelley (1976). This article uses data on 925 cases drawn from the University of Michigan Center for Political Studies' national sample survey of the 1972 election. The estimates of the effect of registration laws are imprecise, perhaps because of the limitations of the Michigan sample for this purpose.
14. In 1962, five percent of the black voting-age population of Mississippi and 13 percent in Alabama were registered to vote. Ten years later the figures were 59 percent and 55 percent. Sources: for 1962, Peirce (1974); for 1972, Lewis and Allen (1972, p. 119).
15. Data on turnout come from replies to this item: "This month we have some questions about whether people voted in the November 7th Presidential Election. Did (you) (this person) vote in the election held on November 7th?" For almost half the sample turnout data were provided by the respondent for another family member. Such second-hand interviewing raises the possibility of misreporting, as Tufte (1977, p.

306) suggests. This fear seems unjustified, however. Respondents who reported their own vote had a turnout rate of 66.7 percent. People in the sample for whom voting was reported by another family member had a turnout rate of 67.7 percent. We also estimated the effect of second-hand reporting by entering a dummy variable (1 = second-hand reporting) in the probit equation summarized in Table 4-2. The resulting estimate was .007 with a standard error of .010. This number is substantially zero, and no change occurred in the coefficients reported in Table 4-2. In short, we feel justified in assuming that any errors in the reporting of turnout (whether first-hand or second-hand reports) are uncorrelated with registration provisions.

16. The weighting procedure is described in Bureau of the Census, "Documentation of the Annual Demographic File," 1975, Appendix A, pp. 4-12.
17. *CPS 1972 American National Election Study* (Ann Arbor, Michigan: Center for Political Studies, 1973), Variable 4.
18. Bureau of the Census, "Voting and Registration in the Election of November 1972," p. 13. For additional information on sampling procedures see Bureau of the Census, *Current Population Survey: A Report on Methodology,* Technical Paper No. 7, U.S. Department of Commerce, 1963; and "Documentation of the Annual Demographic File," Appendix A; and Center for Political Studies, *1972 Study,* p. xii.
19. Information on sampling error in the Census survey and the procedures for adjusting the standard error of estimates for groups of states below the regional level can be found in "Documentation of the Annual Demographic File," Appendix A, pp. 13-45, 62-66; and "Voting and Registration in the Election of November 1972," pp. 13-16.
20. U.S. Senate, Committee on Post Office and Civil Service, as reported in the *Congressional Record,* 8 March 1972, pp. 7530-31; Robert Thornton, "Election Legislation," in *The Book of the States, 1972-73,* 19 (Lexington, Ky.: Council of State Governments, 1972), pp. 25-30; Reitman and Davidson (1972); and League of Women Voters Education Fund, "Registration and Absentee Voting Procedures by State, 1972" (Washington, D.C., 1972).
21. One exception is the list compiled by the Congressional Research Service. Printed just after *Dunn* v. *Blumstein,* this publication claims that every state's residency requirement is governed by the 1970 VRAA for presidential elections and by *Dunn* for other elections. This blanket description proved to be wide of the mark. See Library of Congress, Congressional Research Service, *Election Laws of the Fifty States and the District of Columbia,* April 1972.
22. In Arizona, for example, a recent county registrar of voters required prospective deputy registrars to take a rigorously graded examination. His successor brought about a substantial increase in the number of registrars by relaxing these standards. (We are indebted to Bruce B. Mason of Arizona State University for this information.)
23. The frequent erroneous responses in our mail survey of state election officials suggest that it would be virtually impossible to gather accurate information on how state laws are administered in the nation's thousands of counties and cities.
24. Using the entire sample would have required about 50 *minutes* of computer time for each probit equation estimated. Although we did not use all respondents for the crucial stage of our analysis, it should be noted that a national sample of such magnitude is necessary to provide adequate state-by-state subsamples.
25. Other things being equal, increasing the variance decreases the standard error of the estimate (Theil, 1971, pp. 90-91; Finney, 1971, pp. 33-37).
26. We excluded respondents in the District of Columbia from all data analyses reported hereafter. Since their franchise is limited and an inordinate number of District residents maintain legal voting residences elsewhere, we thought we would avoid unnecessary complications.

27. See Theil (1971, chap. 8). All probit equations were estimated on the subsample of 7,936 actual respondents. While the case weight provided by the Census Bureau should be applied for descriptive purposes (e.g. cross tabulations), it is not appropriate to apply it for purposes of estimation (Koch, Freeman, and Freeman, 1975; Porter, 1973).
28. Our initial analysis also included these variables: (a) the number of days before the election an absentee ballot had to be obtained; (b) whether the absentee ballot had to be notarized; and (c) whether voting machines were used. These variables had less than a one percent impact on the probability of voting and their coefficients were not statistically significant. We deleted them after this early stage of the analysis.

    In addition, estimates were made for nonlinear functions of the residency requirement and closing date. This did not appreciably improve the fit. We also estimated interaction terms between each provision and education, between deputy registrars and county registration, and between deputy registrars and irregular office hours. All were insignificant.

    Finally, we examined the independent effect on turnout of income and party competition. Poorer people, of course, are less likely to vote, and party competition is often said to result in higher turnout. Thus any estimates of the relationship between registration laws and turnout that omitted consideration of these two variables might lead to a spurious conclusion.

    We used the following procedure to determine whether these two variables in the error term should be included in the analysis. For one of these variables to bias the coefficient of a particular registration provision (which we will call X_1), two conditions had to be met: After controlling for the other independent demographic variables, the variable in question had to be correlated both with X_1 and with turnout. If either of these conditions were not met (i.e., if one of the partial correlations was zero), then the variable could safely be left out of the analysis without biasing the estimated coefficient for variable X.

    Using this procedure, we found that income was not correlated with any registration provision, once education, region, and age had been controlled. The average magnitude of the partial correlations of the registration provisions was .029. The partial correlation between competition and turnout was −.009. Therefore, excluding these variables from Equation II does not bias the estimated coefficients for the registration laws. The measure of party competition we used was adopted from Ranney (1972, p. 87).
29. As explained in Appendix C, the estimated effect of an independent variable in probit analysis depends on the probability that the individual would otherwise vote.
30. This reweighting was accomplished by multiplying, for each case, the original weight by the inverse of the sub-sampling proportion for the state from which the case was selected. This yields a reweighted N of 126,591. This number is slightly less than the weighted N mainly because respondents from the District of Columbia were deleted from the probit analysis and secondarily because of the random selection of cases in the sub-sampling procedure.
31. For each respondent, Equation II was used to compute a probit estimate which was then converted to a probability by evaluating that number on the cumulative standard normal distribution. (The International Mathematical and Statistical Library includes a fortran subroutine which will compute this value.) The same procedure was followed, altering the values for the variables in Equation II to simulate changes in the registration provisions. For each respondent these two probabilities were subtracted. The arithmetic mean of these individual probabilities is the estimated aggregate percentage.

32. The standard error of this estimate is 2.1. Thus there is only a 5 percent chance that the true coefficient is less than 4.9 percent or more than 13.3 percent.
33. North Dakota did not require registration at all in 1972. There were not enough respondents from this single, sparsely populated state to permit precise estimates of the effects of its unique voting laws. By 1976 four other states permitted election day registration.
34. Table 4-4 also shows the effect of liberalized registration laws by income and age. Poorer people would be most affected, as we would expect because of the relationship between education and income. The variation among income categories is much smaller than among people with different educational attainment, however. This reflects the much stronger relationship between education and turnout. Variations by age are small. People in the age groups with the highest turnout would be affected only slightly less than those with the lowest voting rates—citizens under 32 and over 78.
35. For representative comments, see Polsby and Wildavsky (1976, p. 129). For a dissenting view, emphasizing "the general insensitivity of partisanship to large changes in turnout," see Converse (1966c, p. 29).
36. *San Francisco Chronicle,* 16 May 1977, p. 38. The Republican National Committee formally opposed Carter's plan, and a Gallup Poll in the spring of 1977 revealed that rank-and-file Republicans were more hostile to it than Democrats, who themselves were unfavorable to the proposal. (*San Francisco Chronicle,* 9 May 1977, p. 8.) The pronounced partisan cleavage on this issue among congressmen is described in *Congressional Quarterly Weekly Report,* 14 May 1977, pp. 909-11.
37. The composition of the actual electorate was estimated by using Equation II to compute a probit estimate for each respondent. The probit estimate was then converted to a probability. The percentage of the electorate comprised of people with a given characteristic (e.g. a college education) was computed in the following manner:

$$\frac{\sum_{j=1}^{j} \text{Probability of Voting}}{\sum_{n=1}^{n} \text{Probability of Voting}} \times 100$$

where j = the number of respondents with a given characteristic (i.e. in that category on the variable); and n = the total number of respondents. The same procedure was used to calculate the projected composition of the electorate, with the values for the registration provisions altered to simulate the liberalized conditions.

We used Equation II rather than the reported turnout to estimate the composition of the actual electorate. If we had used the reported turnout, then the difference between the projected electorate and the actual electorate would be due both to the simulated changes in registration laws and the residual for each individual in Equation II. These residuals cancel out if Equation II is used for calculating the composition of both the actual and the projected electorates.

38. The data were made available by the Inter-University Consortium for Political Research.
39. These projections, as well as those summarized in Tables 4-6 and 4-7, are based on the 1972 National Election Study of the University of Michigan Center for Political Studies. For this sample we used Equation II to estimate both the actual and projected composition of the electorate, as described in note 37. We deleted 13 cases from this sample: the 10 respondents from the District of Columbia and 3 respondents whose education was not reported, and for whom turnout therefore could not be predicted.

Equation II correctly predicted turnout for 74.3 percent of the cases in this sample, compared to 71.4 percent of the cases in the Current Population Survey subsample. The differences between the actual and projected electorates summarized in Table 4-5 can be replicated within 0.4 percentage points by using Equation II with the Michigan data.

40. This classification is based on Keith, et al. (1977).
41. Candidate popularity was measured by the proportion of those rating McGovern higher than Nixon on the candidate "feeling thermometers."
42. For extended discussions of this problem see Clausen (1968-69); Andrews (1966); Roper (1961); "Voting and Registration in the Election of November 1972," pp. 7-8; and Campbell, et al. (1960, pp. 94-96).
43. Bureau of the Census, "Projections of the Population of Voting Age for States: November 1972," *Current Population Reports,* March 1972, Series P-25, No. 479, pp. 1, 3.
44. Ibid., p. 3; Clausen (1968-69, pp. 589-91); Meyer Zitter and Donald E. Starsinic, "Estimates of 'Eligible' Voters in Small Areas: Some First Approximations," *Proceedings of the Social Statistics Section of the American Statistical Association,* 1966, pp. 368-78; and Andrews (1966, pp. 642-44).
45. Campbell, et al. (1960, pp. 94-95), and "Registration and Voting in the Election of November 1972," p. 8.
46. Clausen (1968-69, pp. 592-96); "Voting and Registration in the Election of November 1972," pp. 8, 13; and Campbell et al. (1960, pp. 94-95).
47. Clausen (1968-69, pp. 596-98, 601). For other estimates see Campbell, et al. (1960, pp. 93-96); and "Voting and Registration in the Election of November 1972," p. 7.
48. These were drawn from Clausen (1968-69, pp. 594-95).
49. Center for Political Studies, *1972 Study,* p. xiii; and Bureau of the Census, "Voting and Registration in the Election of November 1974," *Current Population Reports,* Series P-20, No. 293, p. 89.

DETERMINANTS OF THE VOTE

5. WHAT DETERMINES THE VOTE?

A continuing question in voting behavior is what determines the vote. Are peoples' votes primarily issue-determined, with voters choosing between candidates on the basis of the great issues of the day—or, for that matter, the minor issues of the moment? Are votes primarily based on reactions to political candidates? Is voting really party-based, with voters choosing on the basis of habitual affiliation with a particular party? Or is voting based on age-old social cleavages, such as social class, religion, or ethnic divisions?

Much research has been devoted to sorting out the relative importance of these different causes of the vote. This research has typically found that party and candidate factors are the most important, with issues only occasionally being found to play much of a role. This has led to much controversy in the field, since voting on the basis of issues seems more "rational" to some observers than does voting on the basis of candidate characteristics, partisan appeals, or group divisions, and these observers want to show that political man and woman are rational actors. In addition issue voting provides an interesting intellectual puzzle because there are numerous kinds of issues, only some of which may affect the vote. Thus the controversy in this chapter revolves around two questions—are issues important, and if so, which ones are important?

Parties, Candidates, and Maybe Issues

The original view was that voting must of course be based on issues, since parties and candidates spend so much time during election campaigns discussing and debating issues. The early empirical voting studies, however, found that the public had very limited knowledge of issues, so that the other determinants must be more important.

The Columbia University studies of 1940 and 1948, for example, found that voters often decided how to vote before the campaign, and thus before issues were raised. And they found that voters often perceived the issue positions of candidates incorrectly, so that issues could not be important. Similarly, *The American Voter* reported that on 16 different issues in 1956 only 18–36 percent of the electorate satisfied what the authors considered three prerequisites for issue voting: being familiar enough with the issues to have an opinion, knowing what the government is doing on the issue, and believing the parties differ on the issue. Converse's (1964) conclusion that some issues were marked by "nonattitudes," with respondents answering questions virtually randomly so as to satisfy the overinsistent interviewer, further emphasized the lowly role of issues in voting.

If voting was not issue-based, then social groups, party, and/or candidate factors must predominate. The Columbia research stressed the social group factors, as was explained in the introduction to this book. Even today, many reports on elections give considerable attention to how different groups voted. But most students of American voting behavior agree that it is necessary to delve deeper into the voter's political attitudes in understanding the vote, rather than just to observe the person's demographics.

The American Voter pioneered in emphasizing the importance of party identification in the vote decision. Most Americans generally consider themselves either Republicans or Democrats and vote accordingly in most elections. Not only is long-term partisanship a direct cause of the vote, but it also affects the way people view the candidates and the issues, which are short-term influences on the vote. Some observers might view party voting as less rational than issue voting, but that need not be the case: if people initially choose to identify with a party because they generally agree with it on the issues, then they can later use their party identification as a short cut in deciding how to vote at later elections without taking time to research all the issues of those elections. As will be seen in later sections of this book, issues can also still be important in changing a person's partisanship—a person may change from one party to another if the other party is seen to be better on the issues over the course of several elections. Thus issues retain some importance in this theory, but voting was seen to be more party-based than issue-based.

The Michigan studies have also emphasized the importance of candidates in voting decisions. After all, if issues are not important and if partisanship and social group factors are very stable, then the dramatic changes in the vote from one election to the next must be due to the changing cost of candidates. This conclusion was first reached by Stokes (1966) in a statistical decomposition of voting results from 1952 to 1964. The Michigan surveys include a set of questions asking people what they like and dislike about both major parties and presidential nominees. The responses are categorized in terms of six "components" of the vote: attitudes toward the Republican candidate, the Democratic candidate, domestic issues, foreign issues, parties as managers of government, and group-related issues. To determine the relative impact of these six attitudes on the individual vote decision, Stokes used "regression analysis," which essentially shows the effect of each attitude on the vote when the effects of the other attitudes are statistically "held constant." He then multiplied the effect of an attitude on the vote by the average value for that same attitude (which reflects whether more people liked the Republicans or Democrats on that matter and by how much) to determine the effect on the election result. Stokes found that the domestic issue component and group-related issues favored the Democrats from 1952 to 1964, while party performance and foreign issues helped the Republicans (except in Goldwater's 1964 campaign), but the greatest variation was due to the candidates. The candidate factor varied from so strongly pro-Republican in 1956 as to reelect Dwight D. Eisenhower in a landslide to so strongly Democratic in 1964 as to give Lyndon B. Johnson his landslide victory. The candidate factor clearly provided the dynamism of electoral politics.

Miller and Wattenberg (1981) have updated the Stokes analysis. Table 5-1 shows the findings through 1980. The group factor remains strongly pro-

Table 5-1 Net Impact ($b_i \cdot \bar{X}_i$) of the Six Components on the Vote, 1952-1980

	Election Year							
	1952	*1956*	*1960*	*1964*	*1968*	*1972*	*1976*	*1980*
Domestic Policy	−1.34[a]	−0.88	−0.54	−2.36	1.10	1.35	−0.69	3.13
Foreign policy	3.30	2.46	1.80	−0.25	1.00	3.23	0.40	2.77
Party Management	5.40	1.18	1.20	−0.30	1.50	0.04	0.17	.59
Group Benefits	−4.29	−5.50	−4.01	−2.59	−3.60	−4.55	−4.53	−4.46
Democratic Candidate	−1.18	0.17	−1.99	−3.93	0.90	4.29	−0.05	−.41
Republican Candidate	4.37	7.60	5.70	−2.60	1.60	3.98	2.24	−.50

[a] A negative value indicates a Democratic vote advantage; a positive value, a Republican vote advantage. The entries can be interpreted as the percentage of the vote moved in a given partisan direction as a result of the particular component.

Source: Arthur H. Miller and Martin P. Wattenberg, "Policy and Performance Voting in the 1980 Election," Paper presented at the 1981 Annual Meeting of the American Political Science Association, New York, New York. Reprinted with permission of the authors.

Democratic. The Democratic advantage on domestic issues dissipated after 1964, favoring the Republicans in the Nixon campaigns and especially in 1980. The party management and foreign policy components returned to being pro-Republican after 1964, though the impact of party performance has been negligible after 1968 (and foreign policy had minimal impact on 1976). But the wild gyrations in the candidate factor remain, with the strong Republican advantage giving Nixon a landslide victory in 1972. It is evident from these data that the Republicans have been able to win the White House so frequently since the 1950s, despite the Democratic lead in party identification, largely because they generally managed to put up a better-appreciated candidate. But the 1980 data show a contrary pattern, with the Republicans winning because of the issues, and suggesting that the importance of issues should not be dismissed prematurely.

Is the importance of the candidate factor necessarily an indication of voter irrationality? Not really. If the candidate factor simply reflected whether or not the voter liked the candidate's smile, then the candidate emphasis would be a sign of lack of rationality. However, the studies indicate that reactions to the candidates are generally more meaningful. For example, it is fully rational to vote against a candidate who is seen as not competent to carry out his issue promises. Popkin, Gorman, Phillips, and Smith's (1976) analysis of George McGovern's 1972 defeat thus showed that his loss was due more to questions about his competence than to his issue positions. As a result, it is important to disentangle the separate dimensions underlying the candidate factor. Markus's (1982) analysis of new candidate trait questions included in the 1980 election study shows that candidate competence and candidate integrity are separate, independent dimensions of reactions to presidential candidates. Subsequent analysis of a 1983 pilot study also distinguished separate dimensions of managerial competence and general charisma. Voting on the basis of the competence, integrity, and/or managerial competence of the candidate would certainly be rational, even though it is not issue voting.

Can the relative influences of the party, candidate, and issue factors be further disentangled? A causal model of the vote decision that attempted to determine the relevant importance of these different forces was first offered by Goldberg (1966) for the 1956 election. Partisanship was portrayed as affecting issue positions, candidate evaluations, and the vote; issue positions were seen as affecting both candidate evaluations and the vote; and candidate evaluations affected the vote. Goldberg found the candidate factor to be much more important than issues. Partisanship, however, was the most important causal factor in 1956, both directly and indirectly through its effects on the way people view the candidates and the issues. The first edition of this book reprinted an article by Schulman and Pomper (1975) in which they extended Goldberg's analysis to 1964 and 1972. They found that the importance of issues was increasing over the years, while correspondingly partisanship was declining in importance. Their work heartened those who were looking for issue effects on voting, while providing added evidence to those who were arguing that the American party system was dealigning (see the last section of this book). Hartwig, Jenkins, and Temchin (1980) have now filled in the results for 1960, 1968, and 1976, as shown in Table 5-2. There is evidence here of increased importance of issues and declining role of party, though neither changed as sharply as Schulman and Pomper reported when they looked at only three elections. Even summing direct and indirect effects, the issue factor is always the least important of the three, and party is always first.

Table 5-2 Comparison of Path Coefficients for Six Elections

Path	*1956*	*1960*	*1964*	*1968*	*1972*	*1976*
Party Identification						
to Issue Index	.235	.336	.301	.092	.249	.309
to Candidate Evaluation	.549	.482	.356	.496	.340	.337
to Presidential Vote	.448	.379	.364	.397	.310	.341
Issue Index						
to Candidate Evaluation	.114	.205	.203	.177	.312	.292
to Presidential Vote	.060	.114	.224	.116	.233	.162
Candidate Evaluation						
to Presidential Vote	.365	.415	.377	.442	.366	.419
R^2	.548*	.581*	.570*	.607*	.478*	.535*
N	763	833	1111	766	827	1102

* $p < .001$

Source: Frederick Hartwig, William R. Jenkins, and Earl M. Temchin, "Variability in Electoral Behavior," *American Journal of Political Science* (1980) 24:554, Table 1. Reprinted with permission of the publisher.

This early causal model of the vote soon proved more simplistic than our evolving theoretical understanding of voting. For one thing, its emphasis on determining the relative importance of party, candidate, and issue factors ignores the fact that they do not operate separately. It is difficult to disentangle their separate effects, and their combined effects may be of greater interest. For example, dissatisfaction with an incumbent's handling of a problem may be both a candidate and an issue factor at once, as is concern with the competence of a challenger to handle a particular issue. Thus, concern with McGovern's "foolish" proposals in 1972 (such as his proposal to give every person in the United States one thousand dollars) or concern with Carter's competence (his inability to get back the hostages from Iran) were simultaneously candidate and issue factors, and any attempt to allocate them to just one category is artificial.

Furthermore, the early causal model of the vote was simplistic in treating causation as unidirectional, not exploring effects of voting on partisanship (which will be examined more carefully in a later section of this book) or effects of candidate orientation on issue views. Brody and Page (1972, reprinted as chapter 13 of the first edition of this book) showed that the relationship between issue position and voting could be due to three different processes. True "policy voting" would occur if voters first decide how they stand on the issues and then choose to vote for the candidate nearest them on the issues. If voters first decide which candidate they like and then just assume their preferred candidate agrees with them on the issues, then "projection" is causing the correlation between issue position and the vote. If the voters first decide which candidate to support and then modify their own issue positions to conform to those of that candidate, then policy "persuasion" is causing the issue-vote correlation. If we want to determine the true importance of issue voting, we must first remove the confounding effects of projection and persuasion. Beyond that, projection and persuasion effects are interesting to study in their own right, since they represent the combined effects of candidate and issue factors working together, a sort of interactive effect that was missed in the early causal models. Because Goldberg's causal model assumed only unidirectional causation with issue position affecting candidate evaluation but not vice versa, he was unable to test for projection and persuasion effects. To test for reciprocal causation requires moving beyond the "recursive" (one-way) causal models to more complicated "nonrecursive" (two-way) models.

Jackson (1975b) provided the first such model of the vote decision in 1964. In his model, party identification affected both issue positions and evaluations (of the candidates), with the latter affecting both party identification and vote decision. Because the relationship between partisanship and evaluation was portrayed as reciprocal, the model could not be estimated with regular regression analysis ("ordinary least squares"). Instead, a special "simultaneous equation" procedure was required, adding several other predictors to the model that would affect one of the variables caught in the reciprocal causation but not the other (such as finding demographic variables that theoretically should affect partisanship but not issue position or candidate evaluation directly). These are termed "exogenous" variables in that they are outside the model, affecting variables inside the model but not being affected by them. Jackson used demographic variables for a two-stage least-squares analysis. He found issues to be important, while partisanship's effect was limited to voters' not perceiving party differences on any issue. In addition, Jackson found that partisanship is affected by evaluations of the candidates on the issues, so that treating partisanship as a wholly exogenous variable as in earlier causal models was incorrect. Jackson's analysis is widely seen as an advance over previous models of the vote but as necessarily limited by the exogenous variables available in the 1964 election study. The results of the two-stage procedure depend very much on the quality of the available exogenous variables, and sufficient useful exogenous variables were not included in that study. In addition, this model also permitted reciprocal causation, but it did not allow for the impact of candidate evaluations on issue positions.

The readings in this section by Page and Jones and by Markus and Converse are state-of-the-art causal models of the vote decision. The Page and Jones chapter (6) analyzes 1972 and 1976 data. Their model permits a full range of reciprocal relations between party, candidate, and issue terms, while recognizing the further direct impact of the candidate's personal characteristics on the candidate evaluation. Methodologically, as with Jackson's model, the only way to determine the relative importance of the reciprocal paths is to include some exogenous variables in the model, variables that are assumed to affect some of the political variables in the model but not others. For example, Equation 2 and Figure 7 of Page and Jones assume that the respondent's relative closeness to the two candidates is affected by the respondent's race, age, sex, education, and income, but these demographic variables are assumed not to affect directly their relative evaluations of the candidates or their current partisanship. They treat vote as a function of only relative candidate evaluation, feeling that any increase in explanation that partisanship would provide is just a reflection of the imperfections of the candidate rating data that underlie the relative candidate evaluation calculation. Comparative candidate evaluations are found to affect comparative policy evaluations, showing that projection, persuasion, and other rationalization mechanisms do affect the issue term in voting models. The issue factor was found most important in 1976, with personal qualities of the candidates a close second, and partisanship third. By contrast, in the "clear choice" election of 1972, the issue factor predominated so much that the other variables can provide little further explanation.

The Markus and Converse chapter (7) employs the more powerful 1972–1974–1976 panel study to examine the determinants of voting in 1976. By using panel data Markus and Converse can incorporate reciprocal causal effects through lagging variables—as by assuming that issue stands at one point in time affect issue stands at a later time. They are also able to model both projection and persuasion effects, seeing how respondents' issue stands at an earlier time are affected by their candidate evaluations. They find projection effects to be low but significant, persuasion effects on three of their five issues, and projection a fifth stronger than persuasion. Candidate evaluations are found to depend on perceived candidate personalities, partisanship (which also has a substantial indirect effect through perceived candidate personalities), and issues. Vote is portrayed as basically dependent on candidate evaluation, with partisanship having a direct impact only when respondents are fairly neutral between the candidates.

The Markus and Converse methodology is more complicated than that of most previous studies, because it includes lagged variables and interaction terms in many of its equations. This may make their study more appropriate than previous studies, but it also makes its results harder to interpret. Fortunately, Markus and Converse generally include extra tables to help interpret the results. For example, Table 7-1 of their chapter can be used to understand their findings on the determinants of 1976 party identification. According to their Equation 7, partisanship in 1976 is affected by the respondent's partisanship in 1972 as well as by whether and how the respondent voted in 1972. The table shows that 1976 partisanship is predicted to be most Democratic (as indicated by the most negative value in the table) for those strong Democrats in 1972 who voted for McGovern in that year.[1] Strong Democrats who did not vote in 1972 were somewhat less Democratic in their 1976 identification, while strong Democrats who voted for Nixon in 1972 were even less Democratic in their 1976 identification. All in all, looking down the columns of Table 7-1, whether and how people voted in 1972 affected their 1976 partisanship by less than a point (on the seven-point partisanship scale). By contrast, looking across the rows of that table, the person's 1976 partisanship is determined more by his or her 1972 partisanship, with more than a three point difference between 1972 strong Democrats and strong Republicans in 1976 partisanship, regardless of how they voted in 1972.

The differences in results of these two chapters for the 1976 election reflect the difficulties inherent in such modeling. A large number of decisions must be made as to which variables affect which others and how to operationalize the variables with questions from the surveys. The exact specification and operationalization decisions have a great effect on the results of simultaneous equation modeling. The Page and Jones piece is particularly sensitive to the choice of exogenous variables. For example, should not race in their model be affecting partisanship as well as policy preferences, since blacks are much more Democratic in their partisanship than are whites? Also, the models incorporate partisanship in very different ways and operationalize the issue factor differently. Finally, they differ in that Page and Jones treat candidates evaluation as equivalent to the vote, while Markus and Converse are interested in the increment that partisanship adds when the person is approximately indifferent between the candidates.

What is more important, though, is to emphasize the similarities between these two efforts. They agree that a simultaneous equation approach is necessary. They both recognize the existence of projection and persuasion effects, though only Markus and Converse are able to provide separate estimates of each. They both represent much more complex attempts to incorporate party, candidate, and issue factors into a model of voting than did the previous models, although Markus and Converse find candidate characteristics to have the largest direct effect on candidate evaluations in 1976 while Page and Jones find issues of greater importance. In any case, they both accept the need to incorporate party, candidate, and issue terms in voting models.

In a later study, Markus (1982) used panel data for 1980 to develop a dynamic model of the vote decision in that year. Projection effects are again evident, while persuasion effects are not. Evaluations of both Jimmy Carter and Ronald Reagan were strongly affected by their perceived competence. Candidate integrity also was important as regards evaluations of Reagan, whereas dissatisfaction with Carter's performance strongly detracted from ratings of Carter. Issues in the sense of policy distances also worked against Carter to a small degree, but dissatisfaction with Carter's performance (which Markus treats as an issue factor) was the dominant influence.

Research on voting in other nations differs in several respects from the type of analysis discussed so far. For one thing, the candidate factor is typically given much less attention, especially for countries in which the public votes for members of parliament rather than directly for a president or prime minister. This difference makes concern over reciprocal causation between issue position and candidate evaluation less serious. At the same time, there is more interest in other countries in the impact of social characteristics on the vote. The party system in many of these countries is based on social distinctions, which Lipset and Rokkan (1967a) argue reflect the cleavages of earlier days—among them center-periphery (including linguistic conflicts), and state-church, land-industry, and owner-worker cleavages. Often researchers feel that partisanship need not be considered per se, since it is simply a reflection of these social cleavages. These concerns—the role of social cleavages and the relevance of party identification—will be taken up in chapters 26 and 21 respectively.

Baker, Dalton, and Hildebrandt, however, do provide a causal analysis of voting outside the United States. Their work is reprinted here as chapter 8. They view the vote in West Germany as dependent on issues, party, and social characteristics, where the latter also affects issues and party. Social characteristics are found to be of decreasing direct importance over the years, though with an important indirect effect. Partisanship predominates in most of the elections, although with issues being equally important in 1969. The researchers explain the growth in issue importance as being due to New Politics concerns (such as environmental and women's issues), especially among young voters.

Overall, the literature reviewed to this point indicates that parties, candidates, issues, and social cleavages are all important in determining the vote. None can be ignored, and their relative importance varies from one election to another. If anything, however, parties, candidates, and perhaps social cleavages predominate over issues, according to most of the studies reviewed, probably because of the apparently limited issue awareness of most voters. But has all this understated the role of issues? That is the major continuing controversy in this field.

Issues, Issues, and Particular Issues

While much of the analysis of voting determinants focuses on the relative importance of parties, candidates, and issues (and often finds that issues are the least important of the three), the other side of this debate emphasizes the importance of issues—albeit sometimes just particular types of issues. The importance of issues has been emphasized most by those observers who want to view the voter as a rational political actor and who view issue voting as more rational than voting on the basis of party or candidate considerations. As argued in the preceding pages, it often is entirely rational to employ party and candidate considerations in deciding how to cast one's vote, but the more general argument would be that issue voting best demonstrates the seriousness of the citizen when choosing how to vote. The first chapter of this book gives an outline of the rational voter approach, particularly Downs's (1957) work. Briefly, rational voters would be expected to calculate how much they differ from each candidate on the issues and then vote for the candidate to whom they are closest. This approach is incorporated in the Page and Jones and the Markus and Converse chapters in this section, though they differ in how important such issue calculations turn out to be. The major controversy in this field, once again, revolves around whether issues are as unimportant as the early Michigan studies proclaimed or whether issues have the importance that the rational-voter approach tries to claim.

The first empirical work to argue that voters are calculating observers was a posthumous book by V. O. Key, Jr. (1966), *The Responsible Electorate.* Key argued that vote change between elections was due to voter satisfaction or dissatisfaction with the performance of the administration. As an example, three-fifths of the 1956 Eisenhower voters who became dissatisfied with Eisenhower's performance as president voted for John F. Kennedy in 1960. According to Key, this showed that "voters are not fools"—they can vote on the basis of issues, and particularly satisfaction with the administration. While Key's emphasis on issues led to important reexamination of this subject by political scientists, his own evidence had limitations. It relied on respondents' recall of how they voted in the preceding election, a recall that is not always accurate. And it does not handle the projection problem raised above—people may decide how to vote on other grounds and then report satisfaction or dissatisfaction with the incumbent administration so as to be consistent with that planned vote. This problem is most apparent when Key's data (1966, p. 46) show that voters who were dissatisfied with the Roosevelt farm policy were most likely to switch their votes in 1940, whereas few historians would regard that election as a major referendum on Roosevelt's farm policy.

Key's book also introduced an important concept into the issue literature. He reminded us that issues would be important only when the parties (or candidates) differed on them. He called this the "echo chamber effect"—that the electorate can just echo back whatever alternatives they are provided. If the candidates do not really differ on the issues, then they will be unimportant—and elections such as that of 1956 show this to be the case. On the other hand, when the candidates present stark issue contrasts, as in recent elections such as 1964 and 1972, then the electorate does respond. From Key's perspective, then, the lack of issue voting is not a fault of the electorate; it is a fault of a party system that does not provide the electorate real issue choices.[2]

Whereas Key used Gallup data for his evidence on issue voting, RePass (1971) made use of the Michigan data in his reconsideration of issue importance. RePass pointed out that the Michigan findings of low issue voting were based on questions that did not really concern issues. When respondents were asked what they liked and disliked about the parties and candidates, their attention was being directed away from issues. Consequently, the low level of issue responses should not be a surprise. Even when the voters were asked about issues, they were all asked about the same issues, and ones decided on in advance by the questionnaire writers rather than the voters themselves. According to Converse's (1964) discussion of "issue politics," one would expect that different citizens would be most concerned about different issues—Americans of Eastern European descent would be concerned about foreign policy with respect to that region of the world, and so on. Yet the evidence against issue voting was largely based on the assumption that the same issue should concern everyone. RePass instead made use of a question asking people to name the "most important problems" facing the government in Washington. He found that people listed problems, perceived party differences on those problems, and recognized party positions on those issues fairly accurately. He found that issues were about as important as party in 1964, but in the absence of the proper questions he could not tell whether this would have been true in the elections studied in *The American Voter.* Nor does this mean that even the 1964 election provided Johnson an issue mandate on any single issue.

Whereas RePass's focus was primarily methodological and might alter the interpretation of the 1950s, Pomper's (1972) was more substantive and was directed to change over time. Pomper's analysis of the 1956–1968 surveys showed that issues became more important after 1960. Beginning in 1964 there were large differences in the proportions of Democrats and Republicans who took liberal positions on issues, more people perceived differences between the parties on the issues, and more people perceived the Democrats as more liberal on those issues. Pomper explained this change as being due to greater differences between the parties in the 1960s than in the 1950s, an explanation in keeping with Key's echo chamber argument.

This evidence was somewhat controversial, as when Margolis (1977) showed that large numbers of respondents were not asked the questions that Pomper was analyzing because they were not at all familiar with the issues involved. However, a large volume of work—epitomized by *The Changing American Voter* (Nie, Verba, and Petrocik, 1976)—supported the proposition that the public became more issue-oriented in the 1960s. The times had changed; the politically quiescent 1950s were followed by a turbulent decade marked by the Civil Rights Revolution, urban riots, and a land war in Vietnam and protest against it. The issues still would not matter if the candidates took ambiguous stands on them as in 1968 (Page and Brody, 1972), but in general the importance of issues seemed to have increased.

Recently there have been three major restatements of the importance of issues in voting. The first is by Carmines and Stimson in their paper reprinted in this section (chapter 9). It makes an interesting distinction between "hard" and "easy" issues. Hard issues are more difficult for voters to comprehend than are easy ones, so hard issues will be important only for voters with high levels of political information, while easy issues will also be important for voters with low information levels. Carmines and Stimson argue that there is a large amount of issue voting when easy issues are involved in an election. They use the racial issue as an example of an easy issue, arguing that it had a major impact on some recent elections even though it was not raised explicitly. Finally, they claim that realignments are more likely to occur around easy issues, and in their more recent work (see chapter 29) they suggest that a realignment occurred in the 1960s and 1970s around the racial issue.

A second major recent statement of the importance of issues is Fiorina's (1981b) analysis of "retrospective voting." Fiorina distinguishes between prospective voting, in which citizens vote for the candidate or party making the best promises for the future, and retrospective voting, in which citizens vote on the basis of past party performance. With an argument reminiscent of Key's, Fiorina argues that it is rational for citizens to vote against a party when it has not performed well in office. Indeed, it may be more rational to vote restrospectively than to cast a prospective vote on the basis of campaign promises that the candidate will not keep.

Fiorina models the vote as a function of retrospective evaluations and future expectations,[3] with past partisanship (in the previous election) controlled. His results emphasize the importance of the retrospective terms, both directly and working through future evaluations. For example, Fiorina finds evaluations of Gerald Ford's presidential performance, feelings about the Nixon pardon, future expectations on inflation and unemployment, relative trust of Carter and Ford, and a judgment about which has the most appropriate presidential personality to have significant effects on the vote in 1976 once 1974 partisanship is controlled, where future economic expectations are based on retrospective evaluations of the government's economic performance and evaluations of Ford's presidential performance are "mediated" retrospective evaluations. Miller and Wattenberg (1981) offered a retrospective interpretation of the 1980 election, arguing that Reagan won more out of citizen dissatisfaction with Carter's performance (retrospective voting) than out of a preference for Reagan's conservative policy promises (prospective voting).

The third recent treatment of the importance of issues consists of a large and growing literature on a particular set of issues: economic issues. The recent literature on voting has been heavily influenced by a form of economic determinism. There are actually several different aspects to this literature, not all of which are directly relevant to our present concern. The first argument is that government approval (often operationalized by a question on approval of the president or prime minister) is strongly influenced by the status of the economy, either the respondent's own financial status or the overall economic situation. The second argument is that the economy affects voting, although along with this is a countertheme that administrations manipulate the economy near election dates so as to maximize their chances of reelection. The final argument is that left and right parties differ in their economic policies, so that the electorate is indeed making real economic choices when it votes. In terms of voting determinants, all this amounts to a strong case for the importance of economic issues in voting. We shall not consider the full case here but focus instead on the extent to which economic variables influence government evaluations, and thus the vote.

Much of the work is intuitively straightforward, although mathematically very complex. The dependent variable is most often the proportion of the public expressing support for the incumbent president or political party. In the United States, for example, Gallup "approval ratings" of the president are used. In Great Britain, the question asks which party a person would vote for "if there were a general election tomorrow." The advantage of these measures is that they are available frequently, often monthly, whereas elections are much more episodic. However, these scores are obviously autocorrelated (approval in one month being heavily dependent on approval a month earlier), and the survey question is dichotomous while approval is a matter of degree. This accounts for the complexity of the statistical models and estimation procedures.

The independent variables typically include measures of unemployment, inflation, and real personal income, or a subset of these. Dummy variables represent each administration to account for the fact that some incumbents are consistently viewed more positively than others. Sometimes other economic variables are included. For example, Hibbs (1982a) includes a term for changes in the exchange rate of the pound "since British governments of all stripes have been preoccupied for most of the post-war period with defending the international role of sterling" (pp. 436-37). Occasionally noneconomic variables (in addition to administration) are included, especially in models of the United States where early work by Mueller (1970) and Stimson (1976) located relevant noneconomic factors. But modifications are also required elsewhere, to take account, for example, of the Grand Coalition of the CDU and SPD parties in Germany from 1966 to 1969.

Results from studies using this approach have produced a variety of conclusions, but they agree in two important senses. First, the models explain the support scores extremely well (in a statistical sense). This is true even if only economic variables and variables representing each administration are included. Second, it is consistently the case that (some or all of) the economic variables have an effect on support. As Hibbs (1981, p. 8) says in the introduction to a recent book, "considered as a whole, the empirical evidence . . . indicates rather convincingly that public support for political authorities in a wide range of institutional settings responds quite systematically to macroeconomic conditions."[4]

Models of this sort have been proposed most extensively by Hibbs and by Frey and his associates.[5] All together, applications have been made to nearly a dozen countries—the United States, Great Britain, West Germany, France, Denmark, Sweden, Norway, Switzerland, Japan, and Australia—often over a 10 or 20 year period. We represent this approach by reprinting (chapter 10) an analysis by Hibbs of the popularity of the French president. Hibbs's methodology can become very complicated, and the formal presentation of his model in the appendix is difficult. Fortunately, Hibbs's words and figures do a nice job of explaining his approach and results.

In addition to this aggregate analysis, individual-level analysis also lends some support to the economic influence literature. Kiewiet (1981), for instance, finds that "there was a mass of (survey) evidence showing voters reacting to their concern over unemployment by voting more Democratic" (p. 459). Also, as just described, Fiorina shows that a variety of economic factors—both retrospective judgments about past performance and expectations about future behavior—influence voting behavior.[6] In addition, both these individual-level analyses along with some aggregate analyses of U.S. behavior (for example, Fair, 1978) show directly that economic variables influence the vote and not just popularity scores. Both types of analysis, but especially the individual-level ones, also demonstrate convincingly that economic factors retain their explanatory power when noneconomic variables are included in the equations.

The work on economic issues can be challenged, even though the great majority of studies do document economic effects. For example, a recent study (Norpoth and Yantek, 1983) of French and American data that corrected for the inevitable autocorrelations within the economic variables (such as the correlation of unemployment in one time period with unemployoment in the previous time period) found no significant lagged effects, so that changes in presidential popularity were not associated with changes in the economy. In addition, regardless of their statistical significance, Golden and Poterba (1980) have argued that economic effects are too small to matter in most cases. In particular, they find that "a one percentage point rise in the rate of inflation leads to about a one point fall in popularity, assuming the inflation is maintained for six quarters" and "a one point increase in unemployment reduces popularity by less than one point. . . ." (p. 698). Madsen (1980) found little relationship between economic conditions and voting in Denmark and Norway, and Whiteley (1980) discovered no relationship in Great Britain. Finally, there are questions as to the specifications of the economic effects equations. Even Hibbs (1981, p. 8) points out that "there is no consensus about the appropriate theoretical specification for the economy-political behavior linkage." In fact, there are almost as many variations in specifications as there are articles.

As noted above, both economists and political scientists have now "turned around" the economic effects equations, arguing that there are political influences on economic policy. Unemployment, inflation, transfer payments (for example, social security), trade agreements, and so on are all used to generate support for the incumbent administration, as when administrations time increases in transfer payments to fall close to the election date. In some instances the influence is benign, as when "governments pursue macroeconomic policies broadly in accordance with the objective economic interests and subjective preferences of their class-defined core constituencies" (Hibbs, 1977, p. 1467). Examples of studies showing such effects include Bunce's (1980) demonstration that budget allocations to health and social welfare tend to be higher under left governments than right governments, Hibbs's (1977) evidence that unemployment rates tend to be lower when Democrats/left governments are in power while inflation rates tend to be lower under Republicans/right governments, and Cowart's (1981a, 1981b) data showing that governments of the left and right differ more in their use of monetary policy than fiscal policy. Since there are always trade-offs involved so that not everyone can benefit equally in economic terms, it is to be expected that parties and governments represent the economic interests of their supporters. In fact, this is what democratic government is all about.

But others view at least some government actions as manipulations in the worst sense of the term. Tufte (1978, p. 143), for example, charges that:

> The electoral-economic cycle breeds a lurching, stop-and-go economy the world over. Governments fool around with transfer payments, making an election-year prank out of the social security system and the payroll tax. There is a bias toward policies with immediate, highly visible benefits and deferred, hidden costs—myopic policies for myopic voters. Special interests induce coalition-building politicians to impose small costs on the many to achieve large benefits for the few. The result is economic instability and inefficiency.

Despite some evidence to support such strong charges, studies of political influences on the economy are still in their infancy. The most firmly established conclusion is that there is no very simple short-run relationship between political and business cycles. Nonetheless, given the responsiveness of the voters to economic factors, it would be surprising if there were no attempts to manipulate economy policy to the benefit of political leaders. Thus we can expect to see growing evidence that there is at least some political control of the economy. A number of efforts to identify a general political-business cycle have concluded that none exists (Thompson and Zuk, 1983; Dinkel, 1981; Golden and Poterba, 1980; Paldam, 1981; McCallum, 1978). Even if one looks for effects only in the immediate preelection period, positive results are not always found (Beck, 1982b; Brown and Stein, 1982). And Hibbs's attempt to link left- versus right-wing parties with differing unemployment levels has been questioned in separate and quite distinct analyses (Beck, 1982a; Madsen, 1980, 1981). It would appear, as Golden and Poterba (1980, p. 713) conclude, that political leaders try to influence economic outcomes, but whether they do so successfully is not yet clear.

Thus, while the area is itself controversial, there has been considerable recent emphasis on economic issues in voting. Whether stated in terms of easy issues, retrospective voting, or economic determinants of presidential popularity, there is a much greater emphasis on the role of issues in voting today than there was a decade ago.

Conclusion

In the mid-1970s one would have guessed that a clear judgment on the relative importance of the determinants of voting would be obtained as soon as better data and more powerful analysis techniques were employed. Now that has been done, but without achieving any consensus as to the relative importance of the different voting determinants.

First, the use of more complicated models and better data do not necessarily provide definitive conclusions. Instead, these models prove very dependent on their exact assumptions, whether these are the simultaneous equations models of Page and Jones and Markus and Converse, or the economic models of Hibbs. A different set of assumptions would yield different results. Similarly, a different set of operational indicators could yield different results. The models are always going to be vulnerable to these matters of assumption and operationalization, and so consensus now seems beyond reach.

At the same time, there is a growing consensus on some considerations. Individual-level modeling now accepts that rationalization processes affect the measurement of policy voting, and they agree that projection is more common than persuasion. Voters are more likely to assume the candidate they like agrees with their issue positions than to accept the issue positions of the candidate they like. The results also show that effects are reciprocal, so that simple one-way causation models no longer suffice.

The models also seem to agree that policy voting has some role, even if they disagree on its exact nature. The issue term can no longer be left out of the equation, even if there is disagreement as to whether it is all-important. And whether economic determination explains everything is a major area of dispute.

There is more disagreement on the importance of partisanship in the equation. Some models find major partisanship effects (and the dynamic models are most likely to do so), other models find minor partisanship effects, and some models omit the partisan term completely.

Finally, the original emphasis on determining the relative importance of party, candidate, and issue factors may have been misplaced. As we have seen, they do not necessarily operate separately (as in the case of projection and persuasion effects), and they can be difficult to disentangle. Beyond this, the more complex causal models of the vote are more interesting in terms of development of a theory of voting than are simplistic attempts to separate party, candidate, and issue factors. Thus, we are left indeterminacy, but at the same time we have available some very useful attempts to construct general models of voting.

NOTES

1. The value of this entry can be calculated from the results the authors present for Equation 7. Remember that they scored partisanship −3 (strong Democrat) to +3 (strong Republican), voting 0 (abstainers) and 1 (voters), and Democratic and Republican voters 0 (No) and 1 (Yes). Then for a strong Democrat who voted for McGovern, ID 1976 $= -.37 - .20(1) + .49(0) + (.63 + .10(1))(-3) = -.37 - .20 + (.73)(-3) = -2.76$.
2. Downs's (1957) spatial model of party competition shows that, under specified assumptions, the optimal issue positions of the parties converge to the median voter's position, so rational behavior by the parties can lead to their not offering real choices to the electorate. More recent work also shows that ambiguity is useful for politicians, in that more voters can then think those politicians agree with them on the issues (see especially the discussion of ambiguity by Page, 1978).
3. Fiorina differentiates between two types of retrospective evaluations. Simple restrospective evaluations (SRE) include the person's satisfaction with such things as personal financial situation, foreign policy, civil rights, and so on. By contrast, mediated retrospective evaluations (MRE) are summary judgments that are influenced by the respondent's prior dispositions and information sources. MREs include evaluation of presidential performance and government economic performance. They are affected by the SREs and by prior partisanship. Fiorina also makes allowance for future expectations (FE), such as which party the voter expects to handle economic problems better in the next four years, which presumably are based on retrospective evaluations and partisanship.
4. Having shown the relevance of economic factors, some of the literature is now beginning to address more refined questions of varying influence over time and across categories of respondents. Hibbs (1982a), for example, argues that economic influences were greater in the United States, Great Britain, and West Germany in the 1970s than in the 1960s (see also Frey and Schneider, 1981, pp. 18-19). Hibbs (1982b, 1982c) and Frey and Schneider (1980) also address the question of class differences in response to economic variables in Britain and the United States, finding that blue-collar or lower-income workers in both countries are more sensitive to unemployment than are white-collar and higher-income employees.

   These more refined analyses are interesting because they speak to questions about economic influences that have been raised in other contexts. For example, Hibbs uses his results to argue strongly that while there have been fluctuations in the relationship of class to voting, "there is no evidence of a persistent decline in the fundamental occupational class alignment of political support for Labour and Conservative governments" (1982b, p. 268). Thus, Hibbs very directly, and others often implicitly, argue that economic thinking is still the foundation stone of mass political behavior. If there is change over the last decade or so in the way the public views politics (see the discussion of New Politics in the last section of this book), the performance of the economy is still the primary basis on which elections turn.

5. Recent summaries can be found in Hibbs and Fassbender (1981), Whiteley (1980a), and Frey (1978, chapter 11).
6. Other individual-level analyses have concentrated on congressional voting with some positive results. See chapter 11.

FURTHER READINGS

The Role of Issues

Benjamin I. Page, *Choices and Echoes in Presidential Elections* (Chicago: University of Chicago Press, 1978). Emphasizes role of ambiguity of candidate positions in elections.

Bo Särlvik and Ivor Crewe, *Decade of Dealignment* (Cambridge: Cambridge University Press, 1983). Decomposition of importance of specific issues in change in voting results from 1974 to 1979 British elections.

Impact of Economy on Government Popularity and Voting

Douglas A. Hibbs, Jr., and Heino Fassbender, eds., *Contemporary Political Economy* (Amsterdam: North Holland, 1981). Part II on the effects of the economy on political support in the United States and Europe.

Douglas A. Hibbs, Jr., with R. Douglas Rivers and Nicholas Vasilatos, "On the Demand for Economic Outcomes," *Journal of Politics* (1982) 44:426-62. Comparative analysis for United States, Britain, and West Germany.

D. Roderick Kiewiet, *Macroeconomics and Micropolitics: The Electoral Effects of Economic Issues* (Chicago: University of Chicago Press, 1983). Personal and especially national economic experiences influence voting behavior.

Effects of Party Choice on Macroeconomics

Douglas A. Hibbs, Jr., "Political Parties and Macroeconomic Policy," *American Political Science Review* (1977) 71:1467-87. Choice of governing political party affects government economic policy.

Andrew Cowart, "The Economic Policies of European Governments," *British Journal of Political Science* (1978) 9:285-312, 425-40. Two-part analysis of monetary and fiscal policy differences between left and right governments in Europe.

Valerie Bunce, "Changing Leaders and Changing Policies," *American Journal of Political Science* (1980) 24:373-95. Effects of party change on budget allocations.

Nathaniel Beck, "Parties, Administrations, and American Macroeconomic Outcomes," *American Political Science Review, (1982) 76:83-93.* Presidential administration is more important than party in determining government action on unemployment.

Francis G. Castles, ed., *The Impact of Parties* (Beverly Hills: Sage, 1982). Comparative studies of the effects of politics on economic policy in industrialized nations.

Political Manipulation of Government Economic Policy

Edward R. Tufte, *Political Control of the Economy* (Princeton: Princeton University Press, 1978). Makes the case for an electoral-economic cycle.

Thad A. Brown and Arthur A. Stein, "The Political Economy of National Elections," *Comparative Politics* (1982) 14:479-97. Argues against Tufte's evidence.

Nathaniel Beck, "Does There Exist a Political-Business Cycle?" *Public Choice* (1982) 38:205-09. No political-business cycle.

Mancur Olson, *The Rise and Decline of Nations* (New Haven: Yale University Press, 1982). A theory of interest groups and their effects on economic growth and constraint.

James E. Alt and K. Alec Chrystal, *Political Economics* (Berkeley: University of California Press, 1983). Overview and summary of political influences on the economy.

Kristen R. Monroe, ed., *The Political Process and Economic Change* (New York: Agathon Press, 1983). Examines several innovative topics connecting politics and economics.

6. RECIPROCAL EFFECTS OF POLICY PREFERENCES, PARTY LOYALTIES AND THE VOTE

Benjamin I. Page and Calvin C. Jones

Students of political behavior have long been interested in the extent of "policy voting," that is, the degree to which citizens take account of the public policy stands of candidates when they cast their votes. They have sought to discover the importance of policy orientations in voting, and how they compare with such factors as long-term partisan loyalties and perceptions of the character and personal qualities of the candidates. Answers to such questions are thought to bear not only upon the workings of individual psychology, but also upon theories of democratic politics (in terms of the rationality and cognitive capacities of the citizenry) and upon various theories of the decision process in voting.

Unfortunately, more than 30 years of research have left many issues unresolved. Varying conceptions of the central variables and differing methods of measurement and analysis have led to widely divergent conclusions, even on such apparently straightforward matters as whether policy positions, party loyalties or candidates' personal characteristics were more important in a given election, or whether or not policy concerns increased in importance in the 1960s and 1970s in comparison with the 1950s.[1] It is our purpose to further this research with some new empirical evidence. In doing so we must also complicate matters, suggesting that virtually all past voting studies have erred by ignoring the possibility of reciprocal causal effects among the central variables of the electoral process.

Among the few exceptions is the work of Jackson (1975b), whose non-recursive voting model of the 1964 election specified causal interdependence between partisan affiliations of voters and their evaluations of the public policy stands of the parties and candidates. Although we argue below that Jackson's model omits certain crucial reciprocal linkages, it was the first instance of a

---

Authors' Note: We are grateful for research support from the National Science Foundation, the Social Science Research Council, and the Social Science Research Committee of the University of Chicago. The origins of this study owe much to Richard A. Brody and Hayward R. Alker, Jr. A number of helpful criticisms and suggestions were offered by John Ferejohn, John Jackson, Herbert Kritzer, Merrill Shanks, Arthur Stinchcombe and others. Robert Y. Shapiro provided able research assistance. The data were made available through the Inter-University Consortium for Political and Social Research; the responsibility for analysis and interpretation is our own.

Source: *American Political Science Review* (1979) 73:1071-90. Reprinted with permission of the publisher.

system of structural equations to consider the roles of partisanship and policy orientations as dependent, as well as independent variables, and represented a major step forward in electoral research. More recent papers by Achen (1976) and Markus (1976) also allow for some reciprocal causal links.

Within the last several years survey data have become available which allow researchers to design and test sophisticated electoral process models. Yet, while a great many scholars have seized upon these data to improve their operationalizations of central electoral variables, few seem to have recognized all of the implications of the newer constructs (e.g., the "proximity" measures of candidate policy evaluations) for the task of specifying the equation, or system of equations in their statistical models. We will present below a full non-recursive voting model. For data we have turned to the 1972 and 1976 presidential election surveys conducted by the Center for Political Studies (CPS) at the University of Michigan. These are the first election studies to include the measures we believe necessary for constructing an adequate model of the electoral process.

One-Way Causation: Recursive Models of Voting

Most published voting studies to date, from the simplest to the most complicated, have been based upon some form of recursive model of the voting decision. Causation in these models is assumed to operate in one direction only, typically from policy preferences and/or party affiliation and/or candidate evaluations to the vote.[2] We intend to specify and estimate a non-recursive model, in which causation may be reciprocal, simultaneously operating in both directions among several pairs of variables. For comparative purposes, however, we first consider some typical recursive models and their results. We begin with a simple bivariate model which postulates that citizens' policy preferences uniquely determine their voting choice.

We conceptualize the voting choice somewhat differently from usual. Most past researchers have focused on a dichotomous dependent variable—the respondent's prospective or retrospective report of his or her vote for one of the major party candidates. We prefer to analyze the respondent's net comparative evaluation of the opposing candidates, as measured by the arithmetic difference between the scores given to each of the candidates on the CPS "feeling thermometer" scales.[3] The candidate thermometer scores can be argued to represent rather well what utility prospective voters think they would gain or lose from the election of a given candidate. The difference between thermometer scores for Democratic and Republican candidates, then, represents the net gain (or loss) in utility which the citizen would expect to receive as a result of the election of the Republican rather than the Democratic candidate. In this sense, it closely resembles Downs' concept of the "expected party differential" (1957).

Past empirical work has shown that such comparative evaluations of candidates, whether measured by the difference in thermometer scale scores or by a net count of positive and negative open-ended comments about the parties and candidates, are excellent predictors of voting decisions (Brody and Page, 1973; Kelley and Mirer, 1974). In both 1972 and 1976, according to our own analysis, over 95 percent of the voters who scored one candidate higher than the other on the thermometer scale reported voting for that candidate. Ordinary least squares regression of the binary vote measure upon a trichotomization of the net comparative evaluation measure resulted in standardized regression coefficients or betas of .81 for 1976 and .87 in 1972, with corresponding gammas of .95 in both years (see Figure 6-1).

It can be argued that party loyalties have some direct effects upon the vote in breaking ties when citizens evaluate the opposing candidates equally. We would contend, however, that here partisanship is as likely to be a dependent variable, if anything, and that the apparent additions to explanatory power by party and other variables may merely reflect the imperfection of thermometer scores as measures of the overall utility expected from the election of candidates.

Comparative evaluations, in other words, are so closely related to the vote that they can be substituted for the binary measure in our analysis. Such a substitution has the advantage of providing a continuous variable which can be related to other continuous variables without need for transformations such as logit or probit—which in fact would conflict with our theoretical specification of an expected utility decision rule—in order to capture more accurately the underlying mathematical function associated with the vote for a particular candidate. It also has the advantage (important for our non-recursive models below) of clearly conceptualizing the attitude immediately proximal to the voting act as one which can conceivably affect, as well as being affected by, other attitudinal variables. Put most simply, we believe that the voting intention is not only a dependent variable, but may be an independent variable as well.

We will now consider several alternative measures of issue orientations, in each case—for the sake of simplicity—dealing with a summary measure of many policy preferences rather than trying to estimate separate effects for different policies. The first, which we will call the "Policy Preference Index," is a weighted linear composite of respondents' scores on a series of closed-ended policy items: the CPS self-rating scales. It resembles the policy index used by Nie, Verba and Petrocik (1976).

Figure 6-1 Effects of Comparative Candidate Evaluations on the Voting Decision, 1972 and 1976

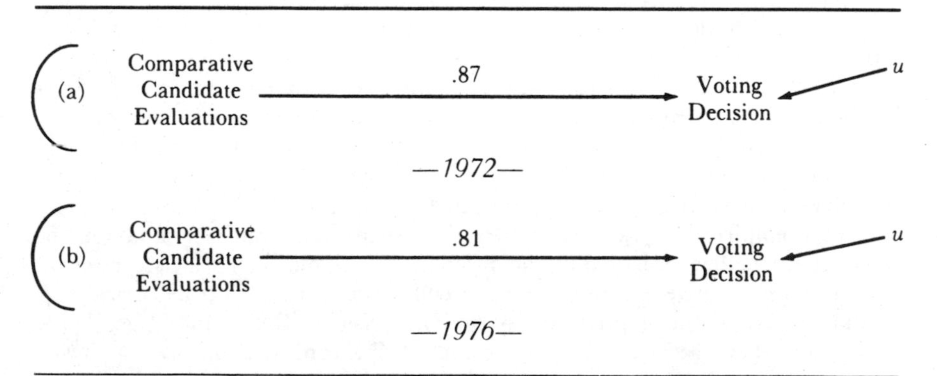

Source: 1972 and 1976 national election studies, Center for Political Studies, University of Michigan.

A second approach to measuring policy orientations makes use of a simple net count of pro-Republican minus pro-Democratic policy-related comments offered in response to the CPS open-ended questions concerning likes and dislikes for the major parties and candidates. It is similar to the policy variables used by Stokes (1966). This measure (which we have labeled "Net Policy Comments") allows respondents to define their own policy concerns, rather than imposing the same scales of policy alternatives upon everyone: it counts policy orientations as meaningful only when they are salient enough to be mentioned spontaneously by a respondent.[4]

We need a third measure of policy orientation in order to take account of the theoretical literature on spatial modeling which has grown out of the work of Hotelling (1929), Downs (1957), Davis, Hinich and Ordeshook (1970), and others. This literature specifies precisely how policy voting could occur in terms of an individual's decision calculus. It argues that voters take into account their perceptions of the policy proposals of the candidates as well as their own preferences, and that they vote for the candidate whose policy stands are perceived to be closer to their own preferences. Depending upon where the candidates actually stand and where the voters perceive them to be, there might or might not, according to these theories, be a linear relationship between voters' policy preferences and their intended vote. There should, however, always be a direct relationship between comparative policy distances and evaluation of the candidates.

Accordingly, we computed an indicator of "Comparative Policy Distances" between candidates and voters. There are various ways to construct policy distance measures; ours uses the CPS closed-ended, self-rating policy preference scales together with the associated perceptions of candidates' stands to construct a single, relative distance between the respondent and both candidates. That is, absolute distance measures were computed between the voter's preferred position and the perceived positions of the Republican and Democratic candidates on each policy scale. For each voter, distance from the Republican was then subtracted from his or her distance from the Democrat, and the resulting signed, algebraic scores were weighted and summed over all policy scales. The result tells which candidate a voter feels closer to, and by how much.[5]

Ordinary least squares estimates (standardized) of the effect of issues upon the vote, using each of these three policy measures and the simple bivariate model, are given in Figure 6-2. Plainly it makes a difference how policy orientations are measured. The first two estimates, based on simple policy preferences and open-ended policy comments, are similar and of moderate size. The latter is slightly larger, suggesting that policy comments may indeed more accurately reflect issues of real concern to voters. But more striking is the fact that the third estimate, using policy distances, is considerably larger than the other two. On the face of it, this seems to support the argument that spatial models do a superior job of specifying the form and process of the voting decision. However, there is an alternative explanation which we will deal with later: namely, that distance or proximity estimates of policy voting may be artificially inflated when the possibility of reciprocal causation is ignored.

In order to round out the bivariate approach to explaining the vote, we included in Figure 6-2 separate estimates of the effects of two non-policy

Figure 6-2 Bivariate Recursive Models of Voting Behavior, 1976

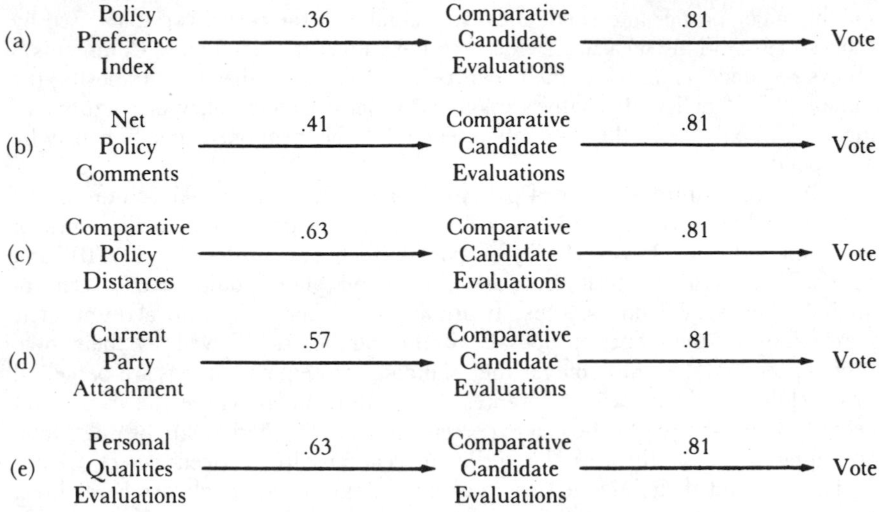

(a)	Policy Preference Index	.36 →	Comparative Candidate Evaluations	.81 →	Vote
(b)	Net Policy Comments	.41 →	Comparative Candidate Evaluations	.81 →	Vote
(c)	Comparative Policy Distances	.63 →	Comparative Candidate Evaluations	.81 →	Vote
(d)	Current Party Attachment	.57 →	Comparative Candidate Evaluations	.81 →	Vote
(e)	Personal Qualities Evaluations	.63 →	Comparative Candidate Evaluations	.81 →	Vote

Source: 1976 national election study, Center for Political Studies, University of Michigan.
Note: Symbols for disturbance terms are omitted for the sake of clarity.

variables, subjective party attachments and evaluations of the candidates' personal and leadership qualities. Subjective partisanship is measured by the usual CPS seven-point classification of "party identification" based on whether, generally speaking, respondents consider themselves Democrats, Republicans, Independents or whatever. In magnitude, the effect of partisanship ranks between the estimates for "Policy Preferences" and "Policy Comments," on the one hand, and "Comparative Policy Distances," on the other. This result highlights a problem faced by scholars interested in the relative importance of partisanship and policy concerns in the voting process. Obviously, a great deal depends upon how one defines and measures policy orientations at the outset.

We measured reactions to candidates' personalities by counting the net number of pro-Republican minus pro-Democratic comments in response to the CPS open-ended questions, including only those comments focusing on personal or leadership qualities and quite devoid of policy or partisan content. The standardized estimate of the effect of candidates' personal qualities on evaluations is bigger than that for subjective partisanship, policy preferences or policy comments, and equal in size to the bivariate coefficient for our comparative policy distance measure.

The most obvious objection to all these estimates is that they take account of only one independent variable at a time. If policy orientations, partisan commitment and evaluations of candidate character each have some independent influence on the voting decision, and if these variables are even moderately collinear, then the bivariate estimates will be biased. Under the usual circumstances (i.e., positive correlations among the regressors), the bias would be upward, so that bivariate methods are quite likely to overestimate the extent of policy voting—or, for that matter, the extent of party or candidate voting (Johnston, 1972). Some of the work of Boyd (1972), Pomper (1975), Aldrich (1975), Miller et al. (1976) and others is subject to this criticism. Particularly vulnerable is the issue-by-issue "normal vote" technique, since issues may be collinear with each other as well as with other variables.

Of course, most analysts are aware of this problem and incorporate two or more independent variables in their voting models. It is common, for example, to include one or another measure of policy orientations together with partisan loyalties.

Some estimates for such models are shown in Figure 6-3. As expected, the estimates for both policy orientations and partisanship effects are somewhat lower

Figure 6-3 Multivariate Recursive Models of Voting Behavior of 1976 with Policy Orientations and Partisanship as Independent Variables

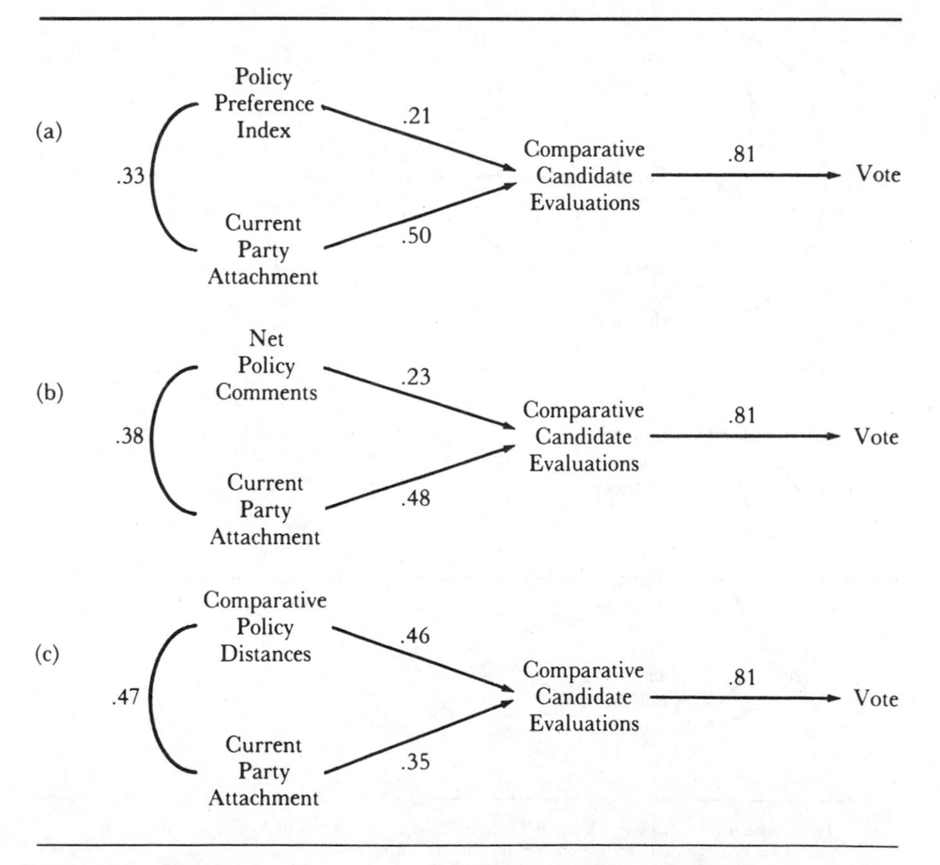

Source: 1976 national election study, Center for Political Studies, University of Michigan.
Note: Symbols for disturbance terms are omitted for the sake of clarity.

Figure 6-4 Multivariate Recursive Models of Voting Behavior for 1976 with Policy Orientations, Partisanship, and Personal Qualities Orientations as Independent Variables

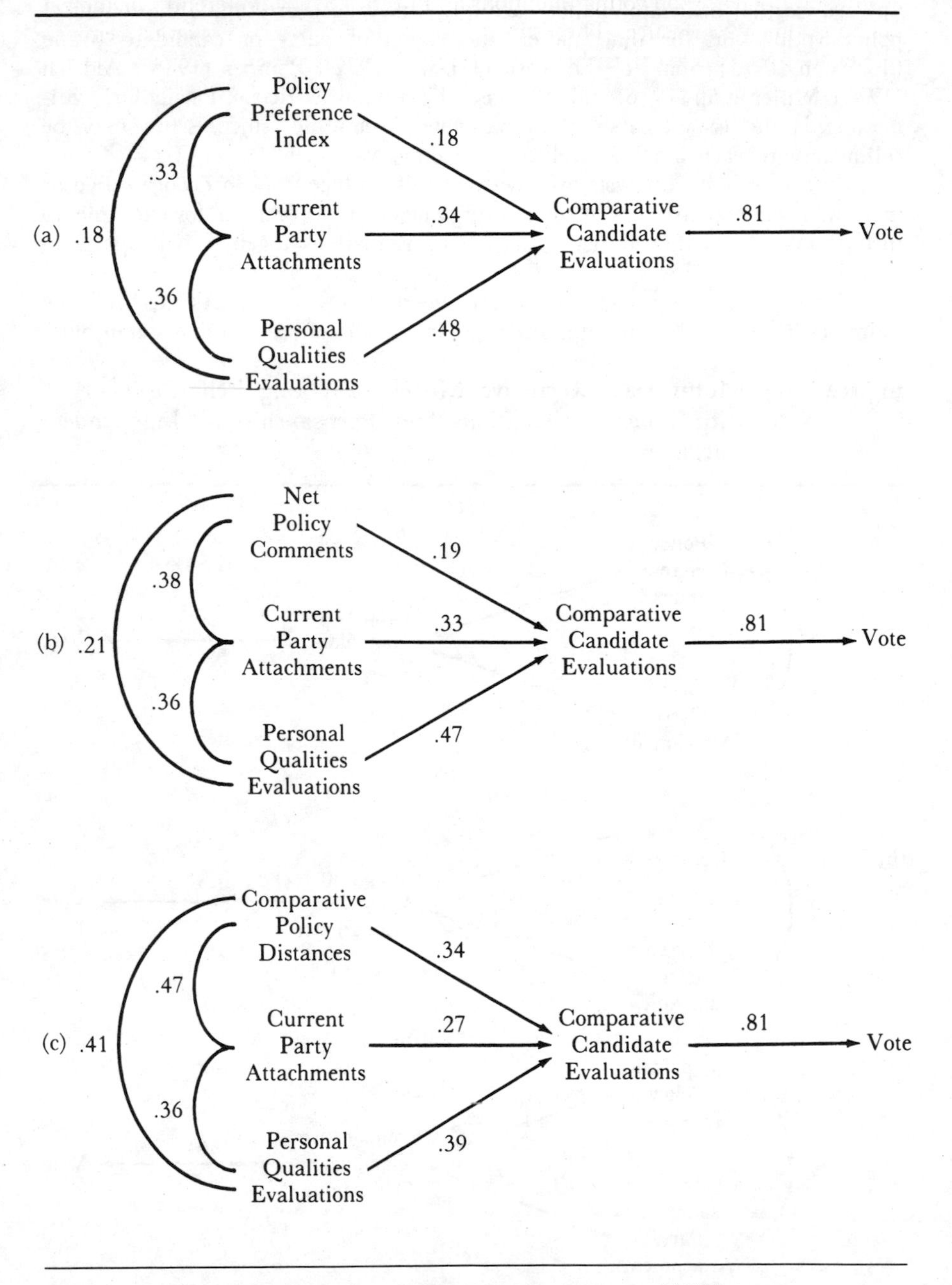

Source: 1976 national election study, Center for Political Studies, University of Michigan.
Note: Symbols for disturbance terms are omitted for the sake of clarity.

than those in Figure 6-2. Party attachments now appear to exert more than twice as much influence upon voting intentions as do either policy preferences or the net policy comments measure. The estimate for policy distances, however, remains higher than that for partisanship when both variables are included, although the disparity is not large.

One can easily add evaluations of the candidates' personal qualities to these models, as in Figure 6-4. The introduction of an additional explanatory variable results in still further reduction of the estimates for each separate effect. Yet, in relative terms, the initial findings continue to hold: in 1976 voters' evaluations of the candidates' personal attributes appear substantially more important than their partisan attachments in determining the vote choice. Furthermore, both current partisanship and candidates' personal qualities seem to carry far more weight in the voting decision than do policy considerations when the latter are measured by either the index of policy preferences or the net count of policy-oriented comments. If policy concerns are conceptualized as relative distances from the candidates, however, we arrive at a different conclusion. Then, policy considerations seem to be just about as important as personal qualities evaluations in the determination of intended votes. The effect of partisanship is substantially lower.

An important variant of the models in Figure 6-4 is that formulated by Stokes (1966), which resembles Figure 6-4b except that a net count of party-related open-ended comments, conceptualized as a "short term force" like issues or candidate personalities, is used in place of long-term party attachments.[6] Making this substitution decreases the party effect on the vote still further (see Figure 6-5). If we use this specification, the estimate for policy orientations (comments) is twice that for partisanship, while that for candidates' personal attributes increases to almost twice that for the policy measure and is nearly four times as large as the effect of party attachments.

Figure 6-5 Multivariate Recursive Model of Voting Behavior, 1976

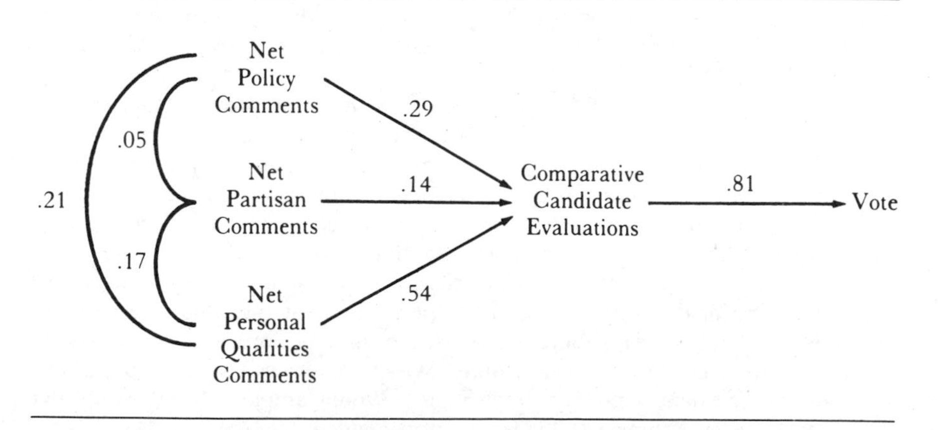

Source: 1976 national election study, Center for Political Studies, University of Michigan.
Note: Symbols for disturbance terms are omitted for the sake of clarity. Policy orientations, partisanship, and personal qualities evaluations measures all based upon net counts of open-ended comments.

Two-Way Causation: Non-recursive Models of the Vote

One problem with the preceding analyses is the multiplicity of conceptualizations and specifications. Undeniably, much of the confusion in debates over policy voting stems from the use of different policy measures, different specifications of equations, and different estimation techniques. Researchers simply talk past one another, treating findings as if they were inconsistent when they are not. In principle this problem is easily solved; it is merely necessary to be precise about what is being claimed, rather than talking in global terms.

A more fundamental problem with such analyses, however—a problem confounding most of the existing literature on voting behavior—is an incorrect assumption of one-way causation. The error of this assumption is most obvious in models employing policy proximity or distance measures. Clearly, citizens may tend to vote for the candidate to whom they feel closest on matters of public policy. Yet it seems to us quite possible—in fact likely—that citizens whose initial vote intentions may be formulated on non-policy grounds, can and do convince themselves that the candidates they prefer stand closer to them on the important policy issues. Just such a pattern is suggested by social-psychologists' studies of "projection" or "selective perception"; it also follows theoretically from the rational calculus of citizens operating with less than perfect information. Lacking other evidence, voters might reasonably infer that a candidate who agrees with them on most matters also would agree with them on any new policy matter that comes up. Thus perceived policy distances may be consequences as well as causes of intended votes. There is some empirical evidence, in Berelson et al., *Voting* (1954) and elsewhere, that overall evaluations of candidates do in fact affect perceptions of candidates' policy stands.

By this logic, two-way causation may have biased upward the estimate of the effects of policy distances upon vote intentions in Figures 6-2c, 6-3c, and 6-4c, and it might well bias upward the estimates of policy voting in any recursive model using proximity measures of this kind, even those which "control" for partisanship and other independent variables (Shapiro, 1969; RePass, 1971; Aldrich, 1975; Miller et al., 1976).

It must be recognized, however, that much the same problem can occur in voting models which employ policy measures that do not explicitly include perceptions of candidates' stands. For example, recall that policy comments are drawn from responses to the CPS questions concerning party and candidate likes and dislikes. Implicit in each response is a judgment—that is, a perception—about where the parties or candidates stand on policies salient to the voter. Despite the open-ended, voluntary character of these responses, they could still be based upon rationalized and/or incorrect perceptions of the candidate or party positions. In other words, policy comments, too, may be consequences as well as causes of overall candidate evaluations, which again could lead to inflated estimates of the extent of policy voting (Stokes, 1966; Campbell, Converse, Miller and Stokes, 1960; Pomper, 1975; Kagay and Caldeira, 1975).

Moreover, we see no reason to assume that voters' policy preferences themselves are unaffected by general candidate evaluations. When an attractive candidate takes a strong stand on a matter of public policy, might he or she not persuade some supporters—especially those for whom the issue is of comparatively low salience—to bring their opinions into agreement? Or, less grandly, might not some of a candidate's supporters, in lieu of genuine opinions, give facile responses to policy questions corresponding to what they think their preferred candidate stands for? Because candidates are often ambiguous, it can be argued that such persuasion effects are likely to be less important than the effects of projection or selective perception, but we see no reason to exclude altogether the possibility that persuasion occurs.

In short, we are suggesting that all analyses which postulate policy variables to be recursive, uni-directional influences on candidate evaluations or vote choices may be overestimating the extent of policy voting. All the previously cited voting studies (except those by Jackson, Achen, and Markus), and many others not cited, are offenders in this respect. Even the pioneering causal model of Goldberg (1966) is entirely recursive and subject to this criticism, as is the recent work of Nie, Verba and Petrocik (1976).

At the same time, we maintain that the many researchers who do not use policy proximity measures or some other means for taking explicit account of perceived candidate positions are likely to *under*estimate the degree of relationship between policy orientations and intended votes. There is no a priori way to tell for certain which direction of error predominates.

To extend this reasoning a bit further, there is no reason to consider subjective partisanship (i.e., "party identification") to be sacrosanct. It seems quite plausible to us that policy preferences—and relative policy distances from candidates—may be both causes and consequences of party loyalties. Just as opinion leadership by party figures might cause some citizens (even perfectly rational ones) to change their policy preferences, we strongly suspect that some voters' policy preferences—especially those touching on economic, social welfare or racial issues—have some effect on their choice of party in the first place. And, indeed, we would argue that policy distances from particular candidates, who may or may not take positions exactly along the lines of older party cleavages (thus reinforcing or weakening traditional policy profiles of the parties), are likely to affect the strength, if not the direction, of subjective partisanship during a given election campaign. Scholars interested in the relationship between partisanship and policy orientations have typically assumed that causation worked exclusively in one direction between the two, usually from party to issues. They may thereby have inflated their estimates of the effects of party identification (Campbell et al., 1960).[7]

Even Jackson's (1975b) pathbreaking non-recursive model postulates that party affects policy preferences but not vice versa. Jackson (1975) and Markus (1976) also rule out any possible influence of candidate evaluations upon policy preferences.

Finally, we must consider the possibility that voters' party loyalties may both affect and be affected by comparative candidate evaluations or intended votes during a particular campaign period. While most researchers have conceptualized partisanship as a sort of blind habit, a relatively long-term exogenous factor affecting vote choice, we expect that to some (perhaps modest) extent, preferences based on a candidate's character or policy stands will affect the intensity—and at times even the direction—of party affiliations. It seems to us an overinterpretation of the temporal stability of partisan attachments to assume that they are altogether impervious to candidate choices in ordinary elections. Candidates, after all, reflect credit or blame upon the parties that nominate them. Thus the many studies of party identification as a determinant of candidate evaluations or voting choices, from *The American Voter* onward, may have overestimated its effect by ignoring the opposite possibility (Campbell et al., 1960). The Michigan Tradition dies hard.

Nor is *The Changing American Voter* immune to this criticism (Nie, Verba and Petrocik, 1976). Comparisons between groups or candidates or over time are also subject to error because the biases in estimates are not necessarily constant from group to group or candidate to candidate or year to year.

We have made the sweeping claim that virtually all studies of policy orientations, partisanship and the vote—certainly including the primitive efforts reported in Figures 6-2 through 6-5—are subject to simultaneity bias and are potentially quite misleading. It is fair enough to ask whether we have anything constructive to add to this work of destruction.

The most appropriate way to handle the problem, we would argue, is through the use of non-recursive, simultaneous equation models which explicitly allow for the possibility of causal processes operating in both directions between variables (Johnston, 1972; Theil, 1971; Hanushek and Jackson, 1977; Duncan, 1975).[8] We can begin to apply such techniques to the voting problem by specifying the central set of variables which we believe to be mutually endogenous—that is, which reciprocally affect each other: comparative candidate evaluations, relative policy distance between the voter and candidates, and current subjective partisanship. We will continue to treat measures of reported vote as direct consequences of overall candidate evaluations.

The relationships postulated among these variables are diagrammed in Figure 6-6. Within the context of this model, we seek to investigate not only the effect of policy orientations upon the vote, but also five other processes of interest:

Figure 6-6 Reciprocal Causal Paths in a Non-Recursive Voting Model

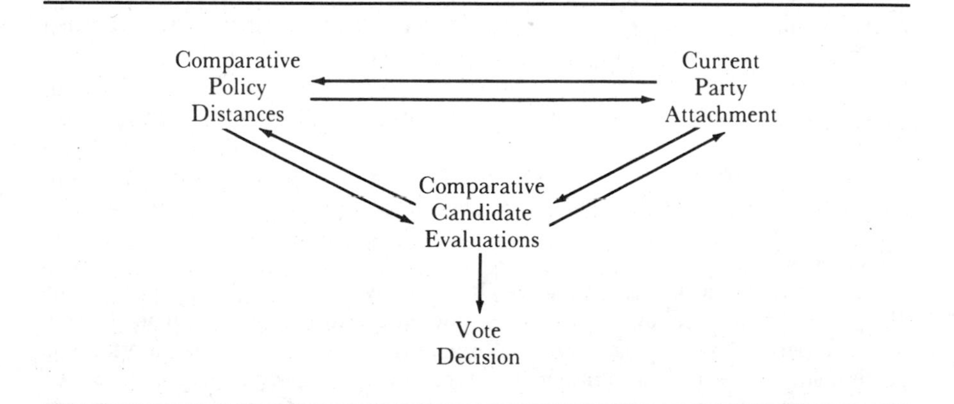

Source: Compiled by the authors.

namely, the reverse effect of overall candidate evaluations upon comparative policy distances, and the two-way linkages between current partisanship and policy distances as well as between party attachments and comparative candidate evaluations.

We cannot estimate any of the coefficients in Figure 6-6, as it stands, because the model is hopelessly underidentified. That is, there are only three empirically observable relationships among the central endogenous variables available to estimate the six causal processes of theoretical interest. Ordinary least squares regression is clearly not appropriate for estimating these causal paths since the required assumptions of independence between the regressors and error terms in each equation cannot be justified. To distinguish between the effects possibly operating in both directions between any two endogenous variables, we must bring additional information into the estimation process. The sort of information needed may be provided by a set of variables which are exogenous to the reciprocal processes specified in Figure 6-6—variables can be assumed (on theoretical grounds) to be unaffected by any endogenous variables, yet which have direct effects on some, but not all, of the endogenous variables (Fisher, 1966).

It is in the search for suitable exogenous variables that difficulties mount, for most of the pertinent social theory is either not very powerful or not universally accepted. The grounds for specifying that a given variable theoretically cannot affect or be affected by another are seldom overwhelming. The situation is worse than usual when one deals with psychological measurements or attitudinal variables, since practically any attitude might conceivably affect any other. There are times when we seem to be studying relationships between mush and slush.

Fortunately, however, it is possible to specify certain exogenous variables for our model with reasonable (and sometimes considerable) confidence, allowing us to identify several of the causal paths. Theory and past empirical research suggest, for example, that the party choices of voters' parents have a direct effect upon their own partisan proclivities, but do not affect their perceived policy distances or overall evaluations of the candidates, except insofar as they act through their own party affiliation. Parents' partisan commitments, therefore, can be specified as operating through uni-directional causal paths upon voters' partisanship only, and their direct effects excluded elsewhere in the model. This will help to identify the effects of voters' partisanship on their policy-oriented evaluations and their vote intentions.[9]

Similarly, we can with some confidence specify that voters' assessments of the character traits and personal qualities of the candidates (as measured by spontaneous responses to open-ended items about candidate likes and dislikes) should have direct effects upon overall comparative candidate evaluations, but should not be substantially affected by overall evaluations in return. In addition, we would argue that character and personality evaluations have no direct links to the voters' policy evaluations of candidates or to their current subjective partisanship, but rather that these effects are transmitted indirectly through the more general overall evaluations of candidates. Thus, the assumption of a recursive relationship from personal qualities assessments to overall candidate evaluations (and the concomitant exclusion of direct effects elsewhere in the model) allows identification of the causal paths from candidate evaluations to both partisanship and comparative policy distances.

Our confidence in this specification depends heavily upon our use only of specific, spontaneous comments about candidates' characteristics, which are far more likely to be causes than effects of candidate evaluations.

It is somewhat more difficult to specify variables which affect voters' comparative policy distances without also affecting the other endogenous variables in the system. We begin, however, by taking advantage of the fact that a number of the voters' background or demographic attributes—factors such as race, sex, age, income and education—affect policy proximities by initially affecting the voters' policy preferences. There is little question that voters' background characteristics are truly exogenous to the electoral process. But the question arises whether they also affect partisanship or general candidate evaluations directly, or whether their effects are transmitted entirely through perceived policy distances. We will assume the latter in our initial model and conduct some tests on the effects of that assumption below.

We have, now, a non-recursive model in which all hypothesized causal paths are identified. The following structural equations are diagrammed in Figure 6-7.

$$\begin{array}{c}\text{Comparative}\\ \text{Candidate}\\ \text{Evaluations}\end{array} = b_1 \begin{array}{c}\text{Comparative}\\ \text{Policy}\\ \text{Distances}\end{array} + b_2 \begin{array}{c}\text{Current}\\ \text{Party}\\ \text{Attachment}\end{array} + b_3 \begin{array}{c}\text{Personal}\\ \text{Qualities}\\ \text{Evaluations}\end{array} + u. \quad (1)$$

$$\begin{array}{c}\text{Comparative}\\ \text{Policy}\\ \text{Distances}\end{array} = b_4 \begin{array}{c}\text{Comparative}\\ \text{Candidate}\\ \text{Evaluations}\end{array} + b_5 \begin{array}{c}\text{Current}\\ \text{Party}\\ \text{Attachment}\end{array} + b_6\,\text{Race} + b_7\,\text{Age} + b_8\,\text{Sex} + b_9\,\text{Education} + b_{10}\,\text{Income} + u. \quad (2)$$

$$\begin{array}{c}\text{Current}\\ \text{Party}\\ \text{Attachment}\end{array} = b_{11} \begin{array}{c}\text{Comparative}\\ \text{Policy}\\ \text{Distances}\end{array} + b_{12} \begin{array}{c}\text{Comparative}\\ \text{Candidate}\\ \text{Evaluations}\end{array} + b_{13} \begin{array}{c}\text{Father's}\\ \text{Party}\\ \text{Attachment}\end{array} + b_{14} \begin{array}{c}\text{Mother's}\\ \text{Party}\\ \text{Attachment}\end{array} + u. \quad (3)$$

Simply providing for identification of path coefficients does not guarantee adequate specification of the causal model, however, and we believe that additional exogenous variables must be included to overcome biases of a different sort. When important independent variables are omitted from any equation of the model, coefficients for the included variables will still be biased if, for whatever reason, the omitted and included variables are correlated. Several such variables are suggested by past research devoted to the individual equations of our model.

The literature on party identification points to five additional potential influences upon current subjective partisanship: the voter's sense of long-term, traditional involvement with a particular party; degree of consistency in party

Figure 6-7 Non-Recursive Voting Model with Incomplete Structural Equations

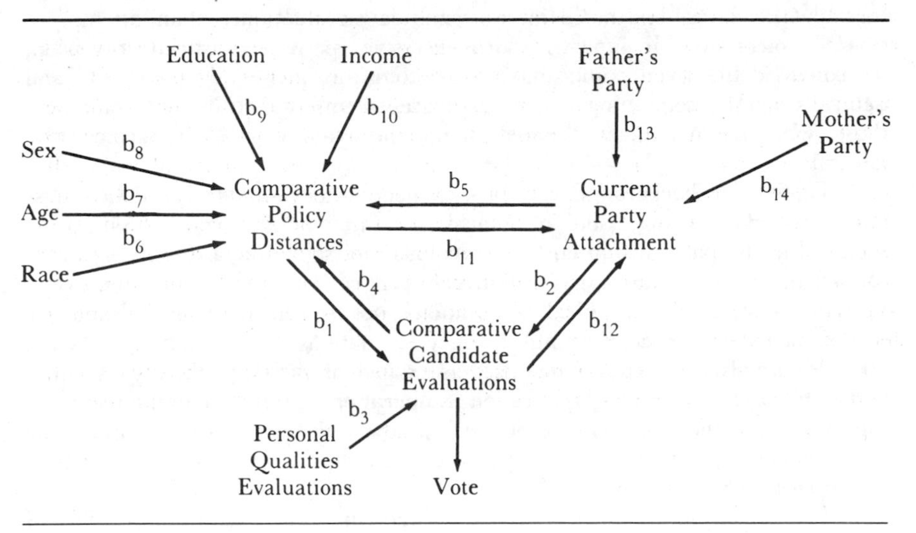

Source: Compiled by the authors.
Note: Disturbance symbols have been omitted for the sake of clarity.

voting for president; religious preference; region of residence; and general ideological leaning. Some of these factors should carry greatest weight among voters whose party loyalties differ from those of their parents or who were not influenced in any partisan direction by their parents; others mediate parental influence.

For many voters, both the direction and strength of current partisanship may be expected to depend in part upon their degree of involvement with their chosen parties, considered either as reference groups to which loyalty is owed, or as information sources providing interpretations and evaluations of the political environment. We measured this sort of involvement by a net count of positive and negative comments which focus only on parties as traditional referents, wholly excluding both policy and candidate personality connotations: "I've just always been (or voted as) a Democrat," or "I like Nixon just because he's a good Republican."

An even stronger factor affecting current partisanship may be our measure of presidential voting consistency, which combines information about citizens' regularity of voting in presidential elections with data on whether they always supported a particular party for president.

In order to take account of socialization or information sources outside the family for those voters with neither a strong sense of partisan tradition nor a history of regular party voting, we included variables which classify citizens according to their region of residence (10-state South versus all other states) and their religious preferences (Catholics, Jews, Fundamentalist Protestants and those with no religious preference versus all others). Finally, for those voters whose partisanship derives from their view of the parties as purveyors of more or less coherent social and economic programs, we included a simple trichotomous classification of their ideological leaning based on their self-placement on the CPS closed-ended liberal/conservative scale. Rather than attempt to classify voters on this indicator with excessive (perhaps artificial) precision, we collapsed the seven points into a trichotomy of "pro-left," "pro-right" and neutral positions, combining voters who placed themselves at the mid-point with those who did not place themselves on the scale at all, as ideologically neutral.

To the five background variables exogenous to Comparative Policy Distances, we added a single additional measure—the same ideological classification included in the partisanship equation. Inclusion of so simple a classifying index allows us, without undue worry about reciprocal causation to estimate the extent to which voters, philosophical orientations not rooted in racial, sexual or socioeconomic differences may affect policy evaluations of the candidates. While attitudes are always suspect when used as exogenous variables, the high salience and stability of voters' self-classification as liberal or conservative to the moderate number of respondents who embrace such a label bolsters this specification. The direction of such a stance is considerably less subject to electoral influence than is the intensity of commitment.

The special nature of the Carter candidacy in 1976 raised the possibility of two additional factors which might have independent effects on comparative candidate evaluations, namely Carter's southern origins and his highly religious outlook. Therefore, we included in the equation for overall candidate evaluations two more exogenous variables. The first is the same indicator of region of residence which appears in the partisanship equation; the second is the dichotomous classification of citizens' religious preferences which also appears in the partisanship equation.

With the addition of these exogenous variables, our model may be described by structural Equations (4) through (6) (diagrammed in Figure 6-8):

$$\begin{matrix}\text{Comparative}\\ \text{Candidate}\\ \text{Evaluations}\end{matrix} = b_1 \begin{matrix}\text{Comparative}\\ \text{Policy}\\ \text{Distances}\end{matrix} + b_2 \begin{matrix}\text{Current}\\ \text{Party}\\ \text{Attachment}\end{matrix} + b_3 \begin{matrix}\text{Personal}\\ \text{Qualities}\\ \text{Evaluations}\end{matrix} + b_4\,\text{Region} + b_5\,\text{Religion} + u. \qquad (4)$$

$$\begin{matrix}\text{Comparative}\\ \text{Policy}\\ \text{Distances}\end{matrix} = b_6 \begin{matrix}\text{Comparative}\\ \text{Candidate}\\ \text{Evaluations}\end{matrix} + b_7 \begin{matrix}\text{Current}\\ \text{Party}\\ \text{Attachment}\end{matrix} + b_8\,\text{Race} + b_9\,\text{Age} + b_{10}\,\text{Sex} + b_{11}\,\text{Education} + b_{12}\,\text{Income} + b_{13}\,\text{Ideology} + u. \qquad (5)$$

$$\begin{matrix}\text{Current}\\ \text{Party}\\ \text{Attachment}\end{matrix} = b_{14} \begin{matrix}\text{Comparative}\\ \text{Policy}\\ \text{Distances}\end{matrix} + b_{15} \begin{matrix}\text{Comparative}\\ \text{Candidate}\\ \text{Evaluations}\end{matrix} + b_{16} \begin{matrix}\text{Father's}\\ \text{Party}\\ \text{Attachment}\end{matrix} +$$

$$b_{17} \begin{matrix}\text{Mother's}\\ \text{Party}\\ \text{Attachment}\end{matrix} + b_{18} \begin{matrix}\text{Traditional}\\ \text{Party}\\ \text{Involvement}\end{matrix} +$$

$$b_{19} \begin{matrix}\text{Partisan}\\ \text{Voting}\\ \text{History}\end{matrix} + b_{20}\ \text{Region} + b_{21}\ \text{Religion} +$$

$$b_{22}\ \text{Ideology} + u. \qquad (6)$$

Since each equation of the model includes overidentified paths, we estimated the standardized coefficients for the model using two-stage and three-stage least squares programs.[10] These estimates are also presented in Figure 6-8.

To us, the most striking aspect of the estimates in Figure 6-8 is the extent to which they differ from the corresponding coefficients obtained using simple recursive models. Comparative policy distances now appear to be the strongest single factor affecting intended votes, with a standardized, partial (3SLS) regression coefficient of .44. This estimate is greater than that produced by any of the multivariate recursive models examined above; it is roughly comparable in magnitude to the bivariate coefficient for the net policy comments measure (recall Figure 6-2b above), although it would be wrong to conclude that recursive models using comment counts necessarily give good estimates of policy voting generally, in all elections.

This major role played by policy orientations in the voting decision is, of course, very much in the spirit of rational-man spatial models. It is noteworthy

Figure 6-8 Full Non-Recursive Voting Model with Overidentified Structural Equations, 1976

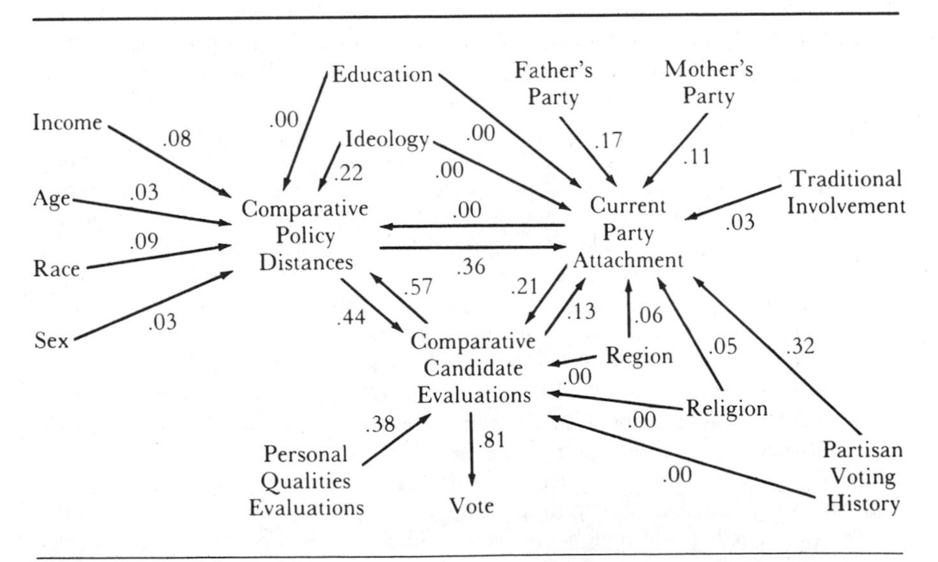

Source: 1976 national election study, Center for Political Studis, University of Michigan.
Note: Disturbance symbols and inter-correlations among exogenous variables have been omitted for the sake of clarity.

that our estimation procedure, which takes explicit account of theory by using policy proximity measures, reveals a greater extent of policy voting than do most other methods. At the same time, however, evaluations of the candidates' personal and leadership qualities run a close second in importance, with a standardized coefficient of .38 (about equal to the estimate derived from the recursive model depicted in Figure 6-4c). Indeed, we cannot be sure that the policy effect was significantly greater than that of candidate personality. Spatial models in their narrowest form, postulating exclusively policy-oriented voting, are plainly inadequate. But we would argue that this does not reflect badly on the citizenry. In a presidential system, rational individuals must pay attention to leadership characteristics, if only to ensure that their favored candidate is competent to carry out the promised policy stands.

In 1976, citizens' party attachments had much less direct influence upon vote intention than either policy orientations or evaluations of personal qualities. The coefficient of .21 is lower than that for any of the recursive estimates presented above (except that for the attenuated partisan comments measure in Figure 6-5). Party loyalties, in other words, had some independent effect on the vote—again contrary to narrow notions of voter rationality, but not to a broader conception. (Surely citizens are well advised to view the parties to some extent as governing teams, with records of past performance which bear upon future prospects. What V. O. Key called the "standing decision" to support one or another party—subject, of course, to modification in the light of experience—is an efficient and generally reliable aid in voting.) Yet our estimate indicates that partisanship was by no means a straitjacket. It was clearly not the most important factor affecting the vote, as has been alleged of the 1950s and early 1960s.

Despite the special features of Carter's campaign, in 1976 the estimated coefficients for both region and religion did not differ significantly from zero. We suspect that this result follows from the fact that evaluations of personal qualities and current partisanship already take account of such effects. With these variables included in the candidate evaluations equation, the region and religion variables are superfluous.

Two important findings, which can emerge only from a non-recursive model like ours, concern the reciprocal effects of both intended votes and policy distances upon current partisanship. When all of the customary influences on the formation and maintenance of party attachments are allowed for, intended votes still show a modest independent effect (.13) on voters subjective partisanship. In 1976, then, partisanship was not an exogenous influence on the vote, impervious to other electoral stimuli. Instead citizens apparently alter their party loyalties when the parties nominate especially desirable or undesirable candidates, just as sensible voters would be expected to do. By ignoring this effect of overall evaluations of the presidential candidates upon partisanship, many scholars have overestimated the effects of party affiliation upon voting decisions.

What may be more surprising to some is the much stronger effect (.36) of comparative policy distances from the candidates upon party attachment. Conceptually, it seems logical enough that voters who see their policy interests served much better by one candidate than another might be inclined to consider themselves supporters of that candidate's party. The question arises, however, why such a judgment on policy grounds would not be translated into an overall positive evaluation of (i.e., an intention to vote for) that candidate, and only then go on to influence partisanship. The answer seems to involve the fact that policy judgments form only one of many independent dimensions of candidate evaluations; preference for one candidate on policy grounds does not guarantee a favorable evaluation overall. In fact, in 1976, over 15 percent of the survey respondents fell at the neutral or indifference point on our measure of comparative candidate evaluations. While 65 percent were classified as being closer to Carter on policy matters (35 percent closer to Ford), only 33 percent preferred Carter's personal and leadership qualities and 40 percent preferred Ford's. Thus even when comparative policy distances did not automatically lead to vote intentions, they appear to have influenced voters' feelings of attachment to the political parties.

For a given election, the overall magnitude of either of these endogenous effects on partisanship would depend, of course, upon citizens' partisan attitudes before the start of the campaign and upon their various evaluations of the nominees. The effects are not overwhelmingly large; we would not argue from these findings that major shifts of pre-existing party allegiances result from a campaign like that of 1976. The several variables which we specified as exogenous to current party attachment have significant (and in some cases, sizeable) coefficients, clearly indicating the presence of powerful stabilizing influences. The effects of parental socialization and of consistency in party vote for president, for example, no doubt serve to anchor some voters against the ebb and flow of campaign developments. Yet change in party attachment, whether through the weakening or strengthening of former ties, or by the creation of a sense of partisanship among new voters, clearly followed from evaluations of campaign stimuli. This finding, we hope, will help lay to rest the notion that partisanship can be treated as an unmoved mover in the analysis of voting behavior.

Perhaps the most theoretically important of all our estimates is the strong effect (.57) of overall candidate evaluations upon perceived policy distances. The existence of such an effect squarely controverts the assumptions of spatial models, which specify that voting decisions are the result of calculations of policy proximities or distances from the candidates, and that the policy preferences and perceptions of candidates' stands used in these calculations are independently arrived at. The evidence is clear that influence runs both ways: voters' evaluations of Carter's and Ford's policy stands were strongly conditioned by their overall judgments about the candidates. Those who generally favored Carter, let us say, tended to locate themselves and Carter close together on the policy scales; those who disfavored a candidate tended to place themselves and that candidate farther apart. This finding goes against the fixed-preferences and perfect-information assumptions widespread in economists' views of politics (and, for that matter, economics as well). It calls for considerable rethinking of some notions of electoral democracy.

At the same time, it would be quite erroneous to conclude that we have found voters to be irrational or deficient with respect to some democratic ideal. In the first place, the influence of candidate evaluations upon perceived policy distances from candidates encompasses a complex bundle of processes (projection, persuasion, rationalization), in which either voters' policy preferences or their perceptions of candidate stands are affected by their evaluations of the candidates. Some of these processes are useful or even essential to the workings of democracy; we cannot at present sort out which are operating. (To distinguish the effects on perceptions from those on preferences would require a four-equation model with two complicated nonlinear equations.) In the second place, most if not all of these processes are best understood as reactions by rational citizens to the problems of obtaining political information. To the extent that some reactions interfere with electoral democracy, much of the blame must fall upon the political environment and the kinds of information made available (or lacking), rather than upon the voters themselves.

It is quite possible—and compatible with our findings—that some voters who have no information about the candidates' policy stands, but who have developed a preference for one candidate (based on party ties or personal attributes) project their own preferred policy positions onto their favorite candidate, especially when pestered to answer survey questions about where candidates stand. In addition, there are no doubt voters for whom policy considerations are of sufficiently low salience that they blithely adopt as their own the policy prescriptions of whichever candidate they have come to prefer for non-policy reasons. Yet persuasion (i.e., a candidate's influence upon policy preferences) can take a much less casual form—a form equally compatible with our findings—when citizens listen to information and argument about policy and are genuinely convinced by a candidate they trust. In a complicated world of imperfect information, rational citizens must be open to persuasion.

Moreover, the existence of strong effects of policy orientations upon candidate evaluations suggests that few voters, if any, rely exclusively upon simple rationalization in arriving at their final evaluations of the presidential contenders' policies. It is much more likely that a given voter will have had at least some realistic notion of his or her comparative distances from the candidates which conditioned more general evaluations in the first place. Lacking perfect information, such voters might then combine what data they have on policy distances with party cues and judgments about the candidates' personal attributes into a preliminary comparative evaluation of the nominees, which they then may use to infer their ultimate net distance from the candidates over a wider range of policy areas. In this light, what at first seemed to be rationalization may in fact be rationality.

Again, we would emphasize that if voters make foolish and easily avoidable errors about candidates' policy stands (and no evidence yet establishes this to be so), this probably results as much from the obscurity and ambiguity of what candidates say as from limitations of citizens' cognitive processes (Page, 1978, Ch. 6).

All the findings we have discussed so far pertain to the 1976 presidential election. Both as a check on our methods and for its own substantive interest, we present in Figure 6-9 comparable estimates for 1972. All measures were constructed in precisely the same way as for 1976, and the series of alternative specifications used for testing purposes were identical.

Comparison of Figures 6-8 and 6-9 reveals many similarities in overall structure, especially in the effects of exogenous variables. This increases our confidence in the model and the estimation procedure. At the same time, the

Figure 6-9 Full Non-Recursive Voting Model with Overidentified Structural Equations, 1972

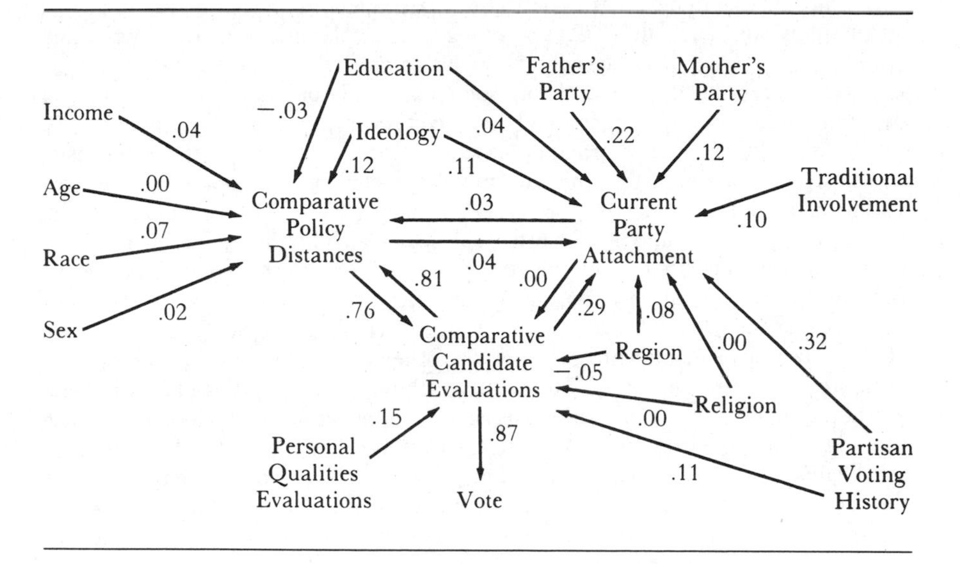

Source: 1972 national election study, Center for Political Studies, University of Michigan.

Note: Disturbance symbols and inter-correlations among exognous variables have been omitted for the sake of clarity.

comparison uncovers some sharp differences, which are readily interpretable in terms of differences in the electoral environment. Plainly the Carter-Ford contest and the Nixon-McGovern campaign differed in ways which aroused dissimilar reactions among the voters.

As in 1976, we find in 1972 clear evidence of reciprocal causation between policy orientations and overall candidate evaluations. Many citizens voted on policy grounds, but many also were influenced in their assessment of policy distances by their overall evaluations of the candidates. As in 1976, the effect of candidate evaluations upon perceived policy distances (.81) appears slightly stronger than the effect in the opposite direction (.76), but this difference was much smaller in 1972 than in 1976 and is not statistically significant. No doubt the projection or rationalization of issue stands was relatively more difficult in the "clear choice" setting of 1972.

What stands out most strongly is the much greater magnitude of both roles of policy orientations (as both independent and dependent variables) in 1972. The Nixon-McGovern election was truly an issue-oriented affair; no other factor approached the importance of public policy orientations in affecting voting decisions. Indeed, this feature of the election was so marked that it can be discerned no matter how crudely the data are analyzed, as when we replicated for 1972 various simple recursive models. Yet, at the same time, the clarity of the choice on policy grounds evidently did not prevent a very substantial amount of alteration in perceptions of candidate stands and/or policy preferences in response to feelings about the candidates.[11]

The impact upon votes of citizens' evaluations of personal qualities was surprisingly low (.15) in 1972, suggesting that explanations of the vote which emphasize McGovern's allegedly poor judgment and personal instability as important direct factors are probably somewhat wide of the mark. According to our estimates, policy distances had an effect over five times as great as did reactions to the candidates' personal attributes. Still, this finding is not inconsistent with the possibility that the outcome of the election (as opposed to the total variance in voting decisions) was heavily influenced by judgments about the candidates' personal and leadership qualities. Calculations of Stokes-type net effects, which take account of the strongly anti-McGovern drift of this factor, indicate that it was quite important (Popkin et al., 1976).

Among the most noteworthy aspects of Figure 6-9 is the nearly total absence of any effect of party attachments upon the other two endogenous variables. Our estimates reveal that in 1972—quite unlike 1976—party loyalties played no part in the formation either of voting decisions or perceptions of closeness to the candidates on policy matters. McGovern dramatically dissociated himself from the Democratic party's mainstream; and, by the same token, the central core of the Democratic party abandoned McGovern to his own devices. Party *per se* had no independent effect at all on the vote. Furthermore, the absence of a significant effect of policy distances upon partisanship, together with the very strong impact of policy distances upon intended vote, indicates that the policy choices around which voting decisions revolved (the Vietnam War, urban unrest, campus disturbances, alternative life styles) cut across the grain of the older party cleavages.

There was, on the other hand, apparently some effect of intended votes upon partisanship. That is, although party loyalties did not affect votes, intended votes did affect partisanship—presumably because some Democratic defectors to Nixon felt their Democratic affiliations to be weakened. There are, however, some doubts about this finding. In spite of the moderate size of this coefficient (.29), the conventional significance test (which is asymptotically valid for two- and three-stage least squares estimation) indicates that it is not significantly different from zero at the .05 confidence level. Examination of the intermediate two-stage calculations reveals a high degree of collinearity between the "decontaminated" versions of the policy distance and candidate evaluations variables. This results in high standard errors of estimates for the respective coefficients (i.e., lowers their precision), which substantially raises the difficulty of disentangling the independent effects for these two variables. Since we presently lack any satisfactory way to deal with multicollinearity in the second stage of two-stage least squares, it is necessary to reserve judgment on the significance or insignificance of the 1972 impact of intended vote upon partisanship.

Among the exogenous factors in 1972, there are also some differences from 1976 related to the nature of the candidate pairings in those two years. For the most part, however, the exogenous variables—especially those which represent stable characteristics of respondents—exerted roughly comparable amounts of influence in both elections. In general, the overall structural similarity between the estimated models for 1972 and 1976 is an encouraging sign that the estimates are correct and not subject to vagaries of the estimation technique or arbitrary variations with independent data sets.

Thus the variation in the effects of ideological orientations is easily exhausted in terms of the differences in the kinds of policies at issue during the two campaigns. In 1976, policy debates tended to line up much more with older, New Deal notions of liberalism and conservatism than was the case in 1972. Our measure of ideological leaning (which relates most closely to voters' attitudes on New Deal type issues) therefore had a greater effect on policy distances in 1976 than in 1972. In addition, whereas in 1972 voters' ideological orientations affected both policy distances and party attachments directly, in 1976 the effects of ideology were passed entirely through policy distances, affecting partisanship indirectly via the path from policy distances to partisanship.

Changes in the pattern of effects for partisan voting consistency are of a similar nature. In 1972, party attachments had no discernible effect on comparative candidate evaluations. Yet the more consistently citizens had voted for the same party for president, the more likely they were to prefer that party's candidate to the opposition in 1972. Presumably it took a rather special kind of partisan attachment rooted in a firm history of voting support to make Democrats (independently of other factors) prefer McGovern to Nixon. In 1976, however, we find that the direct path from voting history to comparative evaluations no longer functioned. Again, controlling for other factors, voting history directly affected only current party attachments, with candidate evaluations being affected only indirectly.

Finally, it seems to us that the differences in the effect of personal qualities evaluations between the elections is largely due to the great differences in the intensity of the effects of policy issues in the two campaigns. Policy distances were so overwhelmingly important in 1972 that judgments about personal attributes were left with relatively little independent explanatory power.

Conclusions

The clearest implications of our findings concern errors inherent in recursive voting models. In the first place, researchers who rely on single-equation techniques simply fail to reproduce faithfully the underlying complexity of the electoral decision process. Beyond this, even if multiple equations are specified in elaborate hierarchical recursive models, the estimated coefficients are still subject to simultaneity bias.

This defect is most damaging when recursive models are used with variables (such as the policy distance measures) which are especially likely to have been influenced by the very factors of which they are presumed causes. Our results suggest that the use of such measures should be restricted to non-recursive simultaneous equation models and that only those estimation techniques appropriate for such models should be applied. Yet practically all studies of issue voting, party identification and the like have specified uni-directional causal relationships without having theoretical justification for doing so. Our findings indicate that the degree of error introduced by mis-specification and simultaneity bias in such models can be quite substantial.

Our most important empirical discovery involves the reciprocal causal paths between policy orientations and overall candidate evaluations. In both 1972 and

1976 there was a high degree of policy-oriented voting—considerably more than is revealed by some less powerful analytical techniques. The identification in both years of a substantial effect from intended votes to policy distances, as well, confirms what many theorists have suspected for some time: policy-based evaluations of presidential candidates are endogenous to the electoral process.

We have argued that the effect of intended votes upon policy distances is consistent with individual rationality, since it may be perfectly rational to be persuaded by a favored candidate's policy stands, or even to infer a candidate's positions on policies (and, hence, one's degree of proximity to them) from other characteristics. We have pointed out, however, that this is inconsistent with simple spatial models of voting behavior, in which preferences are assumed to be fixed, and perceptions of candidate stands are assumed to vary only randomly (if at all) among the electorate.

In addition, the estimates from our two data sets imply that the effect of partisanship on the vote varies considerably across elections, depending largely upon the nature of the candidate pairings and the extent to which current policy issues conflict or coincide with established party cleavages. When the policy debates of a campaign are such that the parties are seen to have relatively distinct and internally coherent positions, and when the presidential nominees are perceived as being reasonably typical representatives of their respective parties' interests and stands (as was largely the case in 1976), then voters' current party attachments may both affect and be affected by policy orientations and overall candidate evaluations. When these conditions are not met (and surely 1972 was a quintessential case where they were not), partisanship is isolated from the electoral process.

Further, when party loyalties do enter in, they do not function purely as fixed determinants of the vote; those loyalties can themselves be affected by attitudes toward the current candidates. Even short of major realignments, party affiliations are effects as well as causes in the electoral process.

We have contended that non-recursive simultaneous equation models are necessary in order to eliminate substantial, systematic biases from estimates based on cross-sectional data. At the same time, we must concede that the modeling procedures and estimating techniques we advocate are by no means free from specification problems. One of the chief difficulties is locating variables in existing data which are genuinely exogenous—that is, which are truly free from reciprocal influence by their target endogenous variables, and which can be excluded on persuasive theoretical grounds from having direct effects on certain other endogenous variables. In the search for plausible and identifiable specifications, researchers must be quite careful to state their theoretical justifications, and also to make clear, by the use of sensitivity testing, just what the consequences of alternative specifications would be.

Simultaneous equation analyses are, to an important extent, dependent for their success upon the decisions of those who design survey instruments and collect the data. If important variables are not measured or are measured poorly, one cannot place much confidence in empirical findings. By "important variables," we mean not only those of major theoretical and substantive interest, but also potential exogenous variables, some of which may be of little interest in themselves but which have the theoretical properties necessary to assist in estimation.

Lacking tailor-made measures, we have tried to exercise great caution in the specification of exogenous variables—choosing wherever possible items on which voters had fixed characteristics, or had reached established values prior to the campaign under study. Where this was not possible, e.g., in the cases of evaluations of candidates' personal qualities or of voters' ideological leanings, we sought constructs which approached the theoretical ideal as closely as possible. Our measure of personal qualities evaluations, for example, was operationalized so as to minimize the possibility that individual voters' scores would be affected by other factors, while maximizing the probability that they would reflect the true extent to which personal qualities evaluations formed the basis of the voter's electoral decision. We doubt that this construct perfectly satisfies all of the theoretical requirements of an ideal exogenous variable. We believe, however, that it is a defensible specification and that any biases introduced by this type of measure will be small indeed when compared with those resulting from single equation or recursive estimation. The estimates of effects from candidate evaluations to policy distances and partisanship, which depend heavily upon this specification, may be slightly inflated, but we are satisfied that they are very nearly correct.[12]

Future presidential elections will no doubt be accompanied by voter surveys of varying purposes and designs. The opportunities for further developments in non-recursive modeling remain open on a good many fronts. The refinement of existing exogenous measures, the use of panel studies and the incorporation of quasi-experimental designs in future surveys all offer possibilities for improvements in the analytical techniques advocated here. Even limited success in this direction will add far more to our understanding of voting behavior than will repetition of error-ridden, mis-specified models.

NOTES

1. See RePass (1976), Kessel (1972), Brody and Page (1972).
2. The term "recursive"—literally "running back"—is unfortunate, because it gives exactly the opposite of the correct impression. It does not actually describe relationships between variables, but refers to a property of the corresponding system of equations. It is probably too late to undo the confusion resulting from this usage.
3. Thermometer scores range between 0 ("very cold or unfavorable") through 50 ("no feeling at all for candidate") to 100 ("very warm or favorable"). In the 1972 survey, when thermometer questions were asked both before and after the election, we used average scores in order to reduce measurement error.
4. We experimented with a number of coding rules governing which comments to count as policy-oriented, ranging from the vague and general to only the most specific. Inclusion of vague comments led to a much larger, and probably inflated, relationship with candidate evaluations. The estimates reported here are all based upon a narrow, specific definition of policy concerns.

5. We presume linearity rather than the quadratic loss function specified by Davis et al. (1970) because we see the CPS seven-point scales, with their labeled endpoints but unlabeled interiors, as encouraging respondents to report positions and distances in utility units rather than objective policy units. If they do, the linear relationship with candidate evaluations follows directly from the rationality assumptions of spatial models. Observed relationships are very nearly linear.
6. Stokes weights unstandardized regression coefficients by the means of voters' comments to estimate the net effect upon the electoral outcome of each type of short-term force. Throughout this article we report the importance of variables only in terms of standardized regression coefficients (*b*'s) and coefficients of determination (R-squares).
7. A particularly misleading procedure is the "normal vote" technique. It does not attempt to give unbiased estimates of policy and party effects through regression analysis, but simply assigns the joint covariance of policy and party with the vote in two different extreme ways, so that the reader can choose between "long-term" and "short-term" effects. Except by chance, neither of these magnitudes correctly estimates the extent of either policy preferences or party upon the vote (or of party or policy each upon the other); indeed, the technique does not even identify boundaries around the maximum or minimum possible effects. See Boyd (1972).
8. Time-series techniques offer an alternative way to sort out causal orderings, but even when time-series or panel data are available, they offer no panacea. In the first place, whether or not measurements are widely separated in time, there is danger in treating lagged variables as causes of current values of the same variables (e.g., party identification): error terms are often autocorrelated as a result of the omission of other factors (e.g., policy preferences) which affect both, and this biases estimates—usually upwards. To capture distinct stages in the development and change of cognitive elements, to ascertain what changes first, measurements might well have to be repeated almost instantaneously. Moreover, quasi-experimental measurements before and after exogenous events are likely to reveal more about the impact of those particular events than about the net mutual influences of different attitudes in the whole electoral process.
9. Since parents' party is measured in the CPS surveys by the respondent's report, it is conceivable that the reported party affiliation of parents is affected by respondents' partisanship through a conscious or unconscious desire to have it be the same (or different), or simply as an aid to faulty memory. Independent studies based on interviews with parents, however, indicate that the bias in the reports is probably not very serious for our purposes (Jennings and Niemi, 1968). This is particularly true since other proximate influences on partisanship reduce the importance of parents' party in our models.
10. The Statistical Analysis System (SAS) software package was used. The third stage offers improvements in the efficiency of estimates from the previous stage by taking account of the correlations among the equations in the system (Johnston, 1972). In this case, 3SLS estimates differed little from those at the second stage. All variables were standardized before computations were made.
11. In point of fact, the clarity of the choice in 1972, like that in 1964, actually left much to be desired. Nixon's policy utterances were vague throughout, and McGovern gradually retreated into ambiguity after taking unusually specific stands on the defense budget, income redistribution, and the like (Page, 1978).
12. Extensive sensitivity testing was conducted using a series of alternative specifications for each of the three equations. For example, personal qualities evaluations were tested for direct effects in both the partisanship and the policy distances equations, with negative findings. Similar testing showed that the potentially controversial specification of some demographic variables as affecting perceived policy distances but

not (directly) partisanship, has surprisingly little effect upon the estimates among endogenous variables. In fact, so long as parental partisanship was included in the equation, none of the demographic variables was found to have significant effects upon current party affiliations. In the same vein, when our predictors of partisanship were inserted in the equations predicting overall candidate evaluations and policy distances, only those specified in our final models showed significant direct effects.

7. A DYNAMIC SIMULTANEOUS EQUATION MODEL OF ELECTORAL CHOICE

Gregory B. Markus and Philip E. Converse

There is no shortage of studies which focus upon the roles of candidate personalities, partisan leanings, and contemporary issues in affecting the outcomes of elections in the United States. The value of this research is obvious, but it is probably fair to say that too much attention has been paid to the relative importance of factors idiosyncratic to particular elections and not enough effort has been directed toward the development and evaluation of an integrated and generalizable behavioral model of the voter's calculus. The result has been an uncomfortable lack of fit between verbal theories of micro-level electoral dynamics and statistical models of that process.

The goal of this study is *not* simply predictive accuracy, nor the assessment of the "relative importance" of various predictors of the vote. Nor do we intend for this work to be interpreted narrowly as a study of a particular election. What follows is a self-conscious effort at developing a model which is verisimilar to the dynamic cognitive process underlying citizens' electoral decision making. To the extent that we are able to synthesize a scattered set of verbal hypotheses and pre-theories into a precise and testable quantitative structure, we shall consider the effort a success even before confronting a shred of empirical information. Should the data corroborate the hypothesized structure or provide insights into how it might be modified—so much the better.

The model to be presented and evaluated here has two major advantages over previous work: it explicitly embodies the simultaneous interdependence of perceptions and evaluations of political stimuli specific to a particular election; and it is a truly dynamic model in that it depicts how the campaign and the ultimate vote choice modify or reinforce prior orientations. The utility of the model will be assessed by examining its goodness of fit to the 1972-1976 panel data gathered by the Center for Political Studies.

Authors' Note: The research on which this report is based was supported by the National Science Foundation Grant SOC-7707537. We are also grateful to Jean Dotson, Maria Sanchez and Peter Joftis for their aid in data preparation.

Source: *American Political Science Review* (1979) 73:1055-70. Reprinted with permission of the publisher.

Background

Predicting the Vote

A formal model of the voter's calculus which is appealing on both normative and empirical grounds is derived from the idea of minimizing subjective expected loss (Shapiro, 1969; Davis et al., 1970; Riker and Ordeshook, 1973). The loss function is typically assumed to be quadratic, so that the loss associated with candidate j by an individual voter may be defined as:

$$L_j = (X - \theta_j)\ A\ (X - \theta_j) \tag{1}$$

where X is an $mx1$ vector of the voter's preferred positions on evaluation dimensions 1, 2, . . . , m; θ_j is an $mx1$ vector of the jth candidate's positions on these evaluation dimensions, as perceived by the voter; A is an mxm matrix of weights reflecting the relative importance of the dimensions and their covariation.

Once the expected loss associated with each candidate is assessed, the model assumes that the citizen will vote for the candidate with the smallest expected loss, i.e., he or she will vote "rationally." It is worth noting that, from a strictly axiomatic point of view, a choice on the basis of a candidate's personal characteristics is no less rational than one founded on a careful assessment of stated policy positions. Rationality refers to the notion of minimizing expected loss, and the model is utterly indifferent to the criteria employed by the voter in calculating these losses.

Empirically, a behavioral version of the decision rule has been shown to predict individual electoral choice very well, particularly when party identification is used as a tie-breaker in instances wherein the evaluations of the opposing candidates are similar (Kelley and Mirer, 1974; Brody and Page, 1973). Despite the predictive success of this approach, its major drawback is that it says little about the origins of candidate evaluations and thus provides a limited understanding of the broader cognitive process by which an individual arrives at a vote choice. As Brody and Page (1973, p. 10) have pointed out: "Common sense says that people probably vote for the candidate they like best." What remains is to "shift the analytical task away from an explanation of the vote to an explanation of attitudes toward candidates" (Brody and Page, 1973, p. 16). To accomplish this, the decision rule must be embedded within the context of a comprehensive model of electoral choice.

Models of Electoral Choice

In 1966, Goldberg formulated a causal system in which party identification was posited to influence candidate choice both directly and via its impact upon evaluations of parties and issues. This first attempt at modeling voting behavior represented a significant advance over earlier work, but it was flawed by methodological errors and, more importantly, by its lack of correspondence to a well-defined theory of the calculus by which an individual arrives at a candidate preference. Goldberg's causal system was recursive in structure, ruling out feedback from "partisan attitudes" to party identification, but he was nevertheless sensitive to the need to develop more realistic models which allowed for the dynamic interdependence of political orientations.

A major step in this direction was taken by Jackson (1975b) when he presented a model wherein a citizen's policy preferences, partisan attachments, and evaluations of parties' positions were simultaneously related to each other and were, therefore, "endogenous to the electoral process." Testing this model against data from the 1964 Survey Research Center Election Study, Jackson found a triangular causal system operating across the three factors, with party identification influencing the voter's own issue positions, those policy preferences affecting evaluations of the parties and candidates, and they, in turn, impinging upon party identification. The vote itself was the result of an interaction between partisan identification and the evaluations of current political stimuli.

Jackson's work went far toward the development of a realistic and comprehensive model of electoral choice, but it was necessarily limited by the data sources available at the time. For instance, studies have shown that citizens' perceptions of candidate issue stands are correlated with their own policy preferences (Page and Brody, 1972), but neither Jackson's nor any other research to date has succeeded in untangling the causal nexus underlying this relationship. Is it because voters project their preferences onto the candidates, or alter their own positions in response to where they perceive the candidates to stand, or because of some other process? This question has confronted students of voting behavior since the earliest survey investigations (e.g., Berelson et al., 1954), but without suitable measures of the relevant variables—and a properly specified model—any answer has had to be largely speculative.

A second and related point is that models of electoral choice have thus far been almost exclusively static (Jackson, 1975b; Schulman and Pomper, 1975; Declercq et al., 1975; Achen, 1976; Page and Jones, 1979). That is, even when cast in simultaneous-equation form, they have been obliged to focus solely on the relationships among determinants of the vote at a single point in time, leaving unanalyzed the possible ways in which prior orientations and behavior shape reactions to the stimuli of a new election, as well as the modifications produced in those orientations in turn by the new election circumstances. Plainly, the unavailability of sufficiently rich longitudinal data was a major factor in restricting models to static specifications.

Freed from many of the earlier data limitations, this study builds on the work of Jackson and others but offers some significant advances. First, the model incorporates recent thinking about the social psychological processes involved in policy-oriented voting. Second, the model is dynamic, explicitly taking into account not only the simultaneous interplay of political attitudes within the context of a single presidential campaign but also the longitudinal dependence of these attitudes from one election to the next. Among other advantages, a model in this longitudinal form can be given more satisfying specification than one tailored to synchronic measurement. This is so because useful exogenous variables are at hand in states and behaviors actually measured at earlier periods, rather than dredged up by recall. Thus we can say with considerable certainty that evaluations of Carter and Ford as presidential candidates in 1976 cannot have exerted causal influence on expressions of party identification or issue positions in 1972, and hence the latter are suitably exogenous to the nexus of attitudes in 1976. When all measurements are synchronic, it can of course be claimed that certain variables are likely to be exogenous, simply as a tactic to permit the identification of a non-recursive model. However, such arguments must always remain in the final analysis more or less suspect.[1] Our longitudinal data base substantially liberates us from this difficulty.

An Overview of the Model

The preeminence of the trilogy of party affiliation, issue orientations, and candidate personalities as determinants of electoral choice is firmly established in the literature, and the model to be developed here is generally in keeping with this perspective. As Figure 7-1 illustrates, however, we maintain that these factors are not linked directly to the vote.[2] Instead, their confluence yields a set of overall candidate evaluations, on the basis of which a choice is made. More specifically, the model posits that the citizen compares his or her summary evaluations of the candidates and votes for the one most preferred, provided the preference differential is reasonably large. However, the smaller the amount by which the voter prefers one candidate over others, the greater the influence of party loyalty in determining the final choice. For a two-candidate race at time t, the equation linking the probability of a vote for candidate 1 to candidate evaluations and party affiliation is:

$$\text{Cand.}_1 \text{ Vote}_t = a + b_1 (\text{Eval.}_{1t} - \text{Eval.}_{2t}) + (b_2 - b_3 \mid \text{Eval.}_{1t} - \text{Eval.}_{2t} \mid) ID_t + e_t \quad (2)$$

The first explanatory variable in Equation (2) is simply the difference in candidate evaluations, while the second term involves the absolute value of this difference and reflects the hypothesis that the impact of party ties on the individual electoral decision depends on the degree to which one candidate is preferred over the other. Note that when the evaluation differential is small, the amount by which the party identification coefficient is diminished is also small. On the other hand, if one candidate is preferred to the other by a sufficiently large margin, the coefficient for the impact of partisanship may be reduced close to zero. This aspect of the model is consonant with the spirit of the "Decision Rule" devised by Kelley and Mirer (1974) as well as with normative models of the voter's calculus. Its mathematical form is quite different, however.

It should be noted parenthetically that the model is addressed to the topic of choice among candidates and does not deal directly with the question of who votes and who does not. Implicit in this delimitation is the argument that these two concerns may indeed be fairly distinct from one another and, hence, separable for analytical purposes. This argument is made on the grounds that the decision to vote or not in a given election is determined for the most part by fairly stable attitudes toward the act of voting itself and is only secondarily affected by election-specific variables (candidates, issues, etc.). The stream of literature beginning with *The American Voter* and culminating most recently in the works of Riker and Ordeshook (1968) and Ferejohn and Fiorina (1975) supports this contention. As Campbell et al. (1960, p. 93) first put it, and as it has been demonstrated repeatedly since then, "Inquiry into the determinants of voting turnout is less a search for psychological forces that determine a decision made anew in each campaign than it is a search for the attitude correlates of voting and non-voting from which these modes of behavior have emerged and by which they are presently supported."

Figure 7-1 A Model of the Voting Decision

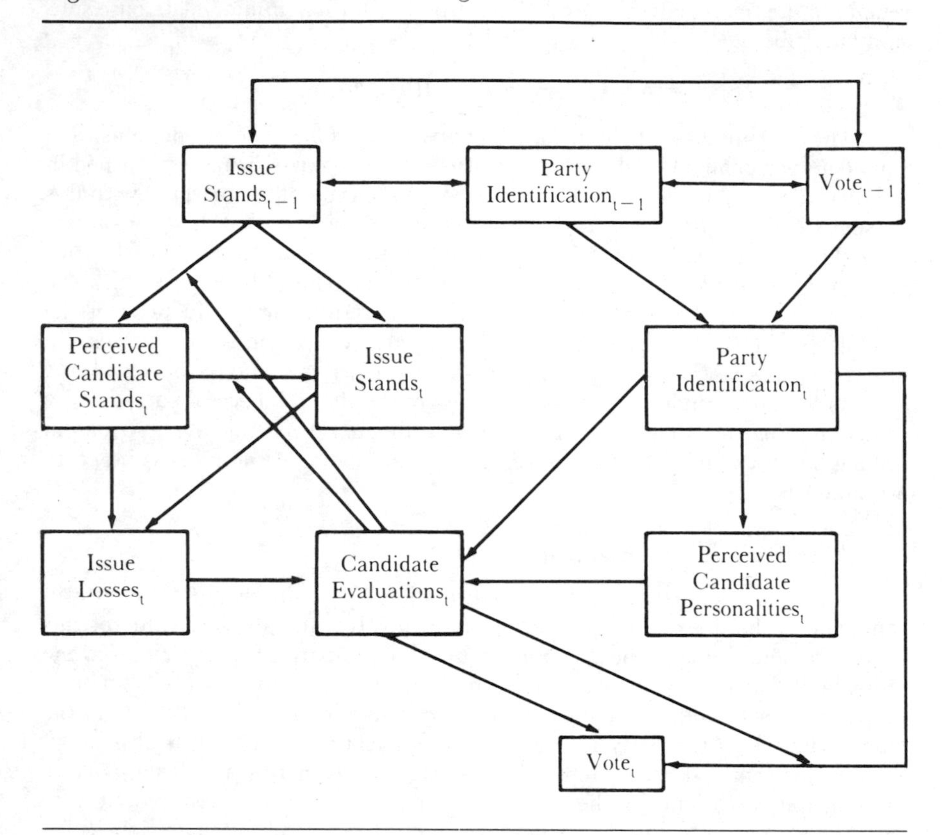

Source: Compiled by the authors.

Issue Orientations

The difficulty with assessing the impact of issues on the voting decision is that perceptions of candidate stands on issues of the day may vary significantly from voter to voter. Some of this variation will be unsystematic, rising from the casual attention most voters pay to campaign information—or arising from the ambiguous nature of the information itself. Against this background of noise, however, how voters perceive candidate policy positions may depend systematically upon their own issue preferences and overall affective orientations toward the candidates. For instance, voters may "project" their own issue stands onto candidates they like on other grounds, and by the same token they may tend to cognize the policy stances of negatively evaluated candidates in such a way as to increase the issue-related distance between themselves and these candidates (Page and Brody, 1972; Brody and Page, 1972).

In addition to the projection hypothesis, there is also the possibility of "persuasion." If a citizen were to alter his or her issue positions to coincide with those of a favorably regarded candidate, then one might say that the voter had been persuaded by the candidate (Brody and Page, 1972). A form of reverse persuasion would occur if a voter changed his or her position so as to contrast it with that of a negatively evaluated contender for office.

Lastly, the summary evaluations of the candidates are likely to be simultaneously interdependent with an individual's own policy preferences and perceptions of candidate positions. Specifically, the hypothesis is that, other things equal, the candidate thought to be most proximate to one's own position in the issue space will be favored.

The projection hypothesis is modeled as follows:

$$\text{Perceived Cand. Stand}_t = \text{Actual Cand. Stand}_t + b_1\,(R\text{'s Stand}_{t-1} - \text{Actual Cand. Stand}_t)\ \text{Eval.}_t + e_t \qquad (3)$$

The equation implies that a voter will cognize a candidate's policy position in such a way as to decrease the issue distance between the voter and a positively evaluated candidate or to increase the distance from a negatively evaluated candidate. Since the voter may enter the campaign period with a set of policy preferences, the respondent's issue self-placements at $t-1$ are incorporated into the equation.

The operationalization of the candidates' "actual" issue stands is problematic. One approach would involve content analysis of campaign speeches (Page and Brody, 1972). Or one might rely on the judgments of a panel of electoral experts. The method employed here is not so ambitious; we shall simply use the sample mean location of each candidate. This procedure is, of course, not without its shortcomings, and it may well be that these average placements do not correspond exactly to the candidates' "true" locations in the issue space. The mean placements nevertheless permit us to ascertain how an individual's perceived locations of the rivals for office differ from where the candidates were seen by the electorate as a whole.

The persuasion hypothesis is modeled for a two-candidate race according to Equation (4):

$$R\text{'s Stand}_t = a + b_1\,R\text{'s Stand}_{t-1} + b_2\,(\text{Perceived Cand.}_1\ \text{Stand}_t - R\text{'s Stand}_{t-1})\ \text{Eval.}_{1t} + b_3\,(\text{Perceived Cand.}_2\ \text{Stand}_t - R\text{'s Stand}_{t-1})\ \text{Eval.}_{2t} + e_t \qquad (4)$$

This equation represents the idea that a voter's issue orientations prior to the campaign may be modified as a function of the candidate's issue stands, as the voter sees them. That is, the voter will move toward a favored candidate's perceived position and/or away from that of a negatively evaluated candidate.

One might question the absence of party identification in Equation (4), particularly since some recent research has suggested an increasing alignment of issue opinions and partisan ties (RePass, 1971; Pomper, 1972). However, a closer examination of the proposed model in Figure 7-1 reveals that the specification does not imply a lack of relationship between partisanship and issue opinions. First, the *long-term* effect of party affiliation on policy preferences is captured in their correlation at $t-1$. In addition, the *endogenous* influence of party ties on issue stances is posited to flow via the effect of such ties on candidate evaluations.

This specification is supported both empirically (Markus, 1976; Converse and Markus, 1979) and by theoretical considerations. With regard to the latter, the argument is that, within the course of a presidential campaign, issues become imbued with partisan qualities insofar as the partisan rivals for office come to be identified with particular policies. The candidates form the link between partisanship and intra-campaign change in policy-related attitudes.

Equation (5) is derived from the ideas underlying the loss function model of evaluation. It posits that the net candidate evaluation differential is a function of issue-based losses and losses (or, in the positive, gains) accruing from preferences in candidate personalities and partisan identification:

$$(\text{Eval.}_{1t} - \text{Eval.}_{2t}) = a + b_1 (\text{Loss}_{1t} - \text{Loss}_{2t}) + b_2 (\text{Personality}_{1t} - \text{Personality}_{2t}) + b_3\text{ID}_t + e_t \qquad (5)$$

Candidate Personality

One would expect that, other things equal, Democrats will tend to prefer the personal traits of a Democratic candidate to those of a Republican office-seeker, and conversely for Republicans. The model, therefore, includes an equation which posits the difference in a citizen's ratings of the candidates' personalities to be a function of partisan ties:

$$(\text{Personality}_{1t} - \text{Personality}_{2t}) = a + b_1 ID_t + e_t \qquad (6)$$

Party Identification

The party identification equation is structured to reflect the possibility that while partisanship is relatively stable through time, it may nonetheless be influenced by prior voting behavior. Thus although the vote is the ultimate dependent variable within the context of a single presidential election, from a dynamic perspective it may feed forward to influence the voter's future political orientations.[3] The model also permits the precursors of current partisanship to interact, with voters and nonvoters differing in terms of the relative stability of party identification through time:

$$ID_t = a + b_1 \text{ Demo. Vote}_{t-1} + b_2 \text{ Repub. Votc}_{t-1} + (b_3 + b_4 \text{ Voted}_{t-1}) ID_{t-1} + e_t \qquad (7)$$

Results

As mentioned earlier, the model of electoral choice was fitted against the CPS 1972-1976 panel data. These data contain information on a national sample of 1286 adult respondents interviewed in the periods immediately following the two presidential elections (see Miller et al., 1976; Miller and Miller, 1977; Converse and Markus, 1979).

Before detailing the results, we should make a few technical comments about our analytical methods. Because of the simultaneous nature of the system of equations, we employed two-stage least squares as an estimator, except in those instances where ordinary least squares estimation appeared justified. Lagged dependent variables were treated as predetermined with respect to the 1976 data, implying a lack of autocorrelation in the disturbances. Although this assumption is perhaps not fully warranted, it is not unreasonable, given the fairly long time lag between waves (cf. Hibbs, 1972). The assumption also finds support in some of our earlier analyses (Converse and Markus, 1979). Finally, the estimation proceeded in modular fashion from equation to equation, rather than being carried out initially for the structure as a whole, and thereby avoids the considerable attrition of case numbers that occurs when cases with missing data on as little as one of the totality of variables in the structure are deleted from any role in the estimation.

Party Identification

The party identification variable ranges in seven integer steps from −3 (Strong Democrat) to +3 (Strong Republican). For purposes of operationalization, the other variables in Equation (7) are coded in a binary fashion, denoting whether the respondent voted in 1972 and, if so, for the candidate of which party. Nonvoters are coded zero on all three binary variables.

Estimation of Equation (7) by ordinary least squares yields the following results (standard errors in parentheses):

$$ID_t = \underset{(.07)}{-.37} \underset{(.10)}{-.20}\ \text{Demo. Vote}_{t-1} + \underset{(.09)}{.49}\ \text{Repub. Vote}_{t-1} +$$
$$(\underset{(.04)}{.63} + \underset{(.05)}{.10}\ \text{Voted}_{t-1})ID_{t-1} + e_t$$

$$R^2 = .64;\ \text{N} = 1252.$$

Party identification is found to be very durable from one election to the next, a result consistent with work on these and other data. Also, as hypothesized, the relationship between prior and current partisanship is somewhat stronger among voters than among nonvoters (with an estimated coefficient of .63 + .10 = .73 for voters versus .63 for nonvoters in 1972). But while partisan attachments move relatively little from one election to the next, they are not completely immune to electoral forces, as demonstrated by the significant coefficients attached to the partisan voting variables.

The feedforward effect of electoral choice on party identification is displayed in Table 7-1, in which the coefficient estimates have been used to generate predictions of party identification at time t for different combinations of past identification and vote. The table shows that when partisanship is not reinforced by consistent electoral behavior, it may weaken. The predicted effect of a deviating vote in a single election is hardly dramatic; indeed, if it were, there would be reason to doubt the analysis. Nevertheless, the cumulative effects of a series of votes running counter to an individual's prior party ties might well lead to a conversion of partisan orientations at the individual level.

Table 7-1 Predictions of Party Identification$_t$, by Prior Partisanship and Voting*

	Party ID$_{t-1}$						
Vote$_{t-1}$	*Strong Democrat*	*Demo-crat*	*Inde-pendent Democrat*	*Inde-pendent*	*Inde-pendent Repub-lican*	*Repub-lican*	*Strong Repub-lican*
Nixon	−2.07 (D)	−1.34 (ID)	− .61 (ID)	.12 (I)	.85 (IR)	1.58 (R)	2.31 (R)
None	−2.25 (D)	−1.63 (D)	−1.00 (ID)	−.37 (I)	.26 (I)	.88 (IR)	1.51 (R)
McGovern	−2.76 (SD)	−2.04 (D)	−1.31 (ID)	−.58 (ID)	.15 (I)	.88 (IR)	1.61 (R)

* Mid-points between scale values were used as cut-points to generate the parenthesized category predictions.

Source: Equation (7), as estimated using data from the 1972-76 Center for Political Studies National Election Panel Study.

Issue Opinions

Five policy domains were selected for study here: social welfare, busing, government assistance to minority groups, tax reform, and women's rights. These issues were chosen because comparable items dealing with them were included in both the 1972 and 1976 Election Studies and because they were issues which were salient to many voters in 1976, as will be illustrated in a moment. For each policy domain, respondents were asked to place themselves and the major party candidates along a seven-point continuum with labeled endpoints.[4]

It is, of course, possible that the inclusion of other issues to the set of five might have altered the results of the analysis significantly, but we deem this unlikely. For one thing, the five issue domains appear to cover most of the public's major policy concerns in 1976. Our evidence for this statement is derived from an open-ended query in the 1976 interview regarding "the most important problem the country faces." Some degree of ambiguity is always inherent in mapping open-ended responses into fixed categories, but by our count over three-quarters of the answers directly concerned one or more of the five issues under study.

Perceptions of where the presidential candidates stood on the issues in 1976 varied with an individual's own policy preferences and affective orientations toward the contenders (see Table 7-2). Generally, a citizen's placement of a favorably evaluated candidate along an issue continuum is positively associated with the individual's own preferred position on the seven-point scale. At the same time, the perceived location of a negatively evaluated candidate is inversely correlated with self-placement. This relationship is by no means invariant across issue domains and candidates, nor do average perceptions of candidate positions float unanchored across the entire seven-point range. Nevertheless, the tabular results display an unmistakable regularity. Table 7-2 does not, however, enable one to gauge the extent of persuasion or projection, since the pattern of association is consistent with either of these hypotheses—or a combination of them. We must turn to the simultaneous equation model for further explanation of the interdependencies exhibited above.

Table 7-3 presents the two-stage least squares estimates of the ten (two candidates x five issues) "projection" equations. The R^2 values associated with these equations are fairly low, but then this is not unexpected: probably most of the variation in perceptions of candidate stands is simply noise arising from the presidential office-seekers' strategy of obscuring their positions on specific issues—especially in 1976.[5] Nevertheless, in all instances save one, the regression coefficient reflecting the extent of projection is significant, hovering around an estimated value of .005. One way of interpreting this value is that it implies that for a very favorably evaluated candidate (i.e., one receiving a translated thermometer score near +50), up to 25 percent of any difference between the candidate's objective issue position and the respondent's favored position would be "projected away." [6] Another way of interpreting these estimates is illustrated in Table 7-4. In that table, predicted candidate placements have been calculated for various combinations of self-placements on the first two issues and feelings toward the candidates. By comparing these predictions with the actual mean scores in Table 7-2, one can see that the mathematically parsimonious projection equations yield aggregate profiles that are consistent with the observed findings.

The two-stage least squares estimates of the equations for voters' preferences on the five issues are presented in Table 7-5. The analysis indicates that issue opinions possess a durability which, although much less than that of party identification, is nonetheless quite significant.[7] There is also evidence of the persuasion or leadership effect with regard to three policy domains: welfare, minority groups, and tax reform. The presidential candidates apparently exerted very little influence upon public sentiments toward busing and women's rights, however.

These findings recall a pattern that emerged in our first cut at these data (Converse and Markus, 1979). In that study, the stability of opinion on various issues was found to be arrayed hierarchically, with attitudes on issues of a moral nature displaying a distinctively higher degree of temporal stability and hence apparently greater crystallization than did opinions on civil rights, domestic policy, and foreign affairs. It stands to reason that attitudes tied closely to one's sense of morality would not be very susceptible to the influence of campaign debate, and that is precisely what we find here.

Lastly, since the dependent and persuasion variables from Table 7-5 are expressed in the same currencies as the dependent and regressor variables, respectively, in the preceding set of equations, the relative effects of projection and persuasion may be compared.[8] Upon doing so, one finds that with respect to both Carter and Ford the projection coefficients are larger than the corresponding persuasion values for all issues but one. The differences are by no means staggering, but they do suggest that projection is about 20 percent stronger than persuasion, on the average. One should bear in mind, however, that under certain circumstances—e.g., a new issue for which public opinion has not yet jelled—the

Table 7-2 Mean Candidate Issue Placement, by Self-Placement and Candidate Feeling Thermometer Score*

	Social Welfare							
	Carter				*Ford*			
R's Location	*Warm*		*Cool*		*Warm*		*Cool*	
1 (Liberal)	2.2	(77)	4.8	(4)	3.4	(31)	6.2	(40)
2	2.5	(48)	3.9	(7)	3.6	(35)	5.9	(21)
3	2.8	(96)	3.4	(18)	3.9	(81)	5.4	(34)
4	3.2	(137)	3.0	(42)	4.1	(149)	5.3	(36)
5	3.8	(103)	2.5	(56)	4.4	(123)	5.0	(32)
6	3.5	(77)	2.2	(48)	4.5	(105)	4.2	(15)
7 (Conservative)	3.7	(87)	2.6	(77)	4.7	(142)	3.7	(28)
Grand Mean	3.2	(625)	2.6	(252)	4.3	(666)	5.2	(206)
eta-squared	.15		.13		.07		.27	

	Busing							
	Carter				*Ford*			
R's Location	*Warm*		*Cool*		*Warm*		*Cool*	
1 (Favor)	3.3	(28)	5.0	(3)	2.5	(10)	6.0	(20)
2	2.7	(27)	5.0	(2)	4.1	(21)	6.1	(8)
3	3.4	(18)	5.0	(2)	4.0	(16)	5.7	(6)
4	3.8	(44)	5.2	(12)	4.1	(39)	5.1	(19)
5	4.1	(32)	3.0	(11)	4.4	(36)	4.4	(14)
6	4.2	(79)	3.5	(35)	4.2	(105)	3.8	(22)
7 (Oppose)	4.2	(318)	3.3	(137)	4.5	(441)	3.3	(120)
Grand Mean	4.0	(546)	3.4	(202)	4.4	(668)	4.0	(209)
eta-squared	.06		.05		.03		.21	

	Tax Reform							
	Carter				*Ford*			
R's Location	*Warm*		*Cool*		*Warm*		*Cool*	
1 (Progressive)	2.6	(109)	3.9	(17)	4.0	(70)	5.3	(44)
2	2.8	(64)	2.9	(20)	3.6	(58)	5.0	(23)
3	3.1	(78)	3.0	(25)	3.9	(77)	4.5	(18)
4	3.3	(96)	2.8	(36)	4.2	(110)	4.4	(25)
5	3.5	(44)	2.8	(18)	4.6	(60)	3.9	(9)
6	4.0	(36)	3.0	(26)	4.5	(46)	4.9	(14)
7 (Same Rate)	4.3	(13)	3.4	(51)	5.0	(133)	4.2	(39)
Grand Mean	3.4	(557)	3.1	(193)	4.3	(554)	4.7	(172)
eta-squared	.17		.04		.10		.07	

R's Location	Minority Groups: Carter Warm		Carter Cool		Ford Warm		Ford Cool	
1 (Government Help)	2.3	(69)	4.0	(7)	2.9	(44)	5.8	(35)
2	2.5	(52)	3.0	(10)	3.3	(45)	4.8	(18)
3	2.9	(102)	3.0	(34)	3.4	(116)	4.6	(22)
4	3.4	(128)	3.0	(41)	3.8	(138)	4.4	(41)
5	3.6	(77)	3.3	(51)	4.3	(112)	4.5	(22)
6	3.8	(73)	3.1	(41)	4.1	(92)	3.3	(22)
7	4.2	(81)	2.4	(60)	4.5	(110)	3.0	(35)
Grand Mean	3.3	(582)	3.0	(244)	3.9	(657)	4.3	(195)
eta-squared	.20		.06		.12		.29	

R's Location	Women's Rights: Carter Warm		Carter Cool		Ford Warm		Ford Cool	
1 (Equal Rights)	2.6	(194)	2.5	(58)	2.3	(181)	3.6	(77)
2	3.0	(83)	3.2	(27)	3.0	(95)	4.1	(21)
3	3.3	(51)	3.6	(18)	3.5	(60)	4.1	(15)
4	3.5	(103)	3.5	(38)	3.7	(122)	4.5	(28)
5	3.9	(43)	3.5	(21)	4.0	(54)	3.6	(14)
6	4.1	(34)	3.0	(11)	4.0	(37)	2.8	(6)
7	4.1	(59)	3.7	(7)	4.0	(48)	2.9	(14)
Grand Mean	3.2	(567)	3.1	(180)	3.2	(597)	3.8	(175)
eta-squared	.16		.12		.23		.09	

* Cool feelings include feeling thermometer scores of 0-49 degrees. Warm feelings are scores of 51-100 degrees.
Source: 1976 Center for Political Studies National Election Panel Study.

Table 7-3 Two-Stage Least Square Estimates for the Perceived Candidate Issue Position Equations

Issue	*Candidate*	*Mean*	*Coefficient*	*Standard Error*	*N*	R^2
Welfare	Carter	3.01	.007	.001	854	.08
	Ford	4.51	.006	.001	869	.02
Busing	Carter	3.84	.005	.001	701	.06
	Ford	4.26	.007	.001	848	.06
Minorities	Carter	3.18	.005	.001	773	.04
	Ford	4.00	.005	.001	813	.04
Tax Reform	Carter	3.32	.000	.000	735	.00
	Ford	4.40	.003	.001	685	.01
Women	Carter	3.20	.002	.001	711	.01
	Ford	3.37	.005	.001	748	.03

Source: 1972-76 Center for Political Studies Election Panel Study.

Table 7-4 Predicted Perceived Candidate Location for Various Combinations of Self-Placement and Candidate Feeling Thermometer Score*

	Social Welfare			
	Carter		*Ford*	
Respondent Position	*Warm*	*Cool*	*Warm*	*Cool*
1 (Liberal)	2.7	3.4	4.0	5.0
3	3.0	3.0	4.3	4.7
5	3.4	2.7	4.6	4.4
7 (Conservative)	3.7	2.3	4.9	4.1
	Busing			
	Carter		*Ford*	
Respondent Position	*Warm*	*Cool*	*Warm*	*Cool*
1 (Favor)	3.5	4.2	3.7	4.8
3	3.7	3.9	4.0	4.5
5	4.0	3.7	4.4	4.1
7 (Oppose)	4.2	3.5	4.7	3.8

* Scores of −25 and +25 degrees were used to represent cool and warm feelings, respectively, on a translated feeling thermometer ranging from −50 to +50 degrees. The former values ae virtually identical to the observed mean feeling scores for the two sets of respondents.

Source: Equation (3), as estimated using data from the 1972-76 Center for Political Studies National Election Panel Study.

influence of political leaders upon the electorate's policy preferences might be substantial.

Candidate Personalities

In 1976, respondents were asked to rate on a seven-point scale the degree to which each of the major candidates had "the kind of personality a President ought to have." The estimated equation linking the difference in ratings of Ford's and Carter's personalities to partisanship is (standard errors in parentheses):[9]

$$\text{(Ford Personality} - \text{Carter Personality)}_t = \underset{(.07)}{.20} + \underset{(.04)}{.60}\, ID_t + e_t$$

The equation accounts for 20 percent of the variation in the dependent variable (N = 1193), equivalent to a standardized regression coefficient of .44 for party identification. On the average, the personalities of both candidates were scored at about 1.4 on a −3 to +3 scale. The unstandardized coefficient estimates show Ford receiving a score about two points higher than Carter among Strong Republicans, however, and about 1.6 points below Carter among Strong Democrats.[10]

Table 7-5 Two-Stage Least Squares Estimates for the Voter Issue Position Equation

	Coefficient	*Standard Error*
Social Welfare		
Constant	2.59	.14
Issue Position$_{t-1}$	.47	.03
Carter Persuasion	.006	.001
Ford Persuasion	.006	.002
R^2 = .29 N = 883		
Busing		
Constant	2.35	.19
Issue Position$_{t-1}$	.61	.03
Carter Persuasion	.002	.001
Ford Persuasion	.003	.001
R^2 = .40 N = 685		
Minority Groups		
Constant	2.25	.14
Issue Position$_{t-1}$	.52	.03
Carter Persuasion	.004	.001
Ford Persuasion	.004	.002
R^2 = .33 N = 764		
Tax Reform		
Constant	2.54	.22
Issue Position$_{t-1}$	.40	.05
Carter Persuasion	.007	.002
Ford Persuasion	.004	.002
R^2 = .16 N = 657		
Women's Rights		
Constant	1.67	.16
Issue Position$_{t-1}$	.41	.05
Carter Persuasion	−.001	.002
Ford Persuasion	.001	.003
R^2 = .21 N = 689		

Source: Data from the 1972-76 Center for Political Studies National Election Panel Study.

Evaluations of the Candidates

Equation (5) posits that a citizen's overall evaluations of the presidential candidates are formed from a mix of policy considerations, partisan predispositions, and beliefs about the personalities of the rivals for office. The operationalizations of the regressors in that equation are by now familiar, with the exception of the issue-loss component. The issue loss associated with each candidate was constructed as the average squared difference between the respondent's self-placement on each issue and his or her perceived location of the candidate. We used an average rather than a simple sum of squares because not all respondents could provide both a preferred policy and a candidate location for all five issues.

This method weights each included issue equally, a procedure which appears to conflict with the notion that all issues may not be equally salient to the voter. A number of considerations render this approach less objectionable than it might seem, however. First, taken as a whole the five issues are salient ones, and the majority of respondents were able to locate themselves and the candidates on each of the issue continua. Moreover, issues that are utterly non-salient to a respondent are given a weight of zero, since both self and candidate placements are required for the issue to be included in the loss calculus. Third, preliminary attempts to devise a weighting scheme based on open-ended and other responses actually led to a slight decrease in explanatory power for the regression equation. This came as little surprise, since a number of recent psychological studies have demonstrated that people are generally quite unreliable in assessing the relative importance of factors in determining their decisions (Nisbett and Wilson, 1977). Moreover, other work indicates that the choice of weights tends to make little difference in the ultimate predictions (Wainer, 1976; Dawes and Corrigan, 1974).

The two-stage least squares estimates for the candidate evaluation are displayed in Table 7-6. The analysis indicates that all three elements—issues, party, and personalities—were important determinants of feelings toward Ford and Carter. Taken together, these three variables account for two-thirds of the variation in the feeling thermometer differential for the presidential rivals.

The results suggest that the perceived personal qualities of the candidates weighed most heavily, at least in the direct-effect sense, in determining the public's overall evaluations of Ford and Carter. The standardized coefficient for the personality differential variable equals .43, and the unstandardized coefficient implies nearly a 40-point difference (6.26 x 6) in the thermometer scores of candidates rated at opposite extremes of the presidential personality scale.

Issues and party ties were about equally important in terms of their direct effect on candidate evaluations, with standardized coefficients of −.30 and .29,

Table 7-6 Two-Stage Least Squares Estimates for the Evaluation Differential Equation

	Unstandardized Coefficient	*Standard Error*	*Standardized Coefficient*
Constant	2.72	.77	
Ford−Carter Issue Loss	−1.34	.38	−.30
Ford−Carter Personality	6.26	.51	.43
ID_t	5.66	.64	.29
R^2 = .67 N = 1013			

Source: Data from the 1972-76 Center for Political Studies National Election Panel Study.

respectively. Keeping in mind that the issue loss differential can range from +36 (favoring Carter) to −36 (favoring Ford), note that the unstandardized coefficient for that variable implies that for each unit increase in Ford's loss value relative to Carter's, the voter's thermometer difference (Ford−Carter) decreased by a little more than one degree, other variables held constant. At the same time, the coefficient for party identification indicates a 20-degree differential favoring Ford among Strong Republicans and a 14-degree contrast favoring Carter among Strong Democrats, *ceteris paribus.*[11]

The fairly modest standardized coefficient for party identification might be somewhat puzzling, given the crucial role that partisanship has been assumed to play in electoral behavior. It is important to remember, however, that in addition to its direct impact on candidate evaluations, party affiliation also exerts a substantial *indirect* influence via its effect upon perceptions of candidate personalities. When this indirect influence is combined with the direct effect, it yields an "effects" coefficient of .29 + .43(.44) = .48, larger than the standardized coefficient for either candidate personalities or issue proximities (see Figure 7-2). This latter value may be more in line with intuitive judgments—and prior evidence—about the impact of partisanship on candidate evaluations. Moreover, under some circumstances party identification may play a significant role in determining the electoral decision quite apart from its influence on feelings toward the candidates, as we shall see in a moment.

Figure 7-2 Candidate Evaluations Segment of the Model of Electoral Choice

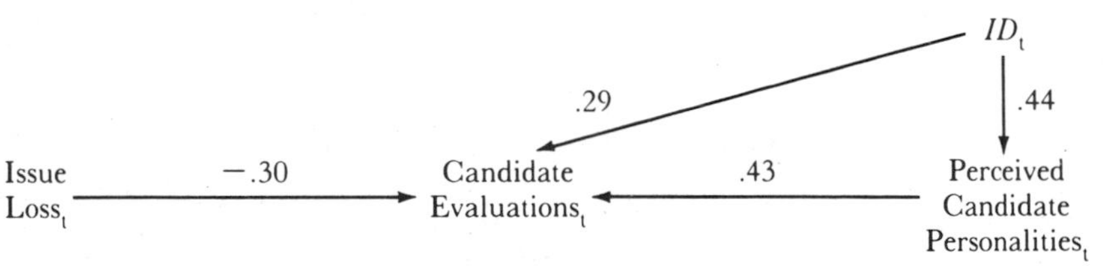

Source: Based on the regression estimates outlined in the text.

The Vote Decision

Least squares estimation of the vote choice equation generates the following results (standard errors in parentheses):[12]

$$\text{Ford Vote} = \underset{(.010)}{.506} + \underset{(.0004)}{.009}\,(\text{Ford Eval.} - \text{Carter Eval.})$$
$$+ (\underset{(.009)}{.141} - \underset{(.0002)}{.0025}\,|\,\text{Ford Eval.} - \text{Carter Eval.}\,|\,)ID_t + e_t$$

The regression analysis lends clear support to the hypothesized vote choice equation. All coefficients have the expected signs and are many times larger than their associated standard errors. The R^2 value for the equation equals .64 (N = 884), but because of the dichotomous nature of the dependent variable, the best measure of goodness of fit is provided by the fact that the equation correctly predicts respondents' votes 90 percent of the time.[13]

Moreover, it can be shown that the direct intrusion of party identification in influencing the vote choice when there is relative indifference in candidate evaluations is the only case in which prior variables in the model affect the vote, save indirectly through the comparative candidate evaluations. That is, the addition of other model variables, including most notably the issue losses and personality ratings, to the simple vote choice regression equation based on differential candidate evaluations and party identification, leads to virtually no increase in predictive accuracy. As a further test, we applied the estimated equation to the data from the 1972 wave of the panel to ascertain its predictive accuracy with regard to the Nixon-McGovern contest.[14] The result was that 97 percent of the voters were correctly classified, a very satisfactory result given that the coefficient estimates are based on an entirely different set of data. Indeed, the predictive accuracy might seem to be *too* good, but the explanation is simply that evaluations of Nixon and McGovern tended to be more disparate than those for Ford and Carter, and hence electoral choice was more predictable than in 1976.

The values of the coefficient estimates possess some charming qualities. For instance, the constant term implies a virtual 50-50 split in the vote of Independents who evaluated the two candidates equally. Furthermore, if one simulates an election wherein net short-term partisan forces (i.e., the evaluation differential) are zero and inserts the sample mean for the party identification variable, the prediction (interpreting the result in aggregate terms) is a 46 percent vote for the Republican candidate—precisely the value of the normal vote (Converse, 1966).

Note that the direct impact of party identification upon the vote decision depends upon the size of the candidate evaluation differential. When both candidates are evaluated identically, each step toward the Republican end of the partisan continuum increases the predicted dependent score (roughly, the probability of voting for Ford) by .14. Once the difference in candidate evaluations reaches about 55 degrees, however, the predicted direct effect or partisanship on the vote is virtually nil, as indicated by its small coefficient: $.141 - .0025(55) = .003$.[15] Although the direct influence of party ties on the vote decision would be negligible under these circumstances, their indirect effect, i.e., their prior impact on the candidate evaluations themselves, nevertheless remains appreciable.

The relative effects of candidate evaluations and party identification on the choice between presidential contenders is illustrated in Table 7-7. As displayed there, the predicted probability of a Ford vote ranges from .00 for Strong Democrats, with a 50 degree evaluation differential favoring Carter, to 1.00 for Strong Republicans, with an equally large pro-Ford difference. The table also illustrates the varying impact of party identification, depending on the contrast in candidate evaluations: when the differential is large, the probability entries do not

Table 7-7 Predicted Probability of a Ford Vote, by Party Identification and Candidate Evaluation Difference

	Party Identification						
Differential	*Strong Democrat*	*Democrat*	*Independent Democrat*	*Independent*	*Independent Republican*	*Republican*	*Strong Republican*
(Pro-Carter) −50	.00	.02	.04	.06	.07	.09	.10
−40	.02	.06	.11	.15	.19	.23	.27
−20	.05	.14	.24	.33	.42	.51	.60
−10	.07	.18	.30	.42	.53	.65	.76
0	.08	.22	.37	.51	.65	.79	.93
10	.25	.36	.48	.60	.71	.83	.94
20	.41	.50	.60	.69	.78	.87	.96
40	.74	.78	.83	.87	.91	.95	.99
(Pro-Ford) 50	.91	.92	.94	.96	.97	.99	1.00

Source: Equation (2), as estimated using the 1972-76 Center for Political Studies National Election Panel Study.

vary much across partisan categories; if the evaluation differential is within the bounds ± 20 degrees, however, the residual impact of partisanship on electoral choice is more potent.

Conclusions

From a substantive point of view, a model is something more than the sum of its parts. We may therefore conclude by moving from an examination of the separate equations comprising the model to a brief summary and discussion of its broader implications.

Perhaps most importantly, the hypothesized model of electoral choice has fared rather well against the 1972-1976 panel data. No alterations in the posited specification were indicated. To the contrary, a number of R^2 values approach what must be their upper bounds, given normal sampling error and other idiosyncratic sources of noise.

The analysis affirms the crucial role of candidates in the dynamics of electoral choice. Candidate evaluations have been shown to be a primary determinant of the vote, with policy considerations and even partisan orientations affecting the vote either exclusively or largely through the way they help to shape feelings toward the presidential rivals. The candidates also mediate the flow of campaign stimuli toward the cognitive predispositions comprising the citizen's network of political beliefs: they serve as the primary vehicle through which policy debate takes on partisan coloration, and through their determining influence on the vote, feelings toward the candidates even act dynamically in at least a small degree to modify or reinforce standing party ties. In the American system of elections, the choice is ultimately between competing candidates.

The fact that comparative candidate assessments are the most potent proximal determinant of the vote decision should not, however, lead us to overlook the causally prior impacts of issues and parties on these assessments. Policy considerations were shown to be significant in determining voters' evaluations of the 1976 presidential candidates. Some of these manifest linkages between issues and candidates turned out to be modestly circular in one sense or another. Thus, for example, a degree of "projection" was uncovered, whereby voters reporting issue positions of candidates they already liked would shade these perceptions toward the issue positions the voter already preferred, while assuming that disliked candidates must have more sharply dissimilar positions. In the same causal nexus it was possible to isolate a persuasion effect as well, whereby the voter appeared to be shifting his or her own reported issue position to conform more closely with that of a preferred candidate, or to distinguish it more sharply from that perceived for a disliked candidate. The persuasion effect was less strong in these data than the projection effect, and furthermore showed signs of variation by type of issue. For issues like school busing or women's rights, where there is independent evidence of sharp crystallization of public feeling, any persuasion effect is negligible. It is chiefly on issues where voters are less personally exercised that the policy position of candidates can sway their admirers' views of the issue.

However intriguing and plausible these side effects may be, the estimates we have derived from the model make clear that they remained no more than side effects in 1976. The policy differences consensually perceived to exist between the candidates, coupled with prior differences in voter positions on these issues, had a noteworthy effect on voters' comparative assessments of the candidates, and through these invidious assessments, the policy terms ultimately left their mark on final voting decisions.

Similarly, the model helps to delineate more clearly than did prior work the important function of partisan predispositions in the processes leading to a voting choice. Earlier investigations limited to static data bases have often tried to assess the relative role of parties, issues and candidates by assigning each a single ultimate regression weight, leading to comparisons which take on the flavor of a simplistic horse race. Viewing the formulation of a voting decision in terms which are more explicitly processual may rob us of such a simple "final score," but may yield redeeming satisfactions due to greater verisimilitude.

In such process terms, the causal role of partisanship appears to be particularly important for two reasons. First, party identifications are much more stable in the intermediate term than other elements in the model. If the game were redefined as one of predicting a voting decision on the basis of political attitudes examined eight years before election day, there would be little contest: the identity of the candidates would be utterly unknown at such remove, some issues to become important later would also be unknown, and voter attitudes on other more abiding issues would be subject to considerably greater flux in the interim.

The second reason shows up clearly in the structure of the model and hinges on the fact that the party component is unique in the way it intrudes at multiple points in the process. Partisan predispositions may be outweighed by other model terms at particular stages, as other research on a static base has shown, but these loyalties keep coming back as determinants while the vote decision process unrolls. For example, Figure 7-2 suggested that neither issues nor partisanship were as important in their direct effects upon ultimate comparisons between the candidates as were simple judgments of their personalities. However, the very same figure makes clear that reactions to candidate personalities have already been shaped by prior partisan predispositions, so that there is an indirect path from party to candidate evaluations which is of imposing proportions in itself, quite apart from the direct path also depicted. Or at a later point, partisanship again enters the model significantly in influencing the final vote when the voter has trouble making sharp affective discriminations between the candidates.

In the same vein, given the durable nature of these loyalties over lengthy periods of time (Converse and Markus, 1979), it may well be that prior partisanship has also intruded at stages too early for adequate representation in our model. Thus, for example, we located an edge of "persuasion" whereby the voters' issue locations were mildly affected by the issue positions perceived for liked and disliked candidates. If such candidate persuasion exists, then it would not be at all surprising if there were an earlier *party* persuasion term of entirely parallel structure accounting for some of the party-relatedness of issue positions at our first time point, yet which is exogenous to our model as presented. Such party persuasion would presumably be operative in the first stages of issue emergence, and hence likely to have more impact on the distribution of attitudes in the electorate than do candidates who arrive on the scene after such issue positions have become at least modestly crystallized.

In short, then, while partisan predispositions are unlikely to dominate the process completely at given stages where the candidates are being assessed, these loyalties appear to make repeated inputs of substantial magnitude throughout the process.

We believe that the model as presented is an integrated and generalizable one that captures most of what is important as voters face elections involving candidate competition. The model could be enlarged to become more general still. It could, for example, add considerations of turnout, representing the fact that voting and nonvoting are for the most part habitual differences, but capturing those margins of turnout variance that are in fact current and dynamic responses to the specific election configuration, such as the likely diminution in turnout that may accompany feelings of sheer disgust about *both* candidates. The model could also be extended more deeply in time, explicating the genesis of the relationships between prior issue positions, prior party loyalties, and prior votes.

Perhaps the most important consideration to keep in mind is that whereas we have used data from the specific period 1972-76 for estimation of model parameters and assessment of general fit, the model per se should be seen as a shell, or a vessel, designed to apply to a wide range of specific elections. Estimates of specific parameters would naturally vary across types of elections, or for specific elections of the same series over time. To seize an example which is too obvious, for candidate elections which are truly non-partisan in fact as well as intent, the coefficients representing the various points of impact of the party term in the model would by definition fall to zero.

It is this conditional variation from one election to another that becomes of subsequent interest to understand. The present model is thus a satisfying vehicle for providing the kinds of parameter estimates that seem to express the voting calculus well in any special case.

NOTES

1. A common tactic with models tailored to static data is to depend on recall of earlier states for exogenous variables. Thus, for example, recall of parental partisanship may be used as an exogenous variable on grounds that current political attitudes cannot act backward causally in time to affect parental partisanship in an earlier period. When no other longitudinal information is available, such an assumption is better than nothing. However, this assumption ignores the possibility that *current* recall of earlier parental partisanship can itself be contaminated by currently evolving political attitudes.
2. In Figure 7-1 we are adopting the convention that an arrow leading to another arrow denotes an interaction or mediating effect. In addition, when the simultaneous equation form of Figure 7-1 is presented, the coefficients and error term in each equation will be subscripted only with respect to that equation (i.e., the constant term for such equation is simply a, the error term is e_t, etc.). The purpose is to keep the notation simple, and it should cause no confusion to the reader.
3. It is important to keep in mind here, as elsewhere in the model equations, that we are less making an assertive assumption that prior votes *do* influence party identification, than merely building a model structure which permits such effects to be discriminated *if they exist*. Earlier recursive models of the Goldberg (1966) type were obliged to pro-

claim by assumption that these reverse effects of vote on party identification did not exist, at least within the time frame of the model. We do not make a contrary proclamation that such effects *do* exist, since a given testing of the model in a special case might show the relevant coefficients to be zero.

4. The text of the issue items may be found in the CPS 1976 National Election Study codebook, available from the Inter-University Consortium for Political and Social Research.
5. Correlations are also probably depressed by the presence of error arising from imprecise instrumentation and the stochastic nature of the latent attitudes being measured (Converse, 1970; Achen, 1975; Converse and Markus, 1979).
6. Multiplication of the .005 average coefficient estimate by the thermometer score of 50 yields the 25 percent figure. The translated thermometer used in estimating Equations (3) and (4) ranges from -50 to $+50$ degrees.
7. See Converse and Markus (1979) for a further discussion of the relative stabilities of political outlooks.
8. We prefer the unstandardized coefficients to standardized ones for two reasons. First, the equations are nonlinear in the variables, rendering the usual interpretation of standardized coefficients may be arbitrarily altered by rescaling the original variables (Allison, 1977). Moreover, since standardized coefficients are by definition variance-sensitive, comparisons of their values across equations—even linear ones—can lead to misinterpretations.
9. The equation was estimated by ordinary least squares, which assumes a lack of correlation between the disturbances in the party identification and personality differential equations. The consequence of this assumption being incorrect would be to overstate the impact of the independent variable. Given the plausibly moderate value of the coefficient estimate, the assumption appears not to have been grossly unreasonable.
10. The predicted dependent variable value is $.20 + .60(+3) = 2.0$ for Strong Republicans and $.20 + .60(-3) = -1.6$ for Strong Democrats.
11. For Strong Republicans, the expected thermometer differential is $2.72 + 5.66(+3) = 19.70$; for Strong Democrats it is $2.72 + 5.66\,(-3) = -14.26$.
12. Both two-stage least squares (2SLS) and ordinary least squares (OLS) estimators were originally employed. Although the methods yielded similar coefficient estimates, the OLS values are preferred here because they yield fewer predictions outside of the allowable 0-1 range and because the 2SLS residuals were only modestly correlated with residuals elsewhere in the system, thus permitting the more efficient OLS estimation. The 2SLS estimates (with standard errors parenthesized) are:

$$\begin{aligned}\text{Ford Vote} = {} & \underset{(.012)}{.503} + \underset{(.001)}{.011}\,(\text{Ford Eval.} - \text{Carter Eval.}) \\ & + (\underset{(.019)}{.157} - \underset{(.0007)}{.0036}\,|\,\text{Ford Eval.} - \text{Carter Eval.}\,|)ID_t + e_t \\ R^2 = {} & .65;\ N = 753.\end{aligned}$$

13. Respondents with estimated dependent variable scores $>.50$ were predicted to have voted for Ford, while those with estimated values $\leq .50$ were classed as Carter voters.
14. This prediction to the 1972 presidential vote refers, of course, to the vote choice equation taken alone. The full model being presented could not be estimated for 1972 separately, for lack of prior panel data in that year.
15. In 1976, 15 percent of all respondents saw no difference in their overall evaluations of the candidates. One half of the sample had evaluation differentials of 25 degrees or less, and nearly 90 percent are included in the ± 55 degree span.

8. A CAUSAL ANALYSIS OF THE COMPONENTS OF THE VOTE

Kendall L. Baker, Russell J. Dalton, Kai Hildebrandt

The postwar period has seen continual change in German partisan behavior. The marked and fairly steady decline in the importance of social cleavages for voting choice raised the question, "What, if anything, is replacing social characteristics as a guide to behavior?" One possible answer is that party identification or a similar political affiliation (like the *tendance* of French politics) is a new cue-giving influence (Shively, 1972, 1979; and chap. 8 [of Baker et al., 1981]). Another answer could be that partisan images, especially issue images, are serving this purpose (Matthews and Prothro, 1966; Trilling, 1976; and chap. 9 [of Baker et al., 1981]).

A change in the basis of voting behavior to either partisanship or issue images can have major implications for the operation of a political system.

In the first place, this transformation can have important consequences for the nature of electoral stability in a political system. A system based on social cleavages is stable only with respect to the citizen's placement in the social structure; his choice of party depends on his view of the party that best represents his social position. Such an elector discriminates little between parties perceived as equally representative of his or her social position. Attachment is primarily to the social group, and hence to a *bloc* of parties that can be seen as representing this group (Shively, 1972). An enduring commitment need not be made to any specific party. If social characteristics were to be replaced by issue orientations, voting would continue to be an instrumental act, but one based on issues rather than group interests: voters would support the party (or bloc of parties) best reflecting their own issue preferences. Again, however, this basis of partisan behavior does not imply continuous support of a single party.

Under both of these conditions—social cleavage and issue-based voting—there is political stability for voting blocs but not necessarily for specific parties. Indeed, despite the discontinuities of Germany's political history a number of researchers have found surprising stability in the electoral support of socially defined voting blocs (Loewenberg, 1968, 1978). Parties have competed for popular support, but apparently voters have switched primarily among parties

---

Source: Kendall L. Baker, Russell J. Dalton, and Kai Hildebrandt. *Germany Transformed: Political Culture and the New Politics*. Cambridge: Harvard University Press, 1981. Reprinted with permission of the publisher.

within one bloc. "Flash" parties may develop in such a system if they can convince their prospective clientele that they represent the interests of the social group better than the existing parties. Shively (1972), for example, emphasizes the instrumental nature of cleavage-based partisanship in accounting for the lack of party stability in the waning years of the Weimar Republic as well as for the sudden rise of the National Socialist party.

A high degree of party identification in a political system leads to opposite expectations. Attitudinal partisanship is not mediated through social groups. These political affiliations contain affective and psychological components that attach the elector directly to a specific party. Since the indirect linkage through social position or issues is replaced by a direct link between the individual and "his" party, attitudinal attachments produce greater individual voting stability and greater stability in the voting results for specific parties, and they limit the rise of new parties (Converse, 1969; Campbell et al., 1966, chaps 2-4, 7, and 10).

In the second place, a shift in the bases of partisan behavior to either partisanship or political issues should affect the relationship between the mass public and political elites. Instrumental voting—voting related to group interests or issue interests—implies a goal-oriented electoral decision. To the extent that election outcomes make such goals explicit, political elites are obliged to respond to the public's policy preferences, or to face the electoral consequences. Obviously the public's issue preferences can be a significant influence on policymaking even when voting is primarily dependent on party identification. In partisanship-based systems, however, the affective element of party identification often blurs the evaluative content of the voting decision (Campbell et al., 1960; Nie, Verba, and Petrocik, 1976; Budge, Crewe, and Farlie, 1976). The weaker presence of an evaluative component means that elites are likely to have more political discretion and freedom of action in such a system; that is, voters elect candidates mainly because they are Social Democrats or Christian Democrats, without specific knowledge of the candidates' (or even the parties') stances on contemporary issues.

The Causal Model

A causal model of voting behavior cannot be an entirely correct or even sufficient explanation for the patterns of change in postwar Germany if it is based either on partisanship or on issue images alone. Both concepts must be used if their relative importance and interrelationship are to be uncovered. To do this, the influences of all three causal forces on the vote—social characteristics as well as partisanship and issue images—must be considered simultaneously and assigned a causal ordering.[1] Although the actual processes determining voting decisions are more complex and subtle than can be reflected in a simple model, the results to be expected from the interaction of these three forces can be made relatively clear.

All three forces have been integrated into the hypothesized causal model of German voting behavior shown in Figure 8-1.[2] Social characteristics are placed at the beginning of the causal sequence. They not only shape both partisanship and issue images, but also exert a direct influence on voting behavior. Both the party-identification hypothesis and the issue-images hypothesis would predict that the direct link between social characteristics and the vote (path C) has been

Figure 8-1 Hypothesized Causal Model of German Voting Behavior

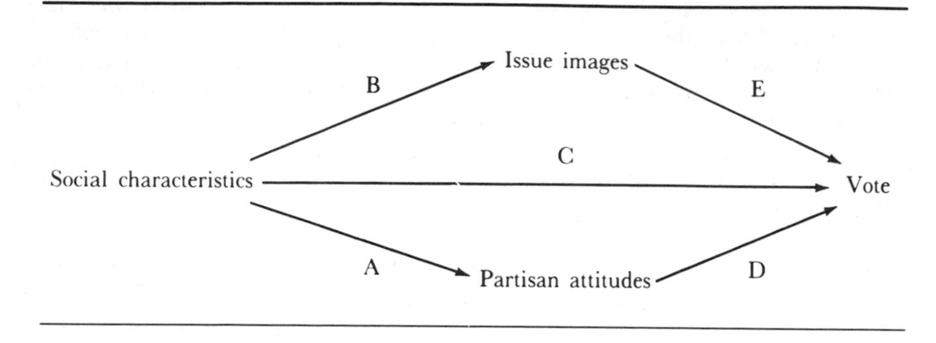

weakening over time, and similarly, the ability of social characteristics to explain both partisan attitudes (path A) and issue images (path B) may also be declining.

As the importance of social characteristics diminishes, the party-identification hypothesis predicts more voters will base their voting decisions on psychological attachment to their preferred party, and consequently the direct link between partisanship and the vote will become stronger (path D). The partisanship measure used here is likely to contain a larger component of short-term affect than a "true" measure of party identification would, but that problem can be lessened by using this partisanship indicator in multivariate analyses across time. Thus, the impact of partisanship can be evaluated in relative terms: relative to itself over time, and relative to social characteristics and issue images. Assuming that the partisan indicator at each timepoint includes this *short-term* affect, the relative change in the path coefficients for partisanship over time can be attributed to changes in the underlying *long-term* component of this indicator. Hence, if the coefficient for path D increases over time, this can be taken as support for the party-identification hypothesis.

The issue-images hypothesis raises a different set of expectations. The independent influence of issue images can be most easily understood in terms of the Old Politics-New Politics dimension of the German political agenda (chap. 9 [of Baker et al., 1981]; Hildebrandt and Dalton, 1978; Inglehart, 1977). On the one hand, issue images may reflect the continued attachment to Old Politics values by some voters, even though their social characteristics or partisanship would dictate different voting decisions. On the other hand, increasing New Politics values may give rise to other concerns that also influence behavior independently of partisanship or social characteristics. In either case, the path between issue images and vote (path E) should generally increase in importance if the issue-images hypothesis is an accurate description of political change in the Federal Republic.

This model as represented in Figure 8-1 does not specify a causal relationship between partisanship and issue images. Both attitudes should be fairly stable and central elements of an individual's belief structure, but it is not clear which of the two attitudes would have a greater impact on the other. Issue images are influenced by attachments to a party, which would imply that the predominant causal flow is from partisanship to issue images. At the same time, however, issue images may work to redefine standing partisan commitments, implying that the causal flow runs at least partially in the opposite direction. In any event, the direction of this causal flow cannot be determined by means of the model in Figure 8-1, whose purpose it is to assess the independent impact of partisanship and issue images on vote choice.[3] Thus, while the correlation between these two concepts will be presented, the linkage between them will not be incorporated into our causal analyses.

To measure the influence of the three causal forces on vote choice, the value of each path coefficient in the hypothetical model has been calculated for every election between 1961 and 1972 (Figure 8-2).[4] Even though caution must be exercised in evaluating the validity of long-term processes in terms of this limited timespan, such a procedure should yield a fuller understanding of the changing bases of German voting behavior. Path coefficients, both unstandardized (presented above the line for each election) and standardized (presented below the line and enclosed in parentheses for each election) are shown in the figure because the causal paths are compared across variables and also across time.

In the 1961 election, the impact of social characteristics on voting is largely mediated by partisanship and issue images. Social characteristics have substantial influence in determining both partisan attitudes (b = 0.41, B = 0.44) and issue images (b = 0.21, B = 0.37), but they show only a moderate direct effect on vote choice (b = 0.02, B = 0.20). As for the two attitudinal variables, partisanship clearly outweighs the issue dimension in causal importance. This probably reflects, in part, the psychological proximity of the vote to the short-term affective component of the partisan indicator. In addition, it reaffirms the finding that party lines were still clearly drawn in 1961, when both the SPD and CDU/CSU campaigned intensely. Furthermore, the policy changes made by the SPD at Godesberg still had not had time to affect the party's popular image.

This causal pattern begins to change in 1965. Social characteristics still show only a weak direct impact on voting behavior, but the relative influence of partisan attitudes and issue images is changing. Affective partisan ties are weakening in the face of the changing content of German politics in the mid-sixties. In step with this new agenda, the path between issue images and vote has nearly doubled since 1961, while the partisanship-to-vote path has declined noticeably. Additional analyses have shown that the increasing strength of issue images reflects a growth in the causal influence of both Old Politics and New Politics items: the persistence of Old Politics values in the face of a changing environment, and the development of New Politics values independent of traditional social and partisan alignments.[5]

The most significant aspect of the pattern for the 1969 election is the extent to which issue images have continued to gain in relative importance, becoming about equal to partisanship in determining the vote. The actions of party elites probably facilitated this increase in the relevance of issue images. The "era of good feelings" surrounding the Grand Coalition minimized the psychological distance between the two major parties, thereby easing partisan conversions and lessening the direct impact of partisanship on vote choice. Moreover, the changing climate of opinion led the SPD to emphasize New Politics alternatives in its party program, typified by the 1969 slogan; "We Create the Modern Germany." The

Figure 8-2 Causal Models of German Voting Behavior, 1961-1972

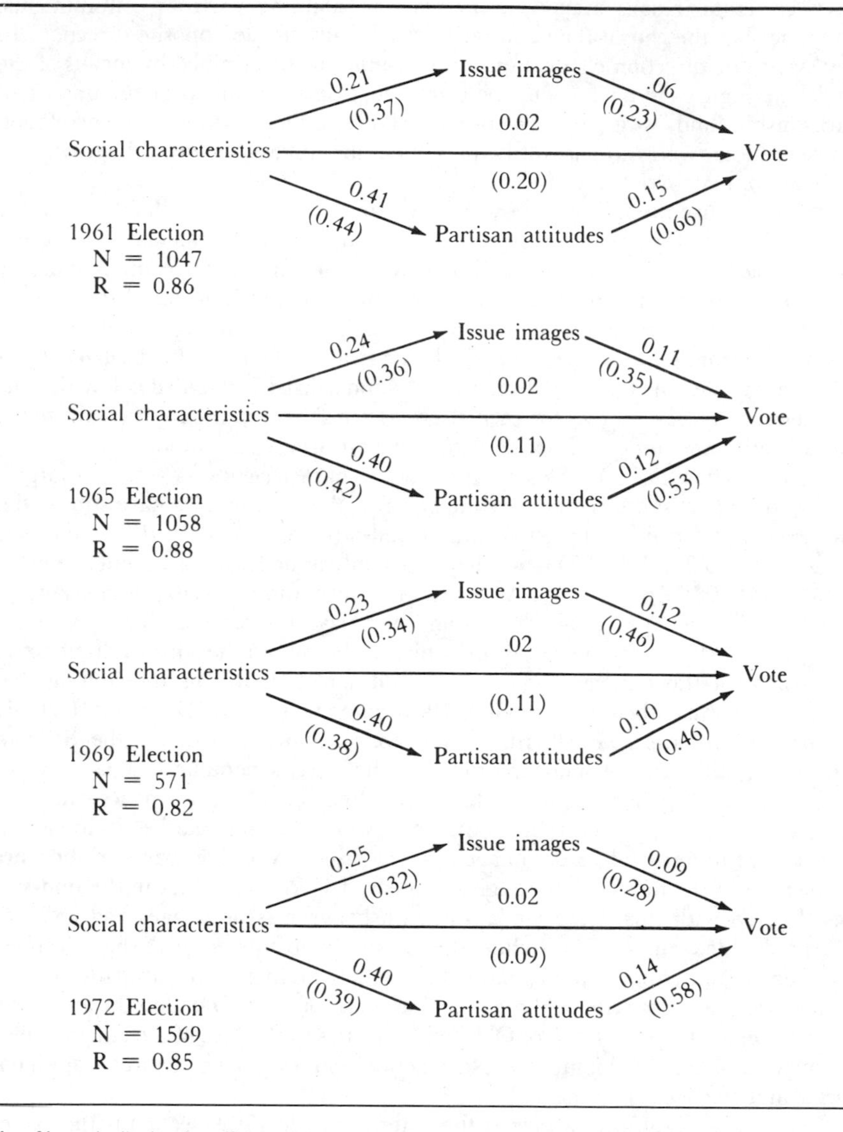

Note: Unstandardized path coefficients (b in text) appear above the arrows; the standardized (B) coefficients appear below the arrows enclosed in parentheses. Listwise exclusion of missing data was used.

SPD's support for New Politics issues such as abortion on demand, educational reform, Ostpolitik, and quality-of-life concerns undoubtedly strengthened the impact of issue images on the vote—especially the New Politics component of these images (Hildebrandt and Dalton, 1978). Indeed, the separation of Old Politics from New Politics issues makes it clear that the overall increase in the causal influence of issues between 1965 and 1969 can be attributed entirely to the New Politics concerns (see note 5).

The span of these three elections (1961-1969) does not provide a basis for very confident conclusions, but the pattern does appear to support the hypothesis that advanced industrialism is changing the values and consequently the partisan behavior of the German public. Because both social characteristics and partisanship decline in importance from 1961 to 1969, electoral changes probably cannot be traced primarily to either of these factors. Rather, these changes seem to be linked to the impact of issue images, which have become increasingly important to voting decisions during the period. Furthermore, New Politics issues, which tap the concerns of an advanced industrial society, have gained most in salience and causal influence.

It could be that issue images have only a short-term influence on voting behavior, but by 1969 the force of these images has become strong enough to suggest that they may be causing a more fundamental change in the nature of German political behavior. The data for 1972 should suggest the form this change may be taking.

In 1972 the direct causal link from social characteristics to vote reflects a weak relationship. More important is the reversal in the trends of the party-to-vote and issues-to-vote paths. For the first time, the causal link between issues and vote decreases, while the path from partisan attitudes to vote increases. Issues are a weaker predictor and partisanship is a stronger predictor than in 1965.

This rise in the importance of partisanship could be attributed to the reassertion of partisan differences after the 1969 election when the Grand Coalition ended and the CDU/CSU went into opposition. But in addition the 1972 election was unique. Voters displayed an intensely affective reaction to the person of Chancellor Brandt, which may appear in the affective measure of partisanship. Furthermore, the CDU/CSU's attempt to oust the SPD/FDP coalition through a "constructive vote of no confidence" led the forces of both major parties to close ranks during the campaign. The 1972 results might, therefore, be explained by specific short-term factors.

The trouble with this idiosyncratic explanation of the 1972 election, however, is that the dramatic shift in the voting patterns of social groups that had occurred in 1969 was also present in 1972, as if issue images were still highly important. For example, the overall level of class voting in 1972 was still far below the pre-1969 level, the new middle class was still giving more support to the SPD, and class voting was still declining among the young. In short, there is a seeming paradox. The weight of partisanship increased in 1972, but the overall evidence indicates that partisanship was not producing the same social alignments and voting patterns as it had in the past. Rather, issue images were influential in 1972, although the causal model would suggest their decline. How can this paradox be resolved?

As Germany has moved toward the postindustrial era, the impact of sociostructural influences on voting behavior has declined. In this situation, the key question to be asked is not "What is replacing social cues?" but "Why are social cues declining?" The answer suggested by the data is that the rise of the New Politics-Old Politics dimension, which runs counter to previous cleavage ties, is at least partially responsible. And as new issues and values develop, the tension between issue images and social characteristics mounts, weakening the impact of social cleavages on voting behavior.

Issue images may well provide a vehicle for changing the more fundamental partisan attachments (Matthews and Prothro, 1966; Trilling, 1976). Ronald Inglehart (1977) suggests that the Old Politics-New Politics dimension may eventually become integrated into partisan attitudes and the party systems of Western Europe. Indeed, the reversed trends in the 1972 issue and partisanship paths shown in Figure 8-2 might suggest that the tension existing in 1969 between issue images and partisanship led to partisan conversion after that election. In addition to the evidence available from the causal model, two pieces of "side information" add weight to this conversion hypothesis. First, issue images became more independent of partisanship between 1965 and 1969 before rising again in 1972.[6] Second, panel data indicate far less stability of partisanship and voting intentions in 1969 than in 1972; in 1969 partisanship was in a state of flux.[7] Taken together, these facts suggest that at least some of the issue component was "absorbed" into more general partisan attitudes between the 1969 and 1972 elections.

It is not clear whether the German party system's response to New Politics concerns or its efforts to provide a partisan outlet for these accumulating forces of change is typical or atypical.[8] The rate of electoral change may have been accelerated because of specifically German conditions. This, of course, has been the primary reason for focusing on Germany as a test case. Nevertheless, after a period of increasing concern with New Politics issues, some segments of the electorate may have developed or adjusted their partisanship to fit this value dimension. Hence partisan attitudes gained a new importance in 1972.

It is difficult, if not impossible, to make a direct test of the conversion hypothesis without long-term panel data. This would require the estimation of the reciprocal causal paths between issues and partisanship, but this reciprocal relationship cannot be estimated with the available data. The conversion hypothesis is therefore an enticing idea that cannot be either empirically confirmed or denied.

It is possible, however, to develop an indirect test of the hypothesis by using the available data. If younger Germans, who are more interested in New Politics issues than the older people, are developing their partisan loyalties on the basis of these concerns, that may partially explain the persistence of partisan patterns associated with the New Politics even after the weakening of issue images in 1972. For the young, partisanship may strongly overlap with New Politics orientations, serving to some extent as a surrogate measure of value priorities.[9]

When the issue indicator is divided into its two component parts—Old Politics and New Politics—generational differences in the bases of partisanship can be examined. In Table 8-1 the partial correlations between partisanship and the two issue domains have been broken down for two cohorts: the young (Federal Republic) and the old (Third Reich, Weimar, and Wilhelmine). As the table shows, the German electorate is primarily oriented toward Old Politics (or materialist) concerns. In all four election years the Old Politics issues are correlated more highly with partisanship for both generations. There are, however, generally consistent differences in the weight given to the two domains by young and old cohorts. In 1961 the partial correlation for Old Politics issues

Table 8-1 Partial Correlations of Issue Competency and Partisanship, 1961-1972[a]

Issue by generation	*July 1961*	*Sept. 1965*	*Nov. 1969*	*Sept. 1972*
Old Politics issues				
Young	0.52	0.55	0.48	0.50
Old	.59	.51	.48	.59
New Politics issues				
Young	.36	.33	.34	.31
Old	.26	.33	.31	.22

a Cell entries are the partial correlations between each index of issue competency and partisanship, controlling for the other issue competency index.

with partisanship is 0.59 for the older cohort and 0.52 (slightly weaker) for the young. For the New Politics index in the same year the opposite pattern emerges: a slightly stronger correlation for the young (0.36) than for the old (0.26). In 1965 the differences between the generations narrow. The partisan loyalties of the young are more closely related to Old Politics issues than are those of the old cohort. With the 1969 election, however, the young place increasing emphasis on New Politics issues. And in 1972 the pattern becomes clearer: the gap between the Old Politics correlations for the young (0.50) and for the old (0.59) is substantial; and New Politics issues are more closely related to partisanship for the young than for the old (0.31 versus 0.22).

These data suggest that when evaluating the two major parties younger Germans place somewhat more emphasis on New Politics issues than do older cohorts. Therefore the partisan attachments of the young are more likely to include both New Politics and Old Politics interests. In this way the partisanship of the young—and presumably of other change-oriented groups such as the new middle class—is helping to perpetuate the impact of the New Politics.[10]

Conclusion

The trends examined in this chapter represent the converging effects of many familiar causal factors: elite actions, economic prosperity, generational change, and general environmental change. Although it is possible that a reversal of these causal forces may alter electoral trends, and although restraint must be exercised in basing long-term hypotheses on relatively short-term data, these empirical findings suggest a pattern of political change that may explain recent German electoral history.

Clearly, sociostructural influences on voting behavior are declining as the postindustrial era approaches. What will replace these cues as a guide for voting behavior? Shively (1972) and others suggest that party identification may serve as an immediate replacement, but this view focuses on the consequences of declining social influences without giving equal attention to the causes of the decline. The evidence of this chapter and of other research suggests that an emerging Old

Politics—New Politics issue dimension is a major factor in weakening the influence of social characteristics. Hence it must be that these issue images (and values) are replacing the old sociostructural cues.

Party identification, on the other hand, might be a long-term consequence of declining cleavage-based voting. After a period of strong issue-based voting at least some segments of the electorate should develop direct psychological ties to a party resulting from their issue preferences; then attitudinal partisanship would increase. In this light, the Old Politics—New Politics issue dimension can be viewed as an intermediate step between a system based on social cleavages and one based on attitudinal partisanship—at least for the cleavage-oriented systems of Western Europe. Thus, the development of party attachments in these systems may partially be a function of Old Politics-New Politics value change and the responsiveness of elites and the party system to this emerging dimension of politics.

NOTES

1. The one obvious factor not included in this model is candidate image. However, because of Germany's parliamentary form of government, candidate image exerts only a minor influence on voting decisions. For over-time analyses see: Klingemann and Taylor (1978); Norpoth (1977).
2. For an application of a similar model to the United States see Goldberg (1966).
3. Separate estimation of the strengths of the reciprocal relationships between issue images and partisanship requires the use of multiwave panel data or instrumental variables. See Markus and Converse (1979); Page and Jones (1979). Several potential instrumental variables were explored without much success. For an introduction to the methodological problems of reciprocal effects see Duncan (1975, chaps. 5-7).
4. The measurement of the components of this causal model were drawn from analyses in the preceding chapters. The indicator of partisan attitudes is the seven-point index developed in chapter 8 [of Baker et al., 1981]. Issue images are measured by an additive index of perceived party competency for the set of four core issues: two related to the Old Politics (price stability and old age security); and the other two related to the New Politics (support for education and relations with the United States). This issue competency measure is used because it taps the direct relevance of valence issues to the party system; it is not intended to serve as an undifferentiated test of issue voting. Including a larger set of issues and weighting competency by issue salience would increase the total predictive power of the issues, but the content of the indicator is of more importance here than maximizing its correlation with the vote. The social characteristics indicator combines all four dimensions of traditional cleavage politics—social status, religion, region, and rural-urban residence—into a self-weighted composite measure of cleavage influences. This measure was obtained by saving the predicted values from an MCA analysis of social characteristics on vote. . . .
5. The following tabulation presents the results of regressing the vote on social characteristics, partisanship, Old Politics issue images, and New Politics issue images. Entries are standardized regression coefficients. For additional discussion of these results see Baker et al. (1975).

	1961	*1965*	*1969*	*1972*
Social characteristics	0.116	0.107	0.105	0.087
Partisanship	.652	.515	.452	.566
Old Politics issues	.157	.302	.282	.222
New Politics issues	.051	.092	.130	.090

6. The Pearson correlation between issue images and partisanship is as follows: 1961 = 0.66, 1965 = 0.72, 1969 = 0.67, 1972 = 0.73.
7. The one-month correlations for election panels in 1969 and 1972 are as follows:

	1st vote	*2d Vote*	*Partisanship*
1969	0.74	0.73	0.63
1972	.86	.89	.81

8. Cameron (1976) argues that the Federal Republic is unique in this respect.
9. For another perspective on generational differences in German partisanship see Baker (1978).
10. In statistical terms there is a large pool of shared variance between the New Politics issue images of the young and their partisan attachments.

9. THE TWO FACES OF ISSUE VOTING

Edward G. Carmines and James A. Stimson

"To speak with precision about public opinion," V. O. Key once observed, "is a task not unlike coming to grips with the Holy Ghost" (1961, p. 8). A similar observation could be made about issue voting, because for all of the recent attention devoted to this political phenomenon, its character has remained as elusive as ever. This is not to say that no progress has been made in untangling the web of uncertainty and ignorance that surrounds our understanding of policy-oriented voting. On the contrary, recent research focusing on elections and voting behavior has pointed to various social, political, and psychological conditions that facilitate the translation of policy preferences into votes. Thus, according to some research, issue voting occurs most frequently during periods of social and economic turmoil, when the policy options provided by the political parties tend to be relatively distinct (Nie et al., 1976, pp. 156-93). And certain individual cognitive and psychological characteristics are similarly thought to be necessary for policy-conscious voting decisions (Broh, 1973; Miller et al., 1973).

But our understanding of issue voting is not likely to be clear, precise, or comprehensive until we know much more about the core "issue" in issue voting, the decision calculus used by voters to link their policy concerns to voting choices. As a first step toward that comprehensive understanding, we need to question whether "issue voting" is a single phenomenon. Our argument is that it is not, that there are two theoretically different and empirically identifiable types.

Issue voting of the first type involves conscious calculation of policy benefits for alternative electoral choices. This "hard-issue" voting has its intellectual roots in the Downsian tradition (Downs, 1957). It presumes that issue voting is the final result of a sophisticated decision calculus; that it represents a reasoned and

---

Authors' Note: Apologies to Bachrach and Baratz for borrowing part of their title. The data used in this article were made available by the Inter-University Consortium for Political and Social Research. The data were originally collected by the University of Michigan Center for Political Studies of the Institute for Social Research, under a grant from the National Science Foundation. Neither the original collectors of the data nor the Consortium bear any responsibility for the analyses or interpretations presented here. For helpful commentary along the way we thank Russell Dalton, James Kuklinski, John McIver, Leroy Rieselbach, Ann Shaw, Ronald Weber, and some kind anonymous readers for the *Review*. The authors would like to thank the National Science Foundation for its support of this research under grant SOC-7907543.

Source: *American Political Science Review* (1980) 74:78-91. Reprinted with permission of the publisher.

thoughtful attempt by voters to use policy preferences to guide their electoral decision. Citizens, after examining the policy positions represented by candidates in a given election, vote for that candidate who is closest to them in some (probably multiple) issue space (Davis et al., 1970; Brody and Page, 1972; Frohlich et al., 1978). Hard-issue voting should be best exemplified, at least in degree, among those who have the conceptual skills to do it well.

The second type of issue voting (which we shall denote "easy") occurs when a particular issue becomes so ingrained over a long period that it structures voters' "gut responses" to candidates and political parties. Because gut responses require no conceptual sophistication, they should be distributed reasonably evenly in the voting population. It can be argued of course that this second type of issue voting is merely a simplified version of the first. But we shall argue that the distinction between them is fundamental, that they involve different decision processes, different prerequisite conditions, different voters, and different interpretations.

The Noncontroversy About Issue Voting

Before we examine in detail these two kinds of issue voting, it will be helpful to put that discussion into perspective by highlighting an assumption upon which all who study the topic seem to agree, that "issue voting" is not a neutral term. On the contrary, the study of issue voting is infused with normative considerations. The common—indeed, universal—view has been that voting choices based on policy concerns are superior to decisions based on party loyalty or candidate image. Only the former represent clearly sophisticated behavior. Indeed, the policy-oriented vote is a defining characteristic of that mythical specimen, the classic democratic citizen. The spatial modeling approach to voting behavior, moreover, is quite explicit in linking issue voting to rationality, an assumption that leads to the conclusion that voting on the basis of other considerations must be nonrational, or at best, less rational.

While scholars have disagreed vehemently about most aspects of issue voting—how it can be measured, whether it has increased in frequency during recent elections—they have never questioned its inherent "goodness." (For a sampling of this literature, see Boyd, 1972; Pomper, 1972; Nie et al., 1976; RePass, 1971; Miller et al., 1976; Margolis, 1977; for a fairly complete bibliography through 1972 see Kessel, 1972.) The issue voter has been universally praised. This assumption has been, in fact, so noncontroversial and such an integral aspect of issue voting that those focusing on the topic have felt no need to justify it. Indeed, it is rarely mentioned at all except for the occasional phrase coupling issue voting with the average citizen having been seen in a more favorable light. Thus, when Key (1966, pp. 7, xiii) announced in the opening chapter of his final, posthumously published work that "the perverse and unorthodox argument of this little book is that voters are not fools," no one should have been surprised that the bulk of the supporting evidence focused on "the parallelism of policy preferences and the direction of the vote." For it is precisely such evidence that would support the notion that "the electorate behaves about as rationally and responsibly as we should expect, given the clarity of the alternatives presented to it and the character of the information available to it" (Key, 1966, p. 7).

This uniformly favorable characterization of the issue voter would be of little consequence except that it has led us to treat all issue-based voting as evidence of voter sophistication. Our inferences about the level of issue voting are not in question here; "easy" issues are still "issues." It is the inferences we draw from the level of issue voting that we are going to call in question.[1]

The idea that all issue voting does not indicate voter sophistication was suggested, perhaps inadvertently, by Survey Research Center (SRC) analysts in their study of the 1968 presidential election (Converse et al., 1969). Stressing the issue distinctiveness of Wallace's supporters, as compared to Humphrey's and Nixon's, they noted that "among the whites who voted for one of the major candidates, only 10% favored continued segregation rather than desegregation or 'something in between'; among Wallace voters, all of whom were white, almost 40% wanted segregation" (Converse et al., 1969, p. 1097). Combining the issue distinctiveness of Wallace voters on a variety of issues with the finding that among the general public favorable and unfavorable evaluations of Wallace had a strong issue coloration led to the conclusion that "the Wallace candidacy was reacted to by the public as an *issue* candidacy" (Converse et al., 1969, p. 1097). While the Wallace voters may have been motivated largely by issue considerations, Converse et al. do not argue (and we have no reason to assume) that they were any more sophisticated—according to any criteria—than Humphrey or Nixon voters. Thus, the SRC analysis of the Wallace candidacy of 1968 represents an initial effort to drive a wedge between issue voting and voter sophistication. But, ultimately, to discover the primary motivation of a candidate's supporters is not likely to reveal much about issue voting for the simple reason that in a strict sense there is no such thing as an "issue candidacy." For any candidate with a modicum of public support will attract voters for all sorts of reasons, many of which have nothing to do with his or her issue positions. Thus, one must agree with Brody and Page (1972, p. 455) that "there is no way to avoid modeling the individual voting decision and still estimate policy voting," a topic to which we shall turn shortly.

The Attributes of Easy Issues

Most of what is written about "issues" is descriptive of what we have called "hard" issues. We focus here, in counterpoint, on the attributes of the easy issue.

If we ask the question, "What makes an issue easy?" we would be asking what makes possible a gut response elicited equally from well-informed and ill-informed, from interested and uninterested, from active and apathetic voters. Three such requisites are these:

1. The easy issue would be symbolic rather than technical.
2. It would more likely deal with policy ends than means.
3. It would be an issue long on the political agenda.

Each of the requisites has a simple rationale. Symbolic conflicts are readily communicated to mass publics. Technical issues are not. As prescriptions for public problems, technical policies require knowledge of important factual assumptions to be appreciated. Symbolic issues may be presented *and understood* simplistically.

Easy issues must almost inevitably concern the ends of public policy rather than the means. In part, this is simply the first requisite restated; the means of public policy are usually more technical than symbolic. In part, it is because preferences about policy ends can arise from the common prejudices of the mass culture. Normative premises are not by definition informed; neither do they need to be articulated.

The easy issue, finally, is likely to be an unresolved conflict long in the public eye. Even if the first requisites were met, a new issue would not be likely to find its way to the "gut" of those paying least attention to politics. Simplicity alone is not enough, but with time and simplicity an issue can permeate the electorate.

A last, more speculative, attribute of the easy issue is not a requisite, but a consequence. The availability of the easy issue for electoral choice we take to be a system-determined attribute. Simply put, sometimes easy issues are offered to the electorate and sometimes they are not. Whether a given easy issue was employed by a given voter in an election depends more crucially upon whether the choice was offered than upon the ability of the voter to make such a choice (Prewitt and Nie, 1971). Hard issues we posit to be always available; the degree to which they are employed is voter-dependent. More interested, more informed, and more involved citizens are more likely to discriminate by hard issues than their less interested, less informed, and less involved counterparts.

This last attribute could form an important link in the solution of the unresolved problem of explaining over time variation in issue voting. But it must remain only an informed speculation here. We turn now to two real-world issues that exemplify the easy/hard distinction.

Desegregation and Vietnam: Easy and Hard

Racial desegregation is a protypically easy issue—in fact, the issue that led us to think about the consequences of easy-issue voting. Although the policy conflicts involved in desegregation can be detailed in great complexity, we think it reasonable to assume that the typical voter sees in it a simple issue. Some support for that assumption can be found in our operational indicator of desegregation attitudes (a factor score derived from a variety of racial materials), which is most clearly defined by items which ask simply for respondent preferences for more or less segregation in American society. Desegregation is symbolic (Sears et al., 1979); there are virtually no technical or pragmatic issues in it. And it has been around a very long time now. The least-informed segments of both black and white communities respond meaningfully to the question of desegregation; it is that easy.

It is an issue, finally, on which parties and candidates have staked out relatively unambiguous positions—most notably in the 1964 presidential election. The clarity of positions on desegregation during that electoral contest can be seen in a simple statistic: the Survey Research Center did not discover a single black Goldwater supporter in its nationwide election survey (cited in Greenstein, 1970, p. 26). The 1964 presidential election, we believe, had a powerful and lasting effect on racial desegregation—perceptions that led to a slow but permanent reshaping of underlying party loyalties (Stimson and Carmines, 1977).

The Vietnam War was quite a different issue. The issue was badly muddled in 1968 when the country was deeply divided about the war (Verba and Brody, 1970) but Nixon and Humphrey took similar positions (Page and Brody, 1972). War and peace are simple enough ends, but the candidates did not offer that choice. Instead, the electorate was presented with alternative plans (one of them "secret") to end the war (Page, 1978). The issue had been changed but not particularly clarified by 1972 (Steeper and Teeter, 1976), when one candidate promised to end the war by immediate withdrawal and the other claimed already to have resolved it by his harder-line approach. While antiwar activists may have seen a wide gulf separating the candidates' position, we believe most voters saw the issue in far more narrow terms, focusing mainly on the speed and conditions of withdrawal. The confusion was heightened, finally, by the fact that Democratic presidents had initiated and vigorously prosecuted the war while the Republican incumbent had sharply reduced the number of U.S. troops in Vietnam. With strong sentiment for ending the war running in the electorate, moreover, the alternative candidate scenarios increasingly focused debate on the return of prisoners of war, American postwar prestige, and the like. The relative efficacy of the not terribly different strategies was the issue.

The pace of withdrawal from Vietnam (the "choice" offered in the 1972 presidential election) was clearly a hard issue by our criteria. The issue, as presented, was pragmatic, not symbolic. It dealt with the best means of ending the war, but with nearly universal agreement on the ultimate end. And it was an issue of relatively brief duration, lasting at most the length of American involvement in the war, but probably a good deal less than that, since the nature of the issue changed as the war evolved.

Our classification of desegregation and Vietnam into theoretical categories rests, in the end, on empirical knowledge. Racial desegregation could be complex and Vietnam simple if the issues had evolved that way in the political system *and if voters saw them that way.* All issues have intrinsically simple and complex facets; which particular facets predominate at a given time is an empirical question. We have no doubt that desegregation was (and is) seen as a simple issue. For evidence that Vietnam was not at all simple in 1972, see Steeper and Teeter (1976).

Desegregation and Vietnam in the 1972 Election

The 1972 presidential election proves to be a useful case study for examining easy- and hard-issue voting. The election is widely described as issue-oriented, perhaps more than any other. It falls in the electoral period of enhanced issue consciousness, a phenomenon yet to be fully explained. And it is particularly convenient for this research because, as we shall soon see, it is dominated by two issues, Vietnam and desegregation, each an exemplification of hard and easy issues, respectively.

Before we can proceed with further analysis, we need (for later purposes) to demonstrate that our two issues had a non-trivial and non-spurious impact on the 1972 contest. This we have accomplished with the multivariate probit analysis of voting choice of Table 9-1.[2] Along with party identification, it includes as independent variables all the (non-racial) CPS seven-point scales administered to both Form 1 and Form 2 respondents and the two racial-attitude factors.

Table 9-1 presents standardized maximum-likelihood estimates (MLEs, analogous to the standardized slope coefficients of regression) along with "z" tests for the null hypotheses that the true MLEs are zero, all for the full sample of is-

Table 9-1 1972 Vote, Party, and Issues

	Standardized Maximum Likelihood Estimate	*Z*
Party identification	−1.733	−15.9
Vietnam withdrawal	− .932	− 9.5
Desegregation	.616	6.3
Guarantee of jobs	− .544	− 5.7
Attitude toward black activists	.410	4.2
Legalization of marijuana	− .218	− 2.2
Rights of accused	− .177	− 1.8
Women's role	.113	1.2
Tax reform	− .045	− .5
Control of inflation	.003	.0

−2 (Log Likelihood Ratio) 832.0
Significance: $P<.001$

Source: Computed from data collected in the 1972 Center for Political Studies election study, University of Michigan.

sues. Vote choice is dichotomous, the seven-point issue scales are the familiar respondent self-placements (not proximity measures) and the two racial scales are factor scores derived from a variety of racial attitude materials (see Appendix A). The first taps attitudes toward desegregation, both in general and in the traditional battlegrounds of schools, jobs, housing, and so forth. The second racial factor, more diffuse and affective, taps attitudes oriented more toward racial protest (and protesters) than the substance of racial policy.

The evidence of Table 9-1 is clear. Both the Vietnam War and desegregation are shown to have influenced the 1972 vote in the face of controls for party identification and a reasonable sample of other possible issues. What is intriguing about Table 9-1 is that racial desegregation emerges as the second best "issue" predictor of voting choice in 1972. For unlike Vietnam, which was a dominant theme in the campaign, racial desegregation was hardly mentioned by either candidate. That it was not emphasized in party platforms and not salient in the campaign but still exerted a substantial influence on the election outcome suggests something about the unusual properties of desegregation as a political issue.

We have talked of issue voting and the distinction between hard and easy issues in largely intuitive and indirect terms, to this point. A more systematic approach is now in order.

Classifying Issue Difficulty

We conceive of issue voting as a two-part multiplicative process requiring at minimum that each voter (1) assess his or her own issue preference and (2) calculate relative positioning of parties and candidates. The second dimension, the spatial mapping process, we believe, distinguishes hard from easy issues. Hard issues are more accurately mapped by the well-informed. Easy issues are accurately mapped by all.

How can we tell empirically whether a particular issue is easy or hard? Our theory suggests simply enough that the relationship between *hard* issues and vote should be *conditional* on level of political information possessed by voters. Issue position should exert a considerably stronger causal influence on the votes of the well-informed because they, more than the ill-informed, accurately map party and candidate issue stances. The ill-informed should show a tendency to mix "correct" responses with "incorrect" ones in the aggregate, and therefore display an apparently weaker[3] relationship between issue and vote. No such distinction should hold if the issue is easy. That the ill-informed can respond appropriately is a defining characteristic of the easy issue.

Figures 9-1 and 9-2 array vote by issue position on Vietnam withdrawal and desegregation, respectively, with voters classified by political information level.[4] Figure 9-1 shows the Vietnam withdrawal scale as a prototypical hard issue.

Figure 9-1 Vote and Vietnam Withdrawal by Political Information Level

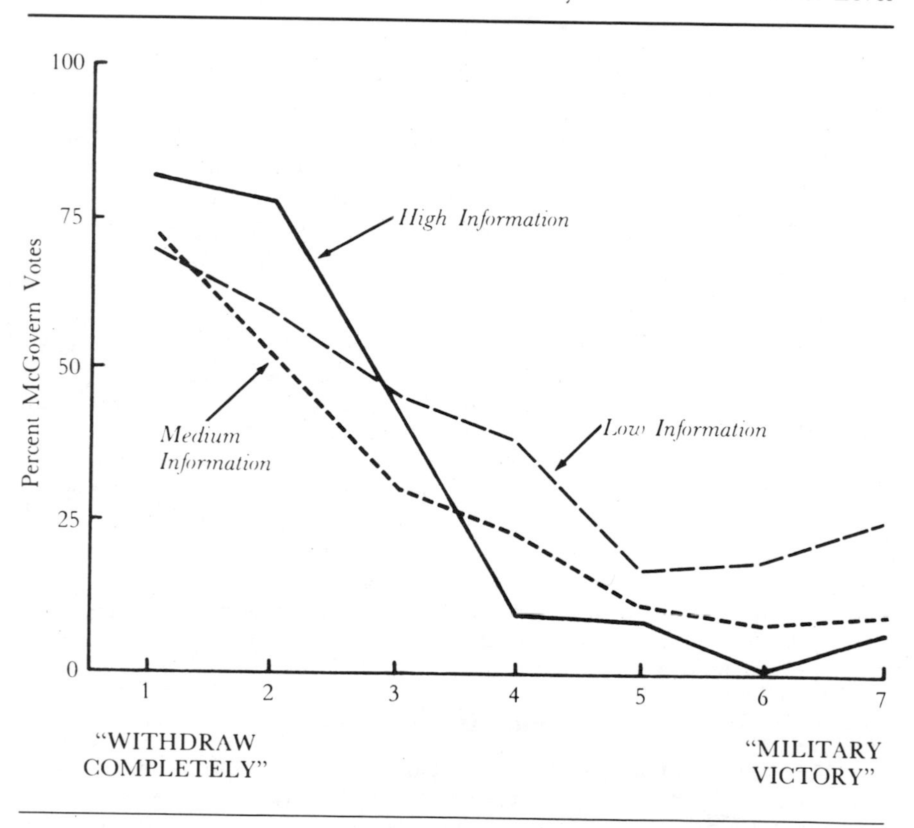

Source: Computed from data collected in the 1972 Center for Political Studies election study, University of Michigan.

Figure 9-2 Vote and Desegregation by Political Information Level

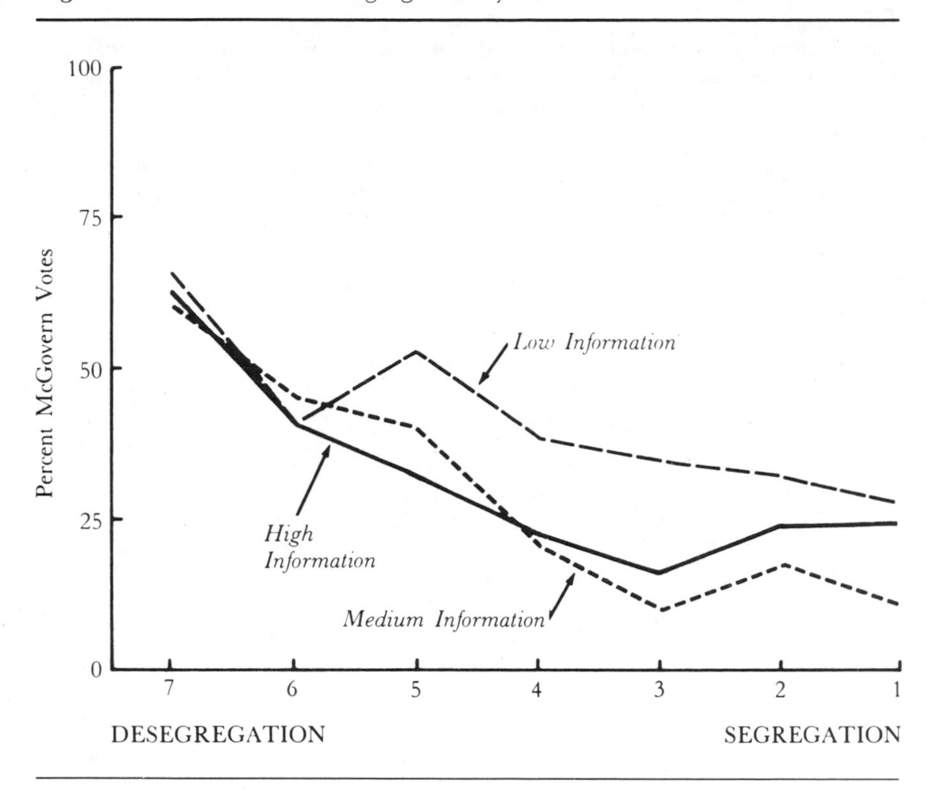

Source: Computed from data collected in the 1972 Center for Political Studies election study, University of Michigan.

Well-informed voters as a group appear extremely sensitive to the issue; the pro-withdrawal segment is sharply pro-McGovern, the "military victory" group almost unanimous in support of Nixon. Those with medium information levels show a still strong but flatter response in their votes; they are less inclined to vote for McGovern if they favor withdrawal, less inclined to vote for Nixon if they advocate the military solution. The least-informed complete the pattern; similar to the medium information group if they favor withdrawal, they are considerably more likely to report a McGovern vote if they take the hard-line position other voters associate with Nixon. The Eta-squared statistic from analysis of variance is a rough summary of the (nonlinear) relationship between issue and vote. For low, medium, and high information groups, respectively, it progresses from .15 to .22 to .46. Voter information makes a difference.

Figure 9-2 demonstrates that the issue/information interaction does not apply to all issues. At the pro-desegregation end of the scale, voters are undifferentiated by information level. Differentiation increases with segregationist sentiment, but it is mixed and intransitive, with the best-informed between the low and medium categories in voting response to pro-segregation attitudes. The Eta squared is similarly intransitive, rising from .06 for the least-informed to .17 for the medium group, and then falling off to .11 for the best-informed. This unpredictability is what we expect of the easy issue; information doesn't structure the relationship between issue preference and vote.

The statistical evidence thus indicates that Vietnam was a hard issue and desegregation an easy one. It may seem paradoxical that the issue which dominated campaign rhetoric was hard and the one undiscussed easy. But we think that is probably normally the case. Easy issues do not require discussion, whereas complicated policy disputes (i.e., hard issues) are not likely to be reflected in electoral response at all unless they are extensively discussed.

Measuring Policy Voting

Although the literature on voting behavior is richly suggestive of where we should look for issue voting—to the well-educated, well-informed, concerned and active segment of the electorate—it has little to offer as a guide to measuring it directly. The presumed causes of issue voting (education, access to information, etc.) are particularly ill-suited as surrogate indicators of it in this research, where it is hypothesized that they are not common to all types of policy voting. This research requires a pure measure of the phenomenon, a yardstick that will allow the categorization of individuals without reference to the presumed antecedents of issue-voting behavior.

To separate issue voting from its antecedents and consequences in order that both may be open to empirical investigation, we define it as voting which is predictable from knowledge about individual policy preferences. That simple definition skirts some theoretical difficulties and is far from easy to render operational, but it does allow for classification at the individual level.

The principal theoretical problem with our simple definition is specifying the proper role of partisanship. Party identification may be conceived as policy-irrelevant loyalty, as a cue to issue preferences, or as an amalgam of the two. It no doubt serves all of those purposes for different subsets of the electorate. It may even of course be the causal result of policy preferences. In the analysis to follow we treat party identification as antecedent to both policy preferences and voting choice. For each individual policy, party identification is used as a predictive baseline against which the presumed influence of issues is judged. Each voter is judged an issue voter if knowledge of the individual's issue position improves our ability to predict his or her vote beyond the level of predictability already achieved by party identification.

The procedure for classifying individuals into issue-voter categories is a good deal less simple than our simple definition; measuring predictability is not as easy as talking about it. The procedure outlined here (and in more detail in Appendix B) is as follows:

1. The best-fitting probit function relating party identification and Vietnam and desegregation attitudes to vote is derived for all voters collectively.

2. Three separate probit predictions are then generated for each of the 1,515 voters. One drops out the two policy attitude variables (by setting them to their

mean values for everybody), leaving party identification as the only predictor variable. One drops out desegregation and predicts from party and Vietnam. And one drops out Vietnam and predicts from party and desegregation.

3. Each of the three predictions is transformed into probability of voting for McGovern.

4. The three probability calculations are compared with reported vote to classify each individual voter into one of four mutually exclusive categories:

> A. Non-Issue Voters: Neither "party + Vietnam" nor "party + desegregation" models have smaller predictive error than "party only," 15 percent of all voters.
>
> B. Easy-Issue Voters: "Party + desegregation" is a better predictor than "party only," but "party" + Vietnam" is not, 19 percent of all voters.
>
> C. Hard-Issue Voters: "Party + Vietnam" is a better predictor than "party only," but "party + desegregation" is not, 24 percent of all voters.
>
> D. Constrained[5]-Issue Voters: Both "party + desegregation" and "party + Vietnam" improve upon the "party only" prediction, 42 percent of all voters.

Our typology is a means to an end; it allows examination of our basic hypothesis, that easy- and hard-issue voting are fundamentally different.

The Attributes of Issue Voters

We have argued thus far that easy issues are different in kind from hard issues. Although we have already presented some evidence for the argument, the most important evidence is to be found in the argument's implication that easy-issue voters are also different from hard-issue voters. We hypothesize that they are. The hypothesis, more specifically, is that hard-issue voters have the characteristics universally attributed in the literature to "issue voters" and that easy-issue voters are no more informed, educated, or active in politics than those who are not influenced by issue considerations at all. The easy-issue voters are genuinely issue voters, but we hypothesize that they share none of the personal attributes traditionally associated with issue voting.

The distinguishing characteristic of the easy issue is that it requires almost nothing of the voter. Those who employ only easy issues would not therefore be expected to be more sophisticated—by any number of criteria—than voters who use such easy alternatives as party loyalty or candidate affect. Similarly, those who employ both hard and easy issues would not be expected to be more sophisticated than those who use hard issues only; the only critical distinction is between using and not using hard issues.

We have chosen three indicators of voter sophistication, "education," "political information," and "political activity," because they are commonly believed to differentiate the issue voter from the non-issue voter. They are central to Berelson's "democratic citizen" (1954, pp. 305-23) and, unlike such other alleged issue-voter attributes as rationality, they can be measured in an unambiguous manner. We take them up one at a time.

Education

The democratic citizen/issue voter is usually considered to be well informed about political choices. We can reasonably assume that formal education contributes to that state of affairs. Table 9-2 displays the levels of education of our four voter types. Of particular note is that the easy-issue voters are far and away the least-educated segment of the voting sample—being even less educated than the non-issue voters, with about 10 percent more who have not completed high school and 15 percent fewer who have attended college.

The constrained-issue voters, also in line with their predicted position, are slightly less well educated than the hard-issue voters (indeed, barely different from non-issue voters), with about 6 percent more reporting less than a high school education. We have predicted that easy voters are *not more* sophisticated than non-issue voters (and constrained-issue voters *not more* sophisticated than hard-issue voters). The outcome with respect to education is stronger than the prediction: those who use race, our easy issue, to aid their decision making appear *less* sophisticated than their counterparts who do not, although the magnitude of difference is small.

Political Information

Knowing "facts" about politics is a second requirement for being well informed. Such factual knowledge can be measured with the political information scale we have already employed. Levels of such political information for our four voter groups are shown in Table 9-3. Easy-issue voters are slightly (but not significantly) better informed by this criterion than non-issue voters, although interpretation is clouded by the presence of fewer easy-issue voters in both lowest and highest information groups. Both easy-issue and non-issue voters are less well informed than voters in the other two groups, which are in turn similar to one another.

Table 9-2 Education and Issue Voting (Percent)

Education	*Non-Issue Voters*	*Easy-Issue Voters*	*Hard-Issue Voters*	*Constrained-Issue Voters*
Less than high school	32.1	41.4	22.6	29.0
High school or equivalent	28.5	34.4	38.0	31.2
Some college or more	39.4	24.2	39.4	39.7
	100.0	100.0	100.0	99.9
N =	(221)	(285)	(371)	(637)

Source: Computed from data collected in the 1972 Center for Political Studies election study, University of Michigan.

Table 9-3 Political Information and Issue Voting (Percent)

Political Information	*Non-Issue Voters*	*Easy-Issue Voters*	*Hard-Issue Voters*	*Constrained-Issue Voters*
Low	41.7	31.7	21.1	23.5
Medium	40.9	54.2	44.3	47.4
High	17.4	14.1	34.6	29.1
	100.0	100.0	100.0	100.0
N =	(115)	(142)	(185)	(344)

Source: Computed from data collected in the 1972 Center for Political Studies election study, University of Michigan.

Political Activism

Political activism is not so much a measure of sophistication as a presumed cause of it. Those who take an active role in politics should develop a more sophisticated understanding of the choices they confront than those whose involvement in politics extends only to the voting booth. To the degree that activism is not a correlate of education, it may well be a substitute for it, an alternative way to learn about the political world.

We measure activism for this analysis with a summary count of respondent reports of engaging in influencing others' votes, attending political meetings, working for a party or candidate, wearing a campaign button or displaying a sticker, giving money, writing to a public official, or writing a letter to a newspaper about politics.

The activism/issue voting relationship is as predicted, as seen in Table 9-4. Non-issue and easy-issue voters look substantially the same on this scale, as do hard-issue and constrained-issue voters. Easy-issue voters, on the other hand, are substantially less active than hard-issue voters, with almost half of them reporting no participation beyond voting; this is the case among less than a third of the hard-issue voters. In sum, all differences are in the predicted direction.

Our analysis to this point has shown but one deviation from the predicted pattern, and that one was statistically insignificant. We turn now to a slight reconceptualization for a summary look at our findings.

The fourfold typology of issue voting can be easily broken down into the two dichotomous variables from which it was created.[6] We decompose it here for a summary analysis of the correlates of using easy issues (variable name "easy"), hard issues ("hard") or both. We do this to present the separable effects individually and to take advantage of the interval scales of two of the criterion variables. The third criterion, education, is recoded to the dichotomy, "high school or less" and "some college or more."

The quality of measurement shows its effect in the low correlations of Table 9-5, but the individual coefficients still tell a clear story. The correlations of

Table 9-4 Political Activity and Issue Voting (Percent)

Number of Participatory Acts	*Non-Issue Voters*	*Easy-Issue Voters*	*Hard-Issue Voters*	*Constrained-Issue Voters*
0	46.1	47.9	31.3	32.9
1	23.3	26.2	27.2	27.6
2	17.8	14.7	20.8	18.6
3 or more	12.8	11.2	20.8	20.9
	100.0	100.0	100.0	100.0
N =	(219)	(286)	(371)	(633)

Source: Computed from data collected in the 1972 Center for Political Studies election study, University of Michigan.

variable "easy" with the three criteria are in all cases trivial, and in two cases go in a negative direction. Whether or not voters are predictable from a hard-issue position, on the other hand, is positively related to our sophistication criteria. To be predictable from a hard issue is to be somewhat better educated, better informed, and more active in politics than the average voter.

Table 9-5 Some Correlates of Easy- and Hard-Issue Voting

	Zero-Order Correlations Voter Dichotomies		*Partial Correlations*	
	"Easy"	*"Hard"*	*"Easy" Controlling for "Hard"*	*"Hard" Controlling for "Easy"*
Education (attended college)	−.045	.086*	−.051	.089*
Information (number of correct responses)	−.013	.207**	−.028	.209**
Activism (number of participatory acts)	.010	.153**	.000	.153**

* $p < .01$
** $p < .001$

Source: Computed from data collected in the 1972 Center for Political Studies election study, University of Michigan.

Partial correlations are displayed on the right side of Table 9-5. They speak to the question of which type of issue voting is associated with sophistication criteria for that large number of voters who are predictable from both hard and easy issues. The first-order partials are virtually identical to the zero-order correlations, an outcome that could have been predicted from the near-zero correlations of the "easy" dichotomy with the criterion variables.

In sum, not all "issue voting" indicates sophistication by these criteria; hard-issue voting does, easy-issue voting does not.

Political Inferences and the Easy-Issue Voter

Political analysts observe issue voting and infer sophistication. That inference is clearly problematic in view of our finding that there is a second type of issue voting that is not sophisticated at all. Indeed, as we have seen, easy-issue voting is found most frequently in the least-sophisticated portion of the electorate. Thus it is clear that issue voting, as it has been traditionally conceptualized and measured, overestimates the amount of sophisticated policy calculation going on in the electorate. This is the most direct implication of our findings. But the question of "how much" issue voting is only part of a larger theoretical quandary that begins with the questions "who?" "where?" and "when?" and ends with "what does it all mean?"

We have seen that some traditionally postulated correlates of issue voting are uncorrelated with easy-issue voting. When the easy-issue voters are included as issue voters, these relationships are weaker than they would be if only hard-issue voters were counted. This suggests that these indicators predict not issue voting per se, but sophisticated calculation (i.e., hard-issue voting). Other theoretically critical correlates of issue voting would be expected to behave the same way.

Some of the meaning of issue voting can be found from studying *where* it occurs. A regional analysis of several recent elections would, for example, point to the South as the homeland of issue voting, an anomaly for current conceptions. The South, with its prevailing low educational levels and politics of one-party factionalism, is hardly the place to search for unusual sophistication in voting behavior. And indeed the South is not unusually sophisticated, because while it contains disproportionate numbers of issue voters, it has disproportionately few hard-issue voters. The difference, of course, lies in the large number of voters—at both ends of the spectrum—who respond only to our easy issue, race.

These findings also shed some light on the debate over whether the lack of issue voting observed in some times and places derives from inherent limitations of the citizen/voter or from inadequacies of choice offered by the political system. It may well be that the two conflicting theories each account for a different kind of issue voting. Sophisticated calculation requires both cognitive ability and attention to political life, neither of which is likely to vary much from year to year. We would expect a gently upward trend in sophisticated calculation over time from the upward trend in mean education level of the electorate. Easy-issue voting, on the other hand, requires neither cognitive ability nor attention to politics, and is free to vary with the availability of easy issues. When easy issues are present, as seems certainly to have been the case for the New Deal era and to a lesser extent, the post-1960 period, increases in issue voting are observed. When easy issues are absent, as in the 1950s, issue voting is considerably more modest because it is concentrated among hard issues.

This suggests that easy-issue voting may occur in waves or surges, as a response to the relatively rare occasions when parties engage in the hazardous behavior of staking out opposing positions on a deeply felt issue. The surge of easy-issue voting is not an encouraging phenomenon for those who would hinge the viability of democracy on the ability of citizens to choose rationally between alternative issue positions of parties and candidates. The surge in issue voting seems likely to occur on a large scale only when choices are simplistic. In light of this account, one should not be surprised that the authors of *The American Voter* (Campbell et al., 1960) did not discover high levels of issue voting for the 1952 and 1956 presidential elections. By that time the easy issues associated with the New Deal had declined in salience but had not yet been replaced by the emerging issue of race.[7] Nor are we surprised by the higher levels of issue voting that researchers have discovered in the post-1960 presidential elections. But the lion's share of this increase, we believe, is owing to the easy issue of race, not to hard issues. Increased issue voting therefore says little about the political sophistication of the American electorate.

Isolating the easy issue and the unsophisticated easy-issue voter is useful, finally, as a bridge between historical accounts of electoral realignment and the modern voting studies. The historical accounts specify a prominent role for the lowest common denominator of the mass electorate in the issue-based overthrow of old party systems. But association of issue voting with voter sophistication in the voting studies would predict that the unsophisticated would be the last to adjust their electoral behavior to an issue cleavage cutting across the party system. The emergence of the easy issue is a plausible resolution of this apparent dilemma. The crystallizing factor that precipitates realignments must, we believe, revolve around easy—not hard—issues. For only easy issues are salient enough over a long enough period to encourage parties to provide relatively clear and simple choices. And these are the only kinds of choices that provide parties the opportunity to change their minority or majority status, to become beneficiaries (or victims) of the unfolding realignment process. Hard issues, on the other hand, are too complicated and too subtle to provide a basis for a *major* reshuffling of party supporters. While their effects on the party system may be dramatic in the short term—as Vietnam was in 1972—their long-term impact is likely to be inconsequential.

Appendix A

The Dimensions of Racial Attitudes:
A Principal Factor Analysis (with Varimax Rotation)*

	Factor 1: Segregation/ Integration	*Factor 2: Attitude toward Black Activists*
Equal employment for blacks	.480	−.244
School integration	.535	−.268
Public accommodations	.577	−.137
Neighborhood integration	−.594	.037
School busing	.385	−.344
Aid for minorities	.459	−.391
Civil rights too fast	−.504	.335
Violence of blacks	−.478	.167
Blacks helped/hurt cause	.461	−.228
Preference for (de)segregation	.615	−.141
Preference for (de)segregated neighborhood	.460	−.211
Equivalence of intelligence	.399	−.098
Feeling thermometers		
Black militants	−.151	.791
Urban rioters	−.120	.776
Civil rights leaders	−.490	.528
Eigenvalue	5.16	1.42
(Percent explained variance)	(34.4)	(9.5)

* The sample consists of 2191 respondents who were interviewed in both pre-and post-election waves.

Source: Computed from data collected in the 1972 Center for Political Studies election study, University of Michigan.

Appendix B

The Issue-Voter Classification Procedure

The PROBIT function derived for all voters—the unstandardized equivalent of Table 9-1, but with "other" issues excluded, is:

$$Z_i = -.44752 - .41236P_i - .28587V_i + .03949R_i$$

where Z_i is the voting prediction for respondent i in standard form,
P_i is party identification,
V_i is Vietnam withdrawal attitude, and
R_i is racial desegregation attitude.

Three alternative predictions are then generated for each respondent by setting combinations of variable values to sample means to eliminate their contributions to prediction:

1. "Party Only" $Z_i = -.44752 - .41236P_i - .28587\bar{V} + .03949\bar{R}$.
2. "Party + Vietnam" $Z_i = -.44752 - .41236P_i - .28587V_i + .03949\bar{R}$.
3. "Party + Desegregation" $Z_i = -.44752 - .41236P_i - .28587\bar{V} + .03949R$.

The three predictions for each respondent are transformed into predictions of "probability of voting for McGovern" by a sub-routine that functions in a fashion analogous to examining "area to the left of z" in a table of areas under the normal curve. The resulting probabilities lie in the interval (0, 1) and, when aggregated, take on the characteristic "S" shape of cumulative probability density functions, but with an asymmetry that reflects the electorate's modal preference for Nixon.

Defining error as the absolute value of the three probabilities minus actual vote, we can then classify by whether or not specific issues contribute to error reduction. Error based on each of the three models can be represented as follows:

e_p is error from the "Party Only" model,
e_v is error from the "Party + Vietnam" model, and
e_r is error from the "Party + Desegregation" model.

The sequence of steps used to classify respondents into the four issue-voter types can then be depicted by the following flow chart [Figure 9-3]:

Figure 9-3

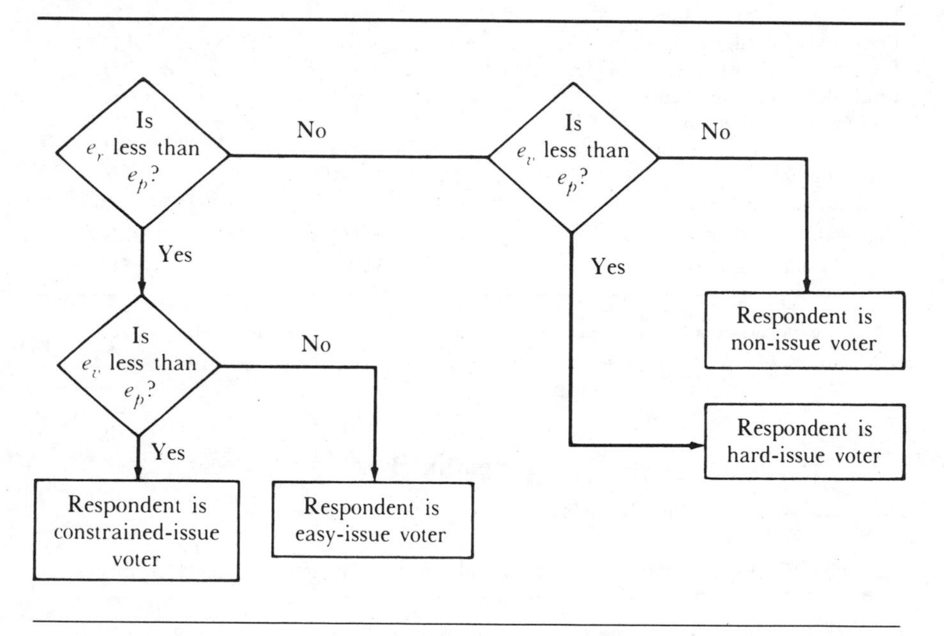

NOTES

1. Our discussion of the distinction between issue voting and voter sophistication parallels the differences between issue voting and rational voting discussed by Converse (1975, pp. 97-100).
2. Our choice of the probit model over regression is based most crucially on our assumption that the S-shaped cumulative propensity function assumed by probit is a

more accurate representation of the impact of issues on vote choice than the alternative linear regression model. It is also important for our yet to be discussed classification procedure that all individual vote choice predictions be bounded by the (0,1) limits of probability. That is the case for probit and is not for linear regression. On these points see Aldrich and Cnudde (1975) and McKelvey and Zavonia (1975). For a very brief discussion of the probit model see Rosenstone and Wolfinger (1978).

3. We use the vague strong/weak terminology here because we expect the relationships between issue position and vote to be cumulative propensity functions—S shapes. If linear regression were appropriate, the argument would be simpler: hard issues would show steeper slopes for the well informed, an interaction effect. Employing a method discussed by Wright (1976), we made such a test, which supports the interpretation presented here. The Vietnam/Vote relationship has a statistically significant information interaction; the Desegregation/Vote relationship does not.
4. Our classification is based upon the number of right answers to a series of six objective questions about American politics administered to the Form 1 subsample. The series includes some questions which are current and relevant to electoral decision making (for example, which party controls Congress?) and some which tap background information (for example, the number of years in a senatorial term). The requirement of objectively correct answers limits the possibility of measuring more directly relevant information. Scores of 0, 1, and 2 are classified "low," 3 and 4 "medium" and 5 and 6 "high."
5. Use of the term "constrained" has the limited connotation that voters seem to use both issues in their voting decision and that both run in the same direction. No other term is a suitable expression of that notion. Whether these voters are "constrained" by other criteria is a question beyond the scope of this effort; we do not wish to imply that they are.
6. Two separate tests are involved in the classification procedures (see Appendix B): (1) whether or not our easy issue contributed to predictions and (2) whether or not the hard issue contributed.
7. That all the early voting researchers had been exposed to the easy-issue politics of the New Deal period may well account for their shock at discovering such a limited role for issues in the post-New Deal period.

10. ECONOMICS AND POLITICS IN FRANCE: ECONOMIC PERFORMANCE AND MASS POLITICAL SUPPORT FOR PRESIDENTS POMPIDOU AND GISCARD D'ESTAING

Douglas A. Hibbs, Jr.
with the assistance of
Nicholas Vasilatos

During recent years the state of the economy has been a very salient issue for the mass publics of the industrial democracies.[1] France is no exception, as the public opinion data in Figure 10-1 indicate. Once the Algerian question was finally resolved in 1962, public concern about the economy moved upward. By the late 1960s, as the long postwar economic expansion was coming to an end, about four out of every ten French voters considered one or more economic issues to be the "most important problem" facing the country. Although the income tax scandal involving Premier Chaban-Delmas diverted public attention from the economy in 1972, economic performance soon recaptured popular attention: following the OPEC supply shock of late 1973, which simultaneously produced inflation and stagnation, more than two-thirds of the French electorate designated an economic issue as the most important national problem.

In view of the importance of economic conditions to the public, it is not surprising that many empirical studies have concluded that mass political support for incumbent political parties and chief executives systematically responds to macroeconomic performance.[2] However, aside from the pathbreaking work of Rosa and Amson (1976) on parliamentary and constituent electoral outcomes, Lafay's important papers (1977, 1981), and Lewis-Beck's (1980) recent article on political support for French executives, we have comparatively little evidence about the impact of economic outcomes on mass support for political officials in France.[3]

Author's Note: The research reported here was supported by National Science Foundation Grant SOC 78-27022. I am grateful to Michael Lewis-Beck, David Cameron, Christopher Pissarides and participants in the conference on political-economic models organized by J. D. Lafay at Poitiers University, January 1981, for comments on an earlier draft.

Source: *European Journal of Political Research* (1981) 9:133-45. Reprinted with permission of the publisher.

Figure 10-1 Aggregate Responses to the Question: "What is the most important problem for France at the present time?" (wording varies)

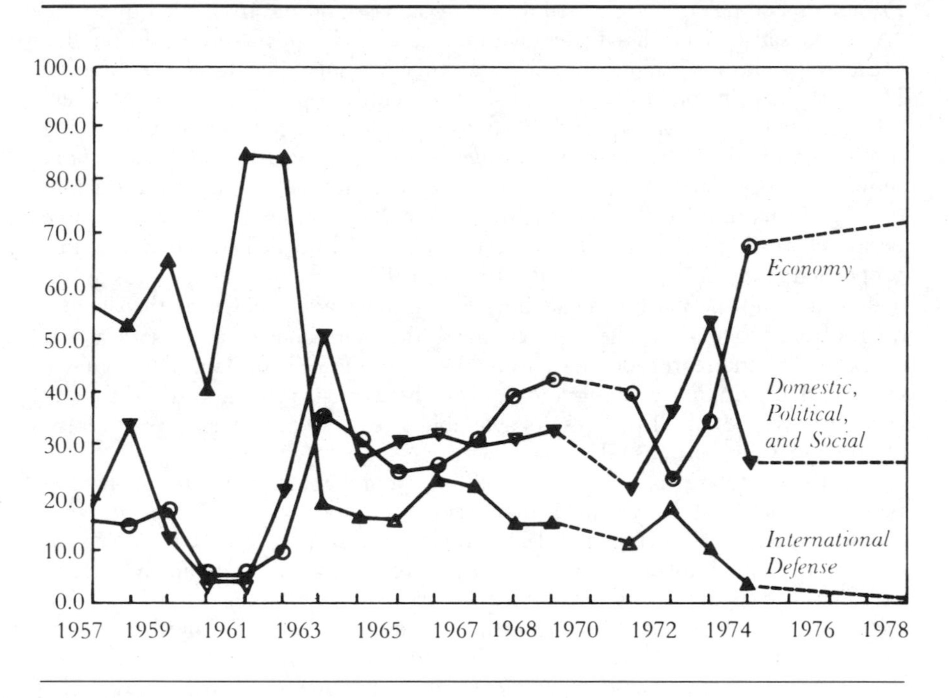

Source: G. H. Gallup, *The Gallup International Public Opinion Polls: France 1939, 1944-1975* (New York, 1976); Lafay 1981.

In this chapter I analyse how popular "satisfaction" with Presidents Pompidou and Giscard d'Estaing was influenced by economic performance. The empirical analyses are based on a model of qualitative political responses, which is described in the following section and, more technically, in the appendix. The most important features of the model are that people evaluate economic conditions relatively rather than absolutely in judging a president's performance, and that the weights people place on current and past economic outcomes decline geometrically, so that current performance contributes more heavily than past performance to the formation of contemporaneous political judgments.

The next section presents empirical results for variations of the model that include as measures of economic performance the rate of inflation, the rate of unemployment, and the growth rate of *per capita* real personal disposable income. The results indicate that the real income growth rate was the most systematic economic determinant of Pompidou's and Giscard d'Estaing's standing with the French public. Estimates of the response of the presidents' poll rating to typical movements in the real income growth rate are presented. The final section of the paper reviews the conclusions and political implications of the study.

The Political Support Model

Opinion surveys typically force people to make discrete, qualitative responses. In the present case, the survey measure of popular satisfaction with Presidents Pompidou and Giscard d'Estaing is based on the IFOP poll question: "Are you satisfied or dissatisfied with _____ as President of the Republic? ("Etes-vous satisfait ou mécontent de comme Président de la République?") However, in principle a person's satisfaction with the president is not a purely qualitative phenomenon, but rather a matter of degree falling on an underlying continuum ranging from strongly positive to strongly negative. As the appendix shows, a reasonable approximation to such a continuously valued satisfaction index is the natural logarithm of the proportion of the survey sample at each time period expressing satisfaction with the president (P_t') divided by one minus this proportion ($1 - P_t'$); that is: $\ln(P_t'/1 - P_t')$. $P_t'/1 - P_t'$ gives the satisfaction odds ratio, and the natural logarithm of this odds ratio, known as the "logit," ranges from $-\infty$ to $+\infty$.[4] The logits comprise the continuously valued satisfaction index used in the regression analyses discussed in the next section. The analyses are based on quarterly observations over the period 1969:4 to 1978:4. The weighted averages of all poll results available to each quarter were used to form the quarterly proportions, P'.

Earlier analyses of economic conditions and popular support for French political officials have assumed that people evaluate economic performance absolutely, and that current political support is influenced only by very recent conditions. These assumptions are overly restrictive. It is unlikely that a president's past record is discounted completely by the electorate, or that conditions during a particular presidential administrature are judged by voters absolutely, that is, without regard to the situation existing when the president assumed office. For example, a president coming to power during the trough of a recession who achieves a modest economic growth rate is likely to be evaluated more favourably than a president with the same economic record who assumed office during a sustained economic boom.

Therefore, the analyses reported ahead are based on equations in which a president's satisfaction rating at each time period is influenced by the *difference between* the cumulated economic performance record of his administration and the economic performance record of previous administrations. However, since the present relevance of the information conveyed by past experiences decays over time, the weights people place on current *versus* past performance outcomes decline geometrically at the rate of g^k: g is a decay rate parameter lying between zero and one. If Z_{t-k} is a performance outcome experienced k periods ago ($k = 0, 1, 2, 3, \ldots$), current and past experiences with respect to Z are weighted Z_t, gZ_{t-1}, g^2Z_{t-2}, g^3Z_{t-3}, and so on.

For example, if the current president has been in office for two periods, then his political satisfaction rating depends (in part) on the cumulated, discounted performance difference

$$Z_t + gZ_{t-1} - g^2Z_{t-2} - g^3Z_{t-3} - \ldots.$$

Of course, voters need not discount past performance outcomes (Z_{t-k}) in exactly this way. As long as people weight past outcomes less heavily than more recent outcomes in making current political evaluations, the geometric weight sequence

g^k will yield a close approximation. Large values of g (approaching 1.0) imply that past outcomes play an important role in current political judgments. Small values of g (approaching 0) imply that voters discount (disregard) the past heavily; only a president's own recent performance matters. If in the regression analyses reported later g was estimated to be actually zero, this would mean that, on average, voters have no effective memory of a president's past performance, and that only the current situation, Z_t, viewed absolutely, has any influence on a president's standing with the public. Clearly, then, g is an interesting political quantity. It defines whether performance outcomes are typically judged relatively or absolutely, and whether past experiences contribute to current political support.

The political support equations include four measures of economic performance. The first is the percentage rate of *unemployment (U)*, that is, the number of unemployed (as adjusted from French sources by the U.S. Department of Labor, 1979) divided by the size of the labour force.[5] The second is the rate of *inflation* (I), that is, the annualized, quarter-on-quarter percentage rate of change of retail prices. The third is the rate of change of the inflation rate ($I_t - I_{t-1}$), that is, the rate of acceleration or deceleration of retail prices. The fourth is the percentage rate of change of *real* household disposable *income per capita (R)*. This variable is formed by taking the annualized, quarter-on-quarter percentage rate of change of nominal household disposable income *per capita* deflated by the retail price index.

The regression analyses also include two binary variables representing discrete political events that were expected to influence (negatively) presidential support in the mass public. The first binary variable, *'Scandal'* (= 1 1972:2 and 1972:3), is designed to estimate the loss of support suffered by President Pompidou when it was revealed in early 1972 that his appointee as premier, Jacques Chaban-Delmas, had exploited tax loopholes to personal advantage. The ensuing scandal over Chaban-Delmas' manipulation of income tax regulations was a source of considerable embarrassment to Pompidou's administration and led to Chaban-Delmas' resignation and replacement by Pierre Messmer in July.

The second binary variable, *"Disorganization"* (= 1 1976:3 and 1976:4), is designed to pick up the loss of public support for Giscard d'Estaing associated with the split between the president and his Gaullist political ally and appointee as premier, Jacques Chirac. During mid-1976 Chirac became seriously disaffected by President Giscard d'Estaing's efforts to restrict his scope for independent action, which was prompted by Giscard's attempt to create a more "presidential" style of government. Although Chirac had played an important role in Giscard's election in 1974, by the summer of 1976 the feud became public and Chirac resigned, complaining that he was unable to confront effectively the nation's problems. Giscard replied in a national broadcast that he ruled out "transferring more power from the presidency to the premier's office, because . . . this is against the institutions of the Fifth Republic." [6] The open feud between the head of state and his prime minister antagonized Gaullist partisans in the electorate and made it obvious to the public that Giscard's administration was severely disorganized. The president's standing in the polls declined during this period as a result.

Empirical Results

Empirical results from the regression analyses of the models described above (and, more technically, in the appendix) are reported in Table 10-1. The regression models are of course nonlinear by virtue of the lag weight decay parameter g. The models were estimated, therefore, by searching the parameter space manually and choosing the least-squares estimate of the nonlinear parameter g that minimized the sum of squared residuals. (A 0.01 grid search for g was used.) Model (1) of Table 10-1 includes all the performance variables described previously. However, since the rate of unemployment is highly correlated with president-specific intercept constants (the correlation of the Giscard constant and the unemployment rate is +0.88), model (1) is specified with a general intercept constant. As anticipated, the Chaban-Delmas tax "scandal" and the Chirac affair ("disorganization") appear to have produced transitory, downward movements in the satisfaction ratings of Pompidou and Giscard respectively. More important for our purposes are the estimates for the economic performance variables. The signs of the coefficients of R and U are consistent with prior expectations: increases in the *per capita* real income growth rate yield upward movements in the public's satisfaction with the president and increases in the rate of unemployment are associated with downward movements in the president's political support.

The rate of inflation enters regression model (1) with a positive coefficient, which of course is a perverse result. However, the parameter estimate for the inflation rate is negligible in magnitude; for practical purposes it may be taken to be zero.[7] This implies that the French public is not averse to rising prices *per se.* As long as money incomes keep pace with the rate of growth of retail prices, there is no political penalty associated with inflation.[8]

Regression model (2) in Table 10-1 drops the unemployment term and is specified with individual intercept constants for the Giscard and Pompidou periods. This model clearly outperforms model (1),[9] which implies that the negative impact of unemployment on public satisfaction with the president is embodied in the difference between the Giscard and Pompidou constants (approximately 0.031 − 0.215 = −0.18). This result is not surprising. We know that unemployment rose sharply in France between the Giscard and Pompidou administrations, but the methods used to estimate movements in unemployment by the French Ministry of Labour and the French National Institute of Statistics and Economic Studies (INSEE) were modified several times during the late 1960s and 1970s, and construction of an accurate unemployment time-series is therefore problematic.[10] Consequently, a model with president-specific constants, which permits the satisfaction index to shift (downward) between the Pompidou and Giscard periods, more satisfactorily picks up the political consequences of increased unemployment.

The parameter estimate for the inflation rate remains incorrectly signed (positive) and of negligible magnitude in regression model (2) and, therefore, it is replaced by the rate of acceleration of retail prices, $(I_t - I_{t-1})$ in model (3). Since the inflation rate in the recent past is among the best predictors of the inflation rate today, $(I_t - I_{t-1})$ is a sensible measure of *unanticipated* movements in prices, which economic theory suggests are the main cause of arbitrary redistribu-

Table 10-1 Least-Squares Coefficient Estimates, Weighted Logit Regression Models (1969:4-1978:4 (standard errors in parentheses))

	Regression Model (1)	(2)	(3)	(4)	*Means (unweighted) of independent variables*
Constants (a_q)					
Pompidou		0.216	0.219	0.219	0.514
		(0.0105)	(0.0105)	(0.0105)	
Giscard		0.031	0.043	0.043	0.486
		(0.109)	(0.0111)	(0.0097)	
General	0.130				1.000
	(0.008)				
Lag Weight Decay Rate					
g	0.8	0.8	0.8	0.8	
Economy					
Unemployment Rate (U)	−0.010				3.630
	(0.0029)				
Inflation Rate (I)	0.004	0.0013			8.689
	(0.0010)	(0.0004)			
Change of Inflation Rate ($I_t - I_{t-1}$)			−0.0001		0.311
			(0.0015)		
Real Personal Disposable Income Growth Rate (R)	0.017	0.014	0.015	0.015	3.261
	(0.0008)	(0.0007)	(0.0006)	(0.0006)	
Noneconomic					
Scandal (Chaban-Delmas tax scandal)	−0.134	−0.195	—0.184	−0.184	0.054
	(0.0129)	(0.0515)	(0.013)	(0.013)	
Disorganization (Chirac affair)	−0.365	−0.331	−0.310	−0.310	0.054
	(0.014)	(0.013)	(0.012)	(0.0115)	
χ^2/df	21.4	15.1	15.5	15.0	

Note: (a) Data on the dependent variable were unavailable for 1970:3, and 1974:2 and, therefore, the regressions are based on 35 observations. Data for the lag functions for the independent, performance variables extend back to 1951:2. Variable means are for the regression estimation range.
(b) The dependent variable is $1n(P_t'/1 - P_t')$; the natural logarithm of the odds ratio.

tions of income and wealth. However, the results for model (3) show that although ($I_t - I_{t-1}$) enters with a negative coefficient, it is indistinguishable from zero. In other words, neither the rate of acceleration nor the rate of change of retail prices appears to have led to significant decreases in the satisfaction rating enjoyed by French presidents. The domestic political consequences of inflation appear, therefore, to be transmitted entirely through the impact of rising prices on the *per capita* real personal income growth stream.

Since I and ($I_t - I_{t-1}$) have little or no impact on presidential support net of movements in R, and because the decline in support attributable to rising unemployment is best captured by specifying president-specific intercepts, the most satisfactory equation in Table 10-1 is regression model (4), which includes only the growth rate of *per capita* real personal income as an explicit measure of politically relevant economic conditions. The success of model (4) in fitting the data is illustrated by Figure 10-2. Practical interest centers on the survey percentages rather than on the logits [$\ln (P_t'/1 - P_t')$] and, therefore, Figure 10-2 shows the actual and fitted *percentages* of the French public satisfied with Pompidou and Giscard at each period. The fitted values track the actuals quite well (the correlation is 0.91) and no serious autocorrelation or other obvious errors in the functional form are revealed by the data.[11]

Notice in Table 10-1 that the optimal estimate of the lag weight-rate of decay parameter g is about 0.8 in all models. This means that the performance outcomes of many past periods influence voters' current political evaluations of the president. The impact of current and past real income-growth rates (R_{t-k}) on the president's popular satisfaction rating in the current quarter is therefore given by the geometric lag sequence:

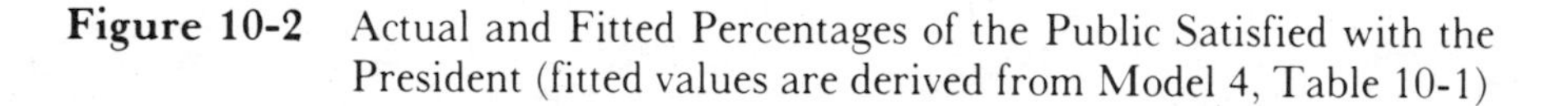

Figure 10-2 Actual and Fitted Percentages of the Public Satisfied with the President (fitted values are derived from Model 4, Table 10-1)

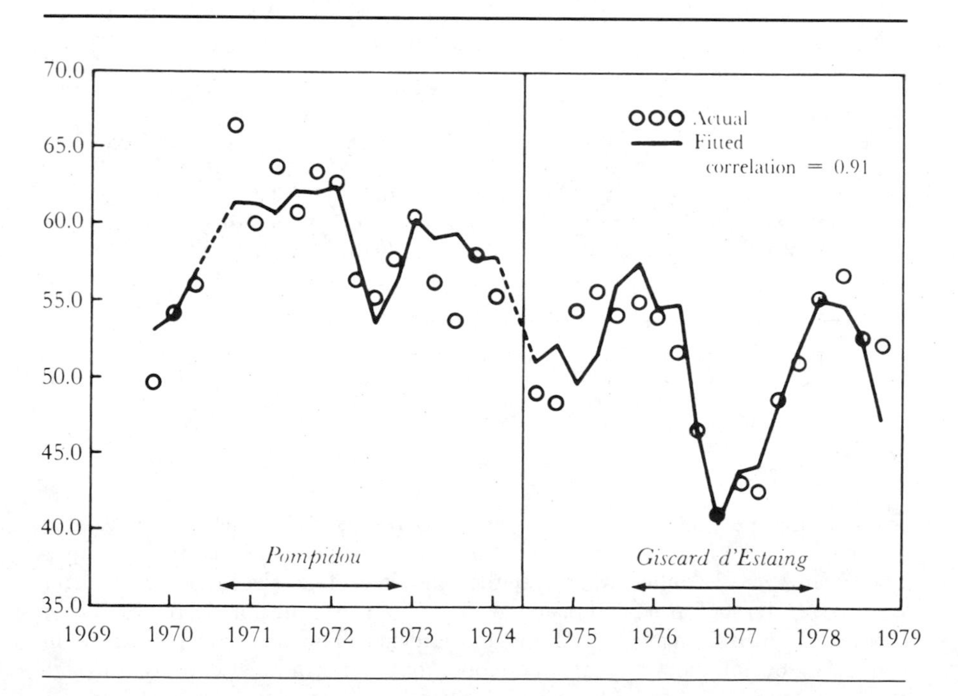

$$0.015 \sum_k 0.8^k R_{t-k} \cdot D_{q,t-k}$$

$$= 0.015 (1.0 R_t \cdot D_{qt} + 0.8 R_{t-1} \cdot D_{q,t-1} + 0.64 R_{t-2} \cdot D_{q,t-2} + 0.51 R_{t-3} \cdot D_{q,t-3} + \ldots).$$

where 0.15 is the contemporaneous impact of R estimated by the regression coefficient in Table 10-1, Model (4), and $D_{q,t}$ is a "switching" variable described in the appendix. If the *per capita* real income growth rate were held at some equilibrium value R* indefinitely, the above implies that the ultimate impact on political support would be

$$0.015/(1 - 0.8)R^* = 0.075 R^*.$$[12]

The percentage of the ultimate impact felt by the kth lag is given by $1 - 0.8^{k+1}$ [13] Therefore, about 20 percent of the total political effect of a sustained change in the real income growth rate is felt immediately, about 60 percent is felt after one year (four quarters), 84 percent is felt after two years (eight quarters), and about 97 percent is felt after four years (16 quarters). Politically, this means that after three to four years in office the systematic part of a president's popular satisfaction rating is based almost entirely on his own absolute performance record. Prior to that time his record in relation to that of his predecessor(s) is an important factor in determining his support in the mass public. This result contrasts sharply with the assumptions of earlier studies that only current performance, viewed absolutely, influences a president's contemporaneous political support.

The coefficients in Table 10-1 pertain to the impacts of movements in the independent variables on the dependent variable in the regression experiments, that is, on the logit $\ln(P_t'/1 - P_t')$. But of course practical interest again centers on the implications of changes in economic performance on the percentage of the electorate satisfied with the president. Since the survey proportions, P_t', are a nonlinear function of the logits, $\ln(P_t'/1 - P_t')$, the effects of practical interest are difficult to judge by direct inspection of the regression coefficients, and they need not, in general, be homogeneous through time.[14] Therefore, to give an idea of the practical political consequences of fluctuations in the *per capita* real income growth rate, I have computed the long-run change in the *percentage* of the French public reporting satisfaction with the president expected at each period from sustained changes in R of one-half and one standard of deviation.[15]

Figure 10-3 displays the time series of these impact measures computed at each period in the regression range. Although, as I noted above, the expected changes in the support percentage associated with movements in the *per capita* real income growth rate may vary over time and across positive and negative changes in R, the data in Figure 10-3 show that such variations are small. Giscard's average satisfaction rating lies close to 0.50 ($P' = 0.51$), and so the effects of positive and negative movements in R were, on average, symmetrical during his presidency. Pompidou's mean satisfaction rating was somewhat higher ($P' = 0.585$), and therefore decreases in R during his presidency had slightly greater effects than positive movements in R, and, on average, these effects were somewhat smaller than the corresponding effects of changes in R during the Giscard years.[16]

Figure 10-3 Changes in the Percentage of the Public Satisfied with the President (P1.100) Expected from Changes in the Per Capita Real Income Growth Rate (R) of One and One-Half Standard Deviation (SD).

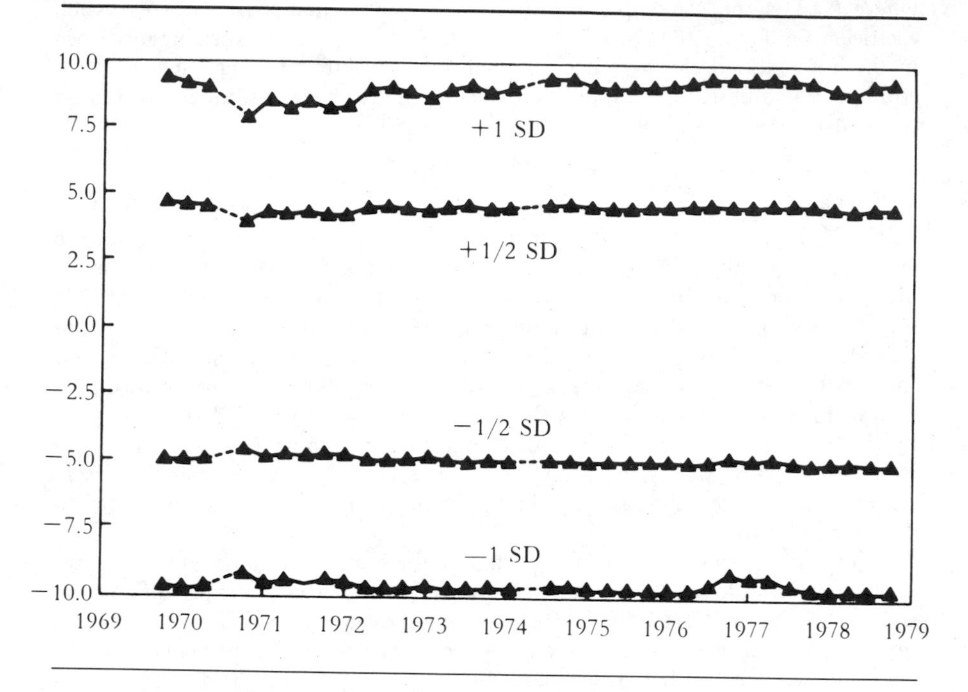

However, these differences are on the whole negligible. The main message of Figure 10-3 is that a movement of plus or minus one-half standard deviation in the *per capita* real income growth rate sustained for four years or more yields changes in presidential satisfaction ratings of just under plus or minus five percentage points. A sustained change of plus or minus one full standard deviation in R produces in the long run a movement in the public's satisfaction with the president just less than twice the former magnitude—between nine and nine and one-half percentage points. If movements on the real income growth rate are accompanied by opposite changes in the rate of unemployment (we know from Okun's law in economics that declines in the real growth rate are accompanied by increases in the unemployment rate), then the political consequences would of course be even more pronounced.

As I pointed out earlier, Giscard's average percentage satisfaction rating was about 7.5 points below Pompidou's (51 *vs.* 58.5 percent). Of course there were dramatic oscillations about these averages, but it is useful to identify the sources of change in the mean or equilibrium support levels experienced by these presidents. Approximate calculations indicate that about 3 percentage points (or 4/10) of the decline in presidential support from Pompidou to Giscard was due to the decline in the real income growth rate, which averaged 4.3 percent per year during Pompidou's administration and only 2.2 percent during the first three years of Giscard's presidency. The effect of the rise in unemployment from the Pompidou to the Giscard years is embedded in the difference between the president-specific intercepts for the reasons discussed previously. Therefore, all we can estimate is the upper limit of the contribution of unemployment to the difference between the mean support levels: it is about 4 percentage points. The remaining one-half percentage point difference is attributable to the difference in the impact of the binary, noneconomic terms. The Chirac affair was slightly more costly for Giscard d'Estaing than the Chaban-Delmas tax scandal was for Pompidou.

The economic effects described above are sizable, but not overwhelming. There obviously is a considerable stability or inertia in the presidential support data stemming from long-standing popular political loyalties anchoring classes of voters to political parties and blocs that is not based on comparative economic performance. A discussion of these factors, however, is beyond the scope of this chapter.

Summary and Conclusions

Since the late 1960s the state of the economy has been quite salient to the French mass public and therefore it is natural to expect that political support for Presidents Pompidou and Giscard d'Estaing was influenced significantly by macroeconomic conditions. The model presented in this chapter incorporates the idea that people evaluate economic performance in relative rather than absolute terms by implicitly comparing a president's cumulative record to that of his predecessors. However, the weights attached to current and economic outcomes ($\sum_k Z_{t-k}$) were estimated to decline geometrically at rate 0.8^k, which as I noted earlier means that after three years (12 quarters), or so a president is judged largely on his own current and past performance record.

The empirical results in Table 10-1 showed that the *per capita* real income growth rate was the principal systematic economic influence on movements in Pompidou's and Giscard's popular satisfaction rating in the IFOP polls. Since the real income growth rate is simply the nominal income growth rate less the inflation rate, price rises lead to declines in political support only to the extent that money incomes lag behind, either relatively or absolutely. This of course has been a persistent tendency in France and elsewhere since the first great OPEC supply shock of late 1973 and 1974, which represented an enormous transfer of real resources from the petroleum-consuming nations to the petroleum producers. Prior to the OPEC shock (over the period 1969:4-1973:3) *per capita* real income in France increased on average at a rate of nearly 5 percent per annum; since then (over the period 1973:4-1978:4) the real growth rate declined to barely 2 percent per year.

The mechanism of the shift in the terms of trade induced by the cartel's actions was of course an inflation, but the economic pain was caused by the real loss, not the price rises it produced. This suggests that deflationary macroeconomic policies sacrificing employment, real output and real personal income in order to achieve price deceleration are not likely to enhance a president's support in the French mass public. Indeed, the estimates graphed in Figure 10-3 indicate that a sustained standard deviation reduction in the *per capita* real disposable income growth rate alone would, on average, yield a decline of 9-9.5 percentage points in the president's satisfaction rating in the polls. In a subsequent paper I hope to develop this point further by explicitly incorporating information about mass political reactions to macroeconomic outcomes in a model of the macroeconomic policy actions taken by French policy authorities.

Appendix

The Formal Political Support Model

The political support model described in the main text is expressed theoretically in terms of an *unobserved,* continuously valued index of the president's popular satisfaction rating, Y^*. Y^* is determined by the cumulated, exponentially discounted performance of the current president's administration *in relation to* the cumulated, exponentially discounted performance of all previous presidential administrations, as well as by a sequence of constants, a_q, representing the unique popularity of the qth chief executive:

$$(1)\quad Y^*_t = \sum_{q=1}^{2} A_q \left(b. \sum_{k=0}^{\infty} g^k Z_{t-k} D_{q,t-k}\right) + a_q + u_t$$

where: Z denotes a vector of performance variables with associated coefficients b;

g is the rate of decay of the lag function weights, $0<g<1$;

$$a_q \text{ and } A_q = \begin{cases} +1 & \text{during the qth presidential administration} \\ 0 & \text{otherwise} \end{cases}$$

$$D_{qt} = \begin{cases} +1 & \text{during the qth presidential administration} \\ -1 & \text{otherwise;} \end{cases}$$

$t = 41, 42, \ldots, T$; and

u_t is an independently distributed random disturbance.

As described in more detail in the main text, equation (1) says that the qth president's satisfaction rating at any time t depends upon the difference between the accumulated performance record of his administration with respect to Z and the performance record of previous administrations. The weights people give to performance outcomes decay exponentially at rate g^k; in other words, it is assumed that in making contemporaneous political judgments people give more weight to current performance than to past performance.

The binary 'switching' variable D_{qt} insures that Y^*_t is indeed based on interadministration performance comparisons. For example, if the qth president has been in office for two periods, Equation (1) yields

$$(2)\quad Y^*_t = b\,.\,(Z_t + gZ_{t-1} - g^2Z_{t-2} - g^3Z_{t-3} - g^4Z_{t-4} - \ldots) + a_q + u_t.$$

Although the lag functions and hence the performance comparisons represented by (1) and (2) imply that the Zs extend back to the infinite past, this is merely a convenient fiction that should be taken to mean that evaluations go back to the beginning of the relevant political era. It is implicitly assumed that knowledge of past performance is transmitted from generation to generation via political socialization.

The model may be expressed in a form suitable for estimation by noticing that (1) may be written

$$(3)\quad Y^*_t = \sum_{q=1}^{2} A_q\left[b\,.\sum_{k=0}^{t-2} g^k Z_{t-k}\, D_{q,t-k} + g^{t-1}E(Y_1)\right] + a_q(1 - g^{t-1}) + u_t,$$

which involves a finite observable lag sequence in the Z_{t-k}. Moreover, because data on the performance variables are available for more than 40 periods (quarters) prior to the first observation on Y* (i.e., prior to Pompidou's first satisfaction rating), g^{t-1} is never larger than g_{40}. Since $g<1$, the terms $g_{t-1}E(Y_1)$ and $-g^{t-1}a_q$ are negligible quantities and therefore may be dropped safely from equation (3) for estimation purposes.

Remember, however, that the continuously valued satisfaction index, y*, is unobserved; the survey data reveal only whether respondents are satisfied or dissatisfied with the president of the French Republic. Hence, we need a model that maps the observed individual binary choices in the surveys onto the unobserved satisfaction index.

Let the observed survey responses in the IFOP surveys be designated by the binary variable Y_{it}:

$$(4)\ Y_{it} = \begin{cases} 1 \text{ for respondents satisfied with the president} \\ 0 \text{ for respondents dissatisfied with the president.} \end{cases}$$

Since this chapter investigates movements through time in aggregated survey responses, it will be assumed here that individuals react homogeneously to presidential performance with respect to Z. Therefore, the Y_{it} are assumed to reflect crudely the underlying continuously valued popular satisfaction index y* such that

$$(5)\ Y_{it} = \begin{cases} 1 \text{ if } Y^*_t > c \\ 0 \text{ if } Y^*_t \leq c \end{cases}$$

where c is a "critical threshold."

Letting f(Z) denote the substantive terms on the right-hand side of equation (3), it follows that the probability (P) of observing a "satisfied" response for individuals at time t is

$$(6)\ P_t = P(Y_{it} = 1) = P[f(Z) + u_t > c] \\ = P[u_t > c - f(Z)]$$

and $(1 - P_t)$ gives the probability of a "dissatisfied" response.

In other words people are satisfied with the president $(Y = 1)$ when Y* exceeds some critical threshold c. The probability of being satisfied therefore hinges on the value of $c - f(Z)$ and the distribution of the random variable u.

The above implies that P_t may be regarded as a cumulative distribution function. Any appropriate distribution for u will yield a well-behaved probability function. It is convenient, however, to assume u logistic (which differs trivially from the normal distribution) with mean zero and scale parameters, which implies the probability function:

$$(7)\ P_t = P[u_t > c - f(Z)] \\ = 1 - \frac{\exp[(c - f(Z))/s]}{1 + \exp[(c - f(Z))/s]} \\ = \frac{\exp[(f(Z) - c)/s]}{1 + \exp[(f(Z) - c)/s]} \\ = L^*[(f(Z) - c)/s],$$

where L* is the logistic operator, $L^*(Z) = \exp Z/(1+\exp Z)$.

Equation (7) means that the response probabilities monotonically approach 1 as f(Z) goes to $+\infty$ (gets large) and monotonically approach 0 as f(Z) goes to $-\infty$ (gets small).

Finally, notice that equation (7) may be manipulated to yield

$$(8)\ L^{*-1}P_t = \ln(P_t/1 - P_t) = [f(Z) - c]/s,$$

which expresses the natural logarithm of the probability odds ratio (the "logit") as a linear function of the logistic model parameters. Replacing the notation simplification introduced in equation (6) with the terms of the original political support model in equations (1) - (3) yields the model used in the regression experiments

$$(9)\ 1n(P_t{}'/1 - P_t{}') = \sum_{q=1}^{2} A_q\ [(1/s)b$$

$$\sum_{k=0}^{t-2} g^k Z_{t-k} D_{q,t-k}] + a_q + e_t,$$

where: $P_t{}'$ = the observed survey proportion expressing "satisfaction" with the president (P_t being the unobserved population proportion); and
$e_t = 1n(P_t{}'/1 - P_t{}') - 1n(P_t/1 - P_t)$.

It can be shown that the error term e has mean zero and variance $1/N_t P_t(1 - P_t)$, where N_t is the number of survey observations used to form $P_t{}'$. This means that efficient least-squares estimates are obtained by weighting each term in equation (10) by $N_t P_t{}'(1 - P_t{}')^{1\ 2}$. These weights were applied in the regressions reported in the main text.

NOTES

1. See, for example, the survey data assembled by Hibbs (1980) showing public concern about economic issues as opposed to international, and domestic political and social questions in the United States, Great Britain and Germany.
2. The literature is too voluminous to reference adequately here. See, however, the papers and citations in two recent volumes: Hibbs and Fassbender (1981), Whiteley (1980a).
3. Lewis-Beck's (1980) paper is discussed further ahead.
4. For further discussion in an earlier issue of this journal, see Muller et al. (1980).
5. A discussion of data sources and all data series are available from the author upon request. All percentage rates of change are annualized quarter-on-quarter changes formed as follows: $1n(Z_t/Z_{t-1})$. 400.
6. *Keesing's Contemporary Archives*, October 1, 1976, p. 27965.
7. Since the dependent variable is the natural logarithm of $(P_t{}'/1 - P_t{}')$, the coefficient magnitudes are difficult to interpret by inspection. I pursue this further ahead.
8. This result contrasts with the findings of Lewis-Beck's (1980) analysis of economic conditions and popular satisfaction with French presidents over the period 1960-80. Lewis-Beck concludes that inflation is the most important economic influence on support for the president in the French electorate. However, Lewis-Beck's model is dramatically different from that proposed here: among other things, it assumes that voters respond absolutely to recent economic conditions alone; it includes an arbitrary trend term; and it excludes the rate of growth of income. Also, Lewis-Beck's calculations of elasticities to compare the relative effects of inflation and unemployment are incorrect.
9. The appropriate goodness of fit test for the validity of the logit specification is the chi square statistic (adjusted for degrees of freedom) obtained from the differences between the observed relative frequencies and estimated probabilities. The smaller the adjusted chi square statistic, the better the fit of the model. In the present case adjusted chi square is simply the sum of the squared weighted residuals divided by the degrees of freedom (χ^2/df).

10. See the discussion in U.S. Department of Labor, Bureau of Labor Statistics, 1979. This volume gives an excellent account of the methods used to compile unemployment estimates in France in comparison to the procedures employed elsewhere.
11. Lewis-Beck's equation applied to these data yields an inferior fit ($r = 0.61$), and substantial residual autocorrelation, which indicates there are problems with his specification. The fitted proportions in Figure 10-2 were generated by $\exp f(Z_t)/1 + \exp f(Z_t)$. Since the equation estimated is of the form $\ln(P_t'/1 - P_t') = f(Z_t) + e_t$, the former expression gives the fitted proportions implied by the logit model estimates.
12. Recall that the sum of the geometric series

$$b(1 + g + g^2 + g^3 + \ldots) \text{ is}$$
$$b/(1 - g), \text{ for } 0<g<1.$$

13. The partial sum of the series $\sum_{k=0}^{\infty} g^k$ is $1 - g^{k+1}/1 - g$. Therefore the partial sum as a proportion of the infinite sum is $(1 - g_{k+1}/1 - g)/(1/1 - g) = 1 - g^{k+1}$.
14. Note that the derivative of P_t' with respect to $f(Z)$ is

$$P_t'(1 - P_t') \,.\, d\ln(P_t'/1 - P_t')\, df(Z)$$

which varies through time and takes its maximum value at $P_t' = 0.5$.
15. Given the model, the change in the proportion of the electorate satisfied with the president at time t, expected from a sustained increase of one standard deviation in the *per capita* real income growth rate, is

$$(P_{t+1}' - P_t') = L^*[\ln(P_t'/1 - P_t') + 0.15/(1 - 0.8) \,.\, 1SD] - P_t',$$

where SD = the standard deviation of R; and L^* = the logistic distribution function, $L^*(Z) = \exp(Z)/1 + \exp(Z)$. The expected long-run political impact of other sustained changes in R are computed in the same way.
16. Again, this simply follows from the fact that the impact of a change in R on P' is greatest at $P' = 0.50$. See notes 14 and 15.

CONGRESSIONAL ELECTIONS

11. WHAT DETERMINES THE CONGRESSIONAL VOTE?

Of all the areas surveyed in this book, the liveliest has been research on congressional voting. Three things account for this. First is the stream of research on the effects of the economy and presidential popularity, especially controversial until recently because the work with aggregate data initially found very weak support in survey studies. Second is the "vanishing marginals," that is, the declining number of closely contested seats in the United States House of Representatives, which researchers felt compelled to explain. Third is the 1978 study by the Center for Political Studies, which for the first time since 1958 focused on congressional candidates rather than on concerns derivative of presidential election studies.

Each of these spawned controversy and a good deal of research. Fortunately, as in the other areas we have considered, progress in the form of relatively firm conclusions has been made, though of course some controversy and some unanswered questions remain. We cannot expect stasis in an area in which so much contemporary research is being done, and even as this book is being written some new analyses and interpretations are being made. Yet most of the research to date can be nicely summarized around the theme of "district level variables versus national political forces" (Jacobson and Kernell, 1981, p. 17).

Congressional Elections as National Events

Those who see legislative elections as basically national events generally stress at least one of three interpretations of these elections: as partisan affairs where only party identification matters, as referendums on the incumbent executive's job performance, or as rewards or punishments for the status of the economy. The local incumbent and challenger are treated as virtually nonentities in these formulations, since the election result is viewed as depending on circumstances beyond their control.

The original emphasis on the role of partisanship in congressional elections is due to a 1958 study by the Michigan Survey Research Center. Stokes and Miller (1966) attempted to study the congressional elections of that year as they had studied the presidential election of the 1950s, but to their dismay they found that voters often could not even recall the names of the candidates and that issues were not playing a part in the evaluations of the candidates the citizens did know. If candidates and issues seemed to play a small role in the election, that left partisanship, which was found to have the same large impact on the vote that it has on presidential voting. Campbell (1960) was able to use this result to construct an explanation of the loss of seats in Congress that the president's party has invariably suffered in midterm elections: that less partisan voters who show up to vote in presidential elections and swing on the basis of short-term considerations to one presidential candidate (and then support his party's ticket for lower offices) are the ones who do not bother to vote at the off-year elections, thus cutting both turnout and the congressional vote for the president's party. Regardless of whether or not one finds this "surge and decline" explanation convincing, survey evidence is clear that party identification is a major correlate of congressional voting.

Still, the partisanship interpretation did not satisfy many scholars. They felt that some issues were of importance—economic issues in particular. And they felt that one candidate was relevant—the incumbent president. One long series of studies, based on analysis of aggregate data, deals mostly with economic variables, including changes in unemployment levels, real income, and the rate of inflation, although some of the contributions also suggest the relevance of overall satisfaction with the president's performance. The series began with an article by Gerald Kramer (1971), in which he showed that a number of economic variables are related to the total congressional vote over the period 1896–1964.[1] A large number of criticisms and reformulations have been made since then.[2] For example, Bloom and Price's (1975) analysis suggested that the president's party is hurt by bad economic times but not helped by good times. More recently, Hibbing and Alford (1982) have found a relationship between economic conditions and U.S. Senate voting, and Lewis-Beck and Bellucci (1982) have extended such analyses to legislative voting in France and Italy. This series is one of the factors that led to the growing corpus of work on economic influences more generally, both here and abroad. These studies were surveyed in chapter 5 and represented by the analysis in chapter 10. Altogether this work—both the congressional series and that surveyed earlier—leaves little doubt that "election outcomes are in substantial part responsive to objective changes occurring under the incumbent party, where for congressional elections incumbency refers to the president" (Kramer, 1971, p. 140).

The impact of the national economy, along with the added factor of presidential performance, was most compellingly stated in an article by Tufte (1975), reprinted in the first edition. Tufte used only two variables, Gallup's presidential approval rating and the yearly change in real disposable personal income per capita, and yet his model achieved an extremely close fit with congressional election figures. Perhaps more than any other article, Tufte's analysis strongly suggested that congressional elections were national phenomena, responding to the national economy and to the performance of the president. This left little room for the candidates themselves, but early survey work on congressional voters suggested that the candidates were hardly known by the voters anyway (see below).

Until recently, the problem with the "economic and presidential popularity" theory was that it could not be directly confirmed by survey-based work. This was especially true of economic factors. Among others, Fiorina (1978) searched diligently for evidence that individual voters considered economic factors in deciding how to vote and came up largely empty-handed (see also Kuklinski and West, 1981; Brown and Stein, 1982). The presumed impact of presidential popularity received somewhat greater support, but even here the results are mixed. Kernell (1977) showed that those who disapproved of the president's performance voted for candidates of their party less often than those who approved of the president's performance even when party identification was controlled. Yet the evidence for 1974—when presidential popularity plummeted—does not suggest a strong connection with congressional voting (Jacobson and Kernell, p. 1981, p. 10). and Ragsdale's (1980) multivariate analysis suggests that presidential evaluations are of no consequence once other relevant variables in addition to partisanship are controlled.

For quite some time, then, there was an impasse. Aggregate studies appeared to show that the performance of the economy and the president were highly predictive of congressional voting behavior, but survey work could find little supporting evidence. Fortunately, a resolution is now at hand. Indeed, there appear to be three distinct ways of reconciling these differences.[3]

One reconciliation comes from work of Kinder and Kiewiet, reprinted here as chapter 12, in which the authors argue that personal economic grievances are not related to congressional voting but that judgments about the national economy are related to both voting and party identification. Though it was not made clear in the series of aggregate studies (since there was no reason to clarify it), the underlying assumption seemed to be that individuals voted their own pocketbooks. For example, those who were unemployed during a Republican administration tended to vote Democratic. This kind of economic voting is what could not be found in survey studies. But Kinder and Kiewiet found that collective (what they called "sociotropic") economic judgments—feelings, for example, about unemployment nationally, irrespective of one's own employment status—were a crucial determinant of congressional voting, not to mention presidential voting and party identification as well. While there is still some debate about just how personal economic factors determine political behavior (Schlozman and Verba, 1979; McIver, 1981), the findings about collective judgments afford one reconciliation of the aggregate-versus individual-level debate (at least with respect to economic variables).[4] A related possibility is that what matters is how the economy has impacted groups (such as the working class, blacks, or elderly) to whom the respondent feels close.

A second resolution to this debate comes from the realization that positive aggregate effects with no individual-level effects are not statistically incompatible. For one thing, if only a portion of the electorate is influenced by economic variables and no other factors vary between elections in a systematic, nationwide fashion, this may translate into a rather strong relationship at the aggregate level. More significantly, Kramer (1983) has demonstrated with a simple but powerful argument that the effects of changes in economic conditions over time might not be picked up by the typical individual-level, cross-sectional analysis. In each of two cross-sectional studies (from different years), there might be little relationship between economic well-being and the vote. Yet between these years there might be a large shift in well-being (for example, many more respondents might feel well off) and a corresponding shift in the vote (for example, many more respondents might vote Republican). The time series would show a strong relationship, but not the cross-section. Kramer also extends his argument to investigations such as Kinder and Kiewiet's, and essentially the same argument could apply to the effects of presidential popularity. Thus there may be largely methodological explanations for the apparent conflict between the aggregate and individual-level studies.

Yet a third way of resolving the apparent conflict involves an important new element in studies of congressional voting—namely the behavior of elites. Elections may have something of a self-fulfilling quality because of the behavior of incumbent representatives, potential candidates, and contributors. As Fiorina (1978, p. 440) put it:

> Take 1974, for example. Everyone expects a Republican disaster. Thus serious Republican candidates wait for a more propitious time before seeking office (or a move to a higher office), and Republican incumbents find voluntary retirement more attractive than usual. Meanwhile Republican contributors hesitate to invest funds in an apparently lost cause. Thus, the Republican ticket is composed of underfinanced cannon fodder. In contrast, the Democrats have a plentitude of enthusiastic candidates lavishly financed by those who know a good investment when they see one.

The beauty of this story is that if elites make their decisions on this basis, congressional and other elections can reflect national forces such as the state of the economy and presidential popularity even if voters do not base their decisions on those factors.

This third reconciliation of the aggregate versus individual conflict is spelled out most elaborately by Jacobson and Kernell (1981).[5] In their book they also provide evidence tending to support the theory. Though this is a relatively new twist, one which we think more theoretical and empirical work needs to be done, it is important enough to be represented in the readings here. Therefore, we reprint an article by Jacobson and Kernell published prior to the 1982 election in which they show how this idea could be applied in that year to modify the predictions of the pure economic and presidential popularity theory, along with a postscript by them reporting on the actual 1982 election results.

Before departing from this theme of congressional elections as national events, we need to return briefly to the role of party identification. There are at least three ways in which partisanship ties in with the theme of this section. First, party identification is surely a national factor as regards congressional elections in that the roots of partisanship are nowhere tied to congressional candidates and constituencies. Except for Canada (Clarke et al., 1979, chap. 5) and possibly some southern Democrats (Hadley, 1983), partisanship seems largely to refer to the national level and to be responsive to national events (Jennings and Niemi, 1966). Second, the existence of a partisan factor is compatible with other theories discussed so far. Tufte's formulation of the economic and presidential popularity theory, for example, was actually modeled so as to predict the deviation from the long-term or expected vote for Congress (as opposed to the actual congressional vote), where the long-term vote can easily be construed to be the underlying partisanship of the electorate. Thus the elite theory includes partisan advantage or disadvantage as an integral component. Finally, while party identification may have been declining as a factor in recent years as the number of partisans declines, that very drop helps explain the increased importance of incumbency that is so prominent in discussions of recent congressional elections *(see below)*. Thus, the almost universal finding in survey studies that party plays a major role in voting[6] offers further support to the argument that congressional elections are best viewed as national political events.

Congressional Elections as Local Events

As just noted, incumbency has increasingly been seen as an important factor in congressional elections, although for a time the significance of this for congressional election theories was not altogether clear. The facts of the matter were first observed in the early 1970s, especially in influential articles by Erikson (1972) and Mayhew (1974b) on the "vanishing marginals." It had long been known that a large proportion of House incumbents win reelection; what Erikson and Mayhew noted was that beginning in the mid-1960s, the margin of victory tended to increase. Hence, candidates from marginal (that is, competitive) districts were vanishing.

Several plausible hypotheses were put forward to explain this change. One was that redistricting had somehow made representatives' districts safer. This hypothesis soon appeared to be unsupported by the evidence (Ferejohn, 1977). Another possible explanation was that as partisanship declined as a voting cue because of the decline in the number of partisans in the mid-1960s, voters substituted incumbency as a kind of necessary guide to voting in these relatively low-information elections. However, as Fiorina (1982, p. 38) points out, this explanation also fails to account for some of the observed evidence.

What turned out to be particularly important about the vanishing marginals observation—and what for the moment at least leads to the best explanation for it—was the emphasis it placed directly on the congressional candidate. It was not enough to look at the state of the economy or the popularity of the president; who the candidate was made a difference as well. In fact, it soon was apparent that focusing only on one candidate factor, incumbency, was itself too narrow a viewpoint. The recognition that the individual candidates are an important factor in congressional elections left the door open to all sorts of new insights. But there was still one obstacle. The traditional view of voters, based largely on the Stokes and Miller (1966) analysis of the 1958 Michigan election study, was that they know little about the candidates. How could the particular candidates be important if voters did not even know who they were? Thus, in explaining the role of incumbency, an attack also had to be made on this traditional view of the congressional voter.

Perhaps the most forceful onslaught against this traditional view was made in a book by Thomas Mann, a portion of which is reprinted here as chapter 14. Mann began by pointing out that much had been made of the fact that many voters could not even recall the names of the congressional candidates. He demonstrated, however, that far more individuals could recognize their names than could spontaneously recall them. Moreover, voters were often able to evaluate candidates. Contrary to the traditional view that "to be perceived at all is to be perceived favorably" (Stokes and Miller, 1966), both positive and negative evaluations were made. Finally, these evaluations were based on policy concerns to a greater degree than the traditional view suggested. While it was true that few constituents had any detailed information about representatives' voting records or policy stands, Mann presented several kinds of information suggesting that voters were often aware of general ideological positions and/or of other pertinent characterizations of the candidates.[7]

Mann's argument went beyond these points, however. In fact, what may be his most persuasive evidence is the fact that there is variety across congressional districts on almost any statistics cited. To take but one example, his survey showed that on average about 25 percent more respondents recognized the incumbent than the challenger. But this figure varied from −2 percent (that is, the challenger was actually better recognized) to +52 percent. Thus, to lump together all incumbents or all of any other category is to fail to see the oftentimes sizable variety across supposedly similar constituencies.

Mann's results were based on special (and not necessarily representative) surveys conducted in 1974 and 1976. However, the basic thrust of his work was substantiated by results of the 1978 CPS election study and other research.[8] Mann himself, in collaboration with Wolfinger, made many of the same points in an analysis of the 1978 study. Their work actually covers so many of the points discussed here, showing how they are supported by the new kinds of data from the 1978 study, that we reprint it as chapter 15.

Further support for Mann's position is found by Hinckley. In a brief survey of post-1978 work, she reports that *"voters' evaluations of the congressional candidates, House and Senate, have a major influence on the vote,* separate from incumbency and party . . ." (1980b, p. 643). No one has replicated Mann's analysis of the range of various statistics (as shown in chapter 14), but Jacobson's (1981a) methodological commentary on the 1978 study makes the point that important variations in candidate (especially challenger) quality existed in that year. Likewise, one of the major distinctions now made between the two houses of Congress is that "there are *two* candidates competing in the [Senate] contests" (Hinckley, 1980a, p. 458; see also Abramowitz, 1980). Challengers in Senate campaigns are relatively well known, but House challengers are often "invisible."

Results showing greater-than-anticipated voter awareness of congressional candidates in general, combined with greater visibility of House incumbents compared to challengers, go a long way toward explaining the vanishing marginals problem. Challengers in recent House elections have been a weak lot; therefore incumbents, being well known and liked, often roll over their opponents with relative ease. But it is not due to some mysterious incumbency effect or simply the substitution of incumbency for party as a voting cue. Incumbency itself contributes little to electoral margins (Hinckley, 1980a, pp. 457-58; Jacobson, 1981, pp. 234-37). What matters is "the very favorable public images members of Congress acquire and the much more negative images—if any—projected by their opponents" (Jacobson, 1981a, p. 237).

This explanation for the incumbency advantage naturally raised a further question: why are incumbents so well known and liked? Attempts to answer that question have led to some controversy, but disagreement or not, discussions of the question seem to revolve around behavior of the candidates themselves, thereby adding to the view of congressional elections as local phenomena.

One answer to the question why incumbents are so popular is that incumbents make considerable and effective use of all the resources at their command. Some of these are fairly traditional: the franking privilege, free transportation to and from their constituencies, personal staffs that can be used for self-promoting activities, and so on. Even in these traditional areas there has been tremendous growth in recent years (Jacobson, 1983, pp. 31-36). About all this there is little disagreement. Fiorina (1977b) has gone a step further, however, and argued that constituency service—casework—accounts for a good deal of the favorable image of incumbents. Here the evidence is generally positive (for example, Epstein and Frankovic, 1982; Yiannakis, 1981) though not entirely so. In one study directed specifically to this question, the authors could find no support for the hypothesis (Johannes and McAdams, 1981). Controversy over that analysis suggests at a minimum that the matter depends to some degree on the theorizing about the processes involved and consequently on the specification of the equations used to test for effects. There is also some suggestion that, as in the study of economic factors, individual-level data may need to be supplemented by other kinds of evidence (Powell, 1982).[9]

Though the matter is not completely settled, evidence in support of the constituency service hypothesis seems sufficiently strong that we devote one of our chapters to the study of this question. Rather than the conventional setting of the U.S. House, however, Cain, Ferejohn, and Fiorina (chapter 16) look at the question in the British House of Commons and conclude that constituency service plays a role there as well. Thus, even in that more party- and leader-oriented system, legislative elections are to some degree local events.

One other answer has also been given to the question of incumbency popularity. This answer stems from Jacobson's observation that *"the more incumbents spend, the worse they do"* (Jacobson, 1978, p. 472). It is not, of course, that money chases away votes. It is simply that many incumbents face weak challengers and consequently win with only small expenditures. Those who face stiff challenges must defend themselves with larger amounts of money. Sometimes they lose, leading to the observation above. Admittedly, this explanation has an element of circularity. It says that incumbents are popular because of weak challengers. How do we know they are weak challengers? Because they win so few votes. Nevertheless, the explanation and the evidence indicate that incumbents are not *always* more visible and well liked. Given a sufficiently strong challenger supported by enough money, the incumbency advantage can be overcome. But some factors—perhaps congressional public relations efforts and casework—make it sufficiently difficult to challenge an incumbent that strong candidates are often unavailable. In any event, it is the candidates that make the difference.

Conclusion

It would be folly to argue that there is no disagreement among congressional researchers. Indeed, we have indicated that there are differences of opinion among supporters of each of the major traditions. Supporters of the economic and presidential popularity theory disagree at a minimum over the precise working of the theory and sometimes over whether there are any effects at all. The work on national versus personal economic factors is new, and there is not yet any widespread agreement about whether the former largely account for the economic part of the theory. There is also some disagreement and uncertainty regarding the local-events interpretation of congressional elections. The role of constituency service, for example, is an unsettled matter, and the degree of policy voting (or the content and meaningfulness of candidate evaluations) is still a matter of some debate. And Fiorina (1981a) raises fundamental questions about how much change has really occurred.

In spite of these controversies, progress has been made in understanding congressional voters and elections. Neither the national nor the local events interpretation has a lock on the truth. To say that both explanations are correct is more than a face-saving compromise, however. As we discussed at some length in the first section, the two interpretations are not incompatible. Elites and voters alike are influenced by the economic situation and by presidential popularity, and if our interest is in studying national swings, we would do best to focus on these factors. (This does not mean that further work is unnecessary. The Jacobson and Kernell article [chapter 12] indicates that additional factors such as party organization can alter anticipated outcomes.) At the same time, the variations across congressional districts, if nothing else, convince us that it makes a difference who the candidates are and what they do. If our interest is in particular congressional races, we would do well to focus on factors related to the candidates themselves.

It is perhaps appropriate to conclude on a normative note. It is fashionable to decry contemporary elections as somehow inadequate and failing. Blame may be attributed to political structures (especially the Electoral College and the very lengthy primary system for nominating presidential candidates), the behavior of elites (they are too self-centered and ambiguous, or the best ones don't run), or voters (they know too little or are too easily swayed by politicians). While some degree of cynicism is appropriate, since we should never be complacent about our political situation, we think that the contemporary balance between national and local factors is better than is often thought to be the case. The increasing local-level influence (or perhaps the awareness of long-standing local-level influence) has rescued the voter from the status of an automaton guided unthinkingly by party identification, economic circumstances, and the behavior of the president. Evaluations of candidates are perhaps based too much on constituency service, but the influence of the national economy and of presidential actions (not to mention limited evaluation of the policies of representatives themselves) suggest that policy and ideology are not irrelevant. Thus, the greater insight into congressional elections afforded by the past decade of studies encourages us to think not only that we are making progress in the discipline, but also that the structure and conduct of congressional elections remains a very meaningful exercise.

NOTES

1. Atesoglu and Congleton (1982) look at the performance of his model since then.
2. A good, two-page summary and list of references is found in Fiorina (1978).
3. Similar conflicting results have appeared in work on German voters. Baker et al. (1981, pp. 96-99) review these studies and suggest resolutions of the differences similar to what we propose here.

4. Not surprisingly, in an area of research as active and as technically complex as this, some contradictions are to be found. In an analysis published in the same year as the Kinder and Kiewiet article represented here, Kiewiet (1981) observes that there has been a change over the past few decades. Between 1958 and 1978, "it seems clear that voters' perceptions of national economic problems have come to have virtually no impact upon their voting decision in congressional elections" (p. 458). Whatever the ultimate resolution of these points, the distinction between personal and national economic problems and their possibly very different effects are important enough to warrant inclusion of this article.
5. Still a fourth possible resolution of a sort is that economic factors have complex direct and indirect effects. See Fiorina 1981c, 1983; Hibbing and Alford, 1981. Rosenstone (1982, p. 43) notes that individual-level models may be inaccurate because they omit the influence of economic variables on turnout.
6. This includes recent studies of congressional voters (for example, Hinckley, 1980a, esp. pp. 456-57; Kuklinski and West, 1981, pp. 441-42; Fiorina, 1981d, p. 556).
7. Fiorina (1981a) raises the interesting methodological question of whether congressional voters in the 1970s and 1980s really are that different from 1950s voters. New and altered questions in 1978 make it appear on the surface as if respondents in that year were more informed than respondents in the 1958 congressional study. Yet a careful, though necessarily inclusive, comparison indicates that the differences may not be as widespread or as dramatic as sometimes suggested.
8. A dissenting note with respect to voters' knowledge of candidates' policy positions is found in Hurley and Hill (1980).
9. Fowler, Stonecash, and Carrothers (1982) argue that casework is not a factor in state legislatures.

FURTHER READINGS

Determinants of Voting for Congress

David R. Mayhew, "Congressional Elections: The Case of the Vanishing Marginals," *Polity* (1974) 6:295-317. Original statement of the increasing incumbency advantage.

Thomas E. Mann, *Unsafe at Any Margin: Interpreting Congressional Elections* (Washington, D.C.: American Enterprise Institute, 1978). Emphasizes insecurity of congressional incumbents despite the well-known incumbency advantage.

Barbara Hinckley, "The American Voter in Congressional Elections," *American Political Science Review* (1980) 74:641-50. Summarizes results from the 1978 National Election Study.

Gary C. Jacobson and Samuel Kernell, *Strategy and Choice in Congressional Elections*, 2nd ed. (New Haven: Yale University Press, 1983). Full statement of their theory of strategic decision making by candidates and potential candidates.

Keith Krehbiel and John R. Wright, "The Incumbency Effect in Congressional Elections: A Test of Two Explanations," *American Journal of Political*

Science (1983) 27:140-57. Partisan dealignment does not account for safer congressional seats.

Economic Effects on Congressional Voting

Gerald H. Kramer, "Short-Term Fluctuations in U.S. Voting Behavior," *American Political Science Review* (1971) 65:131-43. Original statement of the relationship between the state of the economy and voting behavior.

Edward R. Tufte, "Determinants of the Outcomes of Midterm Congressional Elections," *American Political Science Review* (1975) 69:812-26. Congressional elections are based on the economy and presidential popularity.

D. Roderick Kiewiet, *Macroeconomics and Micropolitics: The Electoral Effects of Economic Issues* (Chicago: University of Chicago Press, 1983). Electoral effects of economic issues are less consistent for congressional than for presidential voting.

Effects of Constituency Service

Morris P. Fiorina, *Congress, Keystone of the Washington Establishment* (New Haven: Yale University Press, 1977). Strong statement of the constituency service role of representatives.

John R. Johannes and John C. McAdams, "The Congressional Incumbency Effect: Is it Casework, Policy Compatibility, or Something Else?" *American Journal of Political Science* (1981) 25:520-42. Questions the effects of constituency service.

Diana E. Yiannakis, "The Grateful Electorate: Casework and Congressional Elections," *American Journal of Political Science* (1981) 25:568-80. Casework is important, especially for swaying the challenger's supporters.

Effects of Constituency

Warren E. Miller and Donald E. Stokes, "Constituency Influence in Congress," *American Political Science Review* (1963) 57:45-56. Impact of constituency on roll-call voting by members of Congress.

Morris P. Fiorina, *Representatives and Roll Calls* (Lexington Mass.: Lexington Books, 1974). Formal analysis of constituency electoral characteristics and their impact on voting in Congress.

Samuel H. Barnes, *Representation in Italy* (Chicago: University of Chicago Press, 1977). Attitudes and linkages between voters, communal councillors, and parliamentary deputies.

Christopher H. Achen, "Measuring Representation," *American Journal of Political Science* (1978) 22:475-510. Pitfalls of the correlation coefficient for measuring representation.

Philip E. Converse and Roy Pierce, "Representative Roles and Legislative Behavior in France," *Legislative Studies Quarterly* (1979) 4:525-62. Differing roles taken by legislators in France.

Lynda W. Powell, "Issue Representation in Congress," *Journal of Politics* (1982) 44:658-78. Reevaluates the impact of constituency on legislative behavior.

Financing of Congressional Elections

Gary C. Jacobson, *Money in Congressional Elections* (New Haven: Yale University Press, 1980). The role of money in congressional elections, especially for nonincumbents.

Gary C. Jacobson, *The Politics of Congressional Elections* (Boston: Little Brown, 1983). Overview of recent work on all aspects of congressional elections.

12. SOCIOTROPIC POLITICS: THE AMERICAN CASE

Donald R. Kinder and D. Roderick Kiewiet

American elections depend substantially on the vitality of the national economy. Prosperity benefits candidates for the House of Representatives from the incumbent party (defined as the party that controls the presidency at the time of the election), whereas economic downturns enhance the electoral fortunes of opposition candidates (Kramer, 1971; Kramer and Lepper, 1972; Lepper, 1974; Tufte, 1975, 1978; Bloom and Price, 1975; Li, 1976). Short-term fluctuations in economic conditions also appear to affect the electorate's presidential choice (Meltzer and Vellrath, 1975; Fair, 1978; Tufte, 1978) as well as the level of public approval conferred upon the president during his term (Frey and Schneider, 1978; Kernell, 1978; Monroe, 1978; Lewis-Beck, 1980). By this evidence, the political consequences of macroeconomic conditions are both pervasive and powerful. But just how do citizens know whether the incumbent party has succeeded or failed? What kinds of economic evidence do people weigh in their political appraisals? The purpose of our paper is to examine two contrasting depictions of individual citizens—one emphasizing the political significance of citizens' own economic predicaments, the other stressing the political importance of citizens' assessments of the nation's economic predicament—that might underlie the aggregate entwining of economics and politics. Ours is an inquiry into the political economy of individual citizens.

Strictly speaking, the aggregate results are of course compatible with any number of propositions about individuals. Yet in setting up their analysis and in interpreting their results, aggregate-data analysts have gravitated naturally to one characterization of the individual voting act—to pocketbook voting (Bloom and Price, 1975; Tufte, 1978). In reaching political preferences, pocketbook voters are swayed most of all by the immediate and tangible circumstances of their private

---

Authors' Note: Data for this paper were provided by the Inter-University Consortium for Political Research, University of Michigan. The Consortium of course bears no responsibility for our interpretations or conclusions. A preliminary version of this paper was delivered at the annual meeting of the American Political Science Association, New York, 1978. We would like to thank the journal's two anonymous referees, Jack Citrin, Faye Crosby, Robert Jervis, Richard Merelman, David Sears, Steven Weatherford, and particularly Janet Weiss for their helpful comments and criticisms.

Source: *British Journal of Political Science* (1981) 11: 129-61. Reprinted with permission of Cambridge University Press.

lives. Citizens preoccupied with their pocketbooks support candidates and parties that have advanced their own economic interests and oppose candidates and parties that appear to threaten them. From this angle, it is easy to see why the party in power stumbles during recessions. During economic downturns, more voters encounter increasingly serious economic difficulties in their own lives; they then march to the polls to turn the rascals out.

The pocketbook prediction draws partly on common sense for its widespread appeal: personal experiences—personal *economic* experiences in particular—are compelling in ways that vicarious experiences cannot be. Moreover, a political calculus based on personal experience substantially reduces the costs that are normally incurred by becoming informed about the political world. Popkin and his colleagues (1976), in expounding their "investment voter" theory, make precisely this point: "Usable political information is acquired in the process of making individual economic decisions: housewives learn about inflation of retail prices; homebuyers find out the trends in mortgage loan interest rates, and owners of stocks follow the Dow-Jones averages." Pocketbook politics requires little in the way of political expertise. Knowing who the incumbents are, where the polling place is located, and a few other details are all that is needed. Given the uneven and intermittent attention the American public pays to politics, the minimal informational demands placed upon voters by pocketbook politics contributes materially to its attractiveness.

So it should come as no surprise that pocketbook-like assumptions have long informed political analysis and continue to do so. Several distinguished examples can make this point. Kramer's (1971) formative aggregate study of the electoral consequences of macroeconomic performance was inspired by Downs's (1957) rationality axiom that "each citizen casts his vote for the party he believes will provide him with more benefits than any other." And to calculate such expectations voters need only review their own economic circumstances: "Rational men are not interested in policies *per se* but in their own utility incomes. If their present utility incomes are very low in their own eyes, they may believe that almost any change likely to be made will raise their incomes. In this case, it is rational for them to vote against the incumbents, i.e., for change in general." [1]

A similar theme is sounded by the authors of *The American Voter* in their discussion of the psychological underpinnings of public opinion. Policy preferences, they claimed, often reflect little more than "primitive self-interest" (Campbell et al., 1960). Working-class citizens generally support social welfare policies, putatively because the benefits of such programs accrue to them, while the middle class, operating on the same grounds of self-interest, opposes them. That the public is customarily indifferent to the details of policy is then ascribed to the remoteness of most policies to citizens' private lives. When policies intrude upon private life—when they become "doorstep issues"—then interest and attention escalates (Converse, 1975a).

In their reappraisal of the American voter, Nie and Andersen (1974) nevertheless preserve the self-interest theme. Attempting to explain the apparent increases in consistency of policy beliefs shown by the American public in the middle 1960s, they point to "the changing nature of politics from the 1950s to the 1970s and, as a result of these changes, the growing sense on the part of the mass public that politics has a significant effect on their lives" (p. 571).

As a final illustration, the pocketbook assumption also surfaced in the "end of ideology" argument, common some years ago, that continued prosperity would dampen ideological conflict and produce a consensual basis for liberal democracy. As LaPalombara (1966) characterized this argument, citizens of western democracies, swept away by "an avalanche of washing machines, automobiles, and television sets," would come to feel only profound affection for their governments. Additional examples abound, but the general point should be evident. Pocketbook politics, in the guise of economic self-interest, narrowly defined, figures heavily—and rather uncritically—in social science thinking about politics.

That the pocketbook assumption is popular does not make it true. An alternative to it is what we shall call *sociotropic* prediction.[2] In reaching political preferences, the prototype sociotropic voter is influenced most of all by the *nation's* economic condition. Purely sociotropic citizens vote according to the country's pocketbook, not their own. Citizens moved by sociotropic information support candidates that appear to have furthered the nation's economic well-being and oppose candidates and parties that seem to threaten it. Thus the party in power suffers at the polls during hard times because voters act on their negative assessments of national economic conditions—quite apart from the trials and tribulations of their own economic lives.

It may seem at first that a sociotropic politics places unrealistic informational demands upon voters, especially in contrast to pocketbook politics. We think not, however. It is not necessary for sociotropic voters to undertake a sophisticated analysis of the economy, or to entertain subjective probabilities of the consequences of economic policies pursued by rival governing teams. Rather, voters must only develop rough evaluations of national economic conditions, and then credit or blame the incumbent party accordingly.[3]

One final point is needed by way of introduction. The distinction between pocketbook and sociotropic politics is *not* equivalent to the distinction between a self-interested and an altruistic politics. To be sure, it is difficult to imagine a motive other than concern for self-interest driving the preferences of voters who choose between alternative candidates on the basis of their own economic circumstances. The motives that underlie sociotropic voting, on the other hand, are not so transparent. Sociotropic voting may proceed out of altruistic concern for the well-being of all Americans. Alternatively, sociotropic voting may be totally self-interested. Prototypic sociotropic voters may construe the incumbent administration's handling of the economy as a public good, and thus use information about the national economic condition as a superior indicator of the incumbent's ability to promote (eventually) their own economic welfare—and only incidentally that of fellow citizens as well. What evidence is currently available cannot convincingly distinguish between these two possibilities. In the meantime, differences between the pocketbook and sociotropic characterizations of citizen politics should be regarded not as one of *motivation*, but as one of *information*. Pocketbook voting reflects the circumstances and predicaments of personal economic life; sociotropic voting reflects the circumstances and predicaments of national economic life.

This difference carries implications for political analysis construed more broadly. As we have tried to suggest, the pocketbook assumption is well-entrenched in contemporary social science thinking. The sociotropic voter hypothesis therefore represents a challenge to conventional thinking. Replacement of pocketbook politics with a sociotropic politics could have widespread ramifications, forcing a reappraisal of our understanding of citizen rationality, of elections as devices of democratic control, and more generally of the link between citizens and their governments. We shall say more on each of these points later.

The Limitations of Prior Research

Perhaps because of its manifest plausibility, the pocketbook prediction has seldom been subjected to pointed empirical testing. The relevant evidence comes from a handful of recent studies, all drawing on the election surveys conducted by Michigan's Center for Political Studies (formerly the Survey Research Center). The empirical verdict for congressional elections is clear: voting for Congress (from 1956 to 1976) was influenced only faintly by personal economic grievances. Voters unhappy with change in their own financial circumstances or those who had recently encountered employment difficulties, were not thereby moved to support opposition party candidates (Logan, 1977; Fiorina, 1978; Kinder and Kiewiet, 1979; Klorman, 1978). Evidence in favour of this proposition is somewhat more positive, although erratically so, for presidential voting (Campbell et al., 1960; Fiorina, 1978; Klorman, 1978; Tufte, 1978; Wides, 1976).

Thus economic conditions (in the aggregate) do affect electoral outcomes (also in the aggregate), but the link between the two is evidently not supplied in any important way by economic deprivations and disappointments suffered in private life. Although this conclusion fits the available evidence, it is premature: the literature is limited in several important respects. In the first place, research that tests the pocketbook prediction has so far been dominated by the Downsian hypothesis—that the citizens whose own economic fortunes have deteriorated will vote for change (i.e., against incumbent party candidates). But personal economic discontents can take many forms, and precisely how citizens define their own economic problems may shape their political repercussions. Consider citizen Smith, for example, whose financial status is deteriorating. The simple version of the pocketbook hypothesis predicts that Smith will be inclined thereby to vote for the opposition party. But if Smith's economic unhappiness is traced to fears of being laid off, and if Smith believes the Democrats to be particularly concerned with problems of unemployment, then Smith may be led, *ceteris paribus,* to vote Democratic. By the same logic, if Smith's complaints are due to being forced to take a second job to keep up with inflation, then Smith's economic discontent might lead to a Republican vote. In short, pocketbook voting may be policy-oriented instead of incumbency-oriented, and hence go undetected in analysis that tests only the Downsian hypothesis.[4]

A second limitation of the literature is its reliance on cross-sectional analysis.[5] Although personal economic grievances are weakly correlated with political preferences when they are assessed simultaneously, they might be linked dynamically. A voter who supported a Republican congressional candidate in 1974, for instance, and whose economic circumstances then worsened, might end up voting for a Democratic candidate two years later, all in accordance with the pocketbook voter hypothesis. Such shifts could be systematic and politically important, but show up as mere traces in cross-sectional analysis.[6]

These limitations suggest that the pocketbook prediction may have been short-changed; and that support in its favour could be demonstrated if only the appropriate evidence could be secured. Part of our purpose here is to provide a fairer and more complete test of pocketbook politics.[7]

The sociotropic hypothesis has so far attracted less attention than the pocketbook voter, although the initial findings are more encouraging. In our analysis congressional voting did indeed derive partly from citizens' sociotropic judgements (Kinder and Kiewiet, 1979). Such judgements were of three types: assessments of recent trends in general business conditions; evaluations of how well the government was managing economic problems ("government performance"); and judgements about which party was the more competent in economic matters ("party competence"). So defined, sociotropic judgements were consistently and occasionally powerfully related to congressional voting—even with stringent controls on partisanship.

Evidence on sociotropic voting is encouraging, then, but hardly definitive. A third and more general limitation of this literature—which applies with somewhat greater force to the sociotropic hypothesis but is relevant to pocketbook voting as well—is simply that we do not know very much. What we do know is confined largely to research on congressional voting. A second major purpose here is to extend the assessment of the pocketbook and sociotropic predictions beyond the congressional context, and in so doing, to push further the debate between these two conceptions of the American voter.[8]

Overview

Our analysis comes in three parts. The first section reopens the question of the possible link between personal economic grievances and congressional voting. It first pursues a refinement of the simple pocketbook hypothesis, which takes into account how citizens define their personal economic problems. This analysis draws upon an open-ended question included in the 1972, 1974 and 1976 CPS National Election Surveys that asked respondents to name their most important personal problems. To maintain the distinction between personal grievances and sociotropic judgements, we also examine a parallel question that asked respondents to indicate the most serious *national* problems. Our questions here are: does inflation-related distress produce votes for Republican congressional candidates? Does unemployment-related discontent become translated into support for the Democrats? And most important for the contrast between pocketbook and sociotropic voting, is it citizens' definitions of their own economic problems, or their conceptions of economic problems confronting the nation, that are associated with their votes for Congress?

The second part of the re-examination of congressional voting then takes up several dynamic possibilities, in a pair of analyses made possible by the availability of the 1972-74-76 CPS panel study. Here we ask: do personal economic interests produce shifts in congressional voting over time?

The second and third sections of the analysis then expand the comparative investigation of the pocketbook and sociotropic predictions beyond congressional voting, as promised. We again draw principally on the 1972, 1974, and 1976 National Election Surveys, largely because they include a uniquely rich complement of measures of both personal grievances and sociotropic judgements. Our questions here are: to what extent is presidential voting responsive to personal economic interests? To what extent to sociotropic interests? And, in the final section, do pocketbook economic interests affect partisanship—especially the intensity of partisanship? To what extent is partisanship affected by sociotropic economic judgements?

Congressional Voting and Personal Economic Grievances: Reopening the Case

A first step in testing the refined version of the pocketbook prediction is simply to examine what sorts of things citizens mention when asked about their own problems. This first step is more arduous than might appear, however, because the coding scheme developed by CPS for the personal problem question turned out to be unsuitable for our purposes.[9] It was therefore necessary first to develop a new coding scheme for the personal problem question (although, fortunately, not for responses to the national problem question), and then to return to the original protocols. The results of such efforts are displayed in Table 12-1.

Not surprisingly, economic concerns figured prominently in both personal and national life during the period 1972-76. As regards *personal* economic problems in particular, inflation was named most often on each of the three occasions (by 19 percent in 1972; 37 percent in 1974; and 28 percent in 1976). This category included references both to high prices and to rising prices. Technically inflation means a rising general price level, of course, not high prices. But as many economists have suspected, the public evidently does not differentiate much between the two. Respondents appeared to use the terms interchangeably: complaints such as "high foood prices—inflation in general" and "the high cost of living—rising heating costs" were common. The inflation category also included references to declining real income, such as complaints about eroding purchasing power, the failure of wages to keep pace with prices, and so forth. (Such references made up a relatively small share of all inflation responses, roughly one-fifth in each of the National Election Surveys.)

Unemployment, in contrast, was mentioned as a personal problem by relatively few CPS respondents. The unemployment category included people who complained that they or someone close to them were laid off, unable to find work, unable to work as many hours as they would like, or worried by the threat of unemployment. As shown in Table 12-1, such complaints were expressed by only a handful of respondents—roughly 3 or 4 percent in each survey.

How citizens defined *national* problems during this period is also reported in Table 12-1. According to the CPS sample, the principal problem facing the country in 1972 was Vietnam, with crime and disorder running a close second. Just two years later, however, with peace declared and the central cities comparatively quiet, these two problems virtually disappeared. Their place in the collective psyche was more than taken up by inflation. With prices soaring in the fall of 1974, inflation emerged as the predominant national problem—completely overshadowing any worries the public expressed about corruption in government. The dominance of economic problems in the public's assessment of the nation

Table 12-1 Personal and National Problems

Most important *personal* economic problems*				Most important *national* problems			
	1972	*1974*	*1976*		*1972*	*1974*	*1976*
Inflation	19.0%	37.0%	28.0%	Inflation	11.8%	41.0%	24.2%
Unemployment	3.4	4.4	4.0	Unemployment	3.7	5.2	28.3
Taxes	5.5	1.3	4.1	Taxes	2.1	0.2	1.3
General or miscellaneous economic problems	18.6	17.6	17.6	General economic problems	4.5	21.8	11.1
Non-economic	32.5	25.9	28.9	Increased government spending needed	5.1	1.3	2.8
No problem mentioned	20.8	13.4	17.2	Decreased government spending needed	1.4	0.7	1.8
				Environmental problems	2.4	1.1	1.3
				Energy crisis	—	2.1	3.5
				Racial problems, civil rights	6.1	0.4	0.7
				Crime and disorder	17.3	6.2	7.2
				National defense, foreign affairs	6.2	5.6	4.6
				Honest, efficient government (lack of)	3.7	9.5	3.4
				Vietnam	24.3	—	—
				Other problems	8.1	1.6	1.5
				No problem mentioned	3.3	3.4	8.4
(N)	(1,109)	(2,523)	(2,415)	*(N)*	(1,109)	(2,523)	(2,415)

* This measure is meant primarily to register personal economic problems. Thus if a respondent mentioned some other problem as the most important one he or she faced, e.g., health, but also mentioned an economic problem, the economic problem was the one that was coded.

Source: 1972, 1974, and 1976 CPS cross-sectional *weighted* samples. Personal economic problem codes differ from CPS codes; see fn. 9.

continued into 1976, with concern about unemployment slightly outstripping inflation-related worries.

By these descriptive data, post-materialism appears as far away as ever. That aside, the essential question here is whether there are systematic relationships between the economic problems people name—personal and national—and their political preferences—in this case, their support for congressional candidates. The following analysis will incorporate additional measures of both personal economic conditions and sociotropic economic judgements that have proved useful in prior research. On the pocketbook side, the personal economic problems that people name are supplemented by a pair of measures: one that taps respondents' evaluations of recent trends in their familiar economic circumstances ("Dissatisfaction with income"); the other that summarizes the family's recent unemployment experiences ("Unemployment experiences").[10] (These measures and those that follow are defined in detail in the Appendix, see p. 232.) The sociotropic side is represented by four kinds of measures. In addition to the problems that people believe are facing the country, the expanded analysis includes: respondents' assessments of recent trends in general business conditions ("Business conditions"); their evaluations of how well the government is managing economic problems ("Government performance"); and their judgements about which party is the more competent in economic matters ("Party competence").

The reader may wonder at this point about the relationship between pocketbook discontents and sociotropic judgements. Are assessments of national economic conditions anything more than generalization of the economic trials and tribulations of private life? They certainly are. Connections between the two are in fact surprisingly tenuous. Having been recently laid off or thinking that things are deteriorating at home have little to do with assessments of the national economy, how well it is being managed, or which party might do a better job. The median Pearson correlation across the two categories—personal grievances and national assessments—was 0.09 in 1972, 0.02 in 1974 and 0.03 in 1976. Other studies of economic perceptions—most notably Alt's (1978) study of economic decline in Britain—have reported identical findings in this regard. More specifically, in recent years the pattern of data has generally been one of individuals expressing much higher levels of satisfaction and optimism about their own economic situation than about the nation's (McCracken, 1973; Yankelovich, Skelly and White, 1975).

The only substantial connection we could uncover was between the particular economic problems citizens cited as most significant in their own lives and those named as the country's most pressing. For example, in the 1974 survey, of those who complained about inflation as a personal problem 52.6 percent named inflation as the most serious national problem, compared with 41.0 percent of the sample as a whole. Similarly, among those CPS respondents who named personal problems associated with unemployment as their most serious, 15.5 percent indicated unemployment as the country's most important problem, as against 4.4 percent of the entire sample. So there is some connection between pocketbook discontents and experiences on the one hand and assessments of national economic conditions, on the other—but it is generally a very loose coupling. Consequently, it is neither hopeless in practical, statistical terms, nor trivial as a theoretical matter, to distinguish and test between the pocketbook and sociotropic predictions.

A complete regression model of congressional voting, which incorporates all these pocketbook and sociotropic measures, is presented formally in Table 12-2. As indicated there, the equation also includes a measure of the respondent's party identification. What we are looking for, then, are deviations from a purely partisan division of the vote as prompted by pocketbook economic grievances, personal economic problems among them, and by sociotropic economic judgements, national economic problems among them.[11]

Table 12-2 makes clear that pocketbook grievances—including the economic problems that people name as their most pressing—bore little relationship to congressional voting in 1972, 1974 or 1976. Considered separately, personal economic grievances accounted for an entirely negligible proportion of variance in voting even in 1974, in the depths of recession ($R^2 = 0.004$. $F < 1$), and hardly better than that in 1972 and 1976 ($R^2 = 0.031$, 0.039, respectively; both $p < 0.05$ by F test). The single pocketbook effect uncovered by the analysis was due to unemployment experiences: respondents whose families had recently run into unemployment difficulties were somewhat more likely to vote for Democratic

Table 12-2 The Effects of Personal Economic Grievances and Sociotropic Economic Judgements on Congressional Voting: Ordinary Least Squares Multiple Regression

	1972 $\left(N = \frac{645}{555}\right)$*	*1974* ($N = 527$)	*1976* ($N = 748$)
Personal economic grievances			
Dissatisfaction with income	−.01	−.02	.04
Unemployment experiences	.05	−.01	.08†
Personal problems—unemployment	−.06	−.02	−.02
Personal problems—inflation	−.06	.01	.01
Sociotropic economic judgements			
Business conditions	.08‡	—	.03
Government performance	.01	.11†	.01
Party competence	—	.14†	.10‡
National problems—unemployment	−.00	−.09‡	−.05
National problems—inflation	−.06	−.04	−.07‡
Partisan attitudes			
Party identification	.59†/.58*†	.50†	.42†
R^2	.387 (est.)*	.362	.283

Note: Entry is β, the standardized regression coefficient. The dependent variable in each case is congressional vote choice, taking the value 0 if the respondent reported voting for the opposition (Democratic) party and 1 if the respondent supported the incumbent (Republican) party.

* In the 1972 split-sample design, $N = 645$ for the personal and national problems estimates, $N = 555$ for the remainder. See fn. 12.

† $p < .01$. ‡ $p < .05$.

candidates, a pattern compatible with both incumbency-oriented and policy-oriented voting. This finding achieved statistical respectability only in 1976, however; traces of it can be discerned in 1972; nothing at all in 1974.[12]

Elsewhere in Table 12-2 the evidence is uniformly bleak for the pocketbook hypothesis. Any impulse to throw the rascals out came no more from those dissatisfied with their family finances than from anyone else. Likewise, there was no convincing support for the hypothesis that voters who mention unemployment as their most serious personal problem would turn to the Democrats, while those feeling pinched by inflation would throw their support to Republican candidates. Thus personal economic grievances, measured in a variety of ways, carried little political punch in these contests—more of a tap, really, than the clout typically assigned to pocketbook interests by social science theories.

Congressional voting *is,* however, responsive to sociotropic concerns. By themselves, the set of variables representing respondents' sociotropic economic judgements predicted a sizeable share of the variance in voting in the three elections (R^2 = 0.049, 0.171, 0.164 in 1972, 1974, 1976, respectively, all $p < 0.01$). As indicated in Table 12-2, that the Democrats were thought better able to manage economic problems (in 1974 and 1976); that the incumbent administration was seen as mishandling economic matters (in 1974); that business conditions were believed to be deteriorating (in 1972)—all of these contributed to voters' support for Democratic candidates, quite apart from their partisan attachment to a political party or their personal economic discontents.

Such effects of sociotropic judgements not only achieve statistical respectability; they are politically significant as well. Consider, for example, the unstandardized regression coefficient of 0.041 for "Party competence" in 1976. Translated into probability terms, it means that with party identification, personal economic grievances, and (all other) sociotropic judgements held constant, voters who thought the Democrats were better at managing economic problems were roughly 0.16 more likely to support Democratic congressional candidates than voters who believed the Republicans to be superior. This is a substantial effect, even in an era of safe seats (Mayhew, 1974a; Ferejohn, 1977, Cover, 1977).

That sociotropic judgements contribute to congressional preferences is not news, of course. What *is* news in Table 12-2 is the evidence on the problems that people name as the country's most serious. As shown there, respondents who so identified inflation were more likely to support Democratic candidates—significantly so in 1976, marginally so in 1972—while respondents who nominated unemployment also tended to vote disproportionately for Democratic candidates—but appreciably so only in 1974. (The comparison or reference group in each case was made up of respondents who named neither unemployment nor inflation.) Thus the political trade-off between unemployment and inflation does not appear to be operating here. Support for the (Republican) in-party diminished among those who emphasized economic problems as the nation's most pressing—whether the problem be unemployment or inflation was by this analysis of little moment.

Although more erratic than one could hope for, the data here are clear on two essential points: how citizens defined national problems was associated with their political preferences; how they defined their own personal economic problems was irrelevant to their preferences.

Before leaving the cross-sectional investigation of congressional voting, we should summarize briefly the results of three additional analyses. The first was undertaken to see whether the estimates of sociotropic judgements might be affected—and reduced—with more stringent statistical controls placed on party identification. They were not. Substituting a set of six dummy variables representing partisanship for the three-way version included in the original regression equation had virtually no effect: not on the overall R^2, nor on the estimates of the individual coefficients representing sociotropic judgements. The second additional analysis was a comparison of the findings presented in Table 12-2, generated by ordinary least squares regression analysis, with estimates provided by probit analysis, a procedure formally more appropriate with a dichotomous dependent variable.[13] We were especially interested in learning whether probit analysis might uncover systematic (if not large) effects of personal economic grievances. It did not. Probit estimates simply recapitulated the regression results in Table 12-2. (This evidence is available upon request from the authors.) Thirdly, we wondered whether voters' pocketbook grievances might "multiply" the effects of their sociotropic assessments; that is, whether people unhappy with their own economic circumstances would, as a consequence, attach more weight to their reading of national economic conditions in reaching congressional voting decisions, while economically more secure voters would weigh such assessments less. They did not. Adding to the regression model a set of multiplicative terms that together represented the interactive effects of pocketbook grievances and sociotropic assessments had virtually no effect: the R^2 did not increase appreciably, and the main effect estimates were undisturbed.[14] By all this evidence on congressional voting, therefore, the pocketbook prediction continues to struggle; the sociotropic prediction, to prosper.

However, one final route needs to be explored: whether personal economic grievances might affect patterns of continuity and change in congressional voting over time. Democratic congressional candidates received the support of 55.9 percent of the CPS respondents in the 1972 election; 61.2 percent in 1974; and 56.9 percent in 1976. Such aggregate stability conceals substantial vote switching at the individual level. For example, of those panel respondents who reported voting for a Republican congressional candidate in 1972, roughly 25 percent switched their support to the Democratic side in 1974; the corresponding "defection rate" for 1972 Democratic voters was significantly less, about 15 percent. For the 1974 to 1976 period, the figures were more symmetrical, with 22 percent of the 1974 Republican voters supporting Democratic candidates in 1976, and 26 percent of 1974 Democratic voters travelling in the opposite direction. The question here is whether such vote switching is predictable from knowledge of voters' personal economic circumstances.

Evidence on this question is provided by a pair of two-stage least squares analyses, done separately for change from 1972 to 1974, and for change from 1974 to 1976. In each case, the dependent variable is congressional vote (in 1974 and in 1976, respectively). The predictor variables include the standard set of our personal economic discontent indicators (as assessed in 1974 and in 1976, respectively), along with a measure representing the citizen's vote in the prior congressional election (1972 and 1974, respectively).[15] The question, then, is whether pocketbook discontents play any discernible role in the dynamics of congressional voting from one election to the next.

The results, displayed in Table 12-3, offer faint support for this version of the pocketbook hypothesis. Personal economic grievances had little to do with shifts in voting. Of the eight coefficients, only one approached statistical significance: voters who thought their own financial condition to be deteriorating (in 1976) were slightly more likely to switch their support from Republican candidates in 1974 to their Democratic competitors in 1976 ($F_{1.528} = 7.77$, $p < 0.01$).[16]

Thus our investigations of vote change simply reinforce the earlier cross-sectional results. By our evidence, congressional preferences respond principally to sociotropic judgements, and rather little to personal economic grievances. The next section examines the same contrast, this time for presidential voting.[17]

Presidential Voting

On several grounds one might expect that both pocketbook and sociotropic interests would play a greater role in presidential voting than in the congressional case. For one thing, each of the 435 congressional campaigns is to some extent unique; each reflects a special mixture of factors: idiosyncratic traditions, particular and sometimes peculiar local conditions, diversity in the "home style" chosen by the incumbent, and so forth (Fenno, 1978). Aggregating across campaigns, as we have done, may have led us to understate the political importance that should be accorded personal economic grievances and perhaps especially sociotropic judgements, oriented as they are to national conditions. But thanks to nationwide news networks, presidential campaigns are much more homogeneous, being roughly the same in Peoria as in Los Angeles. And the unique visibility of the presidency and the enormous attention paid to those who

Table 12-3 The Effects of Personal Economic Grievances on Change in Congressional Voting: Two-stage Least Squares Multiple Regression

	1972-1974 ($N = 468$)	*1974-1976* ($N = 534$)
Personal economic grievances		
Dissatisfaction with income	−.02	.11*
Unemployment experiences	−.03	−.04
Personal problems—unemployment	.00	.03
Personal problems—inflation	−.00	.01
Predicted prior vote	.58	.47
R^2	.34	.24

Note: Entry is β, the standardized regression coefficient. Non-voters on either occasion were excluded.
* $p < .01$.

pursue it may substantially ease the processes by which pocketbook discontents are translated into political preferences; it may also contribute to the public's sense that the president is or at least should be responsible for national economic conditions.

So much for speculation. The evidence, as usual, rewards these common sense extrapolations unevenly—and more importantly, in such a way as both to undermine further the pocketbook hypothesis and to support a sociotropic view of presidential voting.

The relevant evidence is presented in Table 12-4. The first thing to notice there is the paltry effects due to personal economic grievances. Taken just by themselves, pocketbook discontents accounted for about 3 percent of the variance in presidential voting in 1972 and for about 4 percent in 1976, figures comparable to those registered for congressional voting. If anything, the impact of personal grievances was somewhat tinier for presidential voting (compare the regression coefficients arrayed in Tables 12-2 and 12-4). But the essential point is the failure of pocketbook interests to shape presidential preferences. In particular, McGovern's support in 1972 and Carter's in 1976 had nothing to do with citizens' complaints about deteriorating family finances nor with the economic problems they defined as their most pressing. Democratic presidential candidates in both elections did receive somewhat greater support from those voters who had recently

Table 12-4 The Effects of Personal Economic Grievances and Sociotropic Economic Judgements on Presidential Voting: Ordinary Least Squares Multiple Regression

	1972 $\left(N = \frac{760}{658}\right)$*	1976 (N = 913)
Personal economic grievances		
Dissatisfaction with income	.03	.01
Unemployment experiences	.07‡	.05‡
Personal problems—unemployment	−.02	.00
Personal problems—inflation	.05	−.03
Sociotropic judgements		
Business conditions	.06	.06†
Government performance	.27†	.11†
Party competence	—	.40†
National problems—unemployment	−.03	−.05‡
National problems—inflation	.01	−.05‡
Partisan attitudes		
Party identification	.42†/.49*†	.33†
R^2	.394 (est.)*	.599

Note: Entry is β, the standardized regression coefficient. The dependent variable in each case is presidential vote choice, coded consistently with congressional voting (see note for Table 12-3).

* In the 1972 split sample design, N = 760 for the personal and national problems estimates; N = 658 for the remainder. See fn. 12 for further detail.

† p <.01. ‡ p <.05.

suffered unemployment difficulties, and in about the same (modest) measure. Thus, as in congressional voting, the political effects of personal economic grievances were faint, and they were carried principally by experience of unemployment in the family.[18]

Our common sense extrapolations fare somewhat better when we turn to the role of sociotropic judgements in presidential voting. As is also shown in Table 12-4, voters' reading of national economic conditions were strongly linked to their support for presidential candidates, more so than in congressional voting, and particularly in 1976. Carter's support in 1976 came substantially from those voters who thought that business conditions were declining, and who gave the current (Republican) administration bad marks as economic problem solvers. As in the case of congressional voting, there was no indication here of a political trade-off between unemployment and inflation: Carter's votes came disproportionately and in equal measure from those who believed unemployment *or* inflation to be the most serious national problem.[19]

These various conclusions survive intact the results of three additional analyses. Firstly, replacing the three-way measure of partisanship with a set of six dummy variables did not alter the estimates of the effects due to sociotropic economic judgements. The regression model was then further expanded to include measures of voters' evaluations of the two contending candidates (based on CPS thermometer ratings) plus their comparative evaluation of the two major parties (the difference between voters' evaluations of the Republicans and the Democrats, both derived from thermometer ratings). Following this procedure—which deliberately over-controls on partisanship—sociotropic judgements continued nevertheless to contribute substantially to presidential voting. Secondly, estimates provided by probit analysis again simply corroborated the OLS results. In particular, the slight role played by personal economic grievances in presidential voting was confirmed by probit analysis. Thirdly, in following the same procedure outlined in the preceding section, we could find no evidence of interactions between pocketbook grievances and sociotropic economic judgements. The public's reading of national economic conditions was an important ingredient in presidential voting, as much for voters who were financially secure and satisfied as for those who were themselves struggling with economic problems.

One final point: we suggested earlier that research on presidential elections has generally been kinder than investigations of voting at other levels to the pocketbook prediction. Studies involving a variety of analytic techniques have reported consistent relationships between citizens' retrospective judgements about their own economic condition and their vote for president. Klorman's (1978) normal vote analysis, Fiorina's (1978) logit analysis, Tufte's (1978) contingency table analysis, and Wide's (1976) correlational analysis all make this point. So too does our own regression analysis, summarized in Table 12-5. In the six most recent elections, presidential preferences were consistently, if modestly, linked with citizens' judgements about their family's financial position in accordance with the pocketbook voter hypothesis. Table 12-5 also presents estimates of the effects due to experience of unemployment on presidential voting, again from 1956 to 1976. The evidence here is ragged, with the estimate fluctuating erratically from one election to the next, reaching statistically reliable levels in two of the six elections.

Table 12-5 The Effects of Personal Economic Grievances on Presidential Voting Controlling on Partisanship: 1956-1976

	1956	*1960*	*1964*	*1968*	*1972*	*1976*
Pocketbook economic grievances						
Dissatisfaction with income*	.062‡	.019	.018	.047‡	.032§	.034‡
Unemployment†	.043	.040	−.095§	.005	.101	.150‡
(N)	(806)	(788)	(914)	(724)	(622)	(763)

Note: Entry is *b*, the unstandardized regression coefficient. For the personal economic grievances variables, a positive coefficient means that greater discontent is associated with the opposition party, with controls on partisanship. Partisanship was represented in this analysis by a pair of dummy variables, with pure Independents serving as the suppressed reference group.

* The exact question is: Would you say that you (and your family) are better off or worse off financially than you were a year ago? (or, in 1956, 1960, and 1964, *two* years ago?). Variable coded: 'worse' = 1; 'same' = 0; 'better' = −1.

† A dichotomous variable coded: head of respondent's family unemployed recently = 1; otherwise = 0. 'Recently' means in the preceding two years in 1960, 1964 and 1968; the preceding year in 1972 and 1976; and refers to current status in 1956.

‡ $p < .01$. § $p < .05$.

And on one occasion—1964—the effect was the opposite of that forecast by the pocketbook prediction.[20]

Thus in some presidential elections, but not in others, voting will reflect in some modest measure the economic circumstances of voters' personal lives. And it is indeed in modest measure; adding both measures of personal economic grievances to a regression model that included only partisanship improved the predictability of presidential voting across the six elections by an average of less than 1 percent (range = 0.2 percent to 1.5 percent). Our intensive analysis of the 1972 and 1976 presidential elections, summarized in Table 12-4, does nothing to alter this uninspiring conclusion, but it does provide a fresh perspective on it: for presidential voting even more completely than for congressional voting, citizens' assessments of national economic conditions—their sociotropic judgements—overwhelm economic grievances encountered in private life.

Partisanship

This final section searches for links between citizens' economic concerns—pocketbook and sociotropic—and their partisanship, relying in each case on cross-lagged correlation analysis.[21] The first proposition to be tested is that citizens who have suffered economic hardships during 1972-76, with a Republican occupying the White House, will come to feel less strongly identified with the Republican Party (if they entered the period as Republicans) or more allegiant to the Democratic Party (if they started out as Democrats).

We should be clear about our expectations here. Converse's (1976) cohort analysis, Brody's (1977) preliminary exploration of the 1972-74 CPS panel, and more recently still, Converse and Markus's (1979) first cut at the full 1972-74-76 panel, all suggest in different ways that the effect of personal economic grievances on partisan identification are likely to be modest, if they show up at all, producing adjustments in the strength of identification rather than wholesale changes. It is one thing for Republican voters who believe their financial situation to have deteriorated during a Republican administration to feel less enthusiastic about their party; quite another to embrace the opposition. Shifts in strength of identification prompted by pocketbook grievances, although less glamorous than conversion from one party to the other, would still be politically important—if we could find them.

Evidence on this question is shown in Figure 12-1, which displays one representative portion of a more comprehensive cross-lagged panel correlation analysis. Figure 12-1 presents correlations between partisanship on the one hand and unemployment experiences and dissatisfaction with the family's financial position, on the other, for the period 1972-74. These are *partial* correlations, with age, race, sex, and socioeconomic status serving as control variables in an effort to improve stationarity.[22] Partisanship is coded here into one of five values, reflecting both a directional and a strength component: strong Republicans; weak Republicans plus Independents leaning toward the Republican Party; pure Independents; Independents leaning toward the Democratic Party plus weak Democrats; and strong Democrats.

Defined in this way, partisanship was virtually unrelated to citizens' experiences of unemployment, as shown in the top panel of Figure 12-1. Partisanship and unemployment were uncorrelated in both 1972 and 1974 (the synchronous partial correlations were 0.01 and −0.04, respectively); the cross-lagged correlations were also negligible. This perfect pattern of non-findings, moreover, continued in a comparable analysis of the 1974-76 panel.

Matters improve for the pocketbook hypothesis—but only slightly—when dissatisfaction with income is examined (consult the bottom panel of Figure 12-1). There the synchronous partial correlations at least hovered close to statistical

Figure 12-1 Personal economic grievances and partisanship, 1972-1974

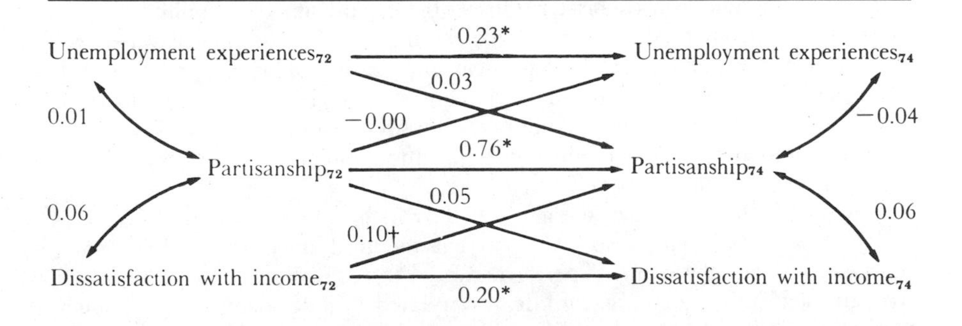

Note: Entry is Pearson *partial* correlation, with simultaneous controls on age, sex, race, and socioeconomic status, all as assessed in 1972.

*$p < .01$. †$p < .05$.

significance (in 1972 partial $r = 0.06$, $p < 10$; in 1974, partial $r = 0.06$, $p < 0.05$). And the cross-lagged correlations suggest that citizens who felt that their own financial situation was declining shifted their allegiance away from the Republicans (thereby corroborating Brody's preliminary finding). The difference between the cross-lagged correlations did not reach statistical significance, however ($t = 1.08$, $p > 0.25$).[23] More telling, perhaps, is that the differential cross-lagged correlation pattern shown in Figure 12-1 did *not* recur in the 1974-76 panel.

Here as elsewhere, then, we could uncover little in the way of political effects arising from pocketbook grievances. Economic hardship in personal life does not seem to influence voters' partisanship, just as it does not seem seriously to impinge on congressional and presidential voting.

This brings us finally to consider the interplay between citizens' partisanships and their sociotropic economic judgements. In so doing, we confront squarely a worry that continues to nag the sociotropic hypothesis, embodied in the charge that such assessments are only rationalizations for party identification. According to this argument, which has its parallel in the issue-voting controversy, judgements of government performance or party competence are hopelessly confounded by a more fundamental loyalty to party.[24] Economic conditions become a kind of projective test, subject to gross misperception in the service of preserving and cementing partisan identity.

No doubt some of this does go on—events in the United States rarely take on political significance without being interpreted and filtered through a partisan lens. The question is really whether sociotropic judgements are *only* superficial masks for partisan identification. The availability of panel evidence affords an opportunity to investigate this possibility, which we shall call the rationalization hypothesis. In so doing, we shall also present evidence that bears on the alternative possibility: that assessments of national economic conditions have an existence separate from partisanship, and, moreover, that changes in sociotropic assessments produce changes in partisan identification (rather than the reverse).

Once again we rely on cross-lagged panel correlation analysis, but with one important amendment. Brody's (1977) analysis of the 1972-74 CPS panel study suggested that changes in strength of identification from 1972 to 1974 appeared to be reliably associated with short-term forces principally among Republicans. The prescription for our analysis is clear: we should examine the interplay between economic concerns and strength of partisanship for Republicans and Democrats separately. We did so for personal economic grievances, but without learning anything not already revealed by the pooled analysis (summarized in Figure 12-1). We also followed this procedure in analyzing national economic assessments, this time with a genuine payoff.

This evidence is shown in Figure 12-2, which concentrates on 1974-76, as the CPS surveys from those years carried identical measures of both party competence and government performance. First of all, among Democrats, strength of identification was significantly related to judgements of government performance and to evaluations of party competence, in both 1974 and 1976, and in the expected direction. Moreover, the cross-lagged correlations suggest that voters' assessments of national economic conditions causally dominated their intensity of identification. That is, across the 1974-76 period, Democrats became

Figure 12-2 Sociotropic Economic Judgements and Partisanship, 1974-1976

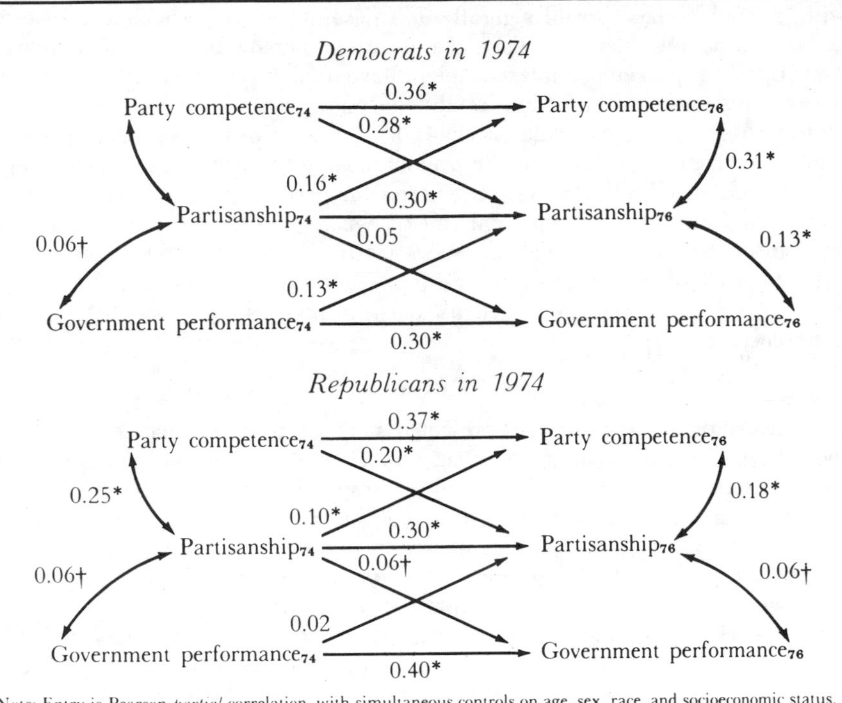

Note: Entry is Pearson *partial* correlation, with simultaneous controls on age, sex, race, and socioeconomic status, all as assessed in 1974.
* p <.01. † p <.05.

more strongly identified with their party to the degree that they held a dim view of the current government's performance on economic problems (t = 1.48, p <0.20) and to the degree that they felt the Republicans to be inferior economic problem solvers (t = 2.18, p <0.05). This held for the Democrats in 1972-74 as well and just as strongly, although this analysis was necessarily limited to the government performance measure.

Unfortunately Republicans resist this neat pattern. Figure 12-2 shows that among Republicans in 1974-76, strength of identification was essentially unrelated to judgements of government performance in cross-sectional analysis; the cross-lagged correlations are similarly uninspiring (this pattern is replicated in the 1972-74 panel). However, evaluations of party competence and strength of identification among Republicans were correlated. And here the cross-lagged correlations follow the pattern established by the Democrats: judgements of party economic competence influenced the intensity of identification, not the reverse (t = 1.39, p <0.20). Republicans (in 1974) who thought their party to be proficient on economic problems became stronger Republicans; those who thought the Democrats more able became weaker Republicans.

The evidence presented in this section thus sustains the theme that we began with, and which has run through all our analysis. Personal economic grievances do not appear to influence partisan identification, thereby foreclosing one indirect route by which pocketbook interests might have impinged on political preferences. Assessments of national economic conditions, on the other hand, were intertwined with partisanship, in particular strength of partisanship. Furthermore, we could find no evidence to support the rationalization hypothesis that sociotropic judgements (specifically ratings of government performance and evaluations of party competence) merely represent an expression of partisan loyalties. Quite the reverse: on balance, our evidence suggests that how the public sizes up the national economic scene constitutes an important short-term political force of its own, which acts on (and through) partisanship, as well as shaping vote preferences directly.[25]

Resumé

According to the evidence presented here, American voters resemble the sociotropic ideal, responding to changes in general economic conditions, much more closely than the pocketbook ideal, responding to the circumstances of personal economic life. In the first section of the analysis we reopened the case of congressional voting, prompted mainly by an interest in providing a fairer test of the pocketbook prediction than previous congressional election research, including our own, had done. This re-examination merely added to the prior evidence against pocketbook congressional voting. Whether voters were preoccupied in their personal lives with rising prices or with unemployment had no effect on their votes for Congress. And personal economic grievances played at best a minor role in accounting for patterns of stability and change in congressional voting over time, the second basis for our re-examination. Moreover, the many failures of the pocketbook prediction were hardly confined to the congressional case. As demonstrated in the second and third parts of the analysis, pocketbook interests were weakly and erratically related to presidential voting, and had virtually nothing to do with partisanship.[26]

The evidence was much stronger at each point for the sociotropic prediction. We found that voters' definitions of national economic problems correlated with their political preferences. Moreover, voters' judgements of recent trends in general business conditions, their ratings of the incumbent administration's handling of economic matters, their evaluation of which party was better equipped or more inclined to solve national economic problems, all contributed to their decision about which congressional candidate to support; substantially influenced their presidential voting; and affected even the most central of political predispositions, party identification. Political preferences thus seem to be shaped by citizens' conceptions of national economic conditions, not by the economic circumstances of their personal lives. Politics is carried on sociotropically, not at the level of the pocketbook.[27]

What, then, are the implications of a sociotropic politics? In this final section, we would like to explore several, including: (1) differences within the somewhat miscellaneous collection of judgements that we have so far lumped together under the label of "sociotropic"; (2) the rationality of sociotropic voting; and (3) speculations about the psychological underpinnings of sociotropic politics.

Types of Sociotropic Judgements

Until now, we have made no effort to distinguish between types of sociotropic judgements. Definitions of national problems, general business conditions, government performance, and party competence have been treated indiscriminately. For the purpose of comparing pocketbook and sociotropic models of voting, this has been a sensible strategy. There are nevertheless important differences between the various sociotropic indicators, and their roles in the voting decision could well vary from one context to another. It is instructive to consider Downs's (1957) argument at this point. According to Downs, in a presidential election between an incumbent and a challenger the public has much "harder" evidence on the former than the latter, i.e. how things have been and how well they have been handled during his tenure in office. Thus the president will be evaluated largely on the basis of his performance in office. Not surprisingly, a significant share of the president's campaign will be given to glorifying his record and defending it from the scurrilous accusations put out by the opposition (Page, 1978). By comparison, the challenger has no comparable history available for public scrutiny.

If Downs is correct, different types of national economic assessments should have different relevance for the two candidates. Voters' evaluations of the incumbent president should be closely tied to their judgements of recent trends in business conditions and their evaluations of government performance. But business conditions and government performance should be tied less strongly to evaluations of the president's challenger. On the other hand, judgements of each party's economic competence should be bound up at least as tightly, perhaps more so, with evaluations of the challenger than with evaluations of the incumbent. The challenger has no record; therefore, voters may rely more on their expectations of how well the challenger will perform. Such expectations, in turn, may be based substantially on their general sense of the relative ability of the two parties to manage economic problems—what we have called party competence.

These predictions were neatly borne out in the 1972 and, even more, the 1976 election. As shown in Table 12-6, voters' assessments of government performance were correlated much more sharply with evaluations of the incumbent than with evaluations of the challenger (evaluation was measured in each case by the re-election thermometer rating). A similar pattern emerged, although less sharply, for the public's assessment of business conditions. This pattern was reversed for judgements of party competence, as predicted. Evaluations of the comparatively unknown Carter in 1976 were closely tied to citizens' impressions about the parties' abilities to deal with economic problems; this was less true for the incumbent, President Ford.[28]

There appears to be a concordance, then, between the habits of the sociotropic voter and those emphasized by Downs in his formulation of voter rationality. The sociotropic voter rewards incumbents for good performance and punishes them for bad; the sociotropic voter is inclined to support challengers to

Table 12-6 Relationships Between Sociotropic Economic Judgements and Evaluations of Presidential Candidates

	1972		*1976*	
	Nixon	McGovern	Ford	Carter
Government performance	−.289*	.142*	−.378*	.112*
Business conditions	−.105*	.093*	−.156*	.087*
Party competence	—	—	−.304*	.414*
Thermometer score: Mean	66.0	49.1	61.0	62.8
Thermometer score: S.D.	27.1	29.3	23.7	26.4

Note: Entry is Pearson *partial* correlation, with simultaneous controls on party identification (three-way), age, race, sex, and socio-economic status. Evaluations of candidates are supplied by standard CPS pre-election thermometer rating. In 1972, *N* ranges from 899 to 918; in 1976, 2,036 to 2,119.
* $p < .01$.

the degree their party has delivered prosperity in the past, and is less apt to when the challenger's party has produced (or at least been associated with) bad times. All of this makes good sense and is at a general level compatible with Downs's formal depiction of the rational voter. The twist, of course, is that the ingredients that figure in political preferences are not pocketbook interests—not the voter's own personal economic circumstances—but rather sociotropic interests—the voter's assessment of national economic conditions. The sociotropic voter asks political leaders not "What have you done for *me* lately?" (Popkin et al., 1976), but rather "What have you done for the *country* lately?" and, "What are you likely to do for the *country* in the future?"

Rationality of Sociotropic Voting

This shift—from pocketbook to sociotropic interests—carries with it questions that have far-reaching ramifications for the debate about voter rationality. We emphasize two here. The first touches upon how well-informed about politics rational voters can and should be.[29] At the outset we agree with Downs, that for citizens to become absorbed in politics would in most cases be politically irrational. The development of this argument is indeed one of the strengths of Downs's formulation of voter rationality. And the facts on this matter are absolutely clear: three decades of public opinion research demonstrate overwhelmingly that most citizens are indifferent to and generally poorly informed about much of what happens in political life (Converse, 1975a; Sears, 1969).

Our picture of the sociotropic voter is fully consistent with Downs's allegations and with these facts. That sociotropic judgements impinge on political preferences most assuredly does not mean that voters must undertake a sophisticated analysis of macroeconomic policy, nor that they need identify and appreciate the subtle differences that might separate the economic policies advocated by leading candidates. What is required of the voters is much more tractable: merely that they form impressions of how the economy is performing, of what national problems seem the most pressing, and of how the incumbent administration is handling economic issues and problems. In short, sociotropic voting does not place unreasonable informational demands on citizens, does not demand of them an irrational hunger for political knowledge. This implies the *possibility* of a rational sociotropic politics.

A second set of questions implied by our results bears even more directly on the voter rationality debate. These questions pertain to the *sources* of sociotropic judgements: how, in fact, do citizens arrive at such judgements? How faithfully do sociotropic judgements reflect economic reality? These are essential questions in a descriptive sense, in elaborating further the sociotropic voter hypothesis; and in a normative sense, in appraising the desirability of elections shaped by sociotropic judgements.

At one rather preliminary level, our findings can be construed to mean that some significant portion of the electorate is sensible (perhaps even rational). That is, in forming political preferences, citizens tend to rely on information about the economy as a whole, instead of information about their own perhaps idiosyncratic experiences. But how well do they do this? To what extent do sociotropic judgements reflect citizens' realistic appraisals of national economic conditions? Sociotropic judgements do *not,* as we saw earlier, serve to rationalize partisanship, nor do they represent mere extrapolations from pocketbook experiences. Moreover, fragmentary aggregate evidence suggests that the electorate is remarkably responsive to changes in general economic conditions (Hibbs, 1979; Kernell, 1978; Kinder and Kiewiet, 1979). However, firm conclusions about the quality of sociotropic decision-making are not yet possible. There remains considerable room for confusion on the citizen's part, distortion on the part of the media, and orchestration and manipulation by the politician. Having demonstrated the political weight carried by sociotropic judgements, an obvious next step is to understand their antecedents.

Psychological Underpinnings of Sociotropic Politics

To demonstrate the failure of pocketbook politics and the success of sociotropic politics is one thing; to account for this pattern is quite another. That personal economic grievances are—or seem to be—compartmentalized away from political preferences is a particularly striking finding, and we have no pat explanation for it. We do have speculations of course, of two broad types.

The first centers upon citizens' explanations for economic outcomes—their own and the nation's. We suspect that the causal accounts people offer for their own economic problems seldom have anything to do with the political world, but focus instead on such proximate factors as local business conditions and idiosyncratic circumstances at the workplace. They may also include elements of self-blame, a reflection of the pre-eminence of individualism in American society (Sniderman and Brody, 1977; Schlozman and Verba, 1979). Such explanations are privatistic. To the extent that people locate the causes of their economic problems either in the immediate environment or in their own failings, personal discontent is unlikely to have political consequences. But there is a flip side to this first speculation: that in accounting for national economic conditions, the public *will* often point to political factors, the president and Congress most of all. Thus beliefs about the causes of economic problems—personal and national—may channel economic discontent. The ramifications of personal economic problems are turned inward; those of national economic conditions are directed to the political system.[30]

Our second speculation begins with the observation that there are qualitative differences in the character of information about personal economic experience, on the one hand, and national economic conditions, on the other. In objective terms, personal economic experiences are vivid, immediate, and concrete. And as Lane (1962) has pointed out, they are likely to remain so in their subjective representations. People "morselize" their private experience: the events and details of daily life are typically not interpreted as instances of broader themes, political or otherwise. Such morselization is an enormous obstacle to the politicization of private experience. At the same time, information about national economic conditions is at least available in a quite different form. From the mass media, such information comes pre-digested, comparatively coherent, and abstract. Packaged in this way, evidence about national conditions may be very difficult to integrate with evidence about personal experience. That is, there may be fundamental psychological incompatibilities in the ways the two different kinds of information are processed.[31] And of course, information about national conditions is typically conveyed at a level of abstraction appropriate to nationally-oriented political judgements. This may substantially ease the processes by which sociotropic judgements are translated into political preferences.

Both lines of speculation refer to psychological processes—a legitimate and even propitious place to begin. But any psychological explanation that survives empirical examination must at some point be joined to a more broadly-gauged analysis, one that is persistently sensitive to normative considerations. In this more ambitious sense, our speculations represent a modest beginning, one point of departure for our future research.

Appendix

Question-Wording

	CPS Survey		
	1972	*1974*	*1976*
Personal Economic Discontents			
Dissatisfaction With Income			
We are interested in how people are getting along financially these days. Would you say that you (and your family) are better off or worse off financially than you were a year ago?	X	X	X
Are you making as much money now as you were a year ago, or more, or less?	X		
How satisfied are you with the income you (and your family) have?		X	
How satisfied are you with your standard of living—the things you have like housing, car, furniture, recreation, and the like?		X	

Unemployment Experiences			
Working at present, never out of work in the past year (+4). Working at present, but out of work sometime in the past year (−1). Temporarily laid off at present, but had not been out of work in the past year (−3).	X	X	X
Unemployed at present, but had worked sometime in the past year (−4). Unemployed at present, and had not worked anytime in the past year (−5).			
Personal Economic Problems			
We like to have people tell us what sorts of problems they have to deal with in their daily lives. Can you tell me what some of the problems are that you face these days in your life? . . . Anything else?	X	X	X
Sociotropic Economic Judgements			
Party Competence			
Do you think that the problems of inflation and unemployment would be handled better by the Democrats, by the Republicans, or about the same by both?		X	X
Do you think inflation would be handled better by the Democrats, by the Republicans, or about the same by both?			X
Do you think the problems of unemployment would be handled better by the Democrats, by the Republicans, or about the same by both?			X
Government Performance			
As to the economic policy of the government—I mean steps taken to fight inflation or unemployment—would you say that the government is doing a good job, only a fair job, or a poor job?	X	X	X
Thinking about the steps that have been taken to fight inflation—would you say that the government has been doing a good job, only fair, or a poor job?			X
Now how about the government's economic policy dealing with unemployment—would you say the government has been doing a good job, only fair, or a poor job?			X
Business Conditions			
Would you say that at the present time business conditions are better or worse than they were a year ago?	X		X
National Problems			
What do you think are the most important problems facing this *country*? . . . Anything else?	X	X	X

Coding

The first four predictor variables represent voters' pocketbook interests. *Dissatisfaction With Income* takes a positive value if the respondent's personal economic condition has recently improved, 0 if stable, and a negative value if it has declined. *Unemployment Experiences* assumes a positive value if the respondent's head of household has experienced no employment difficulties in the recent past, and negative values if the household head has been unemployed recently. *Personal Unemployment Problems* and *Personal Inflation Problems* are then a pair of dummy variables that together index citizens' definitions of their most important personal economic problems. (The suppressed reference group is made up of respondents who named neither unemployment nor inflation as their most serious personal problem.)

The next set of five variables represents the voters' sociotropic interests. *Business Conditions* measures the respondent's judgement of recent trends in business conditions in general, scored so that a positive value indicates that respondents believe business conditions to be on the upswing, a negative value that conditions have deteriorated. *Government Performance* taps the respondent's evaluation of the current administration's dealing with economic problems. A positive score on this measure corresponds to a favourable evaluation, a negative score means an unfavourable rating. *Party Competence* is a measure of the respondent's judgement of the relative ability of the two parties to manage economic problems. It takes a positive value if the Republicans were thought to be more capable, and a negative value if the Democrats were thought to be more capable. Finally, *National Unemployment* and *National Inflation* are a pair of dummy variables representing respondents' judgements about serious national problems, patterned after the personal problem variables.

The regression model also includes a measure of partisanship, derived from the standard CPS question. *Party Identification* takes a value of 1 if the respondent is a Republican (strong identifier, weak identifier, or an independent 'leaning' toward the Republican Party), 0 if the respondent is an independent, and −1 if the respondent is a Democrat.

NOTES

1. Downs (1957, p. 42). To be sure, Downs's formulation does permit voters to take into account considerations other than their own personal economic circumstances: "It is possible for a citizen to receive utility from events that are only remotely connected to his own material income. . . . There can be no simple identification of acting for one's greatest benefit with selfishness in the narrow sense because self-denying charity is often a great source of benefits to oneself. Thus our model leaves no room for altruism in spite of its basic reliance upon the self-interest axiom" (p. 37). Thus our empirical probings of the pocketbook predictions should not be equated in any simple way with testing Downs's analysis of voter rationality. The pocketbook hypothesis should be construed rather as an expression of a central theme of Downs's analysis.
2. This term was used originally in Meehl (1977).
3. Both the pocketbook and sociotropic predictions—at least as we have characterized them—describe voters who react *retrospectively*. The concept of retrospective voting has a distinguished heritage—see Downs (1957); (Key 1966). For a recent and extensive treatment of retrospective voting, see Fiorina (1981b).
4. The argument that voting in response to economic issues might be policy-oriented was made by Stigler (1973). Furthermore, several studies of Western democracies suggest that macroeconomic policy is a function of the extent to which the executive branch has been controlled by parties of the Left as against parties of the Right. In particular, according to Hibbs (1977), long periods of control by right-wing parties are associated

with higher rates of unemployment. Control by left-wing parties, in contrast, is associated with larger and more rapidly growing public sectors, and with downwardly redistributive tax systems—see Cameron (1976a, 1978). To act in a policy-oriented fashion voters would need to have registered these differences. It should be noted, however, that as regards the issues of inflation and unemployment, policy-oriented voting does *not* require voters to believe in the existence of a trade-off between these two maladies. It only requires that they perceive differences between the amount of effort and/or skill the two parties are able to apply against whichever of the two problems they find especially troublesome.

5. An exception is Weatherford (1978).
6. This is due to the fact that previous studies have all, in one way or another, controlled for party identification. It could be that considerations which prompt individuals to change their votes might also prompt them to change their avowed partisanship; by controlling for partisanship the impact of such considerations, including unfavourable economic conditions, would fail to be detected. There is, after all, considerable evidence indicating that party identification is susceptible to just this sort of change—see, for example, Brody (1977); Shively (1977); Page and Jones (1979). Most analyses to date have been quite sensitive to this issue, but it is certainly prudent to probe more deeply for potential problems. For this reason, the analyses in this paper will examine both changes in voting and changes in partisanship, as later discussion will reveal.
7. It should be noted, however, that several recent investigations into a number of different domains have also found personal concerns and discontents of various kinds of negligible political consequences. See, among others, Gatlin, Gile, and Cataldo (1978); Kinder and Sears (1981); Lau, Brown, and Sears (1978); Sears, Hensler, and Speer (1979); Sears and Kinder (1971); Sears, Tyler, Citrin, and Kinder (1978); Sears, Lau, Tyler, and Allen (1980).
8. Although our attention will be confined to pocketbook and sociotropic conceptions of politics, these two certainly do not exhaust the possibilities. For example, one alternative perspective emphasizes social group identification, essentially arguing that much of American politics is carried on at a level intermediate between pocketbook and sociotropic interests. This is a venerable idea; we are happy to notice indications of its revival; see, for example, Miller, Gurin, and Gurin (1978); Rhodebeck (1980).
9. One of the major problems was that in 1976 complaints about unemployment were lumped together with all other job-related references, which ranged from despising the public (mentioned quite often by sales clerks) to having to work too many hours. Only about half of the references in the employment related category were about unemployment. It also turned out that the many complaints in 1976 about taxes were coded as "other or less specific economic woes." Furthermore, the 1972-74 codes often contained a hodge-podge of various and sundry responses. One category, for example, contained references to inflation, governmental waste, and the cost of college. We obviously needed to disaggregate these responses.

   The staff at CPS was extremely accommodating and helped make the task of reading the interviews much less arduous than it might have been. We would like to thank Warren Miller for his approval of the project, and Ann Robinson, Alice Hayes, and Maria Sanchez for their valuable assistance. A more detailed analysis of the political consequences of personal economic problems and perceptions of national economic problems appears in Kiewiet (1981).
10. Despite superficial appearances these measures are not at all mutually redundant. The family's recent experience with unemployment was indeed correlated with the respondent's subjective assessment of personal economic problems but quite imperfectly (this evidence is described in detail in Kinder and Kiewiet (1979). In any case, it makes absolutely no difference whether the set of pocketbook interests are included together in the regression analysis or whether their effects are estimated separately.

11. The major determinant of voting in congressional elections is the citizen's partisan attachment to a political party (see Campbell et al., 1966). Thus it is essential to remove the possible confounding effects of partisan identification. At the same time we must avoid over-controlling for partisanship. Two recent analyses have implied that "nominal party identification"—i.e. identification as a Republican, an Independent, or a Democrat—is a stable, enduring characteristic for most citizens. Strength or intensity of partisanship—for example, the difference between strong Republicans and weak Republicans—is much more responsive to a variety of short-term forces (see Brody (1976) and Converse (1975)). We have therefore operationalized partisanship in its nominal form for the purposes of these vote analyses. The third section of our analysis takes up more directly the causal interplay between partisanship and economic discontents, both pocketbook and sociotropic.

    We also ran the regressions with a set of social background measures included—age, sex, race, and a composite measure of socioeconomic status. Unless otherwise noted in the text, adding these variables as additional controls had no effect on the pattern of results.
12. The 1972 interview schedule was split into two overlapping but non-identical forms, with each administered to half of the full sample. This was done in order to increase the total number of questions that could be asked, and was accomplished in such a way as to ensure that the resulting sub-samples each constituted a representative cross-section of the electorate. As a consequence of this procedure, questions representing some elements of the basic regression model were asked of the entire sample—vote choice and partisanship, in particular. Other questions were asked only of one half-sample or the other. The major complication here is that the personal and national problem questions were posed to one half-sample, the remainder of the personal economic grievances and national economic assessments to the other. This rules out the possibility of any genuine multivariate analysis. Rather than putting the 1972 study aside altogether, we generated estimates for the personal and national problems separately from the rest. We would be much more reluctant about presenting these findings if the personal and national problems people name were highly correlated with other predictor variables. From the 1974 and 1976 studies, we know that they are correlated, but quite modestly so—see D. R. Kiewiet and D. R. Kinder (1978).
13. The probit analysis program used was written by McKelvey and Zavoina (1975). For a very readable, less technical description of probit analysis, see Wolfinger and Rosenstone (1980, App. C).
14. For a good introduction on the specification and interpretation of interaction terms in multivariate analysis see Cohen and Cohen (1975).
15. The latter term is actually an estimate of the respondent's vote in the previous election. Based on an OLS regression, it is the first stage of the two-stage procedure. Substituting this estimate for the actual reported vote solves the estimation problems resulting from autocorrelated error. Any good econometric text discusses this procedure. For a very readable introduction to these problems and procedures see Markus (1979).
16. Essentially the same pattern held for sporadic voters as well. Among citizens who failed to vote for Congress in 1972 but did so in 1974, their choice in that year had nothing to do with economic misfortunes suffered in private life; the same is true for voting in 1976 among 1974 non-voters.

    Nor did the evidence improve when we examined a second change hypothesis: that voters whose pocketbook experiences *worsened* from one election to the next would be inclined to switch their votes from the in-party to the opposition. We could find only traces of support for this hypothesis. Voters whose unemployment experiences worsened between 1972 and 1974 were somewhat more inclined to switch their support to Democratic candidates during the same period. But in general the collective effects due to changes in pocketbook experiences were at least as frail as those reported in Table 12-3.

17. So far we have neglected the question of pocketbook discontents and *turnout*. It has been argued that the economically aggrieved will turn to the political system for reparations and, consequently, will participate more, other things equal, than economically secure citizens; see, for example, Lipset (1960). Others contend that pocketbook discontents are largely irrelevant to conventional political activity, for example, Meltzer and Vellrath (1975) and Schlozman and Verba (1979). The most persuasive evidence, however, is found in Rosenstone (1982). Analysing data from the Census Bureau Current Population Survey, Rosenstone finds that personal economic adversity suppressed congressional turnout in 1974. Preoccupation with personal economic problems appears to diminish somewhat the resources that can be allocated to politics. Rosenstone's results corroborate our own analysis of congressional turnout. We find, too, that personal economic discontents have slight (and erratic) dampening effects on participation. The economically aggrieved evidently do not look to the national political system for solutions—another blow to the pocketbook prediction.
18. This effect of unemployment experiences on presidential voting may be less robust than it appears. When a set of social background variables (age, race, sex, socio-economic status) is added to the basic regression model, the effect vanished in 1976 (although not in 1972).
19. Kiewiet (1981) extends this analysis of personal and national level concern about inflation and unemployment back to the 1956 election. Evidence of voting in response to unemployment specifically was uncovered early in the series, for example, 1958. This does not imply, however, that a political trade-off between unemployment and inflation used to exist, because during these years very few voters perceived inflation to be a serious problem.
20. Although the evidence on unemployment and presidential voting shown in Table 12-5 constitutes little in the way of support for the Downsian "throw the rascals out" hypothesis, it is more compatible with the alternative formulation that also emphasizes voters' pocketbook interests: namely, that the unemployed look to the Democratic party for solutions to their problem, and therefore support the Democratic presidential candidate, regardless of which party controls the White House.
21. A good exposition of this technique can be found in Kenny (1975).
22. For details of this procedure see Kenny (1975).
23. The *t*-statistics reported in this section are associated with differences between cross-lagged correlations. Again, see Kenny (1975) for an explanation of how they are calculated.
24. There is a voluminous literature on issue-voting, but most of the major points of contention are addressed in Brody and Page (1972) and in Niemi and Weisberg (1976).
25. Sociotropic economic judgements may not always play such an active role, of course. When times are unequivocally good or (perhaps especially) unequivocally bad, then economic conditions are less subject to misperception. When economic signals are less clear, rationalization is encouraged. A similar argument presumably applies to issue voting. When candidates take ambiguous positions on issues, as they often do, the public's tendency to ascribe opinions to them so as to reinforce or rationalize its own view is enhanced, thereby subverting the possibility of genuine issue-based voting. See Brody and Page (1972), Kinder (1981), and especially Page (1978).
26. One way to account for the pocketbook prediction's dismal record here is to explain the findings away. Perhaps we have measured economic grievances inadequately; if so, the frail relationships between political preferences and pocketbook interests would not

reflect the true state of affairs at all, but rather deficiencies in our assessment of personal economic grievances.

This is a legitimate criticism but not a telling one: substantial evidence supports the construct validity of our measures. Part of this evidence is drawn from the CPS surveys themselves, in that replies to the questions on personal economic grievances did show the expected degree of consistency. People who complained about unemployment or declining real income, for example, were also likely to express dissatisfaction with their family's financial condition (Kiewiet and Kinder, 1978). More persuasive, perhaps, is evidence drawn from external sources, such as Klorman (1978). Analysing data from an Institute for Social Research (University of Michigan) income dynamics panel survey, he found strong relationships between citizens' retrospective judgements of their financial progress, on the one hand, and changes in family income, on the other. For more corroborative evidence based on still another data source, see Rosenstone, Wolfinger, and McIntosh (1978). And at the aggregate level such retrospective judgements fluctuate (if sluggishly) with changes in national economic conditions. From 1956 to 1976, for instance, the proportion of respondents who reported improvements in their family's financial condition was greatest in 1964 (41 percent), also the year registering the sharpest increase in real per capita disposable income; the survey question recorded the least satisfaction in 1974 (25 percent), when decline in real income was the most pronounced. Over the eleven election surveys spanning this twenty-year period, the Pearson correlation between change in real income and retrospective judgements of family financial progress was 0.68. Finally and most tellingly, improving the measurement of personal economic adversity does nothing to alter our verdict on the pocketbook's minimal political effect. We have recently developed an extensive battery of questions to tap personal economic experiences and worries. Aided by a more comprehensive, sensitive, and reliable gauge of pocketbook grievances, we nevertheless find virtually no support for the pocketbook prediction—see Kinder, Denney, and Hendricks (1980). The measurement of personal economic grievance does not seem to be the problem. The measures are up to customary methodological standards. But the discontent they tap seldom gets expressed in political judgements.

27. For further corroboration see Denney, Hendricks, and Kinder (1980); Kiewiet (1981); Kinder (1981); Kinder, Denney, and Hendricks (1980); and Sears, Lau, Tyler, and Allen (1980).
28. The same incumbent-challenger asymmetry characterizes the evidence on personal economic grievances. In 1972, for example, evaluations of Nixon were correlated with voters' employment experiences (partial $r = -0.047$, $p < 0.05$, with simultaneous controls on party identification, age, race, sex, and socioeconomic status) and their retrospective judgements regarding their own financial conditions (partial $r = -0.115$, $p < 0.01$). Both indicators were essentially unrelated to evaluations of McGovern (partial $r = 0.021$, n.s.; 0.059, $p < 0.05$, respectively). Virtually identical results were obtained in 1976.
29. This, of course, is a central question in both normative and empirical democratic theory, addressed, among other places, in Downs (1957), Converse (1975a), and Lippman (1922).
30. This speculation implies both that pocketbook voting will be more likely among those citizens who see their own problems as having social or collective causes, and that sociotropic voting will be enhanced among those who define national economic problems as having political causes and political solutions. Both implications are borne out in our preliminary analysis of new national survey data from the United States, reported in Kinder, Denney, and Hendricks (1980).
31. Some provocative evidence on this point is reported in Nisbett, Borgida, Crandall and Reed (1976).

13. STRATEGY AND CHOICE IN THE 1982 CONGRESSIONAL ELECTIONS

Gary C. Jacobson and Samuel Kernell

Common to both political folk wisdom and political science is the idea that the midterm congressional election is a referendum on the performance of the current administration. The more popular a president and the more successful his policies, the better his party does at the midterm. The president's party almost invariably loses some congressional seats in off-year elections (since the Civil War the president's party has added House seats only once—in 1934—though it occasionally picks up Senate seats). But the extent of its losses varies widely (from one to 56 House seats in postwar midterms), depending, so the theory goes, on how the electorate rates the administration's performance.

The 1982 congressional elections will, in this view, be a referendum on President Reagan's administration and in particular on his economic policies, which have been a focus of political attention since inauguration day. If this is true, then economic conditions prevalent through the spring of 1982 (a potentially devastating combination of deep recession, high unemployment, and high interest rates) and Reagan's shaky support in the polls (less than 50 percent approving his performance in all Gallup surveys during the first four months of 1982), portend a Republican disaster of major proportions in the fall.

Remarkably, almost no one is seriously predicting anything of the kind. And it may indeed be a mistake to bet on enormous Republican losses—partly, we will argue, because they are *not* widely anticipated. Our purpose here is to explain why this is so. The explanation arises from a particular theory of how national forces are translated into aggregate election results; indeed, the 1982 elections promise to provide a test of the theory against its rivals.[1]

The idea that midterm elections are referenda rests on a solid empirical base. Kramer (1971), Tufte (1975; 1978), and others (Arcelus and Meltzer, 1975; Bloom and Price, 1975) have shown aggregate congressional election results to be highly responsive to national conditions. The state of the economy, variously measured, and the popular standing of the president are strongly related to shifts in the distribution of the national vote for House candidates. The more positive the responses to the president and the better the performance of the economy, the better the administration's party's candidates do on election day. The electorate

Source: *PS* (1982) 15:423-30, with postscript by the authors. Reprinted with permission of the publisher and the authors.

behaves, collectively, like V. O. Key's (1964, p. 567) "rational god of vengeance and reward."

Most scholars (Tufte is an exception) have been quick to take collective rationality as evidence of individual rationality: people cast votes for House candidates on the basis of their own economic experiences and feelings about the president. The problem with this interpretation is that studies of individual voting behavior in congressional elections turn up surprisingly little evidence of rationally grateful or vengeful voting. Economic effects on individual voting decisions are particularly hard to find. In some election years feelings about the president were evidently related to voters' congressional choices, but in others they were not. Even Watergate-related attitudes had little apparent effect on voting behavior in 1974.[2]

What survey studies did discover was that, with the possible exception of partisanship, the most important influences on individual voters are familiarity with and evaluations of the two candidates running in the district. The better a voter knows and likes a candidate, relative to the opponent, the more likely he or she is to vote for that candidate. This means that the relative quality of candidates and vigor of campaigns is a crucial factor affecting the outcome of congressional contests. Each specific pair of candidates and campaigns presents a particular choice, and the voting decision depends heavily on the alternatives offered. In contests between incumbents and challengers, the choice is largely determined by the quality and resources of the challenger. Attractive, well-financed challengers can seriously threaten incumbents; most incumbents are reelected easily because they do not face such challengers.

The predominant importance to voters of candidates and campaigns is consistent with an alternative theory of how national forces affect aggregate congressional election results. This theory, which we present in detail in *Strategy and Choice in Congressional Elections,* argues that politically active elites—candidates and those who recruit and finance them—provide an essential connecting link between national conditions and individual voting decisions.

If we accept that politicians are not fools, it is clear that variations in the quality of candidates and the quantity of resources they can mobilize for a campaign cannot be random. Ambitious career politicians looking to enter or move up the hierarchy of elective offices are likely to be the most formidable challengers. But they also have the most to risk in the attempt; defeat is at best a setback, at worst ends the career. Thus the best candidates will also be the most cautious in deciding when to run for higher office. They will be most sensitive to the odds on winning and most aware of the factors that affect those odds.

One of those factors is of course the availability of money and other resources for the campaign; astute politicians know how important it is. People who control campaign resources must also make strategic decisions about deploying them. And these, too, are strongly affected by electoral odds. Although a variety of motives inspire contributors to political campaigns, most are more likely to give to campaigns of agreeable candidates who seem to have some plausible chance of winning. Among the things they consider is the quality of the candidate. Good candidates attract money, just as the availability of money attracts good candidates.

If politicians believe that things like the state of the economy or the popular standing of the president strongly influence congressional voters—and there is plenty of anecdotal evidence that they do—their assessments of such conditions will influence their strategic career decisions. National conditions that are thought to affect election results will govern the perception of election odds. When conditions appear to favor a party, more of its stronger potential challengers will decide that this is the year to make their move. The shrewder and more ambitious politicians of the disadvantaged party will reach the opposite conclusion; the longer odds will convince them to sit this one out.

Suppliers of campaign resources will similarly adjust their strategies to the anticipated prospects of their preferred party. If signs are positive, they will put more into the campaigns of challengers, who enjoy improved chances of winning. If portents are ominous, they will instead concentrate on defending threatened incumbents, giving up on challengers as lost causes. The strategies of candidates and people who control campaign resources are again mutually reinforcing. Because the effects of campaign spending are asymmetrical—the marginal return on campaign spending is much greater for challengers than for incumbents—intersecting offensive and defensive strategies produce a net benefit for challengers of the favored party.

The aggregate consequence of these strategic choices is that the party expected to have a good year will field a larger proportion of high-quality challengers with well-financed campaigns, while the opposing party is stuck with a disproportionate number of feeble challengers lacking the resources for a serious campaign. The choice between pairs of candidates across congressional districts in an election year varies systematically with the strategic decisions of potential candidates and associated activists. The strategic decisions are systematically informed by perceptions of national conditions and beliefs about their electoral consequences. Voters need only respond to the choice between candidates at the district level to reflect, in their aggregate behavior, national political forces. Individual-level analogs of national forces—the voter's personal economic circumstances and feelings about the president—need not operate as influences on the vote (though this is not precluded by the theory). The intervening strategic decisions of congressional elites provide a mechanism sufficient to explain how national forces can come to be expressed in aggregate congressional election results.

One important implication of this line of reasoning is that, at the extreme, expectations about a party's electoral performance are self-fulfilling. Choices guided by expectations generate the very conditions that fulfill them. We do not think that this has actually become the case; rather, we argue that electoral prophecies are self-reinforcing. The effects of national forces have been multiplied through the strategic behavior of congressional activists.

We offer in this chapter a variety of evidence supporting the theory. One example of particular interest here is our discovery that economic conditions measured in the first quarter of the election year—the period in which most potential candidates are making final decisions about running—are more strongly related to the fall election results than are economic conditions measured closer to election day. One important test has been lacking, however. In past elections, both our theory and more orthodox economic voting theories have predicted the same result. Only the mechanism was different: economic conditions and presidential popularity might operate directly on individual voting decisions or their effects might be mediated through elite strategies, but the aggregate outcome would be the same. This fall's election promises to be different.

The 1982 Election as a Referendum

If the 1982 election is a referendum on Reagan and Reaganomics and the electorate responds as it has in the past to economic conditions and its assessments of the president, it is hard to imagine a scenario that does not involve dramatic Democratic gains. Consider the possibilities in light of Tufte's analysis. Tufte (1978, pp. 106-15) showed that the division of the House vote in midterm elections is closely related to the state of the economy and the popular standing of the president. He estimated the standardized vote loss of the president's party (measured as the aggregate two-party vote subtracted from the average vote for the party in the previous eight congressional elections) as a function of (1) the percentage change in real disposable income per capita over the year preceeding the election and (2) the president's standing (percentage approving of the way he is handling the job) in the Gallup Poll just before the election. The resulting equation, updated to cover the period 1946 to 1978, is:

$$\text{Standardized vote loss} = -10.56 + \underset{(.143)}{.663}\ \text{Change in Income} + \underset{(.042)}{.130}\ \text{Presidential Popularity}$$

$$N = 9 \qquad R^2 = .84$$

The standard errors are in parentheses.

The equation estimates a vote percentage, but this is easily translated into an estimate of a shift in the number of seats held by a party, for there is a very strong linear relationship between the proportion of votes and the proportion of seats won by parties in postwar House elections:

$$\begin{array}{l}\text{Percentage of Seats}\\ \text{Held by Democrats}\end{array} = -42.5 + \underset{(.16)}{1.90}\ \begin{array}{l}\text{Percentage of Votes}\\ \text{Won by Democrats}\end{array}$$

$$N = 18 \qquad R^2 = .90$$

With these equations we can easily calculate how many House seats the president's party should lose given any combination of economic conditions (measured by change in real income per capita) and presidential popularity. Table 13-1 lists the predicted loss of House seats by Republicans in 1982 for a range of such combinations. The numbers are quite striking. Real income is unlikely to show much increase between 1981 and 1982, though it probably will not fall.[3] Reagan's approval level in the Gallup Poll has ranged from 43 percent to 47 percent during the first five months of 1982; the average is 45 percent. Thus a plausible projection is a one percent increase in personal income and Reagan's approval level at 45 percent. But that should cost the Republicans 50 House seats. And it is easy to imagine worse conditions (for Republicans) holding.

Table 13-1 Projected Republican Losses in the 1982 House Elections at Selected Levels of Presidential Popularity and Real Income Change (Net Number of Seats Lost)

Income Change[a]	*Presidential Popularity*[b]		
	40%	*50%*	*60%*
−2%	72	61	51
−1%	67	56	45
0%	61	50	40
1%	56	45	34
2%	50	39	29

[a] Percentage change in real income per capita between 1981 and 1982.

[b] Percentage approving Reagan's performance in the last Gallup survey conducted prior to the election.

Thus, by the traditional referendum theory, 1982 shapes up as a great Democratic year. But almost no one thinks that it will be nearly this good even if the economy does not turn around dramatically during the summer. Although Democratic leaders have, on occasion, suggested that the "Democrats could rebound in the way they did in 1958" when they won 47 House seats, 13 Senate seats, and 5 governorships,[4] few see this as a serious possibility. The consensus among AFL-CIO leaders, meeting in February, was that Democrats would pick up only about five seats. The most optimistic projection mentioned at the meeting (based on a poll taken for the American Federation of State, County, and Municipal Employees) predicted a shift of about 25 seats.[5] U.S. Representative Tony Coelho, head of the Democratic Congressional Campaign Committee, predicted in January that Democrats would gain "10 seats at a minimum, and, more likely, about 18."[6] *Eighteen is the number of seats Tufte's equation would predict Democrats to gain if income growth and presidential popularity matched their highest points in any postwar midterm election* (1962). This scarcely seems possible. Republican leaders must show a professional optimism, of course; but there are few signs that they secretly expect a drubbing, either. The consensus in both parties in the spring of 1982 seemed to be that the Democrats will pick up a few House seats, but that the election would by no means be a sweep.

These conservative projections are, we believe, entirely justified. Normally our theory would also predict a Republican disaster in 1982. Indeed, our equation modifying Tufte's by using first quarter economic data generates slightly higher estimates of Republican House losses. But the connection, as we see it, depends on the strategic decisions of politicians and campaign contributors. If these are, for some reason, not seriously affected by expectations arising from perceptions of economic conditions and the president's standing with the public, the aggregate of choices offered voters across congressional districts may not systematically reflect national conditions. And so neither may the aggregate vote.

The system depicted in our theory is driven by the strategic choices of individual political entrepreneurs in a decentralized political marketplace. It is well known that individually rational decisions can lead to outcomes that leave everyone worse off than might have been possible with collective action. When a party is expected to have a bad year, the strategic decisions of its candidates and contributors multiply the expected effects. Strong parties might be able to deploy candidates and campaign resources to counteract rather than reinforce the effects of national forces. Our interpretation of midterms is predicated on weak and decentralized parties and on politicians who expect the economy and presidential popularity to influence voters. If a party became strong enough to persuade potential candidates that contrary national conditions would not necessarily be fatal to their careers, the system as we describe it would break down. And this seems to be what is happening in 1982.

The Difference in 1982: Republican Organization

If 1982 is not a Republican disaster, national-level Republican party committees will be the reason. First, they have raised enormous amounts of money to spend on the campaigns. The senatorial committee's budget is $26 million; $37 million is set for House races. The equivalent Democratic committees will be lucky to have one-tenth as much. As of March 31, the Democratic Congressional Campaign Committee (DCCC) had $200,000 on hand; the Republican House committee had $17 million.[7] Republicans have been able to raise so much money because they have spent the last eight years perfecting a direct mail fundraising system. Direct mail has provided Republicans with a steady, predictable income quite independent of fluctuations in the political environment. Add to this the support of cooperative PACs (which take direction from the national party in choosing beneficiaries) and it appears that Republicans, unlike Democrats, will not have to make tough strategic choices about which candidates to fund.

Equally important, Republicans have figured out what to do with their money. They have used it to recruit and train high-quality candidates as well as to help finance their campaigns (the promise of money, of course, helping to recruit strong candidates). Much of the recruiting for 1982 took place in 1981, when Reagan was dominating Congress and talk was of realignment and perhaps a Republican House after 1982. Joe Gaylord, the National Republican Congressional Committee's campaign director, reported that "the identification of good, qualified Republicans is our main priority, and we have spent almost all of 1981 carrying out that priority."[8] When the economy turned sour, committee officials were worried that good candidates might be scared off; "I'd check every day," said Nancy Sinott, the committee's executive director, "but it wasn't happening."[9] Republican consultant Eddie Mahe said in March that "we had so many candidates out so early, we're in pretty good shape. If the heavy decision-making was going on now, we might be suffering" because of the expected impact of the recession. He compared 1982 with 1974, when Watergate and another recession scared off good Republican candidates: "the candidates we had that year couldn't even be the drivers for this year's bunch."[10]

Republican recruitment efforts have, to be sure, sustained some damage from the recession. Three midwestern Republican governors (Milliken of Michigan, Quie of Minnesota, Ray of Iowa) chose not to seek reelection and a fourth (Rhodes of Ohio) declined to challenge a Senate incumbent (Metzenbaum). The economy was a factor in all of these decisions; all of them weaken the Republican ticket.[11] But there is no sign that the damage is widespread, "no evidence of the sort of panicky rededication to the practice of law" [12] observed among potential Republican candidates in 1974.

Republicans have concentrated on recruiting good candidates because they have a clear understanding of how important this is. Representative Vander Jagt, chairman of the NRCC, has argued that "just as they say pitching is 80 percent of baseball, in a Congressional race the candidate is 80 percent of winning. A good candidate can win it, no matter how bad the conditions, and a bad candidate can lose it, no matter how good the conditions." [13] Bernadette Budde, director of political education for the Business-Industry PAC went so far as to argue that "the economy matters for a party only if its candidates think it matters." [14]

Democrats have been slower to adopt this view. Interviewed in February, Coelho expressed the traditional attitude that "a national atmosphere, or a regional atmosphere, that is conducive to your party" is more important than recruiting strong candidates.[15] But only a month later he was saying that "the critical time for the November elections is November through February, when candidates decide to run or not. Whoever has the best candidates usually still wins." [16] Perhaps Coelho found this idea more attractive as Democratic recruitment picked up. He admitted that the Democrats had found it hard to attract good candidates during the first half of 1981 but claimed they had done better since the fall. "Now they're coming to me because they smell victory in 1982." [17]

At present, it appears that both parties will be fielding strong challengers in 1982[18] but for very different reasons. Strong Democratic challengers have been attracted in the usual way: by their belief that serious economic problems and Reagan's declining popularity make it a good year to go after Republican incumbents. Strong Republican challengers have emerged *despite* unfavorable national conditions through the work and money of national-level party committees. The party has managed to organize a strong countercyclical thrust—strong enough to convince many observers of national politics that 1982 will not be an especially good Democratic year.

Just because Republican candidates are *not* following the pattern expected in a bad year for Republicans, the 1982 elections should provide a real test of alternative theories of the midterm referendum. If the vote is a direct response to national forces, Republicans should lose approximately the number of House seats predicted by Tufte's equation. If it is largely a response to particular pairs of candidates and campaigns in each district, Republican losses should be much smaller.

One November scenario is that, with both parties fielding strong challengers (and accepting that the vigor of the challenge is the crucial variable in these contests), a larger than usual number of incumbents from both parties will be defeated. But the Republicans' advantage in campaign resources might minimize Democratic gains in another way. By mounting an unusually large number of formidable challenges, Republicans may compel people and groups that supply funds to Democrats to concentrate their resources on defending incumbents, leaving even attractive challengers underfunded and therefore unlikely to win. An energetic offensive strategy may force a defensive strategy on the Democrats, both strategies working to the benefit of the Republicans.

If we (and Republican strategists) are right, the results of the 1982 election will not reflect the performance of the administration and the popular standing of the president nearly as strongly as they have in the past. The lesson will not be lost on political professionals. The independent value of effective national organization will be unmistakable. And over the long run, repeated demonstrations that candidates' fates are not governed by national forces will foster career strategies that are not nearly so attentive to those forces. As a result, voters, responding now to insulated choices, will no longer reflect in their preferences the strategic advantages national forces once provided.

POST-ELECTION POSTSCRIPT

Had the 1982 election followed the pattern predicted by the standard referendum interpretation of midterm congressional elections, Republican losses would have surpassed those of 1958 and 1974. The economy remained mired in deep recession through election day. Unemployment was at its highest level in more than forty years. Businesses were failing at the highest rate since the Great Depression. The only good news was the inflation rate, which declined sharply as the recession took hold. This, along with the July tax cut and social security increases, kept real per capita income from actually falling despite the recession; it was essentially unchanged from the third quarter of 1981 to the third quarter of 1982. The proportion of Gallup's respondents approving Reagan's performance stood at 42 percent in the October poll. Only Truman had a lower preelection rating (32 percent approving in 1946).

With real income stagnant and Reagan's approval rating at 42 percent, Tufte's model predicts the Republicans to win 41.1 percent of the vote. This would have been a drop of 7.7 percentage points from 1980. The seats/votes equation translates it into a loss of about 58 seats, giving Republicans a projected total of 134 House seats for the 98th Congress. Such an outcome would have exceeded the 1974 debacle, when Republicans won 41.5 percent of the votes and 144 seats.

The 1982 election of course fell far short of the Republican disaster the referendum model predicted. Republicans won 43.5 percent of the vote, higher than projected by 1.7 standard errors (the criterion for $p<.05$, one-tailed, is 1.65). The result was one the model would have predicted only if, given the economy, 60 rather than 42 percent of the public had approved Reagan's job performance or, given Reagan's approval rating, real income had grown by 3.4 percent rather than not growing at all. Democrats actually picked up 26 seats, less than half the number predicted. Their gains were also well below the 39 predicted by the seats/votes equation from the *actual* Republican vote, indicating that Republican votes were distributed more efficiently than usual.

As we expected, Republicans avoided disaster largely through the efforts of their strong and effective national party organization. One important aspect of their success we anticipated: the quality of their challengers was remarkably high, given national conditions; 24 percent of the Republican challengers in 1982 had previously held elective office. This is a higher proportion of experienced Republican challengers than had appeared in the much more promising years of 1972 or 1980.

Only one of these challengers actually won—in part because Republican contributors and party officials adopted a strictly defensive stance as the dimensions of the recession became clear—but they and the abundant funds controlled by the Republicans scared many Democratic incumbents into organizing much more expensive defensive campaigns than circumstances actually warranted. Democratic challengers were of the quality expected when national conditions strongly favor a party; indeed, a larger proportion of them (43 percent) had experience in elective office than had been the case in 1974. But money available to Democrats was absorbed—unnecessarily, as things developed—by worried incumbents. As a result, many of these promising candidacies were inadequately financed and so ultimately came up short.

Many Democratic incumbents who might otherwise have expected weak, underfinanced challengers in a year like 1982 evidently felt compelled to prepare for potentially formidable opposition. Memories of the 1980 election, in which a surprising number of apparently "safe" senior Democrats fell victim to lavishly financed Republican challenges, were still fresh enough to encourage caution. Caution occasionally assumed absurd proportions. As of June 30, Stephen Solarz of New York had $657,364 on hand; Charles Schumer of New York reported $480,711; Dan Rostenkowski of Illinois, $396,332.[19] All three of these incumbent Democrats had won easily in 1980 (the lowest vote share was 74 percent); all three won more than 80 percent of the vote in 1982.

Even if strong opposition did not materialize, enough uncertainty was created to prevent incumbents from relaxing their fundraising efforts until well into the campaign. Challengers were thus starved for funds during the crucial summer months. At midsummer, the average Democratic incumbent had raised seven times as much money as the average Democratic challenger.

As it turned out, an unconscionable amount of the money raised by Democratic incumbents was not even spent on the campaign. Solarz, Schumer, and Rostenkowski were the worst offenders, but they were not alone. The most recent Federal Election Commission figures list no fewer than 32 Democratic incumbents who reported having more than $100,000 on hand after the campaign; their unspent funds alone amount to more than $6.3 million.[20]

Democratic challengers also suffered from their party's relative poverty. Republican House candidates received more than $7 million from national party sources; Democrats were given less than $1 million. Thus the organizations with the strongest direct concern with encouraging successful Democratic challenges—indeed, the only ones that did not flagrantly favor incumbents when doling out assistance—generally lacked the resources to help challengers take advantage of Republican difficulties.

Some revealing summary data on campaign money is found in Table 13-2, which lists the average expenditures (in constant 1982 dollars) in House campaigns since 1972 by party and incumbency status. Compare the pattern of spending in 1982 to that of 1974, the last time national conditions favored Democrats strongly. In 1974, Democratic challengers spent more, on average, than Democratic incumbents; in 1982, incumbents spent twice as much as challengers. Republican money was obviously distributed more defensively in 1982 than in 1980, as we would expect. But Republican challengers were not neglected by contributors, again in sharp contrast to 1974.

Table 13-2 Average Campaign Expenditures by House Candidates, 1972-1982, by Party and Incumbency Status (in thousands of 1982 dollars)

Year and Party	*Incumbents*	*Challengers*	*Open Seats*
1972			
Democrats	115	70	234
Republicans	122	75	213
1974			
Democrats	91	117	204
Republicans	160	42	158
1976			
Democrats	136	77	248
Republicans	165	95	168
1978			
Democrats	167	107	320
Republicans	209	110	288
1980			
Democrats	196	81	223
Republicans	225	131	241
1982			
Democrats	246	127	266
Republicans	286	129	324

Note: Data for 1972-1980 include candidates with major party opposition only; data for 1982 include all general election candidates.

Source: Compiled by the author from data supplied by Common Cause (1972 and 1974) and the Federal Election Commission (1976-1982).

Republican organizational strength paid off in another important way, one which we did not fully anticipate. The Republicans' centralized control of extensive campaign resources allowed them to focus their efforts much more efficiently than would have been possible under the old decentralized campaign finance system (the kind still employed by the Democrats). During the final weeks of the campaign, Republican committees poured money and technical assistance into those races that their frequent tracking surveys told them would be very close. Nearly all of them involved Republican incumbents or candidates for open seats. The National Republican Congressional Committee paid about $2.5 million in bills for its House candidates in tight contests during this period. The post-election consensus among Democratic and Republican campaign officials was that this effort saved the Republicans from ten to twenty seats.[21]

The results of the 1982 election provide, we think, solid support for our theory. Republican losses were half what referendum models predict. To an important extent, national political conditions are transformed into aggregate election outcomes through the medium of elite career and contribution decisions.

In past elections, elite decisions have reinforced the expected effects of national forces; in 1982, in some important respects, they counteracted them.

National-level Republican organizations worked to resist the effect of bad times to the collective benefit of their party. They fostered stronger challenges than would otherwise have emerged and thereby put Democrats on the defensive, inducing incumbents to soak up resources that could otherwise have helped an impressive group of Democratic challengers. They used centralized control over money and skill to focus their effort where it would be most effective, helping threatened incumbents and candidates for open seats in tight races during the final weeks of the campaign. Their intervention manifestly disrupted the usual connection between national conditions and the alternatives presented to voters in individual districts and so helped materially to avoid a disastrous party defeat.

NOTES

1. Our discussion deals almost exclusively with House elections; although the basic arguments should apply to Senate elections as well, the special characteristics of Senate elections, structural and otherwise, make it impossible to perform the kind of systematic analysis we offer here. In 1982, for example, nineteen of the Senate seats up for election are held by Democrats, only thirteen by Republicans (and one by an independent), even though Republicans hold a majority of Senate seats. This will of course make it more difficult for Democrats to gain Senate seats quite independent of national forces.
2. See Jacobson and Kernell (1981) for a full review of these findings.
3. Lower inflation has probably kept real income from falling despite high unemployment and other components of the recession. The income tax cut and cost-of-living increase for social security recipients on July 1 will help add to real income later in the year, so it is reasonable to expect some overall growth in per capita income between 1981 and 1982.
4. Rudy Abramson and Larry Green, "Reagan's Long Coattails May Lead Fellow Republicans on a Bumpy Ride," *Los Angeles Times,* January 19, 1982, p. 9.
5. Harry Bernstein, "'82 Election Odds Not Rosy, Unionists Say," *Los Angeles Times,* February 18, 1982, p. 1.
6. Richard E. Cohen, "Congress: Control at Stake," *National Journal,* January 9, 1982, p. 66.
7. Adam Clymer, "GOP Candidates Lead in Fund-Raising Efforts," *New York Times,* May 16, 1982, p. 16.
8. "GOP Earmarks $63 Million for '82," *San Diego Union,* January 17, 1981, p. 18.
9. Adam Clymer, "GOP Worried About Impact of Job Figures," *New York Times,* January 15, 1982, p. 9.
10. Adam Clymer, "Those Who Recruit Candidates Say the Parties are Running About Even," *New York Times,* March 8, 1982, p. 4.
11. William C. Rempel and Larry Green, "Reagan Policy Facing Test in Midwest Votes," *Los Angeles Times,* March 8, 1982, p. 8.
12. Clymer, "Parties Are Running About Even," p. 4.
13. Adam Clymer, "GOP Recruiting in Missouri for House Contests," *New York Times,* February 13, 1982, p. 8.

14. Cohen, "Congress," p. 60.
15. Clymer, "GOP Recruiting," p. 8.
16. Clymer, "Parties Are Running About Even," p. 4.
17. Cohen, "Congress," p. 66.
18. Clymer, "Parties are Running About Even," p. 4.
19. Adam Clymer, "Light Wallets Weigh Heavily on Democrats," *New York Times,* October 17, 1983, p. E4.
20. See Federal Election Commission, *FEC Reports on Financial Activity 1981-1982, Interim Report No. 3: U.S. Senate and House Campaigns,* May 1983.
21. Adam Clymer, "Campaign Funds Called a Key to Outcome of House Races," *New York Times,* November 5, 1983, p. B10; Richard E. Cohen, "Giving Till It Hurts: 1982 Campaign Prompts New Look at Financing Races," *National Journal,* December 18, 1982, p. 2146.

14. PUBLIC AWARENESS OF CONGRESSIONAL CANDIDATES

Thomas E. Mann

Before assessing the impact of public perceptions of congressional candidates on individual vote choice and on electoral outcomes, I must first document what the public knows about the candidates. Donald Stokes and Warren Miller (1966) were impressed with how many voters in 1958 knew nothing at all about the candidates for the House of Representatives. Since the publication of their findings, no evidence has been presented to dispute the accuracy of this conclusion for the 1958 electorate or to support the view that the level of public information about congressional candidates has increased. The burden of proof is clearly on those who would argue that a significant part of the public is aware of the candidates.

The purpose of this chapter is to investigate the level and nature of public opinion in congressional elections, primarily by using surveys conducted for candidates by the Democratic Study Group in 1974 and 1976. The size of the "attentive public" in congressional elections and the content of their perceptions are the major targets of inquiry. I pay special attention to variations in candidate saliency—between incumbents and challengers, across districts, over time, and in response to the candidates' actions.

Candidate Saliency

In recent years the saliency of a congressional candidate has been taken to mean the proportion of the public that is able to recall his name. Stokes and Miller, however, conceived of candidate saliency in a broader context. The 1958 SRC Election Study questionnaire is the most extensive survey instrument dealing with public perceptions of Congress and congressional candidates ever administered to a national sample of U.S. citizens. In addition to including the item, "Do you happen to remember the name(s) of the candidate(s) for Congress that ran in this district this November?" (which has been repeated in most SRC/CPS election studies since that time), the 1958 questionnaire instructed the interviewers to provide respondents with the names of the candidates when asking them, "Now we're interested in knowing what sorts of persons people think these candidates are. Have you read or heard anything about (name of candidate)?"

The responses to the latter question provided the measure of saliency used by Stokes and Miller; it also served as a screen for a series of additional questions assaying the public's knowledge of the candidates. On its face this measure of saliency appears to be less demanding than the more conventional recall question alluded to above—it is easier to remember reading or hearing about a particular candidate than it is to remember his name. Yet just the reverse was true: more respondents correctly recalled the names of the candidates than indicated having read or heard anything about them.[1] In spite of their use of an "easier" test of saliency, Stokes and Miller might still have underestimated public awareness of the candidates by using this question formula.[2]

Name Recall

Most investigators of candidate saliency since Stokes and Miller have relied upon measures of name recall, not candidate awareness. Gallup and Harris have normally asked, "Do you happen to know the name of the congressman from your district?" while the SRC/CPS format is "Do you happen to remember the names of the candidates for Congress that ran in this district this November?" Table 14-1 contains a number of time series on candidate saliency, all based on

Table 14-1 Congressional Candidate Saliency Measures: Name Recall Data from National Surveys, 1942-1976 (in percentages)

			Ferejohn (SRC/CPS)		*Cover (SRC/CPS)*	
Year	*Gallup, Incumbent*	*Harris, Incumbent*	*Incumbent*	*Non-Incumbent*	*Incumbent*	*Non-Incumbent*
1942	50					
1947	42					
1957	35					
1958			58	38	44	28
1964			63	40	52	32
1966	46		56	38	40	23
1968			64	47	50	34
1970	53		55	31	35	16
1972					36	19
1973		46				
1974					34	16
1976		50				

Note: The Gallup and Harris entries are percentages of all respondents in a national survey who recalled the name of their congressman. The Ferejohn entries are percentages of voters in all contested seats who recalled the names of the candidates. The Cover entries are percentages of all respondents in seats contested by an incumbent who recalled the names of the candidates.

Source: The Gallup data are reported in Cover (1976, p. 56). The Harris data are taken from surveys commissioned by the Congress—in 1973 by the Senate Subcommittee on Intergovernmental Relations, in 1976 by the House Commission on Administrative Review. The Ferejohn data are taken from Ferejohn (1977, p. 170). The Cover data are computed from table 2.9 (1976, p. 58).

name recall. The differences in the findings for a given year stem primarily from differences in the bases used; while Ferejohn's figures are derived from voters in all contested seats, for example, Cover's come from voters and nonvoters in all seats contested by an incumbent. Obviously, Cover's figures are depressed by the inclusion of less attentive (nonvoting) members of the electorate.

Several things are apparent from these data. Incumbents are better known than nonincumbents; their advantage has remained roughly constant, around twenty percentage points, over the last two decades. There has been no increase in candidate name recall over this period; the decline that appears in Cover's data beginning in 1970 might be concentrated among nonvoters. In general, more than half of those voting in congressional elections are able to recall the name of the incumbent and a third or more recall the nonincumbent's name. These figures are slightly higher in presidential election years, when the level of political communication substantially increases.

How do these national figures distribute over congressional districts? Is the name recall advantage of incumbents uniform, or is the distribution about the mean as notable as the mean itself? Table 14-2 summarizes the name recall readings obtained from surveys of likely voters conducted by the Democratic Study Group in twenty-eight margin districts just prior to the 1976 election. (The name recall question used was roughly the same as that used by Gallup and SRC/CPS.) The mean incumbent, challenger, and incumbent-advantage scores computed for the twenty-four districts that were contested by an incumbent are close to Ferejohn's most recent figures, although the DSG figures, since they are taken from preelection surveys, no doubt underestimate the public visibility of candidates, especially challengers, on election day. But the district survey allows us to see the considerable variation in these figures across congressional districts.

Most important, they show that, while incumbents generally have an impressive name recall advantage, in a few cases their advantage is almost nil.

Table 14-2 Congressional Candidate Saliency Measures: Name Recall Data from Preelection District Surveys, 1976 (in percentages; "advantage" figures in percentage points)

Type of Seat and Candidate	*District Mean*	*Range*
Seats contested by incumbents (N = 24)		
Incumbents	50	26 to 78
Challengers	25	5 to 63
Incumbent advantage	25	1 to 45
Open seats (N = 4)		
Candidates	22	11 to 38
Candidate advantage	4	0 to 6

Note: Incumbent advantage is defined as the percentage incumbent minus the percentage challenger. Candidate advantage is the absolute difference between the scores of the two candidates in an open seat.

Source: DSG surveys.

The name recall difference between opposing candidates in open seats, on the other hand, is exceedingly small.

The determinants of differences in levels of candidate name recall are difficult to unravel given the limited number of cases available for analysis. One primary determinant appears to be the nature of the media market in the given congressional district. At one extreme are districts embedded in very large metropolitan areas where public service coverage and paid political advertising of incumbents and challengers are severely restricted. This situation can apply to an entire state—New Jersey has no state-based television programming at all. At the other extreme are congressional districts whose boundaries are contiguous with a natural media market, assuring a reasonable amount of free coverage and cost-effective rates for paid advertising; Toledo, Ohio, is one such. In between these extremes are districts whose media markets present various opportunities and obstacles. A candidate's success in overcoming the obstacles depends in part on the availability of campaign funds and on his public relations skills. The three lowest name recall scores for incumbents were registered in districts that are located in greater metropolitan Los Angeles, New York City, and Chicago, and incumbents from New Jersey were well below the mean. Since all television and daily newspaper outlets in these districts blanket the entire metropolitan area, news coverage of congressional contests is limited and the cost of paid advertising prohibitive. The three highest name recall scores were obtained by congressmen whose districts entirely encompass middle-sized cities that have their own television stations and newspapers. This relationship can be verified by dividing the sample districts into three rough categories according to media access and then computing the mean name recall score for incumbents and challengers in each. The relationship can be verified by dividing the sample districts into three rough categories according to media access and then computing the mean name recall score for incumbents and challengers in each. The resulting figures meet every expectation: the mean name recall score for incumbents in districts with good media access is 61 percent; in districts with fair media access, 50 percent; in those with poor access, 41 percent. The comparable figures for challengers are 42 percent, 24 percent, and 17 percent.

Yet levels of candidate name recall are also influenced by the efforts of the candidates themselves. Another incumbent from the Chicago metropolitan area, who faced the same structural media problems as the congressman referred to above, was twenty-three percentage points ahead of his colleague on name recall. In the Washington, D.C. area two freshmen congressmen whose districts lie side by side had scores twenty percentage points apart. More dramatic evidence of the candidate's impact on his own saliency can be seen from the relative visibility of the challengers. The highest name recall figures for challengers were recorded by former incumbents, former challengers, and first-time candidates who invested heavily in cost-effective mass media. While the lowest challenger scores were found in the major metropolitan areas, many candidates in more attractive media markets also rated poorly on name recall.

There is some evidence that name recall increases with seniority, whatever the structure of the media market, although there are too few senior incumbents in my sample to test this proposition definitively. In several districts, freshman congressmen registered impressive gains in the year preceding their first reelection attempt after they sharply stepped up their use of mass mailings.

. . . [It] is probably unwise to rely exclusively on this single measure of candidate saliency [candidate name recall]. Several scholars have demonstrated that name recall cannot account for the increased ability of incumbents to attract partisan defectors; in the districts surveyed by the DSG, several candidates won in spite of the fact that fewer voters recalled their names than recalled their opponents' names.

An illustration from recent electoral history vividly demonstrates the limitations of this measure. In the summer of 1976 Representative Alan Howe, a first-term member of the House from Utah, was arrested in Salt Lake City for attempting to buy sexual favors from a policewoman disguised as a prostitute. The story attracted immediate national attention, and it remained in the news for some time as the drama of Howe's trial and his decision whether to stand for reelection unfolded. If ever a congressman was "salient," Alan Howe was in the summer of 1976. Yet when asked in August, "Can you tell me the name of your congressman," only 41 percent of a sample of his district's likely voters correctly identified Howe. This measure in no sense captured the level of public awareness of this congressman, nor did it elicit the direction and nature of the public's response to him. Table 14-3 presents figures summarizing Howe's visibility and popularity in November 1975 and August 1976. When presented with his name in August, virtually all respondents indicated that they recognized Howe; 73 percent reacted to him in a negative or positive way; and 65 percent provided a favorable or unfavorable rating of the job he was doing as a congressman. The pub-

Table 14-3 Visibility and Popularity of Representative Alan Howe, November 1975 and August 1976 (in percentages of respondents)

Measure	*November 1975*	*August 1976*
Name recall	19	41
Simple recognition	89	99
Thermometer		
Positive	31	12
Neutral	38	22
Negative	6	61
Job rating		
Favorable	43	29
Unfavorable	25	36

Note: Simple recognition is defined as 100 percent minus those who said they did not recognize Howe when asked to describe their feelings toward him on a five-point feeling thermometer. (They were explicitly instructed to say they did not recognize him if that were the case.) Positive, neutral, and negative scores were obtained directly from the five-point feeling thermometer on which one and two are negative, three is neutral, and four and five are positive. Favorable job rating includes "excellent" and "pretty good" responses to the question, "How would you rate the job Alan Howe is doing as congressman: excellent, pretty good, only fair, or poor?" "Only fair" and "poor" responses constitute an unfavorable job rating. The sequence of these items on the questionnaire was as follows: name recall, thermometer (with no prior mention of office or party), and job rating (with no prior mention of party).

Source: DSG surveys.

lic response to Howe's arrest was just what we would have guessed, but the traditional name recall measure could not accurately record it.

Name Recognition

At the very least, then, saliency measures must allow for the fact that some voters who are unable to recall the name of a candidate can still recognize the name when presented with it and can respond to it in a positive or negative fashion. What is the evidence on simple recognition of incumbents and challengers? The data summarized in Table 14-4 reveal that the electorate is more aware of congressional candidates than was previously thought. In thirty-one congressional districts surveyed by the DSG, virtually all voters recognized the name of the incumbent when they heard it, and most had a positive or negative response.

In 1974 the survey respondents were first read a list of names and asked to indicate whether or not they recognized each; if the answer was yes, they were then asked whether they had a generally favorable or unfavorable opinion of that person. The six districts contested by incumbents were all represented by

Table 14-4 Name Recognition of Congressional Candidates, 1974 and 1976 (in percentages; "advantage" figures in percentage points)

	Simple Recognition		*Positive or Negative Response*	
District Type and Year	*Mean*	*Range*	*Mean*	*Range*
Incumbent-contested seats				
1974 (*N* = 6 districts)				
Incumbents	98	94 to 100	78	66 to 87
Challengers	85	77 to 92	47	38 to 60
Incumbent advantage	14	6 to 22	30	16 to 44
1976 (*N* = 25 districts)				
Incumbents	92	74 to 98	61	35 to 77
Challengers	68	47 to 96	33	20 to 64
Incumbent advantage	25	−2 to 52	28	−1 to 52
Open seats				
1974 (*N* = 4 districts)				
Candidates	76	46 to 97	42	15 to 59
Candidate advantage	21	5 to 44	10	0 to 43
1976 (*N* = 4 districts)				
Candidates	76	62 to 97	41	26 to 63
Candidate advantage	7	0 to 22	10	1 to 30

Note: The 1976 measures of simple recognition and positive or negative response are defined in Table 14-3. The 1974 measures are described in the text. Incumbent advantage is defined as the percentage incumbent minus the percentage challenger. Candidate advantage is the absolute difference between the scores of the two candidates in an open seat.

Source: DSG surveys.

relatively senior Republicans who were subsequently defeated by their Democratic challengers in November. The mean incumbent advantage was fourteen percentage points for simple recognition and double that for recognition with evaluation. In these districts about 20 percent of the respondents in the case of incumbents and almost 40 percent for challengers claimed to recognize the name of the candidate but were unable to express a favorable or unfavorable view of him. This combination of responses is not entirely inconceivable—voters might recognize a candidate but be genuinely indifferent to him. It is likely that some respondents, however, claim to recognize names they don't know in order to appear informed or to please the interviewer. One means of checking this possibility is to see what recognition levels are recorded for candidates with very little or no public exposure. A good example can be found in a normally safe Democratic district in Michigan where in 1974 a senior incumbent faced a political unknown with virtually no organizational backing from his party or civic groups and with total campaign expenditures of under $1,000. A mid-September 1974 survey of likely voters in the district revealed that 84 percent did not recognize the candidate's name and only 4 percent had a favorable or unfavorable view of him. Even if one assumed that in this case the over-reporting of recognition were as high as ten percentage points, the error would not have to be regarded as intolerably high.

In 1976 respondents in twenty-five districts were asked to express their feelings toward the candidates on a five-point feeling thermometer that included an explicit neutral point. (They were instructed to say so if they did not recognize the name.) Twenty of the twenty-five districts were represented by first-term incumbents—hence the slightly lower simple-recognition score than was recorded for the relatively senior incumbents in the 1974 sample; the figures for the two years become comparable when only the five more senior incumbents in 1976 are included. However, the mean differences between 1974 and 1976 in the percentage of those who rate the candidates either positively or negatively stem partly from the different measures used in the two years; the 1976 measure is probably a better indicator of the attentive public. The incumbency advantage in visibility is equally decisive in 1976, although apparently it is possible for as few as a third of the voters to have positive or negative feelings toward an incumbent and a fifth toward a challenger in a marginal seat. Of course, the norm is a good deal higher and the variation across districts is substantial. The constraints on visibility imposed by the structure of the media are less telling for simple name recognition than for evaluative responses to candidates.

The visibility of candidates in open seats was about the same as that of challengers in districts with incumbents running, but the advantage of one candidate over another in open seats was much less than an incumbent's advantage over his challenger in 1976. In 1974 the relationship was just the opposite for simple recognition: the leading candidate in an open seat had a much larger advantage over his opponent than the incumbent had over his challenger in a contested one. Obviously, there are too few open seats in the sample to permit generalization.

The district surveys also reveal that the public awareness of serious and active nonincumbent candidates rises in the course of the campaign; simple-recognition increases of as high as fifty-five percentage points were observed in one district over a six-month period. Shifts are less dramatic for candidates who begin with a measure of visibility—former incumbents, well-known local officials, and so on. Since most of the surveys were conducted anywhere from two to six weeks prior to the election, the figures in Table 14-4 no doubt understate the visibility of the candidates—especially nonincumbents—on election day.[3]

Of course, these measures tell us nothing about the content of the public's perception of the candidates. At this point all I have demonstrated is that most voters recognize the candidates for the House and many are able to express some feeling toward them. How they feel and what they see are different matters entirely. Three types of measures can be used to discern the direction and content of public perceptions of the candidates. Generalized effect is captured nicely by candidate feeling thermometers. Evaluations of the performance of the incumbent in office are gathered by standard job-rating measures. More specific elements of the image conveyed by the candidate to the public—personal characteristics, ideology, positions on issues—require a variety of measures.

Reputation

Donald Stokes and Warren Miller (1966, p. 205), investigating public perceptions of congressional candidates in 1958, found that, "In the main, recognition carries a positive valence; to be perceived at all is to be perceived favorably." Evidence from the 1974 and 1976 district surveys supports an alternative view: while on balance most candidates are viewed positively, some evoke distinctly negative reactions from the electorate. A version of the CPS five-point feeling thermometer, adapted for use in the DSG telephone surveys, was used in 1976 to measure feelings toward the candidates; in 1974 the simpler measure ("Do you have a generally favorable or unfavorable opinion of [name of candidate]") was employed. Table 14-5 shows the range of feelings about incumbents and challengers in thirty-one districts in 1974 and 1976. When interpreting these figures, it is important to bear in mind the differences between 1974 and 1976, both in terms of the sample (senior Republican incumbents who lost in 1974; primarily first-term Democratic incumbents who won in 1976) and in terms of the measures (no explicit neutral point in 1974). The 1974 figures reveal a sizable range in the reputation of incumbents, an incumbent advantage over challengers in the actual percentage of respondents rating the candidates positively, but a clear edge for the challengers in the relative number of positive and negative rankings. The incumbents had both more friends and more enemies than the challengers. In 1976 the incumbents held a clear advantage in visibility and reputation, lending support to the view that incumbents do well at the polls partly because the voters know and like them more than their challengers. These data suggest that public perceptions of challengers are important for understanding both the success of typical incumbents and the exceptions.

When the neutral, don't know, and no answer categories are excluded, the incumbents in 1974 and 1976 have equal ratings while the challengers are twenty percentage points apart; thus the difference in incumbent advantage in 1974 and 1976 stemmed entirely from the challenger ratings. And the latter, higher among the Democratic challengers in 1974 than among the primarily Republican challengers in 1976, is consistent with the strong national Democratic tide in 1974. While partisan feelings may be partly responsible for the high positive ratings of the Democratic challengers in 1974, it is important to remember that

Table 14-5 Feelings Toward Congressional Candidates in 31 Districts, 1974 and 1976 (in percentages; "advantage" figures in percentage points)

	Positive Feelings					
	All respondents		*Respondents excluding neutral, don't know, and no answer*		*Negative Feelings, All Respondents*	
Year and Candidate	*Mean*	*Range*	*Mean*	*Range*	*Mean*	*Range*
1974 (N = 6 districts)						
Incumbents	54	39 to 63	70	53 to 79	24	16 to 35
Challengers	38	32 to 49	81	77 to 84	9	6 to 11
Incumbent advantage	15	6 to 31	−11	−3 to 26	15	5 to 26
1976 (N = 25 districts)						
Incumbents	42	22 to 60	70	55 to 84	18	9 to 29
Challengers	17	8 to 39	51	32 to 76	16	6 to 32
Incumbent advantage	25	4 to 46	19	−7 to 46	3	−10 to 19

Note: The five-point feeling thermometer was used to ascertain positive and negative feelings in 1976; the question, "Do you have a generally favorable or unfavorable opinion of (NAME OF CANDIDATE)," with no explicit neutral point, was used in 1974. The positive and negative entries for all respondents are absolute percentages. The two middle columns, from which neutral, don't know, and don't recognize are excluded, show the balance of positive to negative feelings:

$$\frac{\%\ \text{positive}}{\%\ \text{positive} + \%\ \text{negative}}.$$

Source: DSG surveys.

Table 14-6 Feelings Toward Incumbents, by Party Identification, 1976 (in percentages)

Respondent's Party Identification	*Positive Feelings*		*Negative Feelings*	
	Mean	*Range*	*Mean*	*Range*
Incumbent's party	61	54 to 74	9	4 to 17
Independent	43	32 to 52	16	4 to 28
Challenger's party	30	21 to 41	31	15 to 47
(N = 10 districts)				

Note: Feelings were recorded on the five-point feeling thermometer.

Source: DSG surveys.

the measure of feelings toward the candidates was taken without reference to party or office. If party was a determining force, it was mediated by public knowledge of and feelings toward individual candidates.

The differences in public support among incumbents are not simply an artifact of the number of partisans in each district; the variation is large among incumbent parties, Independents, and those who identify with the challenger's party (see Table 14-6). Incumbents do uniformly well among their own partisans, but their ability to evoke a positive response from Independents and those who identify with the challenger's party varies widely.

Finally, candidate ratings change over time. In 1974, senior incumbents saw their ratings deteriorate in the face of opposition during the campaign. Many first-term incumbents improved their reputations considerably in the year prior to the 1976 campaign. Challengers' ratings improved or deteriorated depending on the visibility and success of their campaigns.

Job Ratings

The public sometimes differentiates between a generalized feeling toward a political figure and an assessment of his performance in office. A good illustration of this is found in public attitudes toward Gerald Ford during his tenure as president: many more people had warm feelings toward him than approved of the job he was doing as a president. Job ratings for six congressmen in 1974 and twenty-two congressmen in 1976 are set forth in Table 14-7. Once again we see that most voters are able to judge the performance of congressmen in office and that their judgments are not uniform. The range in favorable ratings—about twenty percentage points in 1974 and thirty in 1976—is comparable to that recorded on the feeling thermometer. The six senior Republican incumbents in 1974 more than matched the mean favorable job ratings of the twenty-two incumbents in 1976 (eighteen of whom were freshmen Democrats), but the former group were also ahead by an average of eight percentage points in unfavorable ratings. If the four nonfreshmen in 1976 are excluded, the difference is even more pronounced. It seems that senior incumbents in marginal districts

Table 14-7 Job Ratings of Congressmen, 1974 and 1976 (in percentages)

Year	*Favorable*		*Unfavorable*	
	Mean	*Range*	*Mean*	*Range*
1974 (*N* = 6 districts)	55	41 to 62	38	30 to 51
1976 (*N* = 22 districts)	52	34 to 64	30	13 to 42

Note: For the survey question, see Table 14-3. The mean percentage of respondents who were unable to evaluate the job performance of their congressmen was 7 percent in 1974 and 18 percent in 1976.

Source: DSG surveys.

who face serious opposition are more likely to evoke unfavorable public reactions than first-term incumbents in similar situations. Familiarity can breed contempt. Only one of the twenty-eight incumbents received an overall unfavorable job rating: he had become especially visible in 1974 as a member of the House Judiciary Committee asserting the innocence of Richard Nixon, and his job ratings and electoral fortunes had suffered as a consequence.

Candidate Image

Mass public knowledge of congressional candidates declines precipitously once we move beyond simple recognition, generalized feelings, and incumbent job ratings. No clearer demonstration of this fact is to be found than in public responses to open-ended questions about the candidates. Stokes and Miller (1966, p. 207) pointed out some years ago that "the popular image of the Congressman is almost barren of policy content. A long series of open-ended questions asked of those who said they had any information about the Representative produced mainly a collection of diffuse evaluative judgments: he is a good man; he is experienced; he knows the problems; he has done a good job; and the like." Years later Abramowitz (1975, p. 678) found much the same thing in his survey of public opinion in an Oregon congressional district: some respondents mentioned the incumbent's issue positions and constituency services, but half of the comments referred to his personal qualities.

The format and purpose of the DSG candidate surveys prevented consistent use of open-ended questions, but the results obtained in two districts where they were used, both represented by freshmen congressmen, were in accord with earlier findings. Just under half of the respondents were unable to provide a reason for liking or disliking the incumbent. In both districts favorable comments about the incumbent outnumbered unfavorable ones by better than three to one. The respondents who did comment emphasized primarily either personal qualities or relationships with constituents. The number of references to issues was very small by comparison, and they were disproportionately negative, which suggests that when issues are sufficiently salient to affect the public's image of the incumbent, they probably do the incumbent more harm than good.

Another way of getting at the candidates' public images is to ask respondents to judge the accuracy of a series of personal characterizations of the candidates. This might take the form of either, "Do you think Congressman X is ______?" or "Which candidate for Congress, X the Republican or Y the Democrat, do you think is more ______?" This question format allows the researcher to discern whether the public perceives the candidates in terms of the same attributes that the candidates themselves have attempted to present to the public. The difficulty is the confounding presence of nonattitudes—do the responses reflect real perceptions or are they merely guesses? One way of validating the pattern of responses is to look for a high degree of discrimination, either in the respondents' assessments of different characteristics for the same candidate or in their assessments of the same characteristic for different candidates. The degree to which a candidate evokes atypical responses compared to other candidates or responses that are highly differentiated over a number of image components is another measure of candidate saliency.

Of course the initial hurdle—responding affirmatively or negatively to the personal-characterization question or judging which candidate most clearly has the stated quality—must be crossed before a pattern of responses can be analyzed. The percentage of respondents who "don't know" (DK) ranges from 15 to 75 percent, roughly in this order: long-term incumbents, 15 to 25 percent DK; new incumbents, 20 to 45 percent DK; challengers with prior exposure, 40 to 60 percent DK; and new challengers, 60 to 75 percent DK. Specific placement within these ranges is a function of the individual candidate and of the type of attribute. For example, in 1976 the average percentage of respondents who didn't know whether a series of personal qualities accurately fit one freshman congresswoman was 20 percent; the average "don't know" response for another freshman congresswoman was 45 percent. Part of this difference can be attributed to the extent of media access in each district (the latter represented a district in which the use of television was virtually impossible), part to the initiative and skill of the individuals. The number of respondents unable to comment is sensitive also to the nature of the characterization. The percentage responding "yes" or "no" on qualities like "honest" and "hard working" and "listens to the people" is uniformly higher than the percentage for qualities like "doesn't care about the environment" or "is too friendly with the banking industry." The same candidate might evoke only 20 percent DK responses to questions about his character but 50 percent DK to questions about his policy stands. It seems that the public has sufficient information (or is willing to assume the best) about candidates' overall integrity and responsiveness, but that it is largely unaware of these candidates' performance in specific policy areas.

Several examples show that the public is able to judge congressional candidates on several attributes. In 1974 a senior Republican incumbent who had long enjoyed a reputation for excellent constituency service faced a challenger whose campaign focused primarily on "good government" issues—disclosure of campaign contributions and personal income, sunshine in congressional committees, and the like. A survey taken six weeks before the election revealed that while only 6 percent of the respondents took the incumbent to task for not working hard enough and 11 percent found him lacking in honesty, 47 percent believed him to be "too close to special interests." This is precisely the view of the incumbent that had been articulated for many years by his Democratic challengers; it seems that some of the voters were listening.

Another illustration is drawn from a Midwestern urban district represented for many years by a Democrat. After repeatedly winning reelection by wide margins, this incumbent almost lost in 1974 despite the strong national tides favoring the Democratic party. In 1976 he faced the same Republican challenger, whose campaign once again emphasized the importance of change and the need for congressional reform. The Democratic incumbent countered with a strong attack on the personal stability and qualifications of the challenger. A survey of likely voters found that while most believed the Democrat to be "more qualified to hold public office" (55 percent to 16 percent), a large plurality of voters (44 percent to 27 percent) thought the Republican challenger "would try hardest to reform Congress." Once again, public opinion reflected the images articulated by the candidates.

A third example involves a first-term Democrat who had unseated a Republican incumbent after the latter had spent two terms in the House. The Democrat, a political neophyte prior to her narrow victory in 1974, faced the same opponent in her first reelection bid. One month before the election the Republican was perceived to be "more experienced" (55 percent to 18 percent) while the Democrat was judged "more honest" (40 percent to 11 percent) and "more likely to try to help people around here" (58 percent to 20 percent). In this case a large number of voters knew that the Republican had considerable experience in office, at least more than the Democrat. Yet they were able to differentiate experience from responsiveness or attractiveness on other qualities.

In all three cases, the qualities (or alleged qualities) of the candidates that were part of the political dialogue in the constituency became elements of the candidate images perceived by the public. No detailed knowledge of the candidates was required of voters, only the barest recognition and general sense of the candidates conveyed in the media. Obviously the entire electorate did not respond to these images, but at least a third to half were sufficiently aware to hold a multifaceted view of the candidates. It appears that the public was able to discriminate between the contenders and that its views make sense in the light of what we know about the candidates.

In all of these districts the campaigns were lively and hard-fought. The pattern of public responses to candidate images in other districts is much more uniform. In the absence of any controversial actions that focus public attention on the incumbent and lacking a challenger who attacks the personal failings of his opponent or dramatically embodies an alternative, candidate images consist solely of positive or (much less frequently) negative recognition. The range in negative responses to personal characterizations of a single candidate or in the advantage of a candidate over his opponent in these districts is barely ten percentage points, compared with the forty to fifty percentage-point range for the salient candidates discussed above. Incumbents have a distinct advantage in districts where the public's view is undifferentiated; constituents generally believe their representative is honest and responsive and concerned about their problems, and this is usually enough to stem criticism on substantive grounds.[4]

Assessments of the same personal quality over a number of districts seem to vary less. For example, the range in negative assessments of whether candidates were "hard working" was six percentage points and whether they were "honest," ten percentage points. In 1974, larger differences were obtained for "rubberstamp for President Nixon" (fourteen percentage points) and "too conservative" (twenty-two percentage points), neither of which can be explained simply by the number of partisans in each district. Apparently candidates can act to heighten the public's association between themselves and national political figures or broad ideological positions.

Ideology

This raises a related question: To what extent is the electorate aware of the general ideological stance of congressional candidates and how important is this for individual vote choice and for electoral outcomes? In practical politics, the electoral relevance of a candidate's ideology is taken as self-evident. The ideological complexion of a district is thought to impose constraints on a candidate that, if he violates them, mean his defeat. For example, it is often said that, Democrats from the Eastern Shore of Maryland are socially and economically conservative; a liberal candidate hasn't a chance of victory there. Democrats from North Carolina, Tennessee, Indiana, and New Jersey first elected to the House in 1974 by defeating Republican incumbents speak openly of the importance of living within the predominant ideological orientation of their districts, and their voting in Congress reflects that decision.

Yet there are many reasons why we would expect not to find much evidence in public opinion of an ideological influence on congressional voting. The first is the extensive body of research demonstrating the nonideological character of political thinking in the mass public. We know that most citizens' orientation to parties and political figures has little ideological content, changes in the 1960s and 1970s notwithstanding. Second, ideology is not unidimensional. At the very least, ideology encompasses cultural, economic, and foreign policy dimensions, and candidates are often as ideologically inconsistent in these areas as the public. Third, ideology would not enter the electorate's calculus if both candidates were ideologically acceptable. In this sense, ideology serves as a screen in the recruitment of candidates; after the recruitment stage, it is effectively removed from the political debate. Fourth, candidates' ideological stances might be perceived only by the most politically attentive stratum. What reaches the mass public might be a simple positive or negative message devoid of ideological content. Under these circumstances, ideology is very important electorally to candidates, but scarcely a trace of its influence can be detected in public opinion.

No attempt was made in the DSG candidate surveys to determine the levels of conceptualization of the electorate. Rather, respondents were asked either to describe the political views of the candidates as liberal, moderate, or conservative or to judge whether a candidate was too liberal or too conservative. No doubt these labels have very different meanings for different people, but they do provide some measure of whether congressional candidates are ideologically visible to the public. Table 14-8 shows the extent to which congressional electorates were able to describe candidates as liberal, moderate, or conservative. While on the average

Table 14-8 Public Awareness of the Ideological Stance of Congressional Candidates, 1974 and 1976 (in percentages; "advantage" figures in percentage points)

	Respondents Describing Candidate as Liberal, Moderate, or Conservative	
Type of Seat and Candidate	*Mean*	*Range*
Seats contested by incumbents (N = 12)		
Incumbents	73	63 to 89
Challengers		
Former incumbents (N = 2)	69	66 to 73
Other (N = 10)	43	28 to 50
Incumbent advantage	28	−3 to 43
Open seats (N = 12)		
Candidates	42	15 to 43

Note: Incumbent advantage is defined as the percentage describing the incumbent as liberal, moderate, or conservative minus the percentage describing his challenger as liberal, moderate, or conservative.

Source: DSG surveys.

three-quarters of the public was able to label incumbents in this fashion, no more than half could describe the ideological stance of challengers, except when the challenger was a former incumbent. The average ideological-visibility advantage of incumbents over challengers was twenty-eight percentage points; in open seats the mean difference between candidates was twelve percentage points.

Of course, these perceptions might be nothing more than guesses—rationalizations whereby voters project their own ideological views onto the candidates—or routine expressions of partisan loyalties. In fact, there is some evidence of obvious misperception—5 percent of the respondents in one district described a very conservative incumbent as liberal and 6 percent in another district labelled a liberal challenger as conservative. Overall, however, the balance of ideological perceptions for each candidate makes sense.[5] This fact is due partly but not entirely to the mediation of party labels. If we examine only the balance of liberal to conservative ratings, a clear party difference emerges (see Table 14-9). For Democratic candidates the average difference is nine percentage points more liberal than conservative ratings, while for Republican candidates it is sixteen percentage points more conservative; the mean liberal/conservative difference between incumbents and challengers is twenty-five percentage points. (Remember, these percentages are computed on a base of all respondents, including those who describe the candidate as moderate or who "don't know.") Once again, there is considerable variation about the mean for each party. The most conservative Democratic candidate received the most conservative rating among Democrats; the most liberal Republican candidate received the most liberal rating among Republicans. The absolute liberal/conservative difference

Table 14-9 Liberal/Conservative Images of Congressional Candidates, 1976 (in percentage points)

Candidate's Party	*Percentage "Liberal" Minus Percentage "Conservative"*	
	Mean	*Range*
Democrat	9	—10 to 25
Republican	−16	5 to −34
Absolute difference (*N* = 8 districts)	25	0 to 39

Source: DSG surveys.

between incumbents and challengers ranged from zero to thirty-nine percentage points.

The figures reported in Table 14-9 are derived entirely from 1976 surveys in which a three-point liberal, moderate, and conservative scale was used. In 1974 the Republican incumbent who most vocally and visibly advertised his credentials was described by 70 percent of the voters in his district as "somewhat conservative" or "very conservative." The public seems to respond predictably when the signals from the candidates are sufficiently clear.

This difference among candidates is maintained when the form of the question is altered. The percentage of respondents who demonstrated ideological distance from candidates by responding affirmatively to the question "Do you think (name of candidate) is 'too liberal'?" or ("too conservative") ranged from 5 percent to 32 percent.

There is certainly enough evidence here to warrant an investigation of the influence of ideology on congressional voting. . . .

Issues

Assessing the impact of specific issues on voting in congressional elections is more problematic. The requirements for policy voting discussed by Warren Miller and his colleagues (Campbell, Converse, Miller and Stokes, 1960, chap. 8) and by Richard Brody and Benjamin Page (1972) (the issue must be salient to the voters, the candidates must be perceived to take different issue positions, the voters must have real issue preferences, and the voters must choose the most proximate candidate) are much more rarely met at the congressional than at the presidential level. A major stumbling block to policy voting in congressional elections is the requirement that the candidates be perceived to take different positions on a given issue. In order for candidates to be so perceived, they must visibly disagree on issues that are highly salient to the voters. But many of the incentives that influence candidates invite agreement, not disagreement. John Kingdon (1973, chap. 2) has demonstrated that, through the mechanisms of recruitment and "explaining"—justifying their votes before constituent groups—congressmen most often adopt the dominant constituency opinion, in so far as it can be determined. This is especially true for salient local issues such as busing, farm policy, and gun control. Challengers in particular have little to gain by taking opposing positions and articulating their differences with the incumbent.[6] In the absence of the necessary political communication, the public remains unaware of the positions of the candidates. Their becoming aware usually means trouble: as Kingdon (1973, p. 40) puts it, "If constituents were better informed, it would probably be a mark of arousal over something that the congressman did which was out of keeping with their strongly held beliefs."

The public's ignorance of the positions congressional candidates take on issues can be largely explained by the way in which the candidates themselves exploit the issues. In addition to respecting whatever policy constraints are imposed by mass opinion in their constituencies, candidates often avoid taking ideological positions in dealing with issues. They are inclined to emphasize their interest in reducing inflation *and* restoring the economy to full-employment, cutting wasteful government spending *and* maintaining a strong national defense, preventing abuses by public bureaucracies *and* by private corporations. More attention is paid to consensual goals than divisive means. All this does little to educate the public on the respective positions of the candidates. Candidates also use issues more to demonstrate their competence than to spell out clear positions on substance. The manner in which they deal with issues is more likely to be conveyed to the public than the content of their commitments. Of course, elites pay attention to the positions of candidates, and issues are very important for attracting and maintaining core supporters, financial resources, and volunteers. But none of this necessarily informs the mass public about where a candidate stands on a specific issue.

Most of the candidates for whom DSG surveys were commissioned expected policy voting to be relatively unimportant in their races. For this reason no systematic measures of issue proximity were gathered in the DSG surveys. What little evidence is available confirms the view that most voters are unaware of the issue positions of the candidates. I have already discussed the paucity of references to issues in the responses to open-ended questions about the candidates. Even on controversial issues such as abortion and gun control, 70 to 80 percent of the voters surveyed in 1976 did not know the positions of the candidates for Congress. Seven out of every ten voters in a congressional district represented by a very visible Republican member of the House Judiciary Committee did not know what position he had taken on the Nixon pardon, although most were aware of his views on impeachment. At the height of the busing controversy in the Detroit suburbs, two-fifths of the voters in one congressional district had no idea what position their congressman had taken on the issue and three-fourths were unaware of the challenger's position. In this case, the voters' cues were confusing, because busing was both a national *and* a local issue, and because both congressional candidates opposed busing while the Democratic presidential candidate and the senior Democratic senator were on record in favor. The issue worked to the detriment of the Democratic congressional candidates in the Detroit area without the requirements for policy voting being met at the constituency level.

This last example demonstrates that issues can operate in very complex ways to influence the vote for Congress. Ultimately however, we should be able to trace the effect of an issue as it is mediated by feelings toward the congressional candidates or, at the national level, by assessments of the presidential candidates or incumbent administration. A more direct assessment of the role of issues is not possible given the limitations of the data.

Although the public's knowledge of congressional candidates is limited, the evidence presented in this chapter cautions against exaggerating the ignorance of the congressional electorate. The public responds to the political communication about the candidates that reaches its attention. When the major media in a congressional district convey little information about the candidates and when the candidates themselves fail to openly articulate clear differences, public awareness is low. Yet even where information is scarce, incumbents are able to increase their visibility and improve their reputations by plying the tools of their trade: constituency service, newsletters, direct mail, and so on. In many other districts, the constraints on candidate saliency imposed by the structure of the media are not so severe that money and ingenuity cannot overcome them. In these situations challengers as well as incumbents can reach enough of the electorate to move sizable numbers of voters into their column.

Large numbers of voters do have impressions of the candidates, however partial and fragile is the information at hand. Feelings can sour—quickly, in the wake of a devastating and widely publicized event, or gradually, as relations with elite groups become strained and effective opposition is mobilized. The relative visibility and reputation of the candidates condition the electoral influence of such important factors as party identification and the performance of the administration.

NOTES

1. Among voters in contested seats, 56 percent were able to recall the name of the incumbent and 35 percent the name of the challenger; the average name-recall score for candidates in open seats was 42 percent. The comparable figures for those responding affirmatively to the question "Have you read or heard anything about (name of candidate)" are 49 percent for incumbents, 25 percent for challengers, and 34 percent for candidates in open seats. Almost 40 percent of those who correctly recalled the name of the candidate said they had *not* "read or heard anything" about that candidate. These figures are derived from the 1958 SRC election study, which was made available by the Inter-university Consortium for Political and Social Research.
2. It may be that the prefatory sentence, "Now we're interested in knowing what sorts of persons people think these candidates are," led some respondents to think that they were being asked for intimate knowledge of the candidates.
3. For more evidence on changes over time, see the last section of Chapter 4 [Mann].
4. The same cannot be said for public ratings of the Congress itself. We have only begun to understand why ratings of congressmen and the Congress diverge so dramatically. See, for example, Fenno (1975; 1978).
5. The test here and below is the author's knowledge of the positions on issues taken by the candidates in their campaigns and by incumbents in the Congress.
6. Actually, the distribution of public opinion determines the rationality of taking opposing positions. While in homogeneous districts the candidates' positions seem likely to converge, there is some theoretical and empirical evidence suggesting that it is rational for candidates to stake out opposing positions in heterogeneous districts. See Fiorina (1974, chap. 5).

15. CANDIDATES AND PARTIES IN CONGRESSIONAL ELECTIONS

Thomas E. Mann and Raymond E. Wolfinger

During the first generation of research on voting behavior, scant attention was paid to congressional elections. In the 1970s scholars interested in congressional elections quickly exhausted the analytic possibilities of data from the principal source of nationwide sample surveys, the biennial National Election Studies of the University of Michigan Center for Political Studies. Their research provided some interesting findings but also pointed to a need for more and better survey items to explain the gaps and contradictions in the existing state of scholarly understanding.

The Michigan CPS study of the 1978 elections included a number of new questions about public perceptions of congressional candidates and incumbent members of Congress; for the first time scholars have data with which to find valid answers to some of the fundamental questions about how members of Congress are elected. In this chapter we will exploit the new data source to provide answers to these questions: What do voters know about congressional candidates? How do voters decide between candidates? Why are House incumbents so successful at getting reelected by wide margins? Why do Senate incumbents fare less well? How are elections won or lost?

The 1978 National Election Study

The unusually widespread scholarly interest in the 1978 congressional elections stems from the availability of a distinctly new data set rather than from any unusual features of the results. The outcome of the election can be briefly summarized. The Democratic party maintained the majority status in both houses that it has enjoyed without interruption for over two decades. The national net Republican gain in the House of Representatives of 2.8 percent of the votes and 3.4 percent of the seats was modest by midterm election standards, but not wholly unexpected, given several mitigating factors: the absence of presidential

Authors' Note: The data used in this paper were made available by the Inter-university Consortium for Political and Social Research and were originally collected by the Center for Political Studies of the University of Michigan. Neither the ICPSR nor the CPS has any responsibility for our analyses or interpretations.

Source: *American Political Science Review* (1980) 74:617-32. Reprinted with permission of the publisher.

coattails in 1976 (Jimmy Carter ran behind 270 of the 292 Democrats elected to the House in that year); Carter's partial and temporary recovery in the opinion polls following his Middle East Camp David summit meeting; and the electoral advantage of incumbency. Twenty-four House incumbents seeking reelection were defeated—5 in the primaries and 19 in the general election—leaving 94 percent successful. Incumbency was a less obvious advantage in the Senate, where 10 of the 25 senators seeking reelection were defeated—three in the primaries and seven in the general election.[1]

The 1978 elections witnessed the continuation of three additional trends that have been present for several successive elections. First, turnout declined to a postwar low of 35.1 percent. Second, David Mayhew's (1974b) vanishing marginals vanished even further. In 1978, 76 percent of all House races contested by an incumbent were won by a margin of 60 percent or more. Third, the growing insulation of House incumbents from defeat has not led to stability in membership. To the contrary, 18 percent of the House were replaced following the 1978 elections. When added to the shifts following the 1974 and 1976 elections, this means that half the members of the 96th Congress were not in office when Richard Nixon resigned from the presidency. This is equally true for the Senate, where 20 new members entered following the 1978 election and where 49 are in their first term. The answer to this seeming paradox is obvious: retirement has replaced defeat as the primary source of turnover and the number of retirements has been rising since 1972. Once again, 1978 was no exception to this pattern—49 representatives and 10 senators declined to seek reelection. Both figures are as high as any in modern times.

The 1978 National Election Study is the first nationwide survey in 20 years to include more than the most basic questions concerning congressional elections. A substantial portion of the questionnaire was devoted to congressional matters. At the same time, the primary sampling units were changed from counties to congressional districts, which produced a more even distribution of respondents across districts than was the case for the Miller-Stokes 1958 study (Stokes and Miller, 1966). The addition of a substantial body of contextual data permits analysis with the district as well as the individual as the unit of analysis.

A better sense of the opportunities as well as the limitations of working with this new data set can be gained by looking at Table 15-1, which presents the number of respondents, voters, districts and states in the 1978 sample. In the House the major constraint is the total number of respondents in districts with contested races who reported voting for one of the major party candidates—757 where the incumbent ran and 116 where there was an open-seat contest.[2] There are enough voters in incumbent-contested races for most analytic purposes, but it should be remembered that there is an average of fewer than ten voters per district. The small number of voters in elections without incumbents prevents all but the most straightforward presentation of frequencies.

If one has a special interest in races where the outcome is not a foregone conclusion, the sample's limitations are more pronounced. As we indicated above, 24 percent of all House incumbents seeking reelection won with margins of less than 60 percent, which is matched almost perfectly in the sample with 18 "marginal" races out of 77 incumbent-contested races. Although the sample was right on target in this respect, the number of voting respondents in these districts is small

Table 15-1 Respondents, Voters, Districts and States in the 1978 National Election Study, by Type of Election

	Districts or States	*Total Respon- dents*	*Total Voters**	*Demo- cratic Voters*	*Repub- lican Voters*
House of Representatives					
Total	108	2304	1027	590	419
Contested races	88	1803	885	479	394
Democratic incumbent	47	917	432	342	88
Republican incumbent	30	651	334	74	253
Open seat	11	235	119	63	53
Uncontested races	20	501	142	111	25
Democratic incumbent	13	335	103	99	—
Republican incumbent	5	126	26	—	25
Open seat	2	40	13	12	—
Senate					
Total	39	2304	556	284	273
No race	13	1092	—	—	—
Contested races	24	1116	550	272	273
Democratic incumbent	8	256	122	82	39
Republican incumbent	8	558	274	116	157
Open seat	8	302	154	73	77
Uncontested races	2	96	16	12	0
Democratic incumbent	1	37	—	—	—
Republican incumbent	0	—	—	—	—
Open seat	1	59	16	12	0

* Includes all respondents who identified the candidate for whom they voted, not just major-party voters.

Source: 1978 National Election Study, Center for Political Studies, University of Michigan.

for most analytic purposes (178, of whom 170 are major-party voters). Moreover, there is a clear incumbent bias in the voting reports of these respondents. While challengers in all marginal districts averaged 46 percent of the actual vote, less than 35 percent of all the respondents in the sample of these districts reported a vote for the challenger. Any interpretation of the public's view of challengers in competitive districts must take this discrepancy into account.

Actually, an over-report of the vote for incumbents in the sample is not limited to marginal districts. In the universe of districts in which they faced opposition, incumbents won 66 percent of the major-party vote; yet in the CPS sample of these districts 79 percent of the vote was reportedly cast for incumbents.

Only one of the 19 districts in which incumbents were defeated fell within the sample; by chance, we would have expected four or five. We cannot expect the sample to represent such districts; nor would their inclusion have altered substantially the figures for the entire sample. Nonetheless, it is worth observing that a politically and analytically important type of district is under-represented in the sample.

The Senate sample poses much more serious problems. There is no purposive sample of Senate races; what we have is a by-product of designing a national sample of noninstitutionalized adults and of congressional districts. Roughly half the respondents were in states without a 1978 Senate contest. Moreover, the remaining respondents are distributed *very unevenly* across states with Senate elections, ranging from 19 in Iowa to 152 in Texas. There are two major limitations in the data on states where an incumbent senator sought reelection: (1) Fewer than 400 respondents reported casting a vote for a major party candidate. (2) Most of these respondents lived in Illinois, Michigan, or Texas, states in which senior Republican senators were engaged in expensive battles for survival. There are not enough cases for study of any one of these three races, and at the same time we feel uneasy about using respondents from these three states as the principal basis for generalizations about Senate elections. We think it best to use the Senate figures for only the simplest comparisons with the House. This chapter primarily concerns voting in House elections.

The Importance of Party

Because members of Congress are less familiar than the president to most voters, it is easy to accept the proposition that party identification is a far more important determinant of congressional than of presidential voting. This notion can be evaluated by examining Table 15-2, which displays the proportion of

Table 15-2 The Composition of the Vote in Presidential and House Elections, 1956-1978 (Percent)

	House Elections			*Presidential Elections*		
	Party-Line Voters[a]	*Defectors*[b]	*Pure Independents*	*Party-Line Voters*[a]	*Defectors*[b]	*Pure Independents*
1956	82	9	9	76	15	9
1958	84	11	5			
1960	80	12	8	79	13	8
1962	83	12	6			
1964	79	15	5	79	15	5
1966	76	16	8			
1968	74	19	7	69	23	9
1970	76	16	8			
1972	75	17	8	67	25	8
1974	74	18	8			
1976	72	19	9	74	15	11
1978	69	22	9			

[a] Party identifiers who vote for the candidate of their party.

[b] Party identifiers who vote for the candidate of the other party.

Source: National Election Studies, Center for Political Studies, University of Michigan.

voters in every House and presidential election from 1956 through 1978 who were pure Independents, people who identified with a party and voted for that party's candidate, and people who identified with one party and voted for the candidate of the other party.[3]

The first observation to be made is the marked increase in defection in presidential elections in 1968 and 1972, and then the equally sharp return in 1976 to the same modest levels of defection that were found during the 1950s. The trend toward weakening party lines that was so widely discussed in literature based on the 1968 and 1972 elections may well have reflected the candidacies of George Wallace and George McGovern rather than any secular movement in the strength of party loyalties (Nie et al., 1976).

Second, and more interesting for our present purposes, is the continuous increase in the proportion of congressional voters who defect. In 1956, just 9 percent of all those people casting a ballot in a House contest voted for the other party's candidate, compared with 15 percent of presidential voters. The proportion of House defectors crept up slowly and steadily in virtually every election since 1956. Until the most recent elections, however, defection was always lower than in presidential races, and so the contrast between presidential and House voting remained consistent with the proposition that ignorance about House candidates led to greater party-line voting than in presidential balloting, where public familiarity with the candidates produced more defection. But more recently the continued increase in House defection combined with a return to party-line presidential voting to reverse the previous relationship. In 1976, just 15 percent of presidential voters defected; by 1978, a substantially larger number of House voters—22 percent—identified with one party and voted for the other party's candidate. This reversal, whether temporary or permanent, is sufficiently damaging to the conventional wisdom to require further investigation.

Incumbency as an Electoral Force

Defection has not increased in a politically neutral manner. Cover and Mayhew (1977) found that the proportion of defections in favor of House incumbents rose substantially after 1970 and accounted for over three-quarters of all votes cast against party lines in House races. Even in 1974, when national tides ran strongly against the Republican party and 36 Republican representatives were defeated, 74 percent of all defections favored the incumbent. By 1978, challengers received only 11 percent of the defections; two decades earlier the comparable number was 43 percent.[4] These findings suggest that the secular decline in party-line voting observed in Table 15-2 reflects the greater ability of incumbents to attract votes from people who identify with the other party.

The relationship between party, incumbency and vote choice in the 1978 elections can be seen more directly in Table 15-3. Party and incumbency together appear to be an almost unbeatable combination in House elections. Only 5 percent of the voters (19 respondents) who belonged to the same party as their incumbent representative (hereafter called "incumbent partisans") voted for the challenger. When party and incumbency are in conflict, the latter appears as the more powerful electoral force. By contrast, incumbency has a somewhat weaker influence in Senate voting.

Table 15-3 Vote for House and Senate, by Party Identification and Incumbency, 1978 (Percent)

	Party Identification of Voter		
	Incumbent's Party	*Independent*	*Challenger's Party*
Vote for House			
Incumbent	95	79	54
Challenger	5	21	46
n =	(407)	(72)	(277)
Vote for Senate			
Incumbent	89	64	31
Challenger	11	36	69
n =	(179)	(36)	(179)

Source: 1978 National Election Study, Center for Political Studies, University of Michigan.

Before exploring the source of this incumbency advantage, we believe it is worth introducing here a theme to which we return later. The figures reported in the last paragraph are national averages, and they reflect the overwhelming advantage incumbents enjoy nationally. Yet House elections are held in individual congressional districts and the relative influence of party and incumbency may vary from one district to another. One study based on surveys in a number of congressional districts (most of which were in the "marginal" range at one point or another during the last six years) found that some challengers attracted as many as 20 percent of the votes of incumbent partisans, while some incumbents received only 14 percent of the support of challenger partisans (Mann, 1978). Of course, these examples are not representative of districts generally, but no discussion of voting in congressional elections is complete without a consideration of when and how challengers make the best showing against incumbents. Without this understanding, we are in no position to learn the conditions under which change might occur. But with only 19 incumbent partisans voting for challengers in the 1978 data set, there is no variance to investigate. Nonetheless, this need not prevent us from looking for processes of individual decision making that, when certain conditions change, might produce very different results.

The source of the increased incumbency advantage that was registered in the 1960s has been a puzzle to scholars. David Mayhew (1974a) originally suggested three possible explanations: (1) incumbents benefited from favorable redistricting that increased the number of majority partisans in their districts; (2) incumbents gained political support by becoming more adept at advertising, credit-taking, and position-taking; and (3) incumbents benefited fortuitously from the erosion of party loyalties—incumbency replaced party as a voting cue. Mayhew did not explicitly mention a fourth possibility, not unrelated to his third, that the visibility and attractiveness of challengers decreased during this time.

Cover (1977) and Ferejohn (1977) have shown that redistricting does not account for the increased advantage of incumbency, although doubtless there are particular cases where redrawing district lines made incumbents safer. Investigation of the second and third explanations has been constrained by the lack of adequate data on public perceptions of congressional candidates. Cover (1977), Ferejohn (1977) and Nelson (1978) all show that the increase in incumbents' electoral advantages was not accompanied by any increase in the proportion of the population who could recall their names, which suggested that incumbency provided a voting cue unmediated by public awareness of the incumbent. The same conclusion came more directly from Nelson's finding that many voters defected to incumbents whose names they could not recall. This implausible possibility can now be safely dismissed, as we will soon see. But unraveling the other two possibilities—that incumbents are better known and/or better liked now than before, or that the advantage in visibility and reputation long held by incumbents, although not increased, now translates more profitably into votes because party ties are weaker—has been frustrated by the lack of appropriate recognition and reputation measures during the decade when the advantage increased. While we can never adequately investigate this period of change, we can begin to describe more accurately what the public knows about incumbents and challengers today.

Candidate Familiarity

Incumbents are better known than their opponents. Scholars have generally said that incumbents enjoy more "name recognition," and point to repeated findings that incumbents are known to about twice as many people as challengers. What the surveys invariably measure however, is not name *recognition* but name *recall.* The Michigan CPS (1975, p. 124) question in 1974 was: "Do you happen to remember the names of the candidates for Congress—that is, for the House of Representatives in Washington—that ran in this district last November?" Of course, it is far more difficult to recall someone's name without help than it is to recognize a name when it is encountered. Many voters unable to recall the names of their representatives or challengers can nevertheless recognize the names when presented with them, which is the situation they face in the voting booth (Mann, 1978). It seems reasonable to expect, then, that the apparent existence of an incumbent electoral advantage without public knowledge of the incumbent reflects a faulty measure of knowledge, not an ability to impress voters without their conscious awareness.

The 1978 Michigan study for the first time included a true measure of name recognition, one that resembled (although not exactly) the situation voters face in the polling place. This was done with the "candidate thermometer," which elicited responses to a number of public figures, including all major party congressional candidates as well as several national political celebrities. For each person on the list of more than 20 names, the respondents could indicate they did not recognize the name, that they recognized but could not rate the person, or that they recognized and rated the person (see appendix). The thermometer thus measures both name recognition and affect toward the person. Table 15-4 shows the percentage of voters in contested races who recognized and rated the House and Senate candidates, those who claimed to recognize but could

Table 15-4 Candidate Recognition Among Voters in Contested Races, House and Senate, 1978 (Percent)

	Recognize and Rate	*Recognize, but not Rate*	*Don't Recognize*
House			
Incumbents (n = 754)	93	4	3
Challengers (n = 754)	44	19	37
Open seat candidates (n = 116)	72	20	8
Senate			
Incumbents (n = 408)	96	3	1
Challengers (n = 408)	86	7	7
Open seat candidates (n = 158)	88	8	5

Source: 1978 National Election Study, Center for Political Studies, University of Michigan.

not rate the candidate, and those who confessed they could not recognize the candidate.

We see that House incumbents are almost universally recognized by voters in their districts, while the names of challengers are familiar to just under two-thirds of the voters. The lead of incumbents over challengers is more pronounced when we use a more stringent standard of recognition—both recognizing and rating the candidate. Open-seat candidates are substantially more visible than those who challenge incumbents, confirming the general view that open seats are more hotly contested than incumbent-held seats. The contrast with the Senate is instructive, with a caveat for the peculiar nature in the Senate sample. Senate challengers are almost as invisible to the electorate as Senate incumbents, probably reflecting both more serious efforts by the opposition and the publicity that comes automatically to a statewide challenger.

Although most voters know the names of challengers and almost all are familiar with the incumbent, this discrepancy alone does not explain the incumbent advantage. Incumbents' very high victory rate is not fully explained by their greater name familiarity. Challengers have an uphill fight even when the voters know them. This is revealed in Table 15-5, which displays defection by incumbency, party identification, and name recognition. Voters who belong to the incumbent's party are almost sure to vote for the incumbent. Even the handful who do not recognize their representative's name have only a one-in-seven chance of defecting. By the same token, the challenger whose name is known to the incumbent's partisans wins only 7 percent of their voters—and loses fully 46 percent of his or her own partisans. The challenger is better off being recognized, but visibility alone is not enough. Thus we must move beyond simple name recognition in order to understand the advantages of incumbency and the opportunities for challengers.

Table 15-5 Party Defection by Incumbency and Candidate Recognition, 1978 House Elections (Percent)*

	*Voter Recognizes***			
	Incumbent		*Challenger*	
Party Identification	*Yes*	*No*	*Yes*	*No*
Incumbent's party	4	14	7	3
n =	(366)	(29)	(161)	(243)
Challenger's party	57	15	46	63
n =	(257)	(20)	(145)	(132)

* The entry in each cell is the percentage of voters with the indicated characteristics who defected.
** Defined as able to rate candidates on thermometer from 0-100.

Source: 1978 National Election Study, Center for Political Studies, University of Michigan.

Candidate Reputation

The 1978 National Election Study interview schedule gave respondents several opportunities to evaluate the congressional candidates in their district and state. Responses to these questions are all consistent with the proposition that as a class, incumbents are well regarded by their constituents. Table 15-6 shows the percentage of voters who rated the candidates on the feeling thermometer as positive, neutral, negative, or unknown. Almost three-fourths rated the incumbent positively, while less than a fifth made similar evaluations of the challenger.

One can better understand the advantage of incumbency in House elections by contrasting these figures with those for candidates in open House seats and for Senate incumbents and challengers. In the latter cases, the standing of the non-incumbents is relatively high and the gap between the two candidates is relatively narrow.

In addition to thinking highly of incumbents' personal qualities, most voters also feel that their representative is doing a good job. The two sorts of assessments are not always similar. (Sometimes the public combines generalized admiration for a political figure and a low assessment of performance. Jimmy Carter and Gerald Ford come immediately to mind.) Table 15-7 presents the job ratings of House members by party identification and the amount of defection at each category of performance assessment. These figures confirm the well-known point that individual members are highly esteemed despite the public's critical view of Congress as an institution (Fenno, 1975). Nearly two-thirds of all voters think their representative is doing a "good" or "very good" job, and a mere 4 percent have a distinctly unfavorable view. As we would expect, these assessments are affected by party identification; the incumbent's partisans are more enthusiastic than members of the other party. The more important finding, however, is that half the challenger's partisans have a favorable view of the incumbent's performance, and only 8 percent say the incumbent is doing a "poor" or "very poor" job.

The relationship between job assessment and defection is about as strong as we could expect, particularly in light of the handful of incumbent partisans who defected. Incumbents lost no votes at all from members of their own party who say they are doing a "very good" job, and very few from those who rate them "good" or "fair." The numbers are much more striking among challenger

Table 15-6 Voters' Feelings About Candidates, 1978 (Percent)

	Feeling Thermometer Evaluation			
	Positive	*Neutral*	*Negative*	*Can't Rate: Don't Recognize*
House				
Incumbents (n = 754)	73	10	9	7
Challengers (n = 754)	17	18	9	56
Open-seat candidates (n = 116)	50	13	9	28
Senate				
Incumbents (n = 408)	61	15	20	4
Challengers (n = 408)	48	17	20	15
Open-seat candidates (n = 158)	58	16	14	12

Source: 1978 National Election Study, Center for Political Studies, University of Michigan.

Table 15-7 Incumbent Job Ratings, and Defection by Voters in House Elections, 1978 (Percent)

	Rating of Incumbent's Performance					
	Very Good	*Good*	*Fair*	*Poor*	*Very Poor*	*Don't Know*
Percent of all voters rating incumbent	20	44	22	3	1	10
Percent defecting from:						
Incumbent's party	0	4	12	—	—	8
n =	(113)	(180)	(68)	(3)	(2)	(38)
Challenger's party	89	75	35	11	—	21
n =	(28)	(114)	(83)	(19)	(4)	(29)
Percent of Independents voting for challenger	0	11	27	—	—	30
n =	(7)	(36)	(15)	(3)	(1)	(10)

Source: 1978 National Election Study, Center for Political Studies, University of Michigan.

partisans, whose support for the incumbent ranges from 89 to 11 percent, depending on their evaluation of his performance. Support for the challenger among pure Independents is similarly related to the incumbent's job rating.

A final measure of candidate affect comes from the open-ended questions asking respondents if there is anything they like and dislike about the Democratic and Republican House candidates. Predictably, voters' party affiliations shape their answers. Whether incumbents or challengers are the object of the query, the incidence of favorable comments is about 15 percentage points higher among their own partisans. This modest difference is overshadowed by the far stronger relationship of incumbency to favorable assessment, as Table 15-8 shows. Only a fifth of the voters in the challenger's party had anything good to say about the challenger, while three times as many of them expressed favorable opinions about the incumbent in the other party.

The consequences of these assessments for the vote can be seen in the bottom line of Table 15-8. This shows both the importance of candidate image in congressional voting decisions and incumbents' vastly greater success in creating favorable impressions. Differences in defection rates in this table are more pronounced, especially for challengers, than those associated with simple name recognition (Table 15-5). Thus the advantage of incumbents reflects more than just their ability to get their names before the public. It seems likely, moreover, that defection rates would be less loaded toward incumbents if more challengers could make themselves favorably known to voters.

Two final notes on the open-ended comments about the candidates. First, the number of respondents who disliked something about the incumbent or the challenger was relatively small—18 percent for the former, 12 percent for the latter—but higher, particularly for the incumbent, than appeared on either the

Table 15-8 Favorable Comments About House Candidates, Party Identification, Incumbency, and Defection, 1978 (Percent)

	Incumbent				*Challenger*			
	Same Party		*Other Party*		*Same Party*		*Other Party*	
Percent liking something about the candidate	71		56		20		6	
n =	(407)		(277)		(277)		(407)	
	Yes	*No*	*Yes*	*No*	*Yes*	*No*	*Yes*	*No*
Percent defecting	2	12	72	30	16	63	20	3

Note: "Yes" and "no" refer to whether the respondent likes anything about the candidate in the given category.

Source: 1978 National Election Study, Center for Political Studies, University of Michigan.

feeling thermometer or the job rating. Second, the content of the open-ended remarks was highly personalized, with very few references to party, ideology, or issues. Voters appear to judge candidates, and incumbents in particular, on the basis of their perceived character, experience, and ties to the local community. Issues and ideology are subordinated to these personal and particularistic concerns.

Candidate Preference

The evidence presented above makes clear that voting in congressional elections is strongly associated with evaluations of the candidates. Yet up to this point we have analyzed vote choice only as it relates to the assessment of a single candidate. A more likely decision process is for the voters to evaluate both candidates at the same time and to choose the more attractive one. It is possible that a number of voters who rate the challenger positively have an even higher opinion of the incumbent. The reverse is less likely in view of the challenger's lower visibility, but it is possible. In order to deal with this possibility, we must include comparative candidate preferences, not just individual candidate ratings.

Table 15-9 displays the vote for incumbent and challenger by party identification and candidate preference, following a format developed by Richard Brody (1976) for the study of presidential elections. Candidate preference is determined by the relative ranking of the incumbent and challenger on the feeling thermometer. "Don't recognize" and "can't rate" responses are treated as neutral; in cases where one candidate is not recognized or rated, feelings toward the other candidates are decisive. A respondent who does not recognize the challenger but who rates the incumbent negatively is coded as preferring the challenger.

The figures in Table 15-9 confirm the appropriateness of the candidate preference model for congressional voting: 94 percent of all respondents who prefer the incumbent vote for the incumbent; 88 percent of all respondents who prefer the challenger vote for the challenger. In cases where neither candidate is preferred, party identification is the best predictor of the vote, although incumbents fare better among challenger partisans in this situation than we might expect. This is probably best explained by our coding conventions—incumbents who were recognized but rated as neutral on the thermometer were treated the same as challengers who were not recognized, although the former have an edge in recognition.

With the data in Table 15-9 we can divide the vote for incumbents and for challengers into four categories: votes consistent with both party identification and candidate preference, those consistent with candidate preference only, those consistent with party identification only, and those consistent with neither. The results of this exercise, displayed in Table 15-10, demonstrate that routine party support not backed up by express preference for the party's candidate provides a small part of incumbents' total support (22 percent), and a substantially larger part for that of challengers (43 percent). This reflects the failure of most challengers to build a substantial personal following. Yet, overall, most party-line votes are accompanied by a preference for the party's candidate; when partisanship and candidate preference conflict, voters are likely to defect from their party.

Table 15-9 Vote in 1978 House Election by Party Identification and Candidate Preference

Candidate Preference* and Vote	*Party Identification*							
	Incumbent's Party		*Independent*		*Challenger's Party*		*Total*	
	N	%	*N*	%	*N*	%	*N*	%
Prefer incumbent								
Incumbent	258	99	31	91	103	84	392	94
Challenger	2	1	3	9	20	16	25	6
Prefer neither								
Incumbent	123	95	25	81	45	47	193	75
Challenger	7	5	6	19	50	53	63	25
Prefer challenger								
Incumbent	7	41	1	14	2	3	10	12
Challenger	10	59	6	86	58	97	74	88
Total								
Incumbent	388	95	57	79	150	54	595	79
Challenger	19	5	15	21	128	46	162	21

* Determined by the relative ranking of the incumbent and challenger on the feeling thermometer.

Source: 1978 National Election Study, Center for Political Studies, University of Michigan.

Table 15-10 Relationship of Party Identification and Candidate Preference to Each Candidate's Total Vote, House, 1978 (Percent)

Vote Consistent With:	*Incumbent*	*Challenger*
Party ID and candidate preference	44	36
Candidate preference only	23	10
Party ID only	22	43
Neither*	12	11
	100	100
n =	(595)	(162)

* Vote is consistent with neither party identification nor candidate preference.

Source: 1978 National Election Study, Center for Political Studies, University of Michigan.

This analysis of candidate preference is, of course, colored by the relatively low visibility and standing of challengers in our national sample. The 17 cases in the lower left-hand cell of Table 15-9—where incumbent partisans prefer the challenger—are not sufficient to produce confidence in our finding that candidate preference for challengers will override partisanship to the detriment of incumbents. As additional support for our conclusion, therefore, we refer readers to a similar investigation based on surveys in a sample of generally competitive districts (Mann, 1978). That study confirms the ability of more visible and attractive challengers to garner the support of substantial numbers of incumbent partisans.

Why Incumbents are Well Known and Well Liked

We have argued that voting in a congressional election primarily involves choosing between competing candidates; party plays an important role for some voters in determining whether a candidate is attractive and in providing guidance for voters who lack information about the candidate, but it is secondary to the images of the candidates themselves. Incumbents have an enormous advantage over challengers, not because the voters' decision rules are rigged in their favor, but rather because they are more visible and more attractive. Why are members of Congress in such a desirable position?

The data in Table 15-11 move us a long way toward an explanation. Each figure in this table represents the percentage of all voters who had the designated form of contact with incumbents, challengers, or open seat candidates, in the House and Senate. When contrasted with the image of relative anonymity that appeared in the 1958 study of congressional elections (Stokes and Miller, 1966) the figures in this table, especially for incumbents, are staggering. Only 10 percent of all voters had no form of contact with the House incumbent. Almost a fourth met their representative personally, while nearly three-fourths had seen press coverage about him or her via the print media and/or television. By contrast, only 44 percent of these voters had any type of contact with the

Table 15-11 Voter Contact with House and Senate Candidates, 1978 (Percent)

	House			*Senate*		
Form of Contact	*Incum-bent*	*Chal-lenger*	*Open Seat*	*Incum-bent*	*Chal-lenger*	*Open Seat*
Any type	90	44	73	94	82	88
Met personally	23	4	14	9	5	9
Saw at meeting	20	3	13	10	5	13
Talked to staff	12	2	13	6	4	9
Received mail	71	16	43	53	32	47
Read about in a newspaper, magazine	71	32	57	73	63	78
Heard on radio	34	15	28	45	37	49
Saw on TV	50	24	48	80	70	78
Family or friend had contact	39	11	26	—	—	—
n =	(756)	(756)	(121)	(409)	(409)	(158)

Source: 1978 National Election Study, Center for Political Studies, University of Michigan.

challenger. The gap between incumbent and challenger is greatest in mail contacts, which probably reflects the enormous advantage members of the House enjoy in blanketing their districts with mass and specialized mailings. The prohibition on franked (free) mass mailings by representatives for 60 days before an election evidently does not ease the effects of this perquisite of office.

The more one examines Table 15-11, however, the less impressive one finds the argument that the inherent advantages of office adequately explain incumbents' greater visibility. Candidates for open House seats reached a far larger share of voters than challengers did, and in many types of contact were nearly as successful as incumbents. One way or another, open-seat candidates reached 73 percent of the voters, compared to 90 percent for incumbents and 44 percent for challengers. The putative advantages of office are even less evident in Senate races, where voters have nearly as much contact with challengers and open-seat candidates as with incumbents. (Amount of contact is measured by numbers of voters reached, not the number of separate interactions.)

We believe that House incumbents benefit more from the scarcity of serious challenges than from the perquisites of office. Evidence on this point can be found in the data on House and Senate campaign expenditures displayed in Table 15-12. We assume that budgets are a reliable index of total campaign effort, particularly for non-incumbents who must pay for many services that are free to sitting members. The generous spending of candidates for open House and Senate seats helps explain our earlier findings about their visibility to the electorate. In races contested by incumbents, however, the campaign effort and consequently, we believe, the visibility of challengers varies enormously. Just over 70 percent of these elections were won by an incumbent with more than 60 percent of the vote. These campaigns were low-budget productions on both sides. The spending was

Table 15-12 Mean Campaign Expenditures in House and Senate Races, 1978

All Races	*House*	*Senate*
Open-seat candidates	$201,049	$ 820,787
n =	(111)	(25)
Incumbents	111,557[a]	1,341,942[b]
n =	(377)	(22)
Challengers	72,373	697,766
n =	(309)	(21)

Incumbent-Contested Races by Election Outcome	*House*		*Senate*	
	Incumbent	*Challenger*	*Incumbent*	*Challenger*
Incumbent won with 60% or more of vote	$ 93,218	$ 32,564	$ 453,772	$ 47,346
n =	(287)	(219)	(7)	(6)
Incumbent won with less than 60% of vote	161,856	156,445	2,496,484[c]	992,831
n =	(71)	(71)	(8)	(8)
Incumbent lost to the challenger	200,607	217,083	908,348	918,054
n =	(19)	(19)	(7)	(7)

[a] Includes 68 uncontested races.

[b] Includes 1 uncontested race.

[c] Without the $7.5 million spent in Jesse Helms' narrowly successful reelection campaign in North Carolina, this figure would be $1.8 million.

Source: Computed by authors from Federal Election Commission data presented in *Congressional Quarterly Weekly Report*, September 29, 1979.

even more lopsided than the voting, with challengers being outspent three-to-one by the victorious incumbents. Budgets were far larger in the 90 House races decided by smaller margins, particularly for the challengers, who spent an average five to six times as much as their counterparts in non-competitive races.

The pattern is similar in Senate contests—challengers in the closer races spend vastly more than challengers who are defeated decisively—but the frequencies are quite different. Most Senate challengers are big spenders and run competitive races, while the vast majority of House challengers have small budgets and even smaller chances of winning.

The absence of serious challenges to most House incumbents surely owes something to their public standing and their resourcefulness in exploiting the advantages inherent in their office. We suspect that many decisions not to wage a major challenge involve other factors as well, including the vitality of the local opposition party, the high cost of a serious campaign, the difficulty of raising enough money, and some degree of satisfaction with the incumbent among local interests.

Moreover, some House districts have such a lopsided division of Republicans and Democrats that members of the minority party have little chance of winning under any circumstances. This is seldom true of Senate races because statewide constituencies generally are more evenly balanced between the two parties.

Table 15-11 also confirms other bits of conventional wisdom about House-Senate differences. Senators and those aspiring to the office are much more likely than their House counterparts to communicate with the electorate via broadcast media, especially television. Doubtless this reflects the better fit between statewide constituencies and television audiences. In contrast, many congressional districts are such a small portion of a metropolitan television viewing area that their representatives' activities are not very newsworthy. And when the media audience is so large, advertising becomes prohibitively expensive for a candidate who wants to reach only a fraction of it. Also, senators are bigger celebrities than representatives, a result of their smaller number and differences between the impersonal House and the Senate's star system.

The electoral payoff of contact with the voters can be seen from Table 15-13. Among voters who had contact only with incumbents, challengers lose 72 percent of their partisans and attract but 2 percent of the incumbent's partisans. Defection among challenger partisans is 26 percent lower among voters who have had contact with both candidates and 40 percent lower than the handful of respondents who have had contact with neither candidate. These latter results point to the importance of efforts by both incumbent and challenger.

In the face of these striking findings on the extent of candidate contact with voters, the increased advantage of incumbency clearly is not a result only of the errand boy or ombudsman activities of House members (Fiorina, 1977b). Responses to a battery of questions on citizen-initiated contact with representatives let us assess more directly the electoral consequences of these activities. One-fifth of the voting respondents said that they had contacted their representative or someone in the representative's office—to express an opinion, to seek

Table 15-13 Defection in 1978 House Elections, by Contact with Incumbent and Challenger (Percent)

	Contact with:			
Defection from:	*Both Candidates*	*Incumbent Only*	*Challenger Only*	*Neither Candidate*
Incumbent's party	8	2	—	8
n =	(155)	(213)	(0)	(38)
Challenger's party	46	72	—	32
n =	(145)	(103)	(1)	(28)
Support for challenger among Independents	29	7	—	—
n =	(34)	(30)	(1)	(6)

Source: 1978 National Election Study, Center for Political Studies, University of Michigan.

information, or to seek help with a problem, in roughly equal proportions. Virtually everyone received a response, and the vast majority were very satisfied with that response. Yet defection rates between those who contacted their representative's office and those who did not are almost identical. (Actually, the absence of a difference for all voters masks a partisan difference: Democratic incumbents do slightly better among those voters who *have not* contacted their office, while Republican incumbents do slightly better with those who *have* contacted their office.) If we look at just those respondents who wrote to seek help with a problem, we find that a large majority are incumbent partisans; and of the 19 challenger partisans who fell into this category, 11 voted for the incumbent, producing a defection rate identical to that of all challenger partisans in the sample. In other words, responding to constituent requests paid no special vote dividend for House members in 1978.

While the direct payoff for constituent service may have been limited, a reputation for service appears to have been more valuable. Many voters who have not themselves made requests of their congressmen know others who have, and this latter phenomenon is more strongly related to the vote. Moreover, a third of the voters believe their representative would be "very helpful" if asked to help with a problem, and this reputation for service garners the vote of almost 80 percent of the challenger partisans. It is very likely that congressmen build a reputation for service in a variety of ways, exploiting vehicles for mass publicity without limiting themselves to direct servicing of constituent requests. In any case, the reach of other forms of contact with voters extends considerably beyond the constituent service domain.

One final note on additional ingredients in the positive image of incumbents. Richard Fenno (1978) has demonstrated that House members adopt a diversity of "home styles" in presenting themselves in their districts. Some members are highly issue-oriented in their discussions with constituents while others stress their personal identification with the district and make few references to substantive issues. In either case, however, Fenno believes that the result of such encounters with House members is an impression of their personal qualities rather than specific information on their issue positions or voting record. This proposition is confirmed by responses to items in the 1978 study that deal with the member's voting record or positions on issues. Only 15 percent of all voters remembered how their representative voted on any bill in the past couple of years. Fewer than half could say whether they generally agreed or disagreed with the way that representative voted in Washington. In either case, there was very little disagreement with the representative's actions, and the consequent loss in votes was trivial. These data strike a heavy blow at the argument that House members are likely to accumulate enemies because they must take visible stands on many controversial issues. Indeed, only a fraction of all comments about incumbents concern their positions on issues, and the vast majority of these are favorable.

There is somewhat wider awareness of the general ideological posture of representatives—80 percent of voters could place themselves on a liberal-conservative scale and 63 percent could place their congressman. However, only 26 percent were able to classify the challenger. Most ideological descriptions are accurate; Democrats are seen as predominantly liberal, Republicans as conservative. We can gauge the importance of ideological proximity voting by looking at

Table 15-14 Party Defection, by Ideological Distance of Voters from House Candidates (Percent)*

	Voter's Ideological Position		
Party Identification	*Closer to Incumbent*	*Equidistant from Candidates*	*Closer to Challenger*
Incumbent's party	2	6	50
n =	(54)	(18)	(10)
Challenger's party	58	57	15
n =	(12)	(21)	(40)

* Includes only voters who classified their own ideological position and that of the two candidates.

Source: 1978 National Election Study, Center for Political Studies, University of Michigan.

those voters who could place themselves and the two candidates on the scale—roughly a fourth of all voters. Table 15-14 displays the level of defection in House elections by the ideological distance of voters from the incumbent and challenger. The entries confirm the presence of proximity voting, but the sparse number of cases in each cell, particularly those where party and proximity conflict, demonstrate how minimal its effect is.

It would be a mistake, however, to conclude that issues and roll-call voting have no importance for congressional elections. The low salience of issues may reflect in part the efforts of the incumbent to avoid being dramatically out of step with district sentiment. In order to preserve a favorable public image, incumbents may act to forestall vociferous criticism on policy grounds. Incumbents must state positions on issues to satisfy local groups that are important for endorsements, campaign contributions, and volunteers. House members realize that the best way of ensuring their continued reelection is to discourage serious opposition. This requires making peace with those in the district who might otherwise underwrite a vigorous challenge. Finally, most politicians operate at the margin, not at the base. A loss of two or three percent of the vote as a result of a vote or a position taken on an issue will give them pause. Thus the small numbers of cases in Table 15-14 are not conclusive evidence against the proposition that taking positions on issues could affect the outcome of some House elections, and that the prospect of such an influence may well constrain members of Congress.

Midterm Elections as Referendums on Presidential Performance

Several scholars have presented evidence that voting in congressional elections is affected by public assessment of the president's performance. Members of the president's party who like the job the president is doing are less likely to vote for a House candidate of the other party. By the same token, people in the other party who like the way the president is behaving in office are more likely than their fellow-partisans to vote for a congressional candidate in the president's party (Arseneau and Wolfinger, 1973; Kernell, 1977). Using aggregate data, Tufte argues that the size of the losses sustained by the president's party in midterm elections depends on his popularity and how the economy is fairing (1975, 1978). Actually, this latter theory predicts only changes in the partisan division of the national vote for the House of Representatives, either from the preceding presidential year or from some standardized measure of the normal midterm vote. Consequently, at the individual level, we should expect to see its effect only at the margin. And in a year like 1978, when the national swing was less than 3 percent, we should find little evidence of voting in reaction to the president's performance. Moreover, since incumbency seems to insulate House members of the president's party somewhat from adverse judgments of the president's performance (Nelson, 1978), we might expect that the rising electoral effects of incumbency would reduce the referendum effect.

Table 15-15 shows how voting for the House varied according to respondents' judgments of President Carter's performance. Twenty-six percent of Democrats who disapproved of his performance defected, compared to 22 percent of those Democrats who liked his White House record. Republicans who liked the job Carter was doing voted for Democratic House contenders at a rate of 29 percent, compared to 21 percent for Republicans who disapproved. While these differences are miniscule compared to those based on the relative attractiveness of the congressional candidates discussed earlier, they are sufficient to account for the national shift that was observed in 1978. The bottom half of Table 15-15 demonstrates that differences in defection rates are somewhat larger when more refined measures of presidential performance are used.

This finding in no way contradicts a major conclusion of this chapter—that in deciding how to cast their ballots, most voters are influenced primarily by the choice of local candidates. But if we want to explain changes in the national division of the vote from one election to another, especially when those shifts are substantial, we must turn our attention to national forces. How the national swing then translates into swing at the district level and swing in the number of seats, and how important these national forces seem to candidates contesting in local districts, are other questions entirely.

Conclusion

Recent congressional elections can no more be accurately viewed as reflecting standing party decisions than can presidential elections. Most voters have sufficient information about at least one and often both of the candidates to base their decision on something other than party loyalty. Scholars have underestimated the level of public awareness of congressional candidates primarily because of faulty measures. Voters are often able to recognize and evaluate individual candidates without being able to recall their names from memory. At the same time, the content of these evaluations is both thin and highly personalized, with little apparent ideological or issue content.

Incumbents are both better known and better liked than challengers, which accounts for their obvious electoral advantage. No one activity of incumbents—such as the much-heralded ombudsman role on behalf of their constituents—is solely responsible for their popularity. A variety of activities that bring them to the attention of the voters in their districts pay handsome electoral dividends. Yet

Table 15-15 Two Measures of Carter's Job Performance and Voting in House Elections (Percent)

	Democrats		*Independents*		*Republicans*	
House Vote	*Approve*	*Disapprove*	*Approve*	*Disapprove*	*Approve*	*Disapprove*
Democrat	78	74	51	47	29	21
Republican	22	26	49	53	71	79
	100	100	100	100	100	100
n =	336	98	45	19	106	185

	*Democrats**				*Republicans**			
House Vote	*Very Good*	*Good*	*Fair*	*Poor*	*Good*	*Fair*	*Poor*	*Very Poor*
Democrat	87	78	73	72	24	27	20	14
Republican	13	22	27	28	76	73	80	86
	100	100	100	100	100	100	100	100
n =	45	168	214	24	41	169	75	28

* There were too few Democrats giving "very poor" and Republicans giving "very good" ratings to be included in the table.

Source: 1978 National Election Study, Center for Political Studies, University of Michigan.

it is inaccurate to portray congressional voting as simply favorable or unfavorable (but mostly favorable) decisions on the incumbent. Equally important are the public visibility and reputation of the challenger. Most voters make their decision between candidates by judging which one they like better, not by pulling the party lever or turning automatically to the incumbent. In most districts the challenge to incumbents is so inconsequential that the largely favorable images of incumbents prevail. In a much smaller number of districts, challengers stage a strong enough campaign to make the task of choosing between candidates a meaningful exercise. The advantage of incumbency in House elections—in contrast to Senate elections—is enhanced by the absence of a serious challenge and the greater likelihood of a lopsided partisan balance in the smaller and more homogeneous House constituency. The explosion of congressional perquisites has enabled House members to communicate with their constituents far more frequently and directly; and the absence of meaningful party competition at the district level coupled with traditional patterns of local press reporting (Robinson, 1980) works against alternative sources of (negative) information about the incumbent.

Finally, public assessments of the president provide a national dynamic to congressional voting, but the effect is modest compared to the salience of the local choices.

These findings raise as many new questions as they answer old ones. One of us has begun to explore how the conditions of election and reelection outlined here influence the way members of Congress behave in Washington (Mann, 1978, 1980). We won't repeat those arguments. Instead, we conclude with a comment on the research agenda of those who study congressional elections.

If most elections to the House are won for lack of a contest, and the evidence for this is impressive, then we need to know much more about the conditions under which a serious challenge is waged. Incumbent popularity among the voters is certainly an important deterrent to potential opponents and to those who might underwrite their campaign. When an incumbent looks popular, the most attractive candidates are unlikely to waste their time and credibility in a challenge against apparently heavy odds. The same consideration probably keeps contributors' checkbooks closed. Yet local leaders are likely to take other factors into consideration as well, such as the incumbent's record on legislative matters of great interest to them. Fenno reports that incumbents consciously strive to forestall serious opposition. We need to know more about what they do to accomplish that objective, and how these efforts are reflected, if at all, among the mass public. These and other questions relating to the recruitment of candidates and the mobilization of resources should lead us to supplement national samples with surveys of leaders and of contribution patterns at the district level. If most incumbents win reelection before the campaign begins, we should start to find out what happens between elections.

Appendix

This is the candidate thermometer (or "feeling thermometer") question (A16) used in the 1978 Michigan study:

> I'd like to get your feelings toward some of our political leaders and other people who are in the news these days.

I will use something we call the feeling thermometer, and here is how it works:

I'll read the name of a person and I'd like you to rate that person using the feeling thermometer. Ratings between 50 degrees and 100 degrees mean that you feel favorable and warm toward the person. Ratings between 0 degrees and 50 degrees mean that you don't feel favorable toward the person and that you don't care much for that person.

If we come to a person whose name *you don't recognize,* you don't need to rate that person. Just tell me and we'll move on to the next one.

If you do recognize the name, but you *don't feel particularly warm or cold* toward the person, you would rate the person at the 50 degree mark.

NOTES

1. Two of the three senators defeated in the primaries were short-term appointees filling vacant seats, as was one of the seven who lost their seats in the November election.
2. Nine respondents voted for third-party candidates in incumbent-contested elections, as did three respondents in districts with open-seat races.
3. People who initially call themselves Independents and then (in response to the follow-up question) admit that they lean toward one or the other party think and vote like outright identifiers with that party rather than like people who insist that they are Independents (Keith et al., 1977). Therefore we have classified these Independent Democrats and Independent Republicans with the relevant party here and throughout this chapter.
4. Because the 1978 CPS sample over-reported the national vote for incumbents, defections favoring challengers probably were somewhat higher in 1978.

16. THE CONSTITUENCY SERVICE BASIS OF THE PERSONAL VOTE FOR U.S. REPRESENTATIVES AND BRITISH MEMBERS OF PARLIAMENT

Bruce E. Cain, John A. Ferejohn, and Morris P. Fiorina

During the past decade an especially active research area has developed around the study of the advantages of incumbency in U.S. House elections. Erikson (1972), Tufte (1973), and Mayhew (1974b) first called attention to the temporal increase apparent over the course of the 1960s, and numerous succeeding scholars (Burnham, 1975; Cover, 1977; Ferejohn, 1977b; Fiorina, 1977; Hinckley, 1980a; Parker, 1980a) have theorized about the bases and the consequences of the trends identified by Erikson, Tufte, and Mayhew.[1] This outpouring of scholarly effort has produced a reasonable understanding of the multifaceted nature of the incumbency advantage in contemporary elections, although the lack of appropriate longitudinal data hinders efforts to determine precisely what and how much has changed over time (Fiorina, 1981a).

As with much of the congressional literature, a notable feature of the research on incumbency is its exclusively American perspective. In particular, attempts focus on American political institutions and the American political context. Little effort has been made to compare candidate effects in House elections with those that might be present in the legislative elections of other countries,[2] and virtually no effort has been given to abstracting from the American case in an effort to develop more widely applicable theories of the conditions that enhance or depress candidate effects in legislative elections. This article aims principally at the former, empirical, lacuna. Although the significance of any comparative work depends on some basic theoretical ideas that render comparison meaningful and interesting, a detailed comparative theory of voting in legislative elections lies outside our present scope.

Authors' Note: The research reported in this article was made possible through support of the National Science Foundation (grants SOC78-15413 and SES8010662). For comments on earlier versions of this article we thank James Alt, Ivor Crewe, Gillian Peele, Richard Rose, and Graham Wilson; all were helpful, none is responsible.

Source: *American Political Science Review*, (1984) 78:110-125. Reprinted with permission of the publisher.

The Concept of a Personal Vote

By "personal vote" we mean that portion of a candidate's electoral support which originates in his or her personal qualities, qualifications, activities, and record. In legislative elections especially, political science research emphasizes that part of the vote which is not personal—support based on shared partisan affiliations, fixed voter characteristics such as class, religion, and ethnicity, reactions to national conditions such as the state of the economy, and performance evaluations centered on the head of the governing party. This imbalance in emphasis is reasonable enough; most empirical work suggests that factors such as the preceding account for the lion's share of the variation in election outcomes. Only after American scholars realized that the personal vote had reached significant proportions did they really give it much attention.

Still, even if small, the personal vote has potentially great political significance. In contrast with votes based on party or class identifications, religious affiliations, the national economy, or national executive performance, the individual legislator has by definition some impact on the personal vote, and because it is under his control, he may give it disproportionate attention. This in turn has implications for party cohesion in the legislature, party support for the executive, and ultimately, the ability to enforce national electoral accountability in the system.[3] A personal vote reflects a principal feature of the single-member district plurality electoral system: the distinction between the interests and fortunes of an individual representative and those of any collectivity, especially party, to which he or she may belong. It is logically possible for any given representative to win while all fellow partisans are defeated. This simple fact creates an incentive for each representative to build a personal base of support within the geographic district, support not subject to the vagaries of national swings arising from popular reactions to national events, personalities, and conditions. To be sure, myriad features of a political system may work to circumscribe the operation of the individual representative's incentive—the resources available to him, the nomination system, the electoral system (e.g. independent executive or not), the needs, ideologies, and party loyalties of constituents—to name but a few of the more obvious ones. Thus, the gap between individual and collective interests maybe large in some systems (e.g. the American) and virtually nonexistent in others (e.g. the textbook British account). The incentive still exists, however, and fragments of the existing literature gave us reason to believe that it operates even in a system like Great Britain's, although with effects much weaker than those observed in the United States.

The preliminary statistical analysis presented in Table 16-1 illustrates this discussion. The data are from the 1980 NES/CPS American National Election Study and a British Gallup survey conducted after the May 1979 election.[4] The estimates (probit) show the association of party identification, executive performance ratings, and candidate incumbency status (coded from standard sources and merged with the survey files) with the vote for or against the parliamentary and congressional candidates of the incumbent Labour and Democratic parties. Evidently, the American and British findings differ in several respects. First, partisanship exerts a much larger impact, *ceteris paribus,* in British parliamentary voting than in American House voting. Although this difference is expected,

Table 16-1 Summary Vote Equations, Great Britain and United States

		Great Britain (*n* = 1527)	*United States* (*n* = 711)	
Party identification	Strong Con.	−1.86**	−.89**	Strong Rep.
	Weak Con.	−1.43**	−.71**	Weak Rep.
	Other	− .15**	−.46**	Ind. Rep.
	Liberal	− .46**	.40*	Ind. Dem.
	Weak Lab.	1.34**	.40*	Weak Dem.
	Strong Lab.	2.12**	.83**	Strong Dem.
JC job rating	Very good	1.13**	.25	Strongly approve
	Good	1.18**	.06	Approve
	Fair	.80**	.09	Disapprove
	Poor	.09	—	—
	Don't know	1.15**	−.13	Don't know
Incumbency status	Labour	.32*	.78**	Democrat
	Other	− .26*	−.46*	Republican
Constant		−1.59**	−.36	
Correctly predicted		89%	75%	
$\hat{R}^2$		.76	.47	

* $p < .05$.
** $p < .01$.

one would imagine that the difference has increased from what it would have been in the late 1940s, for example. A second even more noteworthy difference between the two equations concerns the importance of Callaghan ratings for the fates of Labour candidates, and the virtual irrelevance of Carter ratings for the fates of Democratic candidates.[5] Again, these results are consistent with the tenor of traditional discussions of British voting behavior, and the more recent studies of House elections. From the standpoint of this article, principal interest attaches to a third difference between the two equations: the much greater importance of incumbency status in American House elections than in British parliamentary elections. The differences here are fully as great, *ceteris paribus,* as those between the effects of party identification and executive ratings.

Still, we daresay that most scholars will be less taken by the difference in the importance of incumbency status in the two countries than by the fact that statistically significant effects appear in Great Britain at all. The estimates show that other things being equal, Labour incumbents ran significantly better than Labour candidates who were contesting open seats, and the latter in turn ran significantly better than Labour candidates seeking to unseat incumbents of any other party (open seats—those for which no incumbent ran—are the omitted reference category for the incumbency status variables). Although significant, these effects are not substantively large; Table 16-2 contains a translation of the

Table 16-2 Estimated Probability of In-Party Vote by Party Identity Executive Performance and District Incumbency Status

	Incumbency		
Great Britain	*Non-Labour*	*Open*	*Labour*
Strong conservative—fair	.00	.00	.01
Weak conservative—fair	.01	.01	.03
No party identification—fair	.15	.21	.32
Liberal—fair	.07	.11	.18
Weak Labour—good	.75	.82	.89
Strong Labour—very good	.92	.95	.98

	Incumbency		
United States	*Republican*	*Open*	*Democratic*
Strong Republican—very poor	.04	.11	.32
Weak Republican—very poor	.06	.14	.39
Independent—poor	.24	.40	.70
Weak Democratic—good	.36	.54	.81
Strong Democratic—good	.53	.70	.90

probit estimates into probabilities of supporting candidates of the incumbent party as a function of the respondent's party affiliation and executive performance ratings, and the incumbency status of the constituency. Each party identification category is assigned the modal executive rating of that category.

As Table 16-2 shows, the impact of Conservative party identification was so strong in 1979 that candidate status made little or no difference among Conservative identifiers (the raw data show that *all* of the 81 strong Conservatives in Labour districts voted against the incumbent). This contrasts sharply with the American case, where a one-third minority of strong Republicans reported support of Democratic incumbents. For those not attached to the Conservative party, however, the effects of incumbency status were more pronounced. Voters offering no party identification, for example, were twice as likely to vote for an incumbent Labour candidate as for a Labour candidate running against an incumbent of another party. The figures are similar for Liberals, and even weak Labour identifiers show a nontrivial effect of incumbency status. In the United States, of course, the general effects of incumbency (looking across the rows) are relatively much stronger, perhaps two-thirds or so as great as the effects of party identification (looking down the columns).

Tables 16-1 and 16-2 suggest that there is indeed a personal vote for us to compare, contrast, and explain. Given the amount of research devoted to American voting, our emphasis in this article will be on the British. By way of introduction, let us briefly consider several of the components of the personal vote identified in American research and how they may or may not apply to the British case. The first and most obvious explanation of the House incumbency advantage arises from the sheer quantity of electorally productive resources provided to all incumbents, such as staff, office space, long-distance telephone privileges and the frank, and travel (Cover, 1977; Cover & Brumberg, 1982; Mayhew 1974a; Parker, 1980b), estimates of the value of which range up to a million dollars per term. This factor can hardly operate in Britain because MPs have very little in the way of personal support. The average MP shares a secretary and may work with a party agent in the constituency.[6] Another partial explanation of the House incumbency advantage focuses on the differential campaign funding of incumbents and challengers (Jacobson, 1980). In Britain, however, campaigns are much cheaper, constituency spending is severely limited, candidates do not raise money individually, and spending decisions are more centralized. Thus, the financial muscle of MPs would seem to be a hypothesis that we can safely dismiss (Pinto-Duschinsky, 1980). Third, some authors have suggested that less tangible factors partially explain the House incumbency advantage. One could argue that strong incumbents deter strong challengers, and that incumbent strength is at least to some extent a self-fulfilling prophecy which results when weak challengers are the only ones willing to make the race (Hinckley, 1980a; Mann, 1978). Here again, the hypothesis would not appear as plausible for Britain. Unlike American candidates who await the proper time to run, many aspiring MPs look for a suitable location—a winnable, if not safe, district. An important qualification for the nomination in such a district is a reputation as a good candidate, and an effective way to earn such a reputation is to wage a strong campaign in a hopeless district. King (1982) reports that in the 1970s Parliaments, one-half of all MPs had lost at least once before winning their seats, and one-fourth had lost twice or more.[7] Thus, it appears that incumbent MPs are less likely to get an electoral free ride than are incumbent congressmen (MCs), given that ambitious challengers in Britain cannot hope to impress future selection committees by merely going through the motions.

All in all, the foregoing considerations suggest that the personal vote in Britain is very personal indeed. Its existence would seem to reflect the particular characteristics and activities of particular candidates. Such a vote is contingent; it depends on who the MPs are and what they do. A likely possibility for an important component of this contingent personal vote corresponds to a fourth partial explanation of the House incumbency advantage—constituency service, by which we mean the nonpartisan, nonprogrammatic effort to help individual constituents in their dealings with the larger government, and to defend and advance the particularistic interests of the constituency in the councils of the larger government. In the next section we present new data on constituency service in Britain, some from the mass survey already introduced, and still more from an elite survey coordinated with the mass survey sampling frame. Analogous American data also will be presented. In the fourth section we report statistical analyses that show the importance of constituency service as an explanation of the personal vote. A concluding section relates our findings to discussions of embryonic developments in the British electoral system.

Constituency Service in Great Britain and the United States

The textbook portrait of British politics leaves little room for a personal vote. Although MPs appear desirous of retaining their office (the retirement rate in 1979 was approximately 10%), and thus have an incentive to fashion a personal vote, the instruments available to them appear too paltry to permit them to do so. Most MPs are faceless troops in the party ranks who vote in accord with the party whip. They have little or no personal power (for example, committee based as in the United States) to procure "pork" for their districts or to provide favors to individual constituents. As mentioned, they have very little staff and office resources, and their campaign spending is both limited and largely out of their control. Their parliamentary careers hinge not only on their continued local renomination and reelection, but also, and more important, on the impressions they make on national party leaders. To cap it all off, their constituents can register a preference for the executive only through their vote decisions for Parliament. Consequently, voters naturally pay scant attention to individual MPs and make their choices on the basis of such general factors as party affiliations, class position, and reactions to top party leaders, particularly those who will constitute the government.

The preceding textbook portrait is familiar to American scholars, many of whom use it to highlight a contrasting textbook portrait of the Congress. Like most textbook portraits, however, the British one is painted in bold relief. Strong tendencies become incontrovertible generalizations, and traces of inconsistent evidence seem to disappear. Knowledgeable observers of British politics have long been aware that MPs are not quite so helpless and electorally irrelevant (or at least don't believe they are) as some textbooks suggest. Moreover, the recent literature increasingly focuses on changes in British politics, changes of a kind different from the generalizations of the older textbooks.

A number of British scholars (Butt, 1967; Chester & Bowring, 1962; Crick, 1970) have observed that in the postwar period the average amount of time devoted by an MP to government legislation has decreased and that devoted to representing constituents against the bureaucracy has increased. Barker and Rush (1970, pp. 183-184) report that Labour and younger members are especially prone to emphasize the "welfare-officer" role. The phrase "a good constituency man" has entered the popular literature on voting (Hartley-Brewer, 1976), and the Liberal-pioneered strategy of grass-rooting has received academic notice (Kavanagh, 1969, pp. 49-50; King, 1974). Relevant data are scarce, however. In an older publication, Dowse (1963) studied an important aspect of constituency relations—surgeries—via a mail survey of 100 MPs. Of 69 responses, only one-fifth of the MPs held no surgery whatsoever, and those with fewer than nine years of service tended to hold them more frequently than more senior members. But Dowse found no relation between electoral margins and frequency of surgeries, and on that basis concluded that constituency work stems from the "genuine desire to win public esteem and to be of service" (p. 336). When queried directly, only one-third of the MPs viewed their activity as electorally profitable.

In contrast to Dowse's findings, our interviews 16 years later indicate that contemporary MPs are considerably more prone to hold surgeries (Table 16-3).[8]

Table 16-3 Comparative Frequency of Surgeries, 1963 v. 1979

	Dowse (1963) %	*CFF (1979)* %
None	17	4
Ad hoc basis	20	3
Less than monthly	—	4
Monthly	23	25
Every three weeks	6	6
Every two weeks	22	32
Three per month	—	11
Weekly or more often	12	15
N =	65	100

As seen, 37% of Dowse's 1963 respondents held no regular surgery; by 1979 only a corporal's guard did not hold surgery on a regular basis. At the other extreme of the distribution, one-third of Dowse's respondents held surgeries at least every two weeks, whereas well over one-half of our respondents did so. In two decades surgery has apparently become the standard aspect of an MP's life.

Surgeries produce contact with constituents, generally those having some request, grievance, or other claim vis-à-vis the government. Our interviews explored at length the topic of casework; several salient features of the responses are of interest before we proceed to the statistical analyses.[9] As government has grown, one would naturally expect that demands in the form of casework would grow commensurately, but some authors (e.g. Fiorina, 1977b) have hypothesized that electoral incentives lead legislators to stimulate constituency demands. To be sure there is a broad range of possibilities, from a simple invitation in a newsletter for constituents to write to a given address, to passing out stamped, preaddressed postcards in nursing homes. At any rate, the interviews showed that at least some level of solicitation is the rule (85%) in the United States. The figure is lower (64%) in Britain, although a clear majority indicates some degree of initiative. In contrast, MPs are more likely (50%) to seek publicity for successful casework. Whereas MCs publicize casework in general terms and in the aggregate, they more often (67%) express the sentiment that publicizing the details of cases would be an invasion of their constituents' privacy.

In the United States the most common types of casework are social security and veterans' benefits (almost universally mentioned). In Britain citizen requests and complaints stem most frequently from housing (mentioned by 85% of our interviewees), pensions (72%), taxes (37%), and immigration (22%). Thus, the single most common source of casework in Britain is a program that is legally a responsibility of local government. An overwhelming majority of MPs (83%) report that they do handle such local casework, although a considerable proportion (33%) do so with reluctance. In contrast, a majority of MCs report

Table 16-4 Number of Cases Handled per Week by MCs and MPs

	Congressmen %	*MPs* %
< 20	9	23
21-40	28	23
41-60	18	14
61-80	6	10
81-100	14	8
100+	16	3
MV[a]	10	19
N	102	101

[a] MV = Refused to answer, didn't know.

they do not handle state and local cases, although they would advise constituents on the appropriate officials to contact.

Obviously, MPs are not geared up to handle casework to the same extent as MCs—they have nothing like the extensive, permanent district operations now common in the United States. Moreover, the much smaller size of British constituencies (about 90,000 people on average, as opposed to 525,000 in the United States) would lead us to expect a smaller case load. However, the estimated case loads reported in Table 16-4 are higher than we had anticipated. Given that some MPs still answer their mail in longhand, their reported workload is quite impressive.

There is, then, a great deal of constituency-oriented activity apparent in Great Britain. And although we have presented data only on casework, MPs are in their constituencies more often than they hold surgery: the model MP returns to the constituency at least weekly (many of them, of course, live in London), and more than 80% go home at least twice a month. Partially as a result of this contact, MPs enjoy high visibility in their constituencies. Referring back to the mass surveys, incumbent MPs enjoyed a spontaneous name recall of 66% in 1979, nearly twice the level achieved by MCs.[10] About an eighth of British respondents claimed to have met their MP personally.

Does the constituency attentiveness of an MP have any electoral payoff? Little in the literature bears directly on the question. As mentioned, only 32% of Dowse's 1963 respondents thought that it did. In our survey, however, 83% (57 of 69) answered definitely yes, and another 16% thought that a limited effect was present. Only one MP flatly denied an electoral effect. This response distribution is virtually the same as that for MCs, although very different from that which Dowse reported. Perhaps there has been a major temporal change, or perhaps Dowse's respondents hesitated to commit a seemingly crass admission to paper. Apropos of the latter possibility, consider that Barker and Rush (1970, p. 177) note that MPs queried in 1967 universally believed that their personal reputations and activities had some impact on the vote.

British academics, however, tend to accept the findings reported by Dowse. Like congressional scholars of the 1960s, British scholars appear reluctant to believe that MPs might be motivated to any significant extent by mundane electoral considerations. The edited transcripts of the King and Sloman BBC interviews reflect (and to some extent underlie) the prevailing consensus; they are worth quoting at some length. The first segment comes from a conversation with Shirley Williams, then a member of the Labour shadow cabinet, and Norman Tebbit, a junior Tory MP, although one from an extremely safe seat. The program was titled, "M.P.s and their Surgeries" (King & Sloman, 1973, pp. 13-14):

> *King:* If it takes up so much time, if M.P.s have to write so many letters, if they sometimes find the work depressing, why do almost all members of Parliament hold surgeries? The cynic would say 'in order to win votes, of course.' But the cynic would be wrong. There is no evidence that this sort of careful individual constituency work makes any substantial difference at the time of a general election, and M.P.s know it. I asked Shirley Williams how far she thought her surgery work helped her win the allegiance of the voters.
>
> *Williams:* I don't think that it makes much difference. All you can say is that perhaps you gradually build up a reputation as a conscientious or reasonably hard-working M.P., and that is of some advantage. But with the individual cases I suspect there's almost no influence at all.
>
> *King:* How much advantage—hundreds of votes, thousands?
>
> *Williams:* At most, hundreds.
>
> *King:* Norman Tebbit seemed surprised even to be asked. Had he won any votes that morning?
>
> *Tebbitt:* Do you know I've never thought of it? I can't say that for me the favorite part of my life as a Member of Parliament is being a social worker, . . . But I just regard it as part of my job and, as to whether it wins votes or not, you know, I'm not really particularly interested.

Similarly, in a segment titled "The Case of Flora Genetio" (King & Sloman, 1973, pp. 26-27), we read the following colloquy between King and Roy Hattersley, then a Labour front-bencher:

> *King:* But in the end doesn't all this constituency work, doesn't the writing of all these letters, the holding of surgeries and advisory sessions, boil down to an effort to win votes, to make sure of getting in next time? Roy Hattersley, and I think most M.P.s, would deny this vigorously. How much help, I asked Roy Hattersley, do you think your constituency work is going to help towards your re-election when the time comes?
>
> *Hattersley:* Very little indeed. My re-election when the time comes depends on the standing of the two parties. I hope I shall poll about nineteen or twenty thousand votes. If two or three hundred of those are the result of my constituency work, I shall have done rather well.
>
> *King:* Why, then, does he do the work?
>
> *Hattersley:* I do the constituency work, not for a political bonus, because there isn't a political bonus in it. I do it because it's part of the job.
>
> *King:* Part of an M.P.s job. The non-partisan, non-speech-making, little publicized part that goes on week in and week out, even when Parliament is in recess.

Evidently, the MPs quoted above do not share the views of most of those MPs we interviewed. Perhaps we were duped, or perhaps our interviewees did not understand the question as we intended it. But then again, perhaps constituency work is a more important concern of backbenchers, who are academically less interesting than frontbenchers. Perhaps, too, prominent politicians are loathe to announce over the BBC that their actions stem from anything but the highest of motives.

At any rate, there are at least three questions that research would do well to keep separate: 1) Do MPs believe that their constituency work has electoral payoffs? Based on our interviews we think the answer is now generally yes. 2) Is the constituency work of MPs motivated primarily by electoral considerations? The academic consensus is probably no, but in any event ascertaining "real" motivations is terribly difficult. 3) Whatever the motivation, does constituency work have an electoral impact? Aside from Dowse, an older study of the electoral strength of "experienced" candidates in 65 marginal seats (Williams, 1966-1967), and a recent study of 18 marginals by Curtice and Steed (1980), there is little research that sheds light on this last question. In the next section we present some findings based on the elite interviews and mass surveys discussed above.

Constituency Service and the Vote: Great Britain and the United States

Both mass surveys pursued at some length the subject of constituency service. Constituents were asked whether they had ever contacted the incumbent and if so, why, whether they had gotten a response, and whether they considered the response satisfactory. In the United States about one in seven respondents (a higher proportion of actual voters, of course) had initiated some communication with their MC; of these, 7% reported that they had requested help, 4% that they sought information, and 4% that they expressed their opinions. In Great Britain 1 in 12 respondents had contacted his MP, with 5% requesting help, 2% information, and as would be expected, fewer than 2% expressing an opinion.[11] Nearly all constituents in both countries reported that they were "very satisfied" with the response, and fewer than 25% reported either no response or dissatisfaction.

In addition to personal experiences, a fifth of the American and a sixth of the British samples claimed they knew of someone else who had contacted his MC or MP (we refer to this as secondhand contact in the discussion that follows). Further, one-fifth of the American sample and one-eighth of the British maintained that they could recall something special the incumbent had done for the district. The probes accompanying this item elicited a very mixed bag of responses by the Americans, with only about half referring specifically to local concerns and programs. In Britain, however, the modal answer, offered by two-fifths of the respondents, is that the MP champions local causes. Smaller, roughly equal proportions mention housing, local industries, aid to individuals in trouble, and the MP's general interest in local affairs.

Each survey included a generalized evaluative item designed to tap the incumbent's relationship to his constituency. First included in the 1978 NES/CPS election study, the item was dubbed "expectation of access." It was intended to capture some aspect of Fenno's (1978) emphasis on the reputation for accessibility and trustworthiness that a representative seeks to develop. We think that the wording of the question makes it a fair general measure of the extent to which a representative is perceived as "a good constituency man." It reads,

> If you had a problem that Representative (your MP) (name) could do something about, do you think he/she would be very helpful, somewhat helpful, or not very helpful to you?

In both countries constituents expressed fairly positive expectations.[12] Some indication that these expectations have real content and are neither purely random nor pure rationalization appears in Table 16-5. The figures in the table are probit estimates for statistical models in which expectations of access are the left side variable. The models presume that incumbents enhance their images by achieving visibility and by actually compiling a good record, or at least one that is

Table 16-5 Expectation of Access Equations, United States and Great Britain

	United States (N = 811)	*Great Britain* (N = 821)
Contact		
Personal	.36**	.56**
Media	.39**	.23**
Secondhand	.24*	− .02
Casework		
Very satisfied	1.07**	.92**
Somewhat satisfied	.17**	− .60*
Not satisfied	−1.22**	−1.39**
Secondhand casework		
Satisfied	.66**	
Somewhat satisfied	.02	.57**
Not satisfied	− .67*	
District service	.38**	.55**
Party identification		
Independent	.02	—
Minor	—	− .44*
None	—	.24*
Same	.19*	.41**
Recall incumbent	.16	.05
Recall challenger	− .05	− .02
Year elected	− .01*	.01
Constant	1.25**	.14
$\hat{R}^2$	.36	.29

*$p < .05$.
**$p < .01$.

perceived as good. In addition constituents may have more positive expectations about an incumbent who shares their party affiliation. Conversely, a visible challenger might dim the luster of the incumbent, given that the former may attack the incumbent's record or person as part of his or her campaign. All of these suggestions are no more than common sense, and all are reflected in the data.

The British and American equations are quite similar. MPs may get more political mileage from personal contacts than MC's,[13] and MCs perhaps more out of secondhand contacts (i.e., contacts with friends, relatives, and co-workers about whom the respondent has heard). After taking reported contacts into account, spontaneous name recall appears to have little effect in either country.[14] Party affiliations are more important, *ceteris paribus,* in Britain, with minor party identifiers significantly less likely to evidence positive expectations than even those who identify with national parties different from the incumbent's (the latter constitute the omitted reference category in the set of dummy variables).[15] Identifiers with the incumbent's party are the most sanguine about the likelihood that he or she would help in a pinch. Finally, in the United States senior incumbents are expected to be more helpful than junior ones; no comparable relationship is apparent in Britain.

However, the largest coefficients in Table 16-5 reflect the effects of the incumbent's previous efforts. Satisfied constituents are highly positive about his or her future potential, and dissatisfied constituents (rare) highly negative (the omitted reference category for these dummy variables comprises those who report no casework experience).[16] Those who recall something already done for the constituency are likewise very positive. Not surprisingly, these figures show clearly that incumbent representatives can behave in a manner calculated to enhance their constituents' images of them, and that conclusion holds for MPs as much as for MCs. As yet, however, we do not know the degree to which positive images translate into supportive votes.

Table 16-6 represents a first attempt at answering the preceding questions. The equations reported in this table treat the vote decision as dependent on the visibility of the incumbent and challenger, the reputation of the incumbent for being "a good constituency man," the party affiliation of the incumbent vis-à-vis the constituent, and evaluations of the executive.[17]

Taking the more familiar American results first, the estimates are consistent with recent accounts of House elections in the academic literature, the popular press, and the laments of political leaders. By achieving visibility and developing a reputation for constituency service, the MC can exert a major impact on his or her electoral fate. All else being equal, a very favorable image as a good constituency representative is more important to the candidate in determining the vote than having the same party affiliation as the voter. As in Table 16-1, the effects of Carter ratings on the House vote in 1980 were nil, even though the present analysis is restricted to incumbents who have a record vis-à-vis Carter.

And what about Britain? The estimates demonstrate much that anyone would have expected, and perhaps a bit that some would not. As in Table 16-1, the effects of party identification are nothing short of massive (recall that "opposite party identifier" is the omitted reference category). How difficult it is for other influences to have an impact in the face of such strong partisan effects is

Table 16-6 Incumbent Vote Equations, United States and Great Britain

	United States (*N* = 644)	*Great Britain* (*N* = 1,111)
Incumbent name recall	.44**	.46**
Challenger name recall	− .77**	− .35**
Challenger contact	− .57**	—
Expectation of helpfulness		
Very	1.76**	.35*
Somewhat	.82**	.07
Don't know	.43*	− .22
Depends	—	− .02
Party identification		
Independent	.57**	—
None	—	.99**
Other	—	.99**
Same	1.19**	2.43**
Executive job rating		
Out-party incumbent		
Approve	.23	.01
Fair/DK	− .47	.34*
Disapprove	− .29	.50*
In-party incumbent		
Fair/DK	− .76	− .20
Disapprove	− .13	− .60**
Constant	− .71**	−1.65**
$\hat{R}^2$	.51	.64
Correctly predicted	80%	86%

shown in Table 16-7. The other major influence on British voting decisions offers a clear contrast to the American results. Ratings of Callaghan's performance have significant effects on the vote for MPs. The omitted reference category is "in-party incumbent, approves Callaghan performance" (the expected effects of Callaghan ratings on the vote are obviously conditional on the party of the incumbent MP). Thus, the estimates show that constituents who disapprove of Callaghan's performance are significantly more likely to vote for a Conservative MP than those who approve; constituents of a Labour MP who disapprove of Callaghan are significantly less likely to vote for the MP than are those who approve of Callaghan.

Of most interest, however, are the variables that capture aspects of the personal vote in Britain. As in the U.S. equations, incumbent visibility has a positive and highly significant impact on electoral support (and challenger visibility has a comparable negative impact). Well-known incumbents do better than unknowns, other things being equal. Of even greater interest is the estimate

Table 16-7 Estimated Probabilities of Incumbent Vote by Expectation of Helpfulness

Incumbent's party	*Voter's identification*	*Not helpful*	*Somewhat helpful*	*Very helpful*
Great Britain				
Lab	Lab	.89	.91	.94
	None/Other	.34	.37	.48
	Cons	.06	.07	.11
Cons	Lab	.12	.13	.20
	None/Other	.56	.58	.69
	Cons	.95	.96	.98
United States				
Dem	Dem	.58	.90	.99
	Ind	.39	.71	.93
	Rep	.20	.49	.82
Rep	Dem	.32	.63	.90
	Ind	.33	.65	.91
	Rep	.58	.84	.97

attached to a reputation for constituency service. Those constituents who hold highly positive expectations of their MP are significantly more likely to vote for him or her than those not holding such expectations. There is no denying, however, that the effects of constituency service are but a shadow of what they are in the United States. Table 16-7 gives some idea of the comparative magnitude of the effects; the variable of interest is the voter's expectation of helpfulness. We examine six configurations obtained by crossing three party-identification categories with two incumbency categories. The figures in the table are calculated from Table 16-6 under the assumption that the voter has the modal value for variables other than expectations of helpfulness. In the British calculations this means that the voter is assumed to recall the incumbent, not recall the challenger, and rate Callaghan good if a Labour identifier, fair if a nonidentifier, and the average of poor and fair if a Conservative identifier. Given these conditions the voters' estimated probabilities of voting for the incumbent MP are given in the top part of the table.

The party identification and Callaghan rating effects are so strong that the vote is almost a foregone conclusion in many cases, but at the margins the effect of being "a good constituency man" emerges. The smallest effect is a .03 increase in the probability that a Conservative identifier would support a Conservative incumbent, whereas the largest is a .14 increase in the probability that a nonidentifier would support a Labour incumbent.[18] These numbers contrast with the American figures in the bottom half of the table.[19] There we see that an incumbent's perceived reputation can have enormous effects. Consider, for example, the range of probability estimates for identifiers of one party who have a MC of the other: these probabilities triple as a function of perceived reputation. All in all, an MC's reputation for helpfulness appears to have a potential impact as great as that of party identification.

How large is the personal vote in Britain? Is it the negligible few hundred that some observers dismiss? Using Tables 16-6 and 16-7 to arrive at a precise estimate is not easy, inasmuch as the estimates vary considerably with voter characteristics and attitudes, but for illustrative purposes imagine some hypothetical races. Looking across our sample we find a constituency quite negative about the expected helpfulness of their MP: 8 electors distributed 0, 1, 7 across the categories "very helpful," "somewhat helpful," and "not very helpful.' Another constituency is distributed in exactly the reverse fashion: 7, 1, 0 (a few constituencies have everyone in the first category, incidentally). Applying the probability estimates given in Table 16-7, and weighting by the actual distributions of party identification in Labour and Conservative incumbent constituencies, respectively, we arrive at estimated differences in expected vote of a little less than 6.5% in the case of Conservative MPs and a little more than 6.5% in the case of Labour MPs. We emphasize that these are *not* estimates of the actual personal vote in 1979, even in an "average" constituency, but rather illustrations of the potential difference between the vote-attracting abilities of MPs with reputations as excellent constituency men and those with reputations as very poor ones. Still, because it is at least partially an MP's decision to become known as an excellent constituency man or a very poor one, the figures represent maximum bounds on the personal vote in contemporary Britain.

We recognize, of course, that some readers may be skeptical of the kind of exercise just reported, inasmuch as it relies on a survey item that measures voter evaluations, and such items always entail a risk of contamination from other evaluative factors. Even given the results in Table 16-5, should we not worry that responses to the expectation-of-access item are in some part rationalizations, that people who plan to vote for a given incumbent naturally say that he would be very helpful? As a precaution against this possibility we report a second analysis based on the elite surveys discussed in the preceding section. Many of our interviewees voiced the opinion that diligent constituency work could dampen swings against their party or augment swings to their party. Given the data they reported, it is a fairly straightforward matter to examine the accuracy of their beliefs. We formulated a simple additive index based on the MP's description of his constituency work. The index gives a value of one for each of the following: does the MP encourage casework, does the MP publicize successful casework, does the MP handle local cases, and does the MP hold surgery more than twice monthly? The 101 districts for which we have interviews range from zero to four on this index.[20] Do these accounts of constituency work bear any relation to objective swings in the vote? Table 16-8 shows that they most certainly do.

A noteworthy feature of the 1979 general election was that the traditional uniform swing was much less uniform than usual: North Britain swung to the Conservatives by 4.2%, whereas South Britain swung by 7.7% (Curtice & Steed, 1980, p. 395). Because of regional variations, recent analyses of British electoral behavior have used regional swing figures rather than a single national average. We follow this practice in the analyses reported in Table 16-8 regressing the swing in our sample districts on the swing in their larger region, several demographic variables previously identified as important (Crewe, 1979), and

Table 16-8 Effect of Constituency Work on Swing[a]

	Conservative Seats		*Labour Seats*	
	(1)	*(2)*[b]	(3)	(4)[b]
Regional swing	.59**	.56**	.83**	.79**
Constituency work	.42*	.44*	− .74†	− .88*
Immigrant (%)	−4.24**	−4.03**	−1.17	—
Metropolitan cities	.19		2.23*	1.92*
Nonmetropolitan cities	− .89	—	.17	—
Constant	1.15	1.22	2.45	3.06
n	55	55	33	33
$\hat{R}^2$	.41	.39	.55	.52

* $p < .05$.
** $p < .01$.
† $p < .10$.

[a] Swing is defined as the average of the gain in Conservative share of the vote and loss in Labour share. The figures are drawn from the *Times Guide to the House of Commons.*

[b] Equations (2) and (4) omit nonsignificant demographic variables included in equations (1) and (3).

their score on the constituency work index.[21] The results are quite indicative. The statistically significant estimates imply that variations in constituency work (0 to 4) account for swings of something between 1.5 and 2% for Conservatives and of something between 3 and 3.5% for Labour. Thus, depending on the party, variations in constituency attentiveness have an electoral effect potentially as large as one quarter to one-half of the observed regional swings. The figure for Labour is almost twice that for Conservatives, consistent with the estimates of Williams (1966-1967) for an earlier period.[22] The estimates are realistic bounds on the actual size of the personal vote, moreover, since it is well within the capability of the average MP to determine where he or she scores on the index of constituency work. We should also note that these estimates are generally in the ballpark, although somewhat larger than those calculated by Curtice and Steed (1980, p. 409) from analysis of 18 "switched" districts.[23]

Discussion

The estimates reported in the preceding section do not show that constituency work is a major influence on the vote in Britain. Rather, our analyses confirm the standard findings that party allegiances and evaluations of party leaders account for the lion's share of the variance in electoral decisions, although it seems clear that party loyalty accounts for less than it once did (Crewe, 1974). Is it the case, then, that constituency service in Britain is of only mild academic interest, not deserving of anything like the attention it has received in the American literature? In our opinion, no.

In the first place, what is of importance to tenured professors seeking to explain variance and what is important to elected officials seeking to win re-election may not correspond very closely. Individual MPs can do little or nothing to alter their constituents' evaluations of party leaders. But individuals can affect their images in the constituency, and the little they can affect may be of greater importance to them than the great deal that they cannot. Moreover, within the ranks of elected officials, there are further distinctions. The minister sitting in a safe seat may share the professor's disdain for a piddling personal vote, but the ambitious politician in a marginal seat may view those one thousand to two thousand votes as the difference between a successful political career and oblivion.[24]

Second, constituency service in Britain might be of more importance than its present impact on the popular vote would indicate, owing to indications that service activity is a growth industry. Our elite interviews contain numerous suggestions that "this sort of thing" has become a larger part of the MP's job in recent years—sometimes to the dismay of older MPs. Constituency parties increasingly require their MPs to establish a local residence. And, as discussed earlier, there has been an increase in the frequency of surgeries. Such indications of increasing constituency orientation have potentially important electoral implications. Whatever the significance of constituency work for electoral behavior today, it might be considerably greater than it was two decades ago, and perhaps considerably less than it might be two decades hence. To explain the importance of that possibly emerging trend, we need to develop a further line of argument.

This chapter presents a simple cross-sectional analysis based on the static theoretical proposition that single-member district electoral systems provide incentives for candidates to cultivate personal bases of support. This proposition is significant in and of itself, we believe, but it takes on even greater significance when embedded in a dynamic theory of the evolution of party systems. In the United States, for example, a number of scholars have argued that the increasing importance of the personal vote and the decreasing importance of party affiliations are not independent phenomena. Burnham (1975) was probably the first to argue that the decline of party provides fertile ground for the growing importance of personal candidate appeals, which in turn further contribute to the decline of party. The argument is a dynamic one which our data are not adequate to test, but a few moments' consideration will demonstrate its plausibility.

Consider a single-member district system perfectly structured by party. Then by definition there is no personal vote: election outcomes simply reflect the automatic support of partisans for candidates of their party. Now if the hold of party should weaken, perhaps because of poor performance by the party in office, or unpopular issue positions by one or more of the parties, then a *context* is created which did not exist before. With some voters willing to employ decision criteria other than partisanship, the personal characteristics and activities of the candidates might, but not necessarily, begin to take on significance. As Fenno writes (1978, p. 211):

> Incumbency is not an automatic entitlement to a fixed number of votes or percentage points toward re-election. . . . Incumbency should be seen as a resource to be employed; an opportunity to be exploited; and the power of incumbency is whatever each member makes of the resource and the opportunity.

But, assume that some incumbents seize the opportunity and work to build personal bases of support. Then we would expect some feedback effect from their activities: observing hardworking incumbents making special efforts to serve their constituents, still more voters will decide that partisanship should matter less and the individual candidates more, thus further weakening thc hold of party. In short, once the dynamic is set in motion it is self-reinforcing; declining parties contribute to increasing personal votes which in turn detract further from the importance of party.

How does the dynamic begin in the first place? Perhaps through some exogenous event(s) as with the aforementioned suggestions of bad performance or unpopular issue stands, or even as a result of more-or-less nonpolitical factors such as a changing media environment, social or technological change, or whatnot. On the other hand an endogenous cause is conceivable. No party system has the kind of complete control posited at the beginning of this argument. There is always some slack in the system. And if incumbents begin to take advantage of such slack—for whatever reason—their resulting electoral benefit may encourage others and thus help weaken the hold of party even in the absence of exogenous disturbances.

What is the upshot of the preceding argument? Are we suggesting that the British party system is undergoing the same sort of decomposition as the American? Not at all. What we are suggesting is that the existence, size, and variation in the personal vote for legislative incumbents are of interest not only for the citizen voting decisions they affect, but also as important indicators of the strength and trend of a nation's party system.[25] And that is a topic that has aroused considerable interest among British commentators. To complete the argument we need refer to nothing so grand as the current Social Democratic challenge to the established Conservative and Labour parties. Less dramatically, Crewe (1974) describes such trends as the declining share of the vote captured by the two major parties, declining turnout, and increasing interelection volatility in the two-party swing. Probably less significant, but even more interesting from the standpoint of the research described in this article, are the reports of departures in the 1979 results from established patterns of British electoral behavior. Consider some selected remarks of Curtice and Steed in their detailed statistical appendix to the most recent Nuffield election study (Butler & Kavanagh, 1980):

> The 1974-1979 swing was not uniform: it varied more from seat to seat than in any other election since 1950 (1980, p. 394).
>
> It is clear that Labour kept down the swing in its marginal constituencies, particularly in those with less than a 2% two-party majority. . . . A major reason for the low swing, particularly the very low swing in the most marginal seats, is the effect of a change in incumbent MP since 1974. Because of the greater attention he can command in the media and the constituency services he can render, an incumbent MP is more likely to be able to establish a personal vote, consisting of those who support him as an individual rather than as a party representative. Where an MP does build such a personal vote in his favour, that vote will be lost if he is defeated. If he does lose, by the time of the next election the new incumbent MP may have acquired his own personal vote. The combined effect of these two personal votes would be a lower swing against the second incumbent at the following election. . . .
>
> These 18 clear cases amount to strong evidence of the personal vote that an MP can build up. The low swing in them is consistent and appears to be independent of location or type of constituency. For the period from 1974 to

> 1979, it would appear that the double effect amounted to around 1500 votes in an average sized constituency. . . . It is, of course, in marginal seats that MPs have the greatest incentive to work for such personal votes (1980, pp. 408-409).
>
> The more important and unexpected change is the reduction in the number of marginal constituencies. The figures . . . show that, on average, about 12 seats would change hands for each 1% swing. However, the equivalent tables produced after the 1964 and 1966 elections showed that about 18 seats would change hands for each 1% swing. This dramatic reduction in the number of seats liable to change hands has undermined the "cube law," which if it holds, does result in practice in about 18 seats changing hands for each 1% swing (1980, pp. 428-429).

Are the 1979 results aberrant? Apparently not. In a later analysis Curtice and Steed (1982, pp. 268-269) view the 1977 results as the continuation of trends which in retrospect began several elections earlier:

> In 1955 the preconditions for the operation of the cube law were still largely met. . . . Between 1955 and 1970 not a great deal of change occurred, except that there was some evidence of a small secular increase in the standard deviation. . . . In the 1970s both major parties won more seats by large two-party majorities: the distribution of the two-party vote widened and flattened. Before 1974 it was unimodal with a peak near its centre; the distribution is now bimodal with peaks where both parties win safe seats by moderately safe majorities. As a consequence of these changes, the exaggerative power of Britain's electoral system has been systematically reduced in the last three elections.

Nonuniform national swings? Incumbency effects? Vanishing marginals? Declining swing ratios? The American student of Burnham, Erikson, Mayhew, and Tufte should be forgiven a sudden rush of déjà vu, although the magnitudes of the changes discussed by Curtice and Steed are but a pale reflection of those observed in American congressional elections. The changes are noteworthy enough, however, that scholars should not blithely dismiss MPs' activities and their associated personal votes. Whatever its current importance, the personal vote may indicate the condition of important features of the larger electoral system and presage future alterations in that system.

NOTES

1. This extensive literature is cited, discussed, synthesized, and otherwise dealt with in two recent books on congressional elections, Hinckley (1981) and Jacobson (1983).
2. Pierce and Converse (1981) is a notable exception, albeit one that focuses on candidate visibility rather than the vote. Also to be noted are Tufte's (1973) cross-national comparison of swing ratios, and Stokes's (1967) contrast of "swing" in the United States and Great Britain. Such aggregate comparisions reflect relative differences in district-level forces, if not necessarily individual candidate effects.
3. For an extended development of this argument, see Fiorina (1980).
4. The 1980 NES/CPS post-election survey included 1,408 respondents. The British Gallup survey included 2,031 respondents interviewed during the week after the 1979 election in a sampling frame covering England, Scotland, and Wales. In consultation

with British Gallup staff we selected a subset of 1978 CPS/NES items and modified them (when necessary) for administration to a British sample.

5. Note, however, that the effects of Callaghan ratings are not nearly linear, nor even monotonic. Relative to the omitted reference category, very poor, those who rate Callaghan fair, good, or very good are significantly more likely to vote Labour. Strangely, the small group of voters who offer no opinion of Callaghan are as positively disposed toward Labour as those who rate Callaghan very favorably. Consistent with the argument of Converse (1966a), these are individuals with lower educational levels and little knowledge of public affairs.
6. Butler and Kavanagh (1980, p. 58, p. 72) report that in 1979 Labour had only 70 full-time paid agents, and in 1978 the Conservatives had 346. In addition, there are part-time, volunteer workers, typically party activists.
7. King finds that in the post World War II period there has been a steady upward trend in the proportions of MPs with previous election defeats in their background.
8. In each country we attempted to procure an elite interview for each constituency in the sampling frame of the mass survey. In the United States we completed interviews for 102 of the 108 districts in the sample. Our target was the congressional administrative assistant who preliminary research indicated would be the best source of information on office organization and activities. In Great Britain we completed interviews with MPs or party agents or both in 101 of the 133 constituencies included in the sample. When reporting the data, of course, we include only one interview for each of the 101 constituencies in the sampling frame, or in some cases only for the 69 constituencies in which we procured an interview with the incumbent MP.
9. The MP responses, along with analogous MC responses, will be discussed at length in a book now in preparation.
10. Approximately 48% of the respondents could recall the name of any challenger for the parliamentary seat, which is much lower than the percentage who could recall the incumbent's, but also more than twice the recall rate for challengers of MCs.
11. Munroe (1977) similarly finds that only a small proportion of constituent approaches to MPs involve general issues as opposed to personal concerns. In addition, Barker and Rush (1970, p. 175) comment that "we noticed that every one of a very varied group of constituencies produced more letters raising personal cases and problems than offered opinions on local or national issues."
12. Across the response categories—very helpful, somewhat helpful, not very helpful, don't know, and depends—the American distribution was 27%, 34%, 10%, 25%, 4%, whereas the British distribution was 28%, 28%, 11%, 24%, 10%. The analyses in Table 16-5 do not include the "don't know" and "depends" responses. The vote analyses in Tables 16-6 and 16-7, however, represent these categories, along with the three ordinal categories, as dummy variables.
13. The contact variables are created from the following survey item: "There are many ways in which MPs (MCs) can have contact with the people from their constituency. On this page are some of these ways (respondent receives card). Think of (name) who has been the MP (MC) from this constituency. Have you come into contact or learned anything about him/her through any of these ways?" Based on Parker's (1981) analysis the responses were used to create two dummy variables: personal contact (met the incumbent, heard him/her at a meeting, talked to staff, agent, secretary or other employee), and media contact (mail, newspaper/magazine, radio, TV).
14. The U.S. equations in Tables 16-5 and 16-6 were also estimated using name recognition in place of spontaneous name recall. Generally the former has a larger and more highly significant coefficient, but other coefficients in the equations are no more than .02 different, and the overall fit of the equations is no better. Thus, in order to maximize comparability we report only the American equations using name recall.

We also included campaign spending in the American equations, but failed to find significant effects. Spending presumably purchases contacts and visibility, but direct measures of the latter already appear in the equations.

15. In Tables 16-5 and 16-6 party affiliations are coded as follows. In the American sample all respondents fall into mutually exclusive classes: same party as incumbent (51%), independent (14%), opposite party from incumbent (35%). In the British sample 38% share the party affiliation of the incumbent, and 17% admit to no party identification. The opposite party category includes adherents of the party whose MP is not of that party—45%. In order to pick up any additional differences between national and party identifiers, an additional dummy variable, minor party identifiers, is included. This variable takes on a value of one for those 2.5% of the respondents who report an identification with other than the Conservative, Labour, or Liberal parties. To avoid statistical degeneracy in the analyses, one category, opposite party identifier, is omitted from each equation reported in Tables 16-5 and 16-6.
16. We did not get a measure of satisfaction with secondhand casework experience in Britain. Thus, the dummy variable takes on a value of one for all those who report knowledge of friend, relative, or co-worker experience. The large and highly significant coefficient suggests that the effects of satisfactory secondhand experience are very strong, given that the estimate in the table is watered down by inclusion of a presumed minority who recall unsatisfactory experiences.
17. In the analyses reported in Table 16-6, the executive performance ratings are collapsed into three categories: approve (very good, good), fair/don't know, and disapprove (very poor, poor). Because the effect of executive approval on the vote will depend on the party of incumbent—relating positively to votes for Labour MPs and negatively to votes for Conservatives—we have formed interaction terms between performance ratings and the party of the incumbent MP, which yields six dummy variables, one of which—Conservative incumbent, disapprove Callaghan—is omitted from the analysis. Analogous procedures were followed in the American case, although the results are completely insensitive to how or even whether Carter ratings enter the equation.
18. That is, .03 is the difference in estimated probability of a Conservative identifier supporting a Conservative incumbent who he believes would not be helpful if a problem arose and that of supporting a Conservative MP who would be very helpful. The other differences mentioned in the text are analogous.
19. The American figures are calculated under the assumption that the voter does not spontaneously recall the incumbent or challenger, approves of Carter's performance if a Democrat, and disapproves if an Independent or a Republican. Again, these assumptions reflect modal responses in the sample.
20. The actual distribution of the 101 districts across the 0-4 scale was 16, 21, 28, 31, 5. The analysis in Table 16-8 utilizes 85 of the 101 cases, excluding retirees, seats won in by-elections during 1974-1979, and seats held by Liberals and Nationalists.
21. The details of this analysis are discussed at length in Cain (1983).
22. Williams's (1966-1967) analysis did not utilize a measure of constituency effort. Rather, he sought more broadly to estimate the personal votes of "familiar" Labour versus "familiar" Conservative MPs. A "familiar" MP was defined as one with eight or more years' service.
23. Bear in mind, however, that Curtice and Steed attempt to estimate the *actual* personal vote in their sample of *marginals*. In contrast, our figures again represent the *potential* electoral difference between a very low level of constituency effort and a very high level, averaged across both marginal and nonmarginal districts.
24. In another article (Cain, Ferejohn, and Fiorina, 1983) we show that electoral marginality is significantly associated with an MP's inclination to engage in a variety

of constituency-oriented activities. Not surprisingly, those whose fates are more dependent on a few votes more actively seek those votes.

25. Of course, happenings in the electoral arena are not the only indicator of the state of the party system. The importance of party in the decisionmaking arena (i.e., Parliament) is of equal if not greater importance, although the two arenas undoubtedly have some connection to each other. In this regard an interesting topic for future research is whether the observations of Norton (1980) and Schwartz (1980) on the 1970s weakening of parliamentary party cohesion bear any relation to the concerns of this chapter.

LONG-TERM FACTORS IN ELECTIONS

I IDEOLOGICAL LEVEL OF THE ELECTORATE

II NATURE OF PARTISANSHIP

III NATURE OF PARTISAN CHANGE

IDEOLOGICAL LEVEL OF THE ELECTORATE

17. DO VOTERS THINK IDEOLOGICALLY?

Major voting studies in the 1950s and 1960s led to the conclusion that mass electorates were very unsophisticated. While political commentary among elites and in the press is traditionally carried out using concepts such as liberalism and conservatism, most voters were found to be blissfully ignorant of these notions, interpreting politics in terms of narrower concepts of group interests instead and often without benefit of any issue-based content whatsoever. But just as the role of issues in voting decisions grew in the 1960s and 1970s (see chapter 5) so the level of ideological thinking might have grown. Moreover, the studies documenting the absence of ideological thought were mostly American, and there was some suggestion that European mass electorates routinely understood the concepts of left and right as applied to politics. Finally, new methodological approaches suggested to some that the assumption of minimal understanding was misleading even for the 1950s. Thus, a considerable amount of writing in the last decade has been devoted to the question of just how widespread ideological thinking is. Fortunately, at least a partial resolution of the controversy seems at hand.

An Unsophisticated Electorate

Most discussions of ideological thinking in the electorate can be traced back to one of two works—*The American Voter* and Converse's (1964) "belief systems" paper. In *The American Voter* (Campbell et al., 1960, chapter 10), the authors categorized individuals into one of four "levels of conceptualization" according to how they discussed politics when asked what they liked and disliked about the two parties and their presidential candidates. Only the top group—a mere 2½ percent of the electorate—was considered to have shown clear evidence of ideological thinking. Others, another 9 percent, showed some form of ideological thought. The remainder of the sample responded to parties and candidates in terms of group benefits (42 percent), the "goodness" or "badness" of the times (24 percent), or incredibly, without any real issue content (22½ percent).

Converse's work was even more devastating. First, Converse found that opinions on policy items often failed to be related to one another. One might have thought that voters with a liberal opinion on one issue would tend to have a liberal opinion on other issues—even if they were not able to describe their views in ideological terms. Yet attitudes were not constrained in this way. Second, Converse found that some respondents failed to express any attitude at all on policy items that were thought to be among the most important at the time. Others gave a response, but the way in which they responded over time suggested that they might be responding randomly. "Nonattitudes" and a lack of ideological constraint were thus added to the characterization of the American voter.[1]

In the past decade the thesis of an unsophisticated electorate has undergone intense criticism, as we shall see shortly. In addition, even writings that lend support to that view often contain qualifications to earlier, unbridled statements about the electorate's abilities. Thus, it is easy to be blinded to the fact that recent research contains numerous indications of very restricted ideological thinking and very limited understanding of ideological concepts and terminology.

A follow-up to Converse's original study, the Converse and Markus article reprinted here as chapter 18, has this dual character. The study reports the results of a panel survey in which respondents were interviewed several times over the period 1972-1976. The study replicated the earlier survey from which Converse had concluded that nonattitudes and lack of constraint were primary features of the electorate.

In their report of the new panel, Converse and Markus emphasize the very high stability of party identification, several new issues on which stability is surprisingly high (suggesting that real attitudes were present), and the intermediate-level stability of candidate evaluations. Yet they make it clear that opinions on many issues were no more stable in the 1970s than in the 1950s. The initial results may have been exaggerated—as when some interpreted the low stability as showing that the vast majority of the electorate was expressing nonattitudes—and the new panel reveals some variability in stability rates that was not previously apparent. But to the extent that the earlier study showed an absence of strong, meaningful opinions on issues, the newer results for these issues support the very same conclusion. Indeed, Converse and Markus refer to the new panel data as "very nearly a carbon copy" of the earlier results. This is rather surprising in light of other changes in the 1960s, above all the apparent increases in constraint over the same period (which we shall describe shortly). As Converse and Markus point out, even if the increased constraint is artifactual, owing to changes in question wording, one might well expect greater attitude stability on the same basis.

Other recent writings contain similar dual results. Levitin and Miller (1979), for example, note that "well over half" the electorate can express some ideological sentiment and that ideological labels have "political significance" for a wide class of voters. Yet they also write of "considerable slippage" in the connection between ideological thinking and electoral decisions. In the end they conclude that perhaps 15-20 percent of the electorate has coherent ideological views, and they write that "our demonstration of the extent to which ideological sentiments do not translate directly into policy preferences is entirely congruent with the research of Converse, Klingemann, Stimson [reprinted in our first edition] and others who have documented the lack of ideological thinking in mass electorates in the United States and Europe" (pp. 769-70).

Klingemann's work is often cited to document increased ideological thinking in the United States and relatively greater understanding of ideological terms in Europe (see below), but the thrust of his major effort is entirely congruent with the quotation above. Klingemann studied the level of ideological sophistication in five European countries surveyed in the 1970s. The results, of course, vary in detail across countries and also demonstrate that voters are not easily packaged into pure categories of ideologues and nonideologues. Nevertheless, summarizing his chief measure of ideology, Klingemann concludes that "the thesis that there is an extraordinarily thin layer of respondents with high ideological competence is thus supported on a cross-national scale" (1979a, p. 245). In fact, from a third (Germany) to two-thirds (Great Britain) of the sample in each country is classified as showing no ideological conceptualization. In a similar vein, Norpoth (1979) observes that voters often rely on party alignments in government rather than on ideology for voting cues.

Also largely supporting the notion of an unsophisticated electorate are papers by Conover and Feldman and by Howell (1983), with the former reprinted here as chapter 19. As in other recent work, Conover and Feldman take it for granted that many voters express feelings about liberals and conservatives and willingly place themselves on a dimension anchored by these terms. What they question is the meaning of these labels for the general electorate. Very often, they argue, ideological labels are "largely symbolic in content and non-dimensional in structure" (p. 369). Individuals respond to ideological terminology, but "causality runs primarily from evaluations of ideological labels to self-identification" (p. 372) rather than the other way around. Howell (1983, p. 2) adds that "ideological identification is not only largely symbolic, but for many is also affected by the very short term events surrounding a particular campaign." Self-identifications changed frequently in 1980 and in a way that suggested that they were responding to candidate evaluations.[2]

Finally, it is imperative that we take note of a series of methodological articles related to the specific question of attitudinal constraint in the general public. As we will note below, Nie and Andersen (1974; reprinted in our first edition) showed an apparently substantial increase in constraint in the 1960s and 1970s compared to the 1950s. Several researchers, however, independently noted that changes in the format of survey questions in 1964 and 1968 might account for these observed increases. Particularly persuasive was the "split sample" study of Sullivan, Piereson, and Marcus (1978), in which the changes observed from the 1950s to the 1960s were replicated at one time point by using both the old one-sided question format and the new balanced format.[3] As a result, this evidence no longer suggests increased constraint.

On another front, Smith (1980) criticized the "levels of conceptualization" measure as both unreliable and invalid.[4] Significantly, Smith concludes that if the "levels" are indeed "false measures of ideological sophistication," then the changes observed in these measures were also misleading. This along with other results imply "that there was a change in the sophistication of the language in which people talked about politics, but no change in the sophistication of the underlying evaluative processes" (p. 695). Collectively, these and other critiques (for example, Margolis, 1977; Hurley and Hill, 1980) raise serious questions about whether or not voters in the issue-laden and polarized 1960s and 1970s were in any sense more sophisticated than those in the issueless and nonideological 1950s.

A (Reasonably) Ideological Electorate

In contrast to the work just reviewed, many recent writings have emphasized that voters are reasonably sophisticated—not budding analysts to be sure, but far from the truly unsophisticated cretins portrayed earlier. Three themes have been emphasized: increased ideological awareness, greater awareness in Europe than in the United States, and more recognition of the importance of ideological terms for the electorate. Each of these will be summarized briefly. In addition, a number of important criticisms have been made of the way in which the early studies measured ideology; these will also be reviewed.

Changes in the electorate are apparent in numerous writings, but they are most forcefully stated in *The Changing American Voter.* Using identical measures from 1952 on, the authors found that the proportion in the electorate who could reasonably be called ideologues (or near-ideologues) was relatively low in the 1950s—reaching its nadir in 1956—but rose substantially during the 1960s. (The level dropped a bit in the 1970s but remained above the 1950s level.[5]) They also elaborated on Nie and Andersen's (1974) apparent finding of substantial increases in the degree to which attitudes were constrained; to a greater extent than before, those who took liberal positions on one issue also took liberal positions on other issues. In both cases—the rise in levels of conceptualization and in constraint—the increase occurred at all levels of education. Thus, the changes could not be attributed to the very considerable increase in education levels in those decades.

As we noted earlier, these analyses have come under serious attack owing to measurement questions. Yet they should not be dismissed too quickly since the apparent increases in ideological thinking were not isolated developments. The dramatic decline in party loyalties and party-based voting and the equally eye-catching increase in issues voting (see chapters 5, 21, and 27) suggest at a minimum that voters in the 1960s and 1970s were paying more attention to the substantive content of political arguments. At an elite level, candidates such as Goldwater, Wallace, and McGovern were describing themselves in ideological terms, creating an atmosphere that made greater understanding by the electorate at least plausible. While these concomitant changes by no means prove that voters were becoming more ideologically oriented, they caution us against too quickly rejecting the direct evidence as methodological artifacts. Moreover, even if the studies are correct in showing that improved survey questions were responsible for the increase in ideological constraint, the appropriate interpretation may be that there was more constraint in the 1950s than was initially realized.

While *The Changing American Voter* contains the most forceful statement of an increasingly ideological electorate, independent analyses also support this trend. For example, codings of the levels of conceptualization that conform closely to the original version yield the same increase in the 1960s and 1970s compared to the 1950s (Hagner and Pierce, 1982, p. 788; Miller et al., 1976, p. 844).[6] The change is especially in the top category as shown in Table 17-1 (although Converse, 1975a, would counter that the proportion of the population in the top two categories combined has remained amazingly stable, as if half the population is permanently consigned to completely nonideological responses). More significantly, perhaps, similar changes apparently occurred in Europe. The direct evidence is very limited, but Klingemann (1979a, pp. 226, 233) found a slight upward trend in Germany between 1969 and 1974 and a probable difference (hampered by different questions and codings) in Great Britain between 1963 and 1974.

Table 17-1 Distribution of Levels of Conceptualization, 1956-1976

Levels of Conceptualization	*1956*	*1960*	*1964*	*1968*	*1972*	*1976*
Ideologues	12%	19%	27%	26%	22%	21%
Group Benefit	42	31	27	24	27	26
Nature of Times	24	26	20	29	34	30
No Issue Content	22	23	26	21	17	24
Total	100%	99%	100%	100%	100%	101%
N	(1,741)	(1,741)	(1,431)	(1,319)	(1,372)	(2,870)

Source: John C. Pierce and Paul R. Hagner, "Conceptualization and Party Identification: 1956-76," *American Journal of Political Science* (1982) 26:377-87.

In a different way the Converse and Markus article reprinted here also supports, if not increased ideological thinking, at least the foundation for such thinking. Recall that the original panel results (Converse, 1964) were widely interpreted as showing that many individuals had "nonattitudes," suggesting that voters hardly thought about issues at all, to say nothing of putting them together in some larger framework. The report of the 1972-1976 panel, while showing similar, low over-time correlations on issues repeated from the 1950s, also found some issues on which over-time stability was quite high. Ideological thinking does not automatically follow, but a basis for it at least existed. Significantly, the issues with the highest stability were moral and racial in nature, the very issues that are arguably the heart of the new ideology (see chapter 18).

At about the same time that researchers were discovering these over-time differences, others were finding evidence of ideological thinking in Europe. Much of the evidence concerns awareness of the terms left/right to describe political conflict. Such an awareness is evidently widespread. Inglehart and Klingemann (1976), for example, reported that in nine European countries, self-placement on a left/right scale was greater than identification with any of the political parties, often as high as 85-90 percent. Similar results are reported by Barnes (1971), Klingemann (1979, p. 279), and Holmberg (1981, p. 196).[7] While the meaning attached to the terms was often vague, many of the respondents were able to place multiple parties on such a scale with a high degree of accuracy (for example, in Holmberg, 1981, p. 201; Sani, 1974). A recent analysis has also shown consistently higher continuity coefficients in Sweden than in the United States (Niemi and Westholm, 1984), including very high stability on left/right self-placement. The authors point out that the results may reflect "stability by proxy," owing to the strong positions taken by the political parties, and may indicate no greater understanding of political arguments. Nonetheless, at a minimum, they indicate recognition and repetition, if not understanding, of ideological terms along with a lower level of nonattitudes. At the extreme, some authors go so far as to interpret findings such as these as indicating that European politics is primarily motivated by ideology, and that ideology plays the role in Europe that party identification does in the United States (van der Eijk and Niemöller, 1983).

We represent this non-American work here with an article by Percheron and Jennings, reprinted as chapter 20. Most directly relevant to the points made above is the authors' argument that the French—even adolescents—make considerable use of the left/right dimension to interpret their complex political world, and that they have a reasonable understanding of that dimension. But the article is useful from other perspectives as well. It is the only one in this book that speaks directly to the issue of political socialization. Since political continuity and change across generations is of considerable concern to the study of voting behavior, it is appropriate that this field of study be at least minimally represented. In addition, continuity in France has been a subject of special concern ever since Converse and Dupeux (1962), erroneously in the view of Percheron and Jennings, offered France as a counterexample of paternal transmission of partisan orientations. Those aspects of the work should not be overlooked. From the perspective of the present section, however, the article represents additional evidence that ideological thinking may play a larger role in Europe than in the United States.

Still a third emphasis in recent work has been on the extent to which ideological terms are related to political behavior. In a sense, this emphasis has its origin in Lane's (1962) early work on personal ideologies. In contrast to Converse's analysis of ideology in relatively short interviews with thousands of respondents, Lane employed in-depth interviews with small numbers of respondents (typically a dozen). Lane's working-class respondents were quite articulate in their discussions of politics, although they did not necessarily put the political world together in the same way that academic political scientists might expect. Instead of using what we might consider the conventional liberal or conservative ideologies, they frequently had their own "personal ideologies." Lane's work showed that ideological thinking was more widespread than mass surveys suggest, but the potential impact on politics is limited when different citizens have their own personal ideologies rather than sharing a more general common ideology.

Lane's focus on what constitutes ideological thinking has led to some controversy over how to interpret *The American Voter*'s findings on levels of conceptualization. For example, are "group benefits" comments nonideological? Or might they be the way in which the working class phrases ideological concerns? After all, saying that one party is better than another for workers or the poor very much expresses the class conflict notion that is fundamental to socialist ideology. Even the usual emphasis on party identification in voting might not be incompatible with an emphasis on ideology. Voters may learn early that one party represents their ideological interests and may subsequently use party identification as a short-cut for ideology.

The recent emphasis on how ideological terms are related to political behavior is most forcibly stated in work by Levitin and Miller (1979). While they make it clear, as noted above, that understanding of ideological terms is often minimal, they nonetheless conclude (p. 769) that "ideological location is an important factor in shaping voters' choices on election day." Or again (p. 751), "those labels [liberal and conservative] have political significance for their [Americans'] political attitudes and election day decisions." Implicit in their formulation is that the importance of ideology goes well beyond the small, sophisticated group of voters commonly referred to as ideologues.

Less explicit about the relationship between ideology and individual voters, but highly influential nonetheless, are macro-level interpretations of recent electoral change. The much heralded "new politics," for example, is often discussed in ideological terms (chapter 26). And since interpretations of day-to-day events are in terms of elite attitudes and behavior, it is easy to forget the lessons of other work, which indicate that elite interpretations may not filter very far down into the general electorate (see footnote 2). Thus, for example, it is tempting to interpret gains by the environmental "Green" party in Germany in 1983 as ideologically based, but in reality those voters might be no more informed about the Greens' policies than were many who voted against Lyndon Johnson in the 1968 primaries.[8] Thus, both academic and popular interpretations of recent events have reinforced the assumption of increased ideological thinking.

Finally, in contrast to the articles cited earlier, some methodological critiques have supported the notion of a reasonably sophisticated electorate. Starting with Achen's (1975) analysis, the main bone of contention is over the meaning of the low correlations observed (as in the Converse and Markus chapter) for attitudes expressed at two or more points in time. The low level of continuity could signify large amounts of real attitude change. However, the low level of continuity in individual attitudes during the panel studies of the 1950s and 1970s was not accompanied by the sharp shifts in aggregate positions that would be expected if real change were occurring. So everyone seems to agree that real attitude change was quite limited. The remaining possibilities are that respondents vacillate because of nonattitudes (Converse's argument, which was discussed at the beginning of this chapter) or that the survey questions are unreliable (so that poor or ambiguous wording causes random fluctuations).

If one is willing to make certain assumptions about the behavior of the measurement errors that occur when one asks survey questions, it is fairly straightforward to "correct" the over-time correlations for the limited reliability of the questions (as Converse and Markus do for party identification). Studies doing so (Achen, 1975; Erikson, 1979; Judd and Milburn, 1980) find that respondents are highly stable in their attitudes despite the variations in their manifest responses. To the degree that these criticisms of the original over-time analysis are correct, the electorate has a strong foundation for an ideological outlook on politics. However, the appropriateness of the assumptions about the measurement errors can be challenged. Thus, in their chapter, Converse and Markus defend their interpretation over Achen's, arguing that the problem lies with the nature of the citizenry rather than with the survey questions.

Conclusion

In concluding their chapter on the levels of conceptualization, Nie, Verba, and Petrocik (1976, p. 122) wrote that "our conclusion must be a middle of the road one: there has been a substantial change in the way the public conceptualizes politics, yet there is evidence for inertia as well." A similar conclusion applies more broadly to the question of whether or not voters think ideologically. On the one hand, empirical research has forever ruined our picture of mass electorates as comprised of idealized good citizens. Along with that fictional person's high levels of political interest, knowledge, and participation, we must discard an all-encompassing ideological view of politics and a clear understanding of political coinage such as liberal/conservative and left/right. Too many results—those cited in the first part of this chapter and others—have found voters like Butler and Stokes's "army" respondent whose understanding and use of ideological thinking are minimal at best.[9] Too many attempts have been made to lower the standards required to declare voters ideological—only to find that many voters still could not qualify.

At the same time, we need not paint a picture of the electorate as unqualifiedly and forever ignorant of ideological perspectives, as perhaps was the impression when *The American Voter* declared that at best 2½ percent of the electorate truly deserved to be called ideologues. The evidence of a reasonably sophisticated electorate, such as the apparent growth in ideological understanding of ideological terms that goes beyond active use of those terms and examples in the United States and abroad of high over-time stability, are too widespread to be dismissed lightly. Similarly, better understanding of our methodology—simply recognizing that there is some unreliability in the survey questions—adds to the understanding that voters are not devoid of somewhat larger, overarching perspectives on the political scene.

Thus our conclusion, like that of *The Changing American Voter,* must be a middle-of-the-road one: voters both here and abroad are neither super-sophisticated nor abysmally ignorant. Individuals form a continuum, with a small group at the very top in knowledge and sophistication, but only a small group as well who are totally uninformed. The only surprise is that it has taken us so long to realize that this truism applies to ideological thinking and all aspects of political knowledge just as it applies to most other subjects.

On the way to this conclusion, we have also learned that ideological thinking varies over time and space. The level of ideological thinking depends in part on the party system, the candidates, and even the specific appeals made in a given year. It is impossible to conclude that some fixed percentage of the electorate is ideological, whatever the definition we use. But it is possible to conclude that ideological thinking ebbs and flows and that it will always play a role, but probably never an exclusive one, in electoral politics.

NOTES

1. There was also some supportive evidence from Great Britain (Butler and Stokes, 1969) and France (Converse and Dupeux, 1962). Evidence of another sort was found in a classic article by Prothro and Grigg (1960). Upwards of 95 percent of their respondents professed agreement with such principles as "the minority should be free to criticize majority decisions," yet far fewer agreed with specific statements that seemed to be logical expressions of these principles.
2. Yet another relevant study is that by Bishop and Frankovic (1981), which replicates Converse's (1964) comparison of an elite sample (congressional candidates) with a cross-section survey of voters. Bishop and Frankovic's data from 1978 and Converse's data from 1958 both show considerably greater attitudinal constraint among the elite than among the general population sample.

3. Some of this work, along with a list of references, can be found in the February 1979 issue of the *American Journal of Political Science.*
4. Though developed in *The American Voter,* the specific versions studied by Smith were from Field and Anderson (1969) and Nie, Verba, and Petrocik (1979).
5. Nie, Verba, and Petrocik (1979). See also the corrections in Nie et al., 1981.
6. Miller et al. did their own coding for 1972 and used the Klingemann and Wright coding for 1968 (first reported in Converse, 1975a). There is a 5 percent discrepancy between Hagner and Pierce's and Miller et al.'s estimate for 1972, about 1 percent of which is probably accounted for by the latter's exclusion of unclassified respondents. For still another measure, see Field and Anderson (1969). These various analyses are not entirely independent, of course, since they rely largely on the same data and often on very similar techniques.
7. It turns out that Americans are also surprisingly familiar with the terms left/right and the more familiar liberal/conservative. However, strict comparisions with European data are hampered by small but important methodological differences (Klingemann, 1979a, pp. 229-30).
8. It was discovered at the time of the New Hampshire primary that ". . . more often than not, McCarthy voters were upset that Johnson had failed to scourge Vietnam a good deal more vigorously with American military might, which is to say they took a position diametrically opposed to that of their chosen candidate" (Converse et al., 1969, p. 1095).
9. His explanation of "left" and "right": "when I was in the Army you had to put your right foot forward, but in fighting you lead with your left. So I always think that the Tories are the right party for me and that the Labour party are fighters" (Butler and Stokes, 1969, p. 209).

FURTHER READINGS

U.S. Studies of Ideology

James W. Prothro and Charles M. Grigg, "Fundamental Principles of Democracy: Bases of Agreement and Disagreement," *Journal of Politics* (1960) 22:276-94. Public acceptance of democratic ideology does not extend to the specifics of democracy.

Angus Campbell, Philip E. Converse, Warren E. Miller, and Donald E. Stokes, *The American Voter* (New York: Wiley, 1960), chapter 10, unabridged; chapter 9, abridged. Analysis of "level of conceptualization" of politics by the electorate.

Philip E. Converse, "The Nature of Belief Systems in Mass Publics," in *Ideology and Discontent*, ed. David E. Apter (New York: Free Press, 1964). Full statement of results about ideology.

Christopher H. Achen, "Mass Political Attitudes and the Survey Response," *American Political Science Review* (1975) 69:1218-231. Emphasis on low question reliability causing apparent lack of ideology.

James A. Stimson, "Belief Systems: Constraint, Complexity, and the 1972 Election," *American Journal of Political Science* (1975) 19:393-417. Reprinted as chapter 8 in our first edition. Politics is viewed unidimensionally by the most able half of the electorate.

Norman H. Nie, Sidney Verba, and John R. Petrocik, *The Changing American Voter* (Cambridge: Harvard University Press, 1976), chapters 7-9. Increased ideological thinking in the 1970s.

John E. Jackson, "The Systematic Beliefs of the Mass Public: Estimating Policy Preferences with Survey Data," *Journal of Politics* (1983) 45:840-65. Complex statistical model showing a coherent and stable systematic component to policy preferences.

Comparative Studies of Ideology

David Butler and Donald E. Stokes, *Political Change in Britain* (New York: St. Martins, 1969), chapter 9. Finds that voter reactions to parties are not satisfied by a single left/right continuum.

Ronald Inglehart and Hans D. Klingemann. "Ideology and Values," in *Political Action*, ed. Samuel H. Barnes, Max Kaase et al. (Beverly Hills: Sage, 1979). "Postmaterialist" ideas, their distribution, and their relationship to political participation in five countries.

Ronald Inglehart and Hans D. Klingemann, "Party Identification, Ideological Preference, and the Left Right Dimension Among Western Mass Publics," in *Party Identification and Beyond*, ed. Ian Budge, Ivor Crewe and Dennis Farlie (London: Wiley, 1976). Use of left/right terminology greater in Europe than in United States.

Richard G. Niemi and Anders Westholm, "Issues, Parties, and Attitudinal Stability: A Comparative Study of Sweden and the United States," *Electoral Studies* (1984) 3:65-83. Greater attitudinal stability in Sweden than in the United States.

18. PLUS ÇA CHANGE . . . THE NEW CPS ELECTION STUDY PANEL

Philip E. Converse and Gregory B. Markus

In some of our sister sciences, publication of frankly provisional findings, even in the most polished of journals, is not considered *déclassé*. This is particularly true where crucial new data bases have freshly come into being. Thus when the first rocks were returned from the moon, a haste spate of publications merely recounted, in the languages of various specialties, what the rocks were like in simple, first-cut terms.

To be sure, more delicate and incisive analyses were to be supplied in ensuing years. However, the function of such early publication for the collective process of inquiry should be transparent. Even the first crude observations as to the apparent age and structure of the rocks, or the presence of water or organic traces, sufficed to shoot down some broad-gauge astrophysical hunches as to what processes, on what time scale, had actually molded the moon's surface. And correspondingly, these primitive observations drew into sharper focus an appropriate research agenda among remaining tenable hypotheses for the months of more probing inquiry which lay ahead. Thus early publication can warn the community in advance which more detailed assays of the new data base are worth, and not worth, making.

Although the metaphor may be a little more dramatic than current political science can sustain, it is in some such spirit thai this chapter is offered. Analysts of the sequence of national election studies generated with National Science Foundation help by the Center for Political Studies at the University of Michigan have been frustrated for some time at the lack of long-term panel linkages—the reinterviewing of the same respondents—in successive replications of the basic study design. The 1976 presidential election marked the completion of the first large-scale panel segment, stretching back to 1972, since the original four-year panel was completed in 1960. These new panel data constitute a fresh and important base which seems worth preliminary report.

Authors' Note: The research on which this report is based was supported by National Science Foundation Grant SOC-7707537. We are also grateful to Jean Dotson, Maria Sanchez and Peter Joftis for their aid in data preparation.

Source: *American Political Science Review* (1979) 73:32-49. Reprinted with permission of the publisher.

Of course the study of electoral change has scarcely withered away in the interim for lack of full longitudinal studies. The use of less expensive independent samples at biennial elections has greatly enriched our understanding of the range of variation in American electoral processes since the first electorate panel in 1960, in part because the intervening period has been one of political change of sufficient magnitude to be plainly visible without the extra sensor of a genuine panel design. However, it is exactly this marked change that has put an increasing premium on the advent of a new round of panel data. Hence it will be helpful background if we review, with a brevity verging on oversimplification, some of the chief findings from the original panel, as well as revisions provoked by subsequent independent samples on into the early 1970s.

The Original 1956-60 Panel and Later Findings

Thanks to the delinquency of the current senior author, the major analyses of the panel-specific data from the 1956-58-60 reinterview sample were never reported in a self-contained monograph. However, some of the more surprising empirical facts to emerge from those analyses played an influential role in his essay, "The Nature of Belief Systems in Mass Publics" (Converse, 1964). Stripped to its essentials, one brute fact which could only have arisen from long-term longitudinal data was the discovery that *at the individual level,* the stability of party identifications in the 1956-60 period vastly outstripped the stability of individual positions on even the most stable of the major political issues of the period.

Such stability of party identification had been suspected for some time on the basis of the noteworthy inertia of marginal distributions for the variable in independent cross-section samples throughout the 1950s. In fact, that suspicion had been central in some of the major theses of *The American Voter* (1960). However, inertia of marginals, or minimal net change, is not at all incompatible with the possibility of high rates of *gross* change, or rapid individual-level "turnover." Indeed, while time series data on distributions of mass opinions on major political issues were somewhat more truncated because of the flux of salient issues from one election to the next, where repeated cross-section measurement did exist for political issues, the marginals were often as inert in the 1950s as those for party identification.

Therefore it was particularly striking to discover that beneath the net stability of party identification lay a very marked degree of gross, or individual-level stability; whereas the inertia or net stability of opinion distribution on major political issues concealed an equally surprising degree of individual-level turnover which appeared to be almost a Brownian motion. Let us be careful not to overstate the case. Party identification was *not perfectly* stable for individuals over the 1956-58-60 panel observations, in the sense that all individuals located themselves in the same one of seven possible categories in each ensuing measurement. Substantial numbers changed to an adjacent location on the continuum, and a very few appeared to move long distances (5-7 "slots") across the continuum. Similarly, it was not true that the individual-level data on issue positions showed no stability whatever. For one thing, there was significant variation from issue to issue, in patterns that seemed decodable; and in any event, even the issues with the greatest individual-level turnover showed some significant degree of continuity, as indexed by the correlation of each issue with itself over time departing reliably above zero.

Nonetheless, the contrasts in stability between party and issue positions remained absolutely stark, and we would find it hard to be impressed with any theory of the dynamics of these political attitudes which failed to encompass such contrasts. One implication seemed to be that party loyalties had a considerable primacy in the attitude systems involved. In the 1950s, at least, issue positions were but weakly aligned with partisanship, in the minds of the voters, in any event. Perceived linkages between parties and issues were, by and large, vague and contradictory as well. We opined at the time (*The American Voter,* pp. 179-83) that a major cause of the confusion might be that "actual" party differentiation on the major issues was at low ebb in the mid-fifties, a guess that later proved to have some merit. However, in the modest degree that partisanship and issue positions did covary, the contrasts in stability from the panel data suggested that it was likely that these issue preferences were more often brought into line with prior partisanship than the reverse. Once again, there is no need to exaggerate the case: surely issue positions could affect partisanship for occasional individuals at any time, and at some occasional junctures might do so for larger fractions of the population. But it seemed well-nigh impossible to square the panel contrasts in party and issue stability with a model in which the preponderant causal flow was, in any intermediate term, from issue position to partisanship, at least in the late 1950s.

Cross-Section Sample Findings from the 1960s

Although no full-blown panels of the national electorate were followed in the 1960s, there was ample sign of major trends in these matters by the middle years of the decade. While change was rapid on many fronts, some of the most impressive evidence involved the party-issue nexus.

Burnham (1968) noted that after a lengthy period in which the aggregate distribution of party identification had remained nearly constant, the first signal change began in the middle 1960s with a rising proportion of the electorate refusing to report identification with either party and insisting on being classed as independents, thereby swelling the neutral middle of the party identification continuum. This apparent erosion in feelings of party loyalty among American voters, caught at an incipient stage by the first Burnham accounts, has since proceeded majestically in the same direction for close to a decade, and certainly must rank by now as change of massive magnitude. The trend has nicely fit Burnham's broader views as to the progressive "decomposition" of the traditional party system in the United States, and has become the subject of a torrent of literature analyzing details of the trend, or speculating as to its implications for partisan realignment.

Where issue positions of the public are concerned, Nie (with Andersen, 1974) has advanced some provocative analyses suggesting that soon after 1960, voter policy preferences began to take on a much firmer "muscle tone" than was characteristic of data from the 1950s. This change is largely indexed by a marked increase in the cross-sectional correlations among issue positions in the 1960s, as opposed to their feeble level of the preceding decade. The reality of the issue trends charted by Nie has been subject to somewhat more controversy than attends the brute empirical facts of erosion in party loyalties, since some (Bishop et al., 1978; Sullivan et al., 1978) have suggested that the changes may be more an artifact of shifts in question format in the Michigan series than true secular change. However this matter may be resolved, the Nie thesis has strong face validity at least, since increased public attention to policy cleavages is almost another way of describing the onset of political turbulence of the type characterizing American politics for the past dozen years.

Moreover, the Nie thesis receives supplementary support from changes observed in linkages between partisanship, issue positions, and voting decisions. For example, Pomper (1972) pointed out that voter perceptions of party differences on policy issues showed more clarity by 1964 than had been true in the first panel period of the late 1950s. The citizen was more likely to see differences between the parties on policy matters, and the alignment between partisanship and issue preferences had heightened as well. In the most exhaustive recapitulation of these trends, Nie, Verba and Petrocik (1976) have shown that the election-by-election correlations between party identification and the vote, as compared with issue-vote correlations, changed after the early 1960s: the apparent weight of partisanship in the voting decision had undergone significant decline, while the weight of policy preferences showed a marked advance.[1]

Again the magnitude of these trends, as well as their durability into the 1970s, remains subject to scholarly dispute (see, for example, Margolis [1977] on Pomper). Similarly, the longer-range import of the differences before and after the early 1960s is subject to basic disagreement. Some see these changes as secular and permanent or even accelerating into the future. Others see one or the other political period as the American norm, interrupted by an era of aberration. Still others see the two periods as local minima and maxima, with a putative normal lying somewhere between.

Nevertheless, some of the component changes are beyond dispute as empirical facts, and taken as a *gestalt,* they have a great deal of intuitive appeal. The parts fit together admirably, and correspond nicely with impressions most of us who lived through both periods would have harbored in any event.

It is against this backdrop that the advent of the new 1972-74-76 panel version of the Michigan election series is particularly welcome. After all, the trends catalogued since 1960 have all been developed without the longitudinal tracing of the same individuals over time. This is not to say the trends are spurious: the movements of marginal distributions and drifts in correlation coefficients estimated within each slice of time would certainly have been duplicated (apart from sampling error and variation due to population replacement) if panel studies had been mounted throughout the era since 1960.

However, one precious class of information—the continuity or individual-level stability of the key variables—cannot be squeezed from the independent-replication design. In fact, it cannot even be deduced from other attendant slice-of-time facts with much reliability, as we shall shortly see. And given the intervening work on electoral change, some of the first-cut expectations as to how the new panel data might look are extremely straightforward. Apparently party is down, and issues are up. The main question to be asked of the new panel data would merely seem to be "by how much?"

We shall reveal the general answer rapidly, for its explication can easily occupy us for the rest of this article. Where party and issues are concerned, and *with respect to those facets of change which a panel design is uniquely equipped to illuminate,* our first-cut explorations show that *the 1972-76 panel data are very nearly a carbon copy of those from the 1956-60 panel!* That is, the individual stability of party identification, relative to that for policy preferences, is just about as great for the latter period as for the former.

We shall spend most of the rest of this article trying to clarify just what those initial results do and do not mean. One thing they do not mean is that no change has occurred over this period. A severe handicap in approaching problems of change consists of the first simplistic assumption that change with respect to a given variable is something monolithic: either the variable changes or it doesn't, in which case we might not want to call it a variable. Such a statement can have merit if we specify it more closely, as we might by referring exclusively to the mean or central tendency of the variable. Then it is undoubtedly true that either the mean has changed or it has not. But more generally speaking, change is multifaceted, even if we are addressing the same variable in its behavior over time.

These multiple facets of change, even with respect to a single variable, are recognized in more formal treatments of process. Although the distinctions are looser than one might like, processes are described as "strictly stationary," only "weakly stationary," or "not stationary at all," according to whether all, some or none of the moments of the univariate distribution are constant. Thus each moment is, unto itself, a facet of change. As we shall see momentarily, there are still further facets of change with respect to a single variable, in addition to the moments, and it is one of these which shows unexpected constancy or stationarity.

It is exactly because impressive changes are known to have occurred in the party and issue variables that the panel discovery of any points of stationarity is particularly exciting. In a period in which multiple facets of change are occurring, the localization of some points of stationarity are theoretically pregnant in diagnosing the nature of the processes underlying the total manifold of observations. To paraphrase Archimedes, they give us "a place to stand" from which other facets in flux can be evaluated.

The Case of Party Identification

We can profitably turn to the case of party identification over the comparative 1956-60 and 1972-76 time segments for concrete examples of the varied facets of change. All too frequently, contradictions appear to arise in the treatments of change carried out on the same variables by different scholars, simply because different aspects of change are being addressed, and for quite different purposes. This potential for confusion is particularly virulent as we approach the panel feature of these change data, so careful description is important.

The most obvious facet of change in a single variable based on aggregated observations over time is the displacement of the mean of the distribution from one reading to the next. Several authors dealing with the first panel have examined changes in the central tendency of the party identification variable in the 1956-60 period. There are various ways such change can be indexed in addition to the obvious integer scoring of the conventional seven-point scale and taking an actual mean. One can deal, for example, with the percentage Democratic (or Republican) of the total sample, or of the more restricted set of those who identify with one party or another. If, for example, we examine the marginal distributions of party identification in the panel years in terms of percentage Democratic (strong or weak) of all *identifiers,* we find values of about 60 percent for 1956, 64 percent for 1958, and 61 percent for 1960. For 1972 the value is 63 percent, for 1974, 65 percent, and for 1976, 63 percent. These are forms of change.

Such statements of change can be conceived as referring to shifts in the mean or central tendency of the party identification distribution, as one facet of change. The shifts are customarily small. If we stick to the percentage Democratic of all identifiers, the median biennial displacement over the whole election study series runs below 2 percent. On the other hand, unless they can be thought of as sampling error, these differences are in themselves evidence that party identification is not perfectly stable down to the last voter. Although they are typically small enough to lie within the tolerances of plausible sampling error, it has long been clear however that these shifts are quite systematic, moving nicely in tune with national short-term tides favoring one party or the other. For example, the three biennial shifts since 1952 which exceed 3 percent are all associated with landslide presidential elections. More impressively still, first differences in these percentages Democratic among identifiers from one biennial election to another show a resounding correlation of .75 with first differences in the Democratic fraction of House seats after the corresponding elections since 1952. Clearly, although these shifts are slight, we are not dealing with mere sampling error in this facet of party identification change. Indeed, Brody (1977) in working with the 1956-58 and 1972-74 segments of the panel studies, focuses a great deal of his attention on these shifts, showing within the panels themselves that shifting has political meaning in terms of other attitudinal dimensions.

How important, theoretically and practically speaking, depends entirely on the more specific class of questions one wishes to ask about change. Certainly for any problems of short-term changes in political tides, they are a crucial indicator, although it must be recognized that a disproportionate share of these swings come from people who do not vote in any event.[2]

On the other hand, if one's research interests concerning change are longer-run in their perspective, then these small shifts are not of gripping interest. This is not simply because they are small, but also because their nature as short-term oscillations around a mean value has historically been quite clear. If the proportion Democratic shifts by 4 percent between two biennial elections, as it did between 1956 and 1958, this is not likely to be an intriguing harbinger of fundamental partisan change, because the odds are very high that the shift will rapidly be reversed. It is as though we were watching reeds growing in a shallow pond. Before an east wind, they tilt to the west. Before a west wind they tilt to the east. When the wind is still, they stand in a middling position. From some points of view the motion is of interest, since it tells us which way the wind is blowing at the moment. From some other points of view it is not of great interest, since we know the reeds are not moving in any absolute sense, but are firmly anchored in a fixed position by their roots.

Speaking more technically, the mean of the party identification distribution around which these small oscillations occur has been almost stationary for the past 25 years. We say "almost" because there appears to have been a glacially slow drift of the mean in a Democratic direction over this period, probably due to population replacement. Even in 25 years, the total ground covered is very small. This secular drift is small by comparison with the amplitude of the oscillations about that mean, even though those oscillations are in turn very small by comparison with the swings of the national popular vote.

It is important to recognize these oscillations for what they are in the panel data, to avoid misinterpretations of the changes they generate. Thus, for example, Brody (1977) discusses the counter-intuitive finding that in *both* the 1956-58 and the 1972-74 segments of the panel studies, Republican identifiers are less "directionally stable" (i.e., more likely to move out of the Republican camp into at least independence if not a Democratic identification) than Democrats, despite the fact that in most other terms Republicans have seemed more "anchored" in their political behavior. This perplexing effect almost certainly arises because both the 1956-58 and the 1972-74 segments bracket major shifts in short-term partisan fortunes from the Republicans to Democrats. Thus even relatively labile respondents who claimed to be Democrats when current winds were favoring the Republicans (1956 and 1972) had little reason to stop being Democrats two years later when the winds had become more supportive. Presumably the reverse partisan contrasts would occur in temporal comparisons where the wind changes were simply reversed.

While the mean of a distribution provides one facet of potential change in a variable, it scarcely exhausts the subject of change where that variable is concerned. Aside from practical problems like ceilings and floors on measuring instruments, the variance of the distribution can move independently of the mean. It can remain stationary while the mean shifts dramatically; or it can shrink or expand dramatically while the mean is stationary. In fact, as we have seen, the most striking change in party identification since 1965 is a shrinkage of the variance by more than 10 percent, as more and more voters cluster toward the independent middle of the distribution. This is again true change in party identification, and has appropriately been treated in the recent literature as having major theoretical interest. Yet this change has occurred rapidly while the mean of the distribution has been essentially constant.

There is no need to do a panel study to monitor change in either the mean or the variance of a distribution. Successive independent cross-section samples can perform this task equally well. The information a panel study uniquely supplies involves the continuity in positioning of the same individuals over time. One index of such continuity is the proportion of the panel on or near the main diagonal of the cross-tabulation of the same variable between waves. While such expressions are commonly used, they are weak summarizations not only because of the arbitrary nature of the category width that constitutes the "stable" diagonal, but also because the resulting proportions are strongly influenced by the number of categories into which the variable is partitioned, so that comparisons across variables of different category "length" become nonsensical. An obvious improvement is to deal with a summary expression of correlation or regression.

We have approached the new panel data on party identification only after a consideration of changes in means and variances for a very simple reason: although novices are constantly confused by the fact, continuity correlations formed on the same variable in two panel waves are as independent of temporal changes in the mean and variance of the distribution as the latter are independent of one another. That is to say, a continuity correlation can range from zero to perfection whether both mean and variance are constant, or one or both shift dramatically between the two time points. This is true by the very construction of the product-moment coefficient, which equates or normalizes the two means and variances, thereby partialling out whatever real change may have occurred with respect to those facets of the variable.[3]

Since continuity correlations can vary independently of changes in means and variances, they obviously tap still another facet of change. It is important to be clear just what facet that is. Obviously, it has to do with stability of individual-level positioning. What is important to remember is that it taps the stability of *relative* individual positions across a population, not absolute ones.

While it is thereby technically quite possible that individual-level continuity correlations for party identification have remained at their high levels of the late 1950s despite the shrinking variance of the distribution, it would not intuitively seem very likely. After all, the descriptors commonly applied to the surge in independence talk of the "erosion" of these identifications, and the "destabilization of partisanship." While such terms are entirely proper, they would certainly seem to imply a major unraveling of individual-level continuities in party preference, even in the stability of relative locations. Moreover, at a less intuitive and more technical level, if error variances remain constant while true variances of a variable decline, then the magnitude of correlations involving the variable will be attenuated.[4] Thus the natural shrinkage of observed variance of party identification might be expected on these grounds alone to dilute the continuity correlations correspondingly.

Some years back we suggested that this might not turn out empirically to be the case with party identification (Converse, 1975a), since the only scrap of a national panel conducted during the 1960s—a couple hundred stray cases reinterviewed between 1964 and 1966—showed continuity correlations which were virtually identical to those estimated from the 1956-60 panel, despite the fact that this panel lapped over into the period in which the variance of identification reports had begun to shrink palpably. Therefore we are not entirely surprised to discover that the continuity correlations calculated for party identification from the new 1972-76 panel are just about as high as they were in 1956-60. In absolute terms they are a hair smaller, but the difference is too slight for statistical significance. Probably the drop is in some degree real, as one would expect from the truncation of variance in the later period. However, the stunning fact is that the decline is simply vestigial: if one could say from the 1956-60 panel that individual-level continuity correlations for party identification with a two-year time lapse ran in the low .80s, one can make exactly the same statement for the 1972-76 panel.

For reasons that should be apparent, the magnitudes of continuity coefficients are specific to the size of the time interval elapsing between measurements. In processes of progressive (that is, not cyclical) change, they can be expected to decline as the interval becomes more extended. Indeed, this property emerges clearly in the party identification data. The four-year correlations are less than those calculated for a two-year interval; and the latter are smaller than correlations formed for measurements separated by only a few weeks in time, as is the case when the party identification item is applied to the same sample in both the pre-election and post-election questionnaires. Therefore continuity correlations in general only have meaning as they are tagged with some specific time interval. If we stick with the two-year correlations in order to encompass comfortably the data from the two-wave, 1964-66 mini-panel, then we find the following best estimates for two-year continuity correlations:[5]

The 1956-60 period	=	.835
The 1964-66 mini-panel	=	.836
The 1972-76 period	=	.813

There are several ways of processing these raw continuity coefficients into more refined components. One of the easiest partitions, dependent on having at least three waves of measurement, is to break the raw coefficients into (1) a reliability component, reflecting the complement of the proportion of error variance; and (2) a "true" stability coefficient, reflecting the degree to which the measurement at two points in time would be correlated if there were not intrusion of unreliability. Such procedures have been described by Heise (1969), and refined a further step by Wiley and Wiley (1970). These manipulations rest, as always, on a series of assumptions about the character of the data and the attendant error structures. One of the less pleasing sets of assumptions—that the measurement reliability (Heise) or the absolute error variances (Wiley and Wiley) are constant from wave to wave in a given panel sequence—can be relaxed in the case of the 1956-60 panel, where instead of three waves of measurement of party identification we can profit from five.[6] While it is regrettable that party identification was measured only three times in the new panel (1972 pre-, 1974, and 1976 pre-), there is sufficiently striking consistency between the two panels to enable us to use the additional information afforded by the first panel to reassure ourselves concerning various assumptions which must be made for the later batch of panel data. Also, of course, we can proceed no further with the mere two waves offered by the 1964-66 mini-panel, although the data presented above also give some assurance that we are dealing with process parameters which have a considerable stability in the intermediate term.

There are other assumptions embedded in calculations of the Heise or Wiley and Wiley type that are not entirely well met by the data. Thus, for example, there is reason to believe that both the measurement reliability and the true stability of the party identification item is less than nicely homogeneous over the population. In later, more complicated assays of these data, we shall take such characteristics into fuller account. Nonetheless, as first-cut approximations, it is worth seeing what can provisionally be estimated concerning the relative proportions of change due to unreliability, as opposed to "true change," in these longitudinal measurements.

Where they can be compared most fully (as in the five-wave panel), calculations of the Heise and Wiley and Wiley type give virtually identical estimates with these data. Both calculations agreed that the main source of the slight decline in overall continuity between the two large panels is a slight increase in unreliability, exactly as one would expect if the main change in the data were a shrinkage in the time variance.[7] In both calculations, the decline in reliability is roughly from (a central tendency of about) .88 in the first panel to about .84 in the second.[8] Once this slight decline in reliability is set aside, as it is when we calculate the true stability coefficients, we find comparisons of the following sort as our best estimates for the two-year interval:

	1956-58-60	*1972-74-76*
Two-year stability (Heise style)	.951	.972
Two-year stability (Wiley style)	.958	.972

The homogeneity of these estimates, both between calculation methods and more especially across two periods in which the nature of party identification has seemed so different, when other facets of change in the variable are considered, is very striking. There are a variety of ways of expressing the implications of these findings. We shall postpone some of the broader theoretical implications for our conclusions. For now, we might briefly consider what the above data imply for the long-term "staying power" of party identifications at the individual level.

If we merely knew that the raw two-year continuity correlation for party identification was about .82 (as a period-free average), then we might be tempted to conclude that over a period of 16 (2^4) years, we could only expect a continuity of .45 (or $.82^4$), a value which would not be entirely impressive. However, if we trust the above estimates as to the proportion of observed change which is mere unreliability of measurement, then we would expect the 16-year *observed* (i.e., error-attenuated) stability coefficient to look something like .73 (or .86 [$.96^4$], where the .86 is the period-free reliability estimate) instead of .45. This is a vastly different picture of the long-term individual-level stability of the variable, especially as it is appropriate to square these two values, yielding a contrast in shared temporal covariance of .53 instead of .26. And we feel considerably less cavalier about cycling hypothetically over longer periods of time in this way, once we have at least some shred of assurance, which the above data give, that the true stability of the party identification measures is remarkably close to stationary across two political periods in which, in other senses, it has been subject to major change.

However, even this assumption is subject to challenge. After all, the decline in reported strength of partisanship has proceeded secularly from 1965 to 1975. While our panel observations in 1964-66 and 1972-76 bracket the beginning and end of this fascinating period, they leave uncovered a crucial segment of time from 1966 to 1972. Perhaps it was in this six-year interval that continuity correlations on party identification might have registered a distinct sag.

Here again we can import a crucial datum which suggests that the stationarity of these continuity correlations has been complete over the past two decades. In 1973 Jennings and Niemi (1977) reinterviewed the parents of their 1965 graduating high school students, who had originally been interviewed in 1965. In principle this is a 1965-73 panel, covering exactly the years that we are missing in our national samples. The difficulty is that these parents cannot be seen as a proper sample of the adult electorate, even though they may be a perfectly honest national sample of a more restricted population.

What the Jennings-Niemi respondents have in common is having been parents of high school seniors in 1965. This means that they are a very homogeneous age cohort, relative to the electorate as a whole. The group lacks newer and younger voters completely and, given their association with children not dropping out of high school, they should show higher than normal social status. Now it can be calculated that if such respondents were really representative of the full electorate, and if our panel continuity coefficients were truly stationary in the long run, then over an eight-year span these respondents should show a continuity correlation for party identification of .76. However, the age and class bias of the Jennings-Niemi respondents would lead one to expect a slightly higher figure. It turns out that the observed figure for the party identifications of the Jennings-Niemi parents over the 1965-1973 interval is .79. This value is either right on target or, if anything, a shade high: certainly an hypothesis which maintains that continuity sagged between our panel points of 1966 and 1972 finds no comfort whatever in these data. All of the available evidence, then, suggests that there has been no change in the individual-level continuity of party identification over the past 20 years, despite an incontestable change in the likelihood of reported partisanship.

The Continuity of Policy Preferences in the '50s and the '70s

A comparative examination of the individual-level stability of preferences on political issues poses somewhat different analysis problems, chiefly because while the two major parties have long been constants of the political scene, the objects of issue orientation are in perpetual evolution. The issue positions which seemed central to political controversy in the early 1970s were somewhat different from those central in the late 1950s. Moreover, the election studies have been for some time measuring issue positions in a different format than was used in the late 1950s, and there are reasons to expect that these pure methods changes should affect some of the process parameters which interest us (Bishop et al. and Sullivan et al., 1978).

Hence strict comparisons of issue continuities are impossible. Nevertheless, there are some matches between issue items from the panel studies of the two periods which are tighter than others, so that some rough comparisons are possible. Moreover, the continuity correlations for issue positions in the original panel fell within a range which was vastly different from the values for party identification, and therefore it is of interest to see how even the newer issues are behaving in these terms in the more recent panel. We shall begin with a few of the closer matches and then summarize the general trends over all of the new panel issues as a set.

One issue item in the later panel was worded identically to the original 1956-58-60 study. This is a foreign policy question, in agree-disagree form, intended to tap isolationism:

> "This country would be better off if we just stayed home and did not concern ourselves with problems in other parts of the world."

Despite the identical wording of questions, there were minor variations in format. Most notably, the item responses were handled dichotomously in the new panel, whereas they had been spread out into four main points ("strong agree" to "strong disagree") in all waves of the original panel. Also in the last two waves of the first panel, a "filter" was added to assess whether respondents felt they had an opinion on the matter. Both of these format differences would seem likely, by conventional wisdom at least, to dull the correlations surrounding the more recent application of the isolationism item, other things equal.

Unfortunately, this foreign policy item was asked only in 1972 and 1976 in the second panel, so we can only make direct comparisons with the four-year (1956-60) continuity correlation from the first panel. Since the same limitation applies to the only other plausible foreign policy item match, we shall take that item in the same breath, even though item wording is much less parallel. Both panels had an item on foreign aid, although with the following variation in wordings:

> (1956-60) "The United States should give economic help to the poorer countries of the world even if those countries can't pay for it."
>
> (1972-76) "The United States should give help to foreign countries even if they don't stand for the same things we do."

The same differences in response categories pertain for these foreign aid items as for the isolationism item.

The four-year continuity correlations for these foreign policy items are as follows:

	1956-60		*1972-76*	
	r	*(N)*	*r*	*(N)*
U.S. Stay Home	.347	(1086)	.309	(1113)
Foreign Aid	.292	(1009)	.264	(1039)

The similarities between the two panels are quite impressive. And if there is any merit in our a priori expectation that format differences would tend to attenuate the more recent panel results by some small amount, it would be hard to argue that these continuity estimates are any less stationary than those for party identification, although of course they fall at a totally different level of correlation.

In the original panel, foreign policy preferences tended to be among those issue items of lesser individual-level stability. We shall see that the case is exactly the same in the new panel. Domestic issues in the old panel fell into two substantive domains: social welfare policy and civil rights policy. Both domains are represented with three-wave issue items in the new panel, although the item format is always different, and the wording shows greater or lesser variation.

The nearest thing to a match among the social welfare items involves questions about government guarantees of employment. The old agree-disagree item has been changed to a forced-choice format, with two contrasting substantive alternatives. Moreover, in this case—in contrast to the foreign policy items—response alternatives for the new panel are *more* numerous than for the old, with a 7-point rating scale being used to replace the four-category agree-disagree form. Thus, by the same reasoning as used before, we might expect slightly higher correlations with the new panel than with the old. Despite such differences in form, the intent of the two items is surely identical:

> (1956-60) " 'The government in Washington ought to see to it that everybody who wants to work can find a job.' Now would you have an opinion on this or not? (IF YES) Do you think the government should do this?"
>
> (1972-76) "Some people feel that the government in Washington should see to it that every person has a job and a good standard of living. Suppose that these people are at one end of this scale—at point number 1. Others think the government should just let each person get ahead on his own. Suppose these people are at the other end at point number 7. And, of course, some other people have opinions somewhere in between. Where would you place yourself on this scale, or haven't you thought much about this?"

For these items, asked in all three major waves of both panels, the average two-year continuity correlation in each study is:

	1956-60	*1972-76*
Government Job Guarantee	.457	.493

Again, we may well be struck by the similarity in values between the two periods, especially by comparison with the much more stable party identification items, or the visibly less stable foreign policy questions. Or if we want to pay attention to the small differences in absolute values between the two estimates, the value for the new panel is in fact slightly higher, as format changes would have led us to believe.

In civil rights, an item on school desegregation occurs in both panels, although it is another instance in which the question was only asked twice (1972 and 1976) in the second panel. The latter item is a forced-choice version of the earlier form, with those respondents claiming no opinion being filtered off in both instances.

> (1956-60) "The government in Washington should stay out of the question whether white and colored children go to the same school."
>
> (1972-76) "Do you think the government in Washington should see to it that white and black children go to the same schools, or stay out of this area as it is not its business."

In general we would expect the forced-choice version to produce slightly more discriminating measurement and hence higher correlations; yet the item in the second panel was only scored as a dichotomy, instead of the four-point agree-disagree scale used originally. Therefore there are no very clear expectations as to pure methods differences in the continuity correlations. The actual four-year correlations are, however, very similar:

	1956-60		*1972-76*	
	r	*(N)*	*r*	*(N)*
School Desegregation	.397	(1059)	.410	(714)

By this time it will not be surprising if the reader is beginning to find the parallels between all of these panel results, despite a decade and a half of intervening political change, as eerie as these parallels have seemed to us.

We have by now exhausted all of the issues for which very close matches in wording and intent, if not in format or in letter, are available.[9] While the similarities in individual-level stability for these well-matched items are striking, we should not conclude that the issue materials from the new panel more generally look just like those from the earlier data set. This is true chiefly because there are new issues present in the 1972-76 panel which are not inheritances from the past; and these items sometimes have a different cast in continuity terms.

A good example is provided by the civil rights issue concerning school busing to promote racial integration. This issue was not even in the air at the time of the earlier panel, so that its absence from those interviews was not at all a matter of editorial oversight, but rather a token of a truly different environment of policy debate. The issue is also of particular interest because casual observation would suggest that this issue, probably more than any other in the civil rights area or, for that matter, the total arena of policy debate, has had an inflammatory or polarizing quality that has bitten deep into even relatively inattentive segments of the public. In other words, if as we have earlier suggested, it is true that the general levels of these continuity correlations reflect the degree to which items tap into more or less thoroughly crystallized attitude structures (where the limiting case of no crystallization whatever is the "non-attitude"), we would expect rather substantial continuity correlations for the busing items. This expectation is sustained. The best estimate of the two-year continuity correlation is .575, a value still falling very well below the corresponding value for party identification, but nonetheless significantly higher than that registered for any issue items in the whole 1956-60 panel.

There are at least two other issues new to the 1972-76 panel which show even higher continuity values. These items are not only new: together they seem to stand for a coherent *class* of issue which was not even of much salience in the 1950s. One is a 7-point scale where the extremes involve the legalization of marijuana at one end, and the setting of higher penalties for its use at the other. The other is an item on abortion, in which the respondent is asked to choose between four levels of lenience in availability, essentially bounded by "under no circumstances" at one end and "at any need" on the other. Neither of these items was asked in the middle wave in 1974, so that only estimates of the four-year continuity correlations are available. As we have pointed out, coefficients over this time lapse tend to run lower than their two-year counterparts. Thus, for example, if the school busing issue runs about .574 for a two-year lapse, it stands at .535 for a four-year lapse. The only two issues which exceed it are marijuana and abortion, with *four*-year coefficients of .640 and .617, respectively.

These are high values, and they seem clearly associated with a class of moral issues of the kind brought to salience by the counterculture confrontations of the preceding decade. Indeed, the only other specific issue item with a four-year continuity correlation over .50, in addition to marijuana, abortion and busing, is an item on whether women should have an equal role with men in business and government, or should keep their place in the home (.519). Again, this is an item which pits the cutting edge of new mores against an array of traditional values.

For those who have worked in other political cultures, it is not entirely surprising that such moral issues should have a deeper resonance among those not normally attentive to much political controversy than is true for policy debates of most other kinds. Perhaps these uncommon magnitudes represent something other than a sharper crystallization of attitudes across a larger fraction of the electorate than is true of other issues, but for the time being such would seem to be the most plausible diagnosis.

There is one other item, not referring to a specific policy issue or for that matter any "new" issue at all, but relevant to a large range of issues, which also shows a four-year continuity correlation over .50, although the high value occurs under a special configuration of circumstances important to make clear. This item is the ideological item involving self-placement on a 7-point liberal-conservative scale, with a four-year continuity correlation of .564. The special circumstances arise because the correlation is being figured on a much more limited fraction of the population than is true of any of the other specific issues. This high attrition occurs because such a continuity correlation can only be computed for those respondents who choose some content response at both years involved in the correlation. On items like the abortion question, almost all respondents choose a content alternative, so that the continuity correlation refers to a quasi-totality of the electorate. On the liberal-conservative item, however, over one-third of the population must be set aside at the outset as missing data, either because they say they do not know their position or because they accept a "no-opinion" filter.

It may seem surprising that only as few as 35 percent or so fail to give content locations on two successive administrations of this ideological scale, and hence do not figure in the continuity correlations, when for many years items asking people what the labels "liberal" and "conservative" mean have shown some 40 percent or so who do not know. The implication is either that some people who would not profess to know what political difference is intended are nonetheless choosing a location on the continuum, or that the 40 percent value has changed, although it had not changed even after we were deep into the turmoil of the 1960s. Unfortunately, the item tapping the meaning of the terms was never asked in any of the five waves of the new panel. However, work in Western Europe has made it clear that people who locate themselves on an analogous left-right scale despite confession that they do not understand what the terms mean politically, tend in large numbers to place themselves at the exact midpoint of the continuum offered (e.g., Converse and Pierce, 1970). This is an easy solution when one is unsure of the significance of the extremities. And indeed, the midpoint of the United States scale is very well populated also. In fact, in the turnover cross-tabulations of the liberal-conservative scale, the cell which marks the exact center on both administrations tends to be two to three times as populous as any other cell in the matrix.

Hence the special circumstances which appear to sustain the high liberal-conservative continuity correlations seem to be that better than one-third of the population is removed at the outset; and among the remaining two-thirds, substantial numbers express their uncertainty by persistently locating themselves at dead center, thereby not adding to the continuity correlation, but not detracting much from it either. It is likely that for those with truly crystallized positions on the liberal-conservative continuum, the individual-level stability of position is very high, even as high or higher than party identification. But this fraction of the population is likely to be quite limited.

In our discussion we have introduced a number of issues or meta-issues which were not present in the original panel, but are new entrants in the 1972-76 period. All of these items discussed show higher levels of continuity than the most stable issues in the original panel. This might lead to a conclusion that levels of continuity in issue positions are up quite notably, if not because of heightened continuity from issues that can be specifically matched across the panels, at least because issues newly arisen in the real world are of a kind that tap more sharply crystallized opinion.

One can defend a very modest version of this argument if one limits attention to the two or three moral issues. However, a number of other "new issues" in the panel have not been discussed, and these generally show levels of continuity that are utterly redolent of issues in the 1956-60 period. Thus, for example, two items which have overtones of the "law and order" themes of the past decade—one dealing with repercussions of urban unrest, another dealing with protection of the rights of accused persons as opposed to stopping crime at all costs—show two-year continuity coefficients of about .36 and .45 respectively, values which are very middling relative to the range "normal" for domestic issues late in the 1950s. An item addressed to the possibility of a more or less progressive taxation rate shows a four-year value of about .31, and the figure is only .28 for an item asking whether the federal government has become too powerful. The latter figures are *lower* than any parallel figures to be found for domestic issues in the original panel.

To summarize, then, we have found that where specific issues can be directly matched, continuity values seem amazingly stationary across the two panels. One type of issue not salient in political debate in the late 1950s—moral or counterculture issues—do show signally higher continuity values than any other specific issues in either panel. Once beyond these moral issues, however, even new issues do not in general show any higher levels of continuity than the old.

A great deal of work of a more probing sort can be done with these issue materials. For example, more intensive investigations of the apparent substantial error structures in these responses are possible, particularly as some few of the new panel issues have been applied on four waves instead of merely three. Such empirical wedges are important to arrive at a proper diagnosis as to what these error structures really mean. Achen (1975) has concluded that the low levels of continuity marking issue responses occur simply because the items are unreliable, probably because of poor wording. It was the amazingly low "test-retest" reliability of the 1956-58-60 panel issues that touched off our earlier investigations as to why this degree of unreliability occurred, and led to our conclusion that the low apparent reliabilities were not simply a function of the items themselves in a shoddy-wording sense, but rather were a joint function of the substance of the items and the variable degree of attitude crystallization which more and less attentive respondents brought to the particular substance (Converse, 1964, 1970).

We still feel our interpretation is preferable to Achen's revision. Among other things, Achen's explanation does not give as much help in understanding why high political elites show higher continuity coefficients and hence apparently higher reliabilities than does the mass public, even when asked to respond to the very same simplistic issue items, although this difference is the most direct corollary of our original interpretation. Nor does the Achen interpretation prepare us to expect that the same team of question-writers who manage to word questions quite effectively regarding personal morals cannot find comparably effective wording when asking about foreign policy debates. Again, we need only imagine that disagreements about personal morals grip more people more vitally than do debates over foreign affairs in order to fold the new findings nicely into our original interpretive structure.

The important point is that the new panel data base offers a challenging field for investigating some of these differences more thoroughly.[10] For the moment, however, it seems fair to conclude that the individual-level relative stability of issue positions in the American public has changed only slightly between the two panels, and that no significant change whatever can be discerned where the same issue substance can be matched across the two eras.

Evaluations of Political Figures

Of the original Survey Research Center triad of parties, candidates and issues, all empirical work of a panel type has focused to date on parties and issues, for the simple reason that the 1956-60 period bridged two presidential elections with no continuity of candidates. The same lack of continuity marks the 1972-76 interval. However, the new panel does include multiple evaluations, on a thermometer scale, of the most prominent partisan political figures in the land, even if not running for president. It is naturally of interest to ask how stable these personality evaluations are, by comparison with the high stability of party identification and the relatively low stability of personal positions on political issues. Therefore we shall close our review of some of the first panel findings with a brief consideration of these raw continuity results.

Ratings of Hubert Humphrey, Ted Kennedy, Scoop Jackson, Richard Nixon and George Wallace were drawn in 1972, 1974 and 1976. In addition, a rating of George McGovern was applied in 1972 and 1976. Over all instances, the 100-point thermometer scale was explained and then names were offered *seriatim* as stimulus words for evaluation. The continuity correlations available for these political figures are summarized in Table 18-1. A number of provisional observations about this array are fairly obvious.

One is that the levels of continuity correlations across six of the most prominent political figures of the era covered by the new panel show a very wide range of variation. While it is not perfectly certain in what currency such comparisons should be made, we find it reasonable to square the above correlational values and speak in terms of the proportions of temporal covariance

Table 18-1 Continuity Correlations in the 1972-76 Panel Six Major Political Figures

	Continuity Correlations	
	Average, 2-Yr. Ests.	*4-Yr. Ests.*
Edward "Ted" Kennedy	.722	.671
George Wallace	.683	.609
Hubert Humphrey	.592	.531
Richard Nixon	.585	.461
George McGovern	—	.554
Henry "Scoop" Jackson	.445	.343

Source: 1972-74-76 panel study of the national electorate carried out by the Center for Political Studies, University of Michigan.

involved in the various evaluations. In this currency, evaluations of Kennedy appear some 2½ to 4 times more stable than evaluations of Jackson. Given such variation, it is tempting to try to explain its sources. One hypothesis might be that the stimulus words "Henry 'Scoop' Jackson" are more poorly worded as question items than the stimulus words "Edward 'Ted' Kennedy," and that hence the Jackson item is simply less reliable. A plausible rival hypothesis, and one that we considerably prefer, is that more American voters bring more meaning to the Kennedy name than to the Jackson name, have more crystallized attitudes toward it as a stimulus, and hence respond more stably to it. The apparent reliability is not, by this construction, a function of the measuring instrument taken in a vacuum, but rather a product of the interaction between content and the variable degree of meaning this content has for various citizens.

However, a second observation helps to keep us from considering these continuity correlations too woodenly as though they were test-retest reliability coefficients. Although it may not dazzle the unaided eye, the pattern of continuity coefficients for evaluations of Richard Nixon are quite unique relative to all other contents of the new panel discussed to date. We know from the panel marginals (as if we needed them!) that true change in evaluation of Richard Nixon between 1972 and 1974 or 1976 was of massive proportions. In 1971, according to the Gallup Poll, the American people considered Richard Nixon the most admirable person in the entire world. His thermometer ratings in the 1972 wave of the panel confirm this level of adoration, since he received a mean rating of 65-66 in that year, relative to a rating of 52 or 53 for popular figures like Kennedy or Humphrey. By 1974 he had tumbled into the high 30s, and by 1976 to 31.

Thus there is a major injection of real change in the Nixon case, although as we have seen, it may or may not have been a type of change that affects the stability of relative individual positions. That is, it remains possible that people who were wildly enthusiastic about Nixon in 1972 merely were reduced to lukewarm feelings about him by 1976; and those just mildly warm were reduced to cool feelings, etc., such that there was little leap-frogging of individual positions. What is peculiar about the Nixon pattern, however, is that a good deal of true change (in the latter sense) was touched off by the Watergate drama. If we make the relevant Heise calculations for the Nixon case, we find that quite uniquely relative to all other panel materials, true change competes on nearly equal terms with unreliability in explaining why the raw continuity coefficients are as low as they are.

A final observation concerning Table 18-1 returns us to the main themes of this essay. We introduced the panel data on personages by way of asking where "candidates"—broadly construed—fit in the hierarchy of continuities defined up to now by parties and issues, given prior panel material. If we are correct in our interpretation of the reasons why Kennedy evaluations are so much more stable than those for Jackson, then it should be clear that we could generate variations in these continuity coefficients for political leaders almost at will, by playing with the known prominence of such figures. In the limiting case, we could probably generate a continuity coefficient approaching zero with a stimulus like "Senator Zablocki," although it is reasonable to imagine that a persistent "ethnic vote" might keep such coefficients from actually touching zero.

Nevertheless, while it would be a chimera to imagine that some restricted range of continuity coefficients could reliably encompass any political figures whatever (by comparison with parties or issues), it is reasonable to limit our attention to the few truly prominent (in a mass-public sense) political personages in the land, just as the authors of the voting surveys try to restrict their issue measurements to the most salient policy cleavages of any particular period. And if we make such a limitation, then the data in Table 18-1, coupled with those cited earlier for parties and issues, might strongly suggest that in the hierarchy of continuity that these panel data help to establish, evaluations of major political leaders might properly be wedged in between parties as the most stable objects of orientation in terms of relative voter positioning, and issue positions as the least. Thus major political personages in any given epoch may serve as important cynosures of attention for the electorate, and as significant cues for other more substantive forms of political evaluation.

Summary and Implications

Figure 18-1 provides a handy graphic summary of the continuity correlation information that we have reviewed. In a nutshell, this summary says that apart from the emergence of some political cleavages having to do with traditional moral values in the later period, there has been scarcely any change in the comparative continuity of party and issue positioning between the two eras, despite manifold reasons to expect not only change, but change of major proportions. The individual-level continuity of party attachments continues to dwarf that for issue positioning in the 1972-76 period, as it did in 1956-60. And affection and dislike for the most prominent political leaders of the epoch seem to show levels of continuity which—again absent the moral issues—clearly lie between parties and issues.

The display in Figure 18-1 is rich with implications, some few of which we shall develop here. First, however, let us consider an apparent implication or two that should *not* be drawn, particularly with regard to the surprising information

Figure 18-1 Continuities in Public Response to Parties, Leaders, and Issues

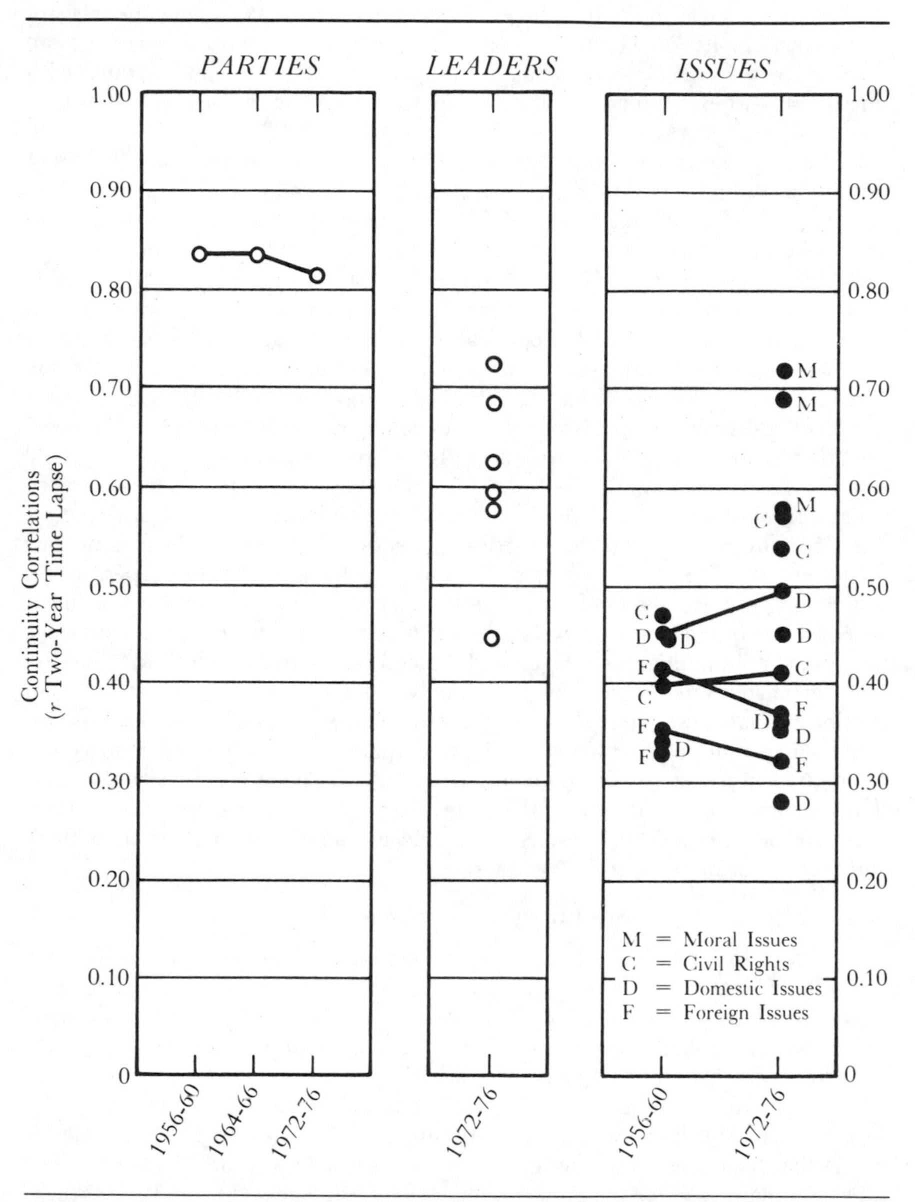

Note: Where items can be plausibly matched between panel segments, the respective data points are linked by a trend line. The whole figure is expressed in the currency of *two*-year continuity correlations. Where only four-year correlations are available, plausible two-year interpolations have been made to permit inclusion of a maximal number of observations.

Source: 1972-74-76 panel study of the national electorate carried out by the Center for Political Studies, University of Michigan.

concerning the continuities in party identification. We have emphasized before that these continuities do not mean that evidence of weakening partisanship, as registered by change in the party identification marginals since 1965, is somehow imaginary or meaningless. It should be kept clear that Figure 18-1 does not even address this facet of change in any direct way, even though it is very tempting to confuse the two.

Thus, for example, one improper implication to be drawn from these data is that since the individual-level continuity for panel respondents remains high while partisanship is weakening, it must mean that the weakening is all attributable to new entrants into the electorate who do not figure in a long-term panel table. Hence it would seem that one major point to these data is that the weakening can be traced entirely to population replacement processes. However, such a conclusion again involves a subtle confusion between the two facets of change. Clearly generational replacement has made a major contribution to the weakening of aggregate partisanship, especially in the later portions of the past ten years. But with equal clarity, persons already in the electorate before the decline began have also made further important contributions to it, and have continued to do so all the way to 1975 (Converse, 1976). Such persons do figure in our panel tables, and indeed they show a weakening of partisanship even within those tables: over all segments, including 1964-66, 1965-73 and 1972-76, later observations on these people show lesser variance in partisanship than earlier ones, although continuity levels remain intact.

Thus the decline in reported strength of party identification over the past decade remains an important but virtually independent fact. Moreover, there is evidence that defection rates for given levels of identification strength have been higher in recent years than they were in the 1950s. Both changes attest to a weakening of partisanship in the electorate. Both are thoroughly documented, and both have had real effects on the operation of the American political system.

For many analytic purposes and prognostications, the weakening of partisanship can be more important information than the near-constancy of continuity correlations summarized in Figure 18-1. For other purposes, however, the reverse is true, and it remains for us to suggest what some of the genuine implications of Figure 18-1 would seem to be.

Some of these implications are relatively technical or methodological. Thus for example, the kind of cycling of coefficients over time periods that we carried out with respect to party identification on p. 338 makes sense only if the facet of change indexed by the continuity coefficients is essentially stationary, as we have found it to be. More generally, the virtual lack of period dependency of the kind of estimates we have generated from the panel can provide a potent assist for a variety of structural modeling ventures aimed at sorting out in a more satisfactory way the causal interplays between evaluations of parties, issues and candidates. To be carried out effectively, such enterprises presume knowledge of things like measurement reliability. Since such information is rarely available, investigators often plug in quite fanciful guesses in order to proceed. The panel data in themselves provide better-grounded estimates. And the fact that these estimates seem quite invulnerable to changes in period—even when one would least dare to expect them to be, as in the case of partisanship, 1964-76—can be an important liberating fact for the conduct of further research.

The findings have provisional implications for research methods which are broader still. For some time, the cost-benefit ledger for panel designs, as opposed to less expensive independent replications, has been subject to some dispute. One can learn a good deal about important facets of change without making the extra investment in a multi-wave panel. However, other facets of change, such as those central to this respect, can only be observed with the help of a panel. One swallow does not a summer make, and it would obviously be premature to conclude that the stationarity of continuity coefficients which marks these political data would emerge for panel studies in all periods with any subject matter. On the other hand, these continuities seem so pervasive across a variety of types of variables in the election panels that the hint of universality is hard to miss. And if there is some generality to the findings, then the premium that might be placed on doing panels persistently over a series like the election studies is at least somewhat reduced, although occasional panel links would remain important.

The findings also have strong bearing on various substantive questions. For example, one of the points of most vigorous theoretical ferment in the past decade in electoral politics has involved the nature of partisan realignments. The subject has captured uncommon scholarly interest not merely because of its obvious importance in any theory of elections, but also because of the seeming imminence of such a realignment after 1964 or so. Given past periodicities, the time was ripe. Much more to the point, several key ingredients associated with past realignments had begun to emerge.

Very crudely put, the most important of these ingredients was the outbreak of uncommonly galvanizing political turmoil, of the sort which certainly marked the late 1960s and early 1970s. More finely drawn, we have the excellent effort of Sundquist (1973) to reconstruct the internal dynamics of a partisan realignment, with stress upon crucial emergence of important cross-cutting cleavages which the leaderships of the extant traditional parties bound to older cleavage lines, fail to articulate. Again, such ingredients were present, par excellence, by the late 1960s. That these new cleavages were gripping for common voters is attested to at least indirectly by the high continuity values associated in the new panel with items like busing and the life-style or moral issues. That these new issues posed cleavages which were truly cross-cutting (i.e., relatively orthogonal to or uncorrelated with prior lines of party alignment) is clearly demonstrated by Miller and Levitin (1976, p. 82), who show the lack of much association between voter persuasions on the newer issues and their party identifications.

One must insist that the new issues be cross-cutting ones to set the stage for a realignment, since otherwise the emergence of new issues more or less aligned with old ones would merely reinforce existing party differences. In the late 1960s and the early 1970s, some Democrats were affronted by counterculture trends while others were not; likewise, some Republicans approved while others disapproved. What is important about these differential within-party affinities is that if potent enough, they should produce changes in partisanship of a leap-frogging kind, disturbing the relative ordering of individuals on the continuum of partisan loyalties. However, it is exactly this possibility of leap-frogging that our continuity correlations are admirably designed to register, however insensitive they may be to other forms of change. And they give us the message that the leap-frogging type of change in partisanship was scarcely more prevalent over the whole of this period than it had been in 1956-60. Hence while the emergence of cross-cutting cleavages seems to have been real enough, it also seems clear that they did not produce the relevant changes in partisanship in this period, even of the compensating kind which leaves the net balance of partisanship in the aggregate unaffected.

Another set of implications flows from the panel data patterns of the issue items. Our original theorizing led us to imagine that constraint among belief elements measured at a point in time and the stability of those beliefs for individuals across time would tend to covary, although no empirical test of this assumption between periods of time has been possible until the new panel. In effect, if Nie's (1974) demonstration of increased constraint in the recent period has substantive merit, then we would be obliged to expect the stability of these types of items to advance in the new panel as well.

The fact that no such increase is observed poses an interesting problem. One possibility is that the original assumption, which sees variations in attitude crystallization as producing variations both in constraint and in stability, is simply wrong and needs to be rethought. Another possibility which, as we have seen, has already been raised (Bishop et al., 1978; Sullivan et al., 1978) is that the Nie displays are largely a product of changes in question format, rather than true increases in constraint. At first glance, the accrediting of such challenges might seem to solve the problem by removing the weight of the expectation that issue stabilities should have advanced in the new panel. However, even if the Nie results were in fact largely due to question format, one might still expect comparable variations in stability on the same base. Now we saw as we passed through the issue items that small changes in continuity values did appear to follow in expected ways along lines of shifts in question format. However, these latter tests were few and at points equivocal, so that not a great deal should be made of them. But in any event, even these changes were of very limited magnitude. Thus some fundamental problems remain which challenge further research, at least some of which can be carried out with other probings of the new panel data set.

A final cluster of implications which is of great theoretical importance flows from the hierarchy of continuities across parties, leaders and issues suggested in Figure 18-1, and is relevant for controversies over the prevalence of issue voting. It is not hard to imagine that attitudes which show higher individual-level stability have causal primacy relative to less stable attitudes. If this simple surmise is meaningful, then it would seem that where political evaluations are concerned, a party —> leader —> issue flow may be dominant, even across periods as disparate as those before and after 1960.

It must be kept in mind that the new panel data are merely suggestive in this regard, rather than definitive. Even the gross discrepancies in continuity between partisanship and issue positioning cannot guarantee that party identification is nearly always causally primary when party feelings are discovered to be aligned with issue preferences. Among other things, we must remember that there are only two major parties, whereas the number of political issues which may exercise one or another voter is legion. Thus it would always be possible, if indeed a bit strained, to imagine that the typical voter might be viscerally gripped by one issue out of some 30 in the active universe in some period, with very uncrystallized attitudes on the other 29. If party positions on such crucial but idiosyncratic issues remained constant over long periods of time, these policy preferences might totally dictate party identifications, at the very same time that measurement over a dozen or so of the 30 potential issues might show very high aggregate instabilitiy, since only one voter in 30 would, on the average, be gripped by each.

While such a model remains conceivable, it is obviously not the most plausible reading of current data. The huge discrepancies in individual-level continuities between party loyalties on one hand and issue positions on the other, particularly in view of what now seems to be their long-term constancy, argues for an overwhelming primacy of the party term when party-issue congruence does occur. However, further causal modeling work with the new panel, profiting from some of the kinds of estimates presented in this report, can mold more incisive conclusions from what must remain only suggestive ones at this point.

The additional fact, also made clear by the new panel data, that reactions to political leaders display levels of continuity intermediary between partisanship and policy preferences, raises a number of further interesting possibilities. Such a data configuration may, for example, suggest a significant margin for policy leadership available to major political figures, whereby admirers are quite susceptible to influence leading them to adopt policy positions more congruent with those espoused by their heroes. Or again, the greater continuity in evaluation of leaders as compared with issue positions may simply reflect the fact that party attachments anchor *both* leader assessments and issue positions, but do so more effectively in the case of leaders because the common voter can maintain much more firm and unequivocal cognitive links between parties and their most prominent leaders than between parties and positions on various issues.

This is obviously not the place to begin sorting out such possibilities. However, the first-cut results from the new CPS panel are striking indeed. They already rule out some constructions which might be placed upon the electoral history of the past decade, and begin to draw into focus a number of new research questions which, with more refined "milling" of the panel data, we may well be able to answer effectively.

NOTES

1. Presidential voting in the 1976 election seems to be the first major reversal of this trend.
2. For a more extended discussion of the significance of these oscillations, see Converse (1976), pp. 126-30.
3. Obviously, one can restore some of this information in relatively compact form by shifting from correlation coefficients to raw or nonstandardized regression coefficients plus intercept terms. For some purposes this is exactly what one should do, although such statements operate in a metric-bound currency which can impede communication for those unfamiliar with the variable. For simplicity we shall deal here with continuity correlations.
4. Note, however, that this expectation is contingent on an error variance which is gaining in size relative to the true variance. In the more general case, the continuity

correlation is in theory independent of the variances of the component distributions.

5. All correlations are calculated on the basis of party identification as a seven-point, integer-scored scale. Here as at some other points in this article, precise numbers of cases are difficult to provide, since the estimates are more often than not "synthetic," resting on multiple bases. Thus, for example, the value of .835 is based on an averaging of four different estimates available in the 1956-60 panel for the correlation after about a two-year interval. While all of these values are very similar in appearance, each is based on a rather different number of cases.
6. In addition to the full-blown fourth wave present on ICPSR tapes due to a full-sample application of the party identification item in the post-election as well as the pre-election study for 1960, a stray set of 165 cases were re-asked the party identification question in the 1956 post-election study as well. Estimates from this mini-sample are of course less stable than their counterparts in the four other waves. However, where comparisons are possible, they are so gracefully consistent with what can be learned from the pre- and post-1960 waves that we do not have much hesitation in using them to yield the additional degrees of freedom provided by a fifth wave. Naturally, in all relevant calculations, we take account of the fact that the points of observation are very unequally spaced in real time.
7. Actually, our detailed calculations show not only no shrinkage in the error variance, but if anything a slight absolute increase. Thus the decrease in reliability (or the proportion of true variance to total variance) has a double source.
8. Throughout this chapter we are providing mere "bottom-line" estimates that conceal more detailed consideration of angularities in the data. These will be dealt with more explicitly in subsequent technical articles. One such angularity being momentarily ignored in this statement, although dealt with in our calculations, is the presence of some systematic progression of the unreliability term across waves of the same panel.
9. There is one other pairing, also in civil rights, where a somewhat rougher match might be made. In the first panel, a question inspired by the FEPC legislation of the time asked about the appropriateness of the government attempting to ensure that Negroes get "fair treatment in jobs and housing." In the second panel, respondents were asked whether the government should make "every possible effort to improve the social and economic position of blacks and other minority groups." These are divergent questions, both in substance and in group of reference, although there is some obvious kinship between them. The first item was in four-point agree-disagree form; the second was in forced-choice, seven-point scale form. The average two-year continuity correlations in the first instance was .468; in the second, a somewhat higher .535.
10. We postpone consideration of the detailed partitioning of the issue items into reliability and stability components until a subsequent technical paper, since a proper treatment requires taking account of differing response variances in different population segments. These complications are too elaborate for space available here. However, it may be of interest to note that a simple partitioning of these issue items, ignoring the complications, suggests that the unreliability component of responses greatly outruns a true change component, just as was true for the original panel.

19. THE ORIGINS AND MEANING OF LIBERAL/CONSERVATIVE SELF-IDENTIFICATIONS

Pamela Johnston Conover and Stanley Feldman

Over the last 20 years, one of the enduring questions characterizing the study of mass electorates has been whether or not there is ideological thinking in terms of the liberal/conservative continuum. Curiously, though research on this question has been both abundant and controversial, it has tended to ignore—or perhaps take for granted—the meaning of liberal/conservative self-identifications and their impact on political behavior. Typically, it has been assumed that the logical links between ideological self-identifications, on the one hand, and general political orientations and specific issue positions, on the other hand, do in fact exist. Only in the past few years have researchers begun to probe the wisdom of such traditional reasoning. Notably, Levitin and Miller (1979, p. 751) recently explored "the use of the terms 'liberal' and 'conservative' as they are applied by citizens to describe themselves, the political parties, presidential candidates, and positions on issues of public policy." Along similar lines, Holm and Robinson (1978) have compared the impact of partisan and ideological identifications on voting behavior. Finally, from a cross-national perspective, Klingemann (1979a, 1979b) has studied both the use and meaning of the terms "left" and "right."

Generally, these researchers have concluded that, although many members of the public may lack a complete understanding of such ideological terms as traditionally conceptualized, these labels and related self-identifications nonetheless have considerable impact on political perceptions and behavior. Thus, these studies have succeeded in establishing the political significance of ideological labels and identifications. At the same time, however, they have left in doubt the dynamics of the process underlying the influence of such identifications. In

---

Authors' Note: The order of the authors' names is alphabetical. An earlier version of this article was presented at the 1980 annual meeting of the Midwest Political Science Association, Chicago, April 24-26, 1980. The data analyzed in this article were collected by the Center for Political Studies and made available through the Inter-university Consortium for Political and Social Research, neither of which bears any responsibility for the interpretations presented here. We would like to thank Robert Weissberg, Herbert Asher, Herbert Weisberg, and two anonymous reviewers for their constructive comments on this article.

particular, in order to understand why liberal/conservative identifications are as influential as recent researchers have claimed, it is necessary to explore the meaning they hold for members of the public, a task which is undertaken in this paper. In so doing, we attempt to bridge the gap between the more traditional research on mass belief systems and the recent work on the political impact of ideological labels.

The Meaning of Ideological Labels

It is our contention that in order to understand fully the nature of ideological self-identifications, it is first necessary to uncover the meaning of the "liberal" and "conservative" labels. In this regard, implicit in much of the mass belief system's literature are two questionable assumptions: (1) that the meaning of ideological labels is structured in dimensional terms; and (2) that the content of such meaning is largely issue oriented. Clearly, these assumptions are not unreasonable given the predominant direction of research on mass belief systems. Nonetheless, there is substantial reason to doubt their validity.

The Structure of Meaning

Traditionally, it was assumed that the meaning of ideological labels and self-identifications could be easily summarized in terms of a single dimension: the liberal/conservative continuum. In recent years, however, this viewpoint has undergone some modification. The decade of the 1970s ushered in a variety of "social" issues—abortion, marijuana use, the Equal Rights Amendment—which did not fit easily into the traditional liberal/conservative spectrum. Because of this, many researchers now posit that the meaning of ideological labels and self-identifications must be interpreted within the context of two liberal/conservative dimensions: one economic and one social (Asher, 1980; Miller and Miller, 1977; Weisberg and Rusk, 1970).

Whether one assumes the presence of a single or several liberal/conservative dimensions does not fundamentally alter our argument. From our perspective, what is critical is the assumption of bipolarity which is common to *both* dimensional interpretations. That is, both the single- and two-dimensional conceptualizations assume that with regard to a particular dimension of meaning the liberal perspective is simply the opposite of the conservative one. In effect, liberals and conservatives are depicted as sharing the same perceptual framework(s); all that differs is that their view is from opposite sides of the field. Because of such shared meaning, voters ought to be able to compare candidates, issues, and parties, and subsequently evaluate such objects using their own identification as an anchoring point.[1] But, recent works reveal that many voters are unable to make accurate comparisons of candidates and issues in liberal/conservative terms (Erikson et al., 1980; Levitin and Miller, 1979). Furthermore, this tendency is especially pronounced in the case of issues, where, based on traditional conceptualizations, one might logically expect to find the clearest liberal/conservative distinctions. For example, Erikson et al. (1980, p. 57) note a Harris poll which revealed that only 50 percent of the electorate was able to "correctly identify the liberal and conservative sides of major political issues." Similarly, Levitin and Miller (1979) found that on some issues even so-called

.s had difficulty in distinguishing the liberal position from the conserva- .e. One interpretation of such findings is that most members of the elec. ate attribute relatively little meaning to the terms "liberal" and "conservative." An alternate interpretation, however, is that researchers have erred in their basic assumption that the meaning of ideological terms is necessarily structured in dimensional terms. Both empirical findings and theoretical arguments suggest that the latter interpretation is the more valid one.

To begin with, those studies (Asher, 1980; Weisberg and Rusk, 1970) which posit the existence of two liberal/conservative dimensions raise a possibility which paradoxically conflicts with a dimensional interpretation of the meaning of ideological terms. Namely, for some voters, one dimension might be significantly more salient than the other in determining the meaning associated with such terms. Some people, for example, might define ideological labels almost exclusively in terms of social issues while, at the same time, others may base their interpretation entirely on economic issues. Were this to occur, different groups of people would have fundamentally different, rather than opposing or bipolar, ideological perspectives. More generally, several studies have found that people organize their beliefs in a multidimensional fashion, with the nature and number of dimensions often varying from individual to individual (Brown, 1970; Conover and Feldman, 1980; Coveyou and Piereson, 1977; Herzon, 1980; Jackson and Marcus, 1975; Lane, 1962, 1973; and Marcus et al., 1974). As a critical by-product of such multidimensionality, the salience of specific beliefs is likely to vary among people, thus creating different frames of reference from which they interpret the meaning of ideological labels (Brown and Taylor, 1973). As a consequence, the ways in which self-defined liberals and conservatives understand those labels may differ in important respects.

Several studies support this hypothesis. Warr et al. (1969), for example, discovered that the political judgements of left-wing, center, and right-wing British respondents were based on different sets of cognitive dimensions. Along somewhat similar lines, Brown and Taylor (1973) found that a group of students differed considerably in how they conceptualized the term "conservatism." Some focused on the "lack of change" which they felt was inherent in the philosophy, while others concentrated on what they perceived to be the "elitist" aspect of conservatism. But, perhaps most relevant to our argument is Kerlinger's (1967, 1972) theory of "criterial referents." Kerlinger posits that attitudes differ in terms of their "referents," or focus; referents that are "criterial" or central to one attitude may be irrelevant to another. With respect to the social attitudes composing political belief systems, Kerlinger (1967, p. 112) suggests that "liberal is not just the opposite of conservative"; rather than representing endpoints on the same continuum, liberalism and conservatism constitute relatively distinct attitude systems based on different criterial referents. Kerlinger's thesis received strong support from his factor analysis which revealed that predesignated "liberal" and "conservative" referents did load on different dimensions, and that there were few negative loadings. Taken together, such findings indicate a distinct lack of bipolarity in the beliefs defining liberalism and conservatism. Thus, based on such evidence it seems quite plausible that the meaning of ideological labels is not structured in bipolar terms. Instead, different referents or concepts may be critical to defining the terms "liberal" and "conservative."[2]

The Content of Meaning

The assumption that the meaning of ideological labels is bipolar typically has been accompanied by a second assumption about the content of that meaning. Specifically, as Levitin and Miller (1979) note, it is traditionally assumed that ideology is based on issue preferences, and consequently that ideological labels are largely issue oriented in meaning. Yet, the findings of several recent studies suggest that the mass public must associate considerable nonissue-based meanings with labels like "liberal/conservative" and "left/right," and that ideological self-identifications may not be determined entirely, or even primarily, by issue stances (Klingemann, 1979a, 1979b; Levitin and Miller, 1979).

If not issue oriented, then what is the meaning associated with ideological labels? Clearly, to some degree such meaning may be partisan in nature, if not origin. Both Levitin and Miller (1979) and Holm and Robinson (1978) note a substantial relationship between partisan and ideological self-identifications; as the former explains, "when people describe themselves as having an ideological position, they also seem to be saying something about their positions on the parties, quite apart from their issue or policy stands" (Levitin and Miller, 1979, p. 768). But, it is unlikely that party identification accounts for all the meaning lent ideological terms, especially given Levitin and Miller's (1979) normal-vote analysis which indicates that liberal/conservative self-placements have an impact on vote choice independent of that of party identification. In any case, to say simply that partisan and ideological labels share some common meaning begs the question in that the nature of that shared meaning remains unspecified. Consequently, we will return to this question once we have explored the meaning of ideological labels.

Our approach to unraveling the meaning associated with ideological labels begins with the assumption that such terms are powerful, political symbols to many members of the public.[3] As symbols, the meaning which people attach to ideological labels, such as "liberal" and "conservative," may be of two types: (1) cognitive—the "objective information or substantive content associated with the symbol," and (2) evaluative—the affect elicited by the symbol (Cobb and Elder, 1973, p. 313). From this perspective, then, much of the previous research has focused on the cognitive content of ideological labels. But, if for many people ideological labels have sparse cognitive meaning, as research seems to suggest, then the symbolic power of such terms most likely stems from their evaluative content: their ability to generate strong positive or negative feelings.

Logically, then, the next step is to focus on the origins of the evaluative meaning of ideological labels. One source may actually be the cognitive content, however little, that is associated with the label. In effect, not only may issue-oriented factors directly define the cognitive content of ideological terms, but they also indirectly influence the evaluation of such terms. For example, an individual may react positively to the term "liberal" because he or she associates favorably evaluated issue positions with it. Alternatively, when cognitive sources of meaning are lacking, ideological labels may derive their effect from other, related symbols whose own evaluations may be influenced by long-standing predispositions. To illustrate, deeply ingrained racial prejudices may prompt a strong negative reaction to the *symbol* of busing (Sears et al., 1979); subsequently, linking that symbol with the "liberal" label should trigger a negative reaction to the latter.

Political symbols differ, however, in their basic nature, and consequently some are more likely than others to be related to ideological symbols such as the terms "liberal" and "conservative." Cobb and Elder (1972, 1973) have argued that political symbols may pertain to four different sorts of political objects: the political community, regime norms, formal political positions, and situational settings involving nongovernmental actors or specific political issues. These various types of symbols play different roles in society; some serve as a foundation for social solidarity while others act as a basis for social differentiation and conflict. For example, symbols of the community (i.e., democracy, freedom) and the regime (majority rule, due process) tend to be sources of consensus and unity in society. In contrast, certain groups (i.e., the Black Panthers, women's liberation) and political issues (i.e., busing, end the war) are symbolic of the lines of conflict in society. Within this context, the traditional nature of ideological concerns suggests that ideological labels should act as a basis for social differentiation. Thus, in the absence of substantial cognitive content, ideological symbols or labels are expected to derive their affect from their association with other symbols of social conflict such as various groups and issues.

A Model of Ideological Self-Identification

Having discarded the assumptions that the meaning of ideological labels is largely bipolar and issue oriented, a different model of the nature and origins of ideological self-identifications may be outlined (see Figure 19-1). A critical element in this model is the specification of the relationship between ideological labels and self-identifications. Based on our earlier discussion, we argue that it is the *evaluative* meaning of ideological labels that is most closely related to self-placement. In effect, it is assumed that identification with an ideological label is associated with a positive evaluation of it. Having made this assumption, we are left with the difficult task of untangling the direction of causality in the

Figure 19-1 Model 1 of Ideological Self-Identification

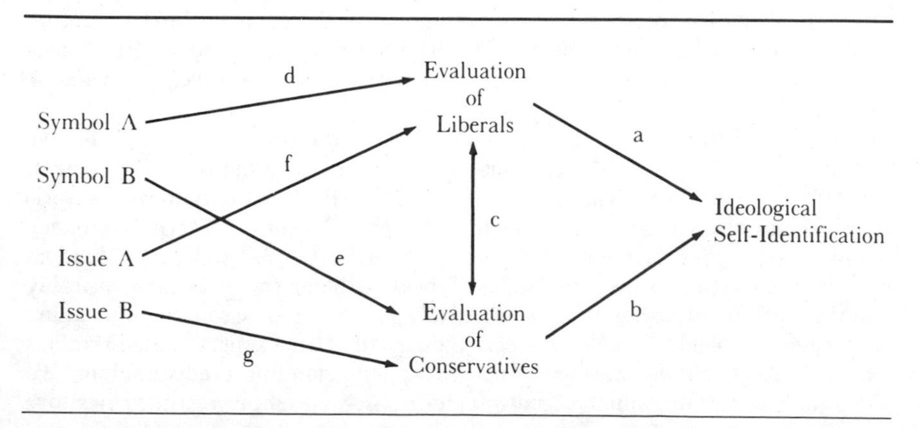

relationship. In addressing this problem, two factors govern our thinking: the presumed lack of bipolarity in the meaning of ideological labels and our conceptualization of self-identification. A presumption of bipolarity is implicit in any causal model in which a single factor, such as ideological identification, is depicted as determining evaluations of both liberals and conservatives. In contrast, a causal ordering in which evaluations of ideological labels influence self-identification requires no assumption about bipolarity or its absence, and is thus consistent with our theoretical argument.

Our conceptualization of self-identification leads us to the same conclusion. If ideological self-placements are thought of merely as acts of social categorization, then considerable research suggests that the more reasonable causal ordering is one in which self-placement stimulates a positive evaluation of the ideological label identified with (for a review, see Hamilton, 1976). If, on the other hand, the act of self-identification is treated as a statement of group consciousness—a declaration of group loyalty—then the reverse causal ordering is more appropriate; that is, a positive evaluation of an ideological group should enhance identification with it (Miller et al., 1978). For our part, we follow the latter line of reasoning by adopting a conceptualization of ideological identification that closely parallels that commonly associated with party identification. Specifically, like Levitin and Miller (1979), we assume that ideological self-placement reflects a "psychological attachment" to a particular group.

In summary, the basic premise underlying our model is that ideological self-placement is determined directly by the individual's evaluation of the two major ideological labels or groups—liberals and conservatives. This relative comparison of evaluations is indicated in the model by parameters *a* and *b*. Furthermore, in the absence of a bipolar structure of meaning, liberals will not necessarily evaluate conservatives negatively and vice versa. Thus, parameter *c* should approach zero, rather than being strongly negative. The direct relationship between ideological self-placement and the evaluation of ideological labels suggests that the meaning of such identifications derives from the meaning of the labels themselves. With respect to the structure of meaning, it was argued earlier that, in the aggregate, liberal and conservative labels have meanings which are not structured in a bipolar or dimensional fashion. Instead, those concepts associated with a positive evaluation of one term are likely to differ considerably from those central to determining a positive evaluation of the other. This lack of bipolar meaning assumes a special significance when considered in conjunction with individual self-identifications. Specifically, it implies that individuals who label themselves as liberals do so for very different reasons than those who call themselves conservatives, in the sense that different concepts or referents are critical in determining their positive evaluations of their respective ideological labels. In essence then, it is posited that liberals and conservatives view the political world not from different sides of the same coin, but rather, if you will, from the perspective of entirely different currencies. In the model this is indicated by the fact that each of the symbols and issues are linked with evaluations of either liberals *or* conservatives, but not both.[4]

Turning to the content of meaning, both cognitive factors and political symbols can influence attitudes towards liberals and conservatives, and thus ideological self-identifications. In the model this linkage is represented by paths *d* through *g*. Individuals may vary, however, in the degree to which they derive their evaluations of ideological labels from cognitive sources such as issue preferences or emotional sources such as political symbols. For some members of the electorate, ideological labels may hold substantial cognitive meaning which complements that derived from various symbols, so that the two sources interact in a consistent fashion to produce the affect associated with the label. Alternatively, lacking issue-oriented information about ideological labels, other individuals are expected to base their evaluations largely on the affective relationship of the label with other political symbols. In both cases, people may attach significant symbolic meaning to ideological labels, and although the sources of the meaning differ, its impact on self-identification, and subsequently behavior, may not.

To summarize, our model specifies a set of causal processes underlying liberal/conservative self-identifications that goes against much of the common wisdom on the subject. As with any model, it is not possible to *prove* that it has been specified correctly. Instead, final judgments about it depend on the theoretical justification of the processes specified, the fit of the model to the data, and the explanatory power of the model. Since we believe that we have established a sound theoretical basis for the model, let us turn now to an empirical assessment of it.

Data and Methods

In testing this model, we had the option of two different research strategies. By focusing on a relatively small group of people, the meaning of ideological self-identifications could be examined on an individual by individual basis. Alternatively, we could take a larger, representative sample and assess the common, or shared meaning of ideological labels. Although individual variations in meaning are important, we have chosen the second route for several reasons. First, this follows the general approach of those studies noted earlier which have raised many of the problems we wish to address. Second, since ideological labels like "liberal" and "conservative" are in large part societally defined, there should be an important component to such identifications that is shared by many people. And finally, looking at the common meaning of such labels provides a basis for assessing their ability to aggregate individual patterns of belief and symbolism. Thus, this approach provides a good first test for the model and ultimately a base line against which group differences may be assessed.

Given this, the data employed in the test of our model are taken from the 1976 National Election Study conducted by the Center for Political Studies. In order to test the model properly, it is necessary to operationalize three categories of variables: (1) ideological self-identification, (2) evaluations of ideological labels, and (3) the cognitive and symbolic sources of the meaning of ideological labels. Let us consider each of these.

Ideological Self-Identification

Ideological self-identification was measured in terms of a standard CPS question which focuses on *political* liberal/conservative identification. Specifically, respondents were asked to place themselves on a seven-point scale whose values ranged from "people whose political views" are "extremely liberal" on one end, to "moderate" in the middle, to "extremely conservative" on the other end. The higher the score, the more conservative the self-identification.

Evaluation of Ideological Labels

Evaluations of the two major ideological labels—liberal and conservative—were measured in terms of "feeling thermometer" ratings. In particular, respondents were asked to rate on a scale from 0 to 100 degrees how warm or cold they felt toward "liberals" and "conservatives"; high scores on each item indicate a positive evaluation of the ideological label.

Cognitive and Symbolic Sources of Meaning

In assessing the cognitive and symbolic sources of the meaning of ideological labels, we were faced with a critical measurement dilemma: whether to employ closed-ended or open-ended questions as the basis for our measures. On the one hand, responses to closed-ended questions dealing with peoples' issue orientations and their attitudes towards various political symbols could be correlated with evaluations of ideological labels in order to identify the meaning of the labels. While this constitutes something of an indirect approach, such closed-ended questions are a relatively clear-cut way of getting at the shared, or aggregate, meaning of ideological labels. In contrast, open-ended questions—such as those asking respondents what the terms "liberal" and "conservative" mean—are a much more direct method of establishing the meaning of ideological labels. However, verbal abilities play a large role in determining whether responses to such questions accurately reflect the meaning associated with ideological labels. Those respondents with lower levels of education may be hampered by the question format so that their responses are not good indicators of the real meaning which ideological labels hold for them. Similarly, because open-ended questions allow for greater individual expression, they make it more difficult to identify patterns of aggregate meaning than is the case with closed-ended measures. All this, taken together with our interest in the shared patterns of meaning, led us to employ closed-ended questions as the primary means of establishing the cognitive and symbolic sources of meaning of ideological labels.

Cognitive Sources. Our assessment of the cognitive sources of meaning is based on the respondents' specific issue positions. In adopting this approach, we acknowledge that measuring the meaning of ideological labels in terms of specific issue positions becomes problematic once we abandon the assumption that belief systems are structured unidimensionally (Coveyou and Piereson, 1977; Jackson and Marcus, 1975; Marcus et al., 1974). In particular, a measure of issue orientation based on a series of issue positions aggregated according to their relationship to a liberal/conservative continuum runs the risk of penalizing those respondents who, in fact, do not structure their attitudes along that dimension. Nonetheless, given that previous research has strongly emphasized the role of issues in determining the meaning of ideological labels and the nature of self-identifications, we considered it necessary to employ specific issue positions in our measure of cognitive meaning, even though in doing so some bias may have been introduced into our analysis.

With that caveat in mind, the respondents' specific issue positions were used to construct three summated rating scales which represent the major domains of domestic policy: economic concerns, social issues, and racial questions (Knoke, 1979). Listed below are the three scales, the issues used in their construction, and their reliabilities (coefficient alpha).[5]

I_1: Economic Issues—health insurance, guaranteed jobs and standard of living, and taxation policy (.54).
I_2: Racial Issues—busing, school desegregation, and aid to minorities (.68).
I_3: Social Issues—marijuana use, abortion, ERA, and sex roles (.62).

In constructing the scales, all the issues were first put in standardized form (mean = 0; standard deviation = 1) and then summed to produce an overall score for the respondent on that scale. In each case, high scores indicate more conservative issue positions.

Symbolic Sources. As noted earlier, to the degree that evaluations of ideological labels are based upon their association with other political symbols, these are likely to be symbols of social differentiation and conflict rather than consensus. Consequently, in measuring the symbolic sources of ideological meaning we focused upon nongovernmental actors or groups that might constitute symbolic representations of various cleavages in American society. Specifically, the respondents' feeling-thermometer ratings of 27 different groups in society were factor analyzed.[6] This analysis produced six factors with eigenvalues greater than one. The interpretation of these factors was based on the assumption that factor loadings of .5 or greater were substantively significant. Based on this criteria, six additive scales were formed from the feeling-thermometer ratings; positive scores on each scale indicate positive feelings towards the groups composing it.[7]

As indicated in Table 19-1, each of the six scales is composed of a distinct cluster of groups which symbolically represent major cleavages in society. The first scale represents the "status quo" and is composed of mainstream groups traditionally associated with the "protestant ethic" and "middle America." The second scale deals with the "radical left": groups symbolic of revolutionary or rapid change such as "black militants" and "radical students." The third scale is symbolic of "capitalism." The "reformist left" is represented by the fourth scale which concerns groups or minorities related to moderate social change. The symbolic meaning associated with the "disadvantaged" segments of society is captured by the fifth scale which pertains to relatively powerless groups such as the "poor" and "older people." Finally, the last scale deals with symbols of "social control" such as the police and military. It is important to recognize that, taken together, these scales symbolically tap the various dimensions of meaning traditionally associated with the liberal/conservative continuum (Converse, 1964; and Klingemann, 1979a). Yet, at the same time, these scales also act as a symbolic representation of some of the new social issues, which emerged in the late 1960s, centered around the agents of social control and the evolution of a counterculture (Miller and Levitin, 1976).

Table 19-1 Six Symbolic Meaning Scales and Their Components

S_1: STATUS QUO Protestants Working Men Whites Men Middle-Class People (reliability = .89)	S_2: RADICAL LEFT Radical Students Women's Liberation Marijuana Users Black Militants (reliability = .73)
S_3: CAPITALISM Big Business Republicans Businessmen (reliability = .77)	S_4: REFORMIST LEFT Blacks Chicanos People on Welfare Jews Civil Rights Leaders (reliability = .77)
S_5: DISADVANTAGED Poor People Older People Women Young People (reliability = .74)	S_6: SOCIAL CONTROL Police Military (reliability = .69)

All reliabilities are coefficient alpha.

Findings

Self-Identification and the Evaluation of Ideological Labels

First, our model suggests that ideological self-placement should reflect evaluations of the two major ideological groups—liberals and conservatives. Our findings confirm this relationship as indicated by the form of the regression equation:

$$\text{Self-Identification} = .309 \text{ evaluations of conservatives} - .422 \text{ evaluations of liberals}$$

(coefficients are beta weights)

Taken together, evaluations of liberals and conservatives explain 36 percent of the variance in ideological self-placement (multiple Pearson's $R = .60$). Furthermore, it is interesting to note that evaluations of liberals have a somewhat stronger impact on self-identification than do evaluations of conservatives. This pattern may reflect the nature of the political environment over the past 20 years. Until quite recently, the "New Left" and the social issues which it championed tended to dominate political discourse in the United States. As a consequence, the "liberal" label may have become more salient and reactions to it more emotionally charged than in the case of the "conservative" label, thus accounting for the relatively stronger impact of the "liberal" label on self-identification. However, with the current emergence of the "New Right" and the concomitant ascendancy of the "conservative" label, evaluations of conservatives may come to have a stronger impact on self-identifications in future years.

The finding that ideological self-identification is strongly influenced by evaluations of liberals and conservatives takes on added significance when considered in conjunction with the following finding: though evaluations of liberals and conservatives are both strongly related to self-identification, they have only a weak negative relationship with one another; Pearson's r equals —.17 for those respondents having an ideological self-identification.[8] This finding runs counter to the argument that the aggregate meaning of ideological labels is bipolar in its structure. Instead, it suggests that evaluations of ideological symbols are relatively independent. In essence, a positive evaluation of liberals does not guarantee a negative attitude towards conservatives, though it does not preclude it either. In more general terms, this finding parallels a pattern uncovered in the study of attitudes towards political parties. Several researchers (Maggiotto and Piereson, 1977; Weisberg, 1980) have found that evaluations of Democrats and Republicans are relatively independent of one another. Taken together, these two sets of findings suggest that the dimensional models so typical in the study of political attitudes be approached with some caution.

Next, our model posits not only that evaluations of ideological labels influence self-identification, but also that they mediate the impact of all other sources of meaning. To test this argument, two regressions were run. In the first, ideological self-placement was regressed on the three issue-position scales. In the second regression, ideological self-placement was regressed on the three issue-position scales, the six symbolic-meaning scales, *and* the evaluations of the two ideological labels (see Table 19-2). A comparison of the two regressions reveals that, with only one exception, all those variables having a significant impact in the first regression had no influence once liberal and conservative evaluations were entered into the regression; only evaluations of liberals and conservatives, and economic issues remained significant in the second regression. Furthermore, although economic issues continued to have some direct effect on self-identification, it is important to note that evaluations of liberals and conservatives had a much stronger impact. Thus, although there remains a weak vestige of what once might have been a strong direct link between New Deal economic issues and ideological identification, by and large our prediction is borne out; both cognitive and symbolic sources of meaning influence ideological self-placement primarily through their contribution to the evaluative meaning associated with ideological labels.

Thus, to this point several key findings have supported our argument that evaluations of liberals and conservatives are the most immediate determinants of ideological self-identification. Despite this, in order for our interpretation to be fully convincing we must consider two major alternatives to our model, both of which seriously question the validity of our causal ordering of the evaluation of ideological labels and self-identification. As illustrated in Figure 19-2, the first alternative, model 2, reverses our causal ordering so that self-identification is depicted as influencing evaluations rather than vice versa. Another alternative conceptualization is represented by model 3 which is based on the assumption

Table 19-2 Regressions of Liberal/Conservative Self-Placements on the Issue-Position Scales, the Symbolic-Meaning Variables, and Evaluations of Liberals and Conservatives[a]

Independent Variables	*Regression 1*	*Regression 2*
I. *Symbolic-Meaning Variables*		
S_1: Status Quo	−.019 (−.0004)	−.018 (−.0008)
S_2: Radical Left	−.113 (−.0027)*	−.037 (−.0009)
S_3: Capitalism	.252 (.0079)*	.067 (.0027)
S_4: Reformist Left	−.232 (.0052)*	−.071 (−.0018)
S_5: Disadvantaged	.009 (.0003)	.009 (.0003)
S_6: Social Control	.095 (.0042)	.076 (.0034)
II. *Issue-Position Scales*		
I_1: Economic	.189 (.131)*	.099 (.069)*
I_2: Racial	.019 (.011)	−.006 (−.003)
I_3: Social	.152 (.070)*	.085 (.031)
III. *Evaluations*		
Of Conservatives	—	.259 (.019)*
Of Liberals	—	−.385 (−.027)*
	(R = .56)	(R = .65)

[a] Unparenthesized entries are beta weights; parenthesized entries are unstandardized regression coefficients.

* $p < .05$ level.

that evaluations of both the "liberal" and "conservative" labels, as well as ideological self-placement, are simply multiple indicators of the same underlying construct, rather than measures of different constructs, as we have assumed. Such a model would be most consistent with the measurement strategy adopted by Levitin and Miller (1979) in their recent examination of ideological identifications.

Both of these alternative conceptualizations lead to certain predictions which can be tested. In particular, model 2 predicts that once ideological self-placement—the intervening variable—is held constant then the symbolic variables and the issue scales should have little or no direct impact on evaluations of liberals and conservatives. This prediction was tested in the following two regressions (coefficients are beta weights and starred coefficients are significant):

$$\text{Evaluations of Liberals} = .07S_1 + .21^*S_2 - .09S_3 + .17^*S_4 - .01S_5 + .09S_6 - .15^*I_1 + .04I_2 - .06I_3 - .33^* \text{ Self-placement } (R = .69)$$

$$\text{Evaluations of Conservatives} = .11^*S_1 + .06S_2 + .42^*S_3 - .02S_4 + .02S_5 + .14^*S_6 + .00I_1 + .17^*I_2 - .03I_3 + .22^* \text{ Self-placement } (R = .71)$$

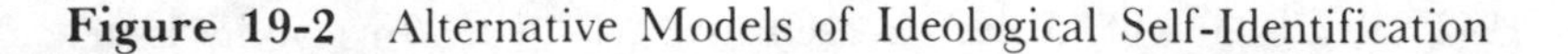

Figure 19-2 Alternative Models of Ideological Self-Identification

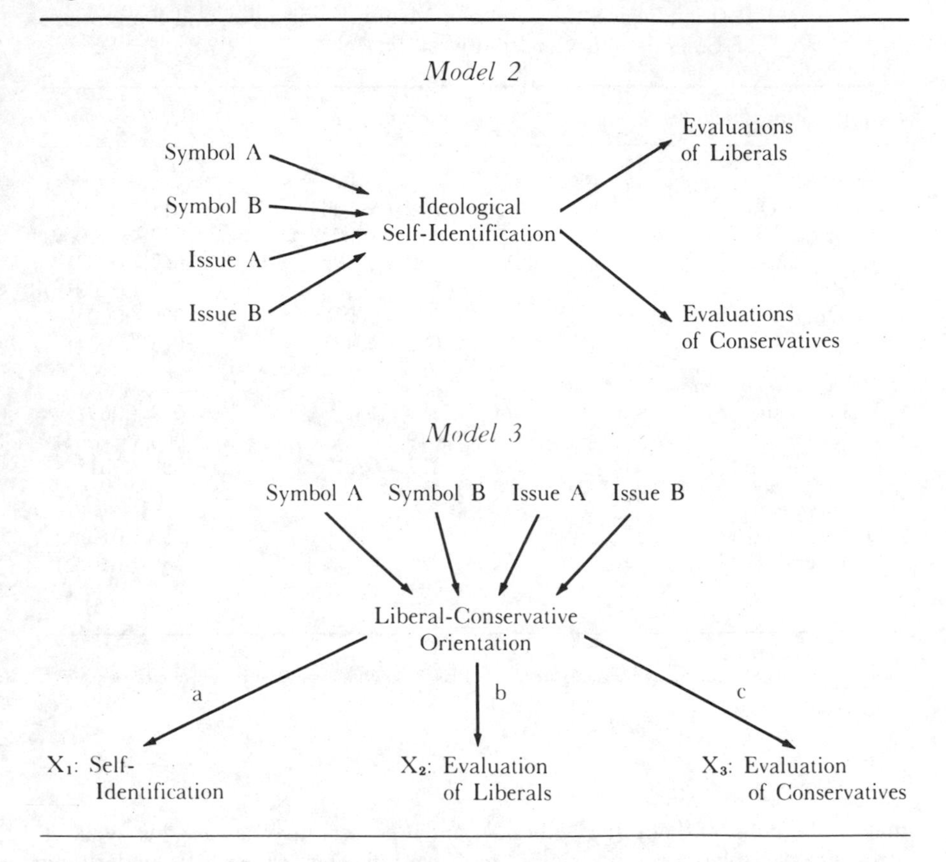

As the estimates show, although self-placement did have an impact on evaluations, the model is clearly misspecified in this form; both the symbolic variables and the issue scales had a substantial direct impact on the evaluations even with self-placement included in the regression. Thus, based on this test, model 2 is not as strongly supported as the original model.[9]

Our test of the third model focuses on the relationship between the theoretical construct of a general liberal/conservative orientation and its three hypothesized indicators—self-placement, and evaluations of liberals and conservatives. In this model, there are three unknowns: the epistemic correlations (*a, b,* and *c*) which represent the relationships between the theoretical construct and its indicators. There are also three known quantities: the observed correlations (r_{12}, r_{13}, and r_{23}) among the indicators. Since there are three unknown and three known quantities, the model is just identified. Consequently, although we can solve for the three epistemic correlations, there is no excess information to test for goodness of fit. Instead, the only weak condition that must be met in order for the model to hold is that the estimates of *a, b,* and *c* not exceed $\pm$ 1, since they are effectively correlations (Duncan, 1972).[10] But, as the following estimates demonstrate, the model fails even this relatively simple test: a = 1.21, b = −.44, and c = .39. Since the estimate for parameter a exceeds one, model 3 cannot be accepted in its present form. In essence, self-identification and evaluations of liberals and conservatives cannot be considered to be indicators of the same theoretical construct.

Thus, in their present forms neither model 2 nor model 3 fits the data very well. Such a relatively poor showing by both of these alternative models bolsters our confidence in our own conceptualization of the nature of the relationship between evaluations of ideological labels and self-identification. Nonetheless, the choice between these various models ultimately must be made on theoretical grounds; no amount of empirical testing can establish the appropriate causal ordering in the absence of a sound theoretical basis (Duncan, 1975). From such a theoretical perspective, any specification of the causal relationship between ideological self-placement and evaluations must be consistent with one's understanding of the nature of those evaluations and their determinants. In this regard, our conceptualization differs critically from the alternative models in our treatment of the question of bipolarity. Because we posit a lack of bipolarity in the meaning of ideological labels, we necessarily must hypothesize structurally *distinct* determinants of the evaluations of such labels. In contrast, the other two models assume bipolarity and therefore are theoretically compatible with the idea of structurally *identical* determinants. This suggests that our judgment as to the appropriate causal ordering between ideological self-identification and evaluations should not be divorced from our assessment of the validity of our broader theoretical framework, particularly our argument concerning bipolarity. Therefore, the next step is to examine the sources of the evaluations of ideological terms.

Sources of the Evaluation of Ideological Labels

As noted earlier, two general types of factors are considered as possible sources of an individual's attitudes towards liberals and conservatives: specific issue positions and other political symbols. To test the relative contribution of each of these types of factors, evaluations of liberals and conservatives were separately regressed on the three issue-position scales and the six symbolic-meaning scales. The results are presented in Table 19-3.

Considering first the content of meaning, symbolic factors clearly played a more important role than issue positions in determining the valuation of ideological labels. Attitudes towards liberals and conservatives were each significantly influenced by four variables; yet, in both cases only one of these was an issue-position scale. Furthermore, for both liberals and conservatives the most important determinants were symbolic in nature. Specifically, positive attitudes towards liberals were primarily a function of positive feelings towards the symbols of the radical and reformist left. Negative sentiments towards the symbol of capitalism and a traditional liberal perspective on economic issues were also significant, though less important, determinants of attitudes towards liberals. In contrast, positive evaluations of conservatives were most heavily influenced by a positive affect towards the symbol of capitalism. In addition, a positive affect towards the status quo and social control symbols, and a conservative stance on racial issues also contributed to a positive evaluation of conservatives.

Table 19-3 Regression of Evaluations of Liberals and Conservatives on Issue Positions and the Symbolic-Meaning Variables[a]

Independent Variables	*Evaluation of Liberals*	*Evaluation of Conservatives*
I. *Symbolic-Meaning Variables*		
S_1: Status Quo	.078 (.019)	.125 (.032)*
S_2: Radical Left	.305 (.073)*	−.022 (−.008)
S_3: Capitalism	−.154 (−.063)*	.473 (.169)*
S_4: Reformist Left	.246 (.080)*	.015 (.004)
S_5: Disadvantaged	−.037 (−.013)	.051 (.016)
S_6: Social Control	.052 (.028)	.192 (.088)*
II. *Issue-Position Scales*		
I_1: Economic	−.132 (−1.28)*	.042 (.326)
I_2: Racial	.029 (.207)	.167 (1.00)*
I_3: Social	−.075 (−.337)	.016 (.083)
	(R = .61)	(R = .69)

[a] Unparenthesized entries are beta weights; parenthesized entries are unstandardized regression coefficients.

* $p < .05$ level.

Even though issue positions had relatively little direct impact on evaluations of liberals and conservatives, it could still be argued that issues have some indirect influence vis-à-vis political symbols. From our perspective, such a causal ordering is theoretically suspect. Nonetheless, we tested this possibility by regressing each of the six symbolic meaning scales on the three issue-position scales. The results of these regressions indicated that issue positions had relatively little influence on the affect attached to the various symbols. On average, the issue scales accounted for only about 11 percent of the variance in attitudes towards the symbols. This suggests that an individual's attachment to political symbols is derived primarily from other, nonissue-oriented sources. Thus, as predicted, ideological self-identifications are largely a product of symbolic affect and only slightly reflect specific issue positions, a finding which strongly confirms Levitin and Miller's (1979) suspicion that issue positions are of limited importance in determining liberal/conservative self-placements.

Turning now to a consideration of the structure of the meaning of underlying the evaluation of ideological symbols, we find ample support for our hypothesis that the structure is not bipolar. Specifically, with only one exception, different referents were central to defining the meaning of the terms liberal and conservative. The one shared referent, the symbol of capitalism, was associated positively with evaluations of conservatives and negatively with those of liberals (see Table 19-3). But, while the capitalism symbol was the most critical determinant of attitudes towards conservatives, it was one of the least important determinants of evaluations of liberals. Thus, for the most part, the aggregate pattern of meaning associated with ideological terms was not bipolar. Rather, the two labels derived their meaning largely from different sources, primarily of a symbolic nature.

The implications of such findings for our understanding of ideological self-identifications are diagrammatically outlined in the path model shown in Figure 19-3.[11] While our findings by no means render the liberal/conservative classification meaningless, they do fundamentally challenge the traditional understanding of this distinction. In particular, our findings indicate that the meaning of ideological labels is largely symbolic in content and nondimensional in structure. Furthermore, our finding of a predominant lack of bipolarity also allows us to

Figure 19-3 Path Model Relating Symbolic Meaning Variables and Issue Positions to Evaluations of Liberals and Conservatives, and Ideological Self-Placement

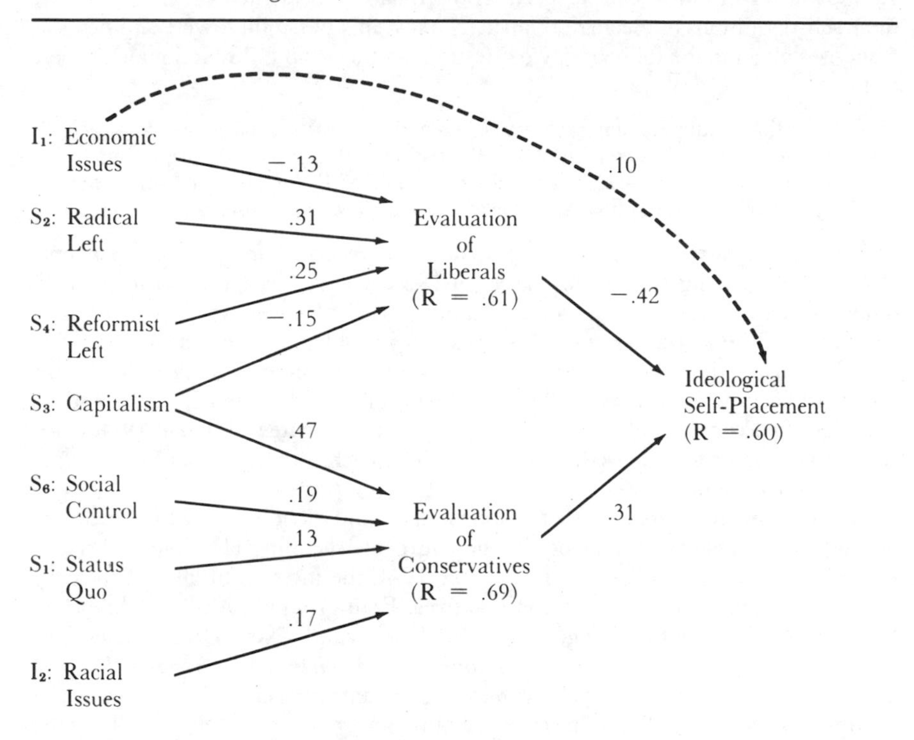

Note: Coefficients are standardized regression weights; all are significant at the .05 level. Only significant paths are shown. The correlations among the seven exogenous variables are:

	S_2	S_3	S_4	S_6	I_1	I_2
S_1	.14	.43	.42	.46	.00	.07
S_2		.03	.47	−.08	−.21	−.31
S_3			.22	.44	.23	.13
S_4				.25	−.30	−.48
S_6					.09	.18
I_1						.39

discount further the viability of the alternative models considered in the last section, since neither of those models is theoretically consistent with such a pattern. Thus, instead of all people viewing the political world from the same perspective, our model suggests that individuals vary in the affect and salience which they attach to political symbols, and this is reflected in how they label themselves ideologically. For the most part, it is likely that conservatives identify themselves as conservatives for quite different reasons than liberals label themselves liberals.

Meaning of Ideological Labels

Even though direct open-ended questions were rejected as a way of initially identifying the meaning of ideological labels, they are nonetheless useful in further testing the viability of our model. If conservatives and liberals really do view politics from different perspectives there should be some evidence of this in their self-definitions of ideological labels. To test this possibility, we examined the responses given to the following two questions in the 1978 CPS National Election Study:

> People have different things in mind when they say that someone's political views are liberal or conservative. . . . What sorts of things do you have in mind when you say that someone's political views are liberal? And, what do you have in mind when you say that someone's political views are conservative?

For each question, up to three answers were coded for every respondent. The original coding scheme for these answers was reduced to 13 categories.[12] Then, for each of the two questions, 13 dummy variables were created which corresponded to the 13 coding categories; these 26 variables were coded "1" if the respondent used the category in *any* of his or her three responses, and "0" otherwise. The percentage of all respondents, of self-identified liberals, and of self-identified conservatives using each category is presented in Table 19-4; since some respondents gave more than one answer to each question, the column totals exceed 100 percent.

To begin, the percentage of respondents using various categories provides one way of assessing whether or not the aggregate meaning of ideological terms has a bipolar structure. As shown in Table 19-4, the ideological labels had some shared meaning for liberals and conservatives. Both groups tended to define both labels with reference to "change," "fiscal policies," and "New Deal policies." *At the same time, however, liberals and conservatives clearly emphasized different categories in their definitions;* there were significant differences between the two groups in their use of all but one category of meaning—minority groups. Thus, as expected, liberals and conservatives did have distinct perspectives on politics which were reflected in the structure of the meaning they lent ideological labels.

Furthermore, the content of the meaning of ideological labels revealed by this analysis accords nicely with our earlier analysis. First, in their definition of ideological labels, liberals made relatively greater use of four categories: "change," "recent social issues," "equality," and "concern with problems." Especially noteworthy is the finding that the liberal viewpoint was dominated by a concern with change; proportionately twice as many liberals as conservatives made reference to "change" and "recent social issues" such as abortion and ERA.

Table 19-4 Frequency Distribution of the Self-Defined Meaning of Ideological Labels[a]

	Meaning of "Liberal"			*Meaning of "Conservative"*		
Category	*All*	*Liberals*	*Conservatives*	*All*	*Liberals*	*Conservatives*
Change	34.9%	52.3%**	23.5%	43.2%	56.8%**	35.5%
Recent Social Issues	7.6	12.7**	6.3	3.0	6.1**	2.4
Equality	4.1	7.5**	2.1	1.6	2.7**	.5
Concern with Problems	4.4	7.5**	3.4	3.1	4.8*	2.1
Group References	4.8	6.6*	3.7	3.9	3.2	3.7
Fiscal Policies	22.7	9.3	33.5**	28.2	12.2	41.8**
Socialism/Capitalism	9.4	7.5	14.7**	11.9	11.3	15.5*
New Deal Issues	14.4	10.9	22.1**	5.5	3.4	9.0**
Foreign Policy	4.0	2.3	7.1**	6.3	4.5	8.7**
Big Government	5.6	5.4	7.6	4.6	4.3	8.1*
Law & Order	3.3	2.3	5.3*	2.2	2.0	3.5
Ideolo. Terms	2.9	1.1	3.1*	2.7	1.8	2.4
Minority Groups	7.3	7.9	8.5	1.7	2.7	1.6
N =	1673	442	620	1673	442	620

[a] Entries are the percentage of respondents mentioning that category; percentages total to greater than 100 percent because some respondents gave more than one answer to the question.

** = The difference between liberals and conservatives is significant at the .01 level, for that category and label.

* = The difference between liberals and conservatives is significant at the .05 level, for that category and label.

This is quite consistent with our earlier finding that a positive reaction to liberals was a function of an attachment to the groups associated with rapid and moderate change in society—the symbols of the radical and reformist left. At the same time, liberals made some use of the various economic categories—"fiscal policies," "socialism/capitalism," and "New Deal issues"—thus, supporting our claim that the symbol of capitalism also influences the evaluations of liberals. But, it is critical to note that liberals made relatively much less use of such categories than conservatives: a finding that confirms our earlier conclusion that capitalism is considerably more important in defining the conservative, as opposed to liberal, perspective.

Turning to the conservatives, we find that they made relatively more references to four categories of meaning: "fiscal policies," "socialism/capitalism," "New Deal issues," and "foreign policy." In particular, the conservative viewpoint was heavily influenced by a strong focus on economic matters; proportionately three times as many conservatives as liberals made reference to "fiscal policies," and twice as many conservatives mentioned "New Deal issues" such as minimum wages and social security. This is consistent with our finding that an attachment to the symbol of capitalism is the most critical factor in producing positive evaluations of conservatives. Similarly, the conservatives' relatively greater use of the "foreign policy" and "law and order" categories supports our contention that the symbols of social control—the military and the police—are relatively more important in defining the conservative, as compared to the liberal, perspective. In summary, our examination of liberals' and conservatives' self-definition of the two major ideological labels strongly supports the conclusion of our earlier analysis. For the most part, liberals and conservatives do have distinct political perspectives which are not simply mirror images of one another.

Conclusions

In summary, in three important respects, our data analysis has provided support for our specification of the processes underlying the development of ideological self-identifications. First, although there may be some reciprocal effects between the two, the data is consistent with our assumption that causality runs primarily from evaluations of ideological labels to self-identification. Not only do such evaluations have a strong impact on self-identification, but they also mediate almost all of the impact which issues and symbols have on such identifications. Furthermore, neither of the two major alternative models of the relationship between self-identifications and evaluations fits the data very well, nor are either of them theoretically consistent with a lack of bipolarity. Second, and related to our first point, three key findings run contrary to the traditional bipolar conception of ideological identifications: the absence of any strong negative correlation between evaluations of liberals and conservatives; the relationship of different symbols and issue stances to those evaluations; and the different emphasis which liberals and conservatives placed on various categories in their definitions of ideological terms. Finally, our analysis indicates that ideological labels, and consequently self-identifications, have largely symbolic, nonissue-oriented meaning to the mass public.

In addition to confirming our model, such findings have other implications as well. Methodologically, our findings suggest that Levitin and Miller's (1979) approach to measuring ideological identifications is simultaneously a step in the right and wrong directions. Recall, rather than relying solely on self-placement on the liberal/conservative continuum, they combine both evaluations of liberals with self-placements in order to arrive at a measure of ideological identification. Such a measurement strategy is an improvement over previous ones in that it draws attention to and takes into account the strong evaluative meaning which our findings suggest is so important to understanding ideological self-identification. At the same time, however, we would argue that their combination of evaluations and self-placement into a single measure is based on an erroneous assumption: namely, that these variables are indicators of the same underlying construct. From our perspective, a more appropriate measurement technique would be one which maintains separate measures of evaluations and self-placement, and then examines, rather than assumes, the relationship between various combinations of the two. Thus, with respect to measurement strategies our work implies both that evaluations of ideological labels are important to understanding self-identifications, and that it is critical to maintain a conceptual distinction between the two.

Several other methodological implications stem from our findings that the meaning of ideological labels is largely based on symbols rather than issues. Specifically, this finding suggests that the common method of using the liberal and conservative labels as stimuli to measure ideological or issue-oriented thinking may be misleading. For the same reason, we should also be cautious of interpretations of political change which rely on shifts in ideological identifications as an empirical indicator of changes in basic issue positions. Our findings imply that major shifts in the distribution of the public's ideological identifications are indicative of fundamental alterations in the symbolic meaning of politics, rather than major changes in issue orientations.

Our model and findings also have several theoretical implications. In particular, one of the major puzzles suggested by both the Levitin and Miller (1979) and Holm and Robinson (1978) studies is why ideological identifications have such an impact on vote choice, even though most voters encounter a great deal of difficulty in labeling which side of an issue is conservative and which is liberal. This is, perhaps, even more curious in a "nonideological" election like 1976 in which voters perceived more of a difference between Ford and Carter in their ideological identifications than on any specific issue position (Page, 1978, p. 98). From our perspective, the symbolic meaning underlying liberal/conservative identifications is the key to understanding these phenomenon. Specifically, even when information about candidates' issue positions is absent or very costly (Page, 1978), the symbolic cues associated with various groups and "easy issues" (Carmines and Stimson, 1980) should still be available. To the degree such symbols are linked to ideological identifications, voters may readily make inferences about the candidates which subsequently influence their evaluations and ultimately their vote choice. Thus, as traditionally argued and empirically confirmed, ideological identifications should act as cues or reference points in the evaluation of candidates. But, contrary to traditional expectations, the basis for these comparisons is largely symbolic, rather than issue oriented, and therefore, may occur in the absence of any true ideological conflict or debate between the candidates.

Similarly, our findings help to unravel the nature of the shared meaning binding together ideological and party identifications. Recall that Levitin and Miller (1979) suggested that such identifications share considerable meaning which, to a large extent, may not be issue based. Given our understanding of the nature of ideological identifications, we now can posit that such shared meaning is primarily symbolic in content. In effect, both party and ideological identifications may represent symbolic ties to the political world which overlap in their meaning. Some insight into the specific nature of this overlap is gained by reviewing the symbolic determinants of evaluations of liberals and conservatives. Specifically, evaluations of Republicans were a component of the capitalism scale—the symbol having the greatest impact on evaluations of conservatives. This suggests that positive evaluations of the conservative label are related to positive evaluations of Republicans, and thus there may be some tendency for self-identified Republicans to also identify themselves as conservatives. At the same time, evaluations of Democrats did not fit into any of our symbolic-meaning scales. Consequently, with no direct symbolic link between evaluations of Democrats and evaluations of either liberals or conservatives, one might expect greater variation in the ideological identifications of Democrats. In fact, this is precisely what Levitin and Miller (1979) found: "Republicans were more homogeneous than Democrats in their ideological self-placement, and they were also much more often unqualified in their ideological commitments" (p. 757). Thus, based on our preliminary findings, we would argue that party and ideological identifications share a common meaning which centers around the symbol of capitalism.

Finally, one criticism of our empirical analysis is likely to be that the results are time bound: the symbolic meaning associated with the "liberal" and "conservative" terms is a consequence only of the recent conflicts and events of the 1960s. But, a closer look at our empirical analysis reveals a basis for drawing more general conclusions concerning the meaning of these terms. The nature of the major symbolic referents that defined each label—the reformist and radical left for liberals, and capitalism, social control, and the status quo for conservatives—indicates that the core symbolic meaning of these labels revolves around elements of "change vs. the preservation of traditional values." In general, liberals seem to favor change and progress even at the expense of government involvement; conservatives, on the other hand, wish to preserve traditional arrangements particularly those threatened by government involvement. This interpretation is somewhat broader than Converse's (1964) "spend-save" characterization of the differences between liberals and conservatives, although there are certainly elements of such a distinction in our analysis. Similarly, Robinson and Holm's (1980) recent description of liberals as being "pro-change" and conservatives as "antigovernment" is compatible with the broad lines of our own characterization.

Given this interpretation of the fundamental differences between liberals and conservatives, it can be argued that at any one point in time the major symbols of change and progress become associated with evaluations of liberals, while the symbols associated with the preservation of traditional values determine evaluations of conservatives. If this is in fact the case, then liberal/conservative identifications should always reflect in symbolic terms the dominant cleavages in society. This would account for the observed changes in the meaning of these terms over time (Erikson et al., 1980); as the cleavages evolve and change so do the symbolic referents associated with each term. Ideological self-identifications, therefore, may serve an important function for the public by providing a symbolic framework which simplifies societal conflicts. Furthermore, these core meanings of change and the preservation of traditional values do capture symbolically the general, more ideological definitions typically associated with these terms. Thus, our analysis suggests that the public's usage of ideological labels is more a simplification than a distortion of reality, and that ideological identifications constitute more a symbolic than issue-oriented link to the political world.

NOTES

1. Even where two bipolar liberal/conservative dimensions are assumed, voters should still be able to compare candidates and parties on those issues relevant to defining that dimension. At the same time, however, assuming the presence of two dimensions does inject some uncertainty into the voter's comparisons, since they may become confused about which dimension they are dealing with.
2. Our examination of the structure of the meaning of ideological labels focuses primarily on their aggregate or shared meaning. In effect, we are suggesting that the public as a whole, does not have a dimensional conception of the two terms. We do not mean to suggest as a general rule that individuals fail to see these terms as opposites, though in some instances there may be a lack of bipolarity at the individual level as well.
3. For a discussion of the various types of symbols, see Edelman (1964).
4. As Kerlinger (1967, 1972) points out, a bipolar structure of aggregate meaning occurs only in one instance: when "conservative referents are criterial to liberals and liberal referents are criterial to conservatives—in both cases negatively" (Kerlinger, 1972, p. 625). This pattern is expected to occur relatively infrequently and primarily among groups of political ideologues.
5. The exact question wording of the items employed in constructing the issue scales is available in the CPS 1976 National Elections Study Codebook. The question numbers are as follows: RACIAL ISSUES, 3257, 3211, 3264; SOCIAL ISSUES, 3772, 3787, 3799, 3796; and ECONOMIC ISSUES, 3273, 3241, and 3779.
6. Specifically, a principal components analysis with oblique rotation was conducted. Consequently, the factors which emerged are correlated to some extent.
7. For each of the six factors, the feeling-thermometer ratings of the specific groups composing it were summed to form a single scale tapping that dimension of symbolic meaning.
8. Some might question whether this finding is an artifact of the "positivity bias" often associated with the thermometer ratings of social groups (Miller et al., 1978). This is not likely. The primary impact of any positivity bias should be to simply shift the mean of the distribution of the evaluations up the feeling thermometer and to reduce the range, but *not* to fundamentally alter the shape of the distribution. Consequently, the transformation produced by a positivity bias should not effect the covariance of the evaluations with other variables. In our particular case, this interpretation is strengthened by the fact that, though there is some positivity bias in the ratings of liberals and conservatives, there is also substantial variance in both sets of evaluations.

... such findings, some might posit a fourth model in which self-identification ...influences evaluations which in turn determine issue positions and the evaluations of political symbols. Theoretically, this model seems to us to be quite weak since it removes from contention the logical determinants of self-identification, and since it does little to specify the manner in which such identifications originate.

10. In order to estimate the parameters, each correlation is first expressed in terms of three parameters: $r_{12} = ab$, $r_{13} = ac$, and $r_{23} = bc$. These three equations can then be solved for each unknown, with the following results:

$$a = \sqrt{\frac{r_{12} \times r_{13}}{r_{23}}} \qquad b = \sqrt{\frac{r_{12} \times r_{23}}{r_{13}}} \qquad c = \sqrt{\frac{r_{11} \times r_{23}}{r_{12}}}$$

For the calculations noted in the text: $r_{12} = -.53$, $r_{13} = .47$ and $r_{24} = -.17$.

11. The full nonrecursive path model was tested; only significant paths are reported.
12. We found that 91.2 percent of all the responses on the "liberal" question and 93.9 percent of all the responses on the "conservative" question were codeable within these 13 categories. The rest of the responses were either uninterpretable or were very infrequently cited reasons. The following constitutes a representative sample of the CPS codes for each category.

(1) *Change*—acceptance/resistance to change, new ideas; slow/rash responses to problems; cautious, irresponsible;

(2) *Recent social issues*—abortion; birth control; women's rights; ERA;

(3) *Equality*—equal rights; elitist; special privileges;

(4) *Concern with problems*—sensitive to social problems, reform; interested/not interested in improving conditions;

(5) *Group references*—all people, working people, common people, middle class;

(6) *Fiscal policies*—government spending; too much spending; tight economic policies; sound money;

(7) *Socialism/capitalism*—socialistic, welfare state; free enterprise, capitalism; big business; rich people;

(8) *New Deal issues*—minimum wage; social security; health insurance; control of utilities; social welfare; poverty programs;

(9) *Foreign policy/national security*—peace/war; internationalist/isolationist; national defense;

(10) *Big government*—centralized government; local government; local initiative;

(11) *Law and order*—hard line/soft line on law and order;

(12) *Ideological terms*—radical; extreme; reactionary; far right; and

(13) *Minority groups*—minorities, black, racist, civil rights.

20. POLITICAL CONTINUITIES IN FRENCH FAMILIES: A NEW PERSPECTIVE ON AN OLD CONTROVERSY

Annick Percheron and M. Kent Jennings

Much dispute has characterized the topic of the transmission of political orientations within the family (Connell, 1972; Jennings and Niemi, 1974; Weissberg and Joslyn, 1977; Dalton, 1980). In one domain, however, consensus has prevailed. The influence of family on the formation of partisan orientations seemed unquestionable. This was a major finding because it was the key to explaining the stability of the party system and of the regime over time according to a very simple causal model: partisan transmission by the parents ——> continuity of partisan preferences from one generation to the next ——> stability of partisan orientations ——> stability of party systems ——> and so forth. This schema certainly seemed true in the United States and, by extension, in a number of other Western nations. France was typically offered as a counter example, as the 1958 study by Converse and Dupeux (1962) apparently demonstrated.

Converse and Dupeux were not primarily interested in political socialization processes; rather, they wanted to explain the instability of the French party system when compared with the stability of the American one. They were struck, however, by the fact that only a minority of their French respondents (45 percent of those who did not refuse to answer the question) expressed any attachment to a given party or broad tendance. They were equally impressed by the fact that even fewer of the respondents could characterize even approximately the partisanship of their fathers. Among the French only 26 percent (against 86 percent in the United States) could link their father with any party or with "the vaguest of tendance." They then concluded, "Where the socialization processes have been the same in the two societies the results in current behavior appear to be the same, in rates of formation of identification. The strong cross-national differences lie in the socialization processess" (p. 14). The major difference stems from the fact that "the French father is uncommunicative about his political behavior before his

---

Authors' Note: The authors would like to acknowledge the helpful comments of Suzanne Berger, Mark Kesselman, and Ezra Suleiman on an earlier version of this article. The first author would like to extend her appreciation to the Department of Political Science and Institute for Social Research at the University of Michigan for facilitating the analysis during her visit in the fall of 1979.

Source: *Comparative Politics* (1981) 13:421-36. Reprinted with permission of the publisher.

children" (p. 13) from which it follows that there are "basic discontinuities in the familial party orientations in France" (p. 13).

One of the weaknesses of their argument came from the fact that they were using recall data. But a few years later, Greenstein and Tarrow (1969), in reviewing a survey of the political socialization of French children, echoed the Converse and Dupeux findings: the great majority of French children fail to acquire any party identification.

Since that time, Converse and Pierce (1970), Cameron (1972), Inglehart and Hochstein (1972), and Inglehart and Klingemann (1976), among others, have raised the earlier estimates. They have concluded that there has been a perceptible increase in the proportion of French people who declare that they feel close to a party. Inglehart and Klingemann give a figure of 59 percent for French people saying that they feel close to a party (data collected in 1973). In the 1975 study that we will analyze in this article 77 percent of a parent sample (adults from thirty-five to sixty years old) declared intentions to vote for a particular party. There has been also an increase in the number of French people who know the political preferences of their parents. Cameron reported that in 1968 some 43 percent (versus 26 percent in Converse and Dupeux) knew their father's partisanship. More recently, in 1973 fully 69 and 67 percent of those questioned could classify their fathers and their mothers, respectively, as being either left or right (*Le Nouvel Observateur,* Feb., 1973).

Nevertheless, the argument about the failure of intra familial transmission has not disappeared. Cameron (1972), for example, explains the increase of partisan identification in France by situational factors such as Gaullism, new generations, and the rise of female political participation. But he does not question at all the problem of transmission fidelity inside the family. On the contrary, quoting Roig and Billon-Grand on one hand and Converse and Dupeux on the other, he argues: "The magnitude of this figure [the number of French identifiers given by Converse and Dupeux] suggests that parental transmission is not a necessary condition for partisanship and that socialization into partisanship is affected by factors other than the parent-child interaction process." Moreover, he says, "it is plausible over time that other factors may have induced changes in the degree of partisan identification even if patterns of parental transmission remained stable" (p. 20).

This article questions these views about the transmission of political preferences within the French family. We are not interested in the stability of the party system as such or in the changing magnitude of partisan identification—though we are interested in the perpetuation of cleavage structure. Rather, we are primarily concerned with the problem of the inheritance of political orientations by children. What we want to demonstrate is that, contrary to what Converse and Dupeux wrote nearly twenty years ago, which, since that time, has been tirelessly quoted, we have to think of France in terms of basic continuities rather than discontinuities of ideological cast across generations. These basic political cleavages in terms of continuities in political tendance are rooted in great part in the perpetuation of family traditions.

We will employ a set of data uniquely suited for such an analysis, a national sample survey of 903 pairs of parents and adolescent offspring (one parent, one child per family).[1] For most purposes we will rely on the 436 pairs that include sixteen-to-eighteen-year-olds. The nature of the data means that we not only have responses by offspring themselves instead of adult recall data, but also that we are able to deal with the ideological preferences of parents as perceived by their offspring and the reverse, that is, the political preferences of offspring as seen by their parents. Finally, drawing on similar data from other countries, we will be able to place the French results within a comparative framework to see if France is, indeed, peculiar.

The Primary of the Left-Right Dimension in France

Thus far we have spoken indifferently, as most people do, about partisan orientations versus other broad ideological orientations. And as a matter of fact the Converse and Dupeux argument is stated in terms of partisan or any other broad tendencies. Here we will deal almost exclusively with ideological orientations as assessed by self-placement on a left-right scale. It is a deliberate choice. We have tried to demonstrate elsewhere why the left-right dimension is the most suitable one for France and more precisely why it is as far as the acquisition of political preferences by young persons is concerned (Percheron, 1978). We may simply recall some of the major arguments.

The most frequently stated reason is the complexity of the French party system. As has been shown by Campbell and Valen (1961), the problem is not so much the number of parties per se. The difficulties, rather, come from the fluidity of the system. Two or three examples will illustrate this point. Just a few weeks before the last legislative elections in 1978 a new movement appeared on the French scene under the name of UDF, which was composed of PR, CDS, and radicals.[2] It was not only a new political organization but a new one with a name very close to another party of the majority (UDR) which, it is true, had itself changed its name since 1976 from RPR. Furthermore, the Gaullist movement since 1958 has taken three different party names. Nor is the Left completely unfamiliar with such practices. The socialist movement since 1958 has been successively known as SFIO, FGDS, and PS, to say nothing about the radicals, now split between the MRG on the left side and the parti radical on the majority side. The situation is made even more complicated by the use of initials rather than full names.

So diverse are the histories of party labelling in France that it seems difficult to think that partisan identification can play its most usual role as a shortcut in helping people cope with the complexities of political phenomena (Miller, 1976). Instead, that role is played by the left-right dimension. The electoral system itself promotes this outcome. The system, with two rounds of balloting, reinforces bipolarization in French politics. For the second and decisive ballot the choice is clearly reduced to a very simple alternative, to vote for the candidate of the Left or for the candidate of the Right. This simple choice delineates the main division in France. The left-right dimension is not simply a surrogate for party identification.[3] The basic cleavage is in fact between the Left and the Right; the very deep current divisions between parties within the Left and the Right are a secondary phenomenon. Of course strong attachment to a particular party tends to intensify this bifurcation.

Three main reasons may help us understand the left-right primacy. The first one comes from the fact that today's ideological preferences are deeply rooted in French history. Siegfried (1949) has shown, for example, that electoral divisions in Ardeche follow the limits of the dioceses before the revolution of 1789. Tilly (1964) has shown the deep impression left by the story of the Chouans in Vendée, and Bois (1960) has demonstrated that Sarthe contemporary electoral choices can be explained by the cleavages that occurred in 1793, when the land of the clergy had been nationalized and sold.

The second reason, also historical, comes from the fact that since the French Revolution, cleavages between the Left and the Right have coincided more or less with cleavages between the Republicans and all others. Third, this line of division is reinforced by the deep and longstanding relationship between religion and politics or, rather, between a dominant Catholic religion and the Right on one side and secularized or minority groups and the Left on the other side. Consequently, using the left-right location rather than party identification is not simply a methodological point.

France in Comparative Perspective

To help place France in perspective it will be useful to draw on data from a large, cross-national study carried out in the early 1970s.[4] We expect that in some countries the transmission between parents and children will take the road of party identification—as in the United States, Britain, and possibly Germany, with their strong two (and one-half) party systems. But in some other countries the transmission will take the form of ideological orientations toward the Left or the Right. Conditions maximizing that likelihood appear to be a conjunction of (1) a multiparty system, (2) a strong leftist party (here communist), (3) a dominant Catholic group, and (4) a strong connection between religiosity and ideological tendance. Italy, France, and possibly the Netherlands are strong candidates for the joint occurrence of these conditions.

Cross-national results point in the hypothesized direction. The correlation between the self-placements of parents and their children on the left-right continuum[5] is moderate to very low in the strong two-party systems: Britain (.29), the United States (.02), and Germany (.11). Perhaps the left-right dimension is an extreme example, at least for the United States. But even on a liberal-conservative scale the American pair correspondence is only modestly higher, being .21 among a national sample of young adults and their parents (Jennings and Niemi, 1974, chap. 4). Should we conclude that in all these countries there is little transmission of ideological leanings within the family? The answer is no, because when a question in terms of party preferences is used instead of the preceding one, and when parties are ordered from left-to-right dimension, the correlations between parent and child choices rise sharply: .80 in Britain, .61 in the United States, and .57 in Germany.

Turning to the other countries, we hypothesized that if we substituted left-right proximities for party identification we would find an extended and strong degree of transmission from parent to child. The Italian case lies in that direction, with a correlation of .45 between the left-wing placements of the sixteen-to-eighteen-year-olds and that of their parents. When party preference is used instead of left-right placement, the correlation is almost identical, but in the latter

Table 20-1 Parent-Offspring Similarity on Left-Right Scale (in percent)*

Offspring	*Parents* Left 1	2	3	4	5	6	Right 7	*Row Total*	*(N)*
Left 1	33	5	1	2	2	3	—	5	(16)
2	17	39	20	6	2	3	12	15	(50)
3	25	29	31	16	19	3	6	21	(70)
4	17	24	34	51	36	28	25	35	(118)
5	4	2	13	17	28	31	12	15	(51)
6	—	—	—	8	9	25	25	7	(23)
Right 7	4	2	—	1	4	6	19	3	(10)
Total	100	101	99	101	100	99	99		
Column Total	7	17	21	27	14	9	5	pair tau-b = .44	
(N)	(24)	(59)	(70)	(90)	(47)	(32)	(16)		(338)

* Based on subset of pairs (78 percent) where both parent and child expressed a preference.

instance 30 percent of the youths are left out (no party preference or no answer) as against 20 percent when the left-right scale is used. Similarly, among the Dutch pairs the left-right correlation is .45, trailed only slightly by that for party identification (.40). However, 45 percent of the Dutch youth professed no party preference compared with only 11 percent offering no left-right placement. The French case is very similar to the Italian and Dutch cases.[6] The pair correspondence (see Table 20-1) on left-right placement is .44, with only 16 percent of the youth being unwilling to locate themselves.

These results are consistent with our hypotheses: (1) across countries the socialization process has to be assessed using coinage appropriate to the political culture and the political system; (2) when indexed by the left-right scale, the level of transmission in the French family approaches or equals that found in other Western countries.

Although we do not have parallel data from our French study about pair similarity in specific party preference, this is not a serious shortcoming. We need not conclude that we would have found low pair correspondence if party identification data had been available. Rather, as in Italy and the Netherlands, substantially more respondents would have been treated as having missing data and, therefore, as people not having, or not having "inherited," an ideological orientation.

An approximation to the relationship may be obtained by correlating the voting intentions of the parents with the left-right scores of their children. Here, the pair tau-b is about the same magnitude (.39) as for left-right location. However, 32 percent of the pairs are now considered to have missing data as against 22 percent when the left-right scores of both parents and offspring are used. We may be sure that the situation would worsen if we were considering party preference on both sides.

We can give further evidence of the differences in the rate of no preference when left-right placement and party identification are used in the French context. Considering first the adult population's expressions of party identification, we have 45-50 percent identifiers in 1958 (Converse and Dupeux, 1962), 59 percent in 1973 (Inglehart and Klingemann, 1976), and 77 percent in 1975 (Percheron et al., 1978). On the other hand, using left-right location in 1966, Deutsch et al. (1966) found 90 percent of the respondents to have an ideological orientation (68 percent filtering out the nominal "centrists," who rank low on political interest); in 1973 Inglehart and Klingemann (1976) observed 78 percent; and in 1975 Percheron (1978) found 92 percent (82 percent if we again filter out the centrists, who score low on political interest).

The differences are even greater among young populations. In a 1973 survey only 56 percent of sixteen-nineteen-year-olds were able to enunciate a party preference (Mossuz, 1979). In 1978 the same was true for 51 percent of a national sample of thirteen-seventeen-year-olds (*Le Nouvel Observateur,* Sept., 1979). By contrast, in the present study 67 percent of the thirteen-fifteen-year-olds and 84 percent of the sixteen-eighteen-year-olds were able to locate themselves on the left-right scale. After we discard those with low political interest, the figures decline but are still higher than when party identification is used; 51 percent for the thirteen-fifteen-year-olds, and 70 percent for the sixteen-eighteen-year-olds. It is worth noting that these frequencies of preference, in addition to being higher when a left-right scale is used, are also almost the same as those for the parents involved in these pairs.

Not surprisingly, the absence of an ideological stance is not randomly distributed. There are families in which successful transmission means transmission of no ideological preferences at all or a pattern of no answer to such questions. We dichotomized the responses according to whether the individual was self-located on the left-right dimension. Among pairs involving thirteen-fifteen-year-olds the tau-b correlation was .18. This figure increased to .28 among the pairs involving sixteen-eighteen-year-olds, primarily as a consequence of a higher rate of self-identification among the older adolescents. In percentage terms 45 percent of those parents without a preference had children without a preference; but among parents with a preference only 13 percent of their offspring reported no preference.

To understand fully the relative significance of pair correspondence on the left-right dimension, we cannot consider that value in isolation nor base a comparison of France and other countries on that dimension alone. Because of the links between religiosity and political orientations, because of the importance attached by parents to the religious socialization of their children, and because of the global nature of both religious attitudes and political ideology, we should compare the pair correspondence between ideological orientation and religiosity.[7] The French results show that the correspondence is slightly higher in the case of religiosity (.52 against .44). Thus, broad political preference is passed on about as well as religious orientation. Turning to the other countries, we find correlations in much the same ranges, aside from a higher one in the Netherlands (.74) and a lower one in Italy (.29). What is striking here is that in those countries (Great Britain, Germany, and the United States) where *party* attachment is the mechanism for intergenerational continuity, the pair congruence in religious orientations approximates that for party attachment. The French case differs only in the sense that left-right attachment rather than party attachment is the political indicator.

The Substantive Content of Left-Right Orientations

So far, the results indicate that the model of lineage similarities and intergenerational continuities fits the French case reasonably well: in fact it fits the French case as well as most other countries examined here. But all that may just mean, as Converse (1975b) once said, that "they know the words without much sense of the tune." For the adults a partial rebuttal is given by the strong correlation (.62) between their left-right placement scale and their party preferences in terms of vote intention. Although it may be true that a good part of the populace is not ideological in a strict sense, it is equally true that the electorate matches reasonably well the melody line of tendance and the lyrics supplied by particular party cluster.

The question is even more crucial for young persons who, some claim, will place themselves on a left-right scale by guessing or by haphazard selection. Actually, the associations between their ideological placement and their attitudes toward different types of political institutions and figures show that the general ideological cast of young people has a high substantive content (Table 20-2). As expected, the correlations are particularly strong (−.65, .55) when the attitude objects are the Left and the Right. But the consistency between general orientation and specific attitudes goes far beyond this and is significant when political leaders, political actions, institutions, or roles are the objects being evaluated. All the correlations are above .20 except for the three political objects that, by definition, are least invested with a left-right component. These three include deputies, political leaders, and political parties on both sides.

Table 20-2 Relationship between Left-Right Position and Attitudes toward Political Objects among French Youths*

Ideologies		*Personalities*		*Institutions and Roles*	
The Left	−.65	Giscard d'Estaing	.48	Minister	.34
The Right	.55	Mitterrand	−.43	Government	.33
Communism	−.47	Chirac	.38	Grievances	−.32
Extreme right	.42	Marchais	−.37	Demonstration	−.30
Socialism	−.40			Union	−.28
Extreme left	−.36			Deputy	.12
Gaullism	.26			Political party	.14
Capitalism	.25			Political leader	.05

* Entries are tau-b correlations between placement on the left-right scale and evaluations of objects (like versus dislike). Average N = 281.

Significantly, and as previously demonstrated, political roles are not perceived separately from their incumbents. (Percheron et al., 1978). For these young people who have only known right-oriented governments, minister and government are political objects with a partisan flavor. Valéry Giscard d'Estaing is not perceived differently than any other (partisan) political figure. He is the president, but he is also a political leader who belongs to the Right. The results seem to underline, too, that in adolescence the left-right orientation links equally well to specific, as well as to more abstract, symbols such as communism, socialism, or even Gaullism. But perhaps the most surprising result, and one that tells most about the rather sophisticated content of the adolescents' ideological preferences, comes from the fact that even institutions or actions such as unions, demonstrations, and grievances are evaluated as political objects in light of the adolescents' own broad political orientations. These are, without doubt, a special part of the left inheritance.

Communications and Perceptions within the Family

Evidence concerning the political content of the ideological orientations of French youth and the degree of transmission within the family supplies only part of the answer to the questions raised by Converse and Dupeux. The other part concerns the pattern of communication inside the French family. Do our results imply that the level of political communication in French families has sharply increased since 1958? And, to go further, what is the degree of perceptual accuracy about political preferences inside the family, and what is the effect of accuracy on the degree of similarity of intergenerational choices?

Our results concerning the frequency of discussion are consistent with those presented by Converse and Dupeux. Sixty percent of the parents and their adolescent offspring agree that they rarely if ever discuss political events, and only 15 percent say they do so often or very often. But is this pattern peculiar to France? In the other nations we have been using for comparison the adolescents were asked how often they talk with their father or mother (two separate questions) about public affairs and politics. Even if the wording is not precisely the same and even if we do not know whether a question means exactly the same thing in different cultures, the non-French materials are close enough to give us a broad basis for comparison.[8]

For each country we present the proportions reporting the equivalents of rarely and never: Britain, 79 percent; Germany, 47 percent; Netherlands, 65 percent; United States, 56 percent; Italy, 64 percent; France, 78 percent. Despite considerable intercountry variations, the results show that low rates of political dialogue seem to be the modal pattern in almost all countries. Nor does France necessarily lead the way in this respect, for the British figure is equally skewed. Thus, it seems difficult to contend that low levels of political discourse are peculiar to France.

But the rate of political discussion is not by itself a sufficient indication whether parents communicate their political preferences. In our study we asked the offspring if they knew the political inclinations of their father and of their mother in terms of a left-right dichotomy. We also asked parents if they knew the left-right preferences of their interviewed offspring. This set of questions enables us to check the accuracy of the perception on both sides and to assess the impact of accurate knowledge on the enunciation of political preferences by the child.

It reveals much about the status of politics as a family matter that 52 percent of the parents think or say that their children have no left or right predilection, especially when we recall that only 16 percent of the adolescents themselves expressed no such sentiment. At first glance this discrepancy might seem to be strong support for the view that partisan orientation is, indeed, poorly passed on in the French family. However, this large gap is fully consistent with American data in the realm of party identification. Whereas all but 1 percent of the high-school seniors in a 1965 national survey professed a party preference (including being an independent), 37 percent of the youths' parents could not characterize their child's party preferences (Jennings and Niemi, 1974, p. 58). Adding to the "no preference" responses those of pure independence (i.e., leaning toward neither party), we find 14 percent of the American youths without a party preference; and now some 50 percent of the parents fail to ascribe a party attachment to their offspring. By coincidence, perhaps, these latter figures coincide almost perfectly with the French figure. If the American example is the archetypical one, the French case resembles it extraordinarily.

Do we find the same distortions when considering the adolescents' perception of their parents' orientations? One could hypothesize that the perceptions will be much better because the child's view will not be confused by the idea that politics is something from which one must protect children in such a way that the political orientations of the children will be denied or negated. Among the youth 70 percent and 62 percent claimed that their fathers and mothers, respectively, had a left-right preference. The "true" figures were 94 percent and 85 percent. Nevertheless, the incidence of perceived *parent* location represents a considerable margin over the 48 percent registered for parental perception of *child* location.

The youth figures are very close to those now given in most surveys by French adults asked to recall their parents' orientations. Nevertheless they fall a bit short of the figures given by Americans of the same age in response to a similar question: 74 and 79 percent of them claimed to know the party preferences of their father and mother, respectively.[9] So it may well be that the orientations inside the French family are less visible, especially regarding women, than in the presumed polar case of the United States. Still, we must emphasize that the differences are far from the magnitude reported by Converse and Dupeux, in which only 26 percent of the French people could describe in even the vaguest sense their father's orientation. Second, we must add that our question is certainly not the best one for capturing the full range of perceived parental leanings. Since the choice was simply between a left or a right preference, no room was left for reporting a centrist position.

If we accept the idea that the level of communication appears to be higher than in 1958 but still far from universal, the next step is to see if only young people who know or claim to know their parents' preferences express political preferences themselves. Our results corroborate the Converse and Dupeux findings, showing that children who "know" either parent's orientations are indeed more ready to develop or to state their own preferences (see Table 20-3). On the other hand, these results indicate that only about a third of the young fail

Table 20-3 Perception that Parents Have Left-Right Position Related to Offspring Having Left-Right Position (in percent)

	Offspring has left-right location?				
	Yes	*No*	*Total*	*Row Total*	*(N)*
Perceive father's location?					
Yes	95	5	100	66	(286)
No	63	37	100	34	(150)
Perceive mother's location?					
Yes	95	5	100	64	(278)
No	65	35	100	36	(158)

to acquire any ideological preferences even when they do not know their parents' orientations. Ultimately, only 13 percent of them do not know the political preferences of their parents and at the same time are unable to place themselves on a left-right scale. That there are so few youths in this category can probably be explained by the impact of a common social environment on not only parents but also children and by the number and importance of indirect cues inside the family. As we have argued elsewhere, children do not need to know explicitly their parents' political leanings in order to inherit them (Percheron, et al., 1978).

That is not to deny the importance of that knowledge or of the accuracy of perception when one moves beyond the acquisition of political orientations to the similarities of the choices inside the family. But before we try to answer that question, we have to determine precisely the degree of mutual accuracy in the perceptions of parents and children. Both generations follow the same rule. First, each correctly perceives the other only moderately well. All cases (including don't-knows) being counted, two-fifths of the adolescents were on target, a figure exceeding the one-fourth proportion for parents.

The second rule is that the further left or right the actual self-location, the better the perception. We may go a little further. Taking into account at the same time left-right scores as well as their voting intentions, we observe that the perceived location of the parents is more accurate when their preferences are more extreme and when they are more consistent, thus more visible. It is when parents place themselves further left and indicate a voting preference for the communist party or when they place themselves on the Right and intend to vote for the republican independents that the offspring's perceptions are the most accurate. From that point of view, the situation of the socialist parents is exemplary. The level of perceptual accuracy by the children, never as good as that found in communist families, nevertheless is better the further left parents place themselves. Sixty-four percent of the socialist parents who place themselves on the Left are perceived as left-oriented by their children as against 24 percent when they place themselves in the center. In the latter case, in fact, 52 percent of the children say that they do not know their parents' preferences.

An interesting corollary here is the fact that adolescents with left orientations are more often perceived correctly than are those with right political orientations. In the former case, 61 percent are correctly perceived by their parents as being left versus a comparable correct figure of 35 percent among parents of right-leaning children. Indeed, some 54 percent of the parents with right-oriented children believed that their offspring had no ideological preference at all. These results, when coupled with those dealing with children's perceptions of parents, suggest that the place of politics has a different standing according to ideological persuasion (Michelat and Simon, 1977). Among left-oriented people politics has a favorable image and seems to be more salient (their higher degree of political interest is well documented). Parents tend to be less reluctant to express their own preferences and to accept the idea that their children have developed their own preferences. Among right-leaning people, on the contrary, politics is perceived as a matter of conflict, as a dirty world from which one must protect oneself and, even more, one's children. Politics becomes less salient in the family, and the parents are less ready to state their own preferences and are even less ready to accept the notion that their children have their own political preferences. Overall, 66 percent of the left-oriented parents versus 49 percent of the right-oriented parents attribute a political persuasion to their children.

These results suggest that the context in which parents exert their influence on their children may vary considerably. Illustratively, we would expect the level of parent to child transmission to vary according to the degree of the child's perceptual accuracy (Tedin, 1974). There are two reasons for this. If we assume that children more often use their parents as positive rather than negative role models, accurate predictions would result in their taking on their parents' political orientations. A second reason is that accurate perceptions are likely to reflect in part the salience of the left-right dimension for the parents and the degree of family communication related to it.

Owing to the nature of the seven-point scale by which respondents classified themselves versus the simple left-right dichotomy by which the youths classified their parents, there is no direct way to determine exactly the youths' perceptual accuracy—especially since the centrist position was not available in the dichotomy. What we have done is to judge leftist perceptions accurate if the parent in fact had a self-location on the three leftward positions of the scale and to judge rightist perceptions accurate if the parent had a self-location on the three rightward positions. All other combinations, including those wherein the parent occupied the exact middle of the left-right scale, were scored as inaccurate perceptions. This would seem to be a conservative procedure. To these two categories of accurate and inaccurate may be added a third—that representing youths who said they did not know their parents' location at all.

The results rather spectacularly support the hypothesized importance of perceptual accuracy (see Table 20-4). In the first place, considering the conservative procedures used, the degree of perceptual accuracy is high. Approximately half of the youths correctly placed their parents as left or right and some portion of the inaccurate ones were so classified because any combination involving "centrist" parents was classified as inaccurate. More significantly, accuracy affects the transmission rates. Recalling that the overall correlation between parent and youth preference was .44, we would conclude that the .62

Table 20-4 Parent-Offspring Similarity, by Offspring Perception of Parent Left-Right Location*

	Pair Correlation	
	tau-b	*(N)*
Perceive parent's location correctly	.62	(168)
No perception of parent's location	.13	(81)
Perceive parent's location incorrectly	−.02	(88)

* Based on subset (78 percent) of pairs where both parent and child expressed a preference.

achieved under circumstances of correct perceptions represents a very substantial improvement. Further attesting to the role of perceptions is the fact that inaccurate perceptions result in essentially no congruence between parent and child. Indeed, there is higher correspondence when the adolescent claims no knowledge of the parent's ideological location. This modest positive relationship suggests that transmission occurs in unrecognized, indirect ways. Our results closely parallel those reported for the United States in both direction and magnitude (Tedin, 1974).

These findings provide a fitting note on which to close yet another reexamination of socialization and partisanship in France. We have argued in general that the object of partisan socialization within the family is country-specific and that for some countries, such as France, an overarching dimension of the left-right variety replaces in part the function served by specific, longstanding party divisions in other countries. In the former situations the individual parties may well be less stable and long-lived but the basic electoral cleavage structures just as durable. Socialization within the French family plays no small role in perpetuating this continuity. Support for this argument was observed in the form of the widespread holding of left-right orientations in France, the fit between these orientations and evaluations of political objects, the fidelity of the reproduction across the two generations, and the existence and consequences of youths' perceptions of their parents' ideological tendance. Where possible we have made comparisons with patterns in other Western countries. In general, France appears to be far less unusual and to present less of a paradox than has been commonly observed. This is not to deny the special characteristics of French (or other) political cultures. Rather, it is to emphasize the commonalities of processes and functions within the diversity of cross-cultural content.

NOTES

1. The data come from a national, representative survey of pairs conducted in November 1975 by IFOP for IFOREP, and directed by Annick Percheron. Parents were from 35-60 years of age; children were 13-18.

2. The following abbreviations will be used: UDF—Union pour la démocratie française PR-Parti républicain; CDS—Centre des démocrates sociaux; UDR—Union des démocrates pour la République; RPR—Rassemblement pour la République; RPF—Rassemblement du peuple français; SFIO—Section française de l'internationale ouvrière; FGDS—Fédération de la gauche démocrate et socialiste; PS—Parti socialiste; and MRG—Mouvement des radicaux de gauche.
3. Inglehart and Klingemann (1976). The issue is a longstanding one. Recent statements supporting the primacy of the left-right dimension are Rosenthal and Sen (1973; 1977). For a sharply contrasting point of view, see Pierce (1980).
4. National surveys of the adult populations, including a subset of parent-adolescent pairs, were carried out in Britain, West Germany, the Netherlands, Italy, the United States, Austria, Switzerland, and Finland. Data from the first five mentioned are employed here for comparative purposes. *N*s for the pairs containing 16-18-year-olds range from 111 to 168. A partial report from the larger study is Barnes, Kaase et al. 1979, chaps. 15-16.
5. The question read: "Many people think of political attitudes being on the 'Left' or on the 'Right.' This is a scale stretching from the 'left' to the 'right.' When you think of your own political attitudes, where would you put yourself." Ten spaces were provided on the scale.
6. The French phrasing was, "Sur le plan politique, á quel endroit de cette échelle, vous situez-vous?" Seven places were provided, anchored on one end by "gauche" and the other by "droite." Although the stimulus differs slightly from that used in the multinational survey, the similarities in wording and the consistent use of left and right as the frame of reference allow for ready comparisons.
7. The indicator of religiosity is frequency of church attendance.
8. In the other five nations the stimulus was "public affairs and politics," whereas in France it was "political events." The alternatives were "several times a week, a few times a month, a few times a year, and hardly ever or never," versus France's "very often, often, not very often, and never."
9. The American figures would undoubtedly have been higher if a directional cue had been included, as was the case in France. Instead the question read: "Which political party does your (father) (mother) favor?" Responses regarding the two parents were averaged.

NATURE OF PARTISANSHIP

21. IS PARTY IDENTIFICATION MEANINGFUL?

It has long been recognized that a person's vote does not depend solely on the candidates and issues of the current election. The formerly strong tendency of southern Americans to vote Democratic year after year (the solid South), the strong association of blacks with the Democratic party since the New Deal of the 1930s, and numerous other examples of persistent regional, linguistic, and religious differences both here and abroad attest eloquently to the existence of a long-term component in voting. Early American voting studies (for example, Lazarsfeld, Berelson, and Gaudet, 1944) and many past and recent studies of voting in Europe treat group attachments such as those mentioned above as this stabilizing element. However, our current understanding of voting behavior was very heavily influenced by the University of Michigan researchers' emphasis on party identification as the most important long-term factor.

The critical insight of the Michigan researchers (Campbell, Gurin, and Miller, 1954; Campbell, Converse, Miller, and Stokes, 1960) consisted of two points. First, just as people identify with religious, racial, and ethnic groups, so do they identify with political parties. Second, parties, like other groups, tend to be quite stable in terms of what they stand for, so that partisanship was appropriately viewed as a long-term component of the political system. In particular, partisanship persists even when people vote contrary to their usual beliefs, as when many Democrats "defected" to Dwight Eisenhower in the 1950s and many Republicans voted for Lyndon Johnson in 1964. However, partisanship was also important because its influence went beyond its *direct* effects on the vote. As portrayed in *The American Voter* (Campbell, Converse, Miller, and Stokes, 1960), party identification affects the other major determinants of the vote—attitudes toward the issues and attitudes toward the candidates. Republican identifiers are more likely to agree with Republican leaders on the issues and to look favorably on Republican candidates. In part this is because partisanship serves a screening function, as citizens selectively perceive political information to the benefit of their preferred party. Republican identifiers are more likely to listen to Republican candidates and to news and advertisements favorable to Republicans; also, they are also more likely to interpret whatever they hear as favorable to Republicans.

Acceptance of the party identification concept was sufficiently strong that most commercial polls, such as the Gallup Poll, now regularly measure the number of Republican and Democratic partisans, and even small fluctuations are subject to journalistic analysis. But recent work has led researchers to wonder just how meaningful party identification is. In the United States, concern initially grew from questions about the stability of partisanship and the degree to which it is affected by short-term forces. As researchers tried to transport the concept to other nations, doubt arose over occasionally low levels of partisanship and was compounded when partisanship seemed to be no more stable than voting behavior. In addition, researchers have recently raised the question: is party identification being measured correctly?

In the first part of this chapter, we will look carefully at the challenges being raised against the notion of partisanship as a universally stable and meaningful component of the vote. Then we will review the evidence in favor of the party identification concept as well as responses to the recent criticisms. Finally, a separate section at the end will address the methodological questions.

Party Identification as Transitory and Meaningless

The first challenge to the meaningfulness of partisanship in the United States is due to evidence that it is less stable than it first seemed to be, at both the aggregate and the individual level. The aggregate stability of party identification has been considerable. Still, there are hints of susceptibility to short-term forces, as when a party's strength falls the year that its presidential candidate suffers a disastrous defeat (such as 1964 for the Republicans and 1972 for the Democrats). More importantly, there was a considerable increase in independence in the 1960s and 1970s (Table 21-1). Not only did this indicate volatility of public

Table 21-1 Party Identification in the United States, 1952-1982

	1952	*1956*	*1960*	*1964*	*1968*	*1972*	*1976*	*1980*	*1982*
Strong Democrat	22%	21%	21%	26%	20%	15%	15%	17%	20%
Weak Democrat	25	23	25	25	25	25	25	23	24
Independent Leaning to Dem.	10	7	8	9	10	11	12	11	11
Pure Independent	5	9	8	8	11	13	14	13	11
Independent Leaning to Rep.	7	8	7	6	9	10	10	10	8
Weak Republican	14	14	13	13	14	13	14	14	14
Strong Republican	13	15	14	11	10	10	9	9	10
Apolitical/Don't Know	4	3	4	2	1	3	1	3	2
Democratic Presidential Vote	44%	42%	50%	61%	43%	38%	50%	42%	
Republican Presidential Vote	55	57	50	38	43	61	48	52	

Note: The classification is based on the following question series: "Generally speaking, do you usually think of yourself as a Republican, a Democrat, an Independent, or what?" If Republican/Democrat: "Would you call yourself a strong Republican (Democrat) or a not very strong Republican (Democrat)?" If Independent: "Do you think of yourself as closer to the Republican or Democratic party?"

Source: Computed from data collected in the 1952-1982 Center for Political Studies election surveys, University of Michigan.

attitudes, but it was literally a movement away from identification with the parties. Also, panel studies showed there was even greater change in individual partisanship that was inevitably concealed in the aggregate figures by compensating changes in opposite directions, with the greatest shifts involving movement into and out of political independence (Converse, 1966; Dreyer, 1973; Table 23-3 of this book).

Evidence of the instability of partisanship led to the possibility that it was not totally long-term but was affected by short-term factors. The early causal models of the vote decision (Schulman and Pomper, 1975), which attempted to derive the separate impact of partisanship, candidate orientation, and issue position on the vote, assumed that party identification was strictly long-term in its effects. By contrast, more recent analyses—most notably that by Page and Jones (chapter 6), but also one by Jackson (1975)—have allowed for the possibilities of reciprocal causation and have found a rather considerable effect of issue and candidate evaluations on current party affiliation.

The view of partisanship as subject to short-term influences is most clearly apparent in the research of Fiorina, a portion of whose work is reprinted here as chapter 22. Fiorina sees partisanship as a running tally of retrospective evaluations, based not only on socialization and historical effects, but also on evaluations of current political happenings. Frequently, he points out (p. 420), there is a considerable degree of continuity in party evaluations. But the fact that partisanship is constantly being tested with information about current politics considerably alters the almost totally static view sometimes gleaned (perhaps erroneously) from the writings of the Michigan researchers.

Another challenge to the meaningfulness of partisanship came when studies in other countries revealed widely differing levels of party identification, with much less identification with parties in some countries than in the United States. Researchers have sometimes concluded that left/right identifications are more important in those countries than party identification (Percheron and Jennings, chapter 20 of this book; Inglehart and Klingemann, 1976; van der Eijk and Niemöller, 1983). Percheron and Jennings' emphasis on left/right identifications in France is not simply a change in the name of the long-term component of the vote. Rather, the fluidity of the party system in France is surely related to the existence of left/right identifications. It is not immediately clear which is the cause and which is the effect—whether a fluid party system causes identification with broad ideological positions or ideological positioning causes fluidity of parties. But if Percheron and Jennings are correct, the secondary status of partisan ties in France at least shows another way in which the original notion of party identification is substantially altered.

The final challenge to the view of partisanship as stable and meaningful asks whether party identification is really distinct from the vote, at least outside of the United States. If partisanship is a long-term identification, then it need not change when people switch their votes from one election to the next. Indeed, most change should be of that form, with partisanship staying the same even when one's vote changes, as is true in the United States. However, analysis for other countries suggests this is often not the case.

The Butler and Stokes (1969) study of *Political Change in Britain* was the first to report that party identification might be less stable in other countries than in the United States, particularly when people do not vote for their own party. (It was still quite stable in Britain, but less so than in the United States.) They explain the national differences by referring to ballot differences: Americans develop party loyalties as they vote for several different offices at the same election, while British citizens cast a vote for only a single office and so are less likely to distinguish between their current party and their current vote. Subsequently, Thomassen's (1976) analysis of Dutch data had a major impact; Thomassen found that people in the Netherlands are actually less stable in partisanship than in vote. (Compare in Table 23-2 the 7 percent of Dutch respondents who voted the same way in 1971 and 1972 but changed their partisanship, and the 4 percent who changed their vote while maintaining their partisanship.) From this Thomassen concluded that party identification in the Netherlands is actually affected by the vote rather than being causally prior to it as in the United States. This severely limits the utility of the concept of party identification in that country. More recent data from Sweden (Holmberg, 1981, p. 177) show a similar pattern there.

Systematic comparisons of partisan stability in fact show that the United States is a unique case in several respects. This is very clear in LeDuc's analysis of four countries (the United States, Britain, the Netherlands, and Canada), reprinted here as chapter 23. For example, changes in party identification were typically two to three times as great in other countries as in the United States, resulting in a quarter or more of the respondents altering their partisanship in no more than a five- or six-year period. And as noted, the stability of partisanship compared to the vote was unusual in the United States.

The extent to which partisanship moves with the vote is so great in some countries, especially West Germany and the Netherlands, that analysts for those countries have frequently dismissed the concept of party identification as irrelevant for them (see, for example, Thomassen, 1976 and the references cited in Baker, Dalton, and Hildebrandt, 1981, pp. 195-98). Some analysts have salvaged the concept by rejecting the direction component while retaining the strength component (Holmberg, 1981), but this seriously erodes the value of the concept. The original notion was that one could obtain a measure of people's predispositions toward the parties independently of their current votes. This may remain true for some individuals (for example, strong identifiers) and in some countries (especially the United States), but in many cases it is unlikely that a measure of partisanship tells us anything different from a measure of how they voted.

Thus, what began as a modest questioning of the view that partisanship was fully stable in the United States and that it was equally important abroad has led to major attacks on the meaningfulness of partisanship in voting. An increasing number of studies argue that it is affected by short-term forces in the United States and is not distinct from the vote in other nations, positions that undermine the utility of the party identification concept as a long-term component in models of the vote decision. However, many (and possibly most) analysts still find party identification a useful concept, because they feel that other evidence shows party identification to be reasonably stable.

Party Identification as Stable and Meaningful

The responses to the several challenges presented above are based on some early data as well as more recent analyses. We shall begin with the American case and move on to the challenges in other countries.

First, the level of stability of partisanship is considerable, even if it is not perfect. There is some ebb and flow, of course, in Table 21-1, but the Democratic lead in partisanship remains intact from 1952 to 1982. In spite of minor fluctuations and even the considerable growth in independence, it is clear that the overwhelming majority of Americans still identifies with (or at least feels closer to) one of the major parties and that the Democrats remain the more popular party.[1]

Further support for the stability of partisanship is found in individual-level data. Across a panel study in which the same respondents were interviewed in 1956, 1958, and 1960, very few respondents changed from Republican to Democrat, or vice versa (Converse, 1966b). Similarly, the report by Converse and Markus in chapter 7 emphasizes the stability of partisanship in the 1970s panel. Early multiyear panel studies in other countries likewise found minimal change across waves (Butler and Stokes, 1969), though LeDuc's chapter clearly shows there is more change in some countries than in others.

As originally viewed by the Michigan researchers, the only significant change in party identification over time (except for critical periods such as the 1930s) involves strength of partisanship, with people becoming stronger partisans as they age (Campbell, Converse, Miller, and Stokes, 1960, pp. 161-69). Similar life-cycle effects were found in other countries (Converse, 1969). A lively debate developed on the existence of such a life-cycle effect in the United States when Abramson's (1975) inspection of "cohort data" failed to find the expected increases in partisan strength. (Cohort data follow a birth cohort through time, for example, comparing the partisanship in 1964 and 1968 of those who were born between 1940 and 1947, instead of just comparing 21- to 24-year-olds in the two years). Converse (1976), however—conceding that events of the mid-1960s caused a modest general retreat from parties—argued that strength increased with age at least for the "steady state" period of 1952-1964. The life-cycle effect is undoubtedly small, but this merely says that stability was greater than anticipated.[2]

The early research also found party identification to be highly stable across generations, especially when compared with other attitudes (Jennings and Niemi, 1968). And again, similar stability was found in early studies of other countries, such as the Butler and Stokes (1969, chapter 3) study of Britain. Later analysis shows that respondents' reports that their partisanship is the same as their parents' must be discounted since respondents frequently misperceive their parents' partisanship (Niemi, 1974). But this problem is avoided in studies based on actual interviewing of parents and offspring (Jennings and Niemi, 1974, 1981), which show frequent slippage across generations into and out of the Independent category but little switching from one party to the opposite party.

As to the effect on party identification of short-term political factors, the question is not *whether* it is affected but how much. Some studies claim a large effect, but two recent studies—while explicitly recognizing that partisanship can be affected by short-term influences—find that the effect is not great. In their dynamic analysis of the 1972-1974-1976 panel study, Markus and Converse (chapter 7) show that partisanship is weakened when a person votes for the other party, but "the predicted effect of a deviating vote in a single election is hardly dramatic" (p. 139). Markus' (1982) analysis of the 1980 panel study provides comparable evidence. In this instance he observed the effect on partisanship in one wave of candidate ratings in the previous wave. Partisanship remained highly stable, with only a modest effect in the latter part of the campaign. However, one could argue that these studies still do not adequately test the short-term hypothesis. For example, Markus and Converse model current party identification as affected by prior partisanship, which is affected by issues, but current party identification is not directly affected by current issues or by candidate factors. Thus, they *assume* partisanship to be long-term, which accounts in part for their finding only small short-term effects. Because of sensitivity to such assumptions, different models are obtaining and probably will continue to obtain different results as regards the importance of short-term effects on partisanship. Minimally, stability may be less than once thought, but the extent of susceptibility to short-term considerations should not be overstated. Even Fiorina's explicit effort to model partisanship as a summary of past influences had to cope with the considerable stability of the measures.

Turning to the challenges from other countries, the differences in the extent of politicization across countries can be seen as a logical result of differences in the countries' histories. Converse and Dupeux (1962) provided the initial recognition that one has to adjust one's understanding of and expectations about partisanship in accordance with a country's past history and present politics. They found that identification with a party was less common in France than in the United States in the late 1950s, but they account for the difference by arguing that intergenerational transmission in the two nations proceeded from different initial levels of parental partisanship. Thus, the transmission process was similar across nations, but France started with a much lower level of partisanship in the parents' generation, which led to a lower level of partisanship in the generation being studied. Percheron and Jennings, in the chapter included in the previous section of this book, disagree with the specific argument of Converse and Dupeux, arguing that what is transmitted in France is not identification with a specific party so much as position on an ideological dimension. Yet this does not destroy the meaningfulness of partisan feelings, so long as one realizes that what appears to be important in France is not one's precise party but one's identifications with left or right tendencies.

Similar points are relevant for studies of other countries. Converse (1969), for example, incorporated different political histories in an explanation of differing levels of partisanship in the five-nation (United States, Britain, Italy, West Germany, and Mexico) study of Almond and Verba. In Germany and Italy, identification tended to increase with age as in the United States and Britain, except that identification was especially low for the age groups most affected by the fascist experience in those countries. Mexico showed a more radical departure from the common relationship between age and partisanship, but this can be accounted for by the fact that Mexican women were unable to cast a presidential vote until a year before the survey was conducted. Sani (1976) and Barnes (1977, chapter 5) also found differences in intergenerational transmission of partisanship in Italy, but they were able to explain the differences by reference to the strong family, organizational, and community ties of Italians. Overall, data from multiple countries make it clear that partisanship will not always be at a uniform level across countries, nor will there be identical relationships with age and other variables. In many of these cases, however, these differences can be explained in terms of democratic experiences, the party system, and other national characteristics.

The final challenge to the notion of meaningful partisanship is in some senses the most serious. If party identification does not "travel" as a concept to other countries, then the logical status of partisanship as a useful concept for the United States would next have to be re-evaluated. The attack on this basis has been most severe from Dutch and West German sources. The Dutch case might possibly be discounted since relationships might be expected to be different in a nation with a dozen political parties, but the West German case is more difficult to dismiss. Kaase (1969), for example, showed partisanship to be less common and less stable in West Germany than in the United States. We reprint the Norpoth chapter here, since it directly addresses the crucial West German case and contains important points to remember when comparing partisanship across nations. Norpoth emphasizes the prosaic problem of translating questions from one language to another and finds that many of the apparent differences are a matter of which survey questions are used. Looking at more comparable partisanship questions leads him to conclude that "durable party attachments are common, though not ubiquitous in the West German electorate" (p. 452). Baker, Dalton, and Hildebrandt (1981) also found that party identification is an appropriate concept for West Germany, although they used party thermometers to construct their measure.[3]

Finally, even if the direction component of partisanship is identical to vote choice in some countries, the strength of partisanship is still a meaningful concept. In Britain, for example, where partisanship and the vote move in tandem to a greater degree than in the United States, Särlvik and Crewe (1983) show that strong identifiers behave differently from those weakly identified with a party. Likewise, Holmberg (1981, chapter 10) shows differences by strength of identification in Sweden.

All this suggests that party identification remains a vital concept, in the United States and probably also in many other nations. Party identification may not be as stable as once thought, but this view is that it is sufficiently stable to be treated as a long-term component of the vote.

Measurement Questions: Is Party Identification Being Measured Correctly?

Recent work has not been limited to analysis of the stability and universality of partisanship. Studies have begun to question how party identification should be conceptualized and measured.

The reconsideration began when Petrocik (1974) called attention to some "intransitivities" in the usual party identification scale. One would expect strength of partisanship to be monotonically related to many other variables, but this was not so in every instance. In many elections, for example, independent leaners were more likely to vote for their preferred party than were weak partisans.

Why might independent leaners behave in a more partisan fashion than weak partisans? One explanation is that independent leaners are actually "closet partisans" who do not wish to admit their partisanship. Brody's (1977) analysis of the 1956-1958 and 1972-1974 panel data supported this position, as did Miller and Miller's (1977) report on the 1976 American national election study. Yet this explanation does not account for all the results since Petrocik, and others have found instances in which the leaners behave as other Independents.

Shively (1977) offered a second possible explanation: that the leaners were really Independents who were reporting how they were planning to vote in the election. The leaners would show up as politically involved in Petrocik's analysis since they were the Independents who were interested enough to vote; at the same time, they would vote for their party more often than weak identifiers since they were responding to the party identification question on the basis of their planned vote. The result of Shively's critical test was that, as expected, leaners more often than partisans changed their party identification when they switched their vote. However, the number of respondents underlying this test is too small to be definitive. And the explanation does not account for the large proportion of leaners who vote for the other party (Miller and Miller, 1977).

The explanation with the most serious potential for our treatment of partisanship is that independence may be a separate dimension from partisanship. The Weisberg chapter (25) summarizes the evidence in favor of this interpretation. Separate dimensions minimally mean that some people can be both partisans and Independents while other people are neither (see Table 25-2). Petrocik's intransitives can then be explained in that some independent leaners are more partisan than are some weak identifiers, even though they call themselves Independents since they are also more independent than are the weak identifiers (Valentine and Van Wingen, 1980). Also, Weisberg's Table 25-7b shows that people who consider themselves neither partisans nor Independents disproportionately fall into the weak identifier category. Consequently, weak partisans might be more partisan than leaners if both categories were purged of people who actually consider themselves neither.

Other studies have also given support to a multidimensional interpretation. Katz (1979) analyzed partisan change over American and British panel studies, using multidimensional scaling to place partisan categories closer together the more respondents switch from one category to another. He found that two dimensions—a direction dimension (Republicans versus Democrats in the United States) and an intensity dimension (partisans versus Independents)—were required to handle the change patterns. Jacoby's (1982) analysis of college students' rank orders of their preferences for the different partisan categories (strong Republican, weak Republican, and so on) found that a third of the sample had preferences that were consistent with a two-dimensional space similar to Katz's, with the other two-thirds fitting the conventional unidimensional scale.

A basic problem in deciding among these explanations is that the standard party identification measure assumed unidimensionality rather than testing for it. However, the 1980 American national election study included several new partisanship questions that were designed to test the multidimensional model and to explore what the traditional party identification questions have been measuring. The Weisberg chapter uses some of these questions to support the multidimensional interpretation. Dennis (1981a) has also extensively analyzed the new partisanship questions, finding three basic components: partisan direction, party system support (Democrats and Republicans are both highly supportive of the party system, while Independents are low on this component) and political involvement (people who are both Independents and partisans are especially high on this component, while those who are neither are especially low). Both Dennis (1981a, 1981b) and Weisberg (1983) have used the 1980 questions to construct and test new party support and closeness typologies.[4]

Once the possibility of multidimensionality of partisanship and independence is recognized, it is also necessary to consider whether there should be separate dimensions for reactions to different political parties. Reactions to the Democratic and Republican parties need not be opposites of one another, as Weisberg argues in chapter 25. Related ideas have been suggested by other researchers. In particular, Maggiotto and Piereson (1977) have examined the "hostility hypothesis" that defection from one's own partisanship depends on one's evaluation of the opposition party. They found that evaluation of the opposition party indeed has an independent impact on the vote. (See also Smidt, 1975, 1981; Guynes, n.d.; Guynes and Perkins, n.d.; Wattenberg, 1982). Additionally, Weisberg (1982) shows that attitude toward a party is the prime variable affecting feelings toward its candidates, with party identification and attitudes toward the other party having little added impact. This suggests a model of partisanship in which the citizen has an identification with each party, based partly on socialization experiences with that party and partly on later satisfaction or dissatisfaction with that party's performance over the years. This model is similar to that which Fiorina offers at the beginning of chapter 22, except that identification with one party need not be the negative of identification with the other party.

This multidimensional approach may also be useful in treating partisanship in other countries. Indeed, the first discussion of partisanship to emphasize the citizen's reaction to each party separately was Crewe's (1976) discussion of "negative partisanship" in Britain. Crewe found it useful to distinguish four types of partisans: "polarized" who are very strongly for their own party and very strongly against the other party, "loyal" who are very or fairly strongly for their own party but are not very strongly against the other party, "negative" who are not very strongly for their own party but are very strongly against the other party, and "apathetic" who are not very strongly for their own party and not very strongly against the other party.

Canadian researchers have also found it useful to adopt a multidimensional measure of partisanship. Clarke et al. (1979, 1980) developed a typology of partisanship based not only on its intensity (very strong, fairly strong, weak), but also on whether or not the party choice is consistent at federal and provincial levels and whether or not it has been stable over time. Strong, stable, consistent partisans are most likely to report always having voted for the same party, while those who "deviate" on all three characteristics are least likely to do so.[5]

As we move toward countries with even larger numbers of parties, we might anticipate ever more complex patterns of partisanship. The Dutch party system may be the epitome of this extreme, with 18 parties having won seats in the lower house of parliament (the Second Chamber) from 1945 to 1981 and high points of 14 parties winning seats in 1971 and 1972. It is perhaps not surprising that van der Eijk and Niemöller (1983) found that close to half the party adherents actually identified with multiple parties. These multiple identifications were consistent ideologically, as when two-fifths of the adherents of both the small right-wing Calvinist religious fundamentalist parties also identified with the other of these parties. Multiple identification based on ideological proximity may be an entirely appropriate response to a fragmented party system and may make the concept of partisanship appropriate where it would not otherwise be.

All in all, it is still too early to draw firm conclusions about these measurement questions. The traditional U.S. party identification question and scale do very well for many purposes, and we have the advantage of a lengthy time-series of their values. Yet they may confound strength of partisanship with independence, so that new measures might be more useful in dealing with party system support and political involvement. The examples of Britain, Canada, and the Netherlands suggest that it is worth extending the treatment of separate reactions to different parties and of multiple partisanship to more party systems. But this should not be read as saying that the case for the multidimensionality of partisanship has been proven. If anything, the controversy is too new to be fully joined, though a recent article by McDonald and Howell (1982) challenges the multidimensional interpretation of American partisanship and Fiorina (p. 422) forcefully argues that the traditional measure can still be used. Clearly these measurement issues will be the topic of dispute for the next several years.

Conclusion

If there was little questioning of the concept of party identification in the years after it was first introduced, there now seems to be no end to the questioning of it. There are disagreements over the nature and measurement of partisanship, disagreements that are unlikely to be settled soon. In part, the question is whether the American treatment of partisanship is useful for studying other countries, but we also ask how we should understand partisanship in the United States itself.

This controversy certainly cautions us about exporting concepts from voting behavior research in one country to studies of other countries. Once a new concept is developed, there is a natural tendency to rush out and try to apply it everywhere. Unfortunately, that may not always work. For one thing, it may be impossible to develop comparable questions in different languages. But the larger problem is that there are meaningful differences between political systems, and these differences may affect the application of concepts across nations. Even if we expect human behavior to be everywhere similar, the differences in political systems and ballot choices yield differences in the stimuli to which citizens react when they vote, and these in turn yield behavioral differences. In particular, there are enough unique factors in the American political system that some concepts developed for the United States may not apply equivalently abroad. At the same time, we should not dismiss problems in applying a concept cross-nationally as irrelevant to the United States. Thus, the problems found in transporting the party identification concept abroad helped alert researchers to the possible theoretical and measurement problems in the American data.

In the end, does the nature of partisanship have real political effects? We think so. If partisanship is solely long-term identification, then political change is likely to occur only at glacial speeds. On the other hand, if partisanship is responsive to short-term factors, then there is a potential for dramatic change that the analyses of the last 30 years have not noticed. This is a very real difference, not only for political scientists but also for practitioners—the politicians who must decide whether the public's partisanship tightly limits the vote for their party or whether it is worth trying to exploit new issues to bring about large voting change. This is a theme to which we will return in the last section of this book, where we examine different interpretations of contemporary political developments.

NOTES

1. Partisanship appears to be such a useful baseline that Converse (1966c) developed the notion of a "normal vote" to describe the results of a hypothetical election in which long-term party identification predominates and short-term issue and candidate factors are negligible. Taking into account both the greater number of Democratic identifiers and the fact that Democrats are less likely to vote than Republicans are, Converse found that the "normal vote" was about 53-54 percent Democratic and 46-47 percent Republican. Those results were for the 1950s, but Miller's (1979) recomputation of the normal vote for the 1960s and 1970s produced virtually identical results.
2. Abramson (1979) questions the strengthening of party identification even during the 1952-1964 period; he argues that changes in overall figures are due to the development of partisan feelings among blacks. See also Converse (1979). Claggett (1981) has argued quite persuasively that some of the differences between Converse and Abramson are due to their ignoring an important distinction between acquisition of partisanship (moving from independent to partisan) and intensification of partisanship (moving from weak partisan to strong partisan), with the two having different dynamic processes.
3. Similarly, although party identification in Britain is closer to the vote than in the United States, Särlvik and Crewe (1983) find the concept useful in their study of British voting in the 1970s. In addition, Cain and Ferejohn (1981) recently showed that the earlier Butler and Stokes result was partly due to their keeping Liberals in the British analysis while omitting Independents from the American data.
4. Weisberg (chapter 25) uses also an alternative measure of partisanship based on thermometer ratings. However, McDonald and Howell (1982) show that this measure is less stable and reliable than the conventional measure, suggesting that it is more susceptible to short-term electoral forces than the traditional measure. If so, Weisberg's party difference measure is not an appropriate validating measure.
5. Another interpretation of the inconsistent partisanship between federal and provincial levels in Canada is offered by Blake (1982), who views it as rational when a person's favorite party at one level of government is not a serious contender at another level. For example, since the Conservative party is very weak at the provincial level in British Columbia, it is entirely reasonable for a voter to be Conservative at the federal level but Social Credit in provincial politics. From this perspective, dual loyalty may not be so

much a matter of inconsistency as a case of multiple identification due to different party systems. There is some evidence of dual partisanship in the United States as well, especially in the South (Jennings and Niemi, 1966; Hadley, 1983).

FURTHER READINGS

The Normal Vote

Philip E. Converse, "The Concept of a Normal Vote," in *Elections and the Political Order*, ed. Angus Campbell, Philip E. Converse, Warren E. Miller, and Donald E. Stokes (New York: Wiley, 1966). Development of the normal vote concept.

Richard W. Boyd, "Popular Control of Public Policy: A Normal Vote Analysis of the 1968 Election," *American Political Science Review* (1972) 66:429-49. Develops summary statistics of the effects of an issue beyond the normal vote.

Christopher H. Achen, "The Bias in Normal Vote Estimates," *Political Methodology* (1979) 6:343-56. Normal vote analysis is misspecified.

Age Effects on Partisanship

Philip E. Converse, *The Dynamics of Party Support* (Beverly Hills: Sage, 1976). Partisan strength increases with age.

Paul R. Abramson, "Developing Party Identification," *American Journal of Political Science* (1979) 23:78-96. Partisan strength does not increase with age.

William Claggett, "Partisan Acquisition Versus Partisan Intensity," *American Journal of Political Science* (1981) 25:193-214. Reexamines aging effect while distinguishing between acquisition and intensification of partisanship.

Richard G. Niemi, G. Bingham Powell, Harold W. Stanley, and C. Lawrence Evans, "Testing the Converse Partisanship Model with New Electorates," *Comparative Political Studies* (1985) 18:300-322. Finds an effect of age that is independent of voting experience.

The Measurement of Partisanship

John R. Petrocik, "An Analysis of Intransitivities in the Index of Party Identification," *Political Methodology* (1974) 1:31-47. Demonstrates the lack of monotonicity in relating party identification to participation.

David C. Valentine and John R. Van Wingen, "Partisanship, Independence, and the Partisan Identification Question," *American Politics Quarterly* (1980) 8: 165-86. Party direction and independence as separate dimensions.

Martin Wattenberg, "Party Identification and Party Images: A Comparison of Britain, Canada, Australia, and the United States," *Comparative Politics* (1982) 14:23-40. Both positive and negative images of the parties are important.

Michael D. McDonald and Susan E. Howell, "Reconsidering the Reconceptualization of Party Identification," *Political Methodology* (1982) 8:73-91. Argues for a unidimensional interpretation of partisanship.

Usefulness of Party Identification in Other Countries

Warren E. Miller, "The Cross-National Use of Party Identification as a Stimulus to Political Inquiry," in *Party Identification and Beyond*, ed. Ian Budge, Ivor Crewe, and Dennis Farlie (London: Wiley, 1976). Defense of the party identification concept.

Jacques Thomassen, "Party Identification as a Cross-National Concept: Its Meaning in the Netherlands" in *Party Identification and Beyond*, ed. Ian Budge, Ivor Crewe, and Dennis Farlie (London: Wiley, 1976). Attacks cross-national use of partisanship.

The Decline of Partisanship in the United States

Jerrold G. Rusk and Helmut Norpoth, "Partisan Dealignment in the American Electorate: Itemizing the Deductions since 1964," *American Political Science Review* (1982) 76:522-37. Decomposition of the increase in Independents into generational and period effects.

Martin P. Wattenberg, *The Decline of American Political Parties, 1952-1980* (Cambridge: Harvard University Press, 1984). Major trend is increasing neutrality toward the parties, not alienation from them.

The Socialization of Partisanship

M. Kent Jennings and Richard G. Niemi, *The Political Character of Adolescence* (Princeton: Princeton University Press, 1974). Reports of independent interviews with high school seniors and their parents.

M. Kent Jennings, Klaus R. Allerbeck, and Leopold Rosenmayr, "Generations and Families: General Orientations," in *Political Action*, Samuel Barnes, Max Kaase et al. (Beverly Hills: Sage, 1979). Reports of interviews with adolescents and parents in five countries.

Russell J. Dalton, "Reassessing Parental Socialization: Indicator Unreliability versus Generational Transfer," *American Political Science Review* (1980) 74:421-31. A multiple-indicator approach to studying intergenerational agreement.

M. Kent Jennings and Richard G. Niemi, *Generations and Politics: A Panel Study of Young Adults and Their Parents* (Princeton: Princeton University Press, 1981). Shows increasing divergence between young adults and parents.

22. EXPLORATIONS OF A POLITICAL THEORY OF PARTY IDENTIFICATION

Morris P. Fiorina

For some two decades the concept of party identification dominated research on American voting behavior as well as accounts of the electoral process premised on that research. A generation of scholars learned to "control" the most commonsensical relationships for party identification and upon doing so often concluded that common sense was in error. Those more concerned with the operation of democratic political processes than with applied psychology resigned themselves to the search for the second, third, and *n*th most important determinants of voting choice.

But while it is fair to say that party identification has played a dominant role in research on voting behavior, it is necessary to add that the nature of that dominance has changed over time. Revolutions—intellectual as well as political—may consume their children. For perhaps a decade the concept of party identification stood unchallenged. It provided the "natural" structure for electoral research. During the most recent decade, however, party ID has increasingly become a target of critical studies. At first hesitantly, then more boldly, revisionists have attacked the old conceptual fortress. That they have only managed to loosen a few stones testifies to the continued strength of that structure.[1]

In chapter 4 [of Fiorina, 1981b] I offered a political theory of party ID, one based on a running tally of restrospective evaluations of party promises and performance. This chapter develops that theory more fully and confronts it with data from the two CPS panel studies. Before presenting that analysis, however, I will briefly examine the concepts of party identification past and party identification present. What was it originally thought to be? How, if at all, has recent research changed our view of what it is? Rhetoric aside, let us briefly consider the nature of the evidence.

The Concept of Party Identification According to Campbell, Converse, Miller and Stokes

The Michigan researchers Campbell, Converse, Miller, and Stokes (1960, p. 121) defined identification as "the individual's affective orientation to an

---

Source: *Retrospective Voting in American National Elections,* New Haven: Yale University Press, 1981.

important group-object in his environment." Given the numerous possible ways of conceptualizing long-term party affiliations (Key's standing decision, for one), what was the basis for the decision to ground party ID in psychological group theory rather than in some alternative conceptual framework? The answer appears to lie in the characteristics of the long-term party affiliations uncovered in the surveys.

There was first the fact that party ID was highly stable. Relying on analysis of a recall question, Campbell, Converse, Miller, and Stokes (1960, p. 150) reported that only 20 percent of the sample had changed party ID during their lifetime, although this refers to a simple three-way categorization rather than to the full party ID scale. Second, there was the fact that assumption of a party ID did not appear to be a concomitant of citizenship or a political coming of age. As later research (Hyman, 1959; Hess and Torney, 1967) verified, party ID appeared to develop early in life[2] and well prior to the development of policy preferences, or indeed policy awareness. Moreover, party ID appeared to strengthen with length of affiliation (Campbell, Converse, Miller, and Stokes, 1960, pp. 161-165; Converse, 1969). These characteristics put one in mind of a religious affiliation. Children learn that they are Catholics or whatever long before they have any understanding or appreciation of church dogma—if they ever do. But for many, the process of maturation brings inclusion in church-related social networks that typically evoke emotional attachments on the part of their members.

The capstone to the preceding line of thought no doubt came from the presumed relationship between party ID and the formation of the partisan attitudes that incorporate the short-term forces of politics. Although recognizing that objective events and conditions could lead to the modification of party ID (Campbell, Converse, Miller, and Stokes, 1960, pp. 133-35, 165), Campbell, Converse, Miller, and Stokes (1960, p. 135) concluded, "In the period of our studies the influence of party identification on attitudes toward the perceived elements of politics has been far more important than the influence of these attitudes on party identification itself." Again, acceptance of dogma follows affiliation rather than vice versa. We are given a picture of party ID as stable, affectively based, and relatively impervious to change except under extremely stressful conditions such as major depressions (Campbell, Converse, Miller, and Stokes, 1960, p. 151).

As one reads the relevant chapters of *The American Voter,* one is struck by the careful, cautious tone of the discussion. Caveats abound, and one feels that revisionist political scientists have not always played fair in their attribution of positions to Campbell, Converse, Miller, and Stokes. Yet that same reading also reveals how sparse the data underlying the Michigan conception of party ID actually were. The evidence for stability came from a recall question that is now treated with considerable skepticism (Brody, 1977, p. 23, n. 13). The aforementioned quotation on the primacy of party ID over partisan attitudes is introduced as a "judgment" and is followed (p. 135) by the remark that "our conviction on this point is rooted in what we know of the relative stability and priority in time of party identification and the attitudes it may affect" and a bit later (p. 136) by the admission that "our statement of causal priorities is in the end an inference." It is both a tribute to Campbell, Converse, Miller, and Stokes and a commentary on the rest of our discipline that such judgments, convictions, and inferences went almost unquestioned for a decade, even given the general availability of a data set whose contents raise fundamental questions about the prevailing conception of party ID.

The Revisionist Critique

Not all political scientists uncritically accepted the prevailing view of party ID during the 1960s, but those who did not had little direct evidence to justify their skepticism.[3] The basis for a serious revision came when scholars turned to an examination of the 1956-58-60 SRC Panel Study. Although the panel had been used to study attitude stability by various scholars (Converse, 1964), its significance for the examination of the prevailing conception of party ID was not fully realized until the 1970s. Then revisionist scholars pointed out some rather surprising results. Far from changing "glacially" at the individual level, party ID showed considerable fluctuation. As seen in Table 22-1, during the two-year periods of the panel, about 15 percent of the respondents (the exact number depends upon how independents are treated) changed *categories* (Democrat, Independent, Republican) on the party ID scale and more than 40 percent of the panel changed at least one place on the full seven-point scale. This was hardly what the prevailing view had led researchers to expect.

Dreyer (1973) suggested that most of the change on the panel could be dismissed as response error. When they were queried at two-year intervals, is it surprising that some previously strong identifiers might report presently weak identifications, or vice versa? But various other analyses (Dobson and Meeter, 1974; Dobson and St. Angelo, 1975; Brody, n.d.) concluded that random fluctuation was not a sufficient explanation for the panel's instability; real change of a systematic nature appeared to be evident.

Very recently the subfield of electoral behavior has come into possession of a second panel study. Its contents are quite consistent with the earlier panel. Consider Table 22-2. If anything, party ID is marginally less stable in the later panel than in the earlier one. On the basis of such data, Brody (1977) cautions that party ID should be treated only as a nominal variable, suggesting that the

Table 22-1 Stability of Party Identification in 1956-60 SRC Panel Study

	1956-58	*1958-60*
Category stable[a]	84.2	85.8
Strength stable	54.3	56.1
Weighted *n*	1,222	1,723

[a] Moves to or from "pure independence" from any other position are treated as categorical (i.e., interparty) change. This produces somewhat higher categorical change estimates than those of Dobson and St. Angelo, who treat moves to and from independence as intraparty, and Brody, who treats moves to independence as interparty but eliminates initial independents from his analysis.

Source: The data are drawn from pre-election surveys in 1956 and 1960 and the 1958 post-election survey. (The party ID item was not included in the 1956 post-election survey.)

Table 22-2 Stability of Party Identification in the 1972-76 CPS Panel Study

	1972-74	*1974-76*
Category stable	80.2	82.0
Strength stable	50.4	54.5
Weighted *n*	1,576	1,155

Source: The data are drawn from pre-election surveys in 1972 and 1976 and the 1974 post-election survey. (The party ID item was not included in the 1972 post-election survey.)

three-point categorization captures whatever long-term component exists but that the full seven-point scale appears hopelessly polluted by the effects of short-term forces.

Change over two- or four-year periods may fail to shake the strongest proponents of the traditional view. They could point out, for example, that a portion of the change is more apparent than real in that some changers come "home" to their original ID after a brief flirtation with the opposition or a brief spat with their own party (Butler and Stokes, 1974). A lot can happen in four years. Consider, then, the observations of Macaluso (n.d.). In the 1960 SRC Election Study the party ID items appeared in both the pre- and post-election surveys, thus yielding a short panel covering a span of at most four months. More than 10 percent of more than 1,700 respondents shifted categories on the party ID scale (see Table 22-3), and fully 40 percent of the respondents shifted at least one position on the full seven-point scale. Meier (1975) reports similar shifts (20 percent on the categorical scale, 40 percent on the seven-point scale) for a local National Opinion Research Center (NORC) panel study in 1972. All in all, it seems difficult to maintain the position that party ID is a deep-seated, stable characteristic of individuals that changes at only a "glacial" rate.

With the scent of blood in the air, the revisionists made the logical leap. Why does party ID change? If change is systematic, then in principle it is explainable. Brody and Macaluso show that changes in party ID relate to short-term forces—attitudes toward candidates, issues, and political conditions. Just as a religious affiliation learned at a parent's knee may give way when one later runs afoul of some particular dogma, so a socialized, affective party ID may crumble in the face of short-term political forces.

Findings like the preceding are positive in the sense of expanding our specific knowledge, but so far as general explanations go, they leave us in a state of

Table 22-3 Stability of Party Identification Pre- and Post-election Measurements in the 1960 SRC Election Study

Category stable	86.7
Strength stable	59.5
Weighted *n*	1,768

uncertainty. To previous evidence that party ID shapes the interpretation of political events and conditions, we now add equally suggestive evidence that such events and conditions modify party ID. Can we ever sort out the causal links? On purely statistical grounds, the answer is probably no, unless the funds become available for panel studies more ambitious than heretofore imagined. An alternative option is to construct more complex theories than those previously accepted, to ascertain whether the empirical regularities we now possess can be subsumed under those theories, and to test any new propositions those theories produce. In other words, a purely empirical effort to pin down the "real" place of party ID in a dynamic model of electoral choice is probably chimerical. All we can do is work toward ever-superior models of voting choice. The models must provide the causality, while the data should keep us from going too far astray.

The enterprise that follows reflects the preceding point of view. In chapter 4 [of Fiorina, 1981b] we proposed a model of party choice based on cumulations of retrospective evaluations. Part of that model was defined as the basis of party ID. The remainder of this chapter explores the empirical evidence in light of that definition.

Party ID as a Running Tally of Retrospective Evaluations

In chapter 4 [of Fiorina, 1981b] we defined party ID as the difference between an individual's past political experiences with the two parties, perturbed by a factor, γ, that represents effects not included directly in an individual's political experiences (e.g., parents' party ID). To repeat the definition,

$$PID(\Theta) = (PPE(\Theta) - PPE(\Psi) + \gamma)$$
$$PID(\Psi) = -PID(\Theta)$$
$$PID = \text{independent if } PID(\Theta) = PID(\Psi) = 0$$

Past political experiences (PPE), of course, are simply the voter's subjectively weighted retrospective evaluations formed while observing the postures and performances of the contending parties during previous election periods.

Based on the preceding theoretical development, the statistical model we use to explain *present* party ID is

$$PID_p = \gamma + \sum_{i=1}^{p} B_i RE_i + u_p, \tag{1}$$

where RE_i is a vector of restrospective evaluations for period i, B_i is the associated vector of coefficients, and u_p is an error term. Owing to the additive structure of the model, equation 1 can be decomposed to

$$PID_p = PID_{p-1} + B_p RE_p + (u_p - u_{p-1}), \tag{2}$$

which is estimable with the panel data previously discussed. Before proceeding to those estimations, however, I would like to emphasize two features of the proposed model of party ID.

First, the model provides an explicit *political* basis for party ID. When a citizen first attains political awareness, the socialization influences summarized by γ may dominate party ID. But as time passes, as the citizen experiences politics, party ID comes more and more to reflect the events that transpire in the world. Granted, those events may not be interpreted exactly the same by all individuals, but why should they be? As human beings we do not perceive ball games, concerts, lectures, or anything else in exactly the same way, either. But that is not to deny the realities underlying our divergent perceptions. Party ID as modeled here reflects evaluations of party activities.

Second, the model provides an explicit mechanism for change in party ID. The traditional conception of party ID suggests that change in identification is a step function of political evaluations: up to a certain severity they have no impact on party ID, while beyond that they shake an individual loose from an existing identification. Clearly, the model we are using allows party ID to vary continuously. As new evaluations form, an individual's identification may wax and wane. Indeed, given that Great Depressions don't happen all that frequently, the pattern of change we would expect is precisely that present in the CPS panel studies: considerable variation in strength of party ID but much less indication of major (i.e., categorical) shifts. Furthermore, any categorical shift that does occur should be disproportionately composed of those whose previous party ID was near the turning point (independent) of the scale. And this, of course, is exactly what happens empirically.

Here is an appropriate place to address a matter that has provoked considerable debate in the literature: the purported relationship between length of affiliation with a party and strength of party ID.[4] If a model like the one proposed here is accurate, the length-strength relationship is probably an artifact. To elaborate, if the parties favor the same sides of various socioeconomic cleavages over time, and if citizens find themselves in the same socioeconomic circumstances over time, then one would expect most citizens consistently to evaluate one party as preferable to the other, which according to our model will produce a continuously strengthening party ID. To the extent that affiliation with a party proxies this kind of consistency in evaluation, an empirical relationship between length of affiliation and strength of affiliation will arise, but there is nothing particularly lawlike about that relationship. If the parties are inconsistent over time, or if social mobility is exceptionally high, or if new issues regularly arise, citizens' PID may fluctuate randomly around some initial level (γ) and neither strengthen nor weaken over time. The length-strength correlation may occur in some countries at some times (U.S., 1930-65) but not in other countries (e.g., India) or at other times (U.S., 1965-) even though the same model applies in all cases (Eldersveld, 1973; Converse, 1976). One must differentiate the general features of a model from the specific values its elements assume at particular times and places.

Finally, a disclaimer. The model allows latitude for a variety of processes to produce a party ID. For example, referring to expression 4-5′, we could have "responsive" party identifiers, those for whom $\alpha_{j-1} < \alpha_j$, $\forall_j \leq p$. For such individuals, increasingly distant political experiences become increasingly less important as time passes. But then again, we could have "traumatized" party identifiers for whom α_j increases with $|U_{j+1} - U_j|$. Such individuals may never forget Hoover's depression or Sherman's march to the sea. Other possibilities exist as well. But we will be unable to examine such subtleties in the analyses that follow. All we have is party ID at time $(p - 1)$ and a few retrospective evaluations from the present (pth) period. We can check to see if certain types of citizens are more sensitive than others to recent events and conditions, but the numerous possible processes at work are hidden in PID_{p-1}.

The 1956-58-60 SRC Panel Study

In the final section of chapter 2 [of Fiorina, 1981b] we presented summary analyses that related various retrospective evaluation items to the vote. This section uses the items listed in table 2.11 [of Fiorina, 1981b] to account for modifications in party ID across the 1956-58-60 SRC Panel Study. These items—financial situation, avoiding war, foreign dealings, and domestic conditions—are all treated as simple retrospective evaluations. I will report two analyses covering the shifts in party ID from 1956-58 and 1958-60, each of which is performed for both the seven-point and three-point versions of the party ID measure.

To account for party ID in 1958, we wish to estimate a model like the following:

$$PID_{1958} = \alpha + b_1 PID_{1956} + b_2 \text{(financial situation same)} + b_3 \text{(financial situation better)} + b_4 \text{(foreign dealings so-so)} + b_5 \text{(foreign dealings good)} + b_6 \text{(domestic affairs same)} + b_7 \text{(domestic affairs better)} + b_8 \text{(head always employed past two years)}.$$

The preceding specification includes a constant term, although none appears in equation 2—there it is incorporated in PID_{p-1}. Given that our indicators of retrospective evaluations are dummy variables, however, the constant term incorporates all the excluded categories. In addition, the preceding specification includes a coefficient on PID_{p-1}, though expression 2 implicitly constrains that coefficient to be one. There are two reasons not to impose the constraint. First, PID_{p-1} is replaced by an instrument (see below) with a scale not comparable to PID_{p}. Second, the changes in party ID are measured over two-year intervals, but the retrospective evaluations often refer to "during the past year" or leave the time span of unspecified length. By freeing the coefficient on PID_{p-1}, we enable the specification to take account of such failures of "fit" among the right-hand-side variables.

The technique of estimation is a maximum likelihood probit procedure. . . . Although much has been written about the robustness of ordinary least squares (OLS) under violations of the traditional assumptions, there is no denying that applying OLS to a limited dependent variable results in biased estimates of the standard errors of estimated coefficients. As a consequence, hypothesis tests involving the coefficients are undependable. Given that the significance of particular coefficients is of crucial concern to this analysis, the trouble and expense of the probit procedure appear justified.

A second complication is apparent from a glance back at equation 2. In decomposing PID_p into $(\text{PID}_{p-1} + \text{RE}_p)$ we obtain a new error term, $(u_p - u_{p-1})$, which, of course, is correlated with PID_{p-1}.[5] This situation might produce biased and inconsistent estimates if we took no remedial action. When using linear regression, the standard remedy for such a problem is a two-stage procedure that first estimates a "purged" variable, PID^*_{p-1}, that then substitutes for the offending variable, PID_{p-1}. An analagous procedure exists for probit analysis. And while the two-stage probit estimates do not have all the desirable properties of the two-stage least squares estimates, they do have the important property of consistency (Heckman, 1978; Nelson and Olson, 1978; Amemiya, 1979). Thus, the estimates in the party ID equations are two-stage probit coefficients. Following Jackson (1975a), the purged version, PID*, of PID is obtained from an analysis in which party ID serves as the dependent variable in an equation with various socioeconomic and demographic characteristics as independent variables. The predicted values, PID*, are then used as input for the second stage of the analysis. (Appendix B contains the details of the first-stage analysis.) Briefly, the data yield no surprises. Party ID is strongly associated with religion, region of residence, union membership, and father's party ID. Occupation and age relate less strongly—but significantly—to party ID, while a variety of other socioeconomic and demographic variables show little by way of genuine association with party ID. The retrospective variables (financial situation, avoiding war, and domestic progress) also relate significantly to party ID. Table 22-4 presents summary statistics on the 1956 and 1958 instruments. The latter are somewhat better, so the analysis of party ID change across the 1958-60 waves rests on firmer statistical foundations than that of change across the 1956-58 waves.

Tables 22-5 and 22-6 contain results that lend considerable credence to the conception of party ID as a running tally of retrospective evaluations. In each case the coefficient of the party ID instrument is quite large and significant: present party ID of course relates strongly to past party ID. But note also the importance of recent retrospective evaluations in accounting for temporal change in party ID. The dependent variable is coded from strong Democrat to strong Republican or from Democrat to Republican. Thus, satisfaction with the incumbent Republican administration should result in movement toward the Republican end of the scale. This is indeed what happens. Republican identification increases significantly among those who believe that the domestic situation has improved, that foreign dealings have gone well, and that our chances of avoiding war have declined. In fact, even a so-so or ambiguous situation seems to be associated with an increase in Republican identification.[6] The financial situation and unemployment variables usually have the right sign, but their effects appear to be smaller and statistically less precise.

Table 22-4 Party ID Instruments, 1956-60 Panel Study

Instrument to replace	$\hat{R}^2$	*Rho (Predicted v. actual party ID)*
1956 Seven-point scale	.26	.46
1956 Three-point scale	.32	.42
1958 Seven-point scale	.41	.61
1958 Three-point scale	.51	.56

Note: *1956 n* = 1,362. 1958 *n* = 1,738.

Table 22-5 1958 PID as a Function of 1956 PID and Recent Retrospective Evaluations, Two-Stage Probit Estimates

	Seven point	*Three point*
Financial situation—better	.06	.12
Foreign dealings—gone well	.23***	.31***
Domestic affairs—better	.54***	.63***
Financial situation—same	.08	.11
Foreign dealings—so-so	.14	.23*
Domestic affairs—same	.27***	.31***
Foreign dealings—don't know	.24**	.20*
Domestic affairs—don't know	.45***	.40***
Head not unemployed in past two years	.11	.19
1956 PID**	1.01***	1.02***
Constant	−.75***	−.88***
$\hat{R}^2$	.32	.39
rho	.52	.48
n	1,062	1,062

* $p < .10$. ** $p < .05$. *** $p < .01$.

Table 22-6 1960 PID as a Function of 1958 PID and Recent Retrospective Evaluations, Two-Stage Probit Estimates

	Seven point	*Three point*
Financial situation—better	.01	−.04
Foreign dealings—gone well	.41**	.45**
Avoiding war—better chance	.42**	.49**
Domestic affairs—better	.58**	.65**
Financial situation—same	−.03	−.02
Foreign dealings—so-so	.20*	.34**
Avoiding war—same chance	.12*	.20*
Domestic affairs—same	.19**	.23*
Foreign dealings—don't know	.06	.00
Avoiding war—don't know	.02	.21
Domestic affairs—don't know	.12	.14
Head not unemployed in past two years	.18*	.09
1958 PID**	.76**	.82**
Constant	−.40**	−.62**
$\hat{R}^2$	.41	.53
rho	.63	.61
n	1,316	1,316

* $p < .05$. ** $p < .01$.

The differences between the 1958 and 1960 party ID analyses are in line with the conventional picture of those campaigns. In 1958 the generalized domestic affairs item has an effect considerably stronger than the generalized foreign affairs item, and the latter is the sole foreign affairs indicator in the analysis, while three domestic affairs items must compete. In 1960 the relative effects of both foreign affairs items are much stronger, although the domestic affairs item still has the largest coefficient. Even though the worst of the recession had passed, perhaps Kennedy's talk of "getting this country moving again" kept domestic affairs in the spotlight.

As explained in appendix A [of Fiorina, 1981b], in probit analysis one cannot discuss the effects of a particular variable in isolation. How much any given variable affects the dependent behavior depends on the values taken on by other variables in the equation. Thus, in order to convey to the reader some indication of the range of effects represented in Tables 22-5 and 22-6, I will examine some hypothetical cases. Consider five individuals, the first with a score on the 1958 party ID instrument equal to the mean of the respondents (μ = .83) included in the analysis, the second and third individuals with scores one standard deviation (σ = .84) above and below the mean, respectively, and the fourth and fifth with scores two standard deviations above and below the mean, respectively. This gives us a set of individuals whose prior party identifications range from very strong Democratic to fairly strong Republican. To make things simple, let us consider the effects of (a) uniformly favorable retrospective evaluations (financial situation, domestic affairs, chances of avoiding war "better," foreign dealings "gone well," and employed); (b) mostly neutral retrospective evaluations ("same" on the four items, employed); and (c) uniformly unfavorable retrospective evaluations ("worse" on the four items, unemployed). Predicted 1960 party ID from Table 22-6, column 1) for each of the five individuals for each of the three conditions is shown below.

	1960 Retrospective evaluations		
1958 ID	*Unfavorable*	*Neutral*	*Favorable*
Average -2σ	Strong Democrat	Strong Democrat	Weak Democrat
Average $-\sigma$	Strong Democrat	Weak Democrat	Independent
Average	Weak Democrat	Independent Democrat	Weak Republican
Average $+\sigma$	Independent Democrat	Independent Republican	Strong Republican
Average $+2\sigma$	Independent Republican	Weak Republican	Strong Republican

Two things are evident from the hypothetical cases. First, retrospective evaluations can play a major role in moving individuals up and down the party identification scale, though we have deliberately structured the examples so that all the retrospective evaluations work in concert. In the less consistent real world, the observed effects will seldom be so powerful as those illustrated above; still, the potential is clearly there. Second, the more partisan an individual, the less responsive his or her reported partisanship will be to retrospective evaluations, although, as the latter cumulate over time, even strong identifiers may eventually cross the threshold of their category.

Readers interested in the effects of any single variable, or in cases other than those examined above, can perform similar exercises using the given data on the mean and standard deviation of the 1958 party ID scores and the threshold values for the 1960 party ID scale listed in the addendum to this chapter.

All in all, Tables 22-5 and 22-6 present a compelling picture: party ID responds to the recent performance of the party in power via a citizen's formation of retrospective judgments. This finding is wholly in accord with the concept of party identification developed in chapter 4 [of Fiorina, 1981b]. Of course, other concepts of party ID are also compatible with these tables. Consider, for example, a Bayesian theory in which past (present) identification reflects a citizen's prior (posterior) distribution of party positions and retrospective judgments reflect the samples of information he or she has acquired in the process of proceeding from prior to posterior.[7] Such a theory is a live competitor. We can never hope to "prove" *the* one correct theory, but the important point concerns what theories can be dismissed. And it appears that we can safely eliminate any theory positing that party ID is either devoid of political content or impervious to change. Granted, party ID may not reflect an elaborate ideology or a wealth of detailed information about current public policies, but at least it reflects the political experiences of the citizen. And while party ID might remain empirically stable for long periods of time, that stability only reflects the empirical consistency of political experiences with previous identification, not the resistance of the latter to change. The underlying theoretical dependence of current party ID on political events and conditions remains.

To this point I have not mentioned the fact that Tables 22-5 and 22-6 contain parallel analyses using both the three- and seven-point measures of party ID. The reason is that it apparently doesn't matter. Whether one looks at column one or two in the tables, the conclusion is the same: change in party ID is predictable from knowledge of an individual's perceptions of recent political events and conditions. Earlier we took note of Brody's then-radical conclusion that the three-category version of the party ID measure captures the presumed long-term essence of a psychological party affiliation, while the seven-place measure is hopelessly "polluted" by short-term forces. If anything, Brody's conclusion is too conservative. The second columns of Tables 22-5 and 22-6 clearly indicate that the categorical measure too is significantly affected by at least one type of "short-term force"—retrospective evaluations. Empirically, we may not see very much by way of categorical change—few political events are sufficiently noteworthy to reverse the sign of a strong Democrat's or Republican's party identification, but over time, movement across the categorical divides appears to follow the same patterns as up-and-down movements in strength of party ID.

At the least, the preceding analysis should give pause to those who would use party ID as a simple "control" of the same order as income, occupation, religion, or race. Variables like the latter nearly always can be treated as purely exogenous in one's analysis: they affect the political behavior of interest but are not themselves affected by it. Party ID is a different matter. It is both cause and consequence of some kinds of political behavior. To take it purely as the former may lead to statistical misspecification and substantive error.[8] At least, that is the import of the analysis of the 1950s panel study.

The 1972-74-76 CPS Panel Study

The major difference between the 1950s panel and the 1970s panel is the presence in the latter of mediated retrospective evaluations such as presidential performance, government economic performance, and the Nixon pardon. Otherwise, this section simply repeats the preceding section with a later data set. Again, the analysis employs party ID instruments estimated from a variety of demographic variables and retrospective evaluations. . . . These instruments are similar to those used in the analysis of the 1950s panel, as seen in Table 22-7.

As specialists in voting behavior will sadly recall, the 1972 survey was partitioned into two forms, with some items appearing on only one form. That is the case with the retrospective evaluations items in 1972, which were asked on only form II of the post-election survey. Thus, in constructing the instruments for 1972 party ID, one-half of the sample is lost at the outset. Deletion of cases with some missing data reduces the set of people for whom we can calculate a 1972 party ID instrument to fewer than 700—about a quarter of the original sample. Then, when the 1972 instruments are used in the 1974 party ID analysis (Table 22-8), deletion of cases with 1974 missing data reduces the base for estimating to just below 400, a situation that is difficult to accept. Therefore, I constructed alternative 1972 party ID instruments based only on 1972 demographic data (requested on both forms of the survey). The statistics on these alternative instruments appear in parentheses in Table 22-7. Although weaker, the alternative procedure permits nearly the entire sample (2,600 +) to receive a 1972 party ID score and nearly quadruples the number of cases available for estimating the 1974 party ID equations (compare Tables 22-8 and 22-9). Fortunately, the substantive conclusions appear unaffected by these alternative manipulations of the data.

Tables 22-8 and 22-9 contain the 1974 party ID equations. Evaluations of presidential performance and the Nixon pardon clearly contribute to the modification of previous party ID, but beyond that, ambiguity reigns. The coefficients of government economic performance switch signs between Tables 22-8 and 22-9, as does that of "financial situation better," though these coefficients are statistically imprecise at any rate. The belief that civil rights progress is too slow appears to contribute weakly to the deterioration of present Republican identification. All in all, though, only evaluations of Ford's performance and his

Table 22-7 PID Instruments, 1972-76 Panel Study

Instrument to replace	$\hat{R}^2$	*Rho (predicted v. actual party ID)*
1972 Seven-point scale	.45 (.30)	.58 (.49)
1972 Three-point scale	.54 (.33)	.58 (.45)
1974 Seven-point scale	.28	.49
1974 Three-point scale	.34	.45

Note: 1972 n = 681. (1972 n = 2,656.) 1974 n = 1,101.

Table 22-8 1974 PID as a Function of 1972 PID and Recent Evaluations, Two-Stage Probit Estimates (1972 PID Instrument Based on Demographic Variables and Retrospective Evaluations)

	Seven point	*Three point*
Ford performance	.25**	.23*
Nixon pardon	.37***	.49***
Financial situation		
Same	.08	.10
Better	.06	.11
Government economic performance		
Fair	.03	−.10
Good	−.43*	−.23
Civil rights		
Too fast	−.04	.00
Too slow	−.07	−.04
Head unemployed in past year	.03	.17
1972 PID**	.86***	.90***
Constant	−.52***	−.51***
$\hat{R}^2$	.46	.55
rho	.64	.57
n	396	396

*$p < .10$. **$p < .05$. ***$p < .01$.

pardon of Nixon appear to be important factors in the temporal transformation of party ID.

As shown in Table 22-10, the estimates for 1976 party ID are quite similar to those for 1974. Again evaluations of Ford's performance and his pardon of Nixon play a clear and important role in modifying past party ID, though the relative importance of the two reverses as the pardon recedes in time and the length of Ford's incumbency increases. Evaluations of the administration's performance on inflation and unemployment also appear to bear some relationship to changes in party ID between 1974 and 1976. But again, simple retrospective evaluations relate weakly and inconsistently to temporal change in party ID.

As before, hypothetical cases may help to illustrate the magnitude of the effects predicted in Tables 22-8 to 22-10. Again, consider five individuals, one with the mean score on the 1974 party ID instrument (μ = 1.01), two more with scores one standard deviation (σ = .63) above and below the mean, respectively, and the fourth and fifth with scores two standard deviations above and below the mean, respectively. Because our two most important variables (Ford performance, the Nixon pardon) are dichotomous rather than trichotomous, let us simply examine the predicted effects of uniformly unfavorable and uniformly favorable retrospective evaluations on the trans-

Table 22-9 1974 PID as a Function of 1972 PID and Recent Retrospective Evaluations, Two-Stage Probit Estimates (1972 PID) Instruments Based on Demographic Variables Only)

	Seven point	*Three point*
Ford performance	.30***	.30***
Nixon pardon	.52***	.64***
Financial situation		
Same	.04	−.05
Better	−.11	−.21**
Government economic performance		
Fair	−.02	.00
Good	.14	.20*
Civil rights		
Too fast	.04	.08
Too slow	−.16*	−.33***
Head unemployed in past year	−.05	.14*
1972 PID**	.87***	.91***
Constant	−.49***	−.51***
$\hat{R}^2$	.32	.39
rho	.52	.47
n	1,535	1,535

* $p < .10$. ** $p < .05$. *** $p < .01$.

formation of party ID between 1974 and 1976. The predicted effects are shown below.

	1976 Retrospective evaluations	
1974 ID)	*Unfavorable*	*Favorable*
Average -2σ	Strong Democrat	Independent Democrat
Average $-\sigma$	Strong Democrat	Independent
Average	Weak Democrat	Independent Republican
Average $+\sigma$	Independent Democrat	Weak Republican
Average $+2\sigma$	Independent	Strong Republican

Again, the potential of retrospective evaluations to modify party ID is major. The example hardly calls to mind a "deep-seated, stable characteristic."

What is the general conclusion to be drawn from Tables 22-8 to 22-10? On the one hand, they reinforce the conclusion drawn from Tables 22-5 and 22-6: party ID waxes and wanes in accord with a citizen's evaluations of the recent performance of the party in power. Yet on the other hand, there is a major difference between the two sets of tables. In Tables 22-5 and 22-6 we see party ID changing in response to evaluations of general *conditions*—international tension, the domestic situation, personal unemployment, and so forth—whereas in Tables 22-8 to 22-10 we see party ID changing principally in response to evaluations of *peo-*

Table 22-10 1976 PID as a Function of 1974 PID and Recent Retrospective Evaluations, Two-Stage Probit Estimates

	Seven point	*Three point*
Ford performance	.52***	.66***
Nixon pardon	.29**	.29***
Financial situation		
Same	.04	−.04
Better	.02	−.06
Government inflation performance		
Fair	.04	.00
Good	.27**	.29**
Government unemployment performance		
Fair	.03	−.02
Good	.20*	.18
Recession	.01	−.03
Business conditions		
Better	.09	.15*
Same	−.20**	−.10
Civil rights		
Too fast	.04	.15*
Too slow	−.16	−.13
1974 PID**	.74***	.77***
Constant	−.14	−.70***
$\hat{R}^2$	.39	.47
rho	.57	.52
n	962	962

* $p < .10$. ** $p < .05$. *** $p < .01$.

ple—Ford and Nixon. One might reasonably suspect that past party ID contributes a great deal to those very evaluations, thus producing a spurious link between them and current party ID. When general conditions rather than political personalities are at issue, the question of spuriousness is much less worrisome.

Throughout the preceding chapters we have treated mediated retrospective evaluations (MREs) gingerly, always admitting the possibility that they do not represent what they seem to on their face. Now, with the interpretation of Tables 22-8 to 22-10 hanging in the balance, we must come to grips with MREs. That is the task of the next chapter [of Fiorina, 1981b]. In order to write a conclusion to this chapter, however, I must offer a preview of the next. We will see that MREs definitely reflect previous party ID, but we will see as well that they just as definitely reflect simple retrospective evaluations. They appear to play the kind of intervening role hypothesized in Figure 4.1 (see chapter 4 [of Fiorina, 1981b]). While one should not interpret them as purely objective judgments, one cannot interpret them as purely subjective rationalizations, either. In light of those findings, I am reasonably sanguine about the interpretation of Tables 22-8 to 22-

10; like Tables 22-5 and 22-6, they indicate that a citizen's party ID waxes and wanes in accord with his/her perceptions of societal conditions, political events, and the performance of incumbent officeholders.

A final caveat. In the preceding pages, conclusions about the nature of party ID have been stated firmly and often. But I will now emphasize a point deliberately understated in the chapter, namely, the empirical continuity of party ID. As Tables 22-5, 22-6 and 22-8 to 22-10 clearly show, present party ID does relate very strongly to previous party ID. There is a pronounced element of continuity, probably enough to merit the shorthand of "habit" or "standing decision." We should never go so far as to deny the existence of some notion of party identification, to treat it as a mere summary for an individual's issue preferences, for example. The tables in this chapter simply support what many of us have believed without adequate evidence all along: there is an inertial element in voting behavior that cannot be ignored, but that inertial element has an experiential basis; it is *not* something learned at mommy's knee and never questioned thereafter.

Addendum: Some Methodological Observations on the Traditional Party ID Measure

. . .[T]he probit procedure assumes that we observe only the ordinal reflection of an underlying cardinal variable. The observed categories are hypothesized to correspond to intervals on the underlying variable, intervals determined by $(n - 1)$ "thresholds" if there are n observed categories. The program of McKelvey and Zavoina provides estimates of these thresholds, normalized so that the lowest one is set at zero. These thresholds, of course, are of interest in their own right in that they provide estimates of the size of, and distance between, the ordinal categories with which we must work.

Most researchers who work with the seven-point party ID measure treat it as an equal-interval scale. That is, before doing their statistical analyses, they code an individual's party ID from -3 to 3 or from 0 to 6. Table 22-11 raises serious doubts about such practices. Let us ignore the strong-identifier categories, which are of infinite length. This is a property of the normal distribution, which matters only if one or more right-hand-side variables is unbounded. Otherwise, there will be some lower (higher) point beyond which no one's party ID scores are predicted to lie. (Theoretically, there is no particular reason to bound party ID scores.) The remaining five categories, on the other hand, are of determinate length, and here we can make relative comparisons. Let us take the 1958 and 1960 estimates first. In each of these years we see that the weak Republican and weak Democratic categories are of comparable length, but they are two and one-half to four times longer than any of the three independent categories. In the 1974 and 1976 data, the weak Democratic and weak Republican categories are again of similar length, but now they are less than twice the length of each of the three independent categories. Put another way, in 1958 independents, broadly defined, occupied a portion of the scale roughly 85 percent as long as that occupied by the weak identifiers. In 1976 broadly defined independents occupied a portion of the scale roughly 150 percent as long as the weak identifiers.

Table 22-11 Estimated Locations of Thresholds Between Party ID Categories

	1958	*1960*	*1974*	*1976*
Strong Democrat				
	.00	.00	.00	.00
Weak Democrat				
	.75	.84	.77	.89
Independent Democrat				
	.95	1.04	1.27	1.29
Independent				
	1.18	1.32	1.66	1.66
Independent Republican				
	1.38	1.62	2.18	2.12
Weak Republican				
	2.10	2.34	2.95	2.88
Strong Republican				

Note: In 1958, .75 marks the boundary between those predicted to be weak Democrats and those predicted to be independent Democrats. In 1976 2.88 marks the boundary between those predicted to be weak Republicans and those predicted to be strong Republicans, and so on.

Table 22-11 suggests two conclusions. First, the seven-point party ID measure is not an equal-interval scale. Consequently, analyses that treat it as such may be misleading.[9] Second, the seven-point measure is not invariant over time; there is considerable movement in the relative sizes of the categories. Thus, diachronic analyses, which treat party ID as an equal-interval scale, may be doubly misleading. The relationship between party ID and some aspect of political behavior might appear to change over time when actually it is the measure that is changing.

As long as we are on the subject of methodological caveats about previous research using the party ID measure, we might as well consider a caveat that potentially applies to this research. Table 22-11 reflects the assumption that party identification is one-dimensional: the probit procedure presumes an underlying cardinal dimension, which we observe only imperfectly as a series of ordered categories. (The unidimensional assumption, of course, is also implicit in treatments of party ID as an equal-interval scale.) Very recently, however, scholars (Valentine and Van Wingen, 1980; Weisberg, 1980) have suggested that responses to the traditional party ID items may require a two-dimensional representation, one measuring attitudes toward the parties, the second measuring attitudes toward "independence." The evidence thus far is sketchy. In evaluating this line of work Kessel (1980, p. 231) notes the strong association between the traditional ordinal scale and the two-dimensional classification, suggesting, "We can continue to use the traditional classification with the caveat that it is an imperfect reflection of more complex attitudes about partisanship and independence."

I am fully in agreement with Kessel's conclusion, and I would append to it the sentiment that we should not let methodology run away with substance. The *concept* of party identification developed by the Michigan group *is* one-dimensional—a bipolar scale anchored by two opposing reference groups. Independents are just that, people who have no particular identification with either party, not those who positively identify with "independence." Similarly, the reconceptualization of party ID proposed in this chapter *is* one-dimensional—the weighted utility difference between past experiences with two parties. Independents are just people who have done equally badly or equally well at the hands of the parties. If the traditional means of *measuring* party ID ("Generally speaking, do you . . .") turns out to elicit multidimensional responses, we have two choices. The obvious one is to clean up the measure. The less obvious one is to reconceptualize party ID as a multidimensional phenomenon including such strange notions as affect toward "independence." [10]

The theory I have proposed is a theory of individual responses to the attitudes-toward-the-parties dimension (if there is more than one) of the traditional ordinal measure. If this measure, in fact, is forcibly combining two dimensions, then replications of my analyses using a purer, one-dimensional measure should yield results even stronger than those reported in this chapter.

NOTES

1. The reader may find it interesting to examine the treatments of party identification in the current American government texts. There the traditional orthodoxy reigns supreme.
2. By fourth grade in New Haven, according to Greenstein (1969).
3. For example, using mostly the aggregate distributions of party ID and the recall item about change in previous identification, John Kessel (1968, pp. 302-08) argues that party ID is at least somewhat responsive to short-term forces.
4. For a review of the debate from the standpoint of one of its principal protagonists, see Converse (1976).
5. Recall that PID_{p-1} would be written as

$$\gamma + \sum_{i=1}^{p} B_i\, RE_i + u_{p-1}$$

6. Usually, one drops the "don't knows" from the analysis, but there are quite a number of them on the foreign-dealings, domestic affairs, and avoiding-war items, so retaining them (easily done in a dummy variable formulation) significantly increases the number of cases usable for estimation.
7. For one illustrative use of such a model, see Zeckman (1979).
8. Regrettably, some of my earlier work is vulnerable to this charge. See Fiorina (1978).
9. When using party ID as a right-hand-side variable, the preferred course would be to represent the seven-point scale by a set of six dummy variables. When using party ID as a left-hand-side variable, the preferred course would be to utilize probit, logit, multiple discriminant, or some other appropriate statistical procedure.
10. This is not to say that "attitudes toward independence" do not exist, not that they are unimportant, only that it is questionable whether they belong under the concept of "party identification."

23. THE DYNAMIC PROPERTIES OF PARTY IDENTIFICATION: A FOUR-NATION COMPARISON

Lawrence LeDuc

The utility of the concept of party identification in voting research, as well as several controversies surrounding its application and interpretation, is well known. American scholars, having observed the erosion of partisanship in the American electorate in the late 1960s and early 1970s, have drawn differing conclusions regarding the implications which these phenomena may have for the theory of party identification as a relatively enduring social-psychological attachment in that country. In cross-national research, scholars have differed widely regarding the applicability of party identification in multi-party systems or in those undergoing fundamental change. At the very least, non-American scholars have agreed that party identification tends to behave differently in different political environments, even where there is no serious problem of conceptual similarity. Butler and Stokes (1969; 1974) first observed the greater tendency of party identification to travel with the vote in Britain than in the United States, even though the over-all level of stability of partisanship was comparable in the two countries. Scholars in some other countries (Meisel, 1975; Thomassen, 1976) have questioned the utility of the concept of party identification in countries where it exhibits a strong tendency to change with vote or is *less* stable than voting behaviour over time.

As these comments suggest, the concept of party identification as originally formulated depends heavily on its relative stability over time. Clearly, in the American case, party identification is more stable than voting choice, whatever may be the other controversies surrounding its interpretation. In part this is because of the unique features of the American electoral system, which demand a number of voting decisions of the individual, and the wide swings which have occurred routinely in American presidential elections since 1964. The stability of partisanship in other countries, however, even in comparison with vote, is less certain. One difficulty in resolving this issue has been the absence of reliable measures of stability, which must normally be derived from panel data collected over more than one national election. Except in Britain, where panel studies have been conducted regularly since 1963, such studies are rare. Slowly, however, a

Source: *European Journal of Political Research* (1981) 9:257-68. Reprinted with permission of the publisher.

sufficient number of panel studies containing comparable measures is becoming available to permit the investigation of the stability of party identification and vote in a truly cross-national context. These studies can help to answer a number of questions, among them being the extent to which other countries exhibit a degree of stability in party identification relative to vote and to the extent to which the United States may in fact be a unique case with regard to the linkage between party identification and voting choice. Only by means of an analysis which includes a range of national cases can such questions be addressed.

Methods and Data

This analysis utilizes survey data from panel studies in four nations—Britain, Canada, the United States and the Netherlands. The criteria for selection of these studies were that they contain equivalent measures of party identification and that they contain non-recall information on individual voting behavior or vote intention collected at three separate time points. In the case of the Canadian and U.S.A. panels, data were collected at the time of three national elections (1974, 1979 and 1980 in Canada, and 1972, 1974, and 1976 in the United States).[1] In the British case, respondents were first interviewed in 1969 and then again following the general elections of 1970 and February 1974.[2] The Dutch panel was begun in 1970, and respondents were interviewed following the Second Chamber elections of 1971 and 1972.[3] Three of the panels are of approximately comparable length, while that for the Netherlands is somewhat shorter, a fact that may be kept in mind in interpreting degree and rates of change.

For purposes of this analysis, a common definition and measure of party identification is employed across the four studies. All of the studies utilize the American-style question to establish direction of party identification, although there are slight variations in question wording, a factor which could cause differences in the level of identification (Kaase, 1976): "Generally speaking, do you think of yourself as Conservative, Labour, Liberal, or what?" The American studies include the option "Independent" in the text of the question, while the others do not. The Dutch surveys use the term "adherent" and do not name the parties in the text of the question: "Do you usually think of yourself as an adherent of a certain party or not? (IF YES) Which party do you like best?" Nevertheless, the measures exhibit a high degree of similarity. Greater comparability can be obtained by imposing a uniform categorization across the studies. All four sets of surveys contain a probe for those respondents who classify themselves as Independents or who refuse a party identification to determine whether they "lean toward" or "feel closer to" any of the parties. In this analysis, all respondents indicating a partisan attachment on any of these measures or probes are classified as party identifiers. In the case of the American and Dutch studies, this reduces substantially the number of Independents and provides greater comparability with the British and Canadian surveys. It is also possible to construct a three-point intensity measure in each of the four countries, although the wording of the intensity question varies slightly among the four cases.

Following these uniform methods of classification, the distribution of party identification shown in Table 23-1 is obtained for the largest sample cross-section survey in each of the four series. The number of non-identifiers (including both self-described Independents and those indicating no party attachment) varies from

Table 23-1 The Structure of Party Identification in Four National Samples

(a) *Britain, Feb. 1974*
(N = 2394)

	Very strong	Fairly strong	Weak/leaning
Conservative	12	18	8
Labour	17	18	9
Liberal	2	7	5
Other[a]	1	1	x
None			4

(b) *Canada, 1974*
(N = 2343)

	Very strong	Fairly strong	Weak/leaning
Liberal	16	23	11
Progressive-Conservative	7	11	6
NDP	4	5	2
Social Credit	1	1	1
None			12

(c) *Netherlands, 1970*
(N = 1813)

	Strong	Not strong	Leaning
PvdA[b]	5	7	8
KVP[b]	6	7	5
VVD	2	3	6
D'66	1	3	7
ARP	2	3	2
CHU	2	2	2
All other	2	1	3
None			23

(d) *U.S.A., 1976*
(N = 2862)

	Strong	Weak	Ind./leaning
Democratic	15	24	12
Republican	11	15	8
Independent/None			15

[a] Includes Scottish National Party and Plaid Cymru.

[b] Includes scattering of mentions of party groupings.

x Less than 1%.

a high of 23% in the Netherlands to a low of 4% in Britain. The proportion of respondents reporting the strongest level of attachment possible within the limits of the survey questions varies from 18% in the Netherlands to 30% in Britain.[4] In both instances, Canada and the United States show a similar pattern and fall near the centre of the distribution. However, these national differences, which can easily be affected by question wording, need not greatly concern us, although they do serve to demonstrate the basic similarities across systems in the pattern of party identification when equivalent measures are employed. Of greater interest is the level of change across time indicated within each of the four national panels, which can be more reliably measured because the question itself is constant across all three waves in each country.

Measuring Change

We begin by examining turnover across a pair of elections by the tabular method most often employed for this purpose. Perhaps surprisingly, the over-all level of stability in the four nations is similar (Table 23-2), with Canada, the

Table 23-2 Turnover of Party Identification and Vote in Four Two-Wave Election Panels (diagonal percentages)

		(a) *Britain (1970-74)* *Vote*		(b) *Canada (1974-79)* *Vote*	
		stable	variable	stable	variable
Party Identification	stable	75	10	70	10
	variable	5	10	5	15
	N[b] =		*795*		*841*

		(c) *Netherlands (1971-72)* *Vote*		(d) *U.S.A. (1972-76)* *Vote*[a]	
		stable	variable	stable	variable
Party Identification	stable	71	4	71	22
	variable	7	18	4	3
	N[b] =		*449*		*539*

[a] For House of Representatives.

[b] Party identifiers and voters in both elections only.

Netherlands and the United States displaying virtually identical proportions of their respective electorates that are stable with respect to *both* party identification and vote across a pair of national elections. The proportion in Britain exhibiting such stability between the 1970 and February 1974 elections is slightly higher than in the other three cases, but exactly equal to the level found by Butler and Stokes for the 1963-66 period. In spite of the similarity in over-all patterns of stability among the four nations, the differing patterns of linkage between party identification and vote come through clearly in the comparison. Party identification in total (considering the upper left and upper right cells together) is more stable in the United States than in Britain, in spite of the greater over-all level of stability (upper left cell only) in the latter country. *Only* the United States among the four displays the classic pattern of partisan stability coupled with vote switching to any great extent, and this cell (upper right) accounts for most of the variation in the American case.[5] As Butler and Stokes observed in the 1963-66 comparison, there is a greater tendency for party identification to travel with vote in Britain compared with the United States, but there is an even greater such tendency in Canada and the Netherlands, a pattern which has been noted in both countries in single-national studies (Jenson, 1975; Thomassen, 1976).

The failure of any of the other three countries to exhibit the American pattern of stable partisanship and variable vote, coupled with the tendency there of partisanship to travel with vote to a greater extent than in the United States does much to illuminate the unique characteristics of the American electoral environment and the special role that party identification tends to play in that setting. Nevertheless, the comparisons of 2 x 2 patterns of party identification and vote shown in Table 23-2 are unsatisfactory for a number of reasons. Firstly, independents or non-identifiers are excluded from these comparisons, a fact which may be particularly significant in the Netherlands and the United States, both of these being party systems which contain many independents and/or "leaning" party identifiers. The movement over time of non-identifiers or marginal identifiers may be an important source of change in these systems and should be examined. Converse (1966b), for example, found that in the United States the proportion of respondents in the 1956-60 panel study moving between a party identification and independence was far greater than the percentage changing parties, and other analysts of American data such as Dobson and St. Angelo (1975) have routinely treated the movement of individuals between independence and identification as equivalent to partisan change. Further, the inclusion of all types of movement in the analysis helps to produce greater measurement equivalence for purposes of cross-national comparison. Cain and Ferejohn (1981) have shown that it is the inclusion of Liberal party identifiers in Britain in the analysis, combined with the exclusion of American independents, which accounts for the observed tendency of party identification to travel with vote in Britain to a greater extent than in the United States. Inclusion in the analysis of partisans and non-partisans alike in all countries will minimize the danger of conclusions which do not truly reflect national differences.

The same point may be made with regard to non-voting. In excluding non-voters from the analysis across pairs of elections as shown in Table 23-2, we arbitrarily eliminate a potentially important source of electoral change. In Canada, for example, Clarke *et al.* (1979) show that movement into and out of the electorate is as important a source of variation in both individual voting behaviour and in electoral outcomes as is direct switching of votes. In the United States, which exhibits substantially higher levels of non-voting than the other three countries, the exclusion of non-voters may mask an important source of change, just as is the case with partisan independents. In any case, given that differences in voting turnout exist among the four countries, the inclusion of both voters and non-voters represents the most clearly defensible comparative analytic strategy.

Finally, it may be noted that the simple two-election comparisons shown in Table 23-2, although useful for purposes of replication, do not take full advantage of available panel data. All of the studies employed in the analysis are three-wave panels, and two of these (Canada and the United States) contain data on voting behavior collected in three separate national elections. The British and Dutch panels, while containing only two election study waves, each contain a third initial wave of interviews with data on party identification and vote intention. The full use of the three-wave panels has a number of advantages, the most important of which is that it permits the investigation of multiple patterns of movement. A respondent who changes party identification, for example, may do so by means of first becoming an independent, for example, old party ——> non-identification ——> new party, a pattern which is suggestive of either a two-stage process of realignment or of general partisan disintegration. In contrast, the pattern old party ——> non-identification ——> old party, although it likewise involves a reported change in each wave, clearly suggests only a short-term disaffection from partisanship and is inconsistent with any hypothesized process of realignment or dealignment over time. In both cases, the two-wave panel will show simply a "change" while the three-wave panel will provide additional clues to the particular nature of that change. The same will hold true with regard to the linkage between non-voting and vote switching across a series of elections. A process in which certain individuals continually move into and out of the electorate but never switch votes is clearly different to one in which individuals switch frequently or in which non-voting and switching combine in various ways.

As is seen in Table 23-3, the inclusion of both non-voters and non-identifiers in the analysis and the use of all three panel waves provide considerable additional information on the movement of partisanship and vote across time in the four nations as well as a more reliable basis for cross-national comparison. Perhaps the most important single observation that can be made is that in all cases the proportion of national samples reporting a stable partisanship *and* vote over time (Table 23-3c) is sharply reduced. In the United States and the Netherlands, for example, it is only 33 percent, less than half the level suggested in Table 23-2. Even in Britain, which is the country showing the highest combined stability of partisanship and vote, the percentage reporting perfect stability falls to 47 percent. Clearly, partisan and electoral stability, measured and analysed in this manner, is considerably less in all four nations than would otherwise be supposed. However, the specific reasons differ quite dramatically in each case. In the United States, the greater instability is due primarily to the high incidence of non-voting in that country. The percentage of American voters who report an actual switch in votes over three elections is slightly lower than in the other three countries, and the percentage reporting an outright change in party

Table 23-3 Summary of Turnover in Party Identification and Vote in Four Three-Wave Panel Studies

	Britain *1969-70-74* (N = 421)	*Canada* *1974-79-80* (N = 791)	*Netherlands* *1970-71-72* (N = 711)	*U.S.A.* *1972-74-76* (N = 772)
(a) *Party identification*				
maintaining the same party identification in three panel waves	64%[a]	59%	36%	68%
changing party identification at least once	27	23	30	11
moving to or from non-identification[b]	12	22	42	24
(b) *Voting behaviour*[c]				
voting for the same party in three elections	51%	49%	49%	39%
switching at least once	33	33	34	30
abstaining at[d] least once	23	24	22	39
(c) *Percent reporting the same party identification AND vote in three panel waves*	47%	41%	33%	33%

[a] Multiple response. Percentages total to more than 100% because categories are not mutually exclusive.

[b] Including respondents who report non-identification in all three waves (Netherlands: 6%, U.S.A.: 4%, Canada: 3%, Britain: less than 1%).

[c] Congressional vote for the United States and Second Chamber vote for the Netherlands. The 1969 British wave and the 1970 Dutch wave are vote intention reports.

[d] But excluding those respondents who report not voting in all three elections. This makes a significant difference only in the case of the United States, in which 18% of the total sample are three time non-voters.

identification is markedly lower. But the very high rate of abstentions, coupled with the substantial degree of movement to non-identification across the panel, produces an electorate with a very high degree of discontinuity over time. In contrast the Netherlands, which shows equally high discontinuity, does not display unusually high rates either of vote switching or of abstention. Rather, the explanation in the Dutch case lies in the high level of movement to and from non-identification with parties. In part this reflects the tendency toward non-identification found in Dutch samples generally, although it should be noted that it is a dynamic rather than a static phenomenon. While 23 percent of the 1970 Dutch sample did not identify with any party (Table 23-1c), only 6 percent of the panel maintained a continuous position of non-identification across the three interviews, even though the period covered by the panel was little more than two years. This suggests that a party tie is more easily accepted and/or abandoned in the Netherlands than in the other three nations, perhaps, as the 2 x 2 comparison originally suggested, tending to travel with vote. Were it not for this high incidence of non-identification, the patterns of change in the Netherlands would be little different from those found in Canada or Britain.

The British case is distinguished by a slightly higher overall level of stability which is in turn brought about by the much lower tendency in Britain for respondents to move between partisanship and non-identification. The British sample contains the lowest proportion of independents at any single time point (Table 23-1a), and the number of respondents who maintain a position of non-identification continuously is negligible. Most British respondents report a party identification, even if not always the same one, throughout all three waves of the panel. The levels of partisan change, vote switching, and abstention in Britain are all comparable to those found in Canada and the Netherlands.

Canada, in some respects, represents the center of the distribution. Its overall level of partisan/vote stability is lower than in Britain, but higher than in the Netherlands or the United States. Levels of vote switching and abstention in Canada are comparable to those found in the other countries, and there is also substantial change in party identification and movement to and from non-identification across the three waves of the Canadian panel. Canada, like the other three nations, displays relatively high rates of change over this six-year period when all possible types of change are considered. Given that the Canadian federal party system is a relatively stable and enduring one, it is evident that its aggregate stability does not derive from any absence of change at the individual level. The same might generally be said of each of the four countries included in the analysis.

As noted earlier, it is possible to identify with three-wave panel data not only the levels of change as shown in Table 23-3 but also particular patterns of change. It is probably not possible over relatively short periods of time positively to isolate patterns of realignment or dealignment, but it is not difficult to identify certain patterns which are inconsistent with either of these phenomena. Respondents, for example, who abandon a party tie only to return to it a short time later are following a classic pattern of deviation, while those who do not return represent one of several possible patterns of positive change (realignment, dealignment, volatility, etc.). Where the change occurs in the second wave of the panel, it is possible to use the third wave to attempt to confirm the nature of that change. Where the change is observed in the third wave, no information exists which would permit more specific classification of the nature of the change. The same sort of scrutiny can be applied to changes in partisanship and in voting behaviour, except that in the latter case it is necessary to provide a specific rule for the classification of non-voters. An individual who follows the voting pattern "party A" ——> abstention ——> "party B" has a positive change pattern which might be associated with volatility or realignment, while one who follows the pattern "party A" ——> abstention ——> "party A" seems more likely to represent a classic mobilization/demobilization pattern than one of positive change. It is possible then to distinguish with some degree of reliability in the three-wave panels two distinctive types of movement in party identification (*deviation* and *positive change*) and three distinctive types of movement in voting behaviour (*deviation, positive change,* and *mobilization/demobilization*). A regrouping of the data to identify these types of patterns for the four nations is shown in Table 23-4.

Table 23-4 Specific Stability/Change Patterns in Partisanship and Vote in Four Three-Wave Panels (column percentages)

	Britain 1969-70-74 (N = 422)	*Canada* 1974-79-80 (N = 854)	*Netherlands* 1970-71-72 (N = 810)	*U.S.A.* 1972-74-76 (N = 784)
(a) *Party identification*				
no change	64%	59%	36%	68%
deviation (change followed by return to former party)	7	8	10	8
all positive change patterns[a]	16	25	38	15
indeterminate changes (third wave only)	12	8	16	9
(b) *Voting behaviour*[b]				
no change[c]	51%	49%	49%	39%
deviation (change followed by return to former party)	4	5	5	6
mobilization/demob. (one or more abstentions but no other positive change)[d]	15	16	15	31
all positive change patterns	20	24	21	15
indeterminate changes (third wave only)	10	6	10	9

[a] Includes continuous non-identifiers (Netherlands: 6%, U.S.A.: 4%, Canada: 3%, Britain: less than 1%).

[b] Congressional vote for the United States and Second Chamber vote for the Netherlands. The initial British and Dutch waves are vote intention reports.

[c] Respondents who report abstention in all three waves are excluded from the analysis.

[d] Including third-wave non-voters who report no other change.

In each of the four countries, a modest amount of the change in both party identification and voting behaviour over time is accounted for by deviation, i.e. a change followed by a return to the former party. In spite of this, a segment of the electorate in all four countries (Table 23-4b) falls into a pattern termed "positive change" with respect to electoral behavior, i.e. a change that might conceivably represent a pattern of realignment or dealignment of the electorate or that is at least a pattern of sustained volatility. The United States, however, stands out in two ways. It is, as noted earlier, the most stable country in terms of party identification and also shows the lowest incidence of "postive change" in voting behaviour as well as in party identification. Secondly, the high level of non-voting in the United States is manifested largely in a "mobilization/demobilization" pattern of electoral behaviour, i.e. movement into and out of the active electorate of persons whose behaviour is otherwise stable. At 31 percent (Table 23-4b), the

United States is substantially higher than any of the other countries in the number of respondents displaying this pattern. In part, this is because of the tendency of voting participation in the United States to decline sharply in the "off year" congressional election.

In both of the comparisons, it is evident that the American pattern of stable partisanship coupled with fluctuation in vote, while not unique to the United States, occurs much more frequently in that country than in any other. It is also evident that all countries, including the United States, exhibit significant changes over time in both voting behaviour and party identification when all possible types of change are taken into account. For the most part, such changes are "real" rather than mere lapses or temporary deviations in an otherwise stable pattern. Nevertheless, party identification is more stable than voting behaviour in all of the countries studied except the Netherlands, although it is only in the United States that it is a great deal more stable.

Party Identification as a Cross-Time Predictor

A useful way of summarizing these data and testing the efficacy of party identification in each of the four national cases is to measure its ability to predict behaviour over time. In theory, party identification as measured in the first wave of a panel study should be a good predictor of identification in subsequent waves. It should be a less efficient predictor of voting behaviour, although such correlations will be influenced by the extent to which party identification travels with vote as well as by the incidence of non-voting. It should not deteriorate over

Table 23-5 Predictive Ability of First-Wave Party Identification Across Three Wave Panels in Four Nations

	Vote			*Party Identification*	
	1st wave[a]	2nd wave	3rd wave	2nd wave	3rd wave
(a) Britain 1969-70-74	.66 (.72)	.47 (.67)	.45 (.56)	.61 (.70)	.53 (.59)
(b) Canada 1974-79-80	.54 (.77)	.38 (.52)	.35 (.50)	.43 (.58)	.44 (.60)
(c) Netherlands 1970-71-72	.72 (.90)	.47 (.65)	.40 (.55)	.42 (.67)	.40 (.51)
(d) U.S.A. (Congress) 1972-74-76	.29 (.58)	.14 (.51)	.24 (.45)	.56 (.80)	.58 (.79)
presidential vote 1972-76	.16 (.27)	—	.33 (.54)	—	—

[a] Vote intention for Britain and Netherlands.

Note: Asymmetric lambda coefficients for all panel cases in each wave. Lambda coefficients for analysis which excludes non-identifiers and non-voters shown in parentheses.

time with respect to either party identification or vote, to the extent that wavering voters or non-voters exhibit a "homing" tendency. A test of these suppositions may be found in Table 23-5, indicating the ability of party identification as measured in the first wave of the panels to predict party identification in the two subsequent waves and voting behaviour in all three waves. The statistic employed for this purpose is *lambda,* which indicates the proportionate reduction of error in prediction when the independent variable (in this case first-wave party identification) is known.[6]

As a predictor of party identification in subsequent waves, first-wave party identification functions significantly better in the United States than in the other three nations, with and without the inclusion of non-identifiers. Predictions are poorest for the Netherlands, and deteriorate significantly between the second and third waves when non-identifiers are included in the analysis, reflecting the high degree of movement in the Netherlands to and from non-identification. The correlations between first-wave party identification and vote, however, present an entirely different picture. The first-wave predictions are high in all cases *except* the United States, and exhibit significant deterioration across the three waves. The American predictions are much lower, even when non-voters and non-identifiers are excluded from the analysis. The correlation between party identification and vote in the 1972 U.S.A. presidential election is particularly low, suggesting the deviant nature of that election. In 1976, however, the correlation *rises* to .54 for identifiers and voters, a level about equal to that of the other three countries. Even for congressional voting, the deterioration across the three panel waves is less for the United States than for the other countries.

The general pattern of high correlations between party identification in subsequent panel waves and low correlation between party identification and vote is that which is most easily associated with the American electoral and party system, and it is noteworthy that it is only the United States which persistently exhibits this pattern. In the other cases, the tendency of party identification to travel with vote produces high initial correlations but rapid deterioration as the various types of movement documented earlier begin to disrupt the predictive power of first-wave identification.

Conclusion

It would be an overstatement to conclude from these analyses that party identification in the sense of an enduring psychological tie to a party is inapplicable outside the United States. Certainly, the electorates of all of the countries examined here contain a mix of partisan types, some of whom will conform very well to a classic reference group model of partisanship.[7] But there are two broad conclusions that are inescapable when the classic concept of party identification is re-examined in a cross-time, cross-national context. First is the fact that all electorates, including that of the United States, display a substantial amount of change over relatively short periods of time when all possible types of change are taken into account. While a considerable amount of this change is to non-identification and/or non-voting, a not insignificant amount in all cases, and a quite substantial amount in the case of Canada and the Netherlands, is of a "positive" quality, suggesting a continuing dynamic rather than a kind of "steady state." While the level of instability of party identification exceeds that of vote only in the case of the Netherlands, the level of instability in both is substantial in all of the cases examined.

Secondly, it should be noted that the American electoral environment appears to be unique in its ability to combine stable party identification with instability of vote, a phenomenon observed in no other case. The concept of party identification, which presumes such a combination as the norm, thus functions much more effectively in the United States than in systems where it displays a marked tendency to travel with the vote rather than to be independent of it. This conclusion is substantiated by the properties of party identification as a cross-time predictor in each of the countries examined here. Although there have been different interpretations regarding the stability of party identification over time in the United States, when statistics measuring cross-time stability of party identification and vote in the United States are examined alongside those for other countries, the unique aspects of the American relationship become more clearly evident.[8]

There is, of course, every reason why this should be expected. Budge and Farlie (1976), for example, found that party identification in the United States behaved in a unique manner in comparison with nine other nations when tested against socioeconomic characteristics as a predictor of vote. It is also often noted that the United States exhibits a larger number of unique institutional characteristics (frequent elections, long ballots, independent executive and legislature) and behavioural ones (low turnout, ticket splitting, etc.). To date, much of the research on party identification has been time-bound and nation-bound, limited to information collected in a single nation at a single point in time. As panel data have become available, the dynamic properties of party identification have become more evident and have engendered debate regarding its utility in electoral research. So, too, the availability of comparable data for a number of nations has permitted new interpretations of the concept and its properties. But such findings do not in themselves challenge the validity and theoretical power of the party identification construct. Rather, they permit greater refinement of the concept and a deeper understanding of political environments. It is only through such comparative and longitudinal inquiry that this understanding is possible.

NOTES

1. The Canadian election studies were conducted by Harold Clarke, Jane Jenson, Lawrence LeDuc and Jon Pammett and financed by the Social Sciences and Humanities Research Council of Canada. The co-investigators are not responsible for the analysis and interpretation of the data presented here. The 1972-74-76 U.S. Panel Study was conducted by the Center for Political Studies, University of Michigan, and made available by the Inter-University Consortium for Political Research and the S.S.R.C. Survey Archive, University of Essex. Neither the principal investigators nor the archives are responsible for the analysis or interpretations presented here. The author is grateful to Mr. Eric Roughley of the S.S.R.C. Survey Archive, University of Essex, for his assistance in subsetting these data.

2. The 1969 and 1970 waves of the British Election Study were conducted by David Butler and Donald Stokes, and the February 1974 wave was conducted by Ivor Crewe and Bo Särlvik. The data were made available to the author by the S.S.R.C. Survey Archive, University of Essex. Neither the principal investigators nor the archives are responsible for the analysis or interpretations presented here.
3. The 1970-73 Dutch Election Study was conducted by Felix Heunks, M. Kent Jennings, Warren Miller, Philip Stouthard, and Jacques Thomassen. The data were made available to the author by the Inter-University Consortium for Political Research and the S.S.R.C. Survey Archive. Neither the principal investigators nor the archives are responsible for the analysis or interpretations presented here.
4. These percentages are not identical to those derived by summation of Table 23-1 due to rounding.
5. If presidential vote rather than congressional vote is used the pattern holds, but the percentage reporting the same party identification and vote is slightly lower (68%). The other cells vary from those shown in Table 23-2d by only 1% in each case.
6. *Lambda* is suitable for use with nominal scale data and its value is not affected by the number of categories (i.e. number of parties). Its upper limit is 1. See Mueller *et al.* (1970, 249-56).
7. A detailed attempt to partition the Canadian electorate in these terms may be found in Clarke *et al.* (1979, 301-19).
8. A thorough review of this literature, together with an analysis of the American panel data, may be found in Converse (1976).

24. PARTY IDENTIFICATION IN WEST GERMANY: TRACING AN ELUSIVE CONCEPT

Helmut Norpoth

To pursue a concept abroad whose value is questioned at home must look like an odd venture. In the land of its creation, i.e., the United States, the notion of "party identification" is increasingly challenged as a guide to electoral behavior. The "end of party politics" has been proclaimed (Burnham, 1969, 1970), with popular attachments to the parties said to be eroding, voting defections from party loyalty to be massive, and young voters to be refusing the party label (Miller et al., 1976). A focus on issues is seen replacing the partisan focus in electoral decision-making (Nie et al., 1976).

Germany, at the same time, would seem ill-prepared for the widespread adoption of party identification. The collapse of the Weimar Republic in the late 1920s and early 1930s and the subsequent Nazi regime severely disrupted both democratic and partisan continuity in Germany. The opportunities for parties and voters to form lasting ties with each other were minimal during these years. A strong undercurrent of antipathy as well as antidemocratic feelings predating the Nazi era, and not entirely gone with it, has further blocked the rise of positive ties between voters and parties in contemporary West Germany.

But apart from the generation most immediately affected by those events and currents, the German electorate, especially voters raised after World War II, have been exposed recently to a political and partisan climate which seems most conducive to the spread of party identification. There are several symptoms pointing in that direction: (1) the high partisan continuity in postwar Germany. Two parties, i.e., the Christian Democrats (CDU/CSU) and the Social Democrats (SPD), have come to dominate the electoral scene since the early 1950s, thereby restricting the partisan "attention span" of the electorate essentially to

---

Author's Note: This article is an expanded version of a paper originally presented at the Southern Political Science Meeting in Nashville, Tennessee, November 6-8, 1975. For any improvement of this version over previous ones I am indebted to Philip Converse, Kai Hildebrandt, Thomas Herz, Jerrold Rusk, Fred Greenstein, and the two anonymous referees as well as the editor. The secretarial and data management assistance of the Zentralarchiv für empirische Sozialforschung in Cologne are also gratefully acknowledged.

Source: *Comparative Political Studies* (1978) 11:36-59. Reprinted with permission of the publisher.

these objects. (2) The high voting stability: the share of the vote of each major party since 1953 has changed by only small amounts between two successive elections (3.1%, on the average, for the CDU/CSU and 3.4% for the SPD). Much of this aggregate stability rests on the steadiness of individual voting decisions, as revealed by the large proportion (70% and more) of voters who say they "always vote that way."[1] When marking their ballots most Germans prove habitual party voters. (3) The transmission of partisan cues within the family, or at least a high degree of partisan transparence within it: about 55% of German voters are able to recall the party their father usually voted for when they were growing up.[2] Family transmission of partisanship, as may be expected, works best among the postwar generation whose share of the population of course, is growing at the expense of that of the older cohorts.

None of these symptoms in any way proves the existence of party identification. Point two may not even rate as a necessary condition for it, since wide fluctuations of vote outcomes do not contradict this notion. But at least it hints at a high degree of partisan acclimatization among the electorate. The combination of points one and three, in turn, create a strong presumption in favor of party identification. In their comparision of American and French electorates, Converse and Dupeux (1962: 279-283) confirm the crucial role of the family as creator of partisan ties. The weak party attachment found in the French public is derived from the failure of French parents to transmit partisan cues to their children, with additional blame falling on the ever-shifting world of French party politics.

The Concept and Significance of Party Identification

"Party identification" in the American context refers to a durable personal tie of a voter to one of the existing political parties (Campbell et al., 1960: 120-168). Being a Democrat or a Republican is part of one's personal identity, a trait of almost life-long quality. Such an identification serves an individual in many ways (Miller, 1976). For one, it provides for an orientation in the changing world of political issues and events. The party an individual identifies with acts as a "reference group" whose norms and positions one can adopt as one's own. This attachment cuts the enormous costs of political information to be borne by the individual voter. By developing positions on political issues, a party aids a voter with the chore of reaching his own position. Party identification has been said to take the place of a fully elaborated political ideology (Hyman, 1959: 35). Moreover, a partisan attachment may guide the individual's evaluation of political candidates and leaders in office. In short, an enduring sense of partisanship supplies an individual with an invaluable cognitive-evaluative guide to the world of politics. As a result of this persuasive assistance, an individual's voting choice at the polls reveals the mark of the partisan stamp. To be sure, not every voter will always obey his partisan "conscience." Certain events and issues may prompt many a voter to view with greater favor the opposite party and its candidates. But even though he may vote for the opposite party, he typically maintains his long-term allegiance. He is capable of distinguishing between his momentary act of preferring another party and the enduring tie to his traditional party.

For the analyst of electoral choice, the concept of party identification is of extreme value because it allows him to disentangle the influence on such choice due to short-run forces unique to a specific election as opposed to long-term forces. The "normal vote" concept, a derivative of party identification, spells out the expected partisan choice of the electorate for any election (Converse, 1966c). This would be an election in which the short-term partisan forces are balanced. By noting the deviation of the actual vote outcome from the normal vote expectation and by relating these deviations to exogenous variables, the analyst can pinpoint the effects of various short-term factors and better grasp the meaning of the electoral "mandate" (Boyd, 1972; Miller et al., 1976).

Aside from creating a standing division within the electorate, party loyalties help assure the stability of the political system. Both the extent to which partisan roots are planted in the electorate and the depth of their reach vitally affect the viability of the system (Converse, 1969). Wherever these roots are weakly or sparsely planted, new parties will find it easy to plant their seeds and disrupt, if that is their goal, the existing political system. The electoral surge of the Nazi party in the Weimar Republic would be hard to imagine in an electorate with pervasive and strong attachments to established political parties. This is not to suggest that partisan attachments would have stemmed the Nazi seizure of power, but the apparent lack of such attachments among wide segments of the electorate augured poorly for the survival of the fledgling Republic in times of severe stress. The question of whether the German electorate after World War II developed durable ties to their parties is, therefore, of more than merely scientific interest.

The Adoption of Party Identification in Europe: Reservations and Confusion

In spite of its theoretical and analytical appeal, the concept of party identification has left many European analysts of voting unconvinced of its value. Measurement difficulties have done their share to strengthen the barrier raised against its adoption. No study, however, can claim to have compellingly disproven its significance, nor has any confirmed it, at least not for the German electorate.

Is It Meaningful?

In questioning the utility of the party identification concept, most European analysts base their opposition on the salience of social, especially class, identifications (e.g., Thomassen, 1976: 77-78; Kaase, 1976: 82-83). The party systems and voter alignments in European politics, unlike that of the United States, are said to have evolved out of deep social cleavages and have been likened to "frozen" landscapes (Lipset and Rokkan, 1967b). The electorates in European societies are segmented into "zuils" (pillars) or "Läger" (camps), to use some native terms, i.e., distinct social milieus with respective organizations as well as ideologies. The political party is just one of the objects within the horizon of a given milieu. But it is neither the most salient one, nor is the latter irrevocably tied to any specific party. Such a model of voter alignments does not require a partisan tie independent of the attachment to the social milieu. Partisan loyalties, though they may flourish in an electorate of that kind, are closely embedded in class-related affiliations (Campbell and Valen, 1961: 267-268).

These social affiliations alone are said to account admirably for electoral stability, provided the voting shares of parties with similar social clienteles are aggregated (Shively, 1972: 1220-1222). Witness in most European countries the fairly constant share of the proletarian parties (Socialists and Communists), on one hand, and that of the bourgeois parties, on the other! Whereas the partisan orientations of voters undergo change, the social orientations remain largely immutable.

While sociostructural determinants may deserve heavy stress in interpreting voting in Europe, it would be highly misleading to imply that party identification in the United States is "class blind" or neutral with regard to social groups. Lazarsfeld et al.'s (1948: chap. 3) attempt at capturing partisanship relied solely on social criteria ("index of political predisposition"). Campbell et al. (1960: chaps. 12 and 13) explored the linkage, however variable, between class and group identification, on one hand, and the party tie, on the other. The social traces may be weaker than in European politics and their impact more dependent on the peculiar circumstances of a given election, but they are not negligible in the American electorate.

Present-day Germany, in turn, presents by no means a model case for sharp social cleavages. In terms of the social cohesion of mass support for the major parties, she ranked near the bottom among Western politics during the middle 1960s (Rose and Urwin, 1969). If anything, this cohesion has weakened since then (Baker et al., 1975; for a dissent, see Pappi, 1976: 22-23).

A caveat of a different sort with respect to party identification in Europe has been voiced by Butler and Stokes (1969: 43), who otherwise are highly supportive of the concept's merits. Their reservation concerns the "prompting" of the partisan attachment through the electoral system, especially the frequency and complexity of electoral contests. On election day the voter in Europe is typically faced with candidates for a single office. He has no way of separately expressing his chancellor preference and his preference for a local representative, assuming they are in conflict. As a result, he is less likely than his American counterpart to grasp the distinction between voting for a party's candidate and being tied to a party in general. He will be inclined to equate the two preferences, thus making the durable component of his choice difficult to disentangle from the momentary one.

Does It Exist?

The conceptual unease of many analysts about "party identification" in the German context is reinforced by a flow of results suggesting that this attitude is neither widespread nor stable across time nor distinguishable from voting choice (Kaase, 1976; Radtke, 1972; Schleth and Weede, 1971). Although noting a host of resemblances between the state of party identification in Germany and the United States, Zohlnhöfer (1965: 158) questions the independent influence on voting choice exercised by party identification in Germany.

Some of these findings, however, are based on measurements of party identification which are not strictly comparable across time, others rely on single cross-sectional surveys and others are simply speculations, however plausible.

The evidence against party identification in Germany presented so far is by no means overwhelming. For a more sanguine, if regionally limited assessment, see Falter (1977).

How to Measure It?

This issue has remained unsettled largely because of difficulties in operationalizing and measuring the central concept. This stands in marked contrast to the ease with which this attitude has been ascertained in the American electorate. Depending on seemingly slight discrepancies in the wording of the question, the results obtained from German respondents are vastly different. Finding the proper translation of "identification" has proved an especially vexing problem. When survey respondents in Germany were queried about whether or not they considered themselves as *Anhanger* (adherent) of one particular party—without party labels being provided as a cue—less than 30% professed an identification of this kind; but when the question included the party labels, slightly over one-half of the respondents named a party tie in one instance (Kaase, 1976: 86-87) and two-thirds did so in another one (Falter, 1977)..

While the suggestion of party cues boosts the overall response figure, the notion of "adherence" still sets a very high hurdle. It appears that adherence captures those partisans whose loyalties are confirmed beyond doubt and who would find it immensely difficult, if not impossible, to vote contrary to their attachment. Such a commitment seems stronger than that implied by the American concept of party identification. By the same token, the question which asks the respondent to name the party "he likes best"—eliciting a positive response from over three-fourths of the electorate—aims too low (Zohlnhöfer, 1965: 133).

A compromise course was pursued by Berger (1973), whose instrument explicitly referred to the tie as having to be durable while allowing for the possibility of occasional deviations from the professed allegiance.[3] This "functional equivalence" approach seems best suited to tap—or trap—party identification in a country like Germany where the literal translation of the American question would confound party membership and subjective identity.

The Plan of the Paper

This paper focuses on three key aspects of party identification in West Germany which thus far have eluded a firm assessment. One of them is the temporal stability of this attitude. If what passes as party identification in interview situations shifts from time to time, clearly something other than durable identification has been ascertained. A second feature of the concept in need of support is its imperturbability in the face of changing vote choices. Perfect harmony between the latter and professed party identification is highly suspect. The third concern of this paper deals with the development of partisan intensity through the life-cycle. Does partisanship harden with the accumulation of electoral experience? The data for the subsequent analysis came from a panel survey conducted in 1972 during the federal election campaign and afterwards.[4] The measure of party identification is the one referred to above (Berger, 1973).

Turnover and Stability of Party Identification

Since the respondents to the 1972 survey were asked about their partisan leanings on three separate occasions, some measure of the stability of this attitude can be obtained. Longer time intervals between interviews, of course, would be required for reaching more definitive conclusions about its long-term stability. The amount and nature of short-term turnover, nevertheless, can tell us a great deal about what to expect in the long run.

Table 24-1 presents the partisanship turnover between successive waves of the 1972 panel. The reports of party identification reveal a high mark of stability

Table 24-1 Turnover of Reported Party Identification: September, October, December, 1972

a) September-October (t_1-t_2)

		t_2 SPD	No Party	CDU/CSU	Total	
t_1	SPD	45.2	3.2	0.6	49.1	
	No Party	6.9	10.5	3.3	20.7	
	CDU/CSU	1.7	3.0	25.5	30.2	N = 990
	Total	53.8	16.7	29.4	100.0%	tau-b = .785

b) October-December (t_2-t_3)

		t_3 SPD	No Party	CDU/CSU	Total	
t_2	SPD	48.6	3.8	1.4	53.8	
	No Party	3.7	10.0	3.0	16.7	
	CDU/CSU	1.3	2.6	25.6	29.4	N = 990
	Total	53.6	16.4	30.0	100.0%	tau-b = .808

c) September-December (t_1-t_3)

		t_3 SPD	No Party	CDU/CSU	Total	
t_1	SPD	44.4	3.1	1.5	49.1	
	No Party	7.2	9.8	3.6	20.7	
	CDU/CSU	1.9	3.5	24.8	30.2	N = 990
	Total	53.6	16.4	30.0	100.0%	tau-b = .751

across time, at least in the short run. Well over 80 percent of the respondents included in the analysis remain steady in their partisanship or their lack of it.[5] Not more than a handful cross over the partisan boundaries between Christians and Social Democrats; 2.3 percent in the first time interval and 2.7 percent in the second.

Just about the only turnover of any visibility occurs between the partisan territories and the partisan no-man's-land in between. Movement away from party does not typically run beyond this no-party land. Many movers return to their party on second thoughts—one of every two, to be precise—and roughly an equal proportion decides to stay. Hardly anyone, therefore, moves on toward a new partisan home: only four of thirty-two respondents among the Social Democrats and one of the thirty among the Christian Democrats do so. Even though some of the defectors from party decide to stay in the partisan no-man's-land, that territory loses between 40 and 50 percent of its population during any given time interval; it cannot count on many permanent residents. The steady independent is as much a stranger in the German political culture as is true for Britain (Butler and Stokes, 1969: 43).

While Table 24-1 has testified to the high stability of partisanship in the short run, it has also revealed some traces of change. The question is whether the observed turnover stems from a true change of mind or whether it must be written off as error. By "error" is meant not so much unreliable measurement, i.e., a property of the instrument, as the response of an individual holding no attitude but professing one nevertheless. Both types of error manifest themselves in change once subjects are queried repeatedly, even though no subject has changed his true position. The notion of party identification offers ample opportunity for respondents to commit errors. An individual lacking a lasting party tie may confuse a momentary preference for a party with long-term allegiance. On the other hand, someone truly holding a long-term attachment to a party should be nearly immune to change. How much of the observed turnover in partisanship, then, belongs to the realm of error and how much to that of genuine change?

Several models have been designed to untangle the amalgam of error and true change, e.g., the "black-and-white" model proposed by Converse (1970), separating stayers (no true change) from movers (random change), or Wiggins' (1973) family of latent structure models allowing for unsystematic (true) change as well as response error. Coleman (1964) introduced a model designed to tap systematic (true) change overlaid by "response uncertainty" (error).[6] This model seems best suited for dealing with turnover in partisanship, for it addresses itself to situations where turnover is neither entirely due to error nor entirely generated by systematic (true) change, but rather is due to a mix of the two.

Change and Response Uncertainty: The Coleman Model

One of the basic assumptions of Coleman's model states that true change follows the rule of a first-order Markov chain. This process implies a constant rate of change across time where the probability of taking a certain position at one time depends only on the position taken at the previous time point (Kemeny et al., 1966: 194-201, 271-291). Stands taken before that time point may show an affinity with one's current stand, but the partial weight of those remote events sinks to zero once the immediately previous position is held constant.

A Markov chain model seems to do great violence to most observed turnovers. Few transitions hew to such a regular pattern over time. The turnover of partisanship, however, seems to be an instance where Markov chains have held (Anderson, 1954; Goodman, 1962; Dobson and Meeter, 1974). In any event, the Coleman model does not tie observed turnover with a Markov chain. It fully recognizes the "random" component of response which makes for non-Markovian change.

Under strict Markovian conditions the turnover from t_1 to t_3—spanning two time intervals—is predicted to be the product of the two separate transitions from t_1 to t_2 and from t_2 to t_3. In the notion of correlations this reads:

$$r_{13} = r_{12}\, r_{23} \text{ (Markov condition).}$$

This equality implies a zero partial, $r_{13 \cdot 2}$, for if r_{13} is equal to the product of r_{12} and r_{23}, the difference between r_{13} and $r_{12}r_{23}$, i.e., the numerator of the partial r, goes to zero. The pure-error model, on the other hand, assumes that turnover between t_1 and t_3 is no more than that between t_1 and t_2, or between t_2 and t_3. Thus, in terms of correlations:

$$r_{13} = r_{12} = r_{23} \text{ (Error condition).}$$

It is quite apparent that the patterns of turnover often fall into the zone right between these extremes. The measured correlation $\hat{r}_{13}$ exceeds the Markovian prediction, but falls short of the error prediction:

$$\hat{r}_{13} > (\hat{r}_{12}\hat{r}_{23})$$

$$\hat{r}_{13} < \hat{r}_{12},\ \hat{r}_{13} < \hat{r}_{23}.$$

In the case at hand (using tau-b as correlation coefficient), the $t_1 - t_2$ correlation (.751) far exceeds the Markovian prediction of .634, i.e., the product of the $t_1 - t_2$ and $t_2 - t_3$ correlations (.785, .808), yet falls below each of the latter two coefficients. The turnover in reported partisanship thus fits Coleman's "empirical regularity."

Coleman suggests that such an instance exhibits a Markovian process whose traces are diluted, though still being recognizable, by response error. In order to see how this model uncovers the transition probabilities of the Markovian process, let us designate the table of observed transition proportions from t_1 to t_2 (Table 24-1a) as P(1,2), that for the $t_2 - t_3$ turnover (Table 24-1b) as P(2,3), and that for the $t_1 - t_3$ turnover (Table 24-1c) as P(1,3).[7] If a Markov chain governs the change process, a matrix of as yet unknown transition probabilities, R, must exist which connects the $t_1 - t_2$ turnover with the $t_1 - t_3$ turnover, according to the rule:

$$P(1,3) = P\,(1,2) \cdot R. \quad [1]$$

That is to say, each observed proportion of the $t_1 - t_3$ turnover is decomposed into observed $t_1 - t_2$ turnover proportions, each of them being weighted by the respective transition probability r_{ij} (no kin of the correlation coefficient). For example, assuming three possible states, the observed turnover from state 1 at t_1 to state 2 at t_3 ($p_{1,2}$) would be expressed as:

$$p_{1,2} = p_{11}r_{12} + p_{12}r_{22} + p_{13}r_{32}.$$

Expression 1 can be solved for R, the matrix of the unknown transition probabilities:

$$R = P(1,2)^{-1}\ P(1,3), \quad [2]$$

and thus yields estimates for the probabilities of Markovian change. Should no Markovian process underly the turnover—with error stripped away—the estimates for some transitions will lie outside the acceptable boundaries of zero and one. To be sure, such transition estimates cannot be distilled out of any set of turnover tables with the aid of Coleman's procedure.

Since the hypothesis regarding long-term party allegiance states that hardly any true change should be at work in the short-run, I would expect a near identity matrix to emerge from the estimates. That this is very much the case can be seen from inspection of Table 24-2. The values in the main diagonal approximate 1.0 and the values in the off-diagonal cells are miniscule by comparison. True change, assumed to be Markovian in nature, is barely visible. This conclusion, of course, applies only to behavior which has been freed of error. When the latter intrudes, turnover becomes conspicuous.

Response certainty, the obverse of error, is defined by the model in terms of test-retest reliability, with the time interval between test and retest shrunk to zero. One postulates a table of instant turnover P(1,1) and applies the same logic to it as was used in expression 1. Thus one obtains:

$$P(1,2) = P(1,1) \cdot R \quad [3]$$

or, after solving for P(1,1):

$$P(1,1) = P(1,2) \cdot R^{-1} \quad [4]$$

Since R, the matrix of transition probabilities, has been estimated already by expression 2, estimates for response uncertainty P(1,1) can now be obtained.

These "reliability" coefficients testify to a high level of certainty for the partisan responses (.938 for SPD and .864 for CDU/CSU). Individuals disposed toward one of these two parties do not waver much in their response. The nonpartisan group, however, with a relatively low value of .545, finds it difficult to stay true to its independent faith. They are a highly volatile group of voters, neither at home in one of the partisan states nor content with independence. If they are seen moving to a partisan side they rarely move for good; witness their

Table 24-2 Transition Probabilities for Party Identification

			t + 1		
		SPD	No Party	CDU/CSU	Total
	SPD	.979	.003	.018	1.000
t	No Party	.041	.923	.035	1.000
	CDU/CSU	.004	.025	.971	1.000

Table 24-3 Coefficients of Response Reliability

	SPD	No Party	CDU/CSU	Total
SPD	.938	.106	−.009	1.035
No Party	.208	.545	.112	.865
CDU/CSU	.040	.103	.864	1.007
Total	1.186	.754	.967	2.907

low values for both transition probabilities and reliability of response! The observed turnover in partisanship thus stems largely from the partisan uncertainty of this group. With uncertainty removed, hardly any change shows up any more and party allegiance proves remarkably steady.[8]

Party Identification Versus Voting Preference

Often times the goodness of reported party identification is questioned when these reports are compared with the stated voting preference. What at first glance may greatly please the observer, namely that the former so well predicts the latter, turns out on closer inspection to be an artifact. Reported party identification is found to vary in tandem with current voting preference; the former registers short-term perturbations as much as the latter. This is the message conveyed by the analyses of Schleth and Weede (1971) as well as Radtke (1972) and Thomassen (1976). A thorough probe of the distinctiveness of party identification vis-à-vis current preference is thus indispensable in order to be able to rule out the "artifact" hypothesis.

The congruence between the reported party identification and voting choice in 1972 is strong, as can be gleaned from Table 24-4. Social Democrats as well as Christian Democrats vote in large number for their respective party lists (second vote), but this fidelity diminishes as the attachment weakens. Within the "weak" columns, one of eight identifiers defect to the opposite party. Defection to the third party, the FDP, while virtually nil among Christian Democrats, also increases with weakening attachment among Social Democrats. This case of defection, however, must be regarded more benignly since FDP and SPD in 1972 ran on a coalition platform, determined to keep governing together after the election.

Is Identification More Stable Than Voting Choice?

The finding that voting fidelity and intensity of reported party identification go hand in hand is a sign of the distinct nature of party identification. But it is not a conclusive one, for one could also expect such a rapport to occur if reported party identification simply tapped a person's momentary partisan preference; the stronger this short-term preference, the more likely a congruent behavior. What is needed is a comparison between the stability of reported party identification and

Table 24-4 Party Identification and Voting Choice, 1972

	Party Identification						
	Social Democrat				*Christian Democrat*		
Voting Choice[a]	Strong	Moderate	Weak	*No Party*	Weak	Moderate	Strong
SPD	93.7	86.9	79.0	53.4	12.9	9.8	2.6
FDP	3.5	7.6	9.3	17.5	0.9	2.2	0.0
CDU/CSU	2.8	5.5	11.7	29.1	86.2	88.0	97.4
Total	100.0%	100.0%	100.0%	100.0%	100.0%	100.0%	100.0%
(N)	(129)	(243)	(117)	(209)	(98)	(130)	(73)

[a] A respondent's *Zweitstimme*, i.e., his vote on the party lists, was used.

voting choice. Lacking data on more than one election, voting intention is substituted for actual choice in the two preelection waves. Across three waves a large variety of turnover patterns can occur, involving party identification and voting preference. Those patterns have been grouped into four types according to a scheme introduced by Butler and Stokes (1969: 41).

It can be gathered from Table 24-5 that both identification and preference are steady in 82.3 percent of the cases, an astonishing figure which, of course, owes much to the short time span covered by the panel. The opposite corner of the table, with 4.3 percent, reveals the miniscule size of that group of voters who shift on both counts. Our interest focuses on the two remaining cells. What is most crucial, on one hand, is the extent to which respondents vary in their voting preference while remaining steadfast in their identification. One of ten voters (10.2 percent) fit that description. On the other hand, there are 3.2 percent who maintain their short-term preference while altering their presumedly long-term partisan affiliation. Surely, with a ratio of 3 to 1, the professed party identification must rate as more durable than the reported voting preference. What a respondent reveals as his party identification is not just a reflection of a momentary partisan preference. With its 3-1 ratio Germany ranks well below the United States, who has enjoyed a long and uninterrupted voting history and a perennial two-party system, its ratio being 8-1 (Butler and Stokes, 1969: 41-42). But Germany seems to qualify for the same league as Britain (2-1 ratio), whose voting history is shorter and whose present two-party system younger than in the American case. The West German electorate, moreover, places well above the fragmented Dutch electorate whose behavior poses an intriguing puzzle: far more voters report stable voting choices along with shifting identification than report stable identification along with variable voting choices (Thomassen, 1976: 71).

A Puzzle and Its Solution

Before leaping to any conclusions about the effect of two-party versus multiparty systems, or of deep versus moderate social cleavages on the develop-

Table 24-5 Stability of Identification and Voting Preference, 1972

		Voting Preference		
		stable	variable	
Party Identification	stable	82.3	10.2	92.5
	variable	3.2	4.3	7.5
		85.5	14.5	100.0% (N = 653)

[a] The base of this table consists of respondents indicating an identification with a party and a voting preference in all three panel waves.

ment of durable partisanship, it should be noted that the German analysis was restricted to respondents who professed an identification with one of the parties at each of the three time points. This decision excluded from consideration a sizeable bloc of voters who on one occasion or another professed no party leanings.[9] Rather than dropping an old party tie or adopting a new one, these are voters who simply waver between an attachment to a party and no attachment; they exhibit high "response uncertainty" about their long-term allegiance. Once this group of voters is included in the analysis the ranks in the two bottom cells to Table 24-5 swell immediately, especially those in the southwest corner. The "vote: stable-identification: variable" group now outnumbers the "identification: stable-vote: variable" group, thus posing the same puzzle as Thomassen's (1976) analysis; namely that short-term voting preference proves more stable than long-term party identification. The resolution of this puzzle, as far as the German electorate is concerned, seems to hinge on those voters who were found wavering between a tie to a party and independence. Many of these voters manage to hold on to the same voting choice in the short-run, their lack of a long-term commitment notwithstanding. It would seem advisable to place these voters into the "no party" bracket and not confuse their volatile response to the identification question with change in long-term leanings. They simply have none.

The puzzle posed by the behavior of this group seems responsible for the ease with which many observers have dismissed the concept of party identification altogether. But this is like throwing the baby out with the bathwater. In fact, once the bathwater is thrown out the baby very much behaves as the model tells it to behave. The short time perspective of the panel at hand, nevertheless, requires a note of caution. Since the days of Lazarsfeld's (1948) voting studies, it is a commonplace that little change typically occurs during the few months preceding an election as compared to the long period between two elections. Many attitudes and perceptions have become firmly established and many decisions have been reached long before election day and largely remain that way until events, issues, and other conditions arising after that date begin to challenge those attitudes and decisions. What appears tied together during the few campaign months may come untangled in the long interval between two elections. Thus, a study conducted during the campaign months may gravely overestimate the extent of stability. On the other hand, voters are never more intensely bombarded by political stimuli and more concerned with politics to prompt many a voter to reexamine convictions held. During the period of observation in 1972, 63 percent of German voters held on to the same party attachments, 7 percent stood firm as independents (no party), and the remainder vacillated between a partisan attachment and no attachment. For some voters with stable party leanings, that stability may rest on nothing more than the same factors prompting their voting choice in 1972. If so, one would expect this type of voter to alter his allegedly long-term allegiance as new considerations arise which motivate a different voting choice. Yet there remains a vast proportion whose steady partisanship will resist such a challenge, bearing out a partisan commitment whose strength may depend on the degree of one's electoral experience.

The Strength of the Partisan Tie and the Life-Cycle

The psychological tie between a voter and a party varies greatly in strength among individuals in the electorate, with predictable consequences for their behavior. Some voters are so firmly entrenched in their partisan loyalty as to preclude any thought of voting for another party, whereas the sense of partisan belonging among other voters is so feeble that they are easily swayed by another party. In the aggregate, the level of partisan strength of an electorate is a tell-tale of the viability of the political system. Where this level is high, competition for power is restricted to the established parties, where it is low, new—and possibly disruptive—parties are provided easy access.

The strength of the partisan tie, this can be safely said for both the American and British electorates, increases in response to electoral participation (Campbell et al., 1960: 161-165; Butler and Stokes, 1969: 55-59). Older voters are said to exhibit a stronger party tie than younger voters because they have accumulated more voting experience. Is this true for partisanship within the German electorate as well?

The Nazi Legacy

The twin fact that democratic rule was abolished by the Nazis and that the German party system was significantly altered in the postwar era has severely hampered the smooth growth of partisan strength. A fairly ragged temporal sequence should be expected. Thus, cohorts coming of age politically at a time lacking electoral and party competition (1933-1945) should not outdo in partisan strength those younger cohorts whose entry into the electorate coincided with the reestablishment of the party system after 1945. Figure 24-1 plots the mean strength values for 11 age cohorts, calculated separately for male and female respondents.[10] Among males, the regular decline of the curve to be expected under normal conditions is interrupted at a crucial turning point. The three age cohorts born between 1915 and 1929 exhibit a steady level of partisan strength which lies below the level of both the cohorts immediately before and after them. This is the "generation" whose adolescent political socialization took place during the Nazi years and whose entry into electoral and party politics was delayed. The

Figure 24-1 Partisan Strength by Year of Birth and Sex

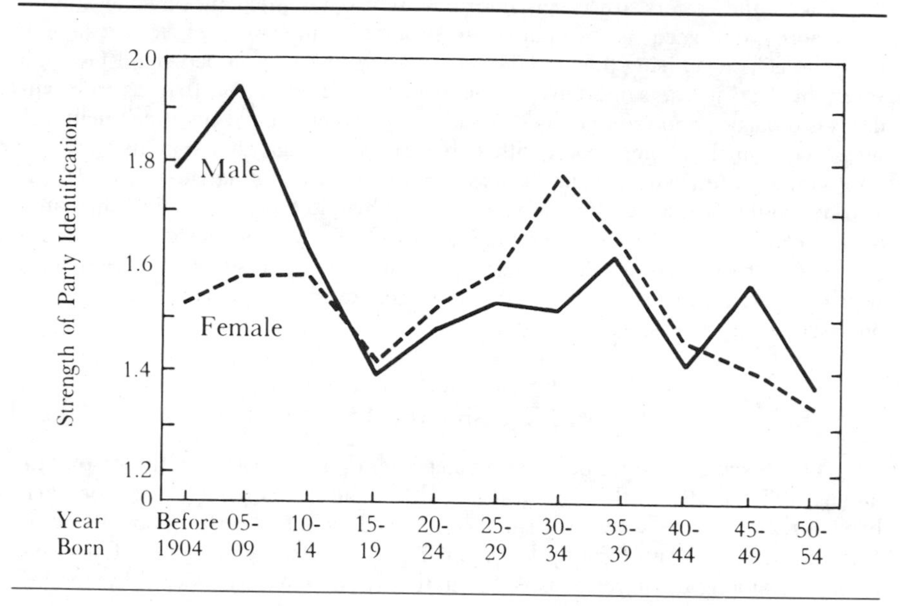

uniformly low level of partisan strength shown by the cohorts of this generation comes as expected. Within this generation, moreover, it appears that the longer the entry into electoral politics was delayed, the more depressed the strength level has become.

The Postwar Decline

Turning to cohorts socialized into politics after the war, i.e., those born after 1930, one can note the resumption of the expected decline in partisan strength. To be sure, this decline is somewhat erratic among male cohorts, but among female cohorts it slopes down monotonically. The combined curve of both cohorts would indicate a regular, though mild decline. It is worth noting that the cohorts socialized in the immediate aftermath of the Nazi defeat are decidedly stronger in their partisan attachment than are the Nazi-socialized cohorts. This difference could be the mark of the Nazi legacy of pronounced hostility affecting the older cohorts toward a competitive party sytem. But it could also stem from the new democratic spirit prevailing in the immediate postwar years and sparking partisan affection among the young cohorts then coming of age politically.

The Pre-Nazi Peak

Cycling back to the oldest cohorts one finds among males the highest levels of partisan strength. On one hand, this is as expected: they have accumulated the most electoral experience. On the other hand, this is surprising, for they have had to cope with a varying cast of partisan actors during their life time, beginning with the parties of the German Empire (1871-1918); after all, electoral experience can only fortify a partisan tie if the partisan stimuli remain fixed. Those parties of the Federal Republic with which the older voters profess to have their current identification are not necessarily the ones they may have adopted way back. Only one current political party—the SPD—has a tradition which goes back that far. Voters who were socially conditioned to this party 50 or 60 years ago could have, indeed, developed an increasingly close tie with that party during the years they had occasion to vote for it. But this cannot be said for those voters whose initially chosen party either faded during the Weimar Republic or did not reemerge after World War II. Why would they, nevertheless, surpass in partisan strength voters first socialized after 1945?

Perhaps this is so because some older voters were able to transfer their old party tie to one of the new parties while maintaining the acquired strength of their former partisan commitment. Certainly, whoever was attached to the Catholic Center Party (*Zentrum*) must have found it painless to adopt the CDU/CSU as a new party. For supporters of other former parties, however, such a transfer may have proved more difficult. How large the share of early SPD and Center supporters is among the older cohorts cannot be computed with the available data. If election returns from that era are taken as a clue, just about one-half of the older voters might fit that description.[11] If so, a sizeable portion of older voters would profess a current party tie which relates to the party of their early socialization. The present partisan strength of the older cohorts, therefore, may largely show the strength of the partisan tie of SPD and Center-turned-CDU/CSU identifiers.

Male versus Female

As for the contrast between male and female cohorts, it is reassuring to note that the two curves, on the whole, run parallel except for that span of time when females were not yet or just enfranchised. While most of the females born after 1904 came of age politically at a time when voting was restricted to males, most of those born between 1904 and 1914 did so after the franchise had been granted to women, but when female participation in politics was still a novelty and far less common than among men.[12] That females born in that era, as a result, even today exhibit a weaker attachment to parties than men of similar age do is not surprising.

Replicating the "Time and Partisan Stability" Model

The overall pattern of development of partisan strength throughout the life-cycle depicted in Figure 24-1 bears witness to a model of partisan stability elaborated and tested on five nations by Converse (1969).[13] The key predictor of that model concerns the amount of electoral experience a voter accumulates(I_p): the greater the experience, the stronger the party attachment! Electoral experience is seen as a function of the length of time a cohort of voters has been eligible to vote, but with several adjustments. One is the actual voting turnout displayed by a given cohort; the other one—most crucial in the German case—is the interruption of the electoral process (1933-1945), postponing the entry of certain cohorts into electoral politics and retarding the growth of partisan strength of older cohorts.[14]

With these adjustments applied, the correlation between I_p, i.e., the accumulation of electoral experience of a cohort, and P_s, its partisan strength, turned out a handsome .603, surprisingly close to the five-nation figure of .558 reported by Converse (1969: 154) for an earlier period. The German voter, viewed from the cohort perspective, has indeed strengthened his partisan tie in a fashion predicted as a result of increasing participation in the electoral system.[15] This adds one more item of support for the proposition that, contrary to the prevailing pessimism, the German electorate fits the party identification mold as well as the circumstances of its history allow.

Conclusions and Postscript

The pieces of evidence assembled above permit the inference that durable party attachments are common, though not ubiquitous, in the West German electorate. A person's report on his long-term partisanship, it has been shown, remains stable among two-thirds of the electorate. While current voting preference and partisan identification go hand in hand among many a voter, deviations of vote from identification are frequent enough to dispel the suspicion that the two are no more than two sides of the same coin. Age-related differences, moreover, highlight the fact that the strength of a voter's partisan tie grows as the result of electoral experience.

These findings, however, are not likely to lay the issue of German party identification to rest. For one, the time span of the panel survey used is not long enough to settle the question of long-term stability. A panel spanning from one election to another one would be required to examine more cogently the interplay between the long-term tie and short-term voting choice. A second point of reservation concerns the quality of the instrument designed to tap long-term partisanship. Even though it explicitly suggests to the respondent the decidedly long-term nature of such a partisanship, it does not keep some respondents from volunteering short-term preferences in return. Measurement problems remain to be solved. Third, the partisan balance suggested by the reports of party identification in 1972 seems distorted. According to those reports, self-styled Social Democrats outnumber Christian Democrats by a 3-2 margin, giving the SPD a potential lead over the CDU/CSU which it has never attained in an actual election. The distortion apparent in the 1972 figures can be blamed on the political climate prevailing in 1972 (Kaase, 1973: 145-150). The CDU/CSU then suffered from being tainted as a disloyal opposition, and its supporters felt reluctant under these circumstances to profess their partisan support during the campaign. In this political climate, the SPD may have temporarily attracted to its ranks some independents whereas the CDU/CSU failed to show its true partisan strength.

Reports of partisanship in Germany are not immune to such instances of intense polarization and politicization. But these distortions remain the exception rather than the rule.

Postscript

Since completion of this paper further data on the partisan distribution became available which cast some light on the 1972 puzzle. Table 24-6 presents

Table 24-6 The Distribution of Party Identification, 1972-1976

Party	*Sept. 1972*	*March 1975*[a]	*Jan.-March 1976*[b]	*June 1976*[c]
SPD	40.7	33.1	30.0	36.2
CDU/CSU	27.4	32.1	33.1	36.8
FDP	3.6	4.4	7.0	5.2
Other	0.1	0.3	0.9	0.7
No party	20.5	23.8	19.6	14.7
Don't know, Refused	7.8	6.4	9.3	6.4
Total	100.1	100.1	99.9	100.0
(N)	(2025)	(2774)	(2934)	(2075)

[a] The 1975 figures were taken from a survey conducted by the Konrad-Adenauer Foundation in Alfter, Germany. Permission to use these data is kindly acknowledged.

[b] The January-March 1976 figures were calculated as a pooled estimate from two separate surveys conducted in January and March 1976 by Professor Werner Kaltefleiter of the University of Kiel, Germany. Permission to use these data is kindly acknowledged.

[c] The June 1976 figures were calculated from a panel survey conducted by the Forschungsgruppe Wahlen e.V. This data set can be obtained from the Zentralarchiv in Cologne (No. 823-825) or from the ICPSR in Ann Arbor.

those figures for three time points since that election, the third of which (June 1976) marks the preliminary phase of the 1976 election campaign. All three sets of figures point to a close partisan balance between the two major parties and thus serve to correct the 1972 impression. The SPD found its excess support trimmed while the CDU/CSU had its share restored.

One may argue that this change stems from the decline of the fortunes of the SPD, as witnessed by setbacks in state elections and culminating in Chancellor Brandt's resignation in May 1974. The disenchantment with this party, so it seems, affected presumedly long-term attachments. As plausible as this may sound one must remember that the 1972 partisan breakdown—along with reports of vote intention and vote cast—is far off the actual electoral mark. Figures for 1972 reveal a strong pro-SPD bias, and any change measure relying on the 1972 baseline is bound to exaggerate the amount of movement. Most of the apparent 1972-1975 change, in my view, must be construed as a correction of this bias. With the political climate cooling off, the "normal" partisan balance reemerged.

The comparatively quiet times between two election campaigns, in any event, are better suited to reveal the long-term partisan breakdown of the electorate than are the moments of intense mobilization, especially when the short-term forces strongly favor one major party over the other one. The high politicization supplied by election campaigns no doubt inflates the partisan ranks, as can also be gleaned from the June 1976 figures. This surge points to the species of "independent leaners" who, with sufficient political stimulation, will temporarily line up with one of the parties. It is imperative to set them aside in order to capture the extent of long-term partisanship.

NOTES

1. These figures are based on surveys of the German electorate in 1965 (Zentralarchiv no. 314, ICPSR no. 7105) and 1969 (Zentralarchiv no. 426, 427, ICPSR no. 7098).
2. This figure is based on the 1969 survey (question V in postelection wave) listed in note 1. Allerbeck (1977: 130-131, Table 4) reports that, of the voters who grew up after World War II, 68.4 percent can recall their fathers' party preference, as compared to 57.5 percent of those who grew up during the Weimar years (1919-1933). For the transmission of partisanship during adolescence, see Baker (1974: 571-572) and Dennis and McCrone (1970: 252, 257).
3. The question reads (in English translation): "Many people in the Federal Republic lean toward a particular party for a long time, although they may occasionally vote for a different party. How about you: do you in general lean toward a particular party? If so, which one?" In the event that the respondent named a party, he was further questioned as to "how strongly or weakly do you lean toward this party: very strongly, fairly strongly, moderately, fairly weakly, or very weakly?" Since the two weak categories were hardly ever chosen, I have combined them along with the middle category and christened this combination as "weak." As a result, the "fairly strongly rubric has been renamed as "moderate" and the top category as "strong."
4. A total of 1,222 respondents was interviewed three times. The first wave ran from September 23 to October 11, the second from October 20 to November 6, and the third (postelection) from December 9 to December 30, 1972. The first wave is denoted in the text as "September" while the second is referred to as "October." The data were originally collected by a research team at the University of Mannheim, Germany. The data were made available for analysis through a joint archival project of ZENTRALARCHIV in Cologne, the ICPSR in Ann Arbor, and ZUMA in Mannheim (Zentralarchiv no. 635-637, ICPSR no. 7102).
5. Excluded from the analysis were respondents professing a leaning toward the third party, i.e., Free Democrats (4.0 percent), along with those refusing to answer the question or saying "don't know" (7.2 percent).
6. A highly readable presentation and evaluation of this model has been given by Beck (1975). A computer program of the model is offered by the OSIRIS package of data analysis programs maintained by the ICPSR, Ann Arbor, Michigan.
7. Note the change in notation. Coleman (1964) refers to P(1,2) as P(0,1), to P(2,3) as P(1,2), and so forth. The notation adopted here seems better to accord with familiar conventions.
8. Compare the matrix of transition probabilities and reliability estimates for the West German electorate with those reported by Beck (1975: 374-375) for the United States (1958-1960):

Transition Probabilities				*Reliability Coefficients*			
	Dem.	Ind.	Rep.		Dem.	Ind.	Rep.
Dem.	.972	.002	.006	Dem.	.912	.128	.054
Ind.	.128	.716	.156	Ind.	.070	.659	.066
Rep.	.021	.017	.962	Rep.	.030	.126	.904

   The match is astonishingly close, with somewhat higher reliability in the United States for the independent response as well as more frequent (true) change from independents to the partisan ranks.
9. The tables presented by Butler and Stokes (1969) and Thomassen (1976) apparently included voters shifting from partisan ranks to independence and vice versa. But neither the British nor the American figures are much affected by that; either because

of the ubiquity of partisanship (Britain) or because few independents are left among the regular voters, especially once off-year elections are included (United States).

10. The levels of partisan strength (recoded) were scored as follows: strong (= 3), moderate (= 2), weak (= 1), no party (= 0). Responses from the first wave were utilized in this part of the analysis in order to minimize the possible effect of voting choice upon the report of one's partisan strength.
11. The combined share of the SPD and the Catholic Center climbed to 46.0 percent in 1898 and stood at 45.0 percent in 1928, that is a generation later. In between those years it fell to a minimum of 37.1 percent (1924) and attained a maximum of 57.6 percent (1919). It should be noted that the share of the BVP (Bavarian People's Party) has been added to that of the Center for the Weimar years.
12. Except for the first election in which women were eligible to participate (1919), the female part of the electorate always lagged behind the male part in voting turnout during the 1919-1930 period, by 8.4 percent on the average. See Lavies (1973: 69).
13. The analysis done by Converse (1969) relied on the data of the five-nation study conducted in 1959 by Almond and Verba (1963). The 1972 data set includes several young cohorts (born after 1940) not available in the earlier data set. This analysis, therefore, was able to include voters socialized into partisanship during the rule of the Federal Republic. Aside from the time frame, the index of partisan strength used here differs from that of the earlier data set. The Almond and Verba (1963: 351) data allowed for a scale of strength ranging from "supporter of any particular political party," including party members (highest level), over "leaner" (intermediate level) to "independent" (lowest level). The German survey of 1972 queried respondents directly about the "strength" of their professed partisan leanings, allowing for five possible grades of strength. For the way they have been recoded, see notes 3 and 10.
14. The variable I_p was constructed in three steps. First, the raw count in 1972 of "years eligible to vote" (Y_e) for a given cohort was adjusted for the voting turnout that cohort displayed at the previous federal election in 1969, the turnout estimates coming from census reports. Second, the resulting variable "years voted" (Y_v), was corrected for the "resistance" (R) encountered by those cohorts given the franchise beyond the age of 21. In the third and final step, the resulting variable was adjusted for the fading of partisan strength during the Nazi period (1933-1945). For the details of this correction (the "forgetting function") as well as the other two, see Converse (1969: 152-154, 159-160, 169-170). In calculating the base Y_e I took the year 1949 as the beginning of voting eligibility after the Nazi regime. While state and local elections were held in the 1945-1949 period, the first federal election in West Germany took place in 1949.
15. The other predictor of the "partisan stability" model, i.e., the partisan push an individual receives during his political socialization (I_f), added little to the prediction of the partisan strength of German cohorts. Although I_f correlated positively with partisan strength (.37), its partial weight in the equation also including I_p proved insignificant. This lack of explanatory power is not surprising in view of the fact that I_f was designed largely to capture "between-country differences in political experience of the parental generation" (Converse, 1969: 155). I am indebted to Kai Hildebrandt for bringing this point to my attention.

25. A MULTIDIMENSIONAL CONCEPTUALIZATION OF PARTY IDENTIFICATION

Herbert F. Weisberg

Contemporary theories of American voting behavior give a prominent position to the role of psychological attachment to a political party in structuring the individual citizen's voting decision. Not only does partisanship affect one's vote, but also it affects one's attitudes toward the issues and candidates, which, in turn, affect one's vote.[1] In recent years, however, the meaning, importance, and measurement properties of party identification have been subject to an increasing challenge.[2] This chapter reexamines the concept and the measure from a dimensional perspective. Simply stated, the argument made here is that party identification involves separate attitudes toward several distinct objects—political parties generally, the Republican party, the Democratic party, and political independence—so a multidimensional view of party identification is required, rather than the traditional unidimensional view. This multidimensional perspective particularly affects our understanding of strength of identification and of political independence, accounting for incongruities on these topics which have recently been discovered.

This chapter begins with a reexamination of the concept of party identification and the survey questions used to measure it. Evidence from the biennial national election surveys taken by the University of Michigan's Center for Political Studies will be introduced, with special emphasis on the new partisanship questions asked in the January-February wave of their 1980 election study.[3]

The Dimensions of Party Identification

Over the years, the party identification concept has acquired many different usages. Some treatments have stressed its affective components, others its cognitive aspects, still others its rational basis, and so on. But if we are to reconsider the concept, it is best to go back to its actual beginnings—the emphasis on group attachment in *The Voter Decides:*

Author's Note: I am indebted to Sandy Davis, Sally Friedman, Tom Boyd, Phil Kramer, and Craig Rimmerman for their skillful assistance in various phases of this research.

Source: *Political Behavior*, Vol. 2, No. 1, 1980, by permission of Agathon Press, Inc.

> The present analysis of party identification is based on the assumption that the two parties serve as standard-setting groups for a significant proportion of the people of this country. In other words, it is assumed that many people associate themselves psychologically with one or the other of the parties, and that this identification has predictable relationships with their perceptions, evaluations, and actions. (Campbell, Gurin, and Miller, 1954, p. 90)

The Michigan researchers amplified this usage of the identification notion in their later study, *The American Voter:*

> We use the concept here to characterize the individual's affective orientation to an important group-object in his environment. Both reference group theory and small-group studies of influence have converged upon the attracting or repelling quality of the group as the generalized dimension most critical in defining the individual-group relationship, and it is this dimension that we will call identification. In the present chapter the political party serves as the group toward which the individual may develop an identification, positive or negative, of some degree of intensity. (Campbell, Converse, Miller, and Stokes, 1960, pp. 121-2)

Political independence has a somewhat ambiguous standing with respect to this psychological attachment meaning of party identification. *The Voter Decides* basically treated independents as only a residual group for those who did not identify with either party, but *The American Voter* adopted a more complex position:

> In using these techniques of measurement we do not suppose that every person who describes himself as an Independent is indicating simply his lack of positive attraction to one of the parties. Some of these people undoubtedly are actually repelled by the parties or by partisanship itself and value their position as Independents. Certainly independence of party is an ideal of some currency in our society, and it seems likely that a portion of those who call themselves Independents are not merely reporting the absence of identification with one of the major parties. (Campbell, Converse, Miller, and Stokes, 1960, p. 123)

This group attachment notion, at least as it is usually treated, unnecessarily constrains the interpretation of party identification in three ways: (1) it assumes that citizens can identify with only a single party, rather than examining more fully their attitudes toward both parties, (2) it assumes that political independence is just the opposite of partisanship, and (3) it assumes the importance of parties, rather than exploring the person's identification with the party system.

A basic concern here is whether a person can identify with more than one group. Multiple identifications certainly exist, as when people consider themselves both Americans and Catholics. Yet, identification with one group generally seems to preclude identification with opposite groups. Thus, we would not expect people to consider themselves both Protestants and Catholics. Yet people can have positive affect toward opposite groups, as by liking both religions. Furthermore, some people might refuse to view the groups as opposites, as when ecumenical Christians who do not accept the denominational distinction identify positively with both Protestants and Catholics.

Additionally, it is possible not to identify with either of two supposedly polar groups. Obviously non-Christians and nonbelievers would not identify with either Protestants or Catholics. What is essential to observe is that lack of identification with either Protestants or Catholics does not foreclose positive religious identification. Nonsectarian Christians can believe in Jesus without identifying themselves with either Catholics or Protestants. And even atheism need not be seen just as a lack of identification with organized religions, for it can instead be a source of positive identification. Altogether, this means that an exploration of religious identification would have to encompass attitudes toward the separate religions, the possibility of multiple identifications, diverse meanings of nonidentification, and attitudes toward the religious system.

Translating this analogy back to the political arena, the argument becomes that party identification can be more complex than identification with a single party. Some people might actually consider themselves both Republicans and Democrats. Some people might be Independents because they dislike both parties, while others might be Independents because they like both parties equally, and still others might be Independents because they positively value political independence. Indeed, some people might consider themselves both Republicans (or Democrats) and Independents, particularly if they generally support Republican issue stands but feel that one should vote on the basis of issues rather than party labels. And some people might be so alienated from the political system that they negatively identify both with political parties and with independence as traditionally conceived.

Some of these identification patterns may seem unreasonable, but the real point is that we know very little about actual identification patterns. *The American Voter* did treat the concept of party identification in very broad terms, but the traditional survey questions do not make allowance for the possibility of multiple identification. Rather than testing for such a possibility, they assume it out of existence. Because our theories of voting have been based on the actual survey questions used to measure party identification, these theories do not handle multiple identification well. Consequently, multiple identifications would necessitate revision in our theories.

Dimensional Models of Partisanship

The above argument is that party identification can be multidimensional. By contrast, the usual view of party identification in the United States is as a single dimension (to be denoted as P^1) with strong Republican identification at one end, strong Democratic identification at the opposite end, and political independence in the middle (see Figure 25-1). This approach makes a series of strong assumptions that have never been explicitly tested: (a) that independence is the

Figure 25-1 The Seven-point Party Identification Scale

Strong Democrats	Weak Democrats	Independents Leaning to Democrats	Pure Independents	Independents Leaning to Republicans	Weak Republicans	Strong Republicans

midpoint of a Republican-Democratic continuum, (b) that Republican and Democratic identification are opposites of one another, and (c) that opposition to political parties is equivalent to independence. These assumptions can be relaxed in a number of different ways, yielding a series of alternative dimensional models of party identification.

In particular, political independence may be a separate object with which citizens can identify rather than merely a neutral midpoint of a Republican-Democratic scale. In fact, citizens could identify with independence regardless of whether or not they are neutral with respect to the two parties. This suggests a two-dimensional interpretation of party identification (to be denoted as P^2): one dimension ranging from Republican to Democrat with neutral in the middle, and the other dimension ranging from independent to not very independent (see Figure 25-2).[4]

Furthermore, Republican and Democratic identification need not be as diametrically opposed as the standard treatment assumes. It is possible for citizens to identify with both parties (or to identify negatively with both parties)—and citizens with such views may or may not identify with independence. This leads to a three-dimensional interpretation of party identification (to be labeled P^3): one dimension measuring attitude toward the Republican party, another measuring attitude toward the Democratic party, and the third measuring attitude toward political independence (Figure 25-3).[5] These three dimensions need not be orthogonal to one another. The degrees of correlation among the P^3 dimensions are best regarded as parameters that can change over time. Negative correlations might be expected immediately after a party realignment, while the correlations might actually be positive during a dealignment.

What is most difficult is to decide how to introduce attitudes toward political parties generally into this spatial presentation. Viewing this as a fourth dimension allows people to like independence and the party system, as well as dislike both, and it allows people to like their favorite party and political parties generally, as well as dislike their preferred party and political parties generally. It is probable that this fourth dimension would be correlated with the others: positively with attitude toward the Republican party and toward the Democratic party, but negatively with attitude toward independence.

Figure 25-2 Two Dimensions of Partisanship and Independence

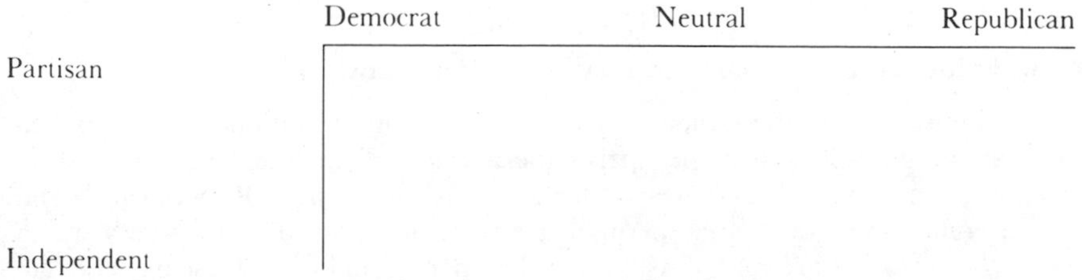

Democrat Neutral Republican

Partisan

Independent

Figure 25-3 Three Dimensions of Party Identification

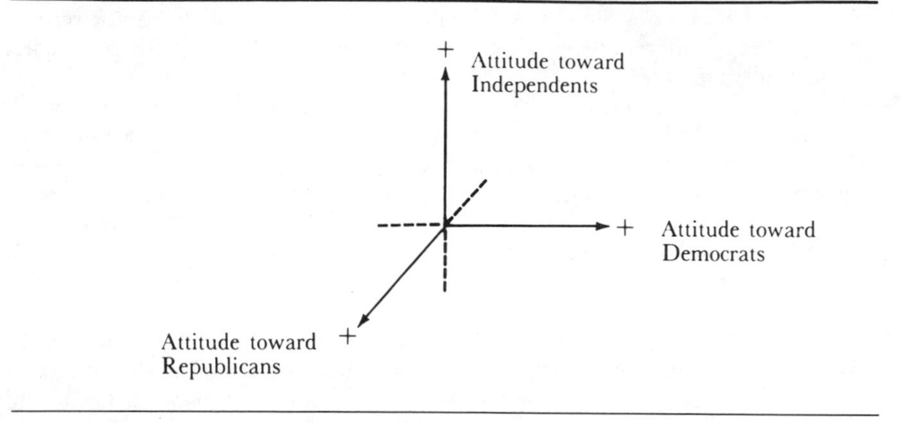

The choice among these dimensional perspectives can directly affect our understanding of voting behavior. For example, the growth in Independents since the 1950s takes on a very different meaning when independence is seen solely as a matter of neutrality between the parties than when it can also mean a positive attraction toward independence or a negative repulsion from the party system, but these distinct meanings are blurred in the conventional P^1 view of partisanship. Similarly, the usual finding of increased strength of partisanship as a citizen ages (Converse, 1976) takes on a very different meaning when it is realized that the usual unidimensional P^1 interpretation combines three aspects that are separate in P^3—how much the person likes his own party, how much more the person likes his party than the opposite party, and how much the person likes political independence—and that it might be that only one of these three aspects really changes with aging.

Fundamentally, the choice among these dimensional views is an empirical issue. The simple unidimensional view may as well be adopted if attitudes toward the parties are unidimensional, but it is also possible that the standard unidimensional treatment of party identification is inadequate. Empirical evidence would be useful, but the usual measuring instrument has been unidimensional, which precludes a separate test of unidimensionality. However, new partisanship measures have provided needed empirical evidence as to dimensionality.

New Evidence on the Dimensionality of Partisanship

An initial test of the standard unidimensional interpretation can be obtained by examining responses to the "party thermometers" included in the national election studies since 1964.[6] Respondents are asked to rate "Republicans" and "Democrats" on a 100 degree thermometer scale, where 100° means very warm feelings toward the group, 50° is a neutral response, and 0° represents very cool feelings. A unidimensional interpretation would imply a very negative correlation between ratings of Republicans and Democrats. Instead, the correlation has ranged from mildly negative to zero: −.38 in 1964, −.18 in 1968, .02 in 1972, .01 in 1976, and −.17 in the January-February 1980 wave (where the stimuli were changed to "the Republican party" and "the Democratic party").[7] These correlations suggest that attitudes toward the two parties are separate dimensions (separated by an angle of something like 90-110 degrees) and not a single dimension.

A further test is provided by the 1980 election study which asked respondents to rate the Republican party, the Democratic party, and "people who call themselves political independents" on the thermometer (see Table 25-1). Under a unidimensional interpretation (Coombs, 1964, chapter 5), Republicans at one end of the dimension would be closer to Independents than to Democrats at the opposite end of the dimension, and so should rate Independents higher than Democrats. Similarly, Democrats at one end of the dimension would be closer to Independents than to Republicans at the opposite end of the dimension, and so should rate Independents higher than Republicans. However, of the respondents who liked either the Republican party or the Democratic party the most, and who gave different ratings to the three groups, only 37 percent preferred Independents to the opposite party. Partisans do not seem to view Independents as being in the middle of a partisanship dimension.

The 1980 study also included a thermometer measure on attitudes toward "political parties, in general." The "political parties" and "political independents" thermometers have a trivial .11 correlation. Not only do some partisans dislike independents and some independents dislike partisans, but also many citizens like both partisans and independents, and many other citizens dislike both. Thus, independence is more than a dislike of parties. The average correlation between the "political independents" thermometer and the Republi-

Table 25-1 Frequencies of Preference Orders Based on Thermometer Ratings of the Democratic Party, the Republican Party, and Political Independents, January-February, 1980

Preference Orders Compatible with Democratic-Republican-Independent Dimension:	
DIR	15%
IDR	14
IRD	10
RID	13
Total	52%
Preference Orders Not Compatible with Democratic-Independent-Republican Dimension:	
DRI	31%
RDI	17
Total	48%

Note: Preference orders are listed in first choice, second choice, third choice order. The total number of respondents with untied preference orders is 507. If each possible preference order on three alternatives were equally likely, two-thirds of the preference orders would be consistent with a single dimension.

can and Democratic party thermometers is .04, with a tendency for people who like Independents to like the Republican party more and the Democratic party less.

Additionally, the 1980 study asked respondents a new set of partisanship questions, including "do you think of yourself as a supporter of one of the political parties, or not?" and "do you ever think of yourself as a political independent, or not?" The correlation between these two new items would be −1.0 if party support and independence were mutually exclusive conditions as the standard unidimensional approach assumes. Instead, the correlation was −.13, showing these are separate dimensions. As Table 25-2 shows, 16 percent of the sample considered themselves both party supporters and Independents. Only 56 percent of the sample consider themselves just party supporters or just Independents. The evidence suggests that the public interprets political independence as more complex than the absence of identification with a party.

Perhaps the most unexpected finding reported here is that a quarter of the respondents consider themselves neither party supporters nor Independents. One would expect that this large group has had unusual difficulty responding to the traditional party identification questions. Presumably these people do not think of politics in partisan terms and probably have little to do with politics, but further exploration is required.

The results reported in this section do not determine definitively the proper dimensional interpretation of party identification, though they suggest that four (sometimes correlated) dimensions are involved. In any case, the results severely challenge the traditional unidimensional conception of partisanship.

The Dimensionality of Party Identification Questions and Scales

If partisanship is multidimensional, then the validity of party identification questions depend on how they relate to that underlying multidimensional space. It is possible to measure party identification along a unidimensional vector even in a multidimensional space, as by showing the respondents a scale which ranges from strong Republican at one end to strong Democrat at the opposite end, and having them place themselves on the scale. Whether a particular party identifica-

Table 25-2 Party Support by Independence, January-February, 1980 (N = 954)

Do you think of yourself as a supporter of one of the political parties?	*Do you ever think of yourself as a political independent?* % Yes	% No	Total %
Yes	16.4	29.5	45.8
No	26.3	27.9	54.2
Total	42.7	57.3	100.0

tion question provides unidimensional measurement depends on the exact question wording.

It is worth examining from this perspective the exact wording of the series of three questions which the Center for Political Studies has traditionally used to measure party identification. The first question is a *direction* question (to be labeled PID_{DIR}): "Generally speaking, do you usually think of yourself as a Republican, a Democrat, an Independent, or what?" PID_{DIR} asks respondents to indicate which of three alternatives is their first choice, and from a theory of data perspective (Coombs, 1964), this preference choice is based on their relative distances from the points representing those three alternatives in the underlying party space. The one indeterminacy here involves independence: not only those closest to independence will respond Independent. In any case, the question does not tell respondents to think of Republicans and Democrats as opposites with Independents in between. Since PID_{DIR} imposes no constraints on the relative locations of the alternatives in the space, the larger dimensional representations are the more general and appropriate.

An important point, generalizing a result of Van Wingen and Valentine (1979), is that PID_{DIR} measures neither strength of partisanship nor strength of independence, as can be demonstrated using Figure 25-4. People below the 45° line in that figure are closer to independence (the horizontal axis) than to their preferred party (the vertical axis), and therefore would respond "Independent" to PID_{DIR}. The standard seven-point party identification scale assumes these independents are less partisan and more independent than are respondents who answer PID_{DIR} "Republican" or "Democrat." However, partisan A in Figure 25-4 identifies with his/her party less strongly than does independent B, and partisan C is actually more favorable to independence than is independent D. The first party identification question is a *direction* question, and its information cannot be used to establish *strength* of partisanship or of independence.

The second party identification question is a *leaning* question (to be referred to as PID_{LEAN}) which is asked of independents and identifiers with other parties: "Do you think of yourself as closer to the Republican or Democratic party?" This question determines whether independents lean toward the Republican party or to the Democratic party or are exactly neutral. Yet it does not assure that independents who lean toward a party are less strongly identified with that party than respondents who identified with that party on the PID_{DIR} question, as the standard seven-point party identification scale assumes.[8]

The third question is a *strength* question (to be labeled PID_{STR}) which is asked of respondents who call themselves Republicans or Democrats on the opening question: "Would you call yourself a strong Republican (Democrat) or a not very strong Republican (Democrat)?" This question explicitly asks respondents how strongly they identify with their own party, not where they would situate themselves on a continuum ranging from Republican to Democrat. That is, it asks people to locate their projection on their preferred axis of P^3; it does not ask respondents to position themselves along P^1 or along the partisan dimension of P^2. The wording of the strength of identification probe is specifically based on P^3.[9]

Figure 25-4 The First Party Identification Question

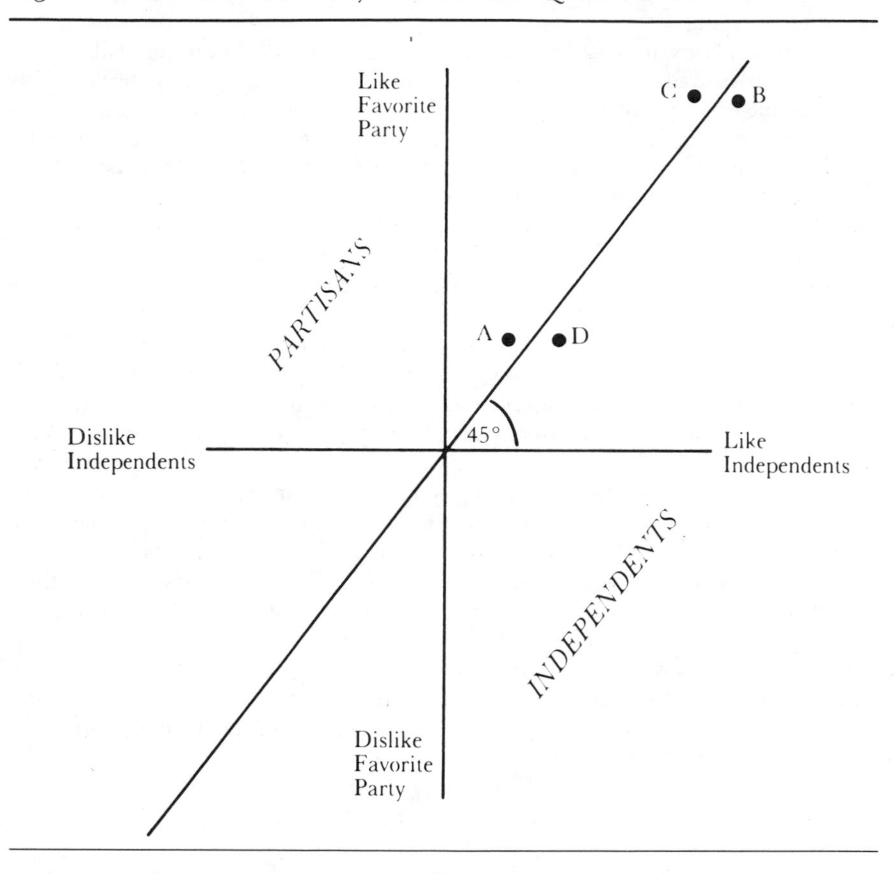

Partisan Categories and Partisan Change

Minimally, a literal reading of the party identification question series is at least as compatible with P^3 as with P^2 or P^1. If that is the case, then how does the standard party identification question divide P^3 into partisanship categories? Figure 25-5 shows the party identification cube that results if the three dimensions are assumed orthogonal.[10] The respondent's position in the space reflects his position on all three dimensions. According to the interpretation of the party identification questions above, the people who will say they are strong Republicans are those closer to the Republican axis than to the other axes and above the plane perpendicular to the Republican axis that differentiates strong and weak Republicans. Weak Republicans are those closer to the Republican axis than to the other axes, but below that plane. Leaning Republicans are closer to the Independent axis than to the other axes, but closer to the Republican axis than to the Democratic axis. Pure independents are equally close to the Republican and Democratic axes; and so on.

Figure 25-5 The Party Identification Cube

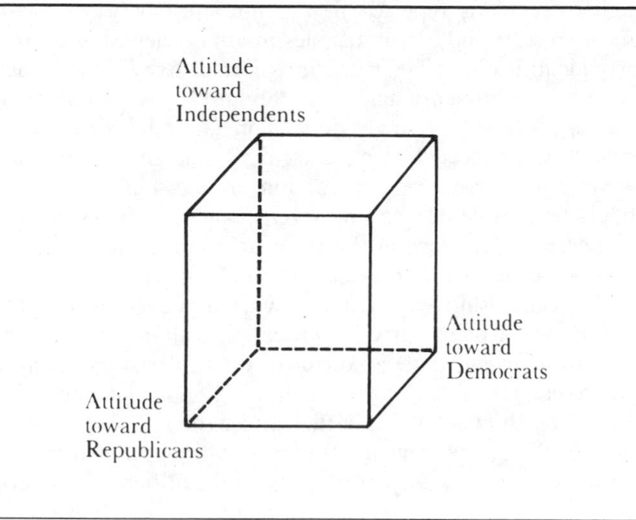

Consider which regions border which other regions in this cube versus the usual P^1 interpretation. In P^1, strong Republicans are next to only weak Republicans, but the standard party identification question series divides P^3 in such a way that the strong Republican region is next to some weak Republicans, some independents who lean toward the Republican party, some pure independents, and some strong Democrats! Weak Republicans adjoin only strong Republicans and Republican leaners in P^1, but in P^3 they also adjoin some pure independents and some weak Democrats.

If partisan change is expected to be mainly between adjacent spatial categories, P^3 leads to a very different view of patterns of partisan change on the standard scale than does P^1. Rather than just expecting shifts between adjacent categories of the seven-point party identification scale, in P^3 we would expect (a) moves between strong partisanship in favor of one party and strong partisanship in favor of the other party, (b) moves between weak partisanship in favor of one party and weak partisanship in favor of the other party, and (c) moves between each partisan category and pure independence.

These expectations can be compared with Katz's (1979) multidimensional scaling of partisan change in the 1956-60 American panel study. Katz finds that change was consistent with an ordering of the seven party identification categories along a horseshoe shape in two-space rather than along the unidimensional P^1. That is, the strong identification categories were closer to one another than P^1 suggests, as were the weak identification categories. P^3 suggests greater movement between each category and pure independence than Katz found, but Brody (1977, Appendix 1) reports enough change of this nature in the panel study to suggest that the P^3 formulation may be correct.

Alternative Partisanship Scales

The high correlations reported in the literature between the seven-point party identification scale and other variables might be viewed as evidence that the standard party identification scale is unidimensional. Even if the "true" partisanship space were multidimensional, the standard scale might compress that multidimensional space into a single dimension fairly faithfully, particularly if most respondents were located along a straight line in that multidimensional space. However, an alternative explanation of the high correlations in the literature should be considered: that the seven-point scale is just highly related to a more unidimensional measure of the partisan continuum. Exploration of this possibility requires examination of some alternative partisanship scales, particularly as to their relationship with criterion variables such as the vote decision.

Whereas the seven-point party identification scale has often been described as the best or most efficient single predictor of voting decisions (Converse, 1975a, pp. 127-128), recent research has shown that it is not monotonically related to presidential vote (Keith *et al.*, 1977; Miller and Miller, 1977).[11] Specifically, for the years 1964 to 1976, an average of 79 percent of independent leaners voted for their party, compared to only 74 percent of weak identifiers. This deviation from monotonicity fits the argument that the seven-point scale is not unidimensional. Furthermore, this deviation suggests that combining responses to the three party identification questions into the standard scale does not necessarily properly order respondents in terms of their partisan strength, the same argument as made in Figure 25-4 above. An alternative measure of partisanship would have to perform better in this regard, particularly in terms of predicting the vote.

A fully appropriate P^3 indicator of the partisan continuum is the *party difference:* how much more the person likes the Republican party than the Democratic party. The best operationalization of this in the Center for Political Studies surveys is obtained by subtracting the feeling thermometer for Democrats from that for Republicans. The Pearson r correlations between the seven-point party identification scale and the party difference in the 1964-1976 studies ranged from .55 to .76, indicating that the measures are highly related but not equivalent. Table 25-3 shows the relationship between party identification and the party

Table 25-3 Average Party Difference Value by Party Identification, 1964-1976

Party Identification Category	*1964*	*1968*	*1972*	*1976*	*Average*
Strong Republicans	42.1	40.6	23.0	26.3	33.0
Weak Republicans	18.5	19.6	13.9	8.8	15.2
Leaning Republicans	14.7	20.9	6.4	6.4	12.1
Pure Independents	− 0.2	5.6	− 0.1	− 3.2	0.5
Leaning Democrats	−20.2	−9.4	−12.6	−11.8	−14.0
Weak Democrats	−23.2	−14.3	−10.9	−15.4	−16.0
Strong Democrats	−48.6	−40.2	−30.5	−30.1	−37.4
Proportion of variance explained (η^2)	53.2	50.5	32.0	38.7	43.6

difference score. The mean party difference score is not always even monotone with the party identification scale, with a problem again for the weak partisan and leaning independent category ordering.

If the P^3 model is correct, the party difference measure would account for the vote better than the seven-point scale does. To provide a sufficient number of cases in each category for a test, the party difference measure has been collapsed into five categories: strong Republicans (31 to 100), weak Republicans (1 to 30), neutrals (0), weak Democrats (−30 to −1), and strong Democrats (−100 to −31). Since having one-third of the sample in the neutral category necessarily detracts from the relationship, a seven-category version of this measure has also been devised, making use of the party identification question to break the neutral category into Republican neutrals, pure neutrals, and Democratic neutrals. The party difference measures have monotonic relationships with vote (see Table 25-4). Table 25-5 shows the proportion of variance in presidential vote explained by each of the partisanship measures for the 1964-1976 presidential elections. The party difference measures consistently explain the vote better than does the party identification scale.

Table 25-4 Republican Vote Proportion of Two-Party Vote by Partisanship, 1976

Party Difference	*% Republican Vote*	*% of Sample*
Strong Republicans (31 to 100)	100	5
Weak Republicans (1 to 30)	94	17
Republican Neutrals (0; Republican PID)	79	14
Pure Neutrals (0; Pure Independent PID)	62	11
Democratic Neutrals (0; Democratic PID)	39	16
Weak Democrats (−30 to −1)	10	24
Strong Democrats (−100 to −31)	3	13
Total		100

Table 25-5 Proportion of Variance in Two-Party Presidential Vote Accounted for by Alternative Partisanship Measures, 1964-1976

	1964	*1968*	*1972*	*1976*	*Average*
Seven-point party identification scale	43.5[a]	49.4	28.0	41.6	40.6
Five-category party difference measure	47.1	53.6	42.0	49.9	48.2
Seven-category party difference measure	49.1	59.0	45.4	54.7	52.0

[a] Cell entries are eta-squares.

Table 25-6 Republican Proportion of Two-Party Vote by Party Difference and Party Identification, 1976

	Party Identification						
Party Difference	Strong Dem.	Weak Dem.	Lean Dem.	Pure Indep.	Lean Rep.	Weak Rep.	Strong Rep.
Strong Rep.	100%	100%	100%	100%	100%	100%	100%
	(1)	(5)	(2)	(2)	(9)	(21)	(56)
Weak Rep.	71	91	71	100	96	93	97
	(11)	(17)	(7)	(12)	(62)	(92)	(115)
Neutral-Rep.					83	73	92
					(87)	(100)	(25)
Neutral-Indep.				62			
				(127)			
Neutral-Dem.	23	43	39				
	(29)	(118)	(78)				
Weak Dem.	4	11	10	15	40	20	
	(113)	(144)	(68)	(17)	(13)	(20)	
Strong Dem.	2	5	0	9		0	
	(106)	(76)	(22)	(12)		(4)	

Note: Values in parentheses are numbers of cases.

The party difference may have the greater relationship with the vote, but party identification could still help account for some of the variance that the party difference leaves unexplained. This possibility can be examined by checking whether party identification affects the vote within categories of party difference, and vice versa. Table 25-6 displays the 1976 vote by combinations of categories on the two partisan variables. Within party identification categories (the columns), party difference has a definite effect—even if one ignores the cells with under ten cases. However, within categories of party difference (the rows), party identification has a minimal effect—except for the neutral category where party identification retains a strong influence on the vote. Party identification seems to have little added impact upon the vote once party difference is taken into account (and would have less were there a probe asking neutrals to which party they felt closer). Furthermore, much of the effect of party identification seems due to its relationship with the party difference.[12]

Two more party direction scales are available in the January-February 1980 election study. First, respondents were asked:

> In your own mind, do you think of yourself as a supporter of one of the political parties, or not? (If yes,) which political party do you support? On this scale from 1 to 7 where 1 means "not very strongly" and 7 means "very strongly," please choose the number that describes how strongly you support the (Republican/Democratic) Party.

With appropriate manipulation, this question series leads to a *party support* scale ranging from −7 for strong Republican support to −1 for weak Republican support to 0 for not supporting either party to +1 for weak Democratic support to +7 for strong Democratic support. Second, respondents were asked:

> (If no on the party support question above), do you ever think of yourself as closer to one of the two major political parties, or not? (If a party supporter on the original question or if yes on the above closeness question,) here is a scale from 1 to 7 where 1 means feeling very close to the Republican Party and 7 means feeling very close to the Democratic Party. Where would you place yourself on this scale?

This leads to a *party closeness* scale from 1 for very close to the Republican Party to 7 for very close to the Democratic Party, with a code of 4 for those not feeling closer to either major party.

We do not yet know how these two new scales perform in comparison with the standard seven-point scale or the party difference measure. After the 1980 election, it will be possible to check which best predicts the presidential vote and other variables of interest. It is clear that these two new scales are highly correlated with one another and with the two older measures (with intercorrelations ranging from .67 to .78). Yet much of this high correlation is due to their all doing a good job of separating Republicans from Democrats. How they differ in dealing with strength of partisanship and with independence will be examined in the following section.

The analysis of this section certainly does not render the standard seven-point scale useless. On the contrary, it has contributed much to our understanding of political behavior and it has a substantial relationship with vote choice, even if the party difference has a somewhat stronger relationship with presidential vote. Apparently the distribution of citizens across the P^3-cube has been such that the seven-point scale transforms the three-space into a single partisan dimension with minimal violence. The party difference may be a somewhat better measure for some purposes, but the differences are small. Given the greater simplicity of the more familiar P^1 representation, it would be foolish to move to a multidimensional representation unless that provided real theoretical and substantive gains. However, before prematurely accepting the conventional scale as adequate, it is essential to consider its measurement of strength of partisanship and independence.

A New Understanding of Independence

If the multidimensional conceptualization is correct and there are multiple dimensions of party identification, then there are also multiple components of strength of partisanship. These several components of strength of partisanship in P^2 and P^3 are thoroughly confounded with one another in P^1. Not only does unbundling these components lead to a far richer conceptualization of partisanship, but it offers an intriguing explanation of the problems with the conventional party identification measure that have recently been demonstrated in the literature. The most obvious difficulty is that independence and strength of partisanship have been measured by the same questions in the Center for Political Studies surveys. Independence is orthogonal to the party dimensions in P^2 and P^3, so these are separate concepts that should be measured separately.

In P^3 there are actually three basic components of strength of identification: the "intensity" with which people like their own party, the degree to which they like their own party more than the other party ("extremity"), and their attitude toward political "independence." These separate meanings are indistinguishable in P^1. For example, strong partisans are viewed as intensely liking their own party, being extreme in preferring their own party over the opposite party, and being least independent. The usual four-point strength of identification scale (strong identifier, weak identifier, independent leaner, pure independent) measures all of the meanings simultaneously in P^1. The three basic strength components are more separate in P^3. For example, people who intensely like one party might strongly prefer their own party over the other party or might like the two parties about equally, and they might be favorable or unfavorable toward independents. No single strength of partisanship measure suffices in P^3; separate measures of the three components are necessary.[13]

These different aspects of strength of identification can be operationalized from the feeling thermometers and the new partisanship questions in the 1980 election study. The intensity with which a person likes his/her own party can be measured by the maximum of the thermometer ratings given to the Republican and Democratic parties, as well as from folding the party support scale described in the previous section into a scale ranging from +7 for strong support of one's own party to +1 for weak support of one's own party and zero for not supporting either party. The degree to which the person likes his/her own party more than the other can be measured by the absolute values of the difference between the thermometer ratings given the two parties, as well as from folding the party closeness scale described in the previous section into a scale ranging from +7 for very close to one's own party to +4 for equally close to the two major parties. Attitude toward independence can be measured by the thermometer rating of political independents, as well as from a new strength of independence question in the 1980 study:

> Do you ever think of yourself as a political independent, or not? (If yes,) on this scale from 1 to 7 (where 1 means "not very strongly," and 7 means "very strongly"), please choose the number that describes *how strongly* independent in politics you feel.

(Respondents not thinking of themselves as independents were assigned the value of zero on this scale.) Additionally, the thermometer rating of "political parties, in general" in the 1980 study gives a mesure of antiparty system views.

The Standard Partisan Strength Scale

The 1980 data can be used to examine what the standard four-point (strong identifier, weak identifier, independent leaner, pure independent) strength of identification scale actually measures. To determine this, the standard scale was regressed on measures of the different aspects of partisan strength discussed above. Multiple regression analysis shows that the standard scale best taps relative closeness to one's own party as against the opposite party (β = .37; r = .61; measured by the folded party closeness scale) and partisan intensity (β = .36; r = .61; measured by the folded party support scale). The contribution is smaller for strength of independence (β = .19; r = -.30; measured by the strength of independence scale). Strength of antiparty feelings (measured by the "political parties" thermometer item) has been dropped from this equation because its coefficient was insignificant. Altogether, these aspects account for just half of the variance in the standard strength of identification scale, so that half of its variance remains unexplained. It is particularly important to note that the standard measure is least related to strength of independence and of antiparty feelings. These are important aspects of strength of identification which are not captured adequately by the standard scale.

A possible objection to this analysis is that strength of independence may itself just be a composite of the other aspects of strength of identification. However, multiple regression analysis shows that not to be the case. Only 3 percent of the variance in strength of independence is accounted for by the folded party closeness scale, the folded party support scale, and the "political parties" thermometer item. Independence appears to be very different from these other aspects of strength of identification.

To compare further the standard four-point scale with some of the new measures, Table 25-7 shows the relationship between the standard strength scale and the new party support and independence questions. Both row and column percentages are shown, as it is interesting to trace through this table in both directions. Many of the findings are obvious, such as that strong partisans nearly always think of themselves as party supporters. But some findings are surprising,

Table 25-7 Partisan Strength by Party Support and Independence, January-February 1980

	Partisan Strength			
	Strong	Weak	Leaner	Pure Independent
A. Column Percentages				
Party supporter only	67%	31%	1%	2%
Both party supporter and independent	19	21	16	2
Only independent	3	17	57	49
Neither	11	31	26	46
Total percent	100	100	100	99
Number of cases	(241)	(369)	(194)	(140)
B. Row Percentages				
Party supporter only	58%	40%	1%	1%
Both party supporter and independent	30	49	19	2
Only independent	2	26	44	28
Neither	10	45	20	25
Total percent	100	100	100	100
Number of cases	(280)	(156)	(250)	(258)

such as that a fifth of strong partisans think of themselves as Independents as well as party supporters. Nearly half of the pure Independents really don't consider themselves either party supporters or Independents, suggesting that the standard party identification question series does not give them a good opportunity to describe their position.[14] Weak partisans scatter across all four categories in fairly equal proportions, suggesting that the weak partisan category is unusually diverse in the nature of its partisanship. Table 25-7B shows that people who consider themselves neither party supporters nor Independents tend to be classified as weak partisans on the standard partisan strength scale, again emphasizing that these citizens who do not accept either partisan or independent labels are not handled well by the standard partisan questions.

This set of results helps to explain why empirical studies of the correlates of independence and of strength of partisanship typically obtain weak and even inconsistent results (Petrocik, 1974; Keith *et al.*, 1977; Van Wingen and Valentine, 1979). In particular, John Petrocik (1974) shows that the conventional four-point strength of identification scale is not monotonically related to other variables which are supposed to be related to strength of identification, with the weak partisans and independent leaner categories often out of their proper order. The dimensional perspective provides an explanation of this anomalous "intransitivity." The usual strength of identification scale is not measuring any concept purely. It synthesizes several related concepts, but this may muddy up its relationship with any other variable that would be expected to have a tidy relationship with one of the components of partisan strength. Strength of identification and independence may be found to have clearer causal antecedents and effects than the current literature shows. And we might find that the different aspects have different correlates—one might be the best predictor of voting turnout, another might best predict political cynicism, another might best predict defection from one's own party to support the candidate of the opposite party, and so on. The 1980 post-election study should permit a fuller map of these relationships. Thus, moving to a more rounded multidimensional picture of party identification may simultaneously yield a more complete understanding of voting behavior.

The Dimensionality of Partisanship

As a final test of the dimensionality of partisanship, the several measures from the January-February 1980 study that have been discussed throughout this paper have been correlated. Factor analysis of the Pearson r correlation matrix yields four principal components, which have been given a varimax rotation. Thirteen different measures have been included in the analysis, with the four components accounting for three-quarters of their total variance.

The variables with high loadings on factor 1 are measures of partisan direction—the party difference index, the usual seven-point party identification scale, the party closeness scale, the party support scale, and the Democrat and Republican thermometers. The variables with high loadings on factor 2 all measure strength of partisanship—the absolute value of the difference in thermometer ratings given the two parties, the folded party closeness scale, the folded party support scale, the standard four-point party identification scale and the maximum thermometer score assigned to a party. The variables with high loadings on factor

4 are the two measures of independence—the strength of independence scale and the thermometer rating of independents. The variables with the highest loadings on factor 3 are the Republican and "political parties" thermometer, with the maximum thermometer score and the Democratic party having the next highest loadings on the factor. The interpretation of factor 3 is the most difficult. A pro-party/anti-party interpretation seems reasonable, though the inclusion of another item measuring attitude toward the party system would be useful in confirming this interpretation. For all factors, the variables not listed above have low loadings on the factors.

It is difficult to display a four-dimensional space, but two two-dimensional planes provide a good understanding of that space. Figure 25-6 plots factor 2 against factor 4. This figure reinforces the argument that political independence is

Figure 25-6 Plot of Factors 2 and 4

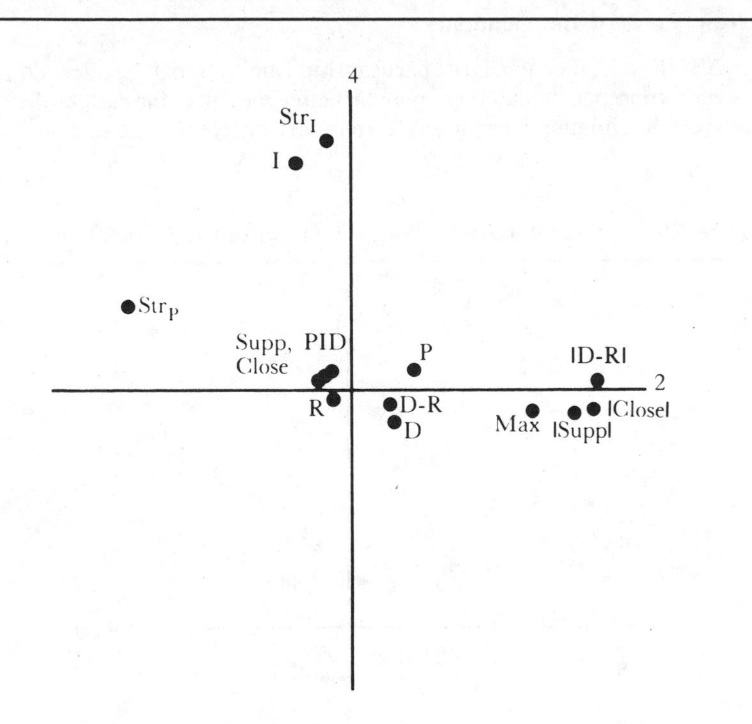

Legend for Figures 25-6 and 25-7

D	Democratic party thermometer	PID	Traditional party identification scale
R	Republican party thermometer	Str_P	Traditional strength of partisanship scale
D-R	Party difference		
|D-R|	Absolute value of party difference	Str_I	Strength of independence
Max	Maximum of Democrat and Republican thermometers	Close	Party closeness scale
		|Close|	Folded party closeness scale
I	Political independents thermometer	Supp	Party support scale
P	Political parties thermometer	|Supp|	Folded party support scale

not measured by the usual strength of identification scale. They are instead separate factors. Figure 25-7 shows the plot of factors 1 and 3.

Putting the four-dimensional space back together, we have evidence of strength of partisanship factor, an independence factor, a partisan direction factor, and a party system factor. The multidimensional perspective adopted in this chapter is confirmed in this factor analysis. At first glance, the standard partisanship direction and strength measures appear to be tapping the same factors as the new measures, but further reflection indicates that the factor analysis cannot be definitive on this issue. The factor analysis does show that there is a single *common element* to the different partisanship strength measures (political independence excluded), but there still may be meaningful differences within both sets of measures. The factor analysis confirms the existence of multidimensionality, but the differences among the variables within each set are better studied by the types of analysis in the previous sections of this chapter.

A New View of Independents

All in all, the standard partisanship and strength scales do measure important concepts, though there may be better measures for each of the concepts. However, the situation for independence is very different—the standard measures

Figure 25-7 Plot of Factors 1 and 3 (see Figure 25-6 for legend)

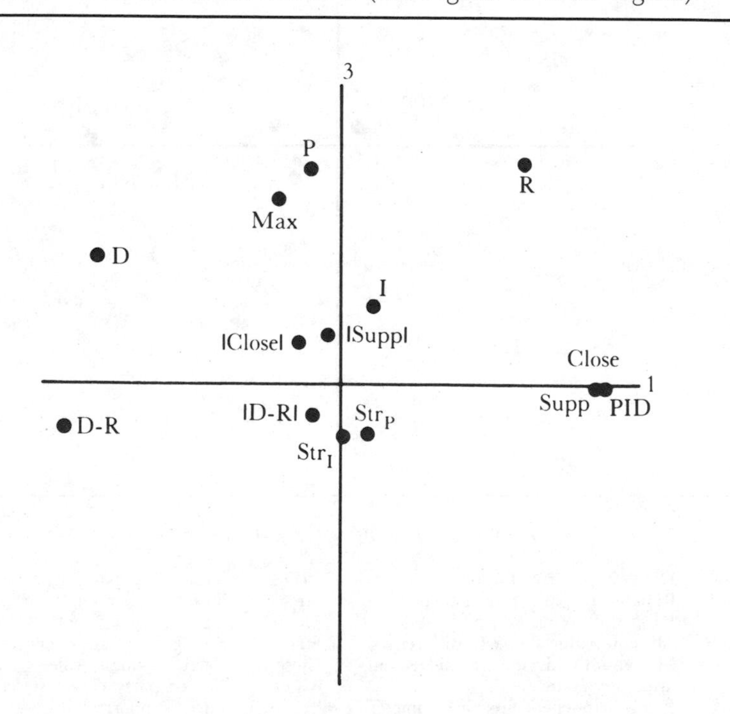

simply do not satisfactorily measure political independence. This calls into question the entire set of empirical findings about the nature of political independents, as well as the literature describing the consequences for the party system of the recent apparent growth in the numbers of independents.

The nature of independents can be examined in the 1980 study, although there are not very many criterion variables in the January-February wave. First, it turns out that people who consider themselves both party supporters and independents are unusually high on a number of measures, including interest in the campaign, talking about the candidates, expecting to vote in the fall election, past voting frequency in presidential elections, and education. People who consider themselves neither party supporters nor independents are unusually low on these same five variables.

Second, strength of independence is also correlated with many of these variables. The usual strength of partisanship measure finds that strong partisans are higher than independents on interest in the campaign, caring about the presidential election outcome, expecting to vote in the fall election, and past voting frequency in presidential elections. However, most of these relationships reverse for strength of independence, with strong independents being higher than nonindependents on interest in the campaign, talking about the candidates, expecting to vote in the fall election, and past voting frequency.

Perhaps the most important result has to do with education. When the election studies first began to study partisanship, one of the surprising results was that independents are not more educated than partisans. This is seen by the small correlation (τ_b = .07) in the 1980 study. This relationship changes dramatically when strength of independence is examined. Strong independents are better educated than weak independents and nonindependents, with a τ_b of .21. In percentage terms, 36 percent of those with college education are strong independents (positions 5-7 on the scale) compared to only 15 percent of those without a high school diploma, while 42 percent of those with college education do not ever think of themselves as independents compared to 76 percent of those without a high school diploma.

These results already begin to suggest that our entire understanding of independence must be revised. Political independence appears to be a complex topic, with many different types of respondents being combined as independents in the standard scales. A more careful examination of independence is likely to show meaningful differences among these different types. Once independence is better understood, the meaning of the "Independent" response to the party identification questions of the past thirty years will also be better understood, and much of the findings and literature of that period may have to be reinterpreted.

Conclusions

A multidimensional conceptualization of party identification has been developed in this chapter. The empirical evidence is limited, but it does suggest that the usual unidimensional interpretation is incorrect. In particular, the usual strength of identification measure so confounds different components of partisan strength that past studies have not been able to study validly the nature of political independence. The new survey questions should lead to better measurement of the full concept of partisanship. Party identification has been the keystone of our understanding of voting behavior. With a little work to bolster its underpinnings, we may find that the concept is even richer and more important than we realized.

NOTES

1. The concept was first discussed by the Michigan researchers in Belknap and Campbell (1952). The question itself was first presented and analyzed in *The Voter Decides* (Campbell, Gurin, and Miller, 1954), where it was treated as a coequal of issue orientation and candidate orientation. It was considered the most important population grouping in Campbell and Cooper (1956), but it was *The American Voter* (Campbell, Converse, Miller, and Stokes, 1960) that pioneered in treating it as the central theoretical concept in the study of voting behavior. By the publication of *Elections and the Political Order* (Campbell, Converse, Miller, and Stokes, 1966), it had been conceptualized as the long-term component of the vote decision which could be used to construct an estimate of a "normal vote" (Converse, 1966c). Knoke (1976) provides a fine treatment of its social bases, while Fiorina (1977a) gives an excellent treatment of its rational basis.
2. The controversy regarding the stability of party identification is reviewed in Niemi and Weisberg (1976, chapter 17), as is the debate as to its relative importance in affecting the vote (Niemi and Weisberg, 1976, chapter 9). Descriptions of important changes since the 1950's in the importance of party identification are given in Burnham (1970), Ladd and Hadley (1978), Nie, Verba, and Petrocik (1976), and Pomper (1975). The use of party identification outside of the United States is severely attacked in *Party Identification and Beyond* (Budge, Crewe, and Farlie, 1976). The most important responses by the Michigan researchers are Miller (1976) and Converse (1975a, 1976). Additionally, measurement problems have been central in papers by Petrocik (1974), Brody (1977), Keith *et al.* (1977), Miller and Miller (1977), Shively (1977), Van Wingen and Valentine (1979) and Katz (1979), which will be referred to later in this chapter.
3. The data have been made available by the Inter-university Consortium for Political and Social Research, which bears no responsibility for the analysis and interpretation presented here.
4. The P^2 model is closely related to Van Wingen and Valentine (1979), whose work first led me to question the dimensional basis of partisanship. A P^2 display format is also used in Nie, Verba, and Petrocik (1976, p. 216ff). Katz (1979) develops a different two dimensional interpretation of party identification, with a strength dimension orthogonal to P^1.
5. This approach is related to the work of Randall Guynes and Jerry Perkins and of Corwin Smidt, but its development here is more so based on generalizing the P^2 approach of John Van Wingen and David Valentine on the basis of my memorandum for the Conference on Party Identification sponsored by the National Election Studies in Tallahassee, Florida on February 23-24, 1978.
6. The party thermometers have been analyzed from a different framework in Maggiotto and Piereson (1977).
7. The stimuli were changed in 1980 to provide less ambiguous referents. The 1979 research and development pilot study conducted by the National Election Studies tried both the group (Republicans) and party (Republican party) versions, and no systematic differences could be found in the responses to the different

stimuli. This seems to be a situation where an intellectual case can be built for expecting response differences, but the stimuli differences are too small to affect the mass public.

8. Shively (1977) instead interprets this question as measuring the intended vote of leaners, an interpretation which does not account for the large number of leaners who instead vote for the opposite party.
9. Of course different respondents may interpret PID_{STR} in different ways. Some may interpret it in the context of the preceding PID_{DIR} question as asking their position on a Republican-Democratic continuum, which is how data analysts have traditionally interpreted the question. Other respondents may interpret PID_{STR} in the context of the preceding PID_{DIR} question as asking their position on a continuum ranging from strong identification with their party to strong independence, which is as plausible as the Republican-Democratic continuum interpretation given the wording of PID_{DIR}. These two interpretations do differ in P^2 and P^3 when independence is viewed as a separate dimension. It would be folly to assume that all respondents interpret PID_{STR} identically. What is important is that these interpretations lead to different understandings of party identification. The remainder of this chapter will develop the implications of the P^3 axis interpretation of PID_{STR}.
10. It might seem that P^3 involves one unnecessary dimension—that the space could be represented in two dimensions with barycentric coordinates, as used for three-party races in McKelvey and Ordeshook (1972, p. 46) or in the fundamental triangle for three person games (Riker and Ordeshook, 1973, p. 131). However, Republican, Democratic, and Independent identification do not exhaust the possibilities, so the three-dimensional representation better allows for the possibility of members of other parties and apoliticals opposing or being neutral to Republicans, Democrats, and Independents.
11. Congressional vote is monotone with party identification, even though presidential vote is not. In any event, party identification is not monotone with one of the most important dependent variables in voting research.
12. An alternative explanation of the better fit for the party difference is that it may measure a more short-term attitude than does the party identification question, as shown by its lower stability in the 1974-76 panel study, an overtime correlation of .61 compared to .83 for the standard party identification scale. This alternative explanation deserves further attention as later work explores measures of party identifications more thoroughly.
13. To understand the P^3 space better, a simulation was conducted. Each citizen was assigned a 1-11 rating for attitude toward Republicans, Democrats, and Independents. A uniform distribution of citizens leads to 1331 logically possible combinations of the 1-11 ratings of three objects. Following the interpretation of the party identification question series earlier in this chapter, a person is classified as a Republican if and only if his highest rating is for Republicans, a Democrat if and only if his highest rating is for Democrats, and Independent otherwise. Party identifiers are classified as strong identifiers if their rating of their own party is 10 or 11, and otherwise as weak identifiers. Independents are classified as leaning to a party if they give that party a higher rating than the other party, or as pure Independents if they give the same rating to both parties.

    The four-point strength of identification scale in this simulation has its highest correlation with attitude toward one's own party ($r = .61$), has only a moderate .50 correlation with extremity, and is least related to political independence ($r = -.37$). Altogether, these three components account for only 56 percent of the variance in the four-point strength scale under the assumption of P^3 with orthogonal dimensions. A principal component analysis of a large number of measures of strength of identification computed for the simulation study obtains three components—intensity, extremity, and independence, with the usual strength scale loading moderately on all three components.

14. The Center for Political Studies convention of coding respondents without a party preference as pure Independents further complicates this relationship.

NATURE OF PARTISAN CHANGE

26. WHITHER PARTISAN CHANGE?

Party politics is always in change. One party does better in a given election than it did in the last, while another loses some support. Some social groups support a party a bit more than they did at the last election, others a bit less. The issues on which a party ran previously are resolved or forgotten and new ones arise to take their place. But most of this change is minor and temporary, just part of the inevitable ebb and flow of politics. Sometimes, however, the change is larger and more permanent, demarcating new eras of political history. Such change is of particular importance, though at the time it is occurring it can be difficult to tell whether a given change is of the more temporary or the more permanent type.

Controversy over partisan change concerns not only the degree of meaningful change that has occurred in the past, but even more the type of change that has occurred. Different analysts look at the same political events and data and see different patterns of change. Some see a decline in the strength of political parties generally, which is termed "dealignment," while others see a change in the relative strength of the parties—"realignment." Of course, this would not be surprising if different types of change were found in different countries. Often, however, there are arguments over the nature of partisan change in the same country—as in controversies in the United States over both historical and contemporary movements. Fortunately, we shall see that there are areas of agreement as well.

One might feel that partisan change is a topic that must be considered separately for every country. Certainly it is true that different countries start out with different party systems, and so their partisan change must be different. However, there is a sense in which major events and broad cultural trends affect many countries simultaneously. Consider, for example, the changes in party trends induced by recent economic problems. In a simpler era, the economies of separate nation-states might have been unaffected by changes in the economies of other nation-states, but today there is an economic interdependence that causes severe recessions or sharp inflation to ravage the economies of many nations at the same time. To the extent that these economic difficulties affect the party system, they are likely to affect several nations in rather similar ways. And it is not just the economy that has this cross-national potential. Increasingly, media diffusion causes many nations to be affected simultaneously by the same concerns, such as the politics of the environment, affluence, and disarmament. These developments can have different impacts on different polities, but we often see remarkably similar developments across nations (such as the growth of the environmentalist "green" parties in several European countries in the early 1980s).

With this possible communality in mind, we can approach partisan changes throughout the developed world. Most of the concern is about changes since the Great Depression of the 1930s, although similar concepts and methods are often used to study earlier periods. We shall see that the controversy is slightly different from those discussed in previous sections. There is broad agreement on the type of change considered first—dealignment. Disagreement enters primarily when we try to go beyond that trend and consider the question of realignments—whether they have occurred already or will occur soon and the nature of such changes.

Dealigning Politics

Most observers agree that there has been meaningful partisan change in the past 40-plus years, at least in terms of movement toward more volatile politics. Voting patterns that once seemed totally stable have now become remarkably fluid. The beginning point for understanding this argument is Lipset and Rokkan's (1967) classic treatment of cleavage structure. Writing in a political sociology tradition, Lipset and Rokkan were intrigued by the development of conflicts in Western societies and their translation into party systems. First, according to their analysis, nation-building proceeded. The national revolution led to conflict in many countries between the "central nation-building culture" and ethnic, linguistic, and/or religious minorities in the peripheries, conflict that remains apparent in Scottish and Welsh separatist movements in the United Kingdom, in linguistic conflict in Belgium and Canada, and in religious conflict in Northern Ireland. In some nations the pattern became conflict between the demands of the government and those of the established church, as in disputes in France over the demands of the church for control over education, marriage and divorce law, and other moral matters. When the Industrial Revolution came, it led to cleavages between urban and rural elements in many nations as well as cleavages between employers and workers.

To Lipset and Rokkan, the party systems of European nations still reflect the interactions of those earlier cleavage patterns. They see a "freezing" of major party alternatives that results in today's party systems mirroring in many ways those of half a century ago. Thus the Christian Democratic, Calvinist, Agrarian, Labour, and many other parties in European countries today are based on cleavages of long ago. The parties may even reflect those cleavages more than contemporary societal cleavages. Nations like France, Germany, and Italy, whose democratic experience was interrupted around World War II by fascist rule and by war, still have party systems that reflect the conflicts of the 1920s. Certainly there have been exceptions, but the beginning point of understanding contemporary partisan change is to realize how much political alternatives had become frozen across a number of countries.

While many contemporary political parties and social conflicts do have long histories, there are several signs of their grip on the current party system loosening. In the United States this has been marked most by the increase in political independence that was pointed to in Table 21-1. In the 1950s most Americans considered themselves either Republicans or Democrats, and less than a quarter called themselves Independents. By the late 1970s, more than a third of the sample called themselves Independents, while the proportion of Republicans had fallen to the level of Independents in the 1950s.[1]

Several aspects of this decline in partisanship are dramatically apparent in *The Changing American Voter* (Nie, Verba, and Petrocik, 1976), a part of which is reprinted here as chapter 27. Fewer citizens now consider themselves strong partisans. More partisans defect to vote for the other party. Increasingly, people vote split tickets rather than voting for candidates of only one party for every office. Presidential candidates are less often evaluated in terms of their party affiliation than in terms of their personal characteristics. Overall, the ties of partisanship are weakening.[2]

This decline in the strength of party has led to increased volatility in the vote, evidenced by the greater uncertainty associated with American presidential elections. Following the New Deal realignment in 1928 and the 1930s, the Democrats were able to win the presidency in five successive presidential elections. But since the 1950s, there has been alternation between the parties: Dwight Eisenhower's Republican White House in the 1950s followed by the John F. Kennedy and Lyndon Johnson Democratic victories of 1960 and 1964, Richard Nixon's Republican victories in 1968 and 1972, Jimmy Carter's Democratic win in 1976, and Ronald Reagan's Republican win in 1980. Even if the party identification majority remains Democratic (see Table 21-1), there is now true volatility in winning the presidency.

Some observers feel that this decline in the strength of party and increased volatility have a potential for leading to an "end of parties." Burnham (1970), for example, speaks of long-term electoral disaggregation and party decomposition. Students of political parties feel that the party organization has been weakened in this century with the decline of the urban political machine, the advent of popular primaries that take decision-making away from party bosses, the institution of federal job and welfare programs that take away many of the benefits that parties could once dispense to the faithful, the replacement of party-based campaigns with media campaigns that are candidate-oriented, and perhaps especially in parts of Europe the massive growth of government bureaucracies to support increasingly socialized public policies. At the extreme, one could imagine a media-based candidate winning major office completely outside traditional party lines (although it must be admitted that writers have long speculated about this possibility in the United States and yet media-based third-party efforts have not shown much success to date).

Still following up on Lipset and Rokkan, one can also ask how much group voting has changed in recent decades. If earlier cleavages are weakening, then the group basis of the parties should be diminishing. The groups that once formed the basis of a party's support would no longer do so—though they would not necessarily shift to the opposite party. Indeed, the question is whether the group basis has declined without a new group basis forming in the meantime.

Here it must be admitted that the evidence is ambiguous. Consider, for example, the data provided by Axelrod (1982). Axelrod decomposed the group contributions to the presidential vote of each party since 1952. The contribution of a group to a party depends on three factors: its size, its turnout level, and its loyalty to its preferred party. A small group necessarily provides a smaller contribution than a larger group, but even a larger group's contribution is limited

Table 26-1 The Democratic Coalition, 1952-1980

	Percentage Contribution						=	(Size						x	Turnout					
Year	P	B	U	C	S	CC		P	B	U	C	S	CC		P	B	U	C	S	CC
1952	28	7	38	41	20	21		36	10	27	26	28	16		46	23	66	76	35	68
1956	19	5	36	38	23	19		25	9	26	25	29	14		40	23	64	72	39	63
1960	16	7	31	47	27	19		23	10	25	25	23	13		46	31	60	74	50	74
1964	15	12	32	36	21	15		19	11	23	26	28	12		45	42	69	72	49	65
1968	12	19	28	40	24	14		16	11	24	26	31	10		44	51	61	68	53	63
1972	10	22	32	43	25	14		12	11	25	31	34	8		37	47	58	65	44	60
1976	7	16	33	35	36	11		9	11	23	30	32	8		32	44	62	55	57	58
1980	5	22	32	32	39	12		5	12	25	31	34	8		31	46	53	52	52	47
Column	1	2	3	4	5	6		7	8	9	10	11	12		13	14	15	16	17	18

	x	Loyalty)						÷	(NTxNL)	
Year		P	B	U	C	S	CC		NT	NL
1952		47	83	59	57	55	51		63	44.4
1956		47	68	55	53	52	55		60	42.0
1960		48	72	66	82	52	65		64	49.7
1964		69	99	80	75	58	74		63	61.1
1968		44	92	51	61	39	58		62	42.7
1972		45	86	45	45	36	61		56	37.5
1976		67	88	63	57	53	61		54	50.1
1980		71	88	50	44	47	69		54	41.0
Column		19	20	21	22	23	24		25	26

P poor (income under $3,000/yr.; $5,000/yr. in 1980)
B black (and other nonwhite)
U union member (or union member in family)
C Catholic (and other non-Protestant)
S southern (including border states)
CC central cities (of 12 largest metropolitan areas)
NT national turnout
NL national loyalty to Democrats

Year	Percentage Deviation in Loyalty to Democrats					
1952	+ 2	+38	+14	+12	+10	+ 6
1956	+ 5	+26	+13	+11	+10	+13
1960	− 2	+22	+16	+32	+ 2	+15
1964	+ 8	+38	+19	+14	− 3	+13
1968	+ 1	+49	+ 8	+18	− 4	+15
1972	+ 8	+49	+ 8	+ 8	− 2	+24
1976	+17	+38	+13	+ 7	+ 3	+10
1980	+30	+47	+ 9	+ 3	+ 6	+28
Column	27	28	29	30	31	32

Source: Robert Axelrod, "Communication," *American Political Science Review* 76 (1982): 394. Reprinted with permission of the publisher.

Table 26-2 The Republican Coalition, 1952-1980

Year	Percentage Contribution						=	(Size						x	Turnout						x	Loyalty)						÷	(NTxNL)	
	NP	W	NU	P	N	NCC		NP	W	NU	P	N	NCC		NP	W	NU	P	N	NCC		NP	W	NU	P	N	NCC		NT	NL
1952	75	99	79	75	87	84		64	90	73	74	72	84		72	67	61	58	73	61		56	57	61	61	57	57		63	55.1
1956	84	98	78	75	84	89		75	91	74	75	71	86		67	64	58	56	69	60		59	59	63	62	60	60		60	57.4
1960	83	97	84	90	75	90		77	90	75	75	66	87		70	68	65	61	71	63		50	51	55	63	50	52		64	49.5
1964	89	100	87	80	76	91		81	89	77	74	72	88		67	66	61	60	68	63		40	42	45	44	38	40		63	38.5
1968	90	99	81	80	80	92		84	89	76	74	69	90		65	63	62	60	66	62		44	47	46	49	47	45		62	43.4
1972	93	98	77	70	73	95		88	89	75	69	66	92		58	57	55	53	62	55		61	66	63	65	60	63		56	60.7
1976	97	99	80	76	67	98		91	89	77	70	68	92		56	56	52	54	53	54		49	52	52	53	49	49		54	48.0
1980	99	99	81	74	67	97		95	88	75	69	65	92		55	55	53	55	55	55		52	56	55	54	51	53		54	50.7
Column	1	2	3	4	5	6		7	8	9	10	11	12		13	14	15	16	17	18		19	20	21	22	23	24		25	26

NP nonpoor (income over $3,000/yr.; $5,000/yr. in 1980)
W white
NU nonunion
P Protestant
N northern (excluding border states)
NCC not in central cities of 12 largest metropolitan areas
NT national turnout
NL national loyalty to Republicans

Year	Percentage Deviation in Loyalty to Republicans					
1952	+1	+2	+6	+ 6	+6	+2
1956	+1	+1	+5	+ 4	+2	+2
1960	0	+1	+5	+13	0	+2
1964	+1	+3	+6	+ 5	−1	+1
1968	0	+3	+2	+ 5	+3	+1
1972	+1	+5	+3	+ 4	−1	+2
1976	+1	+5	+4	+ 5	+1	+1
1980	+1	+5	+5	+ 3	+1	+2
Column	27	28	29	30	31	32

Source: Robert Axelrod, "Communication," *American Political Science Review* 76 (1982): 395. Reprinted with permission of the publisher.

if its turnout rate is low. And even large groups with high turnout make a minimal contribution unless they are loyal to the presidential candidate of their party. Tables 26-1 and 26-2 show the contribution of different groups to the Democratic and Republican vote. The columns showing "percentage deviation in loyalty" are particularly useful since they indicate the difference between the vote cast by a group for a party and the national vote cast for that party.

Several trends are evident in Axelrod's data. The poor, blacks, and central city residents have become increasingly loyal to the Democrats, while union members (and their households), Catholics (and other non-Protestants), and southerners have become less loyal. By contrast, loyalty patterns for Republican groups have changed little. The contribution to the Democratic vote made by blacks increased as black voting rights were protected in the 1960s, and that of southerners has also increased while that of other groups declined. Meanwhile, the contribution of northerners increased while that of other nominally pro-Republican groups has held steady or, in the case of the non-poor and non-central city resident, increased. These figures certainly do not suggest a situation in which party voting no longer exists. On the other hand, changes have occurred in group support, but without a clear realignment of the groups support of each party. We suspect that if a comparable analysis were done for European countries, the same sort of results would be found.

Although it is difficult to tell the precise extent to which dealignment has occurred, there is enough consensus about its existence that the topic should be treated theoretically as well as empirically. For this reason, we reprint a work by Beck (chapter 28) which describes dealignment as part of a cycle of politics. To Beck, realignments are followed by normal politics, which are followed by dealigning periods. Once dealignment has progressed far enough, realignment becomes possible. Beck explains the cyclicity in terms of political generations and socialization theory (see his fuller explanation in chapter 23 of the first edition of this book.) In Beck's analysis, we have moved into a dealigning period, without realignment yet being visible.[3] What is fascinating in Beck's theory is that this cycle affects the entire body-polity of the nation, with different policy implications in each phase. There are alternative interpretations of the events that Beck describes, but it is well worth reflecting on these system-level implications of partisan change.

Discussion of electoral dealignment is not limited to the United States. There have been signs of dealignment in several European countries as well. In some countries this has taken the form of "flash parties," new parties that galvanize popular attention for one or two elections and then fade from view, only to be replaced by an even newer party. For example, in contrast to Lipset and Rokkan's emphasis on the freezing of cleavages, recent elections in the Netherlands have been marked by the emergence of new parties—first the formation of the Democrats 1966 founded on an end-of-ideology platform and designed to break up traditional cleavages, followed only four years later by the formation of the Democratic Socialists '70. In cross-national analysis, Maguire (1983) shows that the vote for the same party in Western Europe became more volatile in 1960-1979 as compared to the entire postwar period, and Pedersen (1979) finds that the volatility of the party systems as a whole increased in the 1970s as contrasted to the 1950s or 1960s.

Särlvik and Crewe (1983) have used the title *Decade of Dealignment* to describe politics in Great Britain in the 1970s. Prior to that, the British system had become one of competition between strong Labour and Conservative parties, with the Liberal party maintaining a distinctively minor presence. But the 1970s was marked by a pulling away from both major parties. Not only did the Liberals benefit (alone or in alliance with the new Social Democratic party in the 1983 election), but also nationalist parties made inroads into the vote in Scotland and Wales (although this in itself was reversed in the 1983 election). Much as in the United States, Särlvik and Crewe's survey evidence shows that strength of partisanship also declined through the decade of the 1970s, falling from 43 percent of identifiers being very strong partisans in 1964 to only 21 percent in 1979.

Rather than view the declining partisanship across a number of countries as coincidental, one can account for the common pattern with a possible common cause—a decline in the importance of class divisions in Western societies. According to this argument, class distinctions were of crucial importance immediately after the Industrial Revolution as well as in the aftermath of the Great Depression. But the 1950s and 1960s were marked by greater affluence among all classes, so there was less necessity for class voting by the 1970s and 1980s. Indeed, trend data for several countries (Inglehart, 1977, chapter 7; Baker, Dalton, and Hildebrandt, 1981, pp. 65-80; Lindstrom, 1982; Borre, 1984) show a decline in class voting in recent decades—though there are occasional increases during periods of economic distress. If politics is class-based and if we are witnessing a decline in the importance of class distinctions, then the end of parties might indeed be possible.[4] That argument presumes, however, that class voting will be completely eradicated. Moreover, the end of parties presumes that class voting will not be replaced by new cleavages. That becomes the element of greatest controversy—are there signs of realignment around new lines of cleavage?

Realigning Politics

While most political scientists agree that party dealignment has been occurring, there is a lively controversy as to whether there has also been party realignment in recent years. The term realignment is meant to describe a situation in which there is an enduring change in relative party strength. This change could be of different magnitudes: from a complete change in the identity of the major parties (as when the Republicans replaced the Whigs in the United States in the 1850s or when Labour and other left-wing parties became major actors in Europe in the late nineteenth and early twentieth centuries), to a change in the party balance (as when the United States shifted from a Republican majority to a Democratic majority in the 1930s), to a long-term increase in the strength of the major party (as when the Gaullists became a dominant force in France in the 1960s), or just the shifting of some social groups from one party to another.[5]

By way of example, there is a consensus among historians that a major realignment occurred in the United States around the 1930s. The Republicans had been the dominant party since the 1890s (as seen by their control of the presidency, except for Wilson's 1912 victory over a divided Republican party and his reelection in 1916), but after the Great Depression the country turned from Hoover's Republicans to Roosevelt's New Deal. The New Deal realignment added the cities and their minority groups (Catholics, Jews, and blacks) to the South, which had been Democratic since the Civil War. The labor union vote and the working-class vote more generally also shifted to the Democrats. The Democrats rapidly became the majority party as a result of these shifts in the group basis of American politics.

Unfortunately, it is difficult to tell when a contemporary realignment has occurred—as one cannot foretell whether political change will be enduring—and it is even difficult to tell exactly when past realignments occurred. Methods have been developed (Burnham, 1970, chapters 1 and 2; Flanigan and Zingale, 1974; Sellers, 1965) that use aggregate data, usually state vote totals, but different methods obtain different results. The consensus among historians (Chambers and Burnham, 1967) is that the five major American party systems are: the competition between Democratic-Republicans and anti-Federalists that ended with the Era of Good Feelings in the 1820s, the competition between Democrats and Whigs from 1828 through the 1850s, the balanced Democratic-Republican competition from the 1860s to 1892, the Republican dominance from 1896 through 1928, and the Democratic dominance since 1928. However, historians would disagree on the exact dates differentiating these eras—questioning, for example, whether the New Deal realignment should be dated from 1932, 1928, 1936, or a "realigning period" throughout the 1930s.

Realignment is generally seen as being issue-based. Perhaps parties change their stands on issues, and voters shift sides accordingly. More likely, new issues arise, and as parties adopt stands on them the basis of party support changes. Sundquist (1973) describes five scenarios that are possible when a new "crosscutting" issue arises that slices across traditional party lines. The issue may prove transitory, affecting one election but disappearing by the next; that is probably the fate of most issues that are potentially realigning. The major parties can take opposing positions on the new issues, thereby each gaining some adherents from the other party—a minor realigning of social groups that does not alter the party balance materially. A third party might be created, with realignment occurring when it is absorbed in one of the traditional parties, as happened in 1896 when the Democrats absorbed the Populist party by nominating its presidential candidate as their own. If none of these less extreme possibilities occur, then a new third party could replace one of the major parties (as the Republicans replaced the Whigs in the 1850s) or, finally, both major parties could be replaced by new parties (a situation that has not occurred in United States history to date).

What issues are urgent enough to lead to such radical changes in a party system? In the American case, the issues causing realignments have been moral (slavery in the 1850s) or economic (severe economic depression in the 1890s and 1930s). It is not clear how severe the economic distress must be to cause realignment, especially since the various recessions and bouts with inflation since the 1930s have not seemed to cause realignment. Nor is it clear what other moral issues can lead to realignment. Racial issues would certainly seem to have this potential, as would abortion and other "life style" issues. Generally, however, the system seems to accommodate these issues before realignment is necessitated.

While this focus on issues suggests how realignments come about, there is no consensus as to how one would tell from survey data that a realignment has occurred. It would be clear that a realignment had occurred if suddenly surveys reported a steady Republican majority in party identification. But party identification might be a lag indicator of realignment, so long-term that it is of the last things to change. Also, the changes that occur in partisanship are sometimes just short-term. For example, in early 1981 several polls reported a swing to the Republicans in party identification, suggesting that a Reagan realignment was in the offing, but that swing proved quite temporary. By the 1982 fall elections the usual Democratic advantage in partisanship was back in place (see Table 21-1).

Since the last agreed-upon realignment occurred before the advent of survey data, it is also difficult to tell the nature of the change processes during a realignment. Do large numbers of people actually "convert," changing their partisanship from one party to another? Or is realignment achieved by "mobilization" of new voters? Andersen (1979) has tried to reconstruct the New Deal realignment from survey reports in the 1950s about whether and when respondents changed partisanship. She finds little evidence of wholesale conversion from Republicans to Democrats in the 1930s. Instead, she shows that large numbers of new voters were mobilized into the Democratic party at that time—both young voters who had not voted before and immigrants who had not previously voted. Her argument is intriguing, as it suggests that a large pool of unmobilized citizens is required for a realignment to take place.

However, Andersen's evidence is not definitive. For one thing, respondents' recall of past partisan change is known to be unreliable, even when a respondent is reporting party change during the brief period of a panel study (Niemi, Katz, and Newman, 1980). Also, Erikson and Tedin (1981) have shown that the *Literary Digest* polls taken in 1928 and the 1930s (which have reliability problems of their own) do not indicate that new voters were distinctively Democratic but instead give evidence of considerable partisan conversion.

Because of the difficulty in determining when a realignment has occurred, analysts have reached different conclusions as to whether or not there has been realignment since the 1930s in the United States. Most books on voting (see, for example, Asher, 1984) assume there has not been, but some analysts argue in favor of a realignment.

In particular, the Carmines, Renten, and Stimson chaper reprinted in this section argues that a realignment occurred in the 1960s as a result of racial issues. Starting in the 1950s the Democrats became less tied to their segregationist southern wing and became the party advancing integration. As the public began to perceive this change, the South became less Democratic while blacks became more solidly Democratic. Total party identification figures changed little in this period, partly because these two types of change were largely compensating in size, but the group basis of the parties changed. Carmines, Renten, and Stimson view this as the essence of a realignment. The total impact on politics was surely not as substantial as that of the 1930s realignment, but Carmines, Renten, and Stimson speculate that the earlier realignment was atypical and that most changes in party alignments are more on the scale of those in the 1960s.

Few other scholars have used the term realignment to describe changes in the 1960s (but for a similar interpretation see Petrocik, 1981).[6] Still, the changed partisanship of southern white Protestants on the one hand and blacks on the other hand have been widely acknowledged (see, for example, Nie, Verba, and Petrocik, 1976, chapter 13). The Carmines, Renten, and Stimson argument is thus controversial, but their chapter is useful in raising questions about the roles of elites and masses in a realignment and about what types of long-term change should be termed realignment.

To this point most of our discussion of realignment has dealt only with the United States. Realignments depend on what the politics already were in a country, and so there is an extent to which they will be country-specific. Other writers have commented on such realignments in other countries in the postwar period. For example, Inglehart and Hochstein (1972) contrast what they see as merely dealignment in the United States in the 1960s with the increasing (re)alignment they find for France over the same period. Whereas Converse and Dupeux (1962) had found low levels of partisanship in France in 1958, partisanship quickly grew after General Charles DeGaulle assumed power and a Gaullist party was formed. Inglehart and Hochstein argue that political conflict in France was relatively unidimensional during this period, and that this encouraged the aligning tendencies, whereas American politics was more multidimensional, with a new issues dimension working at cross-purposes with the traditional party dimension (Weisberg and Rusk, 1970) to produce dealignment. The Inglehart and Hochstein work reminds us that contrary trends can occur in different countries, though often the trends are remarkably similar.

By contrast, the Inglehart chapter in this section (30) is important because it suggests a cross-national basis for party realignment. The last generally acknowledged realignment in the United States and many European nations was due to economic conditions in the 1930s. As prosperity was being achieved in the postwar period, relative affluence may have made people less concerned about economic problems and more interested in other matters. The materialism of previous generations may be in the process of being replaced by a "post-materialism" of the younger generation. Inglehart argues that value change is occurring among the young in Western societies, and that the value change has political ramifications. Politically, the result of this "silent revolution" is a shift to a series of "new politics" concerns—such issues as the environment, disarmament (particularly the nuclear freeze movement), women's status (including such issues as divorce law in some countries and abortion in others), race, and a wide variety of "life style" issues (from gay rights to pornography).[7]

Inglehart is not arguing that a realignment has yet occurred on these new issues, but the potential is there. While his chapter here deals primarily with attitudes, elsewhere Inglehart (1971, 1977) has shown that citizens with post-materialist values vote differently from those with materialist values, which suggests that a realignment may be beginning. Across a number of countries, post-materialists are least likely and materialists most likely to vote for parties of the right, with the largest difference being 43 percent in France and with greater than 20 percent differences in Germany, Italy, and the Netherlands, and the 1972 U.S. presidential vote (Inglehart, 1977, p. 230). Baker, Dalton, and Hildebrandt's discussion of Germany in chapter 8 of this book applies these ideas to contemporary West Germany, arguing that the shifting importance of parties and issues in recent German elections has been due to the way in which new politics issues have affected younger voters.

Inglehart's position remains controversial. Some see the "silent revolution" of which he has written as less than a revolution, while others view it as very temporary. For example, as unemployment increased in the early 1980s, the evidence suggested a natural return to materialistic goals. Inglehart (1983) has responded that this development is natural during a recession but is itself temporary, and he views the long-term trend as toward post-materialism.[8] It remains too early to tell what the long-term direction is, as well as how much effect it will have on party systems. Many European nations experienced the development of strong environmentalist "green" parties in the early 1980s, which would be exactly the impact of post-materialism on party divisions that Inglehart would predict, but it is too early at this point to tell if these are flash parties testifying to the dealignment of politics or whether they represent more permanent realignments of European party systems.

Conclusion

How much has politics changed since the 1930s? Obviously politics has changed considerably. To describe the current day as the same political era that began in the 1930s would be incorrect. The problems of the present are different from the problems of the past. Technology has changed radically, including the technology of political campaigns.

Yet it is equally incorrect to disregard completely the tremendous continuity that exists. Many of the major party doctrines go back to the era of the 1930s, if not further in some cases. There may be change, but there is also substantial continuity.

In any case, there has not been massive convulsive change. There have not been major new parties forming to replace major existing parties. There have not been wholesale movements of political elites and masses from one party to another, as some assume would occur during a realignment. There has been change, but it has been both peaceful and relatively minor.

There are similarities in recent party change trends across a number of countries, but that does not mean that all countries have been affected identically. The different political institutions and party histories in different countries mean that the same event will have different impacts in different nations. There is some gain in considering partisan change cross-nationally, but one must beware of overgeneralizing.

Our own view is that there may well have been some realignment occurring in the United States, particularly in the 1960s. It affected some groups and some policies, but it did not massively change the terrain of party politics. We may also be witnessing some long-term cultural trends of the type that Inglehart describes. But we see dealignment as the major trend. There has been a movement from parties without the polarizing incident that fully realigns the system. To that extent, we would regard the current period as marked more by dealignment than by realignment.

Of course, we realize that political events are bound to overtake these words some day, possibly even in the short run. But we must warn against overinterpreting the events of the present. It is easy to read much into current events, without realizing that they rarely have implications that are truly long-run. A sagging economy can temporarily revitalize the New Deal coalition, but one should not interpret any Democratic win that includes the South as putting back together the New Deal alignment. Such interpretations of Carter's 1976 victory, for example, ignored the fact that his southern success was due more to the black voter than to the white voter (a pattern quite unlike that of the New Deal days), and in any event Carter was unable to keep this coalition together for the 1980 election. Similarly, a victory by a Republican president intent on changing domestic policy priorities may involve some defection from partisanship, but one should not interpret such Republican wins as the death-knell of the New Deal coalition. Such events are minor perturbations that are likely to occur as any political era ages. The drama that leads to large-scale realignment requires much more than these modest shifts.

The pity is that for all our interest in long-term political change, it can only be assessed in the long-term—after it has become old news. It will be much easier to tell whether a realignment began in the United States in 1980, for example, when we look back from the year 2020 to see whether the Republicans maintained control of the White House in 1984, whether they eventually gained control of both houses of Congress, and whether the domestic policy changes initiated by President Reagan remained in force. But by then the topic will be the meat of historians, rather than whetting the appetites of political scientists.

NOTES

1. This evidence on the increased proportion of independents has been cited widely and frequently, but it is less definitive than it might appear. Even in the post-1950 period, most self-declared Independents would admit they were closer to one party than to the other. Consequently, some analysts believe that the increase in Independents just reflected a growing feeling that one should claim to be independent, even if one were really a partisan voter. According to that view, the increase is just a growth in "closet partisans."

   In addition, Miller and Wattenberg (1983) show that much of the increase in Independents starting in 1964 was due to a change in the coding procedure of the Michigan studies, with the people who volunteer to the first party identification question that they have "no partisan preference" being coded as "Independents" if they show some interest in politics.
2. Norpoth and Rusk (1982) trace the sources of the partisan dealignment. They find that the changing age composition of the electorate did little to explain the change. The major sources of change are instead the lower partisan levels of those who entered the electorate after 1964, desertion of parties by adult voters, and the absence of life-cycle increases in strength of partisanship after 1964.
3. Clubb, Flanigan, and Zingale (1980) divide electoral cycles in a related manner: party realignment at a critical election, followed by a stable phase (Beck's period of normal politics), followed by a "midsequence adjustment" and a decay phase. Their analysis of voting patterns over a series of elections suggests that long-term change occurred with the 1948-1954 elections. They regard the period since then as marked by the deterioration of the New Deal alignment.

4. Of course, the decline in class voting does not mean that Lipset and Rokkan's other cleavages have also declined. Inglehart (1977) has shown that preindustrial cleavages, such as religion, language, and race, remain important even as class has diminished as a correlate of the vote. Lijphart's (1979) analysis of the multidimensional party systems of Belgium, Canada, Switzerland, and South Africa shows that religious cleavages remain important in the first three while linguistic cleavages are more important in the latter. Few analyses in the United States or Europe have considered the entire range of cleavages simultaneously.
5. Realignments are seen as important from many differnt perspectives. They illustrate the ultimate importance of issues in voting. They call attention back to the group basis of voting. From a societal standpoint, they represent a peaceful alternative to the regime change by revolution and force that is common in some other countries. The election system remains in force.
6. Relying more on election results, Abramson, Aldrich, and Rohde (1983) conclude that the South now belongs to neither party, that the Democrats are no longer the majority party nationally, and that the Republicans have had the edge in postwar presidential elections. They do not specifically call this a realignment (though it certainly is a different alignment than was true after the New Deal) and appear to see it as the result of dealignment.
7. It is important to recognize that there are two sides to these issues. It is not simply that proponents of these causes are leaving the conventional parties. For example, most people may be "pro-environment," but their support for environmental issues may be tempered by economic considerations. Thus there are people who oppose what they consider extreme environmentalist demands. On the moral issues, there are people who want greater freedom from government, but there are also "moral majority" groups who want new government action to forestall what they see as decadence. Thus new politics means new issues of cleavage.
8. Flanagan (1980) adds a distinction between the respondent's "value-preference" (traditional to libertarian, with the latter being more self-actualizing) and "value salience" (emphasis on economic interests, either materialist or nonmaterialist). He finds value preferences to have a relationship with the vote in Japan, while value salience does not correlate with the vote. Value preferences affect the vote directly only for nonmaterialists, while occupational class directly affects the vote only for materialists.

FURTHER READINGS

Historical Dealignment Trends

Walter Dean Burnham, *Critical Elections and the Mainsprings of American Politics* (New York: Norton 1970). The end of parties?

Jerrold G. Rusk, "The Effect of the Australian Ballot Reform on Split Ticket Voting: 1876-1908," *American Political Science Review* (1970) 64:1220-38. Burnham's trend data is contaminated by institutional ballot changes. See also the continuing Burnham-Rusk debate in the 1974 APSR, pp. 1000-57.

William J. Crotty and Gary C. Jacobson, *American Parties in Decline* (Boston: Little, Brown, 1980). Decline of parties in the electorate, campaigns, and Congress.

Bo Särlvik and Ivor Crewe, *Decade of Dealignment* (Cambridge: Cambridge University Press, 1983). Analysis of the 1979 British general election, with emphasis on dealignment through the 1970s.

Historical Realignment Trends

V. O. Key, Jr., "A Theory of Critical Elections," *Journal of Politics* (1955) 17:3-18. Classic theoretical statement of realigning elections.

William Nisbet Chambers and Walter Dean Burnham, *The American Party Systems* (New York: Oxford University Press, 1967). Review of party systems through U.S. history.

Jerome M. Clubb, William H. Flanigan, and Nancy H. Zingale, *Partisan Realignment* (Beverly Hills: Sage, 1980). Empirical analysis of realignments in American history.

Bruce A. Campbell and Richard J. Trilling, eds., *Realignment in American Politics* (Austin: University of Texas Press, 1980). Current set of readings on realignment at mass and elite levels, including policy consequences of realignment.

Paul Kleppner, Walter Dean Burnham, Richard P. Formisano, Samuel P. Hays, Richard Jensen, and William G. Shade, *The Evolution of American Electoral Systems* (Westport, Conn.: Greenwood Press, 1981). Historical review of conflicts in American party systems.

The New Deal Realignment

Kristi Andersen, *The Creation of a Democratic Majority 1928-1936* (Chicago: University of Chicago Press, 1979). Reconstruction of the dynamics of the New Deal realignment.

Robert S. Erikson and Kent L. Tedin, "The 1928-1936 Partisan Realignment," *American Political Science Review* (1981) 75:951-62. New Deal realignment is due to wide-scale conversion (opposite of Andersen's argument).

Implications for Political Institutions

Richard Funston, "The Supreme Court and Critical Elections," *American Political Science Review* (1975) 69:795-811. Realignment effects on the judicial branch.

Benjamin Ginsberg, "Elections and Public Policy," *American Political Science Review* (1976) 70:41-49. Frequency of policy changes during realignments.

David Brady, "Congressional Party Realignment and Transformations of Public Policy in Three Realignment Eras," *American Journal of Political Science* (1982) 26:333-60. Realignment effects on policy voting in Congress.

Post-Materialism and New Politics

Ronald Inglehart, *The Silent Revolution* (Princeton: Princeton University Press, 1977). Changing values change political cleavages in Western societies.

Kendall L. Baker, Russell J. Dalton, and Kai Hildebrandt, *Germany Transformed* (Cambridge: Harvard University Press, 1981). Change in post-war West German politics, with emphasis on the role of new politics.

Russell J. Dalton, Paul Allen Beck, and Scott C. Flanagan, *Electoral Change in Industrial Democracies* (Princeton: Princeton University Press, 1984). Cross-national analysis of voting change, with emphasis on new politics.

The Electoral Coalition Base of Parties

Seymour M. Lipset and Stein Rokkan, eds., *Party Systems and Voter Alignments* (New York: Free Press, 1967). The relationship between cleavage structure and party systems in Western societies.

Robert Axelrod, "Where the Votes Come From," *American Political Science Review* (1972) 66:11-20. Considers the contribution of groups to a party's vote.

Richard Rose, ed., *Electoral Behavior* (New York: Free Press, 1974). Comparable analyses of the importance of social cleavages for the vote in 12 nations.

Everett C. Ladd, Jr., with Charles D. Hadley, *Transformation of the American Party System*, 2nd ed. (New York: Norton, 1978). Argues class lines have inverted, with the Democrats now being supported by a coalition of the highest socioeconomic status and the lowest.

Seymour M. Lipset, ed., *Party Coalitions in the 1980s* (San Francisco: Institute for Contemporary Studies, 1981). Readings on shifting party coalitions.

John R. Petrocik, *Party Coalitions* (Chicago: University of Chicago Press, 1981). Group realignment has occurred, without a critical election.

27. THE DECLINE OF PARTISANSHIP

Norman H. Nie, Sidney Verba, and John R. Petrocik

Perhaps the most dramatic political change in the American public over the past two decades has been the decline of partisanship. As we have seen party affiliation was the central thread running through interpretations of American politics in the 1950s and 1960s. Citizen attitudes on issues appeared to be only slightly related one to another, and they were unstable enough over time to suggest that a high proportion of citizens had no meaningful issue positions. But party affiliation was a stable characteristic of the individual: it was likely to be inherited, it was likely to remain steady throughout the citizen's political life, and it was likely to grow in strength during that lifetime.[1]

Even more important, party affiliation was connected to other political phenomena. For the citizen, his sense of identification with a party was a guide to behavior; citizens voted for their party's candidates. It was a guide to understanding the political universe; candidates and issues were evaluated in party terms. Parties were objects of affective attachment; citizens expressed positive feelings about their parties. And those citizens with partisan affiliation were the most active and involved citizens; partisanship appeared to be a force mobilizing citizens into political life. Partisanship gave continuity and direction to the political behavior of citizens and to American electoral life.[2]

The weakening of partisanship has been documented many times in the works of political scientists such as Gerald Pomper, Walter Dean Burnham, and Jack Dennis.[3] Much of the data we present in this chapter parallels theirs and will not be new to the student of the subject. It is, however, important to lay out the variety of ways in which the decline of partisanship has been manifested in order to connect these varied changes with other trends we shall discuss. The situation can be summarized as follows: (1) Fewer citizens have steady and strong psychological identification with a party. (2) Party affiliation is less of a guide to electoral choice. (3) Parties are less frequently used as standards of evaluation. (4) Parties are less frequently objects of positive feelings on the part of citizens. (5) Partisanship is less likely to be transferred from generation to generation.

Some Data on Partisanship

Party Identification

Figure 27-1 traces over time the proportion of the population that strongly identifies with one of the political parties, the proportion that weakly identifies with a party, and the proportion that professes independence of the parties. From 1952 to 1964 the proportions remain remarkably stable: a little more than a third of the populace is strongly partisan and a slightly larger group is weakly partisan. The remaining fifth of the population is Independent. The stability of these figures through 1964—despite the wide swings in popular vote from the strong Eisenhower victory of 1956, through the close 1960 race, to the Johnson sweep in 1964—represent convincing evidence of the continuity of partisanship.

From 1964 through 1974, however, the situation changes. The proportion of strong identifiers drops while the proportion of Independents rises. By 1974 only about one out of four Americans can be considered a strong partisan while 38 percent are Independent. Note also that among those who identify with a political party from 1952 through 1964, about equal numbers consider themselves weak and strong partisans. By the 1970s those who consider themselves partisans are

Figure 27-1 Partisan Affiliation, 1952-1974

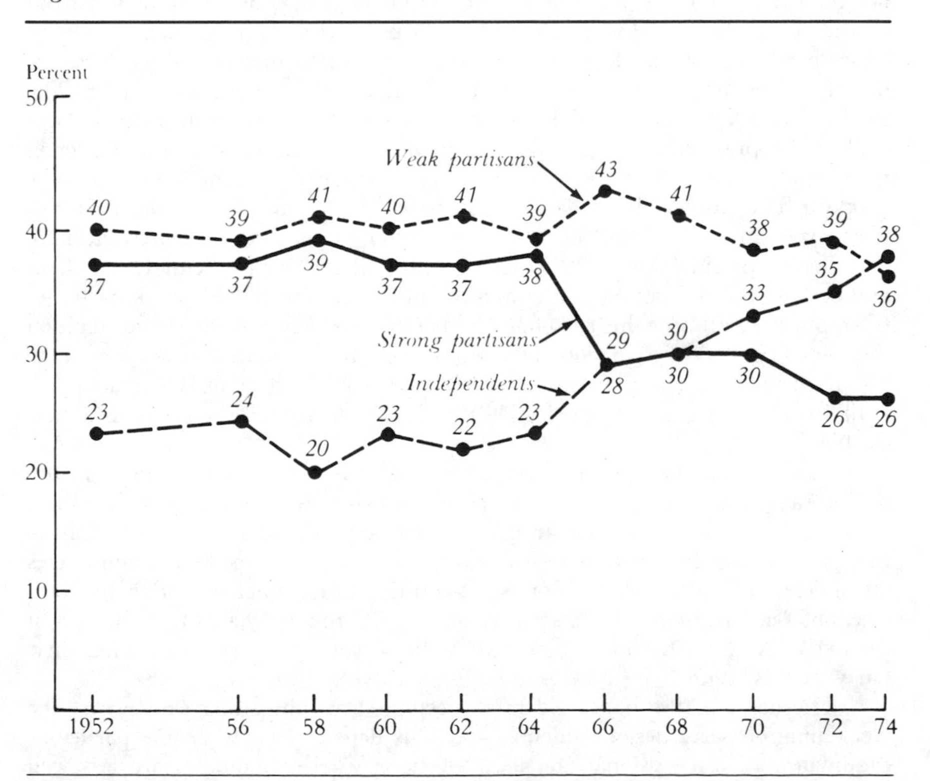

more likely to be weak than strong partisans. The figures indicate a clear erosion of the strength of party affiliation in the American public.[4]

Party and the Vote

In 1956 party identification was the key to the vote. Despite the large number of Democrats who crossed party lines to vote for Eisenhower, 83 percent of those Americans with a party identification voted consistent with that identification in the presidential election; about 90 percent voted consistent with that identification in the congressional elections.

Consider the data in Figure 27-2 which show the proportion of party identifiers who did not vote for the candidate of their party in the elections from 1952 to 1974. The proportion defecting from their party in presidential elections was quite similar from 1952 to 1964, again a stability worth stressing given the heterogeneity of those elections. The defection rate in 1968 was substantially higher (largely a reflection of George Wallace's candidacy) and stayed high in 1972. In 1968 and 1972, more than one out of four party identifiers voted for the presidential candidate of the opposition party. If the group of identifiers who abandoned their party in 1972 to vote for the opposing presidential candidate (they are 17 percent of all voters[5]) is added to the 34 percent who are Independents in that year, one finds that 51 percent of the voting population are not guided by a party affiliation. They either vote against their own party's candidate, or they are Independent with no party ties to guide them.

Presidential voting figures, however, are hard to interpret since they are heavily dependent on the noncomparable exigencies of the particular race. The extent to which the division of the vote is influenced by the characteristics and appeal of the presidential candidates, for example, is well known. The defection rates in other races, therefore, may be essential to interpreting the erosion of party support. The proportion of defectors in both House and Senate elections also rises, especially toward the end of the period. There tends to be somewhat more defection in presidential years because of the pull of the presidential candidates and because the electorate is larger and contains more voters with weak party ties (Campbell, 1960). For this reason, off-year elections may provide clearer data on the role of party. We have plotted the off-year elections separately, and they show a pattern of change similar to that of the presidential elections. Compare 1958 with 1974, for instance. The defection rate in Senate and House elections almost doubles.[6]

Lastly we can look at the defection rates for state and local elections. The defection rates are in general higher in these races since we consider a voter to be a defector if he did not vote the straight party ticket in state and local elections—that is, even one defecting vote for one of the many offices in the election makes one a defector. The number of voters not voting a straight ticket in state and local elections remains more or less steady from 1952 through 1960. From then on, it rises sharply. By 1974 more than half of those voting report abandoning their party at least once.

The data for the nonpresidential elections are compelling evidence of the weakening of party ties. Presidential elections depend heavily on the particular candidates. In congressional and local elections where candidates are less well

Figure 27-2 Proportion of Party Identifiers Voting for Candidate of Other Party, 1952-1974

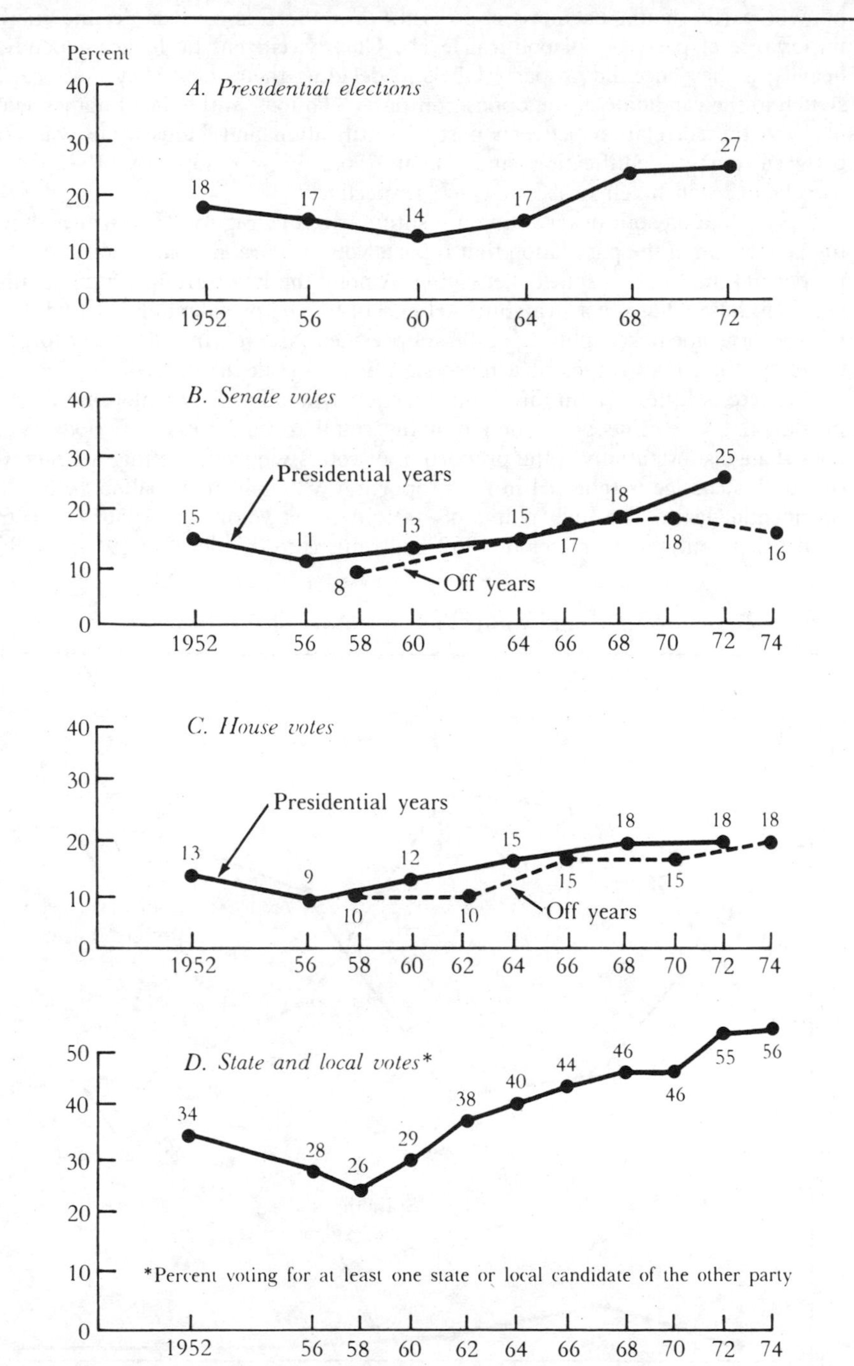

known, party should be more important.[7] Yet there is a clear decline in the importance of party on all political levels. Clearly, citizens no longer depend as heavily as they once did on party labels in deciding their vote. They more easily switch to the candidate of the opposition party. To look at the data another way, in 1956 the correlation between party identification and House vote was .72; between party identification and Senate vote it was .68. By 1972 these correlations had fallen to .55 and .47, respectively.

The data on split ticket voting are summarized in Figure 27-3, which shows the proportion of the population that reports voting a straight party ticket and the proportion that reports split ticket voting. Among the latter group we distinguish between those who vote a straight ticket except for the presidential vote and those who report some ticket splitting at the subpresidential level since the latter form of ticket splitting may represent a more significant break in partisanship.

There is little variation in the proportion who split their ballot only on the presidential vote. The proportion remains small throughout the period. What does change substantially is the proportion of voters who vote a straight ticket. Of course this change is reflected in the proportion who split their ballots below the presidential level. The high points of straight ticket voting are 1956 and 1960. Split ticket voting was greater in 1952 and returns to that level in 1964; in 1968

Figure 27-3 Straight and Split Ticket Voting, 1952-1972

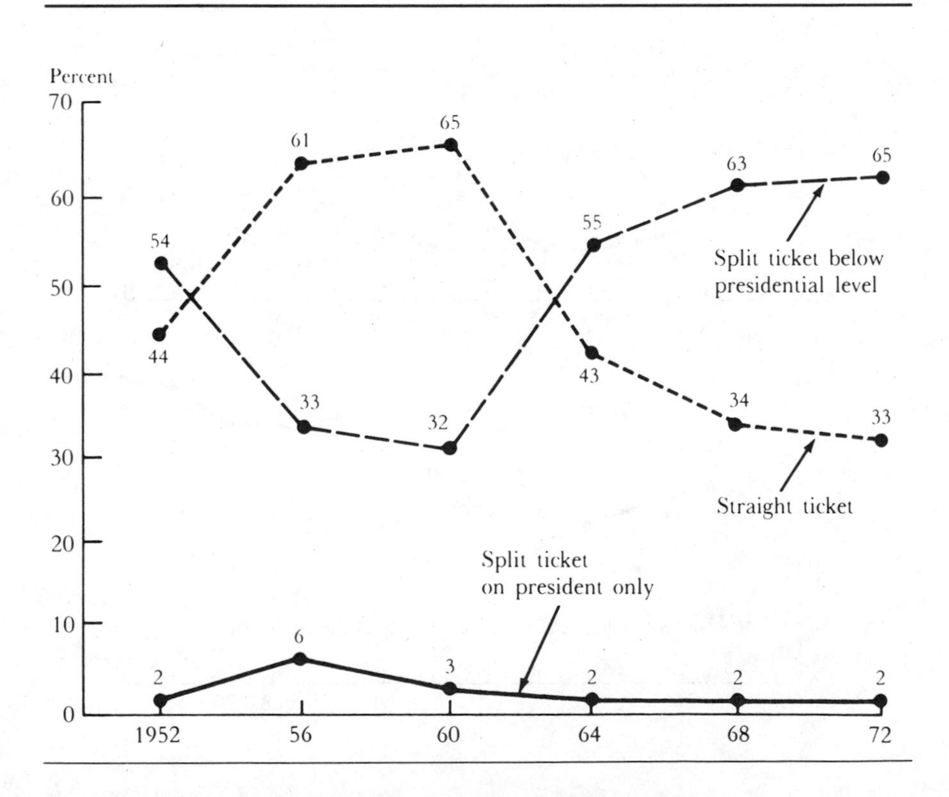

and 1972 it increases even further. The data summarize what has been shown thus far: the 1956 and 1960 elections were high points of party attachment.

The data are particularly striking when one remembers that these are defection rates for those who profess affiliation with a party. Over time the proportion with such self-identification has fallen. One would think that those who remain attached to one or the other of the parties would be those whose commitment was stronger, the less committed having moved into the Independent ranks. Yet even among the increasingly smaller group of party identifiers one finds party affiliation playing a smaller role in determining the vote.[9]

The change in the strength of party ties from the 1950s to the beginning of the 1970s is also apparent in the constancy of party voting from election to election. In each of the elections from 1952 to 1972, respondents were asked whether they always voted for the same party in presidential elections. In 1952, one-third of the voters reported that they had not always voted for presidential candidates of the same party. By 1972, the situation had changed drastically. Over half of the voters reported that their presidential vote had not been constant in party terms (Figure 27-4, dotted line).

The proportion of citizens who are inconstant in their vote—sometimes voting for the presidential candidate of one party, sometimes for the other—can be expected to rise with the rise in the proportion of Independents in the population. Their votes are more likely to move from party to party. But even those who still consider themselves to be partisans are more likely to switch their votes from party to party. The solid line in Figure 27-4 reports the proportion of inconstant

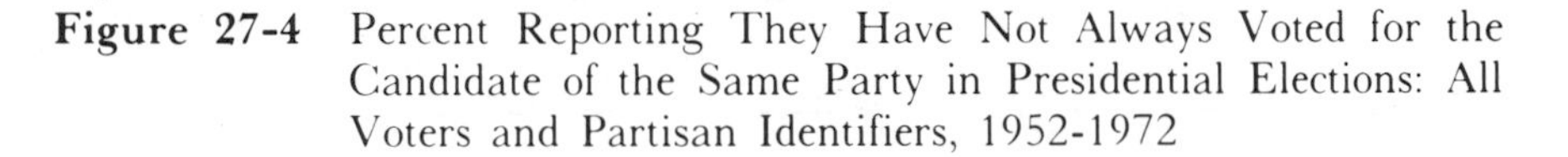

Figure 27-4 Percent Reporting They Have Not Always Voted for the Candidate of the Same Party in Presidential Elections: All Voters and Partisan Identifiers, 1952-1972

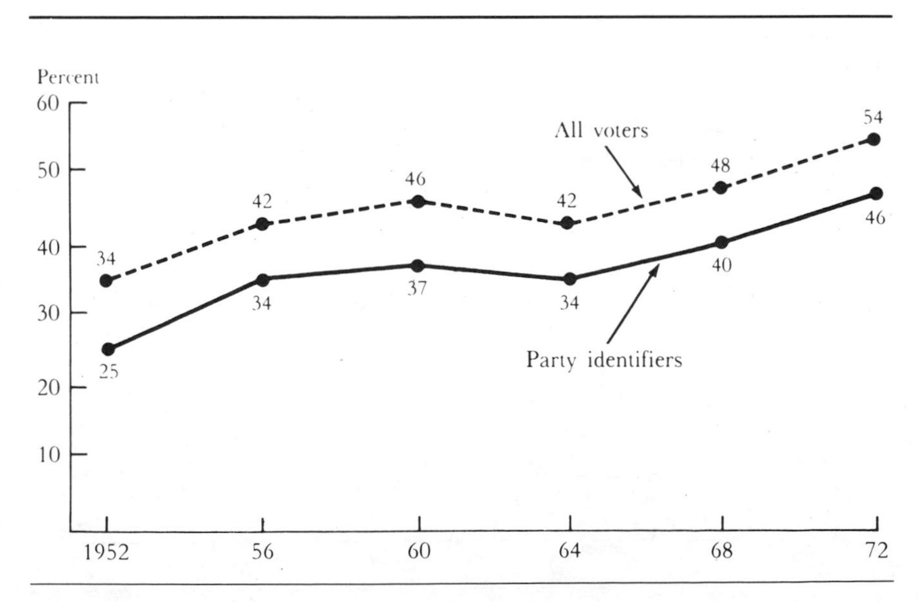

presidential voters only for those with a party affiliation. The inconstancy of presidential voting has increased even among those who have maintained their affiliation. In 1952, only one out of four party identifiers reported inconstancy in the vote. By 1972, almost one out of two identifiers said that they did not always vote for the same party.

The identifiers in the later years—1968 and 1972—ought to be a "hard-core" of partisans since so many of the weaker partisans have taken to considering themselves Independents. But even the hard-core group is weakening in the steadiness with which it follows the party line when it comes to the presidential vote.

Party and Candidate Evaluation

It is clear from these data that citizens are less frequently guided by partisan affiliation in the choice of the candidate for whom they will vote. One can observe this in a somewhat different way by considering what it is that respondents like or dislike about the candidates in presidential races.[10] As noted earlier, almost half of the electorate mention the party affiliation of the candidate as one reason for liking or disliking a candidate: "He is a good Democrat," and so forth. Figure 27-5 shows the proportion that use partisanship as an evaluative standard for candidates from 1952 to 1972. In 1952, 46 percent of the voters cite a party reason for candidate preference. The percentage goes down in 1964 but up again in 1968. By 1972, that figure has dropped to 24 percent. And the proportion of citi-

Figure 27-5 Proportion of Citizens Mentioning the Candidate's Party Affiliation as a Reason for Liking or Disliking Him, 1952-1972

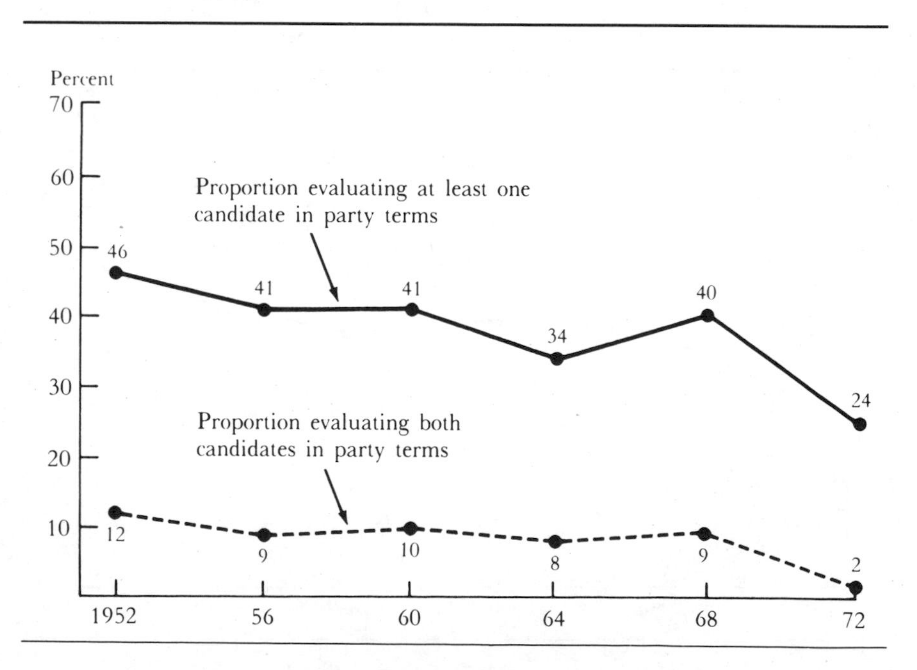

Figure 27-6 Proportion of Democratic and Republican Identifiers Mentioning the Candidate's Party Affiliation as a Reason for Liking or Disliking Him, 1952-1972

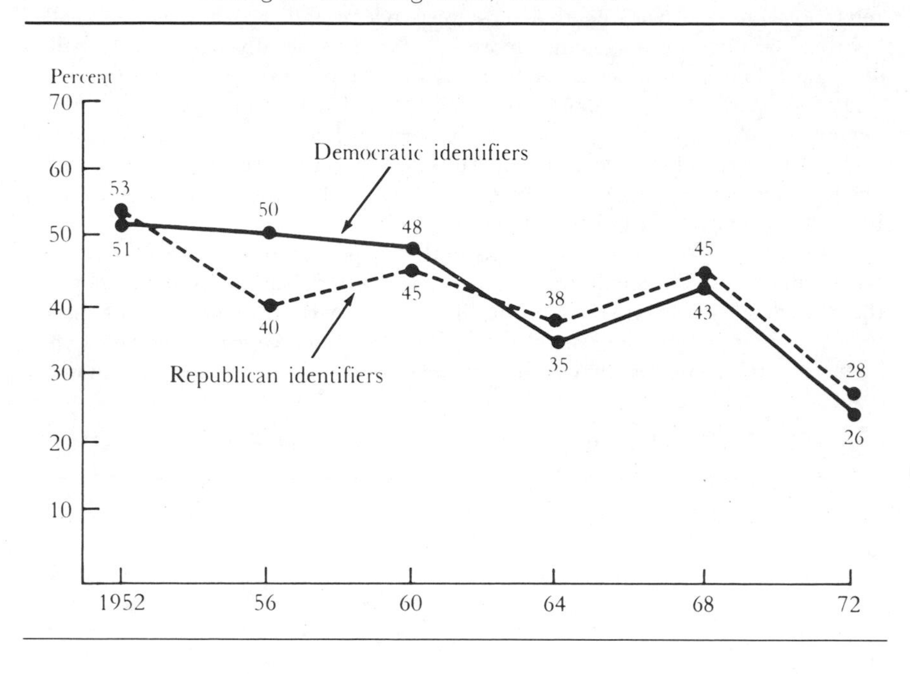

zens who evaluate both candidates in party terms—they like their own candidate because of his party and dislike the opponent because he is affiliated with the opposition—had fallen even more precipitously, from 12 percent to 2 percent.[11]

The decline in the use of party as an evaluative standard is not merely a function of the larger proportion of the populace who have no party ties. The frequency with which candidates are preferred or rejected because of their party ties has declined, even among those who identify with one of the parties (see Figure 27-6).

The data on the use of partisan characteristics of the candidate as a basis for evaluations of the candidate add an important separate confirmation of the erosion of the importance of party. The candidate evaluation questions are open-ended. They elicit whatever standards of evaluation the respondent has in his mind. When party is mentioned it is mentioned spontaneously. The fact that the frequency of such spontaneous mentions declines so rapidly is further evidence that the political centrality of the political party has declined.

Citizen Affection for the Parties

Perhaps the clearest evidence of the erosion of support for the parties is found in Figure 27-7. In each of the election years, the SRC has asked respondents what they like and what they dislike about each of the parties. Earlier, answers to these questions were used to assign respondents to one or another level of conceptualization. These responses can also be used to measure the extent to which respondents have positive or negative views about the parties. Respondents can mention a number of things they like about each party and a number of things they dislike. We compared the rate of positive and negative references. In 1952 we find that most respondents fall in a category we called "partisans": they say on balance more positive than negative things about their own party and on balance are either negative or neutral about the opposition. Sixty-four percent of the population falls into this category. An additional 5 percent says positive things about both parties. The remaining 31 percent of respondents are considered nonsupporters of the party system: they are either negative about both parties, negative about one and neutral about the other, or have no opinion about either.

Figure 27-7 shows what happens to the proportion of these various types of party supporters. The small group that likes both parties remains low throughout the period. More striking is the decline in the partisans and the rise in the nonsupporters. In the elections of the 1950s those who were positive about their own party and combined that with negative or neutral views about the opposition

Figure 27-7 The Decline in Positive Evaluation of Parties, 1952-1972

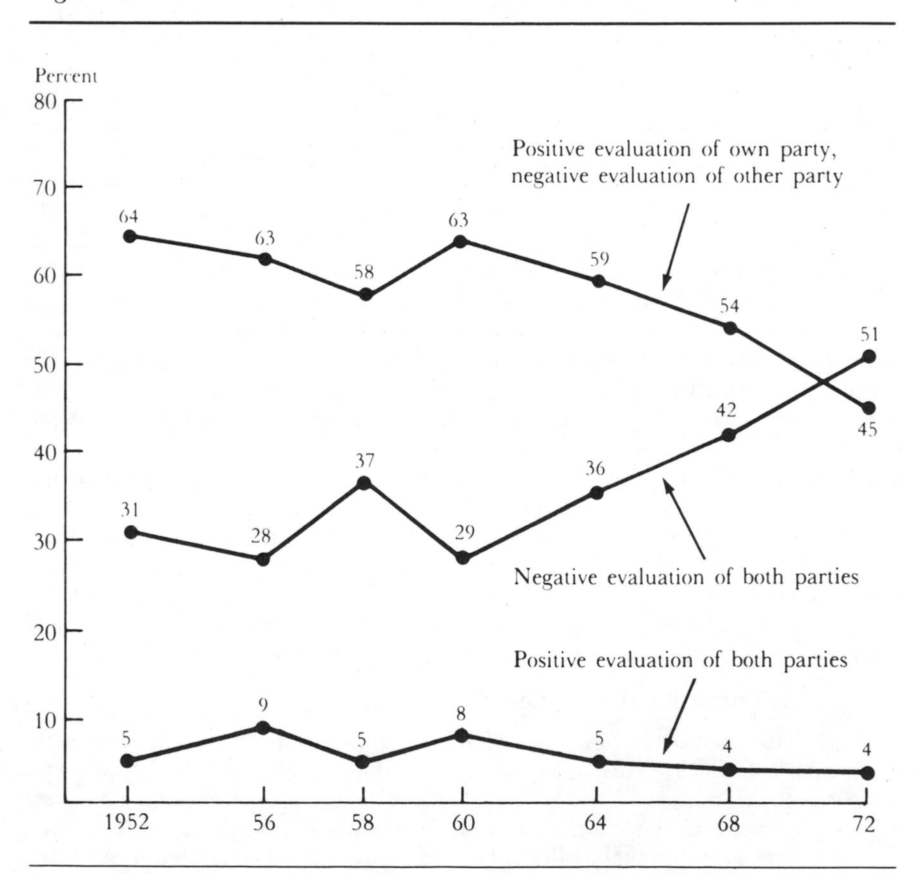

Table 27-1 Proportion of Partisan Identifiers Who Report Changing Their Party Identification During the Previous Four Years, 1952-1974

1952	*1956*	*1958*	*1960*	*1964*	*1968*	*1970*	*1972*	*1974*
3	5	2	3	4	3	3	5	4

outnumbered those who supported neither party by more than two to one. By 1972 more Americans were either hostile or neutral toward the political parties than were supporters of one or the other parties.

In sum, the data show a dramatic decline of partisanship during the two decades we have been tracing. The decline is apparent across a wide range of measures. Citizens are less likely to identify with a party, to feel positively about a party, or to be guided in their voting behavior by partisan cues.

The loosening of party ties, however, is not manifested in a switch of allegiance from one of the major parties to the other. In the SRC studies, respondents are asked if they have switched parties. Table 27-1 shows the proportions who report switching allegiance from one party to the other in the previous four years. As one can see, the proportion is small and remains small even during the period of rapid erosion of partisanship in the late 1960s and early 1970s.[12] The trend appears to be away from parties, not from one party to another.

Sources of the Decline of Partisanship

Partisanship is a habit, the strength of which grows with the length of time one has had the habit. This is one of the main findings of analyses of partisanship across the citizen's life cycle.[13] Older citizens should be more firmly attached to one of the political parties. They have had more exposure to the electoral process and, therefore, more time to acquire and confirm their party attachment. The surge of Independents, this suggests, may come from new entrants into the political system rather than from those who have abandoned already-established party ties. The data in Table 27-2 support this expectation. Table 27-2 presents the proportion of Independents who report having abandoned a party identification in the previous four years. The data are for those Independents who are over twenty-five years of age and who have been in the electorate for the previous four years. As one can see, the proportion who have abandoned a party preference is small in each of the years. More important, the proportions show very little rise in the period of erosion of party ties. In most years, only about 10 percent of the Independents report having had previous party ties. Clearly, the increase in Independents is not attributable in any large part to an abandonment of partisanship by those already in the electorate. The alternative explanation may lie in the replacement of the older electorate with a new one. The young voters who enter the electorate are less likely to have party attachment.

Table 27-2 Proportion of Independents Over 25 Years of Age Who Have Abandoned Party Identification During the Previous Four Years, 1956-1972[a]

1956	*1958*	*1960*	*1964*	*1968*	*1970*	*1972*
8	13	3	8	8	11	10

[a] Question not asked in 1952; asked in a noncomparable form in 1974.

Thus, the source of the rise of independence is found by considering age differences. Table 27-3 presents the proportion of Independents found in different age groups in each of the presidential terms. The data are consistent with the view that the strength of party affiliation grows with age. In each year one finds a larger percentage of the young falling into the category of Independents and a smaller percentage of the older age groups with no party attachment.

The fact of stronger partisan ties among older citizens appears consistently in the various election years, but there is a clear change in magnitude across the years. In the earlier period there is much less difference among the age groups than in the later period. In 1952, the youngest group differs from the over-thirty years of age population by only 3 percentage points in terms of the proportions of Independents. Twenty-five percent of the youngest group and 22 percent of the over-thirty group are Independent. By 1974, there is a 19 percentage point difference between the two age groups; 53 percent of the youngest group is Independent compared with 34 percent of the over-thirty population. The data strongly suggest that the change in the direction of partisan independence comes largely among the younger citizens.[14]

Table 27-3 Proportion Independents by Age, 1952-1974

Age	*1952*	*1956*	*1960*	*1964*	*1968*	*1972*[a]	*1974*[a]
21-25	25	37	39	33	53	51	53
26-30	32	31	26	29	41	50	42
31-40	23	26	27	26	29	40	39
41-50	26	21	25	24	31	30	37
51-65	19	24	21	18	24	26	32
66+	20	13	13	14	15	19	23
Average percent Independent among those over 30	22	22	22	21	26	28	34
Difference between youngest and over 30	3	15	17	12	27	23	19

[a] For 1972 and 1974 the youngest age group is 18 to 25.

The situation can be made clearer by considering changes in some age cohorts over time. The cohorts we compare are:

1. The established voters of 1952. These are the citizens who were twenty-five years of age or older in 1952. In 1956, they are the group that is twenty-nine years and older, and so on until 1974 when they are at least forty-seven years of age. By following their degree of partisanship, we can see what happens to a group that was exposed to the electoral process during the era when partisan ties were stable and firm.

2. The new voters of 1952. This is the age group that enters the electorate between 1949 and 1953. They are twenty-one to twenty-four years of age in our 1952 study; forty-three to forty-five years of age in 1974. They too, have long exposure to the party system by the time the late 1960s come around, though, on the average, not as long as the established voters of 1952.

3. The new voters of 1960. These are the voters who enter the electorate between the 1956 elections and 1961. They do not appear in our 1952 data, of course. They are the twenty-one to twenty-four years of age in 1960, and they are thirty-five to thirty-eight years of age in the 1974 data.

4. The new voters of 1964. This group enters the electorate by the time of the 1964 election, but not by the 1960 election. Members of this group range in age from thirty-one to thirty-four years of age in 1974.

5. The post-1964 voters. They enter the electorate between 1956 and 1973. They are eighteen to thirty years of age in 1974.[15]

Party Identification

Figure 27-8 compares these age cohorts in terms of the proportion Independent across the two decades. Because sample sizes become quite small when one looks at specific age groups, we average the data for pairs of elections—that is, we report the average for the 1956 and 1958 elections, the 1960 and 1962 elections, and so on.[16] The data allow us to examine the relationship between the close and stable partisan ties that characterized the electorate in the 1950s and the forces making for the erosion of such ties in the late 1960s. If the hypothesis that such ties become stronger the longer they exist is correct, we should find differences among the cohorts in the way they react to the challenges to the party system in the late 1960s. The data in Figure 27-8 support the proposition that partisanship solidifies with exposure to the party system. The data also suggest a relationship between long-term commitments to a party and the specific historical events that loosened party ties in the late 1960s. Party affiliation appears harder to shake the longer it has existed. However, such attachment can loosen among those whose party commitment has had less time to become well rooted. More important, the events which erode partisanship seem to have their largest impact on the newest cohort of voters.

Consider the group that was well established in the electorate by 1952: the established voters of 1952. When the challenges to the party system begin in the late 1960s, this group does not respond with an increase in party independence. By the time the parties come under challenge, this cohort has had at least twenty and in most cases many more years to acquire an affiliation. When they first appear on our figure in 1952, 23 percent are Independent. Twenty years later the proportion of Independents among them has risen by only 4 percent.

Figure 27-8 Proportion of Independents by Age Cohorts, 1952-1972

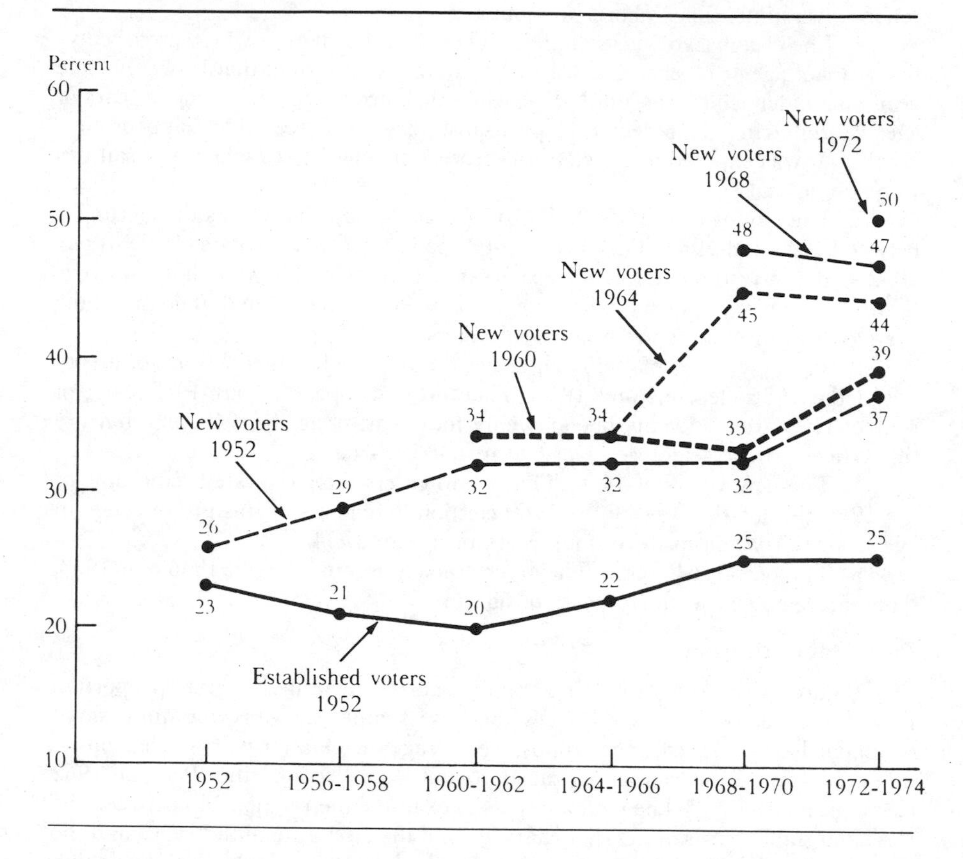

The next cohort to consider is that of the new voters of 1952. When partisanship comes under challenge in the late 1960s, they too have been in the electorate for a long time (about sixteen years), but not as long as those voters who were "established" in 1952. This cohort is not immune from the impact of the challenges to the parties. The proportion who are Independents grows by 11 percentage points over the two decades. At the beginning of the time period, this group was only 3 percentage points more Independent than the established voters of 1952. By the end of the time period they are 10 points more Independent.[17] A similar increase in the proportion Independent is found for the new voters of the 1960 cohort.

The more interesting comparison group is the new voters of 1964 cohort. In 1964-1966 they do not show a level of independence different from the new voters of 1952 or 1960 cohorts. However, these groups diverge in 1968. The new voters of 1964 show a sharp increase in the proportion who are Independent, while the 1952 and 1960 groups do not change. The 1964 cohort, attached to a party for only a few years, has a less firmly fixed party preference and is immediately susceptible to events which erode partisanship.

Still more Independent is the cohort that enters the electorate in 1968, when the forces eroding partisan commitment are strong. This 1968 cohort enters with a remarkably high level of independence—50 percent—and it remains highly Independent through 1972-1974. And the new voters of 1972 enter at a similarly high level of independence.

The data in Figure 27-8 are consistent with the following conclusions: Partisanship is a long-term commitment that once established is hard to shake. The cohort that has been in the electorate for the longest time is largely resistant to the forces that shook partisan identification since the late 1960s. Those who have been in the electorate a shorter time before being exposed to the events of the middle and the late sixties have been more easily moved into the Independent category. The length of affiliation has a delaying effect on party erosion. Those who entered the electorate in 1952 do not begin to abandon party until 1972-1974; those who entered in 1964 begin their exodus in 1968-1970. Finally, those who first entered the electorate during the late 1960s come in at very high levels of partisan neutrality, and have remained there.

Much of the change in the partisan commitment of Americans appears to come from those new voters who enter the electorate in the late 1960s. Their impact is made greater by the fact that young voters have been an increasing proportion of the electorate. In 1952, 8 percent of our sample was between twenty-one and twenty-four; twenty years later 12 percent of the sample falls in that age group (and if one adds the eighteen to twenty year olds, one has an electorate in 1972 in which 17 percent of its members was not eligible to vote in the previous election). The combination of the fact that the new voters are a larger proportion of the electorate and the fact of their greater independence makes clear that these new voters contribute disproportionately to the decay of partisanship.

Changing Strength of Commitment

The members of the cohort who entered the electorate in 1952 tended to maintain their party preference; but does the preference weaken over time? We can answer this question by looking at some of the indicators of strength of partisan commitment among those who are partisans. Figure 27-9 deals with strength of identification. The percentages are the proportion of those who identify with a party who report that they are strong identifiers. As we have seen earlier, that proportion has been falling over time. But as Figure 27-9 indicates, those cohorts who had entered the electorate by the time of the 1952 election have, in general, remained strong partisans. The established voters of 1952 cohort (those who were twenty-four and over in 1952) does not change. About one-half of the identifiers consider themselves strong identifiers in each election during the two decades. The same is true for the new voters of 1952. They also remain relatively steadfast in terms of the proportion of identifiers who have strong identification.

The source of the weakened identification among those who are party identifiers is found in the new cohorts who enter the electorate in the 1960s. Only about one-third of the party identifiers enter the electorate with strong identifications. But unlike the situation in relation to partisan independence, one finds little evidence of decay of partisan strength after the cohort enters.

Figure 27-9 Strength of Party Affiliation by Age Cohorts: Percent of Identifiers with Strong Identification, 1952-1974

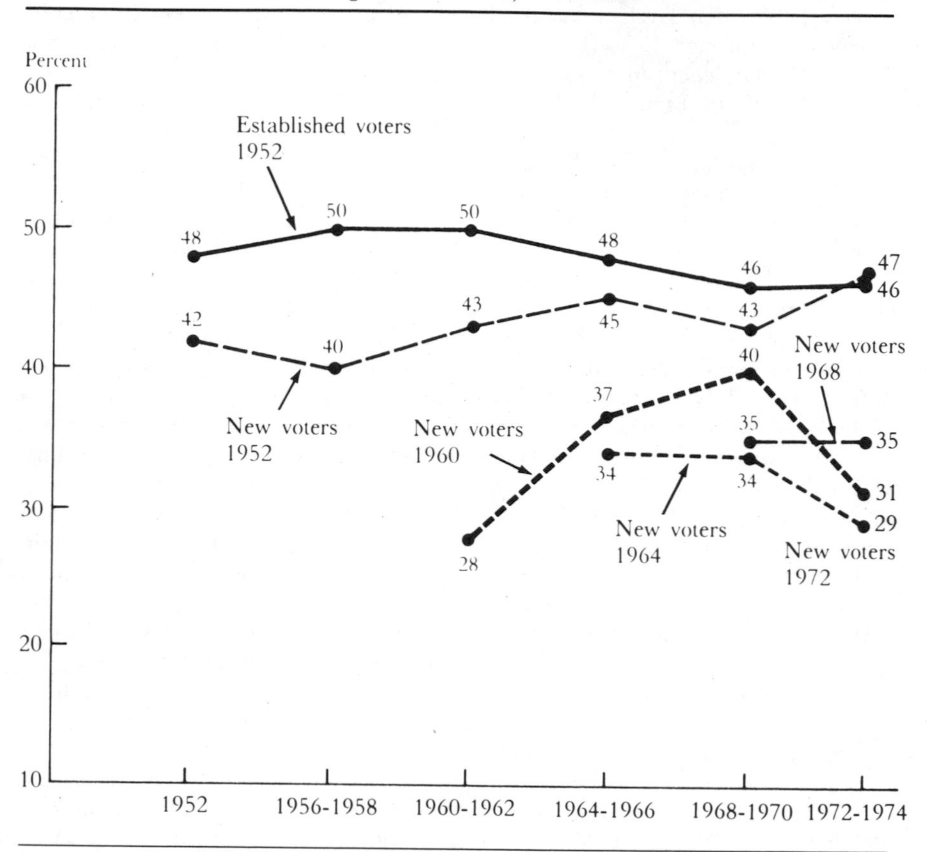

When one compares Figures 27-8 and 27-9, one observes two different ways in which partisanship erodes. The new cohorts of 1960 and 1964 enter the electorate looking like the older cohorts in terms of partisan identification. In succeeding years their partisanship decays. But they enter the electorate with a *strength* of party affiliation already below that of the earlier cohorts—and the strength of identification remains constant. The change in strength of identification appears to result from the replacement of one age group with another.

Partisanship and the Vote

Not all manifestations of weakened partisanship, however, are due to the entrance of new voters. The role of partisanship as a guide to the vote has eroded in a very different way. As we have seen, the proportion of voters who vote a straight party ticket has fallen substantially since 1956 and 1960—the high points of party regularity for the two decades we are studying. Figure 27-10 has data on the proportions of the various age cohorts who vote a straight ticket in presidential years. The data offer a quite different picture from that in relation to party

Figure 27-10 Straight Ticket Voters by Age Cohorts, 1952-1972

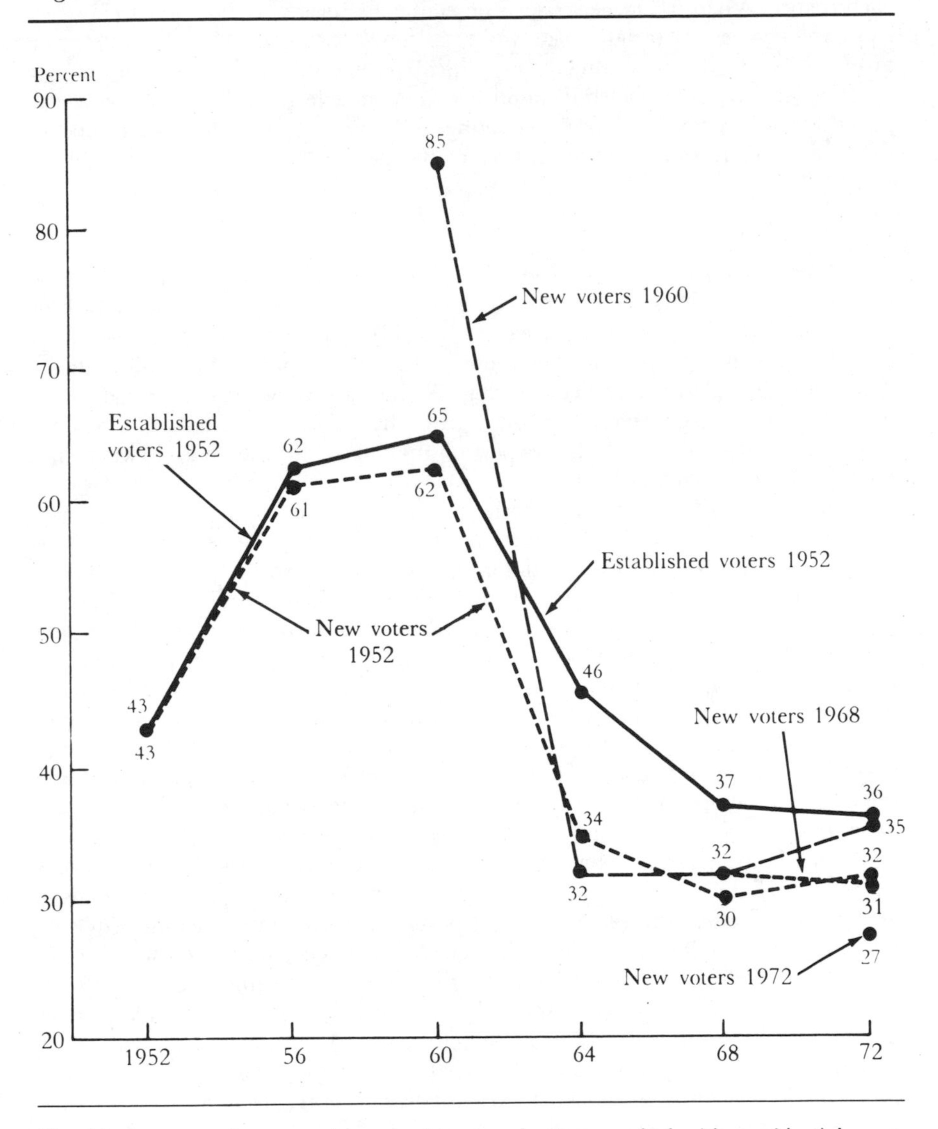

(On this figure we do not combine election years because we deal with presidential years only.)

identification and the strength of that identification. The various cohorts—those who were in the electorate in 1952 as well as the later cohorts—appear quite similar in the proportion who vote a straight ticket at each point in time.

The new and the established voters of 1952 behave identically from 1952 to 1960. In addition, the new cohort that enters in 1960 looks quite similar to the older groups. As straight ticket voting begins to decline after 1960, it declines for each cohort. When the newer cohorts enter the electorate in 1968 and 1972, they show frequencies of straight ticket voting as low—*but not lower*—than the older groups. Clearly the commitment to political parties that kept the older cohorts constant in their strong identification does not impede them from following the general tendency toward split ticket voting. The rise of split ticket voting appears to be more a function of the pressures of the period than the generation of the voter.

Party Evaluations

A similar story is told by the data in Figure 27-11. There we report the proportions of the various age groups who give positive evaluation of one or both of the political parties. As reported earlier, the proportion of the population with generally positive things to say about one or both of the parties falls substantially during the period we have been tracing. At the beginning of our period, more than two out of three Americans had a generally favorable evaluation of at least one of the parties. By 1972, the proportion making such positive evaluations had fallen to less than half.

As Figure 27-11 indicates, positive evaluations of parties fall for all age cohorts, including those who were in the electorate in 1952. The younger groups who enter in 1968 and 1972 are the most negative toward the parties.[18] But the older groups change substantially as well. The established voters of 1952 cohort falls from 72 percent who can be considered positive partisans to 56 percent; and the new voters of 1952 cohort changes even more, from 70 percent positive to 47 percent. The 1952 cohort does not wind up as negative about the parties as are the newer cohorts, but the decline in their affection is substantial. The measure of party evaluation appears to fall between that of frequency of independence and that of split ticket voting. Long-term party attachment has an effect in dampening the decline in affection (as it dampened the rise of independence) but there is still more movement with the times for the established voters.

The data on the attachment of various age cohorts to the political parties sheds some light on the impact of long association with a party on partisan attachment. Those with a long-standing party identification in the late 1960s do not falter in their identification with their party when partisan erosion begins. They remain identifiers, and strong identifiers at that. In this, they differ from those who enter the electorate from 1960 onward. But the partisans who have been in the electorate since 1952 resemble the newer entrants in other respects. When citizens come to evaluate the parties more negatively, the established partisans join them in this. When straight ticket voting declines after 1960, it declines for the established partisans as well.

The data on the older cohorts confirm but also modify our understanding of partisanship throughout the life cycle. They confirm that partisan identification is firmly fixed by long association. But what is ingrained appears to be *self-identification*—one thinks of oneself as a Democrat or a Republican. This does not mean that one cannot vote against that identification—with almost as much ease as does one whose identification is more newly acquired. Nor does it mean that one will not express negative evaluation of one's party along with the newer partisans.

Figure 27-11 Proportion of Positive Partisan Evaluators by Age Cohort, 1952-1972

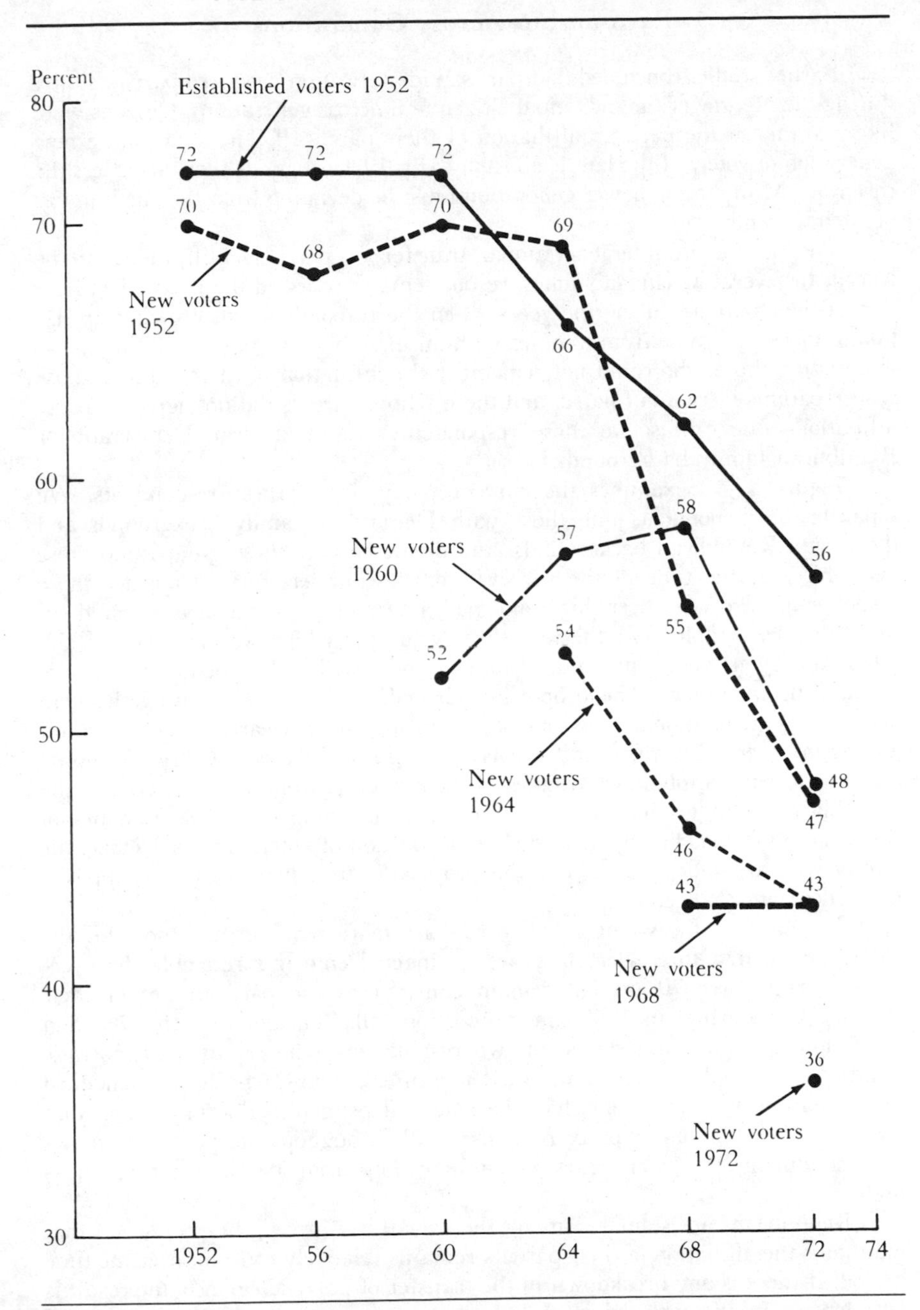

(On this figure we do not combine election years because we deal with presidential years only.)

Partisanship Across Generations

Earlier studies concluded that partisan identification produced party stability during the lifetime of the individual citizen and across generations. Citizens were likely to inherit the partisan affiliation of their parents.[19] The data on the new generation of voters of the late 1960s and early 1970s suggests that this is less the case now. Many in the newer generation must be deviating from the partisan ties of their parents.

The decline in intergenerational transfer of party identification can be traced. In several Michigan studies, respondents were asked the party identification of their parents during the years when the respondent was growing up. By taking those that came from families with an unambiguous partisan affiliation—eliminating those who could not remember the affiliation of their parents, those whose parents were unaffiliated, and those whose parents did not agree on party affiliation—one can isolate those respondents who had clear Democratic or Republican family backgrounds.

Figure 27-12 examines the current party ties of these respondents. We separate the respondents into those with Democratic family backgrounds and those with Republican backgrounds, and divide each of these groups into those over thirty at the time of the survey and those under thirty. Consider those respondents who were over thirty and had a Democratic family background (in the upper left graph). For the first three years for which we have data (1952, 1958, and 1964) about three out of four of those with a Democratic family are Democratic identifiers. The proportion falls about 10 percent during the next decade. Intergenerational transfer of partisan identity is clearly weakening a bit among the over-thirty voters in the early 1970s. But the loss of intergenerational stability does not imply much transfer of the electorate from the Democrats to the Republicans. The decline in the proportion conforming to the partisan ties of their parents is matched by a rise in the proportion of voters from a Democratic family who are Independent. But the proportion that switches to the opposite party does not change.

The data for the younger Democrats are more striking than those for the older. In the first three election years, younger Democrats resemble the over-thirty group—over 70 percent remain constant to the partisan ties of their parents. But starting in 1968, the proportion falls substantially. In 1968 and the following years, almost one in two respondents who report a Democratic family background are not Democratic identifiers. Those who have abandoned the affiliation of their parents have become Independents. The proportion that switch to the Republican party remains small throughout the period. It shows no rise during the later years when defection from parental affiliation is high.

Republicans are similar. Among the over-thirty group, the proportion that maintains the affiliation of their parents remains relatively constant over the time period. If there is any breakdown in the transfer of party allegiance, the result is an increase in the proportion of Independents, not a rise in the number of Democrats. The weakness of intergenerational transfer among Republicans is most extreme among the younger Republicans in the late 1960s. The proportion following in the partisan footsteps of their parents falls to under 50 percent. In

Figure 27-12 Intergenerational party transmission, 1952-1972

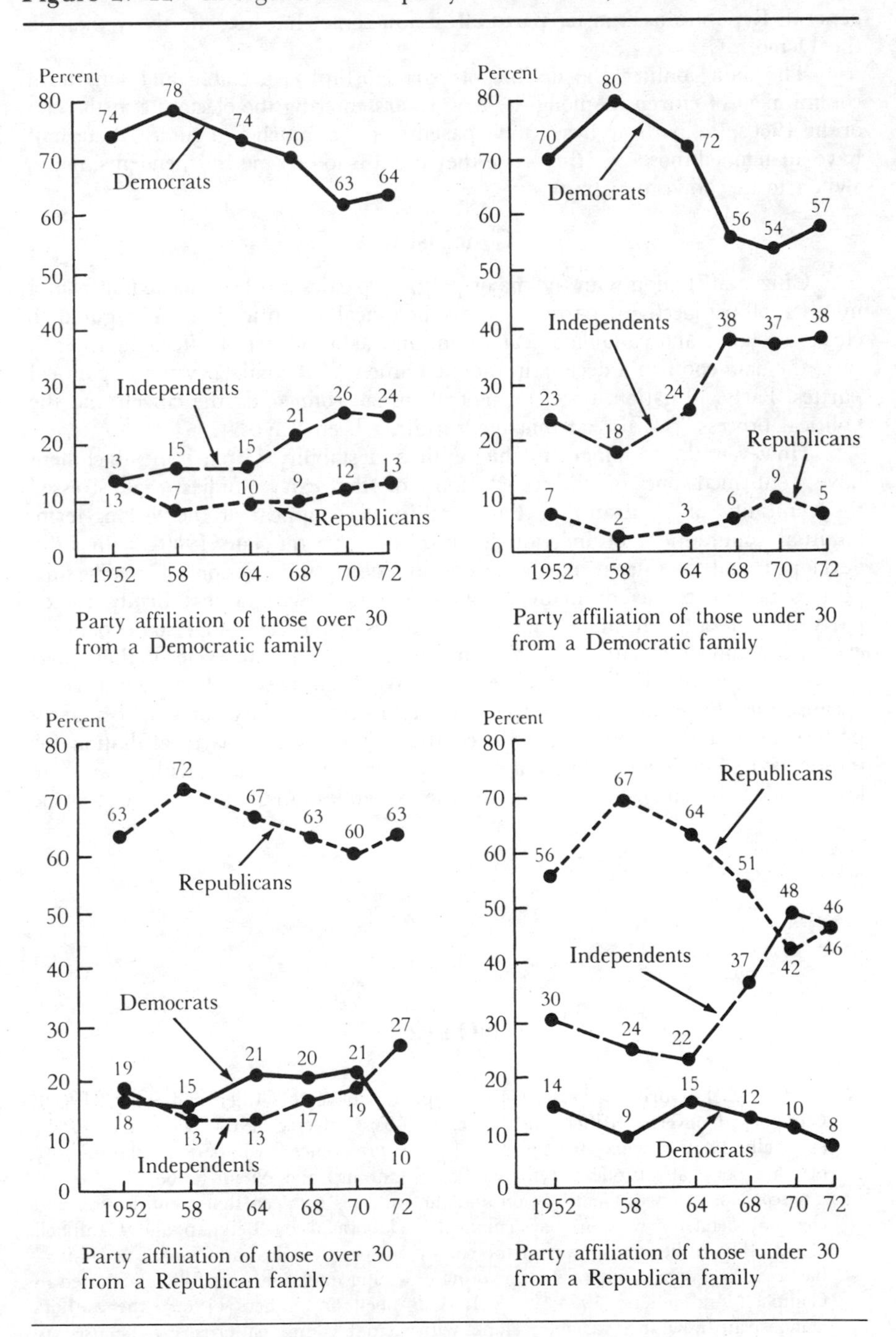

1974 is not included because the appropriate questions were not asked.

general, Republicans transfer party affiliation somewhat less effectively than do the Democrats.

The data confirm the decline of partisanship as a stable and long-term commitment of citizens. Among the new voters entering the electorate at the end of the 1960s, the partisan ties of their parents are not much of a guide. About half have abandoned those ties. But when they do, it is to become Independents, not to switch to the opposition party.

Conclusion

Citizen affiliation with the major political parties has been looked at from a number of perspectives: party as a psychological identification, as a guide to electoral choice and candidate evaluation, and as an object of affection. In each case, the data confirm a decline in the attachment of the citizenry to the political parties. Party affiliation, once the central thread connecting the citizen and the political process, is a thread that has certainly been frayed.

However, these changes in the depth and stability of partisan attachment have confirmed one of the conclusions of the early studies that stressed the centrality of partisanship. Partisanship does appear to be a long-term, habitual commitment of individuals. For those in the late 1960s with fully developed and long-term partisan identifications, the erosion of party support is not nearly as dramatic as it is for those with a less firmly rooted party attachment. The data on recent changes make clear that some political events can interfere with the development through the life cycle of that long-term commitment. Such events seem to have been powerful in recent years because they have not only retarded the acquisition or development of a party preference, but they have also reduced the significance of party affiliation for those who remain identified with a party. Citizens who identified with a party are less guided by their affiliation in the seventies than they were in the fifties.

NOTES

1. See Campbell, Gurin, Miller (1954); Campbell, Converse, Miller, and Stokes (1960); Campbell, Converse, Miller, and Stokes (1966); Converse (1969); Converse (1964), especially 238-240 where the stability of party preference is compared to the stability of other political attitudes; Hyman (1959); Jennings and Niemi (1968).
2. The concept of party identification and the linkages between that identification and electoral behavior was first systematically elaborated by Belknap and Campbell (1952). The utility and power of the concept of psychological attachment to political parties as a property separate from voting or voting intentions was fully elaborated in Campbell and others (1954;1960). In Campbell and others (1966), the authors demonstrate how this variable, along with actual voting patterns, can be used to understand the nature of elections and the flow of the voting in American society. For

the centrality of party identification as a systemic as well as individual concept in American politics see Prewitt and Nie (1971, pp. 479-502).

3. For excellent overviews, parallel to our own, see Dennis (1975) and Pomper (1975, chap. 2). The decline of partisanship is presented in historical perspective in Burnham (1970).
4. This overview of national trends conceals many variations hidden within the data—the South differs from the North, young from old, and so on. We deal with these differences below.
5. That is, they are 27 percent of the party identifiers, but only 17 percent of the voters.
6. For an analysis of the declining importance of party in Senate elections see Kostroski (1973).
7. On the other hand, it is not obviously wrong to assume that the factor of personal recognition does play a considerable role in voting for lower level offices. The "friends-and-neighbors" factor in local voting can be a significant determinant of the outcome of local elections. In a lower level election an individual's reputation can be more important to many voters than his party. The invulnerability of some public officials in otherwise competitive states, counties, and cities can only be attributed to the recognition and positive personal evaluations these officials enjoy. Certainly this is one of the factors which go into giving incumbent politicians an advantage. For some illustrations of the variable importance of party see Stokes and Miller (1966).
8. The correlations reported here are Pearson product moment correlations.
9. There is little evidence that weak partisans have become Independents over the preceding years. Our conclusions about this party change rest upon data which show that most of the change in party identification depends upon the introduction of new populations into the electorate in the last twenty years. Since there does seem to be some small abandonment of party affiliation, however, remaining strong partisans constitute a group which has not relinquished their party loyalties in spite of the relatively great disfavor into which parties have fallen.
10. For early demonstrations of the importance of these feelings see Campbell, Gurin, and Miller (1954); Campbell, Converse, Miller, and Stokes (1960); Campbell and Stokes (1959); Stokes, Campbell, and Miller (1958); Stokes (1966). More recent use of these measures to account for voting choice include RePass (1971) and Kelley and Miner (1974).
11. The decline between 1968 and 1972 may be partly attributable to a change in coding for the 1972 study, but the decline through 1968 leads us to believe that it cannot be completely attributed to coding.
12. The data on recalled switch of parties is quite consistent with a more direct measure of party switching derived from the panel study of voters conducted by the SRC in 1956, 1958, and 1960. If one cross tabulates the party allegiance of voters in 1956 with their allegiance in 1960, one finds that 4 percent report allegiance to one party in 1956 and to the other in 1960. Computed from data in Pierce and Rose (1974, p. 633). For a fuller discussion of the panel data and some recent analyses that seem to contradict this point see Appendix 4 [of Nie, Verba, and Petrocik].
13. See Campbell, Converse, Miller, and Stokes (1960 chap. 7); Converse (1969); Butler and Stokes (1969). Other item specific analyses of the relationship between aging, political preference, and political involvement can be found in Glenn (1969); Cutler (1969); Glenn and Grimes (1968). See also Ryder (1965) and Klecka (1971).
14. Education changes in the past twenty years have frequently been used to explain changes in the social and cultural values of the young, but they cannot explain these changes. The increase in Independents is unrelated to the increasing educational advantages of the young.

Increase in percent of Independents from 1952 to 1974:

25 years or under	+21 points
Did not finish high school	+20 points
Finished high school	+26 points
At least some college	+23 points
26 to 30 years	+18 points
Did not finish high school	+20 points
Finished high school	+15 points
At least some college	+12 points

15. The average age of these cohorts in the different years is presented here.

	1952	*1956*	*1960*	*1964*	*1968*	*1972*
Established 1952	43.4	47.5	51.6	54.4	57.3	60.6
New 1952	22.4	26.5	30.5	34.5	38.5	42.4
New 1960			22.7	26.6	30.3	34.4
New 1964				22.5	26.3	30.3
Post-1964					22.4	23.4

16. For example, the proportion Independent that is reported for the new voters of 1960 for the 1960-1962 data point is the average of the proportion of Independents among those 21 to 24 in 1960 and those 23 to 26 in 1962.
17. The 1972 proportion of Independents for this group is markedly higher than it was in 1968. If the aging hypothesis is correct, one would have expected a steady decline in Independents as this group ages. The fact that they do not change over time suggests that they may be even less committed to political parties than one would ordinarily expect.
18. The data in Figure 27-11 are for both identifiers and Independents. If one eliminated the Independents (who are half of the younger cohorts), the younger age cohorts would not look as different.
19. See Campbell, Converse, Miller, and Stokes (1960); Butler and Stokes (1969); Jennings and Niemi (1968); Goldberg (1969); Dennis and McCrone (1970). Although not very thorough, the data presented by Knoke and Hout (1974) point out the clearly greater importance of parental party preference in the development of party affiliation. See also Converse and Dupeux (1962) and Searing and others (1973).

28. THE ELECTORAL CYCLE AND PATTERNS OF AMERICAN POLITICS

Paul Allen Beck

The relationship between citizens and leaders is the core concern of democratic theory and the primary focus of students of democratic politics. Competitive elections are typically assigned the principal role in structuring this relationship. They are a means by which the public can make government officials accountable and influence the policy directions of government. The case for how elections should link public and leaders is a familiar one. Not so obvious is the strength of this link, particularly the extent to which mass electoral forces may make for fundamental changes in the behaviour of leaders and the policies of governments.

This chapter examines the relationship between changes in mass electoral behaviour and changes at the elite (or government) level of the American political system in the last century and a half. It begins with a model of electoral change which posits the cyclical recurrence of three types of election periods—realigning, stable alignment, and dealigning—throughout American history. The chapter then turns to a consideration of how important features of government politics vary with election periods. Although mass electoral change is certainly not the only contributor to broader government changes, this study suggests that it is a vitally important one.

The Cyclical Nature of American Electoral Change

Research in the past two decades has directed our attention to the existence of different generic types of elections in the American political experience.[1] It is now universally acknowledged that the electoral landscape has been altered visibly at regular intervals by the restructuring of mass party coalitions. During these *realigning* electoral periods, the sources of party support in the electorate undergo substantial change and, usually, but not necessarily, the party balance of

Author's Note: I am grateful to Kristi Andersen, Charles O. Jones, William J. Keefe, Michael Margolis, Morris Ogul, Richard Niemi, and Bert Rockman for their constructive suggestions on an earlier version of this chapter, which was delivered at the 1977 Annual Meeting of the American Political Science Association.

Source: *British Journal of Political Science* (1979) 9:129-56. Reprinted with permission of Cambridge University Press.

power is altered as well. The existence of a second type of electoral period is also widely accepted. During these periods of *stable alignment,* there is little variability in the partisan division of the electorate and little alteration in the bases of enduring support for either party.

Electoral politics of the last decade or so resists classification into either of the familiar electoral periods. It fits a third type, in which party loyalties decline and independence becomes more common. Inglehart and Hochstein (1972) have coined the term "dealigning" to describe this third type of election period. Recognition of the dealigning type has been slow in coming. Many scholars saw the contemporary decay of the New Deal coalitions as the first stage of a new realignment. Because this decay has persisted without leading to realignment for over a decade, however, the need to describe the period as other than realigning or stable alignment has become compelling (Beck, 1977). Evidence will be presented later that such dealigning periods are not unique to contemporary American politics but, rather, have been a constant part of the electoral cycle.

The three different types of electoral period seem to follow one another in regular order. Electoral coalitions form in realigning periods, persist through periods of stable alignment, and then decay during dealigning periods. A new electoral cycle begins when the dealignment is arrested by some exogenous "shock" to the electoral system capable of mobilizing dealigned voters into a new party alignment, built around a new line of conflict. This mobilization, of course, is the substance of realignment.

Each electoral cycle is the political manifestation of a particular line of cleavage in society and reflects fundamental social and economic changes in American life. Social class, centre-periphery, and urban-rural differences have defined the principal cleavage lines in American politics, just as they have in most other Western nations (Lipset and Rokkan, 1967, pp. 1-64). Each has brought certain issues to the forefront of political debate, shoving other issues into the background. The other issues have remained latent sources of political conflict, often cross-cutting the dominant line of cleavage. As long as the latent conflicts are overridden by issues embodied in the prevailing cleavage, the structural contradictions of the party alignments reflected in these latent conflicts will not be exposed. These contradictions become evident, however, in a period of dealignment when the "old" issues are no longer relevant to large numbers of voters. As Schattschneider (1960, p. 74) has put it: "In politics the most catastrophic force in the world is the power of irrelevance which transmutes one conflict into another and turns all existing alignments inside out." This dealigning period ends when some previously latent conflict emerges to forge a new cleavage line or, possibly, when the old cleavage line is reinforced.

American electoral cycles can be charted by beginning each new cycle with the initiation of the realigning period. By common agreement realignments are located roughly at the turn of the eighteenth century; in the late 1820s; in the late 1850s and early 1860s; in the aftermath of the Panic of 1893; and in the aftermath of the Depression of 1929. Each period of realignment seems to have been followed by a long period of stable alignment before the prevailing party system began to decay. Students of electoral politics have often noted the regularity in occurrence of these cycles. With the sole exception of the contemporary period, realignments seem to have appeared about every thirty years.

Elsewhere I have attempted to account for the regularity of electoral cycles and the length of time they last.[2] According to that simple model, the inexorable process of generational replacement produces variations in the composition of the electorate over time. When those who formed party loyalties in the crucible of realignment dominate the electorate, as is the case in the years immediately following a realigning period, a period of stable alignment ensues. Members of this "realignment generation" are likely to hold strong party loyalties, with deep roots in political experience, and are inclined to cling tenaciously to these loyalties for the remainder of their lives.

As time passes since the realigning period which moulded the current party system, individuals whose political identities are only loosely structured by party loyalties enter the electorate. Even for those among them who profess party attachments, the infrastructure of attitudes and perceptions about politics which supports partisan views is likely to be weak. After all, the party system into which they have come is inherited. They did not have a hand in making it, nor did they experience the intense political conflicts which emerged in its making.

Two different generations of post-realignment voters may be distinguished. The "children of realignment" are the offspring of the realignment generation. They are presumed to possess at least some attachment to their inherited party system, as a consequence of parental socialization if nothing else. Their descendants, labelled the "children of normal politics," gain their only political experience during a period of stable alignment, when the conflicts which produced the realignment are much less manifest. Moreover, since they are two generations removed from the realignment even their political socialization into the prevailing party system must be incomplete. The result is enfeebled partisan loyalties among this generation.

For analytical convenience, a dealigning period can be thought of as beginning when the children of normal politics first begin to enter the electorate. With reasonable assumptions about the location of the formative years and the distance between generations, this point comes about twenty-five years after the realigning period has ended. To be sure, signs of dealignment surface earlier than this because even the children of realignment are not firmly wedded to the prevailing party system. In other words, once the generation whose party loyalties were fashioned in the heat of realignment begins to be displaced, underlying strains in the party coalition surface. Until the dealigning period, however, these strains do not threaten immediate damage to the party system. The dealigning period ends when large numbers of young voters, unattached to the now-antiquated party system, are mobilized in a new realignment.

This completes the discussion of election types and the process that moves the system through the electoral cycle. It bears emphasizing that my view is that electoral change results from the impact of generational replacement on the distribution of partisan loyalties in the electorate. The sudden shift from dealigning period to realignment, however, must be attributed to the operation of forces exogenous to the electoral system. In the past, the American electorate formulated new partisan ties on a widespread basis only under the force of depression or civil war and in the presence of creative leadership in exploiting these crises. The generational changes which yield a dealigned electorate, although a necessary condition for realignment, are thus not sufficient in themselves to cause a realignment.

The three electoral periods discussed above are defined most readily by changes in the distribution of party loyalties, although shifts in the sources of party support which maintain the partisan balance would also constitute a realignment. These changes in turn imply other alterations in mass electoral behavior, which are visible even when data on party loyalties are unavailable. Perhaps the most visible of these alterations is a shift in aggregate voting outcomes. Designation of realigning periods in the past is based primarily on such aggregate voting changes.

Additional characteristics of electoral periods may be deduced from the prevailing distributions of party loyalties. A first group of such characteristics reflects the clear differences between periods in the use of party loyalties to guide voting behavior. The more an electorate is tied into the existing party system, the less room remains for electoral success by new parties or political movements. One good index of the utility of party labels, then, is third party electoral strength. And the stronger the links to existing parties, the less willing voters will be to desert the candidates of their party. Thus, a second and a third index of the utility of party labels are split-ticket voting in a single election and party regularity from one election to the next.

A second group of electoral characteristics reflects differences in the intensity of voters' feelings about politics. The most conspicuous index of intensity is the percentage of the electorate which votes in an election. Where current political controversies are deeply felt by large numbers of people, turnout should rise above preceding levels. The more people feel that political issues are remote from their current concerns, on the other hand, the more turnout should decline. In this context it must be recognized that in Western nations politics is largely party politics. This suggests that intensity of public feeling about politics should be a direct function of the extent to which current *party* controversies reflect salient political matters for the electorate. An electorate deeply concerned about issues which are ignored in inter-party conflict is unlikely to be strongly motivated to participate in party-dominated elections.

The preceding passages have identified a recurrent electoral cycle in American politics and have provided the broad contours of an explanation in terms of generational replacement. The following section explores American history for evidence of the realignment/stable alignment/dealignment progression and attempts to pinpoint, for later use, the timing of each phase. Once the broad parameters of each phase of the electoral cycle have been identified, I shall proceed to the central concern of this chapter: the relationship between the electoral cycle and government policies. While the generational replacement theory can account for the regularities of the electoral cycle, it does not need to be accepted for us to recognize the existence of the electoral cycle described here. Thus, I leave consideration of this explanatory theory for another place, to focus only upon the electoral cycle itself and the correlative changes in patterns of American politics.

Identifying Electoral Periods in the American Experience

A definite cyclical pattern of electoral periods appears in American politics since the widespread popular selection of presidential electors in the 1820s and perhaps even since the emergence of political parties in about 1800. The task of this section of the chapter is to identify the parameters of each cycle and the periods within it. Because electoral data are richer for the current period than for the past, I shall begin the task with the present and work backwards. The basic quantitative data for identifying the electoral periods are contained in three figures which will be referred to throughout this section of the chapter. Figure 28-1 displays ticket-splitting between 1900 and 1968. Figure 28-2 shows the minor party share of the presidential vote between 1828 and 1976. Figure 28-3 contains turnout in each presidential election, expressed as a percentage of the eligible adult electorate, from 1856 to 1976.

Figure 28-1 Ticket-Splitting 1900-1968

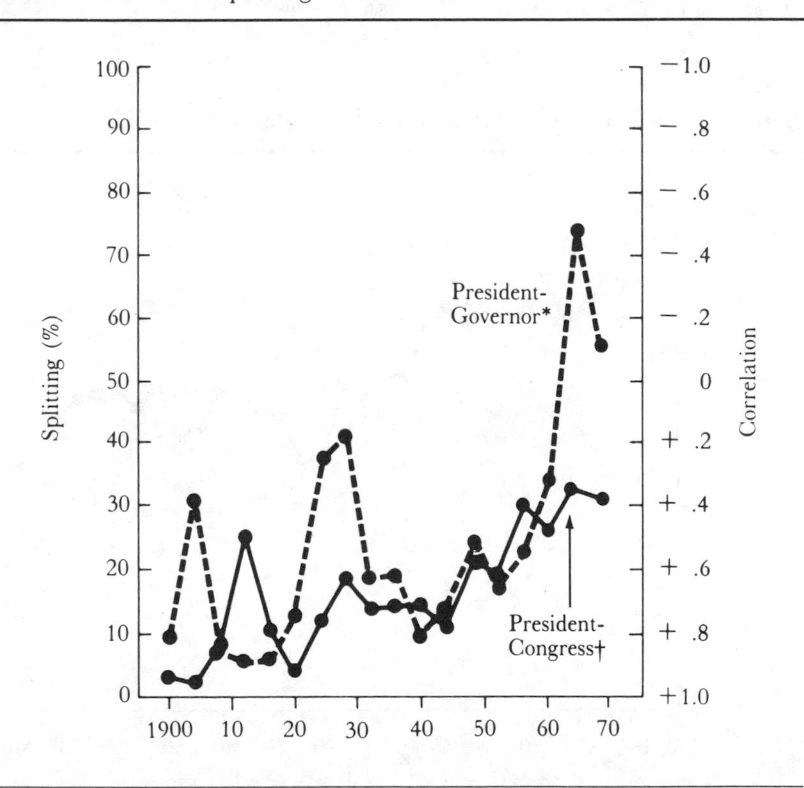

* Correlation of presidential and gubernatorial totals by state (see right-hand axis). Source: Turrett (1971).

† Percentage of split results between congressional and presidential races (see left hand axis). Source: Burnham (1970), p. 109.

Figure 28-2 Minor Party Share of Presidential Vote, 1828-1976

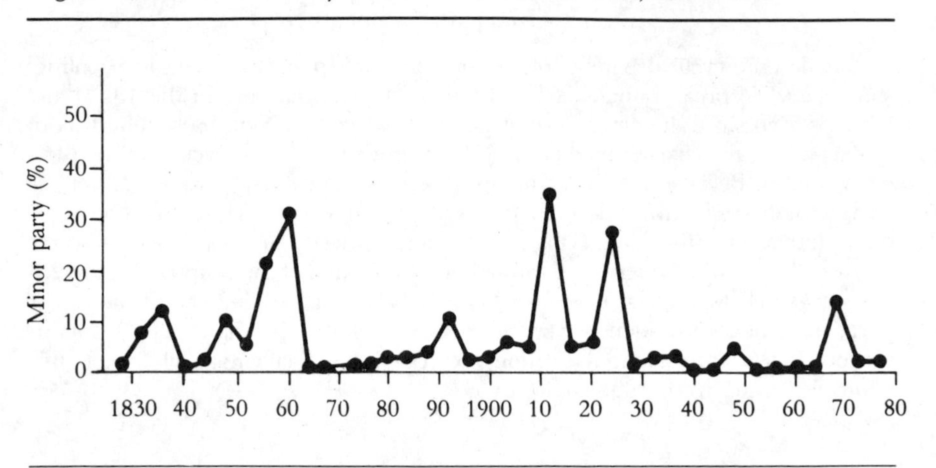

Source: For 1828 to 1972, *Presidential Elections Since 1789* (Washington, D.C.: Congressional Quarterly, 1975); for 1976, *The Statistical Abstract of the United States*, 98th ed., p. 490.

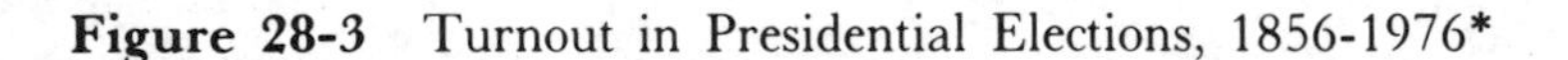

Figure 28-3 Turnout in Presidential Elections, 1856-1976*

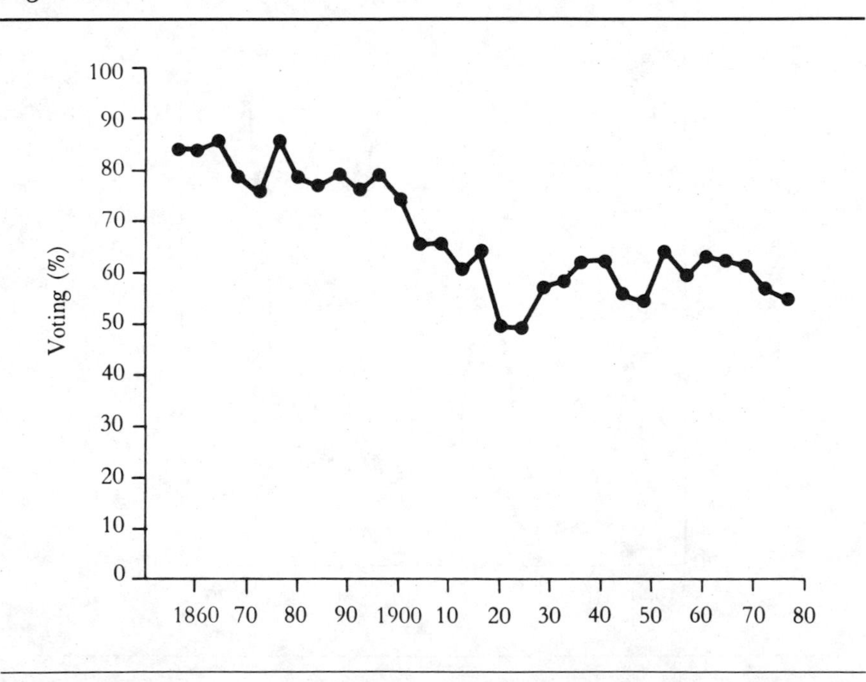

* Entries are the percentage voting of the total adult electorate.
Source: For 1856-1952, Lane (1959), p. 21; for 1956-76, *The Statistical Abstract of the U.S.*, 98th ed., p. 508.

The New Deal Party System

The current cycle of electoral politics began with the realignment of the 1930s. A massive realignment of the American electorate took place along social class lines during this decade, leaving the nation about as Democratic afterwards as it had been Republican before. The New Deal party system seems to have entered its stable alignment phase by the 1940s and to have persisted in this phase throughout the 1950s. But from the mid-1960s and continuing to this day there has been a noticeable deterioration in the New Deal party coalition.

That the present period is a time of dealignment is demonstrated unequivocably in recent distributions of party affiliation. From the remarkably stable distributions of the 1950s, there has been a clear rise in Independents and decline in partisans since 1964, as is shown in Figure 28-4. These changes are neither earthshaking nor precipitous. Alterations which result from generational replacement seldom are. Yet the changes are real, producing by the 1970s an electorate which is about 14 percent less partisan than the electorate of the 1950s.

Corroborating evidence of dealignment is provided by other characteristics of the period. Party labels have become much less useful as guides to electoral behavior since 1964. This evident in the high levels of ticket splitting since then

Figure 28-4 Party Identification, 1952-1976

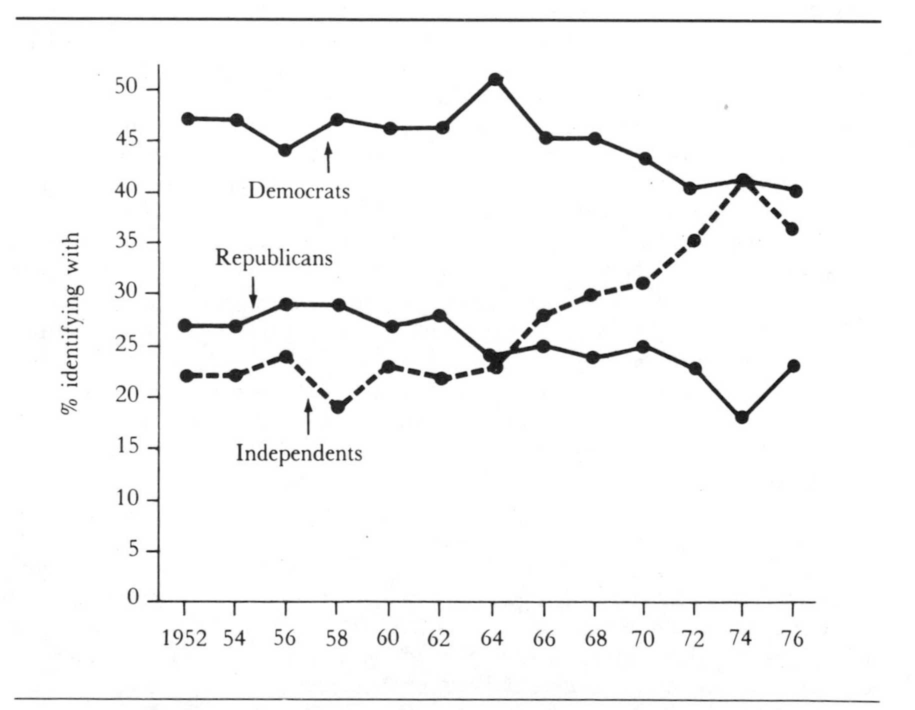

Source: Center for Political Studies, University of Michigan (In response to the question: "Generally speaking, do you usually think of yourself as a Republican, a Democrat, an Independent, or what?").

(see Figure 28-1), especially in the 1972 balloting for president and Congress,[3] and in the high level of third-party electoral strength in the 1968 presidential contest (see Figure 28-2). Inter-year variability in presidential voting has also been high in recent years: Republican *and* Democratic presidential candidates have received between 38 and 61 percent of the vote in the four contests since 1960. Finally, there is ample evidence that the role of party identifications in the voting decision has correspondingly declined since 1964 (Nie, Verba and Petrocik, 1976, pp. 164-73).

Evidence of dealignment is found in the indicators of political intensity as well. Presidential election turnout has declined strikingly since 1964 (see Figure 28-3). This decline is all the more impressive in view of the substantial efforts made during the same period to remove barriers to voting. Legal and cultural impediments to black voting were stripped away throughout the southern states, and residency requirements have been relaxed. Turnout would surely have declined all the more but for these changes. Political involvement, measured by interest in the campaign and attention to the campaign in the printed media, has declined as well (Nie, Verba, and Petrocik, 1976, pp. 164-73).

The period from the late 1940s to the 1960s was a time of stable alignment. The distribution of party identification—the defining characteristic of election periods—was unusually stable across these years. Party labels appeared to be useful guides to electoral behavior for large numbers of voters: ticket splitting was lower even at the time of the two deviating Eisenhower victories (see Figure 28-1 and Nie, Verba, and Petrocik, 1976, p. 67) and third-party movements were either very weak or, where they showed some strength (as in 1948), enjoyed no permanence (see Figure 28-2). Finally, party identification maintained a strong relationship to the vote, in spite of the number of Democrats defecting to Eisenhower (Nie, Verba, and Petrocik, 1976, pp. 164-73). The high level of political intensity of the 1930s had clearly abated by this time. It is unnecessary to labour further what is by now so obvious to students of electoral politics. The electorate of the 1950s is the epitome of a stable alignment electorate.[4]

Although the absence of survey data makes identification of electoral periods more difficult before the Second World War, it seems most plausible to begin the New Deal realigning period sometime after the outbreak of the depression in 1929.[5] Andersen's (in Nie, Verba, and Petrocik, 1976, pp. 74-95) skillful reconstruction of party loyalties during the 1920s and 1930s using the recall of contemporary voters shows slight Democratic mobilization in the 1928 election in comparison with what was to follow. Furthermore, party registration figures in selected areas of four of five northern states show little change until after 1932 (Sundquist, 1973, pp. 204-11). While the seeds of realignment were probably sown by the Crash of 1929 and the ensuing first years of depression, full conversion of Independents to the Democratic banner probably did not occur until the nature of the Democratic alternative became apparent after the 1932 election. In fact, a clear social class cleavage in voting behavior did not emerge until 1936,[6] and the peak levels of turnout were recorded in the 1936 and 1940 elections (see Figure 28-3). The onset of the Second World War offers a convenient demarcation line for the end of the realignment phase.

Other available indicators corroborate location of the realignment period in the 1930s. Split-ticket voting fell in the 1930s from the 1928 peaks (see Figure

28-1). Third-party electoral strength was negligible in the 1930s (see Figure 28-2). Most impressive of all is the pattern of presidential election turnout during this period: by the 1936 election, it had rebounded to the levels achieved before the enfranchisement of women.

The Party System of 1896

The party system destroyed by the Great Depression began abruptly with the presidential election of 1896 and basically reflected a rural-urban cleavage in the electorate. This election ushered in a period of Republican hegemony broken only by the years of the Wilson presidency, which owed more than anything else to a split in Republican ranks. The dissolution of the party coalitions in this party system is not apparent until well into the 1920s.

There is considerable evidence that the period immediately preceding the New Deal realignment was a time of dealignment. One of the most successful third-party movements in American history, La Follette's Progressive party, surfaced during this period, winning almost 17 percent of the popular vote for president in 1924 (see Figure 28-2). Split-ticket voting increased considerably up to the 1928 contest, only to fall off again in the 1930s (see Figure 28-1). Turnout was low in the 1920 and 1924 presidential elections. Although it rose in 1928 and 1932, turnout did not reach its peak for the period until 1940 (see Figure 28-3). Andersen's reconstruction of levels of partisan affiliation in the 1920s nicely complements these data (in Nie, Verba, and Petrocik, 1976). She found that a large number of people who came of voting age in the 1920s had delayed their first vote and their partisan affiliations until the 1930s. This is precisely the kind of behavior we should expect from Independents in a dealigning period who are later mobilized in the realignment.

The beginning of the electoral cycle which culminated in the realignment of the 1920s is placed by common agreement in the brief interval between the Panic of 1893 and the 1896 presidential election. On the eve of the Panic, the parties were almost evenly balanced, as they had been ever since the South gained full admission to the Union in the mid-1870s. The Panic upset this balance, and a Republican landslide was registered in the following congressional elections. What might have been temporary was rendered permanent by populist capture of the Democratic party at its 1896 nominating convention and the presidential election of that year. Never in American history has a realignment occurred so sharply.

Once we leave the twentieth century, even fewer indicators are available with which to reconstruct electoral patterns. The major casualty in moving into the nineteenth century is split-ticket voting. In the 1890s the Australian Ballot system spread rapidly across the United States.[7] By placing control of elections in the hands of government officials rather than the parties, this reform ended the practice of separate party ballots which made ticket splitting so difficult. Before the 1890s, then, the ballot itself restricted ticket splitting, diminishing its utility as a measure of decay in partisanship. Turnout was also affected by reforms in this period, as registration requirements increased the "cost" of voting in addition to reducing fraud.[8]

The remaining indicators of electoral periods all point to the 1893 and 1896 period, and especially the 1896 election itself, as a time of realignment. Turnout peaked in the 1896 election, then fell off precipitously in subsequent years (see Figure 28-3). With the populist capture of the Democratic party, third-party voting virtually vanished from the scene (see Figure 28-2). The regularity of electoral results in the wake of the 1896 contest further attests to 1896 as the beginning of the new party system.

The years between 1896 and the dealignment of the 1920s constitute a period of stable alignment. Turnout levelled off during this period; split-ticket voting in the new "permissive" environment was generally low by later standards; and third-party electoral success was high only in 1912. The 1912 presidential contest is the lone exception to the prevailing stable alignment pattern. While it bears many of the hallmarks of a dealigning period election, it is better explained as the result of a split within the ranks of the majority party over personalities rather than policies. This contest was simply a short-term deviation from the general stable alignment period, not the first stage of an impending dealignment.

The Civil War Party System

The party system which ended with the realignment of 1896 had its beginnings in the regional strife leading up to the Civil War. It was dominated by the new Republican party, victorious in the war and skilled at raising the war issue later, until southern states gained full re-entry to the Union in 1876—after which the system was evenly balanced nationally, being based on sectional party monopolies. The beginning of the realigning period is difficult to pinpoint for this party system, due to discordant patterns of electoral change across the country and the fact that the lines of conflict for the new party system were formed *prior* to the formulation of the new party coalitions. This realignment was consummated only when the electorate found partisan outlets for its extant hostilities.

Evidence of partisan dealignment to end this party system appears in the years prior to 1896. The late 1880s and early 1890s were filled with third-party electoral activity. The Prohibition and Greenback parties were able to garner small shares of the popular vote for president in the 1880s, and the Populist party achieved considerable success in 1892 (see Figure 28-2). Third party candidates polled more than 10 percent of the vote nationwide in that year, winning pluralities in five states and over 20 percent of the vote in seven more. Additional evidence of dealignment comes from the irregularity of electoral outcomes during this period. Only turnout fails to follow the dealignment pattern, perhaps as a result of substantial fraud in this pre-reform era.[9] Corroborating evidence for the view that this was a dealigning period is contained in Jensen's intensive study of midwestern politics from 1888 to 1896. He argues that partisan loyalties were loosened in the pre-1896 years, paving the way for later realignment.[10]

This Civil War party system almost certainly began no earlier than the formation of the Republican party in the midst of the battle over the Kansas-Nebraska Bill in 1854. The realignment had undoubtedly ended by the surrender at Appomattox, although Reconstruction may well have fuelled partisan fires in the South into the 1870s.[11] Without individual-level evidence of changing party identifications, it is virtually impossible to disentangle realigning and dealigning periods unless the realignment is especially sharp, as was the case in 1896. The most persuasive case can be made for beginning the realignment period with the Civil War itself. Characteristics of dealignment were present as late as the 1860 presidential contest. That this was a four-candidate race suggests that partisan divisions were not yet firm, especially in the southern and border areas. While the Republican coalition was largely in place by that time, it took war to make it a majority coalition. Divisions within the southern electorate over the question of slavery surfaced as late as the secession referendums conducted in the months after the presidential election (Lipset, 1960, pp. 372-84). It seems to have taken the war itself to fully realign the electorate.

The Jacksonian Party System

The party system destroyed in the conflict over slavery seems to have been in place by the late 1820s, when its namesake Andrew Jackson became president, and probably began just four years before in the turmoil over denying Jackson the presidency. It reflected the conflict between the traditional East and the new West, between "aristocracy" and "democracy" as guiding principles of American government. This party system was probably as much the result of democratizing trends as of the process of generational replacement which figures so prominently in subsequent realignments. By the time it had faded in the 1850s, the enfranchisement of white males was virtually complete. Never again would an American party system originate from the expansion of the franchise.

The first stages of dealignment in the Jacksonian party system may be found as early as the late 1840s. In the 1848 presidential election, the Free Soil party garnered over 10 percent of the popular vote (see Figure 28-2), drawing its greatest support from the northernmost tier of states from New England to Wisconsin. Like other minor parties in dealigning periods, the Free Soil movement presaged the cleavage which was to become dominant later on. In the aftermath of a seemingly workable compromise on expansion of slavery to the territories four years later, Free Soil support was cut in half. This was only the lull before the storm. Just two years later the party system seemed to explode, destroying the Whig party in the process, over the issue of the extension of slavery embodied in the Kansas-Nebraska Bill. Northerners dissatisfied with both major parties broke off to pursue third-party strategies in many states. Within the short space of two years, diverse third-party movements had coalesced into the national Republican party. No third party has enjoyed greater electoral success than the Republicans. It grew from a small movement to the second party in the system in just two years, and four years later emerged as the dominant party.

Additional signs of dealignment are found in the 1850s. Election results were unusually variable during this time, as is shown in the dramatic changes from Congress to Congress in the composition of state delegations. Not only was the Whig party destroyed because of the slavery issue, but the Democratic party was virtually wiped out in the northernmost states. This wholesale switching of votes from one election to the next and the disintegration of support for major parties in certain areas of the nation surely indicates an electorate with eroded partisan loyalties.

Despite the growing problems in measuring electoral patterns as one goes back in time, it has been shown that the realignment/stable alignment/dealignment cyclical pattern characterizes American electoral politics all the way back to the 1820s. This is not the only regularity in electoral change. Accompanying it is a trend towards ever weaker political parties in the last eighty years. The latter trend may be attributed to persistent hostility towards political parties in the American culture and the antiparty reforms of the late 1800s and early 1900s which that hostility supported. However, the type of electoral change described in the preceding pages seems the *dominant* pattern of American electoral politics. If we are to understand the role of electoral politics in America, we must begin by illuminating the consequences of the electoral cycle for the broader realm of politics.

The Electoral Cycle and Patterns of American Politics

I have traced the cyclical creation, stabilization, and decay of mass electoral coalitions over the last one hundred and fifty years of American politics. It would be remarkable if these changes at the mass level had little effect on patterns of politics within the governing institutions themselves. This would constitute an insulation of leaders from the public that some leaders may dream of and that many studies of elites assume. The major premise of this chapter is that such an insulation does not exist in American politics—that, instead, the American public has had great influence on the nature of government policies and practices. That influence, however, cannot be demonstrated clearly in an isolated snapshot of American political life. To be fully appreciated, the relationship between public and elites must be studied from a diachronic perspective, focusing especially on change in government policies and practices during the electoral cycle.

The remaining task is to explore the relationships between the mass-level electoral cycle and political patterns at the government level. Because this exploration represents an attempt to chart largely unknown territory, and because only four full cycles are available to serve as evidence, the inferences to be drawn are highly tenuous. Even so, the weight of the evidence points to some highly suggestive correspondences between similar stages of the electoral cycle and particular patterns of American politics.

Patterns of Party Politics

Since electoral change has its most direct impact on political parties, it is best to begin with them. We have already seen how the electoral role induces the formation, stabilization, and decay of party coalitions. Its impact may be registered in three additional ways. The most obvious is that internal party life is directly affected by external electoral fortunes. Majority party leaders can be expected to be most harmonious in a realigning era since they represent a newly formed coalition, and least harmonious in a time of dealignment, when the coalition is disintegrating. The minority, by contrast, may exhibit a persistent pattern of intraparty strife in the aftermath of realignment as the party factions battle over whether to resist the policy directions of the realignment or to adjust to them. But it too should show disharmony in dealigning periods, as the basis of even its coalition weakens.

Perhaps the best indicator of intraparty harmony is found in the American parties' primary formal actions as parties—decisions taken at the national presidential nomination conventions. Harmony at conventions may be measured by the number of ballots required to select the party presidential nominee. (These

Figure 28-5 Ballots Required for Presidential Nomination, 1832-1976

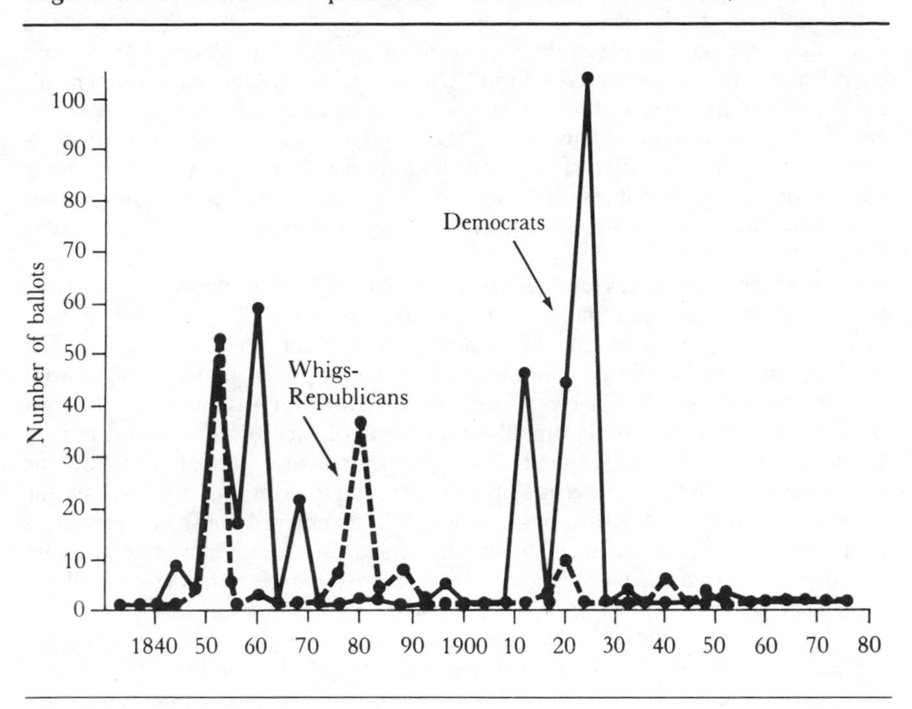

Source: Richard C. Bain and Judith H. Parris, *Convention Decisions and Voting Records* (Washington, D.C.: The Brookings Institution, 1973).

data are presented in Figure 28-5.) For the Democrats and the Whigs and Republicans, convention conflict on nominations shows a tendency to peak during dealigning eras and to fall off during other periods.

Another indicator of conflict is roll-call divisions over the party platform. These have also been most common for the parties during dealigning periods. The percentage of votes for the minority position on the Democratic platform has been highest in 1924, 1972, 1948, 1860, 1968, 1920, 1892 and 1896 in that order. Only one of these years (1948) was not within a dealigning period. For the Whigs and Republicans, recorded splits over the platform are found in nine years (1932, 1912, 1860, 1876, 1964, 1928, 1852, 1892 and 1908). Six of these nine were times of dealignment. While the evidence is not overwhelming, there is clearly some tendency for convention conflict to vary with the electoral cycle.

The electoral cycle also seems to affect political parties through the sustenance various electoral periods provide for party reform movements. Important reform movements in American politics have focused a great deal of attention on political parties, seeking either to alter internal party procedures or to insulate the political system from parties. Ranney (1975) has identified three major periods of party reform: 1820 to 1840, 1890 to 1920, and 1952 to the present. The modern period seems more appropriately located from the mid-sixties to the present, when (as Ranney suggests) the more radical reforms were initiated. Each of these movements for party reform began during a dealigning period. A plausible case can be made that dealigning periods energize the forces for party reform. During such periods mass support for the existing party system falls to its lowest point, as is reflected in the weakening of party loyalties. This allows the negative side of American ambivalence towards parties to surface, providing a mass base for political leaders who wish to attack parties. The opportunities to reform parties may never be greater than when parties are themselves enervated by decay in their mass base.

Whether these opportunities are exploited, of course, depends to a large degree upon forces external to the electoral system. Of particular importance are the political skills of reform leaders and their opponents. The realignment which follows the dealigning period also plays a significant role in the success of a party reform movement. If it catapults the reformers into power, the reforms are likely to be implemented. The reforms may be deflected, on the other hand, if the reformers are pushed aside by the new cleavage. In this connection it is interesting to consider the fate of the reform movement which surfaced in the 1890s. It enjoyed considerable success in its early years and was then side-tracked for a time as the new line of cleavage drove a wedge between populist and progressive elements of the reform movement.

Finally, there is a suggestive covariation between styles of party campaigning and the phases of the electoral cycle. Jensen (1971, pp. 154-77) locates a change from military to merchandizing styles of political campaigning in the early 1890s, when the Midwest was engulfed in partisan dealignment. A parallel change in campaigning styles has been obvious within the current period of dealignment (Agranoff, 1972). Separate candidate campaign organizations, heavy use of the mass media, and polling to ascertain voter preferences are now commonplace in American politics. In both the 1890s and modern times the focus changed from trying to mobilize party loyalists to attempting to persuade independent-minded voters to support a particular party or candidate. Elsewhere, I have shown how county party organization campaign styles are tailored to the local electoral environment (Beck, 1974b). That rule also applies where the national electoral environment is altered over time. In a period of realignment or stable alignment, the best campaign strategy (for the majority party at least) is to emphasize party loyalties. In a dealigning period, on the other hand, both parties and candidates will move over to a strategy which emphasizes persuasion rather than mobilization. The type of campaign practice that proves to be successful depends upon the nature of the electorate as much today as in the nineteenth century.

Thus, the impact of the election cycle on parties may go far beyond the obvious changes in the party coalitions. Intraparty conflict, the impetus of antiparty reform movements, and political campaigning all vary with the electoral cycle. In seeking to explain patterns of each, one should first consider the electoral period that is involved. Even more important, however, is the synchronization of changes in patterns of government in the United States with the changes in the electoral cycle—the topic which will be considered next.

Patterns of Congressional Politics

The electoral cycle is most likely to influence that national governing institution which the framers of the American Constitution made most sensitive to popular pressures, the House of Representatives. Turnover in congressional membership is related to variations in the electoral cycle. Overall turnover is a function of both the willingness of incumbents to seek House careers and their vulnerability at election time. The long-term decline in turnover since the nineteenth century is surely linked to the increasing desirability of these careers as the chamber has become more institutionalized (Polsby, 1968). The vulnerability of incumbents, on the other hand, seems to rise in realigning periods and to fall off at other times. Of the eight general elections between 1872 and 1956 examined by King and Seligman (1974), the percentage of incumbents who were defeated was highest in 1932 and 1896, both within periods of realignment. Incumbent defeats averaged 24 percent for the two realignment years in contrast to 13 percent for the non-realignment years. That incumbents are significantly less safe in times of realignment should come as no surprise. The changes in mass support for parties in these years alter electoral realities for many incumbents, especially when these mass changes reverse relative party strengths within an area.

Incumbent defeats may be expected to be least frequent in a dealigning period. As the utility of party labels declines, the importance of other guidelines for electoral behaviour increases. One of the guidelines is the recognition of name possessed by an incumbent, especially when accentuated by the arsenal of resources available to modern representatives to advertise their names. Data collected since the Second World War provide a single case which supports the hypothesis of greater incumbent success in dealigning eras. Incumbents in the House have become increasingly more successful in their re-election bids. To explain this trend, Mayhew (1971b) has emphasized voter dissatisfaction with party (the dealignment factor) along with greater sophistication by representatives in exploiting the natural advantages of incumbency. Data from a single case, however, are hardly adequate for confirming the hypothesis that incumbent defeats decrease with dealignment. Full understanding of this relationship necessarily awaits examination of the patterns for earlier periods as well.

If the hypothesis that turnover varies with the electoral cycle is valid, then party assumes a variable role in determining an incumbent's fate. Sporting the wrong party label spells trouble for the representative from a realigned district during the realignment, while the right party label is virtually a guarantee of electoral success in stable alignment periods. On the other hand, party seems to make little difference to voters during a time of dealignment. What is operating here instead is the advantage of being known in a less partisan electoral climate—an advantage which has been documented in studies of American non-partisan municipal elections (Williams and Adrian, 1959). Thus, to attribute the increasing success of incumbents in recent years to greater resources for use in campaigning is to overlook the more fundamental factor of dealignment politics: weak partisan ties in the electorate make these resources highly valuable, whereas strong partisan ties may render them superfluous in other times.[12]

An even more obvious link between mass change and elite change appears for party voting in Congress. That congressional party voting should increase with the importance to the public of party labels is an obvious implication of the preceding analysis. There is strong evidence, stretching continuously from modern times back to the 1830s, that this hypothesis is valid. Figure 28-6 presents estimates of party voting, defined as a majority of one party opposed to a majority of the other party, for each Congress between 1835 and 1974. The estimates since 1861 are based on all roll-call votes while the estimates prior to that year are based on selected roll calls.[13]

These data show clearly that levels of party voting rise and fall in a systematic fashion across the electoral cycle.[14] Party voting is typically highest in a period of realignment and then steadily decreases through the dealignment. This pattern has appeared in each electoral cycle since the Civil War, even though there has also been a secular trend towards less party voting over the entire time period. There are traces of the pattern even for the period prior to 1861, where the data are less complete and less reliable. Clubb and Traugott (1977) conclude their analysis of the post-1861 data by stressing how realignments heighten party voting. Others have reached the same conclusion from a more restricted data base

Figure 28-6 Party Voting in Congress, 1835-1974*

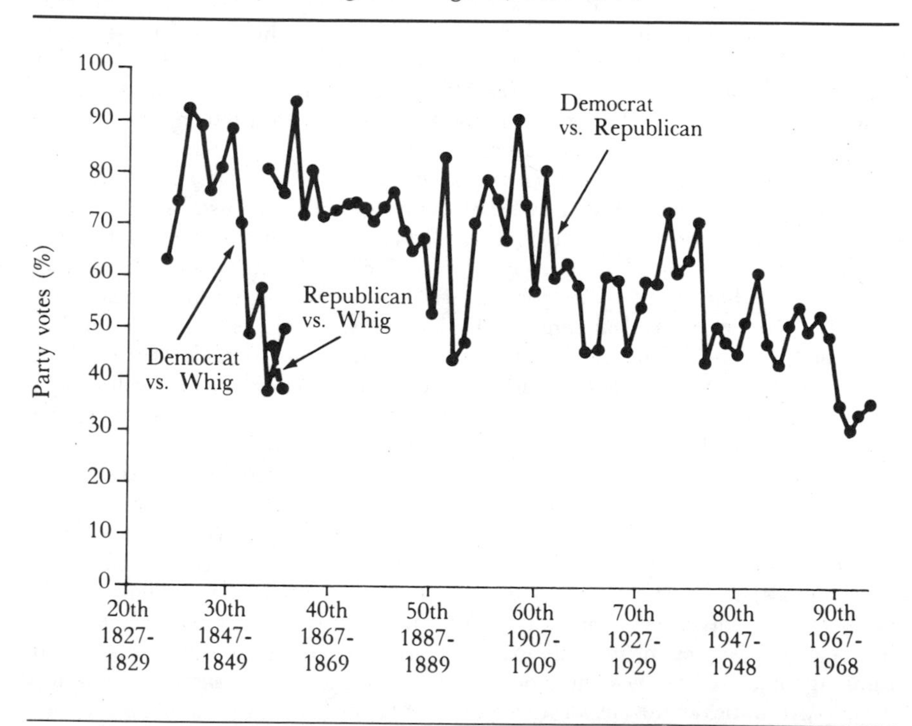

* Entries are the percentage of roll-call votes on which a majority of one party opposed a majority of the other party. Source: For 24th through 36th Congresses, Alexander (1967). For 37th through 93rd Congresses, Clubb and Traugott (1977, pp. 382-83).

(Brady, 1973; Turner and Schneier, 1970). The relationship extends to dealigning periods as well.

To be sure, the different levels of party voting across electoral cycles also suggest the operation of factors unique to each party system. Lower levels of party voting since the late 1890s probably reflect the loosening of structural supports for party accomplished by the widespread reforms of the period. Other contributors may have been the decentralization of power within the House after 1911, the increasingly sharp divergence of southern from northern Democrats since the 1930s, and even perhaps the increasing malapportionment of congressional districts until the mid-1960s.[15] Furthermore, the depth of the dominant cleavage line affects party voting. It is hardly surprising that party voting has never been as high as it was on the eve of the Civil War, when political conflict could not be contained within the political process.

There are compelling reasons for giving this correspondence between congressional party voting and the electoral cycle a causal interpretation. Realigning election periods are times in which party differences as perceived by the electorate appear to be sharpest and, hence, the best guide to congressional voting. From our analysis of turnover, we also know that these are the times in which incumbents are most likely to be displaced. Their replacements in both 1897 and 1933 were more likely to support their party's legislative package.[16] Thus, enhanced turnover during these two periods seems to have contributed directly to greater party voting. Beyond that, it may be surmised that even the behaviour of incumbents will be affected by the changes in the electorate during a realignment period. If candidates for office can be persuaded that voters will rely upon party cues in deciding for whom to vote, it stands to reason that their party loyalty will be greater.

This line of argument may be extended to dealigning periods. As the party coalitions age and the issues which catalyzed them pass from the scene, voters are less likely to rely upon party labels in congressional contests. This point is surely not lost upon representatives in their continual quest for re-election. Further attenuation of party voting may result from the shifting battle lines on important issues, as no clear political agenda dominates the Congress. These tendencies are aptly illustrated in the modern House. Many of the issues which have divided recent congresses have cut across the party lines established by the New Deal political agenda, especially in the first two years of the Carter administration.

The changes in House composition and party voting levels which result from mass electoral change can be expected to have a profound impact on the internal operations of the House. Large infusions of new blood and a new balance of power surely threaten the old rules of the game within the chamber. In this vein it is of considerable interest to consider the institutionalization of the House which occurred in the decade or so after the realignment of 1896. Shortly after this realignment the House became more bounded as its membership stabilized and its leadership specialized, more internally complex as a strong and autonomous committee system evolved, and more universalistic and automatic in its housekeeping decision rules (Polsby, 1968). Furthermore, the institution of the party whip first appeared shortly after 1896 (Nelson, 1977). While most of these changes were registered in the aftermath of the revolt against Speaker Cannon in 1911, it seems likely that they were set in motion before that time. One view is that the realignment of 1896 forced these later changes because it produced a party system with reduced party competition within congressional districts (Burnham, 1970, pp. 100-06). Lower levels of competition, in turn, increased the number of safe seats. It stands to reason that the more veteran chamber which resulted would desire institutionalization, because that would increase its own power and also minimize internal conflict. Greater institutionalization, in its turn, has undoubtedly made the House an even more attractive place to build a career.

Parallel impacts on the internal operations of the House cannot be found for the other realigning periods. Even so, Nelson (1977) identifies the Civil War realignment as one of two important turning points (the other was 1911) in House leadership patterns, as an organized minority-party floor vote in the contest for Speaker appeared for the first time in 1863. It might also be possible to trace the Reorganization of 1946 in part to the increased work load brought on by the New Deal and a larger role for government—an effect of the New Deal realignment which was perhaps delayed by the Second World War.

It is less apparent how dealignment and stable alignment affect the internal operations of the House. Stability in the internal rules of the game is probably a characteristic of stable alignment periods. Informal norms of the chamber should be powerful in these times, with the battle lines well established and the electoral environment fairly predictable. Thus, it is perhaps not coincidental that students of Congress in the late 1950s and early 1960s emphasized a view of Congress as a well-integrated social system rather than a system of conflict. The conflict-system model is much better suited to a realigning period and its immediate aftermath. The integration model serves better to describe a Congress which is more remote from severe changes in the electoral environment. Finally, during dealignment periods one might expect to find a more individualistic House, as the party ties which typically bind members together weaken. While this image seems to fit the current House fairly well, it is difficult to identify such a pattern in earlier dealignment periods.

It has been hypothesized that variations in the electoral cycle affect the turnover, party voting, and internal rules of the game in the House. There is some supporting evidence of each of these hypotheses, and the evidence for the relationship to party voting is particularly strong. But even in the absence of decisive confirmation of the hypotheses it is extremely useful to view the electorate as a crucial agent of change in the behavior of the House. This complements nicely recent studies of voters' influence on congressional behavior at particular points in time (Mayhew, 1974a; Miller and Stokes, 1963).

Patterns of Policy Making

By constitutional design and practice, the American system divides policymaking power among the branches of government and requires joint action by independent legislative and executive branches to enact policy. Such an institutional arrangement makes it difficult to achieve alterations in the policy directions of government. Even with strong presidential leadership, congressional assent and, under certain circumstances, tacit Supreme Court concurrence are required to push through changes. Thus, it is hardly surprising that the American policy process is largely incremental. While the system does not work to slow the pace of change exactly as the framers of the Constitution intended, it nonetheless achieves their goal.

Opportunities for comprehensive policy changes are affected by variations in the electoral cycle. Pervasive party voting by the electorate in a realignment increases the likelihood that both popular branches of government will be controlled by the same party and, of equal importance, that party will be an important cue for political leaders. While its slow turnover introduces some lag, it is usually not long before the judicial branch joins the dominant majority coalition (Dahl, 1957). Intensity of popular feeling about party and partisan issues in a realigning period provides a unified government further impetus for pursuing broad new initiatives.

These conditions are typically absent during a dealigning period. For one thing, the electorate is likely to render a mixed verdict in popular elections, thus preventing single party control of the popular institutions. Different verdicts may also be registered from one election to the next, denying a party the opportunity to sustain governmental initiatives for changes of policy. Even where partisan harmony prevails in the popular branches, the reduced importance of party cues restricts united party efforts on behalf of comprehensive change, as [was] evident in the . . . struggles between President Carter and an overwhelmingly Democratic Congress.

Empirical evidence supports the hypothesis that the conditions for comprehensive change vary systematically with the electoral cycle as described above. Since 1800 control of the presidency and Congress has never been divided in a time of realignment or shortly thereafter. By contrast, divided control of government is found in each dealigning period and was especially pronounced prior to the Civil War and the 1896 election. Dealigning eras are also characterized by alterations in control of the popular branches between parties. Finally, the evidence cited above for both mass party loyalties and party voting in Congress underscores the strength of partisan forces during realignment and their weakness in a time of dealignment.

If opportunities for comprehensive changes of policy are related to the electoral cycle, then what of the occurrence of this change itself? While the evidence is hardly conclusive, my reading of American political history uncovers three periods of comprehensive change in the programmatic thrust of the national government since the 1820s, and each of these periods came during a realignment of the electorate. The most far reaching and familiar changes came during the early years of the Roosevelt administration in the 1930s. Changes of similar scope appeared during and shortly after the Civil War. The institution of slavery was eliminated, and various measures were enacted to guarantee civil rights to the former slaves. Less obvious were important policy changes in the area of economic development. Development policies strenuously opposed by Democrats before the war were adopted during and after the war by Republican congresses. The Morrill Tariff was implemented to protect nascent American industry from foreign competition shortly after the war began. It had the not incidental effect of channelling large amounts of money into the government treasury. With burgeoning tariff revenues in its treasury, the national government was able to fund an extensive program for internal improvements shortly after the Civil War. Railroad and canal construction was supported from the federal treasury and through national land grants.

The Civil War realignment made possible what had been restricted some thirty years before by the Jacksonian realignment. Jacksonians believed the federal government should adopt a low profile, leaving such important activities as internal improvements and banking to the states. Illustrative of the policy thrust of the period is Jackson's destruction of the Bank of the United States, the major target of Democratic opposition. Thus, the major policy changes ushered in by the Jacksonians constituted a sharp curtailment of previous federal efforts to stimulate economic development—a change in direction of policy from activity to passivity.

Only the realignment of 1896 does not appear to have promoted significant policy changes. In part, this is due to the fact that this realignment only increased the hegemony of business-oriented elites. Their hegemony was so widespread before the realignment that it encompassed both parties, as the policy orientations of Cleveland and his Republican counterparts were quite similar, especially on matters of concern to business. Indeed, for the Democratic party to move into a position of policy opposition to the Republicans required a virtual purge of traditional Democratic leaders in 1896. Opportunities for comprehensive changes of policy after the realignment were also neglected because the prevailing ideology prescribed a low profile for government. Aided and abetted by governmental support in its youth, mature American industry now viewed government as more of a potential threat than an ally.

Some empirical support for the hypothesis that comprehensive changes of policy are more likely to occur in a realigning period is provided by Ginsberg (1976). He measured changes in policy directions reflected in federal statutes between 1799 and 1959 and found turning points for national policy in 1805, 1861, 1881, and 1933. Only 1881 is clearly outside a realigning period, and this exception may perhaps be explained by the return of southern states to full political rights. Ginsberg concluded, as I have, that the behavior of voters figured prominently in changes of direction in public policy. Likewise, Hansen (1977) found that changes in tax policy, particularly tax sources, were greatest during realigning periods—made possible by the unified party control of government which accompanies realignment.

In the absence of conditions which favor comprehensive changes of policy, change is likely to be incremental or disjointed. The incremental pattern seems more likely during a stable alignment period, when there is widespread agreement on the political agenda and a "standing decision" on the direction of policy within that agenda. The fact that analysis during the 1950s and 1960s emphasized the incremental character of policy change is entirely consistent with this hypothesis (Wildavsky, 1964). On the other hand, while incrementalism persists into a dealigning period, disjointed policy change would seem to be the more common characteristic of such periods. Variability in election results during this period forces unusually rapid rotation of people with contrasting policy orientations through policy-making positions. Furthermore, in the absence of a dominant political agenda, a bewildering array of issues vie for the attention of politicians and voters alike. Movement in one direction on one issue may be accompanied by movement in another direction on some other. Thus, while there may be policy change in a dealigning era, that change will not be consistent in direction and is much better described as disjointed than as comprehensive.

Empirical testing of these notions using the American political experience is a task of overwhelming difficulty, and I shall not attempt it here. Current patterns of policy making, however, provide the first bit of evidence that disjointed change is a characteristic of a dealigning era. The contrast in policy directions between the Johnson and Nixon-Ford administrations is sharp, especially where domestic issues are concerned. The . . . Carter administration [did not adopt] the policy directions of either of its predecessors. Even more than the Nixon-Ford administrations, Carter [did not] appear to have followed what is a comprehensive and internally consistent policy agenda to most observers. Rather, his policy objectives [had] often seemed unrelated, inviting criticism that they [were] too conservative one day and too liberal the next.

The United States Supreme Court occupies a special place in the policy-making process. Insulated from popular pressures by lifetime appointments, the justices do not always join the dominant national alliance in the immediate wake of a realignment and sometimes manifest hostility to the new governing majority and its policy directions. Funston (1975) found that the Supreme Court has often confronted policy-making majorities in the popular institutions, through exercise of its power of judicial review, in the aftermath of a realignment. Further analysis of his data forces qualification of this conclusion. Only during the early New Deal years did the Supreme Court declare unconstitutional a significant number of laws enacted by "live" majorities.[17] The power of judicial review was seldom exercised in other realigning periods. Prior to the Civil War, the Court seemed to avoid activist intervention in government policy making. By the time judicial activism was fully legitimized in the 1890s, government was in the hands of forces with whom the Court was sympathetic. This leaves only the 1930s as a time in which judicial activism could reasonably have been expected to thwart innovations in federal policy.

Perhaps more important is the possible role of the Supreme Court in periods of dealignment, when the popular branches of government find it difficult to synchronize their actions. There is circumstantial evidence to support the hypothesis that judicial activism surfaces in these times. Three of the four major periods of such activism (the 1890s, the 1920s, the 1930s, and the 1960s and 1970s) are contained in a dealigning era. The infamous Dred Scott decision just before the Civil War provides another example, although an isolated one, of judicial activism in a period of decay in the party system. It may be that room for judicial activism is greatest where there is disarray in the popular branches of government, as the Supreme Court moves in to fill the power vacuum. The justices themselves may perceive more latitude for action, or they may feel that there is a more pressing need for judicial intervention.[18] Whatever the case, it is obvious that decision-making by the Supreme Court is a potentially fruitful area of study from the perspective of the electoral cycle.

Patterns of Elite Circulation

The circulation of elites is a fundamental democratic process. To prevent oligarchy, opportunities must exist for an opposition to form and to gain political power. The public plays the crucial role in elite circulation in a democratic system by determining which team of leaders shall be installed in the government. With the increasing use of primaries in the nominations process, the American public has even come to exercise substantial influence on the composition of the competing teams. It [took] only the election of President Carter, who was not a favorite of the traditional leaders of his party, to bring home forcefully the point that political elites can be replaced as the direct result of mass action.

This circulation of elites can occur in several ways. The most obvious is the replacement of one party by the opposing party. A less obvious change takes place when the leadership (including party officials, elected officials, and appointees) of a party itself is altered, due either to the "natural succession" of younger generations of leaders or to the displacement of the traditional leadership. Natural succession refers to the process whereby old leaders select their replacements; displacement is where the old leaders have little hand in selection. With natural succession, group identifications of new leaders are apt to be similar to the leaders they replaced, although their political outlooks may differ somewhat as a consequence of their different formative political experiences. With displacement, on the other hand, both the group identifications and the political views of the new leaders will usually be different.

These three forms of elite circulation—party change, natural succession, and displacement—vary systematically with the electoral cycle. The usual consequence of a realignment, of course, is that it fosters significant changes in leadership by turning the previous majority party out and putting the previous minority party in. This change is rarely a simple substitution of traditional opposition leaders for incumbents, however, for the leadership of the old minority party has often been displaced in the realigning process. Republicans after 1861 were clearly not Whigs under a new guise, nor were New Dealers the Democratic leaders from earlier times. Only the realignment of 1896 seems to have had little impact on the elite circulation, although it did lead to a change in the Democratic leadership.[19] In the stable alignment aftermath of a realigning period there is usually some circulation of elites. Within the parties, it is best characterized as natural succession, even to the point where older party leaders probably choose to elevate to positions of power those members of the younger generations who are most like themselves. Circulation of elites also occurs in a more obvious manner when the minority party is able to gain temporary control of government in a deviating election. Yet this type of circulation has limited policy consequences, because the minority is rarely willing or in power long enough to challenge directly the majority position on the political agenda.

During a dealignment, it is unlikely that any particular type of elite circulation will predominate. Intraparty displacement of traditional leaders may be most noticeable, as the natural succession processes within the party are eroded by the weakening of party loyalties. This displacement is apt to be intermittent, however, yielding a curious combination of traditional leaders and "newcomers" to the ranks of the party leadership. This would seem to be an accurate depiction of the Democratic party in the contemporary dealignment.

Hypotheses linking elite circulation to the electoral cycle have received little systematic attention from scholars. Nonetheless, a few bits of evidence exist which may be used to provide at least preliminary tests of these notions. King and Seligman (1974) have shown how realigning elections brought new generations of politicians into the House. These new representatives were both younger and from different backgrounds than the incumbents they replaced. From the greater support the newcomers gave to realignment-induced policy changes, it may be surmised that they also were more comfortable with the new political agenda than either those they replaced or the veterans of the chamber.[20]

Additional evidence of patterns of elite circulation may be gathered from presidential appointments to cabinet-level positions. These appointments should go to leaders of the traditional groups within the party coalition during the stable alignment period. In realigning periods, cabinet appointments should be drawn from traditional and still loyal groups as well as from the new members of the party coalition. In both periods the cabinet should mirror the party's electoral coalition. In dealigning periods, by contrast, one might expect sharp departures from the practice of looking to the *party* coalition for cabinet-level appointments. With the growing lack of fit between party and presidential coalitions, presidents are likely to feel that their electoral coalition is embodied in them and does not require sustenance through cabinet appointments. This frees the president to surround himself with top advisors whose prime loyalty is to him or to build a cabinet of technical experts rather than interest group spokesmen. Even where such spokesmen are included in a cabinet, presidents in the dealigning period may be inclined to pay little attention to them.

Cabinet selection and usage over the past decade conforms to the pattern hypothesized for a dealigning period. While the early Nixon cabinet contained its fair share of "political" appointees, they were increasingly isolated from the president as time passed. The second-term Nixon cabinet was composed mainly of people whose political loyalty was to the president and not to some group within the Republican coalition. This pattern of ignoring the party coalition in making top-level appointments [was] followed to some extent by Carter too, although it may be argued that technical expertise rather than personal loyalty [was] a more important criterion of selection for Carter than for Nixon. The brief Ford interlude saw a return to the more traditional party-related practices. This exception supports the general rule, however, because Ford was an unelected president whose political career had linked him tightly to his party.

These rather superficial observations on cabinet-level appointments in the last decade hardly provide adequate tests of the hypotheses presented above. In particular, it may be only coincidental that these practices have appeared during the current period of dealignment. Polsby (1978) attributes them to a qualitative change instead of a cyclical variation in presidential politics. To test these hypotheses adequately requires systematic examination of cabinet selection and usage throughout American history. If there is a pattern to the circulation of elites, it should surface here as well as in the popular institutions of the national government where it is already apparent.

Conclusion

The preceding analysis suggests that changes in American electoral behavior have widespread effects on politics at the elite level. Significant changes take place at the elite level when the electorate enters into a period of realignment. Turnover in elite personnel brings people with new political perspectives and new ideas into the top levels of government. Partisan considerations also become more important in elite behavior: congressional voting follows party lines more, presidential appointments seem to be drawn more from the party coalition, and intraparty conflicts are submerged. "Party government" comes closest to its realization in America. Finally, and of perhaps greatest significance, realigning periods are typically times of comprehensive change in the direction of public policy.

In the periods of stable alignment which follow realigning eras, government policies and practices also stabilize as the conflicts of the realignment become institutionalized. Elections play a different role in this period. They promote incremental movement along the policy agenda established in the realignment when they maintain the majority party in office. They induce only a brief respite from this change when they are of a deviating nature. Electoral changes seem to have their most limited impact on the political system during periods of stable alignment. Because such periods often endure for more than a decade, there is some tendency to view them as the normal pattern of American politics and thus to denigrate the importance of elections. As normal as they may be in terms of their longevity, however, such a view is misleading for it ignores the dynamic quality of the electoral cycle. The very presence of a period of stable alignment politics makes possible, through its lack of formative impact on emergent voters, the transition to the other periods of the electoral cycle.

Scholars have paid little attention to the politics of dealigning periods, probably because the existence of such periods has been recognized only recently. Yet the preceding analysis shows that dealignments too seem to have an important impact on government policies and practices in America. They remove much of the structuring to both mass and elite politics by minimizing the role of political parties. Without this structuring, policy change becomes disjointed and the less democratic forces in the government (especially the Supreme Court) have the opportunity to play a greater role in the political process. It is even conceivable that the democratic components of the system are so withered by dealignment that the presidency becomes the sole repository of popular leadership, dangerously distorting its role in the political process.

All in all, it is reasonable to contend, as Burnham (1970) has argued, that the electoral cycle serves as the mainspring of American politics. Mass politics are surely more intelligible when viewed from the perspective of the theory of electoral change advanced in this chapter. But the most important point of this analysis is that elite politics are much more understandable as well, for they seem to be closely linked to the electoral cycle. The task of specifying clearly and convincingly the exact nature of these linkages remains before us. My hope is that the theoretical perspectives and the hypotheses developed here will both encourage scholars to undertake this task and guide them in their undertaking. Establishing the links between the public and political leaders in a democracy should be, after all, the principal goal of students of democratic politics.

This study has focused exclusively on the United States. The peculiarities of the American system, especially its decentralized political parties and the separation of its executive and legislative institutions, while making the electoral cycle probably more important for American politics, make generalization from the American case to other nations more difficult. Nonetheless, it should not be thought that the model developed from the American experience has no application elsewhere. Both the generational replacement process of electoral change and the particular electoral cycle it spawns may well appear in all well-developed western systems. Recent studies of electoral change in Britain, for instance, have uncovered at least one realignment/stable alignment/dealignment cycle there, even while downgrading the role of generational replacement in the dealignment phase of that cycle (Crewe, Särlvik, and Alt, 1977; Crewe, 1977). Evidence of this electoral cycle also appears in France since 1945 (Inglehart and Hochstein, 1972; Cameron, 1972). The systematic consequences of the electoral cycle in other countries may also bear some resemblance to those in America, although allowance must be made here for the different structural settings. For example, the parallel to American changes in party voting might be the variable incidence of formal party votes in a parliamentary system like Britain's—the implication being that party leaders would force fewer party votes as the time since realignment increased, because party members become progressively more divided on important matters of public policy. Thus, it is my hope that this chapter will stimulate systematic examination of electoral change and its impact beyond the narrow American confines, both to illuminate the nature of democratic politics in other nations and to build towards a general model of the connections between mass and elite change.[21]

NOTES

1. For various typologies of American elections, see Campbell (1966), Lichtman (1976) and Pomper (1967).
2. The evidence for this view is contained in Beck (1974a).
3. Individual-level corroboration of these aggregate results may be found in Nie, Verba, and Petrocik (1976, p. 67).
4. The two Eisenhower presidential victories are the exception which proves the rule. The distribution of party loyalties in the electorate was highly stable during these two "deviating" presidential elections and into the early 1960s.
5. Pomper (1967) and Key (1955) locate the beginning of the New Deal as early as 1928 for selected areas of New England. Virtually all other scholars have preferred later dates. Those locating it between the Crash of 1929 and the 1932 election are: Burnham (1970), Clubb and Allen (1969), Lichtman (1976), and Sellers (1965). A few have even placed the realignment after the 1932 election: Shively (1971), Shover (1974), and Sundquist (1973).
6. See Shively (1971) for data which suggest the class-based realignment case as late as 1936.
7. This ballot had three features which distinguished it from the earlier systems in most of the state: it was prepared and administered by the state, all candidates for office were listed on it, and balloting was done in secret. See Rusk (1970).
8. For the effects of the new ballot system see Rusk (1970). The impact of this and other reforms are discussed more generally in Converse (1972).
9. Converse (1972) makes the case for the impact of electoral fraud on turnout.
10. Jensen (1971, esp. p. 307) describes the movements and countermovements between the two major parties by religious pietists and their liturgical opponents during this period. Early in the period, the Republicans received pietist support. By 1896, however, the pietists had captured the Democratic party, freeing the Republicans of their moralistic fringe and enabling it to attain majority status. Such wholesale

movements from one party to another could only have taken place within an electorate whose party loyalties had eroded considerably.

11. Both Pomper (1967) and Flanigan and Zingale (1973) found that the 1864 election exhibited the aggregate vote pattern characteristic of the culmination of a realignment: discontinuity with election results from preceding years, but continuity with those in subsequent years. The peak levels of turnout for the period were also recorded in 1864 for the states remaining in the Union (see Figure 28-3).
12. The proposition is supported by Cover (1977), who finds little evidence that use of perquisites has improved the chances of House incumbents and who favours a dealignment explanation for greater incumbent success.
13. The source for the data since 1861 is Clubb and Traugott (1977). The earlier data come from Alexander (1967).
14. This conclusion is supported, where the data are available, using an even more restrictive measure of party voting: 90 percent of one party voting against 90 percent of the other. See Brady and Althoff (1974), Lowell (1901), and Turner and Schneier (1970). Thus, while the precise party voting scores are influenced by how party voting is defined, the cyclical patterns of party voting described in this study do not appear to be artifacts of the measure utilized.
15. Brady makes the point about the effects of the decentralization of power in Brady (1972), Brady (1973), and Brady and Althoff (1974). For the possible impact of malapportionment, see Robeck (1972).
16. For 1897, see Brady and Lynn (1973). For 1933, see King and Seligman (1974).
17. This analysis is provided in Lopatto (1976).
18. This point is made in reference to the 1890s by Paul (1960).
19. For documentation of changes within the Democratic leadership, see Hollingsworth (1963).
20. The voting of these newcomers is discussed in Brady and Lynn (1973) and Sinclair (1977).
21. While recognizing the role of leadership in determining the nature of each electoral period, this interpretation clearly presumes that electoral changes are the cause, rather than the effect, of governmental changes. This presumption finds some support in the temporal ordering of the different types of changes, but in most cases it is impossible (as usual) to sort out cause from effect. The important variables in the operation of political systems simply cannot be isolated for causal analysis.

29. EVENTS AND ALIGNMENTS: THE PARTY IMAGE LINK

Edward G. Carmines, Steven H. Renten, and James A. Stimson

Events precipitate changes in party alignment. Whether truth or truism, the events/alignments connection is the bedrock assertion of theories of party realignment. Stripped of all its rich variation, realignment theory comes down to the notion that something happens and the public responds. We can argue about the nature of causal events and, even more vigorously, about the processes that generate the response, but that there is stimulus followed by response is uncontested. How stimulus is connected to response is not quite so obvious, not quite so well understood. Developing and testing a theory accounting for the linkage is our purpose here.

Two theoretical connections are immediately obvious. One is that events, if they are to be realignment stimuli, must be correctly perceived. That implies quite quickly that party images must be the linkage between cause and effect, event and realignment. The second is that the public must care about those images it correctly perceives. Changing party images must carry with them a heavy content of affection and disaffection for the parties if they are to weigh against the stubborn inertia of party identification. We shall follow these two themes where they lead, focusing most of the time on racial desegregation, a case for which we can document cause, effect, and intervening images and affect.

Our theory requires a time-series perspective. Thus our analyses will introduce time series bearing on these questions one at a time, first effect (realignment), then cause (party response to desegregation), and then intervening images and affect.[1] The route from observation to behavior is circuitous and lengthy; a singularly important mediating variable is party image. Party image, we will show, is shaped by events, and in turn, affects party composition.

Partisan attitudes, the sum of what voters say they "like" and "dislike" about the two American political parties, are a heady predictor of voting behavior. This bundle of affect and cognition is highly associated, as would be expected, with "party" measured as self-identification. These empirical linkages were established in *The American Voter,* where proximate attitudes were given the role

---

Authors' Note: This research was supported by the National Science Foundation under grant SOC-7907543.

Source: Presented at the 1982 annual meeting of the Midwest Political Science Association, Milwaukee. Printed with permission of the authors.

of mediator of party identification into vote (Campbell, Converse, Miller, and Stokes, 1960, pp. 18-37). We too assign these attitudes a mediating role, but quite a different one.

Richard Trilling (1975, 1976) has most extensively researched the effects of party image.[2] Trilling defined party image as a mental picture of a political party. Trilling, quoting Matthews and Prothro (1966), argued that this picture is "apt to be vague, often confused and contradictory" (1976, p. 2). The public, largely devoid of extensive ideological frameworks, responds to politics in simple terms (Campbell, Converse, Miller, and Stokes, 1960). To respond simply is often to respond emotively. Because this description fits the American public so well, party image, as we will operationalize it, is admirably suited to predict partisan change.

We are not the first to operationalize party image as simply summary affect toward a party (Trilling, 1976). This definition is also akin to Kelley and Mirer's (1974) "rule." [3] Party image then is simply the algebraic sum of his or her likes and dislikes about each party. We deliberately avoid making use of the *content* of the favorable or unfavorable remarks. To use content would be to stray from the simple definition of image and to lose efficiency in the predictor as well (Trilling, 1976). Neither are we by any means the first to operationalize image "clarity." We borrow both the term and the essential procedure from Pomper (1972). We differ in postulating issue clarity to be an essential linkage in a chain of dynamic causation.

For issues themselves to move voters to change party identifications or bias the recruitment of new identifiers, it must be the case that party images are associated with the issues in question. That is our fundamental thesis, that partisan attitudes are a necessary causal link between issue redefinition at the elite level and mass response. To be meaningful the assertion requires some context.

Issue Evolution: Mass and Elite

This research is a piece in a much larger puzzle. It is a necessary piece; without it, the puzzle has no solution. The thesis flows naturally from a larger theory, and its truth or falsehood reflect directly upon the theory. The theory is "issue evolution," developed for mass political behavior in Carmines and Stimson (1981a) and subsequently refined (1984), and developed for elite behavior in Carmines and Stimson (1981b), with other bits and pieces still in progress.

Issue evolution as description charts the evolving polarization of the national parties (as measured by Senate and House roll-call votes) and of party identifiers (measured by both reconstruction and cross-sectional methods). Interesting in itself as contemporary history, this descriptive evidence is much more valuable as a basis for a theory of the normal process of evolution of realigning sorts of issues.

The evidence suggests a process that has its origins in elite reorientations on contentious issues, followed by a delayed, more inertial reaction of the mass electorate. The reaction, we have argued (in 1984), takes the general form of a "critical moment," when the elite polarization in progress is first squarely confronted by the mass electorate, and an ensuing secular reorientation. The "critical moment" is an electoral response large enough to be noticeable, but considerably less dramatic than the "critical election" of realignment theory. Conversion and mobilization are the causal forces that drive it. The secular reorientation, more substantial in the long run, reflects a delayed recognition of the changed circumstances driven by normal electoral replacement.

If the issue evolution theory is true, it follows that identifiable issue publics should change their attitudes toward the parties and that the change should be temporally bounded between the elite reorientation that is the beginning of the process and the mass issue realignment that is its end. Time ordering is critical. If evolving images of the parties connect elite to mass transformations, they must evolve at the right time. To paraphrase Sen. Howard Baker, our question is, what did the voters know and when did they know it?

If elite policy cues cause a delayed mass issue realignment, the process that connects them must include altered mass perceptions of what the parties stand for. Otherwise we are left to wonder how two related time series evolve in similar patterns, that is, to posit spuriousness. Our first step in demonstrating the existence of issue evolution is to show significant redistribution in public opinion on a policy issue among party identifiers. We begin in Figure 29-1 with the causal effect to be explained, the growing racial attitude polarization of the identifiers of the two parties. Figure 29-1 plots the mean racial attitudes of party identifiers from the SRC/CPS national election series for 1956, 1960, 1964, 1968, 1972, 1976, and 1978. Racial attitudes are scaled with a common metric for all cross-sections and reconstructed backward in time to create a continuous annual series.[4]

Figure 29-1 Reconstructed Desegregation Attitudes, 1931-1980

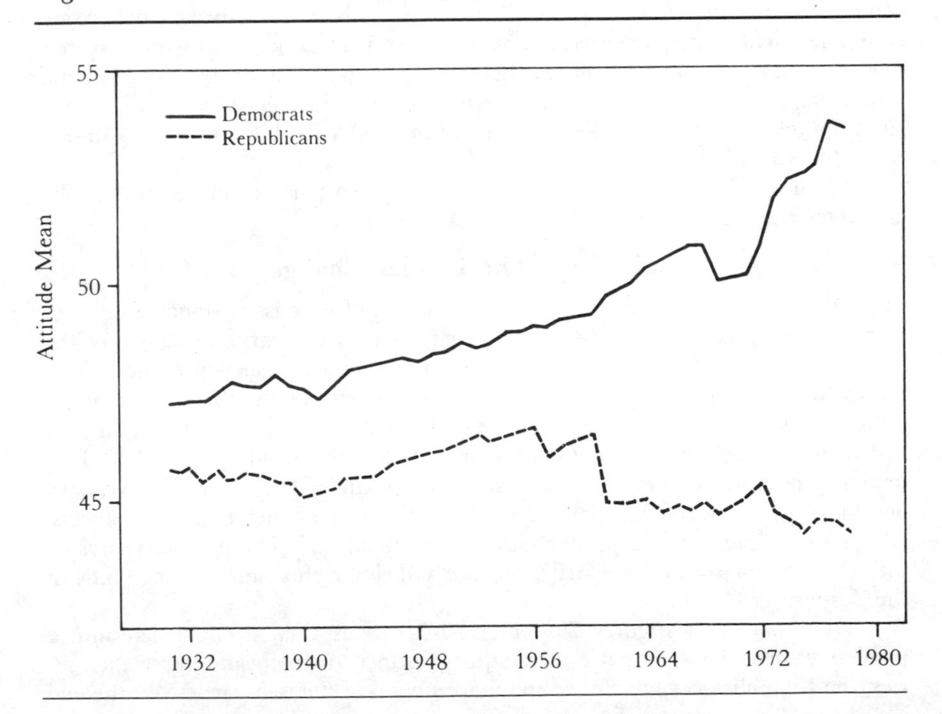

As a number of accounts suggest (see particularly Pomper (1972) and Converse, Clausen, and Miller (1965)), a sharp polarization along racial lines can be seen in the turbulent 1960s. What is less expected—and therefore more interesting—is that the polarization continued to grow during the 1970s when racial issues were no longer prominent on the political agenda.

A pattern of growth *following* the decay of the stimuli that created the initial polarization suggests simply that there is something else going on. Polarization with a self-sustaining dynamic must be more than a response to visible "events." We shall argue that it can be accounted for by (1) real change in party behavior, and (2) dynamic evolutions in perceptions of what the parties stand for, leading finally to (3) self-sustaining issue polarization.

Our theory specifies two ongoing processes. First, there is an image-shaping process. Second, following the newly changed images, there will be a change in affect toward the two major parties.

The image-shaping process specifies a linkage between the nation's political elite and the rank-and-file citizenry. The theory requires that perceived issue images be uniform, which is likely only if the perceived images are "correct." Unless the perception is correct, the second process will not take place as specified.

Several opportunities for falsification of our theory of issue-based alignment evolution exist. The first opportunity for failure comes with the demand that the changes in mass behavior and perception be properly time-ordered. If the mass party images precede elite issue change or if the mass issue change lags too far behind it, there is obviously a fault in our causal model. Another possibility is that the reorientations could take place in both populations simultaneously, but coincidentally rather than causally. Prima facie, this is an absurd model. Aside from its evident illogic, however, it would be a difficult exercise to disprove such a model. A third opportunity for falsification arises with the proposition that the public might simply not be interested in the elite differences we study. This situation (elite change not reflected in mass images) will show up readily in our data. Indeed, this is the null hypothesis.

We deal now with evidence of visible change in party behavior in the roll-call votes cast by senators and house members.

Stage One: The Parties Change

We have chosen to operationalize the notion of elite issue stands with data completely unrelated to the SRC survey data. Given the party structures of the 1950s and early 1960s, and the nature of media coverage since then, it is reasonable to assume that members of Congress constitute a visible portion of the political elite. For the purpose of charting elite policy stands, we have used roll-call votes cast in every session of both houses of Congress from 1945 to 1978. Following procedures developed by MacRae (1970) and Clausen (1973), we have developed standardized racial issue voting scales for all members of Congress, which are aggregated into party means for our analysis.[5] These series represent the issue positions of the two parties on race and civil rights since the beginning of the postwar era.

Examination of Figures 29-2 and 29-3 reveals very strongly determined patterns of behavior. The patterns are quite distinct. At the beginning of each series, the Republicans were clearly the more liberal of the two parties. By the end of the series the parties had reversed their positions. The reversal began in the late 1950s, faltered, revived in the mid-60s, and then completed itself by the late 1960s. Starting around 1970, the differences between the parties began to grow, a process that is continuing. Let us review in depth the series history in the Senate.

The Senate Democrats' stance on civil rights, presented in Figure 29-2, turned sharply to the left after the 1958 elections, almost overtaking the Republicans' on racial liberalism. For a time afterward, differences between the two parties were minor. The leftward impulse appeared again after 1964, and this time the impact was permanent. A few years later the distance between the two parties in the Senate began to increase.

To avoid coming to impressionistic conclusions, we verified our reading of these data through ARIMA modeling (a statistical technique for analyzing time series data). However, because that set of analyses constituted a separate, though related, line of research, we will report the results of the Box-Jenkins modeling only briefly here. The ARIMA models confirmed the description presented in this chapter; there were two significant interventions in the Senate series (1958 and 1964), and a significant dynamic growth process beginning in 1970. The elites of the two parties, as Figures 29-2 and 29-3 demonstrate, have clearly differentiated themselves on racial issues. The congressional series served to operationalize our notion of "elite positions." The series displayed very distinct behavior. Our next question is: did the public perceive that behavior? To answer this question requires an analysis of the public's cognitions.

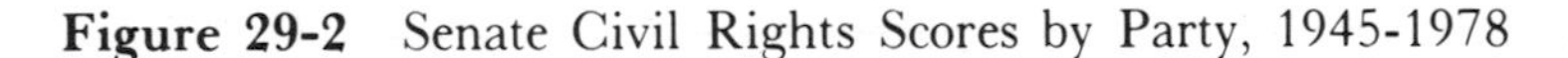
Figure 29-2 Senate Civil Rights Scores by Party, 1945-1978

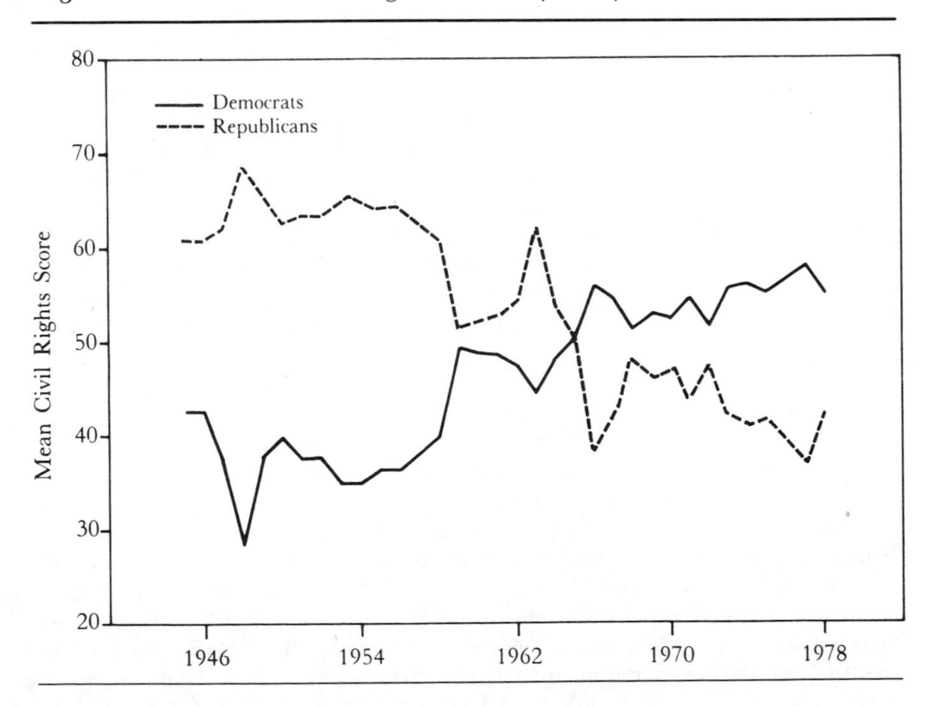

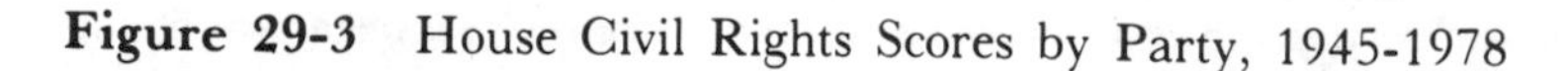

Figure 29-3 House Civil Rights Scores by Party, 1945-1978

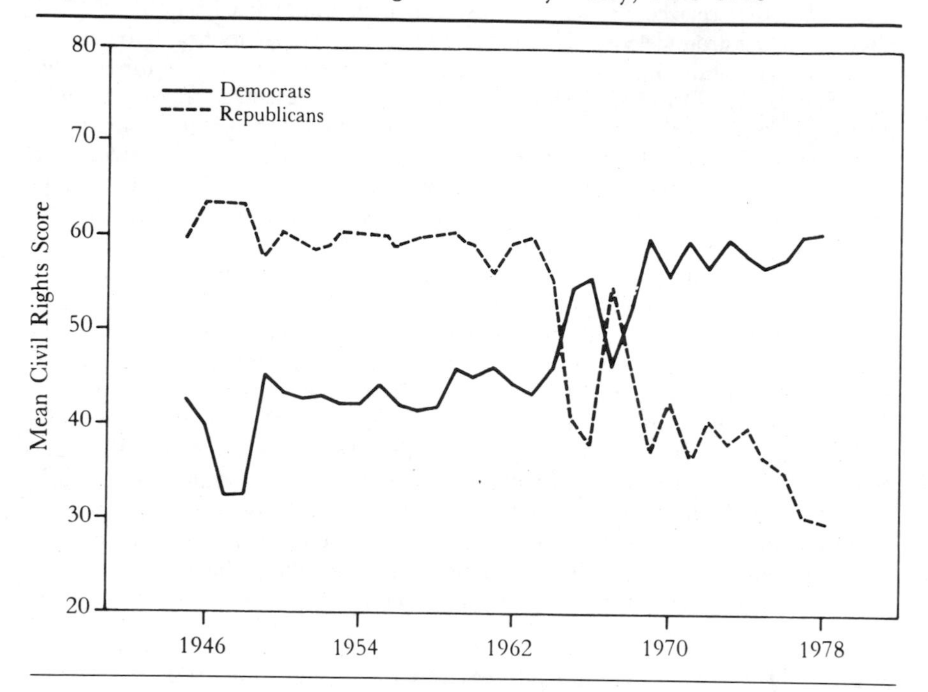

Stage Two: The Public Perceives

For now, then, we must demonstrate that the elite behaviors displayed in Figures 29-2 and 29-3 were correctly perceived by the mass populace. To establish the link between the parties' leadership and the rest of the population, we need an indicator of the public's perception of the parties' stances. For this purpose we employed the CPS/SRC election surveys. The data on party issue positions collected in both the presidential and congressional elections were used. Each data set included questions that required the respondents to deal with party issue positions. As usual, we faced the problem of varying question format.

The variability of the SRC's question format stems from the reasonable desire to incorporate the most current knowledge about question format effects into the data collection effort. Unfortunately, this confounds longitudinal analyses and restricts the conclusions that can be drawn from multiple surveys (Margolis, 1977; Bishop et al., 1978; Sullivan et al., 1978). We were faced with three different question formats spanning three periods, 1956-1958, 1960-1968, and 1970-1980. To ensure comparability of data collected under these varying formats, we reduced the level of measurement to a correct/incorrect dichotomy. Because the 1956 and 1958 surveys did not ask a direct question about where the parties stood on racial policies, an inferential process was used to determine respondent perceptions of party position. While the 1960-1968 studies produced direct respondent orderings of the party positions, the newest (1970-1980) required the reconstruction of order from independent party position ratings.

Figure 29-4 Who is More Liberal on Race Confusion and Clarity

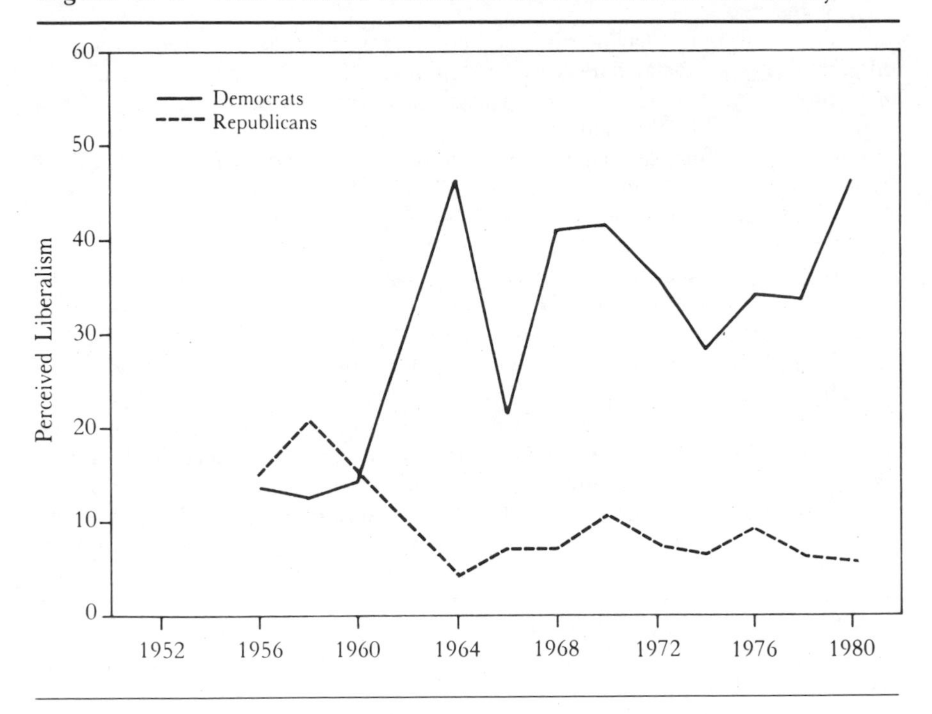

We took considerable care to maintain the conceptual linkages between the early series and the later ones. The empirical evidence bears witness to our success; Figure 29-4 shows both consistent behavior in the series across format changes and impressive variation within common formats.[6] And not least important, the series tracks our *a priori* expectations.

Figure 29-4 is thus both a validation of our measurement strategy and an important step in establishing our general argument. Figure 29-4 displays the result of our attempt to find a link between mass perceptions and party positions. The data reported are the portions of the public regarding each party as the more liberal of the two on racial policies. The Republican party is perceived as the more liberal of the two parties until just before 1964. This parallels the situation found in the Senate and House series. The public appears exceedingly accurate in its perceptions of party stands, at least on this issue. The strength of our claim for correct perception is greatly enhanced by the public's acuity in following the parties' policy reversals in the early 1960s. It would have been possible to justify a claim to accuracy on the basis of the gross pattern of response, even without the acuity. But with this additional twist, we see that the public tracked more than just the barest outlines of the debate; it followed some of the nuances as well. Thus, we have established the vital link between party behavior and image.

A contrast between evolving issues and established issues will add focus to this analysis. Comparison of an evolved issue (jobs) with an evolving one (race) will enable us to assess the relative significance of the newer issue. We can also make some inferences based upon the relative portions of the public responding to each of the two issues.

This comparison will serve other purposes. The observed over-time differences in the racial data series might result from (a) the method artifact of improved survey questions or (b) a general trend toward clarity in perceptions. We have already addressed the question of method artifact, but this second test will further weaken any method artifact argument. The "general trend" hypothesis we have not addressed. By showing the relative independence of the two series, we can refute both arguments. To these tasks we now turn.

We have chosen to contrast the evolving issue of racial policy with the evolved issue of government responsibilities for employment. It is generally conceded that the federal government under Franklin D. Roosevelt had taken upon itself the responsibility for providing jobs to the public in times of need. Although the Populists had proposed similar institutions in the late 1800s (Nye, 1965; Blum et al., 1968), agencies such as the WPA and the CCC changed the federal role. The new role was not one that was universally accepted, however, and thus a cleavage was born for the New Deal party system to nurture. The Republicans traditionally have opposed federal guarantees and the Democrats, to varying degrees, have supported federal employment in times of need. Because the "jobs" issue is fully evolved, we should see in our data either a consistent or a decaying difference between party adherents.

Figure 29-5 presents the results of our analysis of the mass public's perceptions on the "jobs" issue. It is based, like Figure 29-4, on all available SRC/CPS nationwide surveys conducted since 1952. The trend lines display responses to the questions concerning parties and employment policies.[7] The pattern is not in total conformity with our predictions, but it is generally supportive of our arguments. One discrepancy is that the differences in perception do not simply remain stable or decay; they actually grow from 1960 to 1964. An appealing explanation is that Barry Goldwater's campaign of 1964 heightened awareness of both the issue and the relative party stands on it. Goldwater made a concerted attack on government intrusion into the economy and the public responded.[8] This, incidentally, speaks again to the question of accuracy in the public's perception of party stands on policy issues. Goldwater made clear his party's position, and his party's image, clear though it was, clarified itself further.

Another deviation from our theory manifests itself as a "bump" in the mid-1970s. This period, during Gerald Ford's administration, was marked by an economic recession deeper than any since the Korean War. The party differences were heightened in the public's eyes by both rhetoric and action. These deviations notwithstanding, the New Deal-based cleavage appears largely stable since the start of the series.

Several conclusions can be drawn from this comparison of issues. First, it is clear that the two series have very different histories. The jobs issue is much more stable than the race issue; the jobs issue shows a relatively constant difference of about 30 percent. The racial series, on the other hand, shows a difference that first reverses direction and then grows from almost nothing to a gap wider than that of a New Deal issue. This demonstration of the series' independence makes it difficult to maintain that the observed differences in the racial series stem from

Figure 29-5 The New Deal Issue Polarization. Who is More Liberal on Job Guarantees

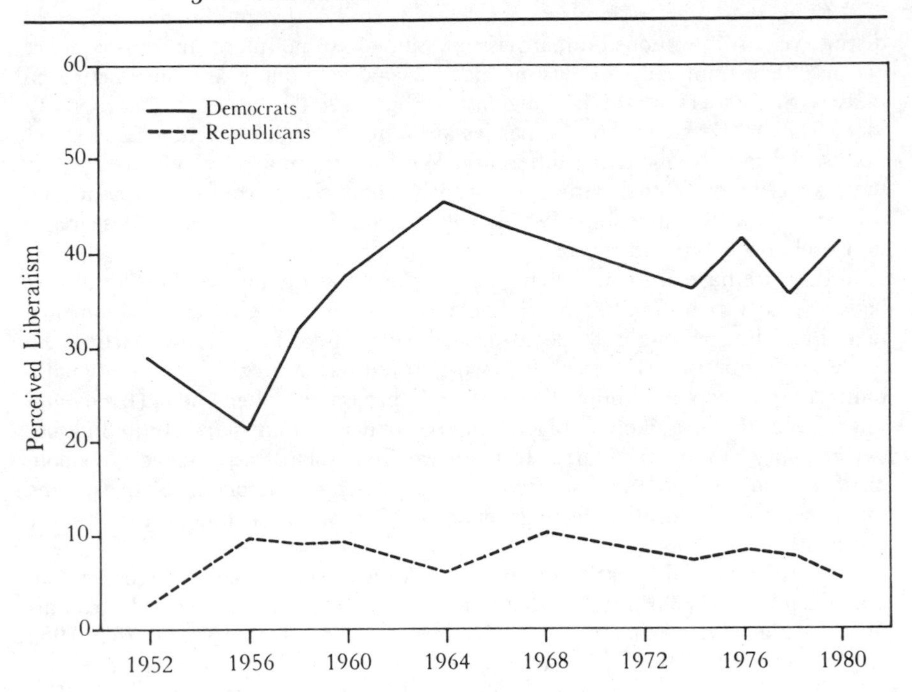

method artifacts or from "general trends" toward clearer perceptions of party stands.

We may also draw some conclusions about the significance of the evolving cleavage. As noted above, the racial issue cleavage now exceeds that of the older jobs issue. This gives us confidence that we have observed the development of a major cleavage in party structures. Because we have based our figures on the *total* sample, rather than on just the segment of the samples that responded to the question, larger gaps mean that more people are responding to the question. This increase has continued despite the use of question filters and format changes. Thus, the parties' positions on the race issue are not only becoming clearer as time goes on, but they are also involving larger numbers of people.

We have seen quite direct evidence of the changing racial images of the Democratic and Republican parties. Whether it *matters* we have not yet seen, for evolving mass party images by themselves are necessary but not sufficient to account for issue evolution. More than clarity of perception is required if evolving party issue positions are to cause systematic issue sorting among the party identifiers; the issue must matter. It must strike home with enough force to divert the citizen from the development of the party identification that would otherwise have been expected.

Stage Three: Citizens Respond to Party Images

Over the quarter-century span of our study, the public has perceived distinctive party positions on many issues. Some have no interesting consequence because they reinforce the existing party cleavage. Others are too fleeting to matter. Still others might be long lasting but lack the power to move party identification. To know that the parties are different on a particular issue is not necessarily to *care* about the difference. We can imagine a hypothetical public that correctly sorts the parties on a particular policy conflict without any consequence for its affections. Whether or not that is the case for the desegregation question is our topic here.

If, as we have argued, evolving party images are the intervening causal link between party policy shifts and the delayed mass response (issue realignment), then those images ought to be associated with affect toward the parties. To address that question we resort to a two-step indirect strategy. It is intentionally indirect to sidestep the "rationalization" and "projection" phenomena (Brody and Page, 1972) that are likely to plague any respondent commentary on the link between policy, affect, and party. Instead, we first isolate respondents who hold distinctive positions on the desegregation issue. Then in a second step we examine the positive and negative feelings expressed for each of the parties by the distinctive issue groups.

To isolate racial liberals and conservatives, we build a scale of desegregation liberalism for every CPS study where measures of both party affect and racial attitude are available (that is, every presidential and off-year study from 1956 onward, excluding only 1958 and 1962).[9] Racial liberals and conservatives are then defined arbitrarily to be the highest and lowest quartiles on the scale. The middle quartiles are excluded on the rationale that "indecisives" on an issue have no grounds for emotional response to party position-taking.[10]

Affection and disaffection for the parties are measured differently—by necessity—for the presidential and off-year studies. For presidential elections they are a summary of all responses to the familiar battery of questions: "Is there anything in particular that you like [dislike] about the Democratic [Republican] party?" "What is that?" "Anything else?" Except for 1972 (when responses were limited to three), the questions elicit as many as five responses for "likes" and "dislikes" for each party. Our affection measure is a summary count of the number of positive and negative references to the two parties, scored in the Democratic direction. In its natural metric the theoretical range of responses runs from +10 (five positive comments about the Democratic Party and five negative remarks about the Republicans) to −10 (for the reverse combination). To eliminate year-to-year variation in *net* affection for the parties, affection scores are adjusted to produce a constant metric (mean: 50, standard deviation: 10). This procedure effectively highlights systematic individual shifts of affection by ruling out the larger aggregate shifts exhibited by a fickle electorate.

The off-year studies force an alternate measurement strategy. Where the open-ended materials are not available, we use the party "feeling thermometers" to tap affective orientation. Rather than asking what they "like" or "dislike" about the parties, the feeling thermometer items instruct respondents to rate the parties on whether they "feel warmly" toward them or "don't feel warmly."

"Liking" and "feeling warm" seem a short conceptual distance from one another. The measurement techniques are, however, different in almost every other regard.[11]

As with the open-ended materials, we subtract Republican scores from Democratic scores to produce net Democratic affection, which is then adjusted to the standard metric.

The net measure, by either standard, allows us to gauge whether citizens with distinctive issue positions reflect their issue biases in their emotional response to the two parties. By pre-1964 standards we might expect racial conservatives to be disproportionately southern and therefore disproportionately favorable toward the not-yet-differentiated Democratic party. Figure 29-6 shows instead a reversed, but nonsignificant, ordering of preferences before 1964. Affect toward the two parties becomes clearly related to issue positions after 1964; in every year segregationists like the Republicans, integrationists like the Democrats. And although the data are altogether independent of the cognitive images of Figure 29-4, the patterns in the two figures are remarkably similar. Peak differences in 1964 and 1968 are followed in turn by a steadily increasing differentiation, leading to a new peak at the end of the series. Affect and cognition on this issue are closely tied. Where American voters have seen party issue differences, they have responded to them. It is but a short step from affection to identification, the consequence of which is issue evolution.

Black Americans fuel the differentiation of affect that appears so clearly in Figure 29-6. Because blacks now constitute a very sizable proportion of the

Figure 29-6 The Net Party Affect of Racial Liberals and Conservatives

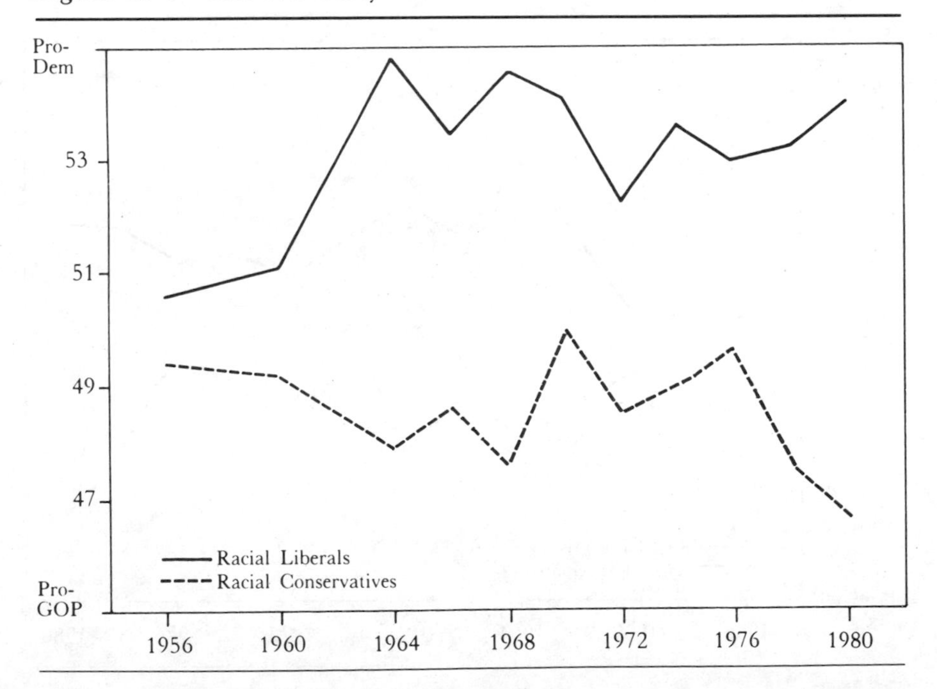

Democratic coalition, their behavior cannot be casually set aside. The Democratic party without blacks would appear quite unlike the real Democratic party. But if the patterns we have observed were entirely explained by the distinctive political behavior of black Americans, we would turn to group identification rather than issue attitudes to explain change (although the two would be collinear). To examine whether issue attitudes alone can account for the affective responses of Figure 29-6, we perform a similar analysis in Figure 29-7 for whites only.

It comes as no surprise that removing blacks from the ranks of racial conservatives produces no change at all. That half of the liberal/conservative mirror image of Figure 29-6 remains. Removing blacks from the ranks of racial liberals, however, leaves the remaining most-liberal quartile less distinctive. That lessened distinctiveness shows up in an over-time response that is itself less distinctive. Figure 29-7 shows the same essential pattern as in Figure 29-6, but it is a little less pro-Democratic and lacks some of the sharp year-to-year variation apparent in the earlier figure. The message of both figures, taken together, is that blacks contribute to the racial issue/party affect association, but they do not determine it.

We have now completed a causal path from observed changes in party behavior (the roll-call series) to accurate mass perception of party position, to different emotional responses to parties based upon issue positions, to—implicitly—mass party realignment, which is where we began. What it means is another question.

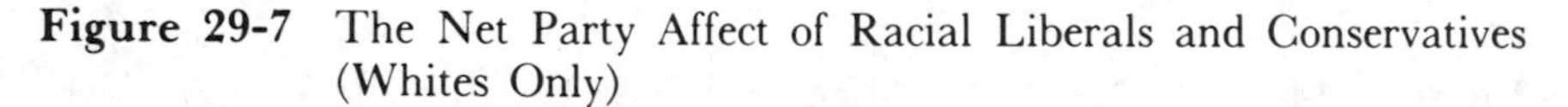

Figure 29-7 The Net Party Affect of Racial Liberals and Conservatives (Whites Only)

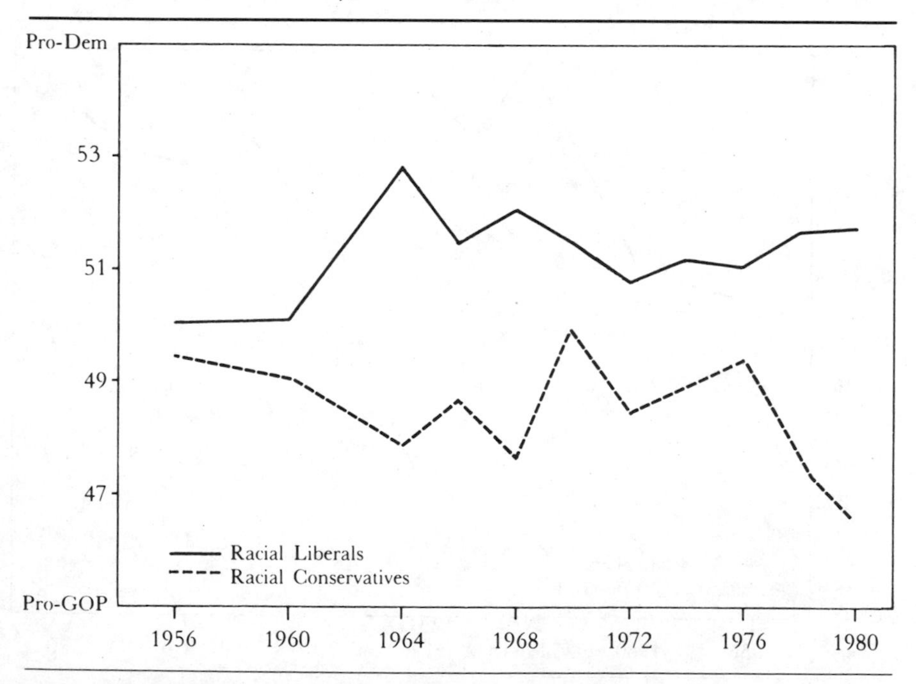

Realignment Reconsidered: Some Reflections on Electoral Change

We inquired in this chapter whether party images in the electorate could connect observable change in the policy orientations of party leaders with the later, more gradual realignment of party identifications. We asked whether the three variables—party behavior, party image, and party realignment— were associated over time, and whether the intervening images were bracketed in time between antecedent behavior and consequent realignment. Our data provide no reason to doubt that the answer to both questions is yes. For one particularly salient issue, party behavior seems to have caused (accurate) changes of party images, in turn leading to mass electoral realignment, but the theory is general. It should be equally applicable to other issues, past and future, that combine great salience with distinctive party movement. So too should it be applicable to other nations; it does not rest on assumptions specific to the American political context.

We look back at our data here and then go on to attempt to reconcile what we have seen with the concepts and expectations of students of realignment. In Figure 29-8 we look at party behaviors (of the congressional series), images, affections, and reconstructed realignment all together. All series are net differences—Democratic minus Republican for the party series, liberal minus conservative for the affect series. All five show the same evolution. Some are dramatic (party behaviors and party images), and some more inertial (affect and realigned

Figure 29-8 Senate, House, Identifier Attitudes, Images, and Affect, 1956-1980

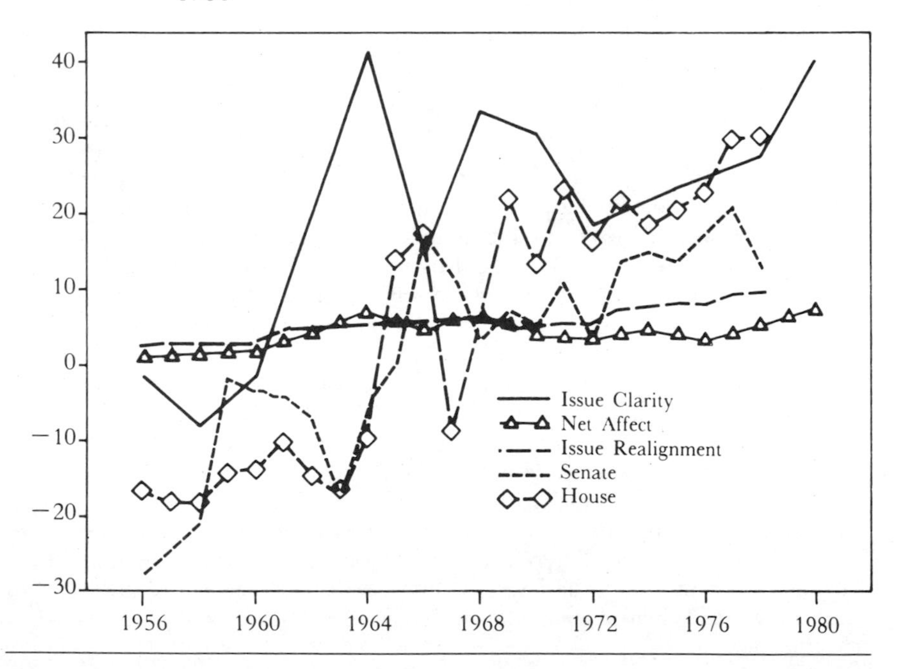

attitudes), but all evolve together. Perhaps equally important, no data we have seen fail to demonstrate the same pattern.

The point of racial policy change of a considerable scale, involving all actors in American politics, is now so evident that the reader may well wonder why we continue to belabor it. The answer is that the across-the-board changes we have seen add up to an electoral realignment, now almost two decades old, while most students of realignment are still waiting for one to happen. "An interesting little change you have there," they might say. "But if we had had a real realignment, we would have noticed."

What then *is* a realignment? Recent scholarship on this question (Clubb et al., 1980; Petrocik, 1981) finds it a more difficult question than was earlier assumed. No longer quite so simple as "first one party was in the majority and then the other one was," the concept has become multifaceted; many criteria are invoked to take its measure. In a fashion drawing on Petrocik, we will examine each of the facets and measure our data against each of the criteria. Why, we shall ask, can scholars look at the changes we have seen and (excepting Petrocik) deny that they belong in the class of events called "realignment?"

Did the parties develop distinctive *new* positions on our issue? Yes, without question they did. Were the distinctive positions perceived by the electorate? We have seen that they were. Did the party identifiers as groups begin to reflect the party issue cleavage? Yes, they did. Writing from the 1972 data, we were compelled to apologize for the weakness of the pattern—and to develop an evolutionary theory that accounted for the weak patterns (Carmines and Stimson, 1981a). Figure 29-1 suggests that we picked our weakest case for the original analysis. The pattern has subsequently become strong; an apology is no longer required.

Have we experienced massive electoral change in conjection with the postulated realignment? We have; the 1964 presidential election, our critical moment, was one of the most lopsided in our history, and there can be no doubt that the outcome was associated with the new racial dimension in American politics. Has the new issue dimension become the focus of political discourse? Here we must answer no, or at least probably no. Open political conflict on racial issues comes and goes. It lacks the continuity of the New Deal issues.

Has the racial desegregation issue created a new majority party? Clearly it has not. It has seemed to work to the detriment of both parties. If there is a *relative* advantage, it would be to the old majority party. Realignment is expected to produce a new majority. But must it be the old minority? The post-1964 Democratic Party is a new majority. Its issues, coalitions, and regional base in the South are forever altered. That seems to fit the meaning of the word realignment.

The most formidable obstacle to recognizing the 1964 realignment is, we suspect, that it did not look like the folk wisdom model of 1932. The coming to power of President Roosevelt seems to have captured our vision of the realignment concept. It was so simple: incensed by a great depression attributed to the old majority, the American people threw over their old party attachments and flocked to the party that offered a "New Deal" for the common man. Like generals preparing for the last war, political scientists are waiting for 1932 to happen again. When a realignment looks like 1932, it will be called a realignment.

There are two problems with using 1932 as a model of realignment. One is that future realignments are unlikely to resemble it, just as future wars will not be modeled on World War II. We should subscript "the 1932 realignment" as an idiosyncratic manifestation—tied to peculiar historical circumstances—of a far more general phenomenon. The other problem is that 1932 did not resemble the folk wisdom of 1932. Realignment scholars have long since rejected the folk wisdom model as descriptive of the New Deal realignment and substituted in its place contentious and complex variations. But it seems to have such a hold on popular thinking[12] that evidence piled atop evidence cannot destroy it.

NOTES

1. The two ends of the causal chain are derivative of earlier work and will be discussed only insofar as it is necessary to understand the linkage processes in the middle.
2. See, for instance, Matthews and Prothro (1966) and Sellers (1965).
3. Kelley and Mirer were concerned with candidate image in their article, but they operationalized this concept in the same way we operationalize party image.
4. The now-controversial reconstruction methodology and its specific application to reconstructing partisan racial attitudes are examined in detail in Carmines and Stimson (1984). That analysis suggests that the much-noted limits of recall are indeed problematic, as is reported "party identification" itself. The specific effect on this reconstructed series is conservative; cross-sectional evidence suggest more dramatic change than is observed in the reconstructed series.
5. See Carmines and Stimson (1981b) for further detail on the scaling procedure.
6. It is noteworthy that the question format changes on respondent positions that confound analysis of changes in the important 1960-1964 period do not occur for the party position questions. The format change in party position questions occurred before 1960. Thus method artifact is ruled out as a possible explanation of the important 1960-1964 changes.
7. The items used concern respondent and party positions on guaranteeing jobs and standard of living. CPS reference numbers are 1952: 46; 1956: 32,34; 1958: 23,24; 1960: 55; 1964: 80; 1968: 67; 1972: 176,177; 1974: 2269,2270; 1976: 3244,3245; 1978: 359,360; 1980: 1009,1010.
8. See Converse, Clausen, and Miller (1965) for corroboration on this point.
9. Items and scales for the presidential studies are the same as those used in Carmines and Stimson (1984) and in Figure 29-1. For the congressional studies and the newer 1980 study similar items are utilized.
10. The data will not be presented, but it can be noted that the middle quartiles always fall between the extremes in ensuing analyses.
11. Differences in technique naturally raise the question of whether the party affection we measure with alternative strategies is the same thing. When both measures are available, as in 1980, they correlate at .57. That association is not high enough to be particularly reassuring on the point, but it might be impressive in the face of the dubious reliability of the open-ended materials. Panel analysis on this question is in progress. We shall refrain from substantive interpretation of apparent differences between presidential and off years in the meanwhile.

12. Political scientists cite Key's (1955) "Critical Elections" article as a seminal contribution, for example, and then proceed to ignore the subversive point of Key's thesis. When Key declared 1928 "critical," he did not just provide an alternate date for the realignment; he provided evidence that is altogether inconsistent with the 1932 model. The 1928 election retained the existing majority party, produced no notable electoral surge and probably no net change in party identification, and—most embarrassing—preceded the event supposed to have caused the later realignment. If the 1932 folk wisdom model of realignment were applied to Key, he would be judged wrong, as would virtually all subsequent scholars of realignment. The 1932 realignment model should long ago have been scrapped; general theories cannot be built atop a single case.

30. POST-MATERIALISM IN AN ENVIRONMENT OF INSECURITY

Ronald Inglehart

A decade ago it was hypothesized that the basic value priorities of Western publics had been shifting from a Materialist emphasis toward a Post-Materialist one—from giving top priority to physical sustenance and safety, toward heavier emphasis on belonging, self-expression and the quality of life. This shift was traced to the unprecedented levels of economic and physical security that prevailed during the postwar era (Inglehart, 1971). Since this first exploration, the Materialist/Post-Materialist value change hypothesis has been subjected to further analysis by dozens of investigators using field work carried out in the United States, Canada, Australia, Japan and 15 West European nations.[1] Measurements at multiple time points are now available for a number of these countries; in all, well over 100 representative national surveys have measured the prevalence of Materialist/Post-Materialist value priorities among the publics of advanced industrial societies. A disproportionate share of this research has taken place in Germany and Japan—two countries that have experienced rapid economic growth in recent decades, and relatively rapid value change. Less evidence has been gathered in the relatively stagnant United States, despite the dominant position this country has held until recently in empirical social research.

Our data now span a decade. Implications for political change that were suggested by the original cross-sectional analysis can be tested in diachronic perspective. We can begin to distinguish between: (1) intergenerational value change, based on cohort effects; (2) life cycle or aging effects; and (3) period

---

Author's Note: The author thanks the following for stimulating comments and suggestions: Samuel Barnes, Russell Dalton, Kenan Jarboe, Max Kaase, Hans D. Klingemann, Shinsaku Kohei, Rex Leghorn, Warren Miller, Ichiro Miyake, Sigeki Nisihira, Tadao Okamura, Jacques-René Rabier, Tatsuzo Suzuki and Joji Watanuki. The European public opinion surveys were sponsored by the Commission of the European Communities; the American data are from the National Election surveys carried out by the Center for Political Studies, Institute for Social Research, University of Michigan. Interviews with candidates to the European Parliament were sponsored by the European Parliament, the Commission of the European Communities and the Volkswagen Foundation. The data used in this chapter are available from the ICPSR survey data archive, the Belgian Archive for the Social Sciences and the Zentralarchiv fur empirische Sozialforschung. This research was supported by grant SOC 79-14619 from the National Science Foundation.

Source: *American Political Science Review* (1981) 75:880-900. Reprinted with permission of the publisher.

effects; in particular, we can ask: have the economic uncertainty and the deterioration of East-West detente in recent years produced a sharp decline in Post-Materialism? As we will see, the answer is No. Overall there was remarkably little change in the ratio of Materialists to Post-Materialists among Western publics. But, like Sherlock Holmes's dog that did not bark in the night, this lack of dramatic change has crucial implications. Much of the literature on Post-Materialism deals with whether it is a deep-rooted phenomenon having a long-term impact on political behavior, or simply a transient epiphenomenon. We will reexamine this issue in the light of recent evidence. If a society's basic values change mainly through intergenerational population replacement, we would expect them to change at a glacial pace. But though short-term changes may be small, close examination of their societal location can provide valuable insight into their long-term implications. Contrary to what some observers have assumed (Kesselman, 1979), Post-Materialism has not dwindled away in the face of diminished economic and physical security. In most countries its numbers grew, and in some way its political influence seems greater now than a decade ago; but its character and tactics have changed significantly.

One of the most important changes derives from the simple fact that today, Post-Materialists are older than they were when they first emerged as a major political factor in the 1960s. Initially manifested mainly through student protest movements, their key impact is now made through the activities of young elites. For the students have grown older, and Post-Materialism has penetrated deeply into the ranks of young professionals, civil servants, managers, and politicians. It seems to be a major factor in the rise of a "new class" in Western society—a stratum of highly educated and well-paid young technocrats who take an adversary stance toward their society (Ladd, 1978; Gouldner, 1979; Lipset, 1979; Steinfels, 1979). The current debate between those giving top priority to reindustrialization and rearmament, versus those who emphasize environmentalism and the quality of life, will not be easy to resolve: it reflects persisting value cleavages.

Reexamining the Theory of Value Change

Before turning to time series evidence, let us reexamine our theoretical framework in the light of recent findings. It is based on two key hypotheses:

1) *A Scarcity Hypothesis.* An individual's priorities reflect the socioeconomic environment: one places the greatest subjective value on those things that are in relatively short supply.
2) *A Socialization Hypothesis.* The relationship between socioeconomic environment and value priorities is not one of immediate adjustment: a substantial time lag is involved, for, to a large extent, one's basic values reflect the conditions that prevailed during one's preadult years.

The *scarcity hypothesis* is similar to the principle of diminishing marginal utility, in economic theory. A complementary concept—Abraham Maslow's (1954) theory of a need hierarchy underlying human motivation—helped shape the survey items we used to measure value priorities. In its simplest form, the idea of a need hierarchy would probably command almost universal assent. The fact that unmet physiological needs take priority over social, intellectual or esthetic needs has been demonstrated all too often in human history: starving people will go to almost any lengths to obtain food. The rank ordering of human needs becomes less clear as we move beyond those needs directly related to survival. But it *does* seem clear that there is a basic distinction between the "material" needs of physiological sustenance and safety, and nonphysiological needs such as those for esteem, self-expression and esthetic satisfaction.

The recent economic history of advanced industrial societies has significant implications in the light of the scarcity hypothesis. For these societies are a remarkable exception to the prevailing historical pattern: the bulk of their population does *not* live under conditions of hunger and economic insecurity. This fact seems to have led to a gradual shift in which needs for belonging, esteem and intellectual and esthetic satisfaction became more prominent. As a rule, we would expect prolonged periods of high prosperity to encourage the spread of Post-Materialist values; economic decline would have the opposite effect.

But it is not quite that simple: there is no one-to-one relationship between economic level and the prevalence of Post-Materialist values, for these values reflect one's *subjective* sense of security, not one's economic level *per se*. While rich individuals and nationalities, no doubt, tend to feel more secure than poor ones, these feelings are also influenced by the cultural setting and social welfare institutions in which one is raised. Thus, the scarcity hypothesis alone does not generate adequate predictions about the process of value change. It must be interpreted in connection with the *socialization hypothesis*.

One of the most pervasive concepts in social science is the notion of a basic human personality structure that tends to crystallize by the time an individual reaches adulthood, with relatively little change thereafter. This concept permeates the literature from Plato through Freud and extends to the findings of contemporary survey research. Early socialization seems to carry greater weight than later socialization.

This, of course, doesn't imply that no change whatever occurs during adult years. In some individual cases, dramatic behavioral shifts are known to occur, and the process of human development never comes to a complete stop (Levinson, 1979; Brim and Kagan, 1980). Nevertheless, human development seems to be far more rapid during preadult years than afterward, and the great bulk of the evidence points to the conclusion that the statistical likelihood of basic personality change declines sharply after one reaches adulthood. Longitudinal research following given individuals over periods as long as 35 years, shows strong correlations (as high as .70) between people's scores on standardized personality scales from young adulthood to middle age, or even old age (Block, 1981; Costa and McCrae, 1980).

Taken together, these two hypotheses generate a coherent set of predictions concerning value change. First, while the scarcity hypothesis implies that prosperity is conducive to the spread of Post-Materialist values, the socialization hypothesis implies that neither an individual's values nor those of a society as a whole are likely to change overnight. Instead, fundamental value change takes place gradually, almost invisibly; in large part, it occurs as a younger generation replaces an older one in the adult population of a society.

Consequently, after a period of sharply rising economic and physical security, one would expect to find substantial differences between the value priorities of older and younger groups: they would have been shaped by different experiences in their formative years. But there would be a sizable time lag between economic changes and their political effects. Ten or fifteen years after an era of prosperity began, the age cohorts that had spent their formative years in prosperity would begin to enter the electorate. Ten more years might pass before these groups began to occupy positions of power and influence in their society; perhaps another decade would pass before they reached the level of top decision makers.

The socialization hypothesis complements the scarcity hypothesis, resolving objections derived from an oversimplified view of how scarcity affects behavior. It helps account for apparently deviant behavior: on one hand, the miser who experienced poverty in early years and relentlessly continues piling up wealth long after attaining material security, and on the other hand, the saintly ascetic who remains true to the higher-order goals instilled by his culture, even in the face of severe deprivation. In both instances, an explanation for the seemingly deviant behavior of such individuals lies in their early socialization.

The socialization hypothesis also explains why certain experimental tests of the need hierarchy have found no positive correlation between satisfaction of a given need at one time, and increased emphasis on the next higher need at a later time (Alderfer, 1972; Kmieciak, 1976). For these experiments are based on the implicit assumption that one would find almost *immediate* changes in an individual's priorities. But if, as hypothesized, an individual's basic priorities are largely fixed by the time he or she reaches adulthood, one would not expect to find much short-term change of the kind that was tested for.

This does not mean that an adult's value priorities are totally immutable—merely that they are relatively difficult to change. Normally, the rewards and deprivations employed in experimental psychology are modest, and the treatment is continued for a fairly brief time. Only in unusual experiments has the treatment been extreme enough to produce evidence of changed priorities among adults. In one such experiment, for example, a conscientious objector was kept on a semi-starvation diet for a prolonged period under medical supervision. After several weeks, he lost interest in his social ideals and began to talk about, think about and even dream about food (Davies, 1963). Similar patterns of behavior have been observed among inmates of concentration camps (Elkins, 1959; Bettelheim, 1979).

Marsh (1975) finds that Post-Materialists do not express higher satisfaction with their incomes than do Materialists. This is illogical, he argues: presumably, the former are Post-Materialists *because* their material needs are satisfied—so why don't they express relatively high levels of subjective satisfaction with their material circumstances? Once again the confusion is based on the implicit assumption that value change reflects an *immediate* response to one's environment. In the short run, one normally *does* experience a subjective sense of satisfaction when one satisfies material needs. But if these needs have been satisfied throughout one's formative years, one takes them for granted and develops higher expectations. In the long run, the fact that one has enough oxygen, water, food and clothing does *not* produce a subjective sense of satisfaction—which is precisely why the Post-Materialists seek satisfaction in *other* realms.

Because their incomes are higher than those of the Materialists, and yet they are still dissatisfied, Marsh concludes that Post-Materialists are actually *more* acquisitive than Materialists. Their emphasis on nonmaterial societal goals reflects mere lip service to fashionable causes, he argues, not their true personal values. Subsequent findings by Marsh himself refute this interpretation. To test his hypothesis, he developed an index of "Personal Post-Materialism"; he finds a correlation of +.22 between it and my index of societal Post-Materialism (Marsh, 1977, p. 180). While his discussion emphasizes the fact that this correlation is "only" .22, the crucial point is that the correlation is *positive*—and not negative, as he argued earlier. When one is dealing with survey data, a product-moment correlation is +.22 is fairly strong, particularly when it is found between two sets of items that were designed with the expectation that they would show a *negative* correlation.

Time Series Evidence from the Postwar Era

Our hypotheses imply that the unprecedented prosperity prevailing from the late 1940s until the early 1970s, led to substantial growth in the proportion of Post-Materialists among the publics of advanced industrial societies. We would need a time machine in order to go back and test this proposition, using the battery specifically developed to measure Materialist/Post-Materialist values. Though this is impossible, some available data *do* seem to tap the relevant dimension.

Data on the priorities of the German public, for example, cover more than 20 years, from 1949 to 1970. In these surveys, representative national samples were asked, "Which of the four Freedoms do you personally consider most important—Freedom of Speech, Freedom of Worship, Freedom from Fear or Freedom from Want?" In 1949, postwar reconstruction had just begun, and "Freedom from Want" was the leading choice by a wide margin. But in the following years, Germany rose from poverty to prosperity with almost incredible speed. In 1954, "Freedom from Want" was still narrowly ahead of any other choice, but by 1958 "Freedom of Speech" was chosen by more people than all other choices combined (EMNID, 1963, 1970).

These changes in the German population's value priorities seem to reflect the concurrent changes in their economic environment. And there is clear evidence of an age-related lag between economic change and value change. In 1962, 59 percent of the Germans from 16 to 25 years old chose "Freedom of Speech"; the figure declines steadily as we move to older groups; among Germans aged 65 and older, only 35 percent chose "Freedom of Speech." The fact that the young are much likelier to give "Freedom of Speech" priority over "Freedom from Want" fits theoretical expectations neatly. The original data have been lost, and it is not possible to perform an age cohort analysis in order to determine how much of this age difference is due to generational change. But the magnitude of the overall shift is so great that each age group must have *deemphasized* "Freedom from Want" as it aged during this period: the age differences *cannot* be attributed to life cycle effects. Further persuasive evidence of an intergenerational shift toward Post-Materialist priorities among the German public is found in the massive and definitive analysis of German survey data from 1953 through 1976 by Baker, Dalton and Hildebrandt (1981).

The most dramatic example of economic change in modern history is Japan—a nation that rose from harsh poverty to astonishing prosperity in a single generation. Indicators of the Japanese public's values are available in the Japanese national character studies carried out at five-year intervals, from 1953 through 1978. Analysis of these surveys indicates that Japanese culture changed along *several* different dimensions during this period, with the perceived sacredness of the emperor declining and emphasis on individuation and political participation rising (Ike, 1973; Hayashi, 1974; Nisihira, 1974; Richardson, 1974; Research Committee on Japanese National Character, 1979; Flanagan, 1979; Inglehart, 1982). One of the changes, it seems clear, was a shift from Materialist to Post-Materialist priorities. Among the available survey questions, the most unambiguous indicator of Materialist versus Post-Materialist priorities is the following: "In bringing up children of primary school age, some think that one should teach them that money is the most important thing. Do you agree or disagree?" In 1953, a strong majority (65 percent) of the Japanese public agreed that financial security was the most important thing. This figure declined steadily in subsequent surveys: by 1978 only 45 percent of the public still took this view. As was true of Germany, the trend is in the predicted direction—but in this case, the original data have been preserved and we can carry out a cohort analysis. Table 30-1 shows the results.

In any given year, the young are a good deal less likely to emphasize the importance of money than are the old. Does this simply reflect an inherent idealism of youth that will disappear as they grow older? Apparently not—for when we follow given age cohorts as they age during this 25-year period, we find no

Table 30-1 Cohort Analysis: Percentage of Japanese Public Agreeing That Financial Security Is Most Important

Age Group	*1953*	*1958*	*1963*	*1968*	*1973*	*1978*	*Change Within Given Cohort 1953-1978*	
20-24	60	—	43	34	22	18		
25-29	66		55	49	36	26		
30-34	63		58	58	42	37		
35-39	62		56	59	43	43		
40-44	65		63	59	46	49		
45-49	66		62	62	46	56 →	− 4	
50-54	72	—	68	65	49	51 →	−15	Mean:
55-59	72	—	72	67	60	56 →	− 7	−6
60-64	77	—	76	66	59	62 →	0	
65-69	78	—	72	73	59	62 →	− 3	
Spread between Youngest and Oldest:	+18	—	+29	+39	+37	+44		

Source: Japanese National Character Surveys carried out by the Institute of Statistical Mathematics, Tokyo.

indication whatever of increasing materialism. Quite the contrary, we find a tendency for a given cohort as it grows older to place *less* emphasis on money: the five cohorts for which we have data throughout the 25-year period show an average shift of six points *away* from giving top priority to money. Almost certainly this was a period effect, with the sharply rising prosperity of the postwar era producing a diminishing emphasis on money within each age cohort, quite independently of generational change or aging effects. As closer examination of Table 30-1 indicates, this period effect operated rather strongly from 1953 to 1973 and then reversed direction, so that from 1973 to 1978 each age cohort came to place slightly *more* emphasis on the importance of money. This pattern reflects changes in the economic environment rather faithfully: the extraordinary rise in prosperity that took place in Japan from 1953 to 1973 was mirrored in a gradual deemphasis on money within each age cohort; and the economic uncertainty that followed the oil shock of 1973 was accompanied by a partial reversal of this trend.

But these period effects are dwarfed by the intergenerational differences. While period effects seem to account for a mean net shift of 6 percentage points away from emphasizing the importance of financial security, we find a difference of 44 points between the youngest and oldest groups in 1978. Since these data show no evidence whatever that aging leads to increasing emphasis on money, there is a strong *prime facie* case for attributing this 44-point difference entirely to intergenerational change. It is conceivable that a life cycle tendency toward increasing Materialism with increasing age *also* exists, but is totally concealed by stronger period effects working in the opposite direction: the complexities of distinguishing between aging effects, cohort effects and period effects are such that we can not totally exclude this possibility (Glenn, 1976; Knoke and Hout, 1976). But belief in such an aging effect must depend on faith alone; it is totally unsupported by empirical evidence.

Indications of intergenerational change, conversely, seem incontrovertible. In 1953, even the *youngest* group showed overwhelmingly Materialistic priorities—because at that time, *all* adult age cohorts had spent their formative years during World War II or earlier. These cohorts show only modest changes as they age during the ensuing quarter-century. It is only from 1963 on—when the postwar cohorts begin to enter the adult population—that we find a clear rejection of financial security as the value having top priority among the younger cohorts. The shift of the Japanese public from a heavy majority giving money top priority, to a minority doing so, seems to reflect intergenerational population replacement above all, with only a minor component due to period effects. By 1978, there was a tremendous difference between the priorities of younger and older Japanese. As the leading example of economic growth in the postwar era, Japan constitutes a crucial case for testing our hypotheses. The time series data are unambiguous: from 1953 to 1978 there was an intergenerational shift away from Materialism among the Japanese public.

Materialist and Post-Materialist Values from 1970 to 1979

Our data from Western countries cover a shorter period than those from Japan, but they were specifically designed to measure Materialist/Post-Materialist value priorities. It is difficult to measure values directly. But their presence can be inferred from a consistent pattern of emphasis on given types of goals. Accordingly, we asked representative samples of citizens from Western nations what they personally considered the most important goals among the following:

A. Maintain order in the nation
B. Give people more say in the decisions of the government
C. Fight rising prices
D. Protect freedom of speech
E. Maintain a high rate of economic growth
F. Make sure that this country has strong defense forces
G. Give people more say in how things are decided at work and in their community
H. Try to make our cities and countryside more beautiful
I. Maintain a stable economy
J. Fight against crime
K. Move toward a friendlier, less impersonal society
L. Move toward a society where ideas count more than money.

Our earliest survey (in 1970) used only the first four items, in six countries. The full 12-item battery was first used in 1973 in the nine-nation European Community and the United States (Inglehart, 1977). Both batteries were administered in numerous subsequent surveys. Items A, C, E, F, I and J were designed to tap emphasis on Materialist goals; theoretically, these values should be given high priority by those who experienced economic or physical insecurity during their formative years. The remaining items were designed to tap Post-Materialist goals; they should be emphasized by those raised under relatively secure conditions. If so, certain respondents would favor Materialist items consistently, while others would consistently emphasize the Post-Materialist ones.

Survey results support these theoretical expectations. Those who give top priority to one Materialist goal tend to give high priority to other Materialist goals as well. Conversely, the Post-Materialist items tend to be chosen together. Hence, we can classify our respondents as pure Materialists (those whose top priorities are given to Materialist goals exclusively); pure Post-Materialists (those whose top priorities are given to Post-Materialist items exclusively); or mixed types based on any combination of the two kinds of items. Though for simplicity of presentation we will usually compare the two polar types, we are dealing with a continuum having numerous intermediate categories.

The predicted relationships with social background are also confirmed empirically. Within any given age group, those raised in relatively prosperous families are most likely to emphasize Post-Materialist items, and the predicted skew by age group is manifest. Figure 30-1 [p. 571] depicts this pattern in the pooled sample of six west European publics interviewed in our initial survey. Significant cross-national differences exist, but the basic pattern is similar from nation to nation: Among the oldest group, Materialists outnumber Post-Materialists enormously; as we move toward younger groups, the proportion of Materialists declines and that of Post-Materialists increases.

A major watershed divides the postwar generation (in 1970, those 15 to 24 years old) from all other age groups. While Materialists are still more than twice as numerous as Post-Materialists among those 25-34 years old, when we move across the World War II watershed, the balance shifts dramatically, with Post-Materialists becoming more numerous than Materialists.

The Materialist and Post-Materialist types have strikingly different opinions on a wide variety of issues, ranging from women's rights, to attitudes toward poverty, ideas of what is important in a job, and positions on foreign policy. Within each age group, about half the sample falls into the mixed value types. On virtually every issue, their position is between the Materialists and Post-Materialists: they seem to be a cross-pressured group that could swing either way.

By 1970, Post-Materialists had attained numerical parity with Materialists *only* among the post-war generation. Furthermore, they were concentrated among the more affluent strata of this age group: among university students, they heavily outnumbered the Materialists. In this light, perceptions of a generation gap in the late 1960s and early 1970s are understandable. Even among the postwar generation, Materialists were about as numerous as Post-Materialists. But in this age group's most articulate and most visible segment—the students—there was an overwhelming preponderance of Post-Materialists. The students lived in a distinct milieu: they had highly developed communications networks with other students but were largely isolated from their non-student peers. The priorities prevailing in this milieu were fundamentally different from those shaping the society as a whole.

The existence of such a milieu can play an important part in the evolution and propagation of a given set of values. Indeed, Habermas (1979) argues that the rise of Post-Materialism is not due to the different formative experiences of different generation units, but to exposure to the specific world views inculcated by distinct communications networks (c.f. Jaeggi, 1979). This explanation seems to complement, rather than substitute for, the one proposed here. It helps account for the spread of values in a given milieu, but provides no explanation why given generation units were disposed to accept given values in the first place, while others rejected them. Nevertheless, it seems clear that in virtually all Western nations, the student milieu of the late 1960s *did* constitute a distinct communications network, propagating a distinctive viewpoint. Given these circumstances, it is not surprising that the student elite saw themselves as part of a counterculture that was engaged in an irreconcilable clash with the culture of an older generation: From their viewpoint, the dictum, "Don't trust anyone over thirty" seemed plausible. Our hypotheses imply that as time went by, the Post-Materialists became older and more evenly distributed across the population. But in 1970, conditions were optimal to sustain belief in a monolithic generation gap, with youth all on one side and older people all on the other.

Clearly, there are large empirical differences between the priorities of younger and older groups in Western Europe (and, as subsequent research revealed, the entire Western world). But one can advance various interpretations concerning the *implications* of this finding. Though our own hypotheses point to intergenerational change based on cohort effects, we must acknowledge that any given pattern of age differences could, theoretically, result from (1) aging effects, (2) cohort effects, (3) period effects, or some combination of all three.

Aging Effects versus Cohort Effects

Perhaps the most obvious alternative interpretation is one based on aging effects. It would argue that for biological or other reasons, the young are inherently less materialistic than the old. As they age, however, they inevitably become just as materialistic as their elders; after 50 years, the youngest group will show the same overwhelming preponderance of Materialists that the oldest group now displays. The aging interpretation, then, holds that the pattern found in 1970 is a permanent characteristic of the human life cycle and will not change over time. The cohort interpretation, on the other hand, implies that the Post-Materialists will gradually permeate the older strata, neutralizing the relationship between values and age.

The most dramatic change from one age group to the next, in Figure 30-1, is the sudden shift in the balance between Materialist and Post-Materialist types that occurs as we move from the second-youngest to the youngest group. Our hypotheses imply the existence of a significant watershed between the postwar generation and the older groups that had experienced the World Wars, the Great Depression and their associated threats to economic and physical security. The gap between the two youngest groups in 1970 fits the historical change theory neatly. But this gap could *also* be interpreted as a permanent feature of the human life cycle. For in 1970, the dividing line between the postwar generation and all older groups happened to coincide with the boundary between those 25 years of age and older, and those who were 24 or younger. Since we know that people tend to get married, have their first child, and begin a permanent career at about this age, it might be argued that what we have identified as an historical watershed between the postwar generation and the older ones, merely reflects the stage in the life cycle when people get married and settle down. Time series data are needed to determine which interpretation is correct.

Period Effects

Both the German data and the Japanese data reviewed earlier show period effects: the economic environment of the period up to 1973 apparently induced *all* age groups to become less materialistic as time went by, quite apart from any processes of aging or generational change. These surveys were executed during a period of dramatic improvement in living standards, particularly in Germany and Japan. But even in the United States (where economic growth was much slower) the real income of the American public approximately doubled from 1947 to 1973.

From 1973 on, however, economic conditions changed drastically. Energy prices quadrupled almost overnight; the industrialized world entered the most severe recession since the 1930s. Economic growth stagnated and Western nations experienced extraordinarily high levels of inflation *and* unemployment. By 1980, the real income of the typical American family was actually *lower* than in 1970.

Western publics were, of course, acutely aware of changed economic circumstances, and responded to them. The most amply documented case is that of the American public, whose economic outlook is surveyed each month. In mid-1972, the University of Michigan Survey Research Center's Index of Consumer Sentiment stood at 95, only slightly below its all-time high. By the spring of 1975, the SRC Index had plummeted to 58—the lowest level recorded since these

Figure 30-1 Value Type by Age Group, among the Publics of Britain, France, West Germany, Italy, Belgium, and The Netherlands in 1970

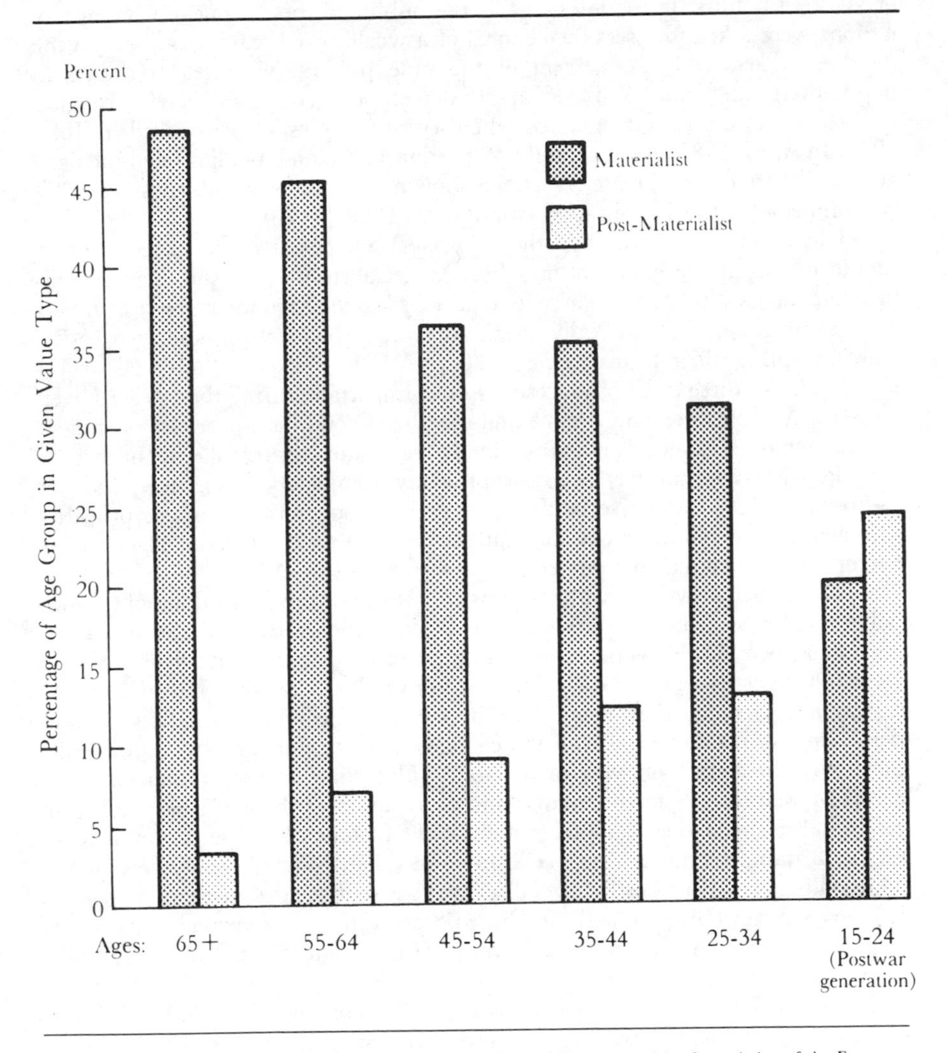

Source: European Community survey carried out in Feb.-Mar. 1970, sponsored by Commission of the European Communities; principal investigators were Jacques-René Rabier and Ronald Inglehart.

surveys were initiated in the 1950s. With the subsequent economic recovery, consumer confidence revived—only to collapse again in the wake of the second OPEC price shock in late 1979; in April, 1980 consumer confidence had reached a new all-time low, with the SRC Index at 53. Similar patterns of declining confidence in the economic outlook were recorded among West European publics (Commission of the European Communities, 1979).

The sense of physical security has also declined. The Soviet arms buildup, their invasion of Afghanistan, and the Western response to these events led to an erosion of East-West detente. This, too, had a pronounced impact on the outlook of Western publics. In the fall of 1977, the publics of the European Community nations were asked to assess the chances of a world war breaking out within the next ten years. Only 26 percent of the nine publics (weighted according to population) rated the likelihood at 50 percent or greater. This was roughly comparable to the results obtained when a similar question was asked in July, 1971. In April, 1980, however, fully 49 percent of the nine publics rated the danger at 50 percent or greater: such pessimism had almost doubled since 1977 (Commission of the European Communities, 1980, p. 16).

Clearly (as the scarcity hypothesis implies), the period effects of recent years should inhibit the development of a Post-Materialist outlook. And the socialization hypothesis implies that current conditions would have their greatest impact on the youngest and theoretically most malleable respondents—those aged 15-24, who are still in their formative years.

Which of these three processes was most important during the 1970s? Given the severity of the economic decline and the almost total disappearance of student protest and other dramatic manifestations of a counterculture, one might assume that Post-Materialism has been swept away completely by a new, harsher environment. Or—as the socialization hypothesis suggests—are these priorities sufficiently deep-rooted among the adult population to weather the effects of the current socioeconomic environment?

Table 30-2 provides part of the answer. It shows the distribution of the two polar value types from early 1970 to late 1979, in the six countries for which we have data covering this entire time span, and in the United States from 1972 to 1980. Of necessity, we use the original 4-item index here. By contrast with the cataclysmic changes that took place in consumer confidence indices and in perceptions of the danger of war, the changes here are remarkably small: for the most part, the shifts from year to year fall within the range of normal sampling error. Moreover, only modest and nonlinear cumulative changes took place from 1970 to 1980, and they vary cross-nationally. In four of the seven countries—Great Britain, Germany, France and The Netherlands—there were fewer Materialists and more Post-Materialists at the end of the decade than at its start. In two countries (Belgium and the United States) there was virtually no change. Only in the seventh country—Italy—do we find a shift toward the Materialist pole.

The fact that Italy is the deviant case is not surprising. During the 1970s Italy not only experienced exceptionally severe economic difficulties, but also severe political disorder. Probably for this reason, there was a substantial net shift toward Materialism among the Italian public. But in the other six countries, the process of population replacement outweighed the effects of economic and physical insecurity. The net result for the seven countries as a whole is that Post-Materialists were slightly *more* numerous at the end of the 1970s than they were at the start.

The impression of remarkable stability that the aggregate national data convey, conceals an extremely interesting underlying pattern. For, as hypothesized, the distribution of values across age groups has changed over time. Table

Table 30-2 Changes in Prevalence of Materialist and Post-Materialist Value Types, 1970-1980 (Percentage falling into the two polar types)

	1970	*1973*	*1976*	*1979*
Britain				
Materialist	36	32	36	27
Post-Materialist	8	8	8	11
Germany				
Materialist	43	42	41	37
Post-Materialist	10	8	11	11
France				
Materialist	38	35	41	36
Post-Materialist	11	12	12	15
Italy				
Materialist	35	40	41	47
Post-Materialist	13	9	11	10
Belgium				
Materialist	32	25	30	33
Post-Materialist	14	14	14	14
Netherlands				
Materialist	30	31	32	28
Post-Materialist	17	13	14	19

	1972	*1976*	*1980*
United States			
Materialist	35	31	35
Post-Materialist	10	10	10

Source: European Community surveys carried out in Feb.-Mar. 1970; Sept. 1973; Nov. 1976; and Nov. 1979; and Post-Election wave of the U.S. National Election surveys carried out in each respective year by the Center for Political Studies, Institute for Social Research, University of Michigan.

30-3 shows this relationship, from early 1970 through late 1979. Figure 30-2 depicts these data in graphic form. As these data reveal, the overall stability shown in Table 30-2 is the result of two opposing processes that largely cancel each other.

On one hand, the youngest group shows a substantial *decline* in the ratio of Post-Materialists to Materialists. In 1970, Post-Materialists were 4 percentage points more numerous than Materialists among this group: in other words, the group showed a Percentage Difference Index (PDI) of +4. This fell to a PDI of −1 in 1973 and fell further to a PDI of −5 in 1976. Although the trend then reversed itself, with a partial recovery to an index of −3 in 1979, this youngest group showed a net shift of 7 points in the Materialist direction during the 1970s.

Table 30-3 Changes in Prevalence of Materialist and Post-Materialist Values, 1970-1979 by Age Group (Percent) (Combined results from six European nations)

	1970		*1973*		*1976*		*1979*	
Ages	*M*	*P-M*	*M*	*P-M*	*M*	*P-M*	*M*	*P-M*
15-24	20	24	21	20	25	20	24	21
25-34	31	13	28	13	29	16	27	17
35-44	35	12	35	9	35	11	33	13
45-54	36	9	39	7	39	8	41	10
55-64	45	7	43	6	47	6	41	8
65 and over	48	3	45	4	52	5	49	5
Total:	35	12	34	10	37	12	35	13
Percent Difference Index:	−23		−24		−25		−22	

Source: Surveys sponsored by the Commission of the European Communities, carried out in Feb.-March 1970; Sept. 1973; Nov. 1976 and Nov. 1979.

But this shift was more than offset by shifts in the *opposite* direction among the older groups. The socialization hypothesis implies that period effects would have their greatest impact on the youngest group. Empirically, it turns out that the youngest group was the *only* group on which period effects had a significant negative net impact: the older ones moved in the Post-Materialist direction. The American data show a similar pattern: younger respondents became more Materialist but the older ones became *less* so. In Europe, this countervailing tendency was especially strong among the second youngest group, which showed a steady rise in the proportion of Post-Materialists even during the depths of the 1970s recession; despite economic uncertainty and the erosion of detente, by 1979 this group had registered a net shift of 8 points toward the Post-Materialist pole.

This seemingly counterintuitive development reflects changes in the composition of the 25-34-year-old group, due to population replacement. In 1970 this group contained no one born after 1945; but by late 1979 its members were recruited entirely from the postwar generation. The World War II watershed now fell between the *two* youngest groups and all of the older ones.

Let us examine Figure 30-2 more closely. In 1970, by far the widest gap between adjacent age groups was that between the youngest and second-youngest groups. This gap was a prominent feature of the value distributions in each of the six nations surveyed in that year. At that point, it was unclear whether this gap should be interpreted as a World War II watershed, or as the reflection of a major life-cycle transition that takes place in one's mid-twenties.

That uncertainty has now vanished. During the 1970s, the still-malleable 15-24-year-old group became progressively more Materialist until the recession

Figure 30-2 Change in Value Priorities in Six Nations, 1970-1979, by Age Group

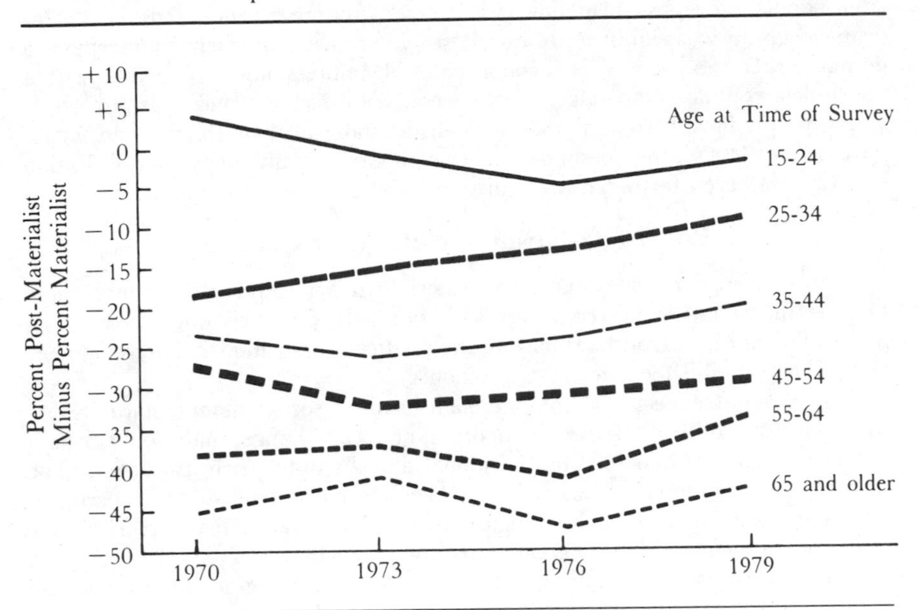

Source: European Community surveys carried out in Feb.-Mar. 1970; Sept. 1973; Nov. 1976 and Nov. 1979 in Britain, Germany, France, Italy, Belgium and The Netherlands: since data from only these nations are available for 1970, only these data are used for the subsequent time points. Surveys were sponsored by the Commission of the European Communities; principal investigators were Jacques-René Rabier and Ronald Inglehart.

bottomed out, and then staged only a partial recovery. But the 25-34-year-old group became steadily more Post-Materialist throughout the 1970s. By the end of 1979 the largest gap no longer was located between these two youngest groups, but between the 25-34-year-old group, and those aged 35-44. This accords perfectly with the fact that members of the postwar generation had now reached 34 years of age.

It is virtually impossible to interpret this pattern in terms of aging effects—unless one believes that the human life cycle changed radically between 1970 and 1979: the crucial life stage transition that took place at age 25 in 1970, had somehow shifted to age 35 in 1979. Furthermore, there is no indication that aging has an inherent tendency to produce a Materialistic outlook. Despite the economic uncertainty of this period, only the 15-24-year-old group became significantly more Materialist; among older groups, the downward pressure of period effects was more than offset by the upward pressure of the population replacement process. Furthermore not even the youngest category showed a *continuous* downward trend: plummeting steeply until 1976, it began to reverse itself with recovery from the recession. It seems far more plausible to attribute this nonlinear pattern to period effects than to the aging process (which presumably is continuous).

The economic and physical uncertainty of the 1970s produced a significant period effect. The net movement toward Post-Materialism that would be expected from population replacement slowed to a crawl. By the decade's end, the 15-24-year-old group was significantly less Post-Materialist than their counterparts a decade earlier had been. This is congruent with impressionistic observations that the student population no longer seems as nonconformist as it once was. For while young people have become more materialistic, those in their thirties and forties have become less so: the notion of a generation gap, already an oversimplification in 1970, was even farther from reality in 1979 due to this convergence.

Post-Materialism and Political Change

The evidence indicates that Post-Materialism is a deep-rooted phenomenon. Despite the recession of recent years, it not only persisted but increased its penetration of older groups. What are the political implications? The remainder of this chapter will focus on that question.

One would expect that, despite their favored socioeconomic status, Post-Materialists would be relatively supportive of social change, and would have a relatively high potential for unconventional and disruptive political action. The reasons can be summarized as follows: (1) Materialists tend to be preoccupied with satisfying immediate physiological needs; Post-Materialists feel relatively secure about them and have a greater amount of psychic energy to invest in more remote concerns such as politics. (2) As a recently emerging minority whose highest priorities have traditionally been given relatively little emphasis in industrial society, Post-Materialists tend to be relatively dissatisfied with the established order and relatively supportive of social change. (3) The disruption and property damage that sometimes result from unconventional political action seem less negative to Post-Materialists, since they threaten things they value less than Materialists do. In short, Post-Materialists have a larger amount of psychic energy available for politics, they are less supportive of the established social order, and, subjectively, they have less to lose from unconventional political action than Materialists. Consequently, the rise of Post-Materialism has made available a new, predominantly middle-class base of support for the left.

Is it empirically true that Post-Materialists tend to be relatively change-oriented and ready to engage in unconventional political protest? One measure of support for social change is now a standard feature of the European Community surveys carried out twice each year. Representative national samples of the publics of the European Community countries are asked:

> On this card are three basic kinds of attitudes toward the society we live in. Please choose the one which best describes your opinion. (1) The entire way our society is organized must be radically changed by revolutionary action. (2) Our society must be gradually improved by reforms. (3) Our present society must be valiantly defended against all subversive forces.

These alternatives might be described as Revolutionary, Reformist and Conservative.

The Reformists constitute a clear majority—63 percent of those responding—in the European Community as a whole, and this holds true for all value types. But there is a pronounced difference between Materialists' and Post-

Table 30-4 Support for Social Change versus Resistance to Social Change, by Value Type, 1976-1979 (percent)

Respondent's Value Type	*Support for Revolutionary Change*	*Support for Gradual Reform*	*Support for Defense of Present Society*	*N*
Materialist	4	57	38	18,292
Mixed	8	62	30	26,694
Post-Materialist	17	69	14	6,098

Note: Results are weighted according to size of each nation's population.

Source: Pooled data from Euro-barometre surveys, 1976 through 1979, from all nine European Community nations.

Materialists' attitudes toward social change. Table 30-4 shows the relationship between value type and attitudes toward social change among the publics of the European Community as a whole. Among Materialists, only 4 percent endorse the Revolutionary option; nearly ten times as many (38 percent) support the Conservative option. Among Post-Materialists, by contrast, the Revolutionary option draws *more* support than the Conservative one. For both, the Reformist option is the leading choice—but Post-Materialists are only about one-third as likely to hold Conservative views as are Materialists, and about four times as apt to favor radical social change.

Despite their relatively privileged social status, Post-Materialists are markedly more favorable to social change than are other value types. But how far are they ready to go on behalf of their values?

A central feature of an eight-nation survey carried out during 1974-1976 was a scale designed to measure an individual's potential for participation in political protest activities (for details of field work, see Barnes, Kaase et al., 1979). This scale is based on whether the respondent has done, or would do and approves of, a series of acts ranging from circulating petitions to occupying buildings and disrupting traffic. Tested and applied in eight countries, the scale has remarkably good technical characteristics and seems to measure, in a straightforward way, just how far an individual is willing to go in order to carry out his or her beliefs.

Do Post-Materialists show a relatively high propensity for unconventional political activities as measured by the Protest Potential Scale? On one hand, Marsh (1975) has argued that Post-Materialist responses tap nothing more than a form of radical chic among a basically conservative elite. If so, the answer would be No. On the other hand, if our typology reflects basic value differences, the answer would be Yes. The Protest Potential Scale was developed, in part, to test whether Post-Materialist values go no deeper than lip service to fashionable goals, or whether they have behavioral implications. The answer is unequivocal.

Table 30-5 shows the relationship between protest potential and value type in each of the eight nations surveyed in 1974-1976. A score of "3" is the cutting point for this table: Those scoring below this level are (at most) ready to circulate

Table 30-5 Protest Potential, by Value Type in Eight Western Nations, 1974-1976 (Percent)

Respondent's Value Type	*The Netherlands*	*Britain*	*United States*	*Germany*	*Austria*	*Italy*	*Switzerland*	*Finland*
Materialist	27	21	38	23	17	20	17	20
Mixed	42	31	48	36	21	38	27	34
Post-Materialist	74	55	72	74	48	69	61	58

Note: Figures represent percent scoring "3" or higher on Protest Potential scale. Values index is based on items A-L cited above.

Source: Eight-Nation survey, carried out 1974-1976; for details of fieldwork and a report of findings from five of these eight nations, see Samuel H. Barnes, Max Kaase et al. (1979).

petitions or to march in peaceful demonstrations; a good many of them have done nothing at all and are not willing to do anything. Those scoring higher are willing to do all of the above *and* engage in boycotts; many are ready to go still further—to take part in rent strikes, illegal occupation of buildings or to block traffic.

As Table 30-5 makes clear, people's value priorities have a strong relationship to their level of Protest Potential. In Great Britain (where the relationship is weakest), only 21 percent of the Materialists are ready to engage in boycotts or go beyond them in protest against some form of perceived political injustice; among the Post-Materialists, 55 percent have done so, or are willing to do so. The linkage between values and the potential for protest is particularly strong in Italy, where only 20 percent of the Materialists rank high on protest potential—as compared with 69 percent of the Post-Materialists. In all eight countries Post-Materialists are far readier to engage in political protest than Materialists.

In multivariate analyses, when we control for the effects of age, education, income, and one's level of ideological sophistication, a strong relationship persists between Post-Materialist values and a predisposition for unconventional protest. A relatively high potential to use unconventional and disruptive techniques in order to intervene in the political process seems to be directly linked with the Post-Materialist outlook; it is not merely a spurious correlate, resulting from the fact that Post-Materialists tend to be young and well educated.

This might seem paradoxical. On one hand, we have seen that the economic uncertainty of the 1970s did not cause Post-Materialism to disappear—on the contrary, its support seems to have grown in most Western countries. On the other hand, the dramatic political protest movements of the late sixties and early seventies have disappeared in the United States (though not in Western Europe): why did this happen, if a relatively high protest potential characterizes the Post-Materialists?

The main answer is that people don't protest in a social vacuum. The Post-Materialists did not protest for the sake of protesting—they responded to specific issues, above all the war in Indochina. The fact that there no longer is a war in

Indochina (or, at least, no *American* war) makes a big difference. Almost nothing can compare with war, in terms of violence, drama and human tragedy, and nothing on the current scene can command sustained mass attention in the way the Vietnam War did. In the absence of any political cause fully comparable to the war, it is only natural that much of the attention and energies of Post-Materialists have been diverted into other channels.

For some, this means seeking self-actualization through development of the inner self, rather than through social action. The human potential movement is an example. For those who remain politically active, this turning inward seems like desertion of the cause; the current crop of youth has been characterized as the Me Generation, practicing a culture of narcissism. There is some truth and even more misapprehension in this view. As we have seen, at the close of the 1970s the 15 to 24-year-old group *was* more materialistic than their counterparts at the start of the decade had been—but the difference was modest. If the potential for political protest generally remained only a potential, it may have been because none of the current political causes were as compelling as those of the earlier decade.

Post-Materialist Penetration of Elite Groups

But another major factor has also affected how Post-Materialism manifests itself politically. It springs from the simple fact that the average Post-Materialist is substantially older than he or she was in 1970. Post-Materialists are no longer concentrated in a student ghetto. They have moved into positions of influence and authority throughout society. Despite their minority status in society as a whole, they outnumber the Materialists in certain key sectors.

Table 30-6 shows how the two pure value types are distributed by age and occupation among the publics of the European Community countries. This table pools the data from six surveys carried out in all nine countries in the late 1970s, in order to provide reliable data for certain small but important elite groups. A national sample survey normally contains only a handful of professionals, for example; but here we have large enough numbers that we not only can compare this occupational category with them, but can break it down by age group.

The pure Post-Materialist type comprises only about 8 percent of the manual workers, and 7 percent of the farmers; in these occupational groups, pure Materialists outnumber Post-Materialists by ratios of at least five to one. On the other hand—despite the recent decline in Post-Materialism among the student-age population—Post-Materialists continue to outweigh Materialists in the student milieu. This is significant but not particularly surprising. What *is* surprising is the fact that among those less than 35 years old with jobs that lead to top management and top civil service posts, Post-Materialists outnumber Materialists decisively: their numerical preponderance here is even *greater* than it is among students. This is all the more astonishing since these young technocrats are older, on the average, than the students. This phenomenon reflects the fact that the young managers and officials are a highly select stratum, recruited according to considerably more demanding criteria than those for admission to a university: there are many more students than young technocrats. In social background, the latter correspond to the students at the most prestigious schools, rather than to the student population as a whole. In general, the more selective our criteria become,

Table 30-6 Materialist versus Post-Materialist Values by Respondent's Occupation and Age Group in Nine European Community Nations, 1976-1979 (Percent)

	Age Less than 35			*Ages 35-49*			*Age 50 and Over*		
	M	*P-M*	*N*	*M*	*P-M*	*N*	*M*	*P-M*	*N*
Top management + top civil servants	20	30	565	22	22	702	28	16	374
Students	20	25	3,800	—	—	—	—	—	—
Professionals	25	21	280	21	19	218	29	12	162
Nonmanual employees	26	18	4,591	34	13	2,918	38	9	1,569
Unemployed persons	24	16	875	38	9	279	48	6	321
Self-employed business persons	35	13	1,329	41	10	1,109	43	7	855
Manual workers	32	11	4,673	40	8	3,264	44	5	2,255
Housewives	38	9	3,469	46	6	3,763	50	5	4,755
Farmers	42	10	347	44	5	528	48	4	778
Retired persons	—	—	—	—	—	—	51	5	7,018

Source: Based on combined data from the nine-nation European Community surveys carried out from 1976 through 1979.

the higher the proportion of Post-Materialists—and the young technocrats represent the elite of the recent university graduates. Already occupying influential staff positions, many of them should reach the top decision-making level within the next decade.

Apart from the students, the young technocrats are the only category in which Post-Materialists hold a clear preponderance over Materialists. But Post-Materialism has also made impressive inroads in certain other elite categories. In the free professions, Post-Materialists are almost as numerous as Materialists—not only in the under-35 age group but in the 35 to 49-year-old category as well. And there is an even balance between Materialists and Post-Materialists among those aged 35 to 49 in top management and top civil service posts.

Among those 50 and older, the Materialists hold a clear preponderance in *every* occupational category. Among self-employed people in business and trades in this age group, Materialists are six times as numerous as Post-Materialists. And even among the self-employed under 35, Materialists predominate by a ratio of nearly three to one: young technocrats may be Post-Materialistic, but young self-employed business people definitely are *not.*

By the end of the 1970s, Post-Materialism had become a powerful influence among technocrats and professionals in their thirties and forties. This does not mean that it will automatically become the dominant influence in Western societies. Post-Materialists remain a numerical minority, better equipped to attain their goals through bureaucratic institutions or the courts than through the electoral process. They may encounter the backlash of resurgent Materialism, as recent political events in the United States suggest. Nevertheless, by the late 1970s, Post-Materialism had not only made deep inroads among young technocrats; but it had *also,* to a surprising degree, penetrated the West European political class.

Table 30-6 may actually *understate* the degree to which younger Western elites had become Post-Materialist. For these data are based on representative national samples; even when we break them down into relatively fine categories as in Table 30-6, even the top management and civil service group is fairly heterogeneous, ranging from relatively modest levels to the truly elite stratum. Theoretically, the latter should be more Post-Materialistic. For an indication of the values prevailing among West European political elites, let us turn to some data from interviews with the candidates running for seats in the European Parliament in 1979. This sample includes candidates from all significant political parties in all nine countries, drawn in proportion to the number of seats each party holds in the European Parliament (for details of fieldwork, see Inglehart et al., 1980). In background, these candidates are roughly similar to members of the respective national parliaments (in which many of them hold seats). Though somewhat younger than the average number of the national parliaments, they seem to provide a reasonably good sampling of the West European political elite.

The candidates for the European Parliament were asked to rank their priorities among the 12-item set of societal goals described above. Those who gave top priority to one Materialist item tended to give high priority to the other Materialist items as well; the same was true of Post-Materialist items. Table 30-7 shows how the 12 items fell into two clearly defined clusters on the first dimension of a factor analysis. The structure of the candidates' choices shown

Table 30-7 Value Priorities of Candidates to the European Parliament, 1979 (First factor in principal components factor analysis)

	Materialist/Post-Materialist (24%)	
Post-materialist goals	More say on job	.660
	Less impersonal society	.478
	More say in government	.472
	Society where ideas count	.408
	More beautiful cities	.315
	Freedom of expression	.254
Materialist goals	Control of inflation	−.436
	Fight against crime	−.442
	Stable economy	−.450
	Economic growth	−.566
	Maintain order	−.588
	Adequate defense forces	−.660

Source: Interviews with 742 candidates for seats in the European Parliament, carried out Mar.-Apr.-May, 1979 as part of the European Election Study organized by Karlheinz Reif. Principal investigators were Ian Gordon, Ronald Inglehart, Carsten Lehman Sorensen and Jacques-René Rabier.

here is virtually identical to that found among the publics of these same nine countries (compare the results in Inglehart, 1977, p. 46). Empirically, all six of the items designed to tap Materialist priorities show negative polarity, while all six items designed to tap Post-Materialist priorities show positive polarity.

The Materialist/Post-Materialist dimension proves to be remarkably robust—not only crossculturally but also across time, and from the mass to the elite level. We used responses to these items to construct a value priorities index, coding those candidates who chose Materialist items for both their first and second priorities as pure "Materialists"; coding those who chose two Post-Materialist items as "Post-Materialist"; and those who chose other combinations as "Mixed." Table 30-8 shows the distribution of value types among our sample of the European Parliament, weighted in proportion to how many seats each party and nationality obtained in 1979.

In the Parliament as a whole, Materialists narrowly outnumber the Post-Materialists. But while Post-Materialists (as defined here) comprise little more than one-eighth of the general public of these countries, they make up nearly one-third of the European Parliament. And when we break our sample down by age group, we find a pronounced skew. Among those 55 years of age and over, Materialists are almost twice as numerous as Post-Materialists. But among those under 55, the Post-Materialists outnumber the Materialists.

Clearly, Post-Materialism is no longer a student phenomenon. When the postwar generation first became politically relevant in the 1960s, the universities may have been the only major institutions in which they were the dominant influence. Their youth, their minority status in society as a whole, and their relative lack of representation at decision-making levels dictated a protest strategy. Post-Materialists had little access to key decision-making posts; but they were highly motivated and articulate. They could not control decision making, but they *could* disrupt it—and they made use of unconventional political protest techniques.

Table 30-8 Value Type by Age Group, among Candidates for European Parliament, 1979 (Percent)

	Ages		
	25-54	*55-86*	*Total for European Parliament*
Materialist	31	43	35
Mixed	34	34	34
Post-Materialist	36	23	32
N =	439	221	660

Note: Percentages are weighted in proportion to actual number of seats each party and nationality had in the European Parliament as of June 1979. Accordingly, candidates from parties that won no seats are excluded from this table. Unweighted Ns appear at foot of each column. One column does not add up to 100 because of rounding.

Source: Interviews with sample of candidates running for seats in European Parliament, interviewed in March-May 1979. This sample includes 62 percent of those actually elected in June, 1979.

Post-Materialism and the Rise of the New Class

The relative youth and powerlessness of the Post-Materialists may have dictated a strategy of student protest in the 1960s. But Post-Materialism has moved out of the student ghetto. By 1980, a Post-Materialist outlook had become more common than a Materialist one among young technocrats, professionals and politicians of Western countries. As experts, congressional staffers and members of ministerial cabinets, Post-Materialists had direct access to the command posts of the sociopolitical system. Protest was no longer their most effective tool. The impact of Post-Materialism was no longer symbolized by the student with a protest placard, but by the public interest lawyer, or the young technocrat with an environmental impact statement.

In recent years, a growing number of Western intellectuals have focused their attention on the rise of "The New Class." In contrast with the establishment-oriented New Class of Eastern Europe described by Djilas (1966), the New Class in the West is an elite characterized by its adversary stance toward the existing social order (Podhoretz, 1979; Bruce-Briggs, 1979); by its "culture of critical discourse" (Gouldner, 1979, pp. 28-29); and by a "new liberalism" (Ladd, 1978, pp. 48-49). Broder (1980) describes the emergence of a new generation of political elites who have many of these characteristics as a "changing of the guard."

There is no clear consensus on the criteria that define the New Class. Ehrenreich and Ehrenreich (1977) describe it as those in the census categories of "professional and technical," plus "managers and administrators"—precisely the categories we have found to be most heavily Post-Materialist. But Ladd (1978) extends its limits to include anyone with a college education. There is even less consensus concerning *why* this well-paid and increasingly powerful stratum of society is critical of the existing economic and political order and participates in leftist political movements. There is a tendency to view an adversary culture as something *inherent* in higher education or in certain occupations, but the reasons are not altogether clear. Highly educated groups have existed for a long time, but in the past they generally were politically conservative. High levels of education and information are the *resource* that enables the New Class to play an important role—but they do not explain why today, an increasing share of the most highly educated and informed strata take an adversary stance toward their society.

I suggest that the rise of Post-Materialism and its subsequent penetration of technocratic and professional elites has been a major factor behind the emergence of the New Class. For this group is distinctive not only in its occupational and educational characteristics, but also in its values. And the ideology attributed to the New Class reflects Post-Materialist values rather closely (Ladd, 1976, 1978). If this is true, it explains why a New Class having these specific characteristics has emerged at this particular point in history.

For the distinctive values of the New Class reflect an historical change that cannot be attributed simply to a changing educational and occupational structure. Rising levels of education and a shift of manpower into the "knowledge industries" have played a major role in the rise of this new elite, as Bell (1973, 1976), Lipset and Dobson (1972), Lipset (1979), and others have argued. But—as Table 30-6 makes clear—an "adversary culture" is not an *inherent* concomitant of the education or adult role of professionals and technocrats. *Older* professionals and technocrats are preponderantly Materialist; it is only among the younger segments of these groups that Post-Materialist priorities outweigh Materialist ones.

Because both the political environment and the social location of Post-Materialists have changed significantly, their tactics have also changed. Though the war in Indochina no longer plays an important role in Western politics, some of the most important movements on the current scene reflect the clash of Materialist and Post-Materialist world views—among them, the women's movement, the consumer advocacy movement, the environmental movement and the antinuclear movement. These movements involve questions of whether one gives top priority to economic growth, or to the individual's right to self-realization and the quality of life.

Environmentalism and Economic Growth

Until quite recently, it was taken as self-evident that economic growth was inherently good; though there were sharp disagreements on how its benefits should be allocated, the pro-growth consensus embraced both labor and management, capitalist and communist. Only recently has this assumption been called into question, with the environmental movement holding that economic growth does not always justify the impact it makes on the environment; and with some segments of the movement arguing that economic growth is now becoming either undesirable or even impossible, because of the scarcity of natural resources. When environmentalism raises questions of environmental quality versus economic growth, it pits Post-Materialist priorities squarely against Materialist ones. Thus in 1977, among the Materialists in the European Community publics, 36 percent expressed a "very high" opinion of the environmental movement—while 53 percent of the Post-Materialists did so. And while 3 percent of the former claimed to be members of some environmentalist group, 7 percent of the Post-Materialists did so.

It is significant that the environmental movement has *not* collapsed, in the post-1973 setting of severe strains on Western economies due to skyrocketing energy costs that exacerbate inflation and drain away immense sums of capital that might otherwise be invested to produce fuller employment. Despite this economic crisis, and a subsequent backlash against environmentalism, environmental protection standards were not abandoned—on the contrary, they became more stringent after 1973, when the energy crisis became manifest. Currently, cross-pressured groups seem to be wavering, but Post-Materialist support for environmentalism remains firm and the movement continues to win some victories. Stricter limitations were enforced on the mining and burning of coal, and on automotive emissions in the late 1970s. Although the amount of hydroelectric power produced in the United States could be doubled fairly readily, environmentalist opposition has made construction of major new hydroelectric projects next to impossible. In 1980, a proposed Energy Mobilization Board—designed to facilitate the development of energy resources in the face of environmentalist opposition—died in Congress; and millions of acres of land were added to wilderness areas that are largely closed to exploration for natural resources.

But the most dramatic and emotionally charged confrontation between Materialist and Post-Materialist priorities was the struggle over nuclear power. One can conceive of a world in which Post-Materialists favored the development of nuclear power on the grounds that it disturbs the natural environment less than coal mines, petroleum wells or hydroelectric dams, and that it produces less pollution and has a better safety record than conventional energy sources. This is conceivable—but the reality is quite different.

Nuclear power has come to symbolize everything the Post-Materialists oppose. It carries connotations of the bombing of Hiroshima, reinforced by fears that nuclear power plants might facilitate the spread of nuclear weapons. Based on complex technology, nuclear power was developed by large corporations and the federal government, in the name of economic growth. Post-Materialists were disproportionately active in the antiwar movement, tend to be suspicious of big business, and big government—and give low priority to economic growth. They form the core of the opposition to nuclear power. And, despite the current energy crisis, opposition to nuclear power plants has not died away—on the contrary, it has brought the development of nuclear power almost to a halt in the United States, West Germany and several other countries. In 1968, nuclear power produced less than one percent of the electricity used in the United States; by 1978 it was providing nearly 13 percent of all electricity consumed. After the Three Mile Island accident this development halted: in 1979 nuclear sources produced only 11 percent of the nation's electricity. Facing protracted and unpredictable delays, no new nuclear power plants are currently being ordered and many of those already ordered have been canceled. In South Korea, where environmental and antinuclear groups have virtually no impact, a nuclear power plant can be built in four years. In the United States, construction time now averages about twelve years. It seems possible that the American power plant industry, which led the world until recently, may shut down completely.

Other nations have chosen to pursue the nuclear option vigorously, and a number of them (including Belgium, Sweden, Switzerland, France, and Great Britain) are already far ahead of the United States in the percentage of electricity they produce from nuclear sources. By 1985 nuclear power plants will supply about 40 percent of Sweden's electricity and 55 percent of France's electricity. The Soviet Union will quintuple its production of nuclear power between 1980 and 1985. The contrasting American record reflects technological problems to some extent, but above all it is a question of political and ideological factors.

Like the environmental movement, the struggle over nuclear power reflects a clash of world views. For Materialists, the use of nuclear energy is viewed as desirable insofar as it seems linked with economic growth and full employment. For them, highly developed science and industry symbolize progress and prosperity. Among Post-Materialists, nuclear power tends to be rejected not only because of its potential dangers but because it is linked with big business, big science and big government—bureaucratic organizations that are evaluated negatively because they are inherently impersonal and hierarchical, minimizing individual self-expression and human contact. The ideologues of the antinuclear movement argue for a return to a simpler, more human society in which energy is used sparingly, and what is needed comes directly from nature—symbolized by solar power (Nelkin and Pollak, 1981).

Tables 30-9 and 30-10 show the relationship between value type and support for developing nuclear energy, among European Community publics and among candidates for the European Parliament. In every country, Materialists are far more favorable to developing nuclear energy than are the Post-Materialists. At the mass level, a majority of the Materialists support the development of nuclear power and a majority of the Post-Materialists oppose it in eight out of nine nations. The differences are even more pronounced at the elite level; a majority of Materialists support nuclear power and a majority of Post-Materialists oppose it among candidates from *every* one of the nine countries. And the percentage spread between Materialists and Post-Materialists is at least 46 points in every country but Italy, where nuclear power has not become a major political issue.

This emerging axis of polarization cuts squarely across traditional left-right lines. On the antinuclear side one finds intellectuals, some socialists—and much of the upper middle class. On the pronuclear side, one finds big business—and the AFL-CIO; Gaullists—and the French Communist party. It is not a traditional class struggle, but a polarization based on Materialist versus Post-Materialist values.

One of the most striking features of the nuclear power controversy is the extent to which well-informed members of the public and even competent experts, when exposed to the same body of information, draw totally different conclusions. We believe this reflects a process of cognitive screening in which given facts are retained and weighted in accord with the individual's basic values. Though support or opposition to nuclear power is usually justified in terms of objective costs, benefits and risks, an underlying factor is a clash of world views.

Materialists take it for granted that economic growth is crucial, and weigh the costs and risks of nuclear energy against the costs and risks of alternative en-

Table 30-9 Support for Development of Nuclear Power Among Nine West European Publics, by Value Type, 1979 (Percent)

	Materialist	*Mixed*	*Post-Materialist*
Britain	79	75	52
France	77	64	44
Germany	69	58	46
Belgium	56	57	46
Italy	57	47	45
Luxembourg	53	59	36
Ireland	52	45	35
Netherlands	59	36	27
Denmark	41	40	20

Note: Figures show percentage who said they "agree" or "agree strongly."
Question: "Could you tell me whether you agree or disagree with ... the following proposal? ... Nuclear energy should be developed to meet future energy needs."

Source: European Community survey (Barometer 11) carried out in April-May, 1979. Values index is based on top two priorities selected from items E-H, cited in text.

Table 30-10 Support for Developing Nuclear Power Among Candidates to European Parliament, by Value Type, 1979 (Percent)

	Materialist	*Mixed*	*Post-Materialist*
France	95	85	49
Germany	98	65	40
Britain	77	54	24
Italy	55	54	44
Belgium	100	40	24
Ireland	54	29	0
Luxembourg	71	25	0
Denmark	86	14	9
Netherlands	64	35	5

Note: Figures show percentage who said they "agree" or "agree strongly." The question about nuclear energy included an "in-between" option (not proposed to the mass publics) that was selected by from 6 to 26 percent of given national samples: only in The Netherlands, Denmark and Luxembourg were pluralities opposed to developing nuclear energy.

Source: European Elections Study survey of 742 candidates for the European Parliament, interviewed in spring, 1979; respondents' value type is based on top two priorities selected from items A-L cited above.

ergy sources. Post-Materialists take economic security for granted and weigh the costs and risks of nuclear power against various no-cost alternatives—among which, reduced material consumption seems not only acceptable but, to some, actually desirable: insofar as it might lead to a more decentralized, less impersonal society that allows freer play for individual self-expression, it has a very positive image (see Schumacher, 1973; Lovins, 1977; Sale, 1980). Thus the debate over nuclear power is based on contrasting visions of the good society, with pronuclear and antinuclear advocates talking past each other because their arguments are implicitly based on different value priorities. To a considerable degree, each side is insensitive to the basic premises of the other.

Conclusion

A decade's time series data indicate that Post-Materialism is a deep-rooted phenomenon with important political consequences. Persisting in an atmosphere of insecurity, Post-Materialism has come to manifest itself in new ways under new circumstances; what was a student subculture in the 1960s has evolved into the ideology of The New Class. And conflict between those seeking materialist and Post-Materialist goals has become the basis of a major dimension of political cleavage, supplementing though not supplanting the familiar polarization between labor and management.

There are ironies on both sides. For generations, predominantly Materialistic elites took it for granted that nature had infinite resources to withstand consumption and environmental pollution, for the sake of industrial development. But growth did *not* inaugurate the "Politics of Consensus in an Age of Affluence" (Lane, 1965). Instead, after a certain lag, it led to the emergence of new sources of discontent while a blind emphasis on growth that depended on cheap oil, undermined its own future.

More recently, some Post-Materialist elites adopted a mirror image of this view, taking it for granted that industry had infinite resources to support taxation, and regulation—sometimes in a needlessly punitive spirit. The irony here was that in the long run, Post-Materialism is contingent on material security; the insecurity of recent years arrested its growth and gave impetus to a renewed emphasis on reindustrialization and rearmament.

The rise of Post-Materialism was accompanied by a wave of legislation designed to advance the cause of human equality, raise social welfare standards, and protect the consumer and the environment. There were pervasive changes in national priorities. Prior to 1965, over half of the American federal budget was spent on defense and only about one-quarter on health, education and welfare. By the end of the 1970s, these proportions had been almost exactly reversed. That reallocation of resources is now under attack.

It would be gratifying to be able to identify one side as totally right and the other as utterly wrong. Unfortunately it is not that simple. Both Materialist and Post-Materialist goals are essential elements of a good society, and neither emphasis is automatically appropriate, regardless of circumstances. A healthy economy, and defense forces adequate to deter attack are essential to the realization of *both* Materialist and Post-Materialist goals. But they are not the only legitimate political concerns. Beyond a certain point, a military buildup tends to generate countermeasures. The Soviet Union is militarily stronger than ever before, and faces suspicion and opposition from China, Afghanistan, Poland, the West and much of the Third World. And beyond a certain point, material production produces growing social costs and a diminishing payoff. When there are two cars in every garage, a third adds relatively little; a fourth and a fifth would be positively burdensome. From this perspective, a shift to Post-Materialist priorities, with more time, thought and resources going into improving the social and natural environment, is simply a rational response to changing conditions.

A statesman's task is to seek a reasonable balance between a variety of social goals. That task is complicated in any case, but all the more so if the goals themselves can change.

NOTE

1. For representative examples, see Ike, 1973; Kerr and Handley, 1974; Marsh, 1975, 1977; Kmieciak, 1976; Lafferty, 1976; Hildebrandt and Dalton, 1977; Zetterberg, 1977; Watanuki, 1979; Inglehart, 1977; Jennings, Allerbeck and Rosenmayr, 1979; Lehner, 1979; Kaase and Klingemann, 1979; Heunks, 1979; Pesonen and Sankiaho, 1979; Kemp, 1979; Flanagan, 1979, 1980; Nardi, 1980.

REFERENCES

Abramowitz, Alan I. "Name Familiarity, Reputation, and the Incumbency Effect in a Congressional Election." *Western Political Quarterly* (1975) 27:668-84.

———. "A Comparison of Voting for U.S. Senator and Representative in 1978." *American Political Science Review* (1980) 74:633-40.

Abramson, Paul R. *Generational Change in American Politics.* Lexington, Mass: Lexington Books, 1975.

———. "Developing Party Identification: A Further Examination of Life-Cycle, Generational, and Period Effects." *American Journal of Political Science* (1979) 23:78-96.

Abramson, Paul R., and John H. Aldrich. "The Decline of Electoral Participation in America." *American Political Science Review* (1982) 76:502-21.

Abramson, Paul R., John H. Aldrich, and David W. Rohde. *Change and Continuity in the 1980 Elections.* rev. ed. Washington, D.C.: CQ Press, 1983.

Achen, Christopher H. "Mass Political Attitudes and the Survey Response." *American Political Science Review* (1975) 69:1218-31.

———. "Issue Voting in the 1950's." University of California, Berkeley, 1976.

Agranoff, Robert. *The New Style of Election Campaigns.* Boston: Holbrook Press, 1972.

Alderfer, Clayton P. *Existence, Relatedness and Growth: Human Need in Organizational Settings.* New York: Free Press, 1972.

Aldrich, John H. "Candidate Support Functions in the 1968 Election: An Empirical Application of the Spatial Model." *Public Choice* (1975) 22:1-22.

———. "Some Problems in Testing Two Rational Models of Participation." *American Journal of Political Science* (1976) 20:713-34.

Aldrich, John H., and Charles Cnudde. "Probing the Bounds of Conventional Wisdom: A Comparison of Regression, Probit, and Discriminant Analysis." *American Journal of Political Science* (1975) 19:571-608.

Alexander, Thomas B. *Sectional Stress and Party Strength.* Nashville, Tenn.: Vanderbilt University Press, 1967.

Alford, Robert R. *Party and Society: The Anglo-American Democracies.* Chicago: Rand McNally, 1963.

Alker, Hayward R., Jr. "Causal Inferences and Political Analysis." In *Mathematical Applications in Political Science,* ed. Joseph Bernd. Dallas: SMU Press, 1966.

Allen, Howard D., and Kay Warren Allen. "Vote Fraud and Data Validity." In *Analyzing Electoral History,* ed. Jerome M. Clubb, William H. Flanigan, and Nancy H. Zingale. Beverly Hills: Sage, 1981.

Allerbeck, Klaus. "Political Generations: Some Reflections on the Concept and Its Applications to the German Case." *European Journal of Political Research* (1977) 5:119-34.

Allison, Paul D. "Testing for Interaction in Multiple Regression." *American Journal of Sociology* (1977) 82:144-53.

Almond, Gabriel A., and G. Bingham Powell, Jr. *Comparative Politics: System, Process, and Policy.* Boston: Little, Brown, 1978.

Almond, Gabriel A., and Sidney Verba. *The Civic Culture.* Princeton: Princeton University Press, 1963.

Alt, James E. *The Politics of Economic Decline.* Cambridge: Cambridge University Press, 1978.

——. "The Dynamics of Partisanship in Britain." Political Science Papers, (1980) No. 55. St. Louis, Mo.: Washington University.

Amemiya, Takeshi. "The Estimation of a Simultaneous Equation Tobit Model." *International Economic Review* (1979) 20:169-81.

Andersen, Kristi. *The Creation of a Democratic Majority, 1928-1936.* Chicago: University of Chicago Press, 1979.

Anderson, T. W. "Probability Models for Analyzing Time Changes in Attitudes." In *Mathematical Thinking in the Social Sciences,* ed. Paul F. Lazarsfeld. Glencoe: Free Press, 1954.

Andrews, William G. "American Voting Participation." *Western Political Quarterly* (1966) 19:639-52.

Arcelus, Francisco, and Allan H. Meltzer. "The Effects of Aggregate Economic Variables on Congressional Elections." *American Political Science Review* (1975) 69:1232-39.

Arian, Alan. *The Choosing People: Voting Behavior in Israel.* Cleveland: Case Western Press, 1973.

Arseneau, Robert B., and Raymond E. Wolfinger. "Voting Behavior in Congressional Elections." Paper presented at the annual meeting of the American Political Science Association, New Orleans, 1973.

Ashenfelter, Orley, and Stanley Kelly, Jr. "Determinants of Participation in Presidential Elections." *Law and Economics* (1976) 18:695-733.

Asher, Herbert B. *Presidential Elections and American Politics.* 2nd ed. Homewood, Ill.: Dorsey Press, 1980, 1984.

Atesoglu, H. Sonmez, and Roger Congleton. "Economic Conditions and National Elections, Post-Sample Forecasts." *American Political Science Review* (1982) 76:873-75.

Averich, Harry, John E. Koehler, and Frank H. Denton. *The Matrix of Policy in the Philippines.* Princeton: Princeton University Press, 1971.

Axelrod, Robert. "Communication." *American Political Science Review* (1982) 76:393-96.

Baaklini, Abdo. *Legislative and Political Development: Lebanon, 1842-1972.* Durham: Duke University Press, 1976.

Baker, Kendall L. "The Acquisition of Partisanship in Germany." *American Journal of Political Science* (1974) 18:569-82.

——. "Generational Differences in the Role of Party Identification in German Political Behavior." *American Journal of Political Science* (1978) 22:106-29.

Baker, Kendall L., Russell J. Dalton, and Kai Hildebrandt. *Germany Transformed.* Cambridge: Harvard University Press, 1981.

Baker, Kendall L., Kai Hildebrandt, and Russell J. Dalton. "Political Stability in Transition: Post War Germany." Paper presented at the annual meeting of the American Political Science Association, San Francisco, 1975.

Baloyra, Enrique A. "Public Attitudes Toward the Democratic Regime." In *Venezuela: The Democratic Experience,* ed. John D. Martz and David J. Myers. New York: Praeger, 1977.

Barker, A., and M. Rush. *The Member of Parliament and His Information.* London: Allen and Unwin, 1967.

Barnes, Samuel H. "Left, Right, and the Italian Voter." *Comparative Political Studies* (1971) 4:157-75.

——. *Representation in Italy.* Chicago: University of Chicago Press, 1977.

Barnes, Samuel et al. *Political Action.* Beverly Hills: Sage, 1979.

Beck, Nathaniel. "Parties, Administrations, and American Macroeconomic Outcomes." *American Political Science Review* (1982a) 76:83-93.

——. "Does There Exist a Political Business Cycle? A Box-Tiao Analysis." *Public Choice* (1982b) 38:205-09.

Beck, Paul Allen. "A Socialization Theory of Partisan Realignment." In *The Politics of Future Citizens,* ed. Richard G. Niemi. San Francisco: Jossey-Bass, 1974a. Chap. 23 in first ed. of this volume.

——. "Environment and Party: The Impact of Political and Demographic County Characteristics on Party Behavior." *American Political Science Review* (1974b) 68:1229-45.

——. "Models for Analyzing Panel Data: A Comparative Review." *Political Methodology* (1975) 2:357-80.

——. "Partisan Dealignment in the Postwar South." *American Political Science Review* (1977) 71:477-97.

Belknap, George, and Angus Campbell. "Political Party Identification and Attitudes Toward Foreign Policy." *Public Opinion Quarterly* (1952) 15:601-23.

Bell, Daniel. *The Coming of Post-Industrial Society.* New York: Basic Books, 1973.

——. *The Cultural Contradictions of Capitalism.* New York: Basic Books, 1976.

Berelson, Bernard R., Paul F. Lazarsfeld, and William N. McPhee. *Voting.* Chicago: University of Chicago Press, 1954.

Berger, Manfred. "Parteiidentifikation in der Bundesrepublik." *Politische Vierteljahresschrift* (1973) 14:215-25.

Berglund, Sten, and Ulf Lindstrom. *The Scandinavian Party System(s).* Lund: Studentlitteratur, 1978.

Berkson, Joseph. "Maximum Likelihood and Minimum X^2-Estimates of the Logistic Function." *Journal of the American Statistical Association* (1955) 50:130-62.

Bettelheim, Bruno. *Surviving.* New York: Knopf, 1979.

Bishop, George F., and Kathleen A. Frankovic. "Ideological Consensus and Constraint Among Party Leaders and Followers in the 1978 Election." *Micropolitics* (1981) 1:87-111.

Bishop, George F., Alfred J. Tuchfarber, and Robert W. Oldendick. "Change in the Structure of American Political Attitudes: The Nagging Question of Question

Wording." *American Journal of Political Science* (1978) 22:250-69.

Blake, Donald E. "The Consistency of Inconsistency: Party Identification in Federal and Provincial Politics." *Canadian Journal of Political Science* (1982) 15:691-710.

Block, Jack. "Some Enduring and Consequential Structures of Personality." In *Further Explorations in Personality,* ed. A. I. Rabin et al. New York: Wiley-Interscience, 1981.

Blondel, Jean. *Introduction to Comparative Government.* New York: Praeger, 1969.

Bloom, Harold, and H. Douglas Price. "Voter Response to Short Run Economic Conditions: The Asymmetric Effect of Prosperity and Recession." *American Political Science Review* (1975) 69:1240-54.

Blum, John H. and others. *The National Experience: A History of the United States since 1865.* New York: Harcourt, Brace and World, 1968.

Bois, Paul. *Paysans de l'Ouest.* Le Mans: M. Vilaine, 1960.

Borre, Ole. "Critical Electoral Change in Scandinavia." In *Electoral Change in Industrial Democracies,* ed. Russell J. Dalton, Paul Allen Beck, and Scott C. Flanagan. Princeton: Princeton University Press, 1984.

Boyd, Richard W. "Popular Control of Public Policy: A Normal Vote Analysis of the 1968 Election." *American Political Science Review* (1972) 66:429-49.

———. "Decline of U.S. Voter Turnout: Structural Explanations." *American Politics Quarterly* (1981) 9:133-59.

Brady, David W. "Congressional Leadership and Party Voting in the McKinley Era: A Comparison to the Modern House." *Midwest Journal of Political Science* (1972) 16:439-59.

———. *Congressional Voting in a Partisan Era.* Lawrence: University of Kansas Press, 1973.

Brady, David W., and Phillip Althoff. "Party Voting in the U.S. House of Representatives, 1890-1910: Elements of a Responsible Party System." *Journal of Politics* (1974) 36:753-77.

Brady, David W., and Naomi B. Lynn. "Switched-Seat Congressional Districts: Their Effect on Party Voting and Public Policy." *American Political Science Review* (1973) 67:528-43.

Brim, Orville G., Jr., and Jerome Kagan, eds. *Constancy and Change in Human Development.* Cambridge: Harvard University Press, 1980.

Broder, David S. *Changing of the Guard.* New York: Simon and Schuster, 1980.

Brody, Richard A. "Change and Stability in Party Identification: A Note of Caution." Stanford University, n.d. Photocopy.

———. "Communication." *American Political Science Review* (1976) 70:924-26.

———. "Stability and Change in Party Identification: Presidential to Off-Years." Paper presented at the annual meeting of the American Political Science Association, Washington, D.C., 1977.

Brody, Richard A., and Benjamin I. Page. "The Assessment of Policy Voting." *American Political Science Review* (1972) 66:450-58. Chap. 13 in first ed. of this volume.

———. "Indifference, Alienation and Rational Decision: The Effects of Candidate Evaluations on Turnout and the Vote." *Public Choice* (1973) 15:1-17.

Broh, C. Anthony. *Toward a Theory of Issue Voting.* Beverly Hills: Sage, 1973.

Brown, Steven R. "Consistency and the Persistence of Ideology: Some Experimental Results." *Public Opinion Quarterly* (1970) 34:60-68.

Brown, Steven R., and Richard W. Taylor. "Perspectives in Concept Formation." *Social Science Quarterly* (1972) 52:852-60.

——. "Frames of Reference and the Observation of Behavior." *Social Science Quarterly* (1973) 54:29-40.

Brown, Thad, and Arthur A. Stein. "The Political Economy of National Elections." *Comparative Politics* (1982) 14:479-97.

Bruce-Briggs, B., ed. *The New Class?* New Brunswick, N.J.: Transaction Books, 1979.

Budge, Ian, and Dennis Farlie. "A Comparative Analysis of Factors Correlated with Turnout and Voting Choice." In *Party Identification and Beyond,* ed. Ian Budge, Ivor Crewe, and Dennis Farlie. London: Wiley, 1976.

Bunce, Valerie. "Changing Leaders and Changing Policies: The Impact of Elite Succession on Budgetary Priorities in Democratic Countries." *American Journal of Political Science* (1980) 24:373-95.

Burnham, Walter Dean. "The Changing Shape of the American Political Universe." *American Political Science Review* (1965) 59:7-28. Chap. 28 in first ed. of this volume.

——. "American Voting Behavior and the 1964 Election." *Midwest Journal of Political Science* (1968) 12:1-40.

——. "The End of American Party Politics." *Transaction* (1969) 7:12-22.

——. *Critical Elections and the Mainsprings of American Politics.* New York: Norton, 1970.

——. "Communication." *American Political Science Review* (1971) 65:1149-52.

——. "Theory and Voting Research: Some Reflections on Converse's 'Change in the American Electorate.'" *American Political Science Review* (1974) 68:1002-23.

——. "Insulation and Responsiveness in Congressional Elections." *Political Science Quarterly* (1975) 90:411-35.

——. "The Appearance and Disappearance of the American Voter." In *Electoral Participation: A Comparative Analysis,* ed. Richard Rose. Beverly Hills: Sage, 1980.

——. "The System of 1896: An Analysis." In *The Evolution of American Electoral Systems,* Paul Kleppner et al. Westport, Conn.: Greenwood, 1981.

Butler, David, and Dennis Kavanagh. *The British General Election of 1979.* New York: Holmes and Meier, 1980.

Butler, David, and Donald Stokes. *Political Change in Britain.* New York: St. Martin's, 1969, 1970, 1974, 1976.

Butt, R. *The Power of Parliament.* London: Constable, 1967.

Cain, Bruce. "Blessed Be the Tie that Unbinds: Constituency Work and Vote Swing in Great Britain." *Political Studies* (1983) 31:103-11.

Cain, Bruce, and John Ferejohn. "A Comparison of Party Identification in the United States and Great Britain." *Comparative Political Studies* (1981) 14:31-47.

Cain, Bruce, John Ferejohn, and Morris Fiorina. "The Constituency Component: A Comparison of Service in Britain and the United States." *Comparative Political Studies* (1983) 16:67-91.

Cameron, David R. "Stability and Change in Patterns of French Partisanship." *Public Opinion Quarterly* (1972) 36:19-30.

———. "Politics, Public Policy, and Economic Inequality: A Comparative Analysis." Paper presented at the annual meeting of the American Political Science Association, Chicago, 1976a.

———. "Postindustrial Change and Secular Realignments." Ph.D. diss., University of Michigan, 1976b.

———. "The Expansion of the Public Economy: A Comparative Analysis." *American Political Science Review* (1978) 72:1243-61.

Campbell, Angus. "Surge and Decline: A Study of Electoral Change." *Public Opinion Quarterly* (1960) 24:397-418.

Campbell, Angus, Philip E. Converse, Warren E. Miller, and Donald E. Stokes. *The American Voter.* New York: Wiley, 1960.

———. *Elections and the Political Order.* New York: Wiley, 1966.

Campbell, Angus, and Howard C. Cooper. *Group Differences in Attitudes and Votes.* Ann Arbor, Mich.: Institute for Social Research, 1956.

Campbell, Angus, Gerald Gurin, and Warren E. Miller. *The Voter Decides.* Evanston, Ill.: Row, Peterson, 1954.

Campbell, Angus, and Donald E. Stokes. "Partisan Attitudes and the Presidential Vote." In *American Voting Behavior,* ed. Eugene Burdick and Arthur J. Brodbeck. Glencoe: Free Press, 1959.

Campbell, Angus, and Henry Valen. "Party Identification in Norway and the United States." *Public Opinion Quarterly* (1961) 25:505-25.

Carmines, Edward G., and James A. Stimson. "The Two Faces of Issue Voting." *American Political Science Review* (1980) 74:78-91. Chap. 21 in this volume.

———. "Issue Evolution, Population Replacement and Normal Partisan Change." *American Political Science Review* (1981a) 75:107-18.

———. "The Politics and Policy of Race in Congress." 1981b. Photocopy.

———. "Racial Issues and the Structure of Mass Political Systems." *Journal of Politics* (1982) 44:2-20.

———. "The Dynamics of Issue Evolution." In *Electoral Change in Industrial Democracies,* ed. Russell Dalton, Paul Allen Beck, and Scott Flanagan. Princeton: Princeton University Press, 1984.

Chambers, William N., and Walter D. Burnham, eds. *The American Party Systems.* New York: Oxford University Press, 1962, 1975.

Chambers, William N., and Phillip C. Davis. "Party, Competition, and Mass Participation: The Case of the Democratizing Party System, 1824-1852." In *The History of American Electoral Behavior,* ed. Joel H. Silbey, Allan G. Bogue, and William H. Flanigan. Princeton: Princeton University Press, 1978.

Chester, D. N., and N. Bowring. *Questions in Parliament.* Oxford: Oxford University Press, 1962.

Claggett, William. "Partisan Acquisition Versus Partisan Intensity: Life-Cycle, Generation, and Period Effects, 1952-1976." *American Journal of Political Science* (1981) 25:193-214.

Clarke, Harold D., Lawrence LeDuc, Jane Jenson, and Jon H. Pammett. *Political Choice in Canada.* Toronto: McGraw-Hill Ryerson, 1979.

Clausen, Aage R. "Response Validity: Vote Report." *Public Opinion Quarterly* (1968-69) 32:588-606.

——. *How Congressmen Decide: A Policy Focus.* New York: St. Martin's, 1973.

Clubb, Jerome M., and Howard W. Allen. "The Cities and the Election of 1928: Partisan Realignment." *American Historical Review* (1969) 74:1205-20.

Clubb, Jerome M., William H. Flanigan, and Nancy H. Zingale. *Partisan Realignment: Voters, Parties and Government in American History.* Beverly Hills: Sage, 1980.

Clubb, Jerome M., and Santa A. Traugott. "Partisan Cleavage and Cohesion in the House of Representatives, 1861-1974." *Journal of Interdisciplinary History* (1977) 7:375-401.

Cobb, Roger W., and Charles D. Elder. "Individual Orientations in the Study of Political Symbolism." *Social Science Quarterly* (1972) 53:79-90.

——. "The Political Uses of Symbolism." *American Politics Quarterly* (1973) 1:305-39.

Cohen, J., and P. Cohen. *Applied Multiple Regression/Correlation Analysis for the Behavioral Sciences.* Hillsdale, N.J.: Erlbaum, 1975.

Coleman, James S. *Models of Change and Response Uncertainty.* Englewood Cliffs, N.J.: Prentice-Hall, 1964.

Commission of the European Committee. *Survey of Consumer Confidence In the European Community Countries.* Brussels, 1979.

——. *Public Opinion in the European Community: Euro-Barometre 13.* Brussels: European Community, 1980.

Connell, R. W. "Political Socialization in the American Family: The Evidence Reexamined." *Public Opinion Quarterly* (1972) 25:323-33.

Conover, Pamela Johnston, and Stanley Feldman. "Belief System Organization in the American Electorate." In *The Electorate Reconsidered,* ed. John Pierce, and John L. Sullivan. Beverly Hills: Sage, 1980.

Converse, Philip E. "The Nature of Belief Systems in Mass Publics." In *Ideology and Discontent,* ed. David E. Apter. New York: Free Press, 1964.

——. "Information Flow and the Stability of Partisan Attitudes." In *Elections and the Political Order,* ed. Angus Campbell et al. New York: Wiley, 1966a.

——. "On the Possibility of Major Political Realignment in the South." In *Elections and the Political Order,* Angus Campbell, Philip E. Converse, Warren E. Miller, and Donald E. Stokes. New York: Wiley, 1966b.

——. "The Concept of a Normal Vote." In *Elections and the Political Order,* Angus Campbell, Philip E. Converse, Warren E. Miller, and Donald E. Stokes. New York: Wiley, 1966c.

——. "Of Time and Partisan Stability." *Comparative Political Studies* (1969) 2:139-71.

——. "Attitudes and Non-Attitudes: Continuation of a Dialogue." In *The Quantitative Analysis of Social Problems,* ed. Edward R. Tufte. Reading, Mass.: Addison-Wesley, 1970.

——. "Change in the American Electorate." In *The Human Meaning of Social Change,* ed. Angus Campbell and Philip E. Converse. New York: Russell Sage, 1972.

——. "Comment on Burnham's 'Theory and Voting Research.'" *American Political Science Review* (1974) 68:1024-27.

——. "Public Opinion and Voting Behavior." In *Handbook of Political Science,* ed. Fred I. Greenstein and Nelson W. Polsby. Reading, Mass.: Addison-Wesley (1975a): 75-169.

——. "Some Mass-Elite Contrasts in the Perception of Political Spaces." *Social Science Information* (1975b) 14:49-83.

——. *The Dynamics of Party Support.* Beverly Hills: Sage, 1976.

——. "Rejoinder to Abramson." *American Journal of Political Science* (1979) 23:97-100.

Converse, Philip E., Aage R. Clausen, and Warren E. Miller. "Electoral Myth and Reality: The 1964 Election." *American Political Science Review* (1965) 59:321-34.

Converse, Philip E., Jean D. Dotson, Wendy J. Hoag, and William H. McGee, III, eds. *American Social Attitudes Data Sourcebook.* Cambridge: Harvard University Press, 1979.

Converse, Philip E., and Georges Dupeux. "Politicization of the Electorate in France and the United States." *Public Opinion Quarterly* (1962) 26:1-23.

Converse, Philip E., and Gregory B. Markus. " 'Plus ca Change. . . :' The New CPS Election Study Panel." *American Political Science Review* (1979) 73:2-49. Chap. 18 in this volume.

Converse, Philip E., Warren E. Miller, Jerrold G. Rusk, and Arthur C. Wolfe. "Continuity and Change in American Politics: Parties and Issues in the 1968 Election." *American Political Science Review* (1969) 63:1083-1105.

Converse, Philip E., and Roy Pierce. "Basic Cleavages in French Politics and the Disorders of May and June, 1968." Paper presented at the Seventh World Congress of Sociology, Varna, Bulgaria, 1970.

Coombs, Clyde H. *A Theory of Data.* New York: Wiley, 1964.

Costa, Paul T., Jr., and Robert R. McCrae. "Still Stable after All These Years: Personality as a Key to Some Issues in Adulthood and Old Age." In *Life-Span Development and Behavior,* vol. 3, ed. Paul B. Bates and Orville G. Brim, Jr. New York: Academic Press, 1980.

Cover, Albert D. "The Advantage of Incumbency in Congressional Elections." Ph.D. diss., Yale University, 1976.

——. "One Good Term Deserves Another: The Advantage of Incumbency in Congressional Elections." *American Journal of Political Science* (1977) 21:523-42.

Cover, Albert D., and Bruce S. Brumberg. "Baby Books and Ballots: The Impact of Congressional Mail on Constituent Opinion." *American Political Science Review* (1982) 76:347-59.

Cover, Albert D., and David R. Mayhew. "Congressional Dynamics and the Decline of Competitive Congressional Elections." In *Congress Reconsidered,* ed. Lawrence C. Dodd and Bruce I. Oppenheimer. New York: Praeger Publishers, 1977.

Coveyou, Michael R., and James Piereson. "Ideological Perceptions and Political Judgment: Some Problems of Concept and Measurement." *Political Methodology* (1977) 4:77-102.

Cowart, Andrew T. "The Economic Policies of European Governments, Part I: Monetary Policy." *British Journal of Political Science* (1978a) 8:285-311.

——. "The Economic Policies of European Governments, Part II: Fiscal Policy." *British Journal of Political Science* (1978b) 8:425-39.

Cox, D. R. *The Analysis of Binary Data.* London: Methuen, 1970.

Cox, Gary W., and J. Morgan Kousser. "Turnout and Rural Corruption: New York as a Test Case." *American Journal of Political Science* (1981) 25:646-63.

Crewe, Ivor. "Do Butler and Stokes Really Explain Political Change in Britain." *European Journal of Political Research* (1974) 2:43-100.

——. "Party Identification Theory and Political Change in Britain." In *Party Identification and Beyond*, ed. Ian Budge, Ivor Crewe, and Dennis Farlie. London, 1976.

——. "Prospects for Party Realignment: An Anglo-American Comparison." Paper presented at the annual meeting of the American Political Science Association, Washington, D.C., 1977.

——. "The Voting Surveyed." *Times Guide to the House of Commons*. London: Time Books Limited, 1979.

Crewe, Ivor, Bo Särlvik, and James Alt. "Partisan Dealignment in Britain, 1964-1974. *British Journal of Political Science* (1977) 7:129-90.

Crick, B. *The Reform of Parliament*. 2nd ed. London: Weidenfiled and Nicolson, 1970.

Curtice, John, and Michael Steed. "Appendix 2: An Analysis of the Voting." In *The British General Election of 1979*, ed. David Butler and Dennis Kavanagh. London: MacMillan, 1980.

——. "Electoral Choice and the Production of Government: The Changing Operation of the Electoral System in the United Kingdom since 1955." *British Journal of Political Science* (1982) 12:249-98.

Cutler, Neal E. "Generation, Maturation and Party Affiliation." *Public Opinion Quarterly* (1969) 33:583-88.

Dahl, Robert A. "Decision-Making in a Democracy: The Supreme Court as a National Policy-Maker." *Journal of Public Law* (1957) 6:279-95.

——. *Polyarchy: Participation and Opposition*. New Haven: Yale University Press, 1971.

Dalton, Russell J. "Reassessing Parental Socialization: Indicator Reliability versus Generational Transfer." *American Political Science Review* (1980) 74:421-31.

Damgaard, Erik. "Stability and Change in the Danish Party System Over Half a Century." *Scandinavian Political Studies* (1974) 9:103-25.

Davies, James C. *Human Nature and Politics*. New York: Wiley, 1963.

Davis, Otto A., Melvin J. Hinich, and Peter C. Ordeshook. "An Expository Development of a Mathematical Model of the Electoral Process." *American Political Science Review* (1970) 64:426-48.

Dawes, Robin, and B. Corrigan. "Linear Models in Decision Making." *Psychological Bulletin* (1974) 81:95-106.

Declerq, Eugene, Thomas L. Hurley, and Norman R. Luttbeg. "Voting in American Presidential Elections: 1956-1972." *American Politics Quarterly* (1975) 3:247-83.

Denney, W. Michael, J. Stephen Hendricks, and Donald R. Kinder. "Personal Stakes and Local Politics." Paper presented at the annual meeting of the American Association for Public Opinion Research, Cincinnati, 1980.

Dennis, Jack. "Trends in Support for the American Party System." *British Journal of Political Science* (1975) 5:187-230.

——. "On Being an Independent Partisan Supporter." Paper presented at the annual meeting of the Midwest Political Science Association, Cincinnati, 1981a.

——. "Some Properties of Partisanship." Paper presented at the annual meeting of the American Political Science Association, New York, 1981b.

Dennis, Jack, and Donald J. McCrone. "Pre-Adult Development of Political Party Identification in Western Democracies." *Comparative Political Studies* (1970) 3:243-63.

Denver, D. T., and H. T. C. Hands. "Marginality and Turnout in British General Elections." *British Journal of Political Science* (1974) 4:17-35.

Deutsch, Emeric, Dennis Lindon, and Pierre Weill. *Les Familles Politiques Aujourd 'hui en France.* Paris: Editions de Minuit, 1966.

Deutsch, Karl. "Social Mobilization and Political Development." *American Political Science Review* (1961) 55:493-514.

Dinkel, Reiner. "Political Business Cycles in Germany and the United States: Some Theoretical and Empirical Considerations." In *Contemporary Political Economy,* ed. Douglas A. Hibbs, Jr., and Heino Fassbender. Amsterdam: North-Holland, 1981.

Dittrich, Karl, and Lars Norby Johansen. "Voting Turnout in Europe, 1945-1978: Myths and Realities." In *Western European Party Systems,* ed. Hans Daalder and Peter Mair. London: Sage, 1983.

Djilas, Milovan. *The New Class.* London: Unwin, 1966.

Dobson, Douglas, and Duane Meeter. "Alternative Markov Models for Describing Change in Party Identification." *American Journal of Political Science* (1974) 18:487-500.

Dobson, Douglas, and Douglas St. Angelo. "Party Identification and the Floating Vote." *American Political Science Review* (1975) 69:481-90.

Downs, Anthony. *An Economic Theory of Democracy.* New York: Harper and Row, 1957.

Dowse, R. E. "The MP and His Surgery." *Political Studies* (1963) 2:33-41.

Dreyer, Edward. "Change and Stability in Party Identification. *Journal of Politics* (1973) 35:712-22.

Duncan, Otis Dudley. "Unmeasured Variables in Linear Models for Panel Analysis." In *Sociological Methodology,* ed. Herbert L. Costner. San Francisco: Jossey-Bass, 1972.

——. *Introduction to Structural Equation Models.* New York: Academic Press, 1975.

Edelman, Murray. *The Symbolic Uses of Politics.* Urbana: University of Illinois Press, 1964.

Ehrenreich, Barbara, and John Ehrenreich. "The Professional-Managerial Class." *Radical American* (1977) 2:7-31.

Eldersveld, Samuel J. "Party Identification in India in Comparative Perspective." *Comparative Political Studies* (1973) 6:271-95.

Elkins, Stanley. *Slavery: A Problem in American Institutional and Intellectual Life.* Chicago: University of Chicago Press, 1959.

EMNID. *Pressedienst.* Cited in *Encounter* (1963) 22:53.

Epstein, Laurily L., and Kathleen A. Frankovic. "Casework and Electoral Margins: Insurance is Prudent Policy." *Polity* (1982) 14:691-700.

Erikson, Robert S. "Malapportionment, Gerrymandering, and Party Fortunes in Congressional Elections." *American Political Science Review* (1972) 66:1234-55.

——. "The SRC Panel Data and Mass Political Attitudes." *British Journal of Political Science* (1979) 9:89-114.

Erikson, Robert S., Norman R. Luttbeg, and Kent L. Tedin. *American Public Opinion: Its Origins, Content and Impact.* New York: Wiley, 1980.

Erikson, Robert S., and Kent L. Tedin. "The 1928-1936 Partisan Realignment: The Case for the Conversion Hypothesis." *American Political Science Review* (1981) 75:951-62.

Eulau, Heinz, and Kenneth Prewitt. *Labyrinths of Democracy.* Indianapolis: Bobbs-Merrill 1973.

Fair, Ray C. "The Effects of Economic Events on Votes for President." *Review of Economics and Statistics* (1978) 60:159-73.

Falter, J. W. "Einmal mehr: Lässt sich das Konzept der Parteiidentifikation auf deutsche Verhältnisse übertragen?" *Politische Vierteljahresschrift* (1977) 18:476-500.

Fenno, Richard F., Jr., "If, as Ralph Nader Says, Congress is 'The Broken Branch,' How Come We Love Our Congressmen So Much?" In *Congress in Change: Evolution and Reform,* ed. Norman J. Ornstein. New York: Praeger, 1975.

——. *Home Style: House Members in Their Districts.* Boston: Little, Brown, 1978.

Ferejohn, John A. "On the Decline of Competition in Congressional Elections." *American Political Science Review* (1977) 71:166-76.

Ferejohn, John A., and Morris P. Fiorina. "Closeness Counts Only in Horseshoes and Dancing." *American Political Science Review* (1975) 69:920-25.

——. "The Decline in Turnout in Presidential Elections." Paper presented at the National Science Foundation Conference on Voter Turnout, San Diego, 1979.

Field, John Osgood, and Ronald E. Anderson. "Ideology in the Public's Conceptualization of the 1964 Election." *Public Opinion Quarterly* (1969) 33:380-98.

Finney, D. J. *Probit Analysis.* 3rd ed. Cambridge: Cambridge University Press, 1971.

Fiorina, Morris P. *Representatives, Roll Calls, and Constituencies.* Lexington, Mass.: Lexington Books, 1974.

——. "An Outline for a Model of Party Choice." *American Journal of Political Science* (1977a) 21:601-26.

——. *Congress: Keystone of the Washington Establishment.* New Haven: Yale University Press, 1977b.

——. "Economic Retrospective Voting in American National Elections: A Microanalysis." *American Journal of Political Science* (1978) 22:426-43.

——. "The Decline of Collective Responsibility in American Politics." *Daedalus* (1980) 109:25-45.

——. "Congressmen and Their Constituents: 1958 and 1978." In *The United States Congress,* ed. Dennis Hale. Proceedings of the Thomas P. O'Neill, Jr., Symposium on the U.S. Congress. Boston College, 1981a.

——. *Retrospective Voting in American National Elections.* New Haven: Yale University Press, 1981b.

——. "Short- and Long-Term Effects of Economic Conditions on Individual Voting Decisions." In *Contemporary Political Economy,* ed. Douglas A. Hibbs, Jr., and Heino Fassbender. Amsterdam: North Holland, 1981c.

——. "Some Problems in Studying the Effects of Resource Allocation in Congressional Elections." *American Journal of Political Science* (1981d) 25:542-67.

——. "Who is Held Responsible? Further Evidence on the Hibbing-Alford Thesis." *American Journal of Political Science* (1983) 27:158-64.

Fisher, Franklin. *The Identification Problem in Economics.* New York: McGraw-Hill, 1966.

Flanagan, Scott C. "Value Change and Partisan Change in Japan: The Silent Revolution Revisited." *Comparative Politics* (1979) 11:253-78.

——. "Value Cleavages, Economic Cleavages and the Japanese Voter." *American Journal of Political Science* (1980) 24:178-206.

——. "Changing Values in Advanced Industrial Societies." *Comparative Political Studies* (1982) 14:403-44.

Flanagan, Scott C., and Bradley M. Richardson. *Japanese Electoral Behavior: Social Cleavages, Social Networks and Partisanship.* Beverly Hills: Sage, 1977.

Flanigan, William H., and Nancy H. Zingale. "Electoral Competition and Partisan Realignment." Paper presented at the annual meeting of the American Political Science Association, New Orleans, 1973.

——. "The Measurement of Electoral Change." *Political Methodology* (1974) 1:49-82.

Fowler, Linda L., Jeff Stonecash, and Robert Carrothers. "The Ties That Bind? Casework and Careerism in State Legislatures." Paper presented at the annual meeting of the American Political Science Association, Denver, 1982.

Frey, Bruno S. *Modern Political Economy.* New York: Wiley, 1978.

Frey, Bruno S., and Friedrich Schneider. "An Empirical Study of Politico-Economic Interactions in the United States." *Review of Economics and Statistics* (1978) 60:174-83.

——. "Popularity Functions: The Case of the U.S. and West Germany." In *Models of Political Economy,* ed. Paul Whiteley. London: Sage, 1980.

——. "Recent Research on Empirical Political-Economic Models." In *Contemporary Political Economy,* ed. Douglas A. Hibbs, Jr., and Heino Fassbender. Amsterdam: North-Holland, 1981.

Frohlich, Norman, Joe A. Oppenheimer, Jeffrey Smith, and Oran R. Young, "A Test of Downsian Voter Rationality: 1964 Presidential Voting." *American Political Science Review* (1978) 72:178-97.

Funston, Richard. "The Supreme Court and Critical Elections." *American Political Science Review* (1975) 69:795-811.

Galli, Giorgio, and Alfonso Prandi. *Patterns of Political Participation in Italy.* New Haven: Yale University Press, 1970.

Gatlin, Douglas S., Micheal W. Giles, and Everett F. Cataldo. "Policy Support Within a Target Group: The Case of School Desegregation." *American Political Science Review* (1978) 72:985-93.

Ginsburg, Benjamin. "Elections and Public Policy." *American Political Science Review* (1976) 70:41-9.

Glenn, Norval D. "Aging, Disengagement and Opinionation." *Public Opinion Quarterly* (1969) 33:17-34.

——. "Cohort Analysis' Futile Quest: Statistical Attempts to Separate Age, Period and Cohort Effects." *American Sociological Review* (1976) 41:900-04.

Glenn, Norval D., and Michael Grimes. "Aging, Voting, and Political Interest." *American Sociological Review* (1968) 33:563-75.

Goel, M. L. "Social Bases of Party Support and Political Participation in India." *Political Science Review* (1974) 13:58-87.

Goldberg, Arthur S. "Discerning a Causal Pattern Among Data on Voting Behavior." *American Political Science Review* (1966) 60:913-22.

——. "Social Determinism and Rationality as Bases of Party Identification." *American Political Science Review* (1969) 63:5-25.

——. *Econometric Theory*. New York: Wiley, 1964.

Golden, David G., and James M. Poterba. "The Price of Popularity: The Political Business Cycle Reexamined." *American Journal of Political Science* (1980) 24:696-714.

Goodman, Leo. "Some Alternatives to Ecological Correlation." *American Journal of Sociology* (1959) 44:610-25.

——. "Statistical Methods for Analyzing Change." *American Journal of Sociology* (1962) 68:57-78.

Gouldner, Alvin W. *The Future of the Intellectuals and the Rise of the New Class*. New York: Seabury, 1979.

Greenstein, Fred I. *Children and Politics*. rev. ed. New Haven: Yale University Press, 1969.

——. *The American Party System and the American People*. 2nd ed. Englewood Cliffs, N.J.: Prentice Hall, 1970.

Greenstein, Fred I., and Sidney G. Tarrow. "The Study of French Political Socialization: Toward the Revocation of Paradox." *World Politics* (1969) 22:95-137.

Guynes, Randall. "Orientations toward the Opposition Party." Emory University, n.d. Photocopy.

Guynes, Randall, and Jerry Perkins. "Notes on a Theory of Partisan Identification." Emory University, n.d. Photocopy.

Habermas, Jurgen. "Einleitung." In *Stichworte zur "Geistigen Situation der Zeit,"* ed. Jurgen Habermas. Frankfurt: Suhrkamp, 1979.

Hadley, Charles D. "Dual Partisan Identification in the Deep South: An Analysis of State Political Party Elite." Paper presented at the annual meeting of the Midwest Political Science Association, Chicago, 1983.

Hagner, Paul R., and John C. Pierce. "Correlative Characteristics of Levels of Conceptualization in the American Public: 1956-1976." *Journal of Politics* (1982) 44:779-807.

Hamilton, David L. "Cognitive Biases in the Perception of Social Groups." In *Cognition and Social Behavior*, ed. John S. Carroll and John W. Payne. Potomac, Md.: Erhlbaum, 1976.

Hansen, Susan B. "Partisan Realignment and Tax Policy, 1789-1970." Paper presented at the annual meeting of the American Political Science Association, Washington, D.C., 1977.

Hanushek, Eric A., and John E. Jackson. *Statistical Methods for Social Scientists*. New York: Academic Press, 1977.

Harrington, Michael. "The New Class and the Left." In *The New Class?* ed. B. Bruce-Briggs. New Brunswick, N.J.: Transaction Books, 1979.

Hartley-Brewer, M. "The Importance of Being a Good Constituency Man." *The Guardian* (1976): 17.

Hartwig, Frederick, William R. Jenkins, and Earl M. Temchin. "Variability in Electoral Behavior: The 1960, 1968, and 1976 Elections." *American Journal of Political Science* (1980) 24:553-58.

Hayashi, Chikio. "Time, Age and Ways of Thinking—From the Kokuminsei Surveys." *Journal of Asian and African Studies* (1974) 10:75-85.

Heckman, James. "Dummy Endogenous Variables in a Simultaneous Equation System." *Econometrica* (1978) 46:931-49.

Heise, David R. "Separating Reliability and Stability in Test-Retest Correlation." *American Sociological Review* (1969) 34:93-101.

Herman, Valentine. *Parliaments of the World.* New York: DeGruyter, 1976.

Herzon, Frederick D. "Ideology, Constraint, and Public Opinion: The Case of Lawyers." *American Journal of Political Science* (1980) 24:232-58.

Hess, Robert, and Judith Torney. *The Development of Political Attitudes in Children.* Chicago: Aldine, 1967.

Heunks, Felix J. *Nederlanders en hun Samenleving.* Amsterdam: Holland University Press, 1979.

Hibbs, Douglas A., Jr. *Mass Political Violence.* New York: Wiley, 1972.

——. "Political Parties and Macroeconomic Policy." *American Political Science Review* (1977) 71:1467-87.

——. "The Mass Public and Macroeconomic Performance: The Dynamics of Public Opinion Toward Unemployment and Inflation." *American Journal of Political Science* (1979) 23:705-31.

——. "Inflation, Political Support and Macroeconomic Policy." Paper prepared for the Brookings Project on the Politics and Sociology of Global Inflation, 1980.

——. "Contemporary Political Economy: An Overview." In *Contemporary Political Economy,* ed. Douglas A. Hibbs, Jr., and Heino Fassbender. Amsterdam: North-Holland, 1981.

——. "On the Demand for Economic Outcomes: Macroeconomic Performance and Mass Political Support in the United States, Great Britain, and Germany." *Journal of Politics* (1982a) 44:426-62.

——. "Economic Outcomes and Political Support for British Governments Among Occupational Classes: A Dynamic Analysis." *American Political Science Review* (1982b) 76:259-79.

——. "The Dynamics of Political Support for American Presidents Among Occupational and Partisan Groups." *American Journal of Political Science* (1982c) 26:312-32.

Hibbs, Douglas A., Jr., and Heino Fassbender, eds. *Contemporary Political Economy.* Amsterdam: North-Holland, 1981.

Hibbs, Douglas A., Jr., and Henrik Jess Madsen. "The Impact of Economic Performance on Electoral Support in Sweden, 1967-1978." *Scandanavian Political Studies* (1981) 4:33-50.

Hibbing, John R., and John R. Alford. "The Electoral Impact of Economic Conditions: Who is Held Responsible?" *American Journal of Political Science* (1981) 25:423-39.

——. "Economic Conditions and the Forgotten Side of Congress: A Foray into U.S. Senate Elections." *British Journal of Political Science* (1982) 12:505-16.

Hicks, Jack M., and John H. Wright. "Convergent-Discriminant Validation and Factor Analysis of Five Scales of Liberalism-Conservatism." *Journal of Personality and Social Psychology* (1970) 14:114-20.

Hildebrandt, Kai, and Russell J. Dalton. "Die neue Politik: Politischer Wandael oder Schönwetter Politik?" *Politische Vierteljahresschrift* (1977) 18:230-56.

———. "The New Politics." In *German Political Studies: Elections and Parties,* ed. Max Kaasc and Klaus von Beyme. London: Sage, 1978.

Hinckley, Barbara. "House Re-elections and Senate Defeats: The Role of the Challenger." *British Journal of Political Science* (1980a) 10:441-60.

———. "The American Voter in Congressional Elections." *American Political Science Review* (1980b) 74:641-50.

———. *Congressional Elections.* Washington, D.C.: CQ Press, 1981.

Hinich, Melvin J. "Some Evidence on Non-Voting Models in the Spatial Theory of Electoral Competition." *Public Choice* (1978) 33:83-102.

Hollingsworth, J. Rogers. *The Whirligig of Politics.* Chicago: University of Chicago Press, 1963.

Holm, John D., and John P. Robinson. "Ideological Identification and the American Voter." *Public Opinion Quarterly* (1978) 42:235-46.

Holmberg, Sören. *Svenska Väljare.* Stockholm: Lieber, 1981.

Hotelling, Harold. "Stability in Competition." *Economic Journal* (1929) 39:41-57.

Howell, Susan E. "Chasing an Elusive Concept: Ideological Identifications in the 1980 Presidential Campaign." Paper presented at the annual meeting of the Midwest Political Science Association, Chicago, 1983.

Huntington, Samuel P. *Political Order in Changing Societies.* New Haven: Yale University Press, 1968.

Huntington, Samuel P., and Joan P. Nelson. *No Easy Choice: Political Participation in Developing Countries.* Cambridge: Harvard University Press, 1976.

Hurley, Patricia A., and Kim Quaile Hill. "The Prospects for Issue Voting in Contemporary Congressional Elections: An Assessment of Citizen Awareness and Representation." *American Politics Quarterly* (1980) 8:425-48.

Hyman, Herbert H. *Political Socialization.* Glencoe: Free Press, 1959.

Ike, Nobutaka. "Economic Growth and Intergenerational Change in Japan." *American Political Science Review* (1973) 67:1194-203.

Inglehart, Ronald. "The Silent Revolution in Europe: Intergenerational Change in Post-Industrial Societies." *American Political Science Review* (1971) 65:991-1071.

———. *The Silent Revolution: Changing Values and Political Styles among Western Publics.* Princeton: Princeton University Press, 1977.

———. "Changing Values in Japan and the West," *Comparative Political Studies* (1982) 14:445-79.

———. "The Persistence of Materialist and Post-Materialist Value Orientations: Comments on Van Deth's Analysis." *European Journal of Political Research* (1983) 11:81-92.

Inglehart, Ronald, and Avram Hochstein. "Alignment and Dealignment of the Electorate in France and the United States." *Comparative Political Studies* (1972) 5:343-72.

Inglehart, Ronald, and Hans D. Klingemann. "Party Identification, Ideological Preference, and the Left-Right Dimension Among Western Mass Publics." In *Party Identification and Beyond,* ed. Ian Budge, Ivor Crewe, and Dennis Farlie. London: Wiley, 1976.

———. "Ideology and Values." In *Political Action,* ed. Samuel H. Barnes et al. Beverly Hills: Sage, 1979.

Inglehart, Ronald, Jacques-Rene Rabier, Ian Gordon, and Carsten J. Sorenson. "Broader Powers for the European Parliament? The Attitudes of Candidates." *European Journal of Political Research* (1980) 8:113-32.

Inkeles, Alex, and David M. Smith. *Becoming Modern: Individual Change in Six Developing Countries.* Cambridge: Harvard University Press, 1974.

Jackson, John E. "Issues and Party Alignment." In *The Future of Political Parties,* ed. Louis Maisel and Paul M. Sacks. Beverly Hills: Sage, 1975a.

——. "Issues, Party Choices, and Presidential Votes." *American Journal of Political Science* (1975b) 19:161-85.

Jackson, Thomas H., and George Marcus. "Political Competence and Ideological Constraint." *Social Science Research* (1975) 4:93-111.

Jacobson, Gary C. "The Effects of Campaign Spending in Congressional Elections." *American Political Science Review* (1978) 72:469-91.

——. *Money in Congressional Elections.* New Haven: Yale University Press, 1980.

——. "Congressional Election, 1978: The Case of the Vanishing Challengers." In *Congressional Elections,* ed. Louis Sandy Maisel and Joseph Cooper. Beverly Hills: Sage, 1981.

——. *The Politics of Congressional Elections.* Boston: Little, Brown, 1983.

Jacobson, Gary C., and Samuel Kernell. *Strategy and Choice in Congressional Elections.* New Haven: Yale University Press, 1981, 1983.

Jacoby, William G. "Unfolding the Party Identification Scale: Improving the Measurement of an Important Concept." *Political Methodology* (1982) 8:33-59.

Jaeggi, Urs. "Drinnen und draussen." In *Stichworte zur "Geistigen Situation der Zeit,"* ed. Jurgen Habermas. Frankfurt: Suhrkamp, 1979.

Jennings, M. Kent, Klaus R. Allerbeck, and Leopold Rosenmayer. "Generations, and Families," In *Political Action,* Samuel H. Barnes et al. Beverly Hills: Sage, 1979.

Jennings, M. Kent, and Richard G. Niemi. "Party Identification at Multiple Levels of Government." *American Journal of Sociology* (1966) 72:86-101.

——. "The Transmission of Political Values from Parent to Child." *American Political Science Review* (1968) 62:169-84.

——. *The Political Character of Adolescence.* Princeton: Princeton University Press, 1974.

——. "The Persistence of Political Orientations: An Overtime Analysis of Two Generations." *British Journal of Political Science* (1977) 8:333-63.

——. *Generations and Politics.* Princeton: Princeton University Press, 1981.

Jensen, Richard J. *The Winning of the Midwest: Social and Political Conflict, 1888-1896.* Chicago: University of Chicago Press, 1971.

Jenson, Jane. "Party Loyalty in Canada: The Question of Party Identification." *Canadian Journal of Political Science* (1975) 8:543-53.

Johannes, John R., and John C. McAdams. "The Congressional Incumbency Effect: Is It Casework, Policy Compatibility, or Something Else?" *American Journal of Political Science* (1981) 25:512-42.

Johnston, J. *Econometric Methods.* 2nd ed. New York: McGraw-Hill, 1972.

Judd, Charles M., and Michael A. Milburn. "The Structure of Attitude Systems in the General Public: Comparisons of a Structural Equation Model." *American Sociological Review* (1980) 45:623-43.

Kaase, Max. "Die Bundestagswahl 1973: Probleme und Analysen." *Politische Vierteljahresschrift* (1973) 14:145-90.

——. "Party Identification and Voting Behavior in the West German Election of 1969." In *Party Identification and Beyond,* ed. Ian Budge, Ivor Crewe, and Dennis Farlie. London: Wiley, 1976.

Kaase, Max, and Hans D. Klingemann. "Sozialstructur, Wertorientierung und Parteiensysteme." In *Sozialer Wandel in Westeuropa,* ed. Joachim Matthes. Frankfurt: Campus Verlag, 1979.

Kagay, Michael R., and Greg A. Caldeira. "I Like the Looks of His Face: Elements of Electoral Choice, 1952-1972." Paper presented at the annual meeting of the American Political Science Association, San Francisco, 1975.

Katz, Richard S. "The Dimensionality of Party Identification: Cross-National Perspectives." *Comparative Politics* (1979) 11:147-63.

Kavanagh, Dennis. *Constituency Electioneering in Britain.* London: Longmans, 1979.

Kearney, R. *The Politics of Ceylon (Sri Lanka).* Ithaca: Cornell University Press, 1973.

Keith, Bruce E., et al. "The Myth of the Independent Voter." Paper presented at the annual meeting of the American Political Science Association, Washington, D.C., 1977.

Kelley, Stanley, Jr., Richard E. Ayres, and William G. Bowen. "Registration and Voting: Putting First Things First." *American Political Science Review* (1967) 61:359-79.

Kelley, Stanley, Jr., and Thad W. Mirer. "The Simple Act of Voting." *American Political Science Review* (1974) 68:572-91.

Kemeny, John G., L. Snell, and Gerald Thompson. *Introduction to Finite Mathematics.* Englewood Cliffs, N.J.: Prentice-Hall, 1966.

Kemp, David A. "The Australian Electorate." In *The Australian National Elections of 1977,* ed. Howard R. Penniman. Washington, D.C.: American Enterprise Institute, 1979.

Kenny, D. A. "Cross-Lagged Panel Correlation: A Test for Spuriousness." *Psychological Bulletin* (1975) 82:345-62.

Kerlinger, Fred N. "Social Attitudes and their Criterial Referents: A Structural Theory." *Psychological Review* (1967) 74:110-22.

——. "The Structure and Content of Social Attitude Referents: A Preliminary Study." *Educational and Psychological Measurement* (1972) 32:613-30.

Kernell, Samuel. "Presidential Popularity and Negative Voting: An Alternative Explanation of the Midterm Congressional Decline of the President's Party." *American Political Science Review* (1977) 71:44-66.

——. "Explaining Presidential Popularity." *American Political Science Review* (1978) 72:506-22.

Kerr, Henry H., Jr. *Switzerland: Social Cleavages and Partisan Conflict.* Beverly Hills: Sage, 1974.

Kerr, Henry H., Jr., and David Handley. "Conflits des Générations et Politique Etrangère en Suisse." *Annuaire Suisse de Science Politique* (1974): 127-55.

Kessel, John H. *The Goldwater Coalition: Republican Strategies in 1964.* Indianapolis: Bobbs-Merrill, 1968.

——. "Comment: The Issues in Issue Voting." *American Political Science Review* (1972) 66:459-65.

——. *Presidential Campaign Politics.* Homewood, Ill.: Dorsey Press, 1980.

Kesselman, Mark. Review of "The Silent Revolution," by Ronald Inglehart. *American Political Science Review* (1979) 73:284-86.

Key, V. O., Jr., "A Theory of Critical Elections." *Journal of Politics* (1955) 17:3-18.

——. "Secular Realignment and the Party System." *Journal of Politics* (1959) 21:198-210.

——. *Public Opinion and American Democracy.* New York: Knopf, 1961.

——. *Politics, Parties, and Pressure Groups.* 5th ed. New York: Crowell, 1964.

——. *The Responsible Electorate.* Cambridge: Harvard University Press, 1966.

Kiewiet, D. Roderick. "Policy-Oriented Voting in Response to Economic Issues." *American Political Science Review* (1981) 75:448-59.

Kiewiet, D. Roderick, and Donald R. Kinder. "Political Consequences of Economic Concerns—Personal and Collective." Paper presented at the annual meeting of the American Political Science Association, New York, 1978.

Kim, Jae-on, John R. Petrocik, and Stephen N. Enokson. "Voter Turnout Among the American States: Systemic and Individual Components." *American Political Science Review* (1975) 69:107-23.

Kinder, Donald R. "Presidents, Popularity, and Public Opinion." *Public Opinion Quarterly* (1981) 45:1-21.

Kinder, Donald R., W. Michael Denney, and J. Stephen Hendricks. "Political Consequences of Inflation." Yale University, 1980. Photocopy.

Kinder, Donald R., and D. Roderick Kiewiet. "Economic Discontent and Political Behavior: The Role of Personal Grievances and Collective Economic Judgments in Congressional Voting." *American Journal of Political Science* (1979) 23:495-527.

Kinder, Donald R., and David O. Sears. "Prejudice and Politics: Symbolic Racism versus Racial Threats to the Good Life." *Journal of Personality and Social Psychology* (1981) 40:414-31.

King, Anthony. *British Members of Parliament: A Self Portrait.* London: MacMillan, 1974.

——. "The Rise of the Career Politician in Britain—and Its Consequences." *British Journal of Political Science* (1982) 11:249-85.

King, Anthony, and Anne Sloman. *Westminster and Beyond.* London: MacMillan, 1973.

King, Michael, and Lester Seligman. "Critical Elections, Congressional Recruitment, and Public Policy." Paper presented at the annual meeting of the Midwest Political Science Association, Chicago, 1974.

Kingdon, John W. *Congressmen's Voting Decisions.* New York: Harper and Row, 1973.

Klecka, William. "Applying Political Generations to the Study of Political Behavior." *Public Opinion Quarterly* (1971) 35:358-73.

Kleppner, Paul. *The Cross of Culture.* New York: Free Press, 1970.

——. "Partisanship and Ethnoreligious Conflict: The Third Electoral System, 1853-1892." In *The Evolution of American Electoral Systems,* Paul Kleppner et al. Westport, Conn.: Greenwood Press, 1981.

——. "Were Women to Blame? Female Suffrage and Voter Turnout." *Journal of Interdisciplinary History.* (1982a) 12:621-43.

——. *Who Voted? The Dynamics of Electoral Turnout, 1970-1980.* New York: Praeger, 1982b.

Kleppner, Paul, and Stephen C. Baker. "The Impact of Voter Registration Requirements on Electoral Turnout, 1900-16." Paper presented at the annual meeting of the American Political Science Association, Washington, D.C., 1979.

———. "The Impact of Voter Registration Requirements on Electoral Turnout, 1900-16." *Journal of Political and Military Sociology* (1980) 8:205-26.

Klingemann, Hans D. "Measuring Ideological Conceptualizations." In *Political Action,* ed. Samuel H. Barnes et al. Beverly Hills: Sage, 1979a.

———. "Ideological Conceptualization and Political Action." In *Political Action,* ed. Samuel H. Barnes et al. Beverly Hills: Sage, 1979b.

Klingemann, Hans D., and Charles Taylor. "Partisanship, Candidates and Issues: Attitudinal Components of the Vote in West German Federal Elections." In *German Political Studies: Elections and Parties,* ed. Max Kaase and Klaus von Beyme. London: Sage, 1978.

Klorman, Ricardo. "Trends in Personal Finances and the Vote." *Public Opinion Quarterly* (1978) 43:31-48.

Kmieciak, Peter. *Wertstrukturen und Wertwandel in der Bundesrepublik Deutschland.* Gottingen: Schwartz, 1976.

Knoke, David. *Change and Continuity in American Politics.* Baltimore: Johns Hopkins University Press, 1976.

———. "Stratification and the Dimensions of American Political Orientations." *American Journal of Political Science* (1979) 23:772-91.

Knoke, David, and Michael Hout. "Social and Demographic Factors in American Party Affiliation: 1952-1972." *American Sociological Review* (1974) 39:700-13.

———. "Reply to Glenn." *American Sociological Review* (1976) 41:905-08.

Koch, Gary G., Daniel H. Freeman, Jr., and Jean L. Freeman. "Strategies in the Multivariate Analysis of Data from Complex Surveys." *International Statistical Review* (1975) 43:59-78.

Kostroski, Lee. "Party and Incumbency in Post-War Senate Elections." *American Political Science Review* (1973) 67:1213-34.

Kousser, J. Morgan. *The Shaping of Southern Politics.* New Haven: Yale University Press, 1974.

Kramer, Gerald H. "Short-Term Fluctuations in U.S. Voting Behavior." *American Political Science Review* (1971) 65:131-43.

———. "The Ecological Fallacy Revisited: Aggregate- versus Individual-Level Findings on Economics and Elections and Sociotropic Voting." *American Political Science Review* (1983) 77:92-111.

Kramer, Gerald H., and Susan Lepper. "Congressional Elections." In *Dimensions of Quantitative Research in History,* ed. William O. Aydelotte. Princeton: Princeton University Press, 1972.

Kraut, Robert E., and John B. McConahay. "How Being Interviewed Affects Voting: An Experiment." *Public Opinion Quarterly* (1973) 37:398-406.

Kuklinski, James H., and Darrell M. West. "Economic Expectations and Voting Behavior in United States House and Senate Elections." *American Political Science Review* (1981) 75:436-47.

Ladd, Everett C., Jr. "Liberalism Upside Down: The Inversion of the New Deal Order." *Political Science Quarterly* (1976) 91:577-600.

———. "The New Lines are Drawn: Class and Ideology in America." *Public Opinion* (1978) 1:48-53.

Ladd, Everett C., Jr., and Charles D. Hadley. *Transformation of the American Party System.* 2nd ed. New York: Norton, 1978.

Lafay, J. D. "Les Conséquences Électorales de la Conjóncture Économique: Essais de Prévision Chiffrée pour Mars 1978." *Vie et Sciences Economiques* (1977) 75:1-7.

———. "The Impact of Economic Variables on Political Behavior in France." In *Contemporary Political Economy,* ed. Douglas A. Hibbs, Jr., and Heino Fassbender. Amsterdam: North-Holland, 1981.

Lafferty, William M. "Basic Needs and Political Values: Some Perspective from Norway on Europe's 'Silent Revolution.' " *Acta Sociologica* (1976) 19:117-36.

Lakeman, Enid. *How Democracies Vote.* London: Faber and Faber, 1974.

Lane, Robert E. *Political Life.* New York: Free Press, 1959.

———. *Political Ideology.* New York: Free Press, 1962.

———. "The Politics of Consensus in an Age of Affluence." *American Political Science Review* (1965) 59:874-95.

———. "Patterns of Political Belief." In *Handbook of Political Psychology,* ed. Jeanne Knutson. San Francisco: Jossey-Bass, 1973.

LaPalombara, Joseph. "Decline of Ideology: A Dissent and Interpretation." *American Political Science Review* (1966) 60:5-16.

Lau, Richard, Thad Brown, and David O. Sears. "Self Interest and Civilians' Attitudes Toward Vietnam." *Public Opinion Quarterly* (1978) 42:464-83.

Lavies, R. R. *Nichtwählen als Kategorie des Wahlverhaltens.* Dusseldorf: Droste Verlag, 1973.

Lazarsfeld, Paul, Bernard Berelson, and Helen Gaudet. *The People's Choice.* New York: Columbia University Press, 1944, 1948.

Lehner, Franz. "Die 'Stille Revolution': zur Theorie und Realität des Wertwandels in hochindustrialisierten Gesellschaften." In *Wertwandel und gesellschaftlicher Wandel,* ed. Helmut Klages and Peter Kmieciak. Frankfurt: Campus Verlag, 1979.

Lepper, Susan. "Voting Behavior and Aggregate Policy Targets." *Public Choice* (1974) 18:67-81.

Lerner, Daniel. *The Passing of Traditional Society.* New York: Free Press, 1958.

Levinson, Daniel J., et al. *The Seasons of a Man's Life.* New York: Knopf, 1979.

Levitin, Teresa E., and Warren E. Miller. "Ideological Interpretations of Presidential Elections." *American Political Science Review* (1979) 73:751-71.

Lewis, John, and Archie E. Allen. "Black Voter Registration Efforts in the South." *Notre Dame Lawyer* (1972) 18:119.

Lewis-Beck, Michael S. "Economic Conditions and Executive Popularity: The French Experience." *American Journal of Political Science* (1980) 24:306-23.

Lewis-Beck, Michael S., and Paolo Bellucci. "Economic Influences on Legislative Elections in Multiparty Systems: France and Italy." *Political Behavior* (1982) 4:93-107.

Li, R. P. Y. "Public Policy and Short-Term Fluctuations in U.S. Voting Behavior: A Reformulation and Expansion." *Political Methodology* (1976) 3:49-70.

Lichtman, Allan J. "Critical Election Theory and the Reality of American Presidential Politics, 1916-1940." *American Historical Review* (1976) 71:317-50.

Lijphart, Arend. "Class and Religious Voting in the European Democracies." Occasional Paper No. 8. Survey Research Centre, University of Strathclyde, 1971.

___. "Religious vs. Linguistic vs. Class Voting: The 'Crucial Experiment' of Comparing Belgium, Canada, South Africa, and Switzerland." *American Political Science Review* (1979) 73:442-58.

Lindstrom, Ulf. "The Changing Scandinavian Voter." *European Journal of Political Research* (1982) 10:321-32.

Linz, Juan J. "Cleavage and Consensus in West German Politics: The Early Fifties." In *Party Systems and Voter Alignment,* ed. Seymour M. Lipset and Stein Rokkan. New York: Free Press, 1967.

___. "The New Spanish Party System." In *Electoral Participation: A Comparative Analysis,* ed. Richard Rose. Beverly Hills: Sage, 1980.

Lippman, Walter. *Public Opinion.* New York: Macmillan, 1922.

Lipset, Seymour Martin. *Political Man.* Garden City, N.Y.: Doubleday, 1960.

___. "The New Class and the Professoriate." In *The New Class?* ed. B. Bruce-Briggs. New Brunswick, N.J.: Transaction Books, 1979.

Lipset, Seymour Martin, and Richard B. Dobson. "The Intellectual as Critic and Rebel." *Daedalus* (1972) 101:137-98.

Lipset, Seymour Martin, and Stein Rokkan. "Cleavage Structure, Party Systems and Voter Alignments." In *Party Systems and Voter Alignments,* ed. Seymour M. Lipset and Stein Rokkan. New York: Free Press, 1967a.

___. *Party Systems and Voter Alignments.* New York: Free Press, 1967b.

Loewenberg, Gerhard. "The Remaking of the German Party System." *Polity* (1968) 1:86-113.

___. "The Development of the German Party System." In *Germany at the Polls,* ed. Karl Cerny. Washington, D.C.: American Enterprise Institute, 1978.

Logan, Mikal Ben-Gera. "Short-Term Economic Changes and Individual Voting Behavior." Yale University, 1977.

Lopatto, Paul. "Realignments and Supreme Court Decision Making." University of Pittsburgh, 1976.

Lovins, Armory. *Soft Energy Paths: Toward a Durable Peace.* New York: Harper, 1977.

Lowell, A. Lawrence. "The Influence of Party Upon Legislation in England and America." Annual report of the American Historical Association, Washington, D.C., 1901.

Luttbeg, Norman. "The Structure of Beliefs Among Leaders and the Public." *Public Opinion Quarterly* (1968) 32:398-409.

Macaluso, Theodore. "The Responsiveness of Party Identification to Current Political Evaluations." University of Kentucky, n.d. Photocopy.

McCallum, Bennett. "The Political Business Cycle: An Empirical Test." *Southern Economic Journal* (1978) 44:504-15.

McCracken, Paul W. "The Practice of Political Economy." *American Economic Review* (1973) 63:168-71.

McDonald, Michael D., and Susan E. Howell. "Reconsidering the Reconceptualization of Party Identification." *Political Methodology* (1982) 8:73-91.

McDonald, Ronald H. "Electoral Politics and Uruguayan Political Decay." *Inter-American Economic Affairs* (1972) 26:25-46.

McDonough, Peter. "Electoral Competition and Participation in India." *Comparative Politics* (1971) 4:77-88.

McIver, John P. "Unemployment and Partisanship: A Second Opinion." *American Political Quarterly* (1982) 10:439-51.

McKelvey, Richard D., and Peter C. Ordeshook. "A General Theory of the Calculus of Voting." In *Mathematical Applications in Political Science, VI,* ed. James F. Herndon and Joseph L. Bernd. Charlottesville: University of Virginia Press, 1972.

McKelvey, Richard D., and William Zavoina. "A Statistical Model for the Analysis of Ordinal Level Dependent Variables." *Journal of Mathematical Sociology* (1975) 4:103-20.

Mackie, Thomas, and Richard Rose. *The International Almanac of Electoral History.* New York: Free Press, 1974.

MacRae, Duncan, Jr. *Issues and Parties in Legislative Voting.* New York: Harper and Row, 1970.

Madsen, Henrik Jess. "Electoral Outcomes and Macro-Economic Policies: The Scandinavian Cases." In *Models of Political Economy,* ed. Paul Whiteley. London: Sage, 1980.

——. "Partisanship and Macroeconomic Outcomes: A Reconsideration." In *Contemporary Political Economy,* ed. Douglas A. Hibbs, Jr., and Heino Fassbender. Amsterdam: North-Holland, 1981.

Maggiotto, Michael A., and James E. Piereson. "Partisan Identification and Electoral Choice: The Hostility Hypothesis." *American Journal of Political Science* (1977) 21:745-67.

Maguire, Maria. "Is There Still Persistence? Electoral Change in Western Europe, 1948-1979." In *Western European Party Systems,* ed. Hans Daalder and Peter Mair. London: Sage, 1983.

Mann, Thomas E. *Unsafe at any Margin: Interpreting Congressional Elections.* Washington, D.C.: American Enterprise Institute, 1978.

——. "Congressional Elections." In *The New Congress,* ed. Thomas E. Mann and Norman J. Ornstein. Washington, D.C.: American Enterprise Institute, 1980.

Mann, Thomas E., and Raymond E. Wolfinger. "Candidates and Parties in Congressional Elections." *American Political Science Review* (1980) 74:617-32. Chap. 15 in this volume.

Marcus, George, David Tabb, and John L. Sullivan. "The Application of Individual Differences Scaling to the Measurement of Political Ideology." *American Journal of Political Science* (1974) 18:405-20.

Margolis, Michael. "From Confusion to Confusion: Issues and the American Voter (1956-1972)." *American Political Science Review* (1977) 71:31-43.

Markus, Gregory B. "Candidates, Parties and Issues: A Feedback Model of the Voting Decision." Center for Political Studies, University of Michigan, 1976.

——. *Analyzing Panel Data.* Beverly Hills: Sage, 1979.

——. "Political Attitudes during an Election Year: A Report on the 1980 NES Panel Study." *American Political Science Review* (1982) 76:538-60.

Markus, Gregory B. "Candidates, Parties and Issues: A Feedback Model of the Voting Decision." Center for Political Studies, Univserity of Michigan, 1976.
in this volume.

Marsh, Alan. "The Silent Revolution, Value Priorities and the Quality of Life in Britain." *American Political Science Review* (1975) 69:1-30.

———. *Protest and Political Consciousness.* Beverly Hills: Sage, 1977.

Martz, John D., and Enrique Baloyra. *The Venezuelan Election of 1973.* Chapel Hill: University of North Carolina Press, 1976.

Maslow, Abraham H. *Motivation and Personality.* New York: Harper, 1954.

Matthews, Donald, and James Prothro. *Negroes and the New Southern Politics.* New York: Harcourt, Brace and World, 1966.

Mayhew, David R. *Congress: The Electoral Connection.* New Haven: Yale University Press, 1974a.

———. "Congressional Elections: The Case of the Vanishing Marginals." *Polity* (1974b) 6:295-317.

Meadows, Donella H., et al. *The Limits to Growth.* New York: Universe, 1972.

Meehl, Peter E. "The Selfish Voter Paradox and the Thrown-Away Vote Argument." *American Political Science Review* (1977) 71:11-30.

Meier, Kenneth. "Party Identification and Vote Choice: The Casual Relationship." *Western Political Quarterly* (1975) 28:496-505.

Meisel, John. *Cleavages, Parties and Values in Canada.* Beverly Hills: Sage, 1974.

———. *Working Papers in Canadian Politics.* Montreal: McGill-Queen's University Press, 1975.

Meltzer, Allan H., and Mark Vellrath. "The Effects of Economic Policies on Votes for the Presidency: Some Evidence from Recent Elections." *Journal of Law and Economics* (1975) 18:781-98.

Michelat, Guy, and Michel Simon. *Classe, Religion et Comportement Politique.* Paris: Presses de la Fondation Nationale des Sciences Politiques—Editions Sociales, 1977.

Milbrath, Lester. "Political Participation in the States." In *Politics in the American States,* ed. Herbert Jacob and Kenneth N. Vines. Boston: Little, Brown, 1965.

Milbrath, Lester W., and M. L. Goel. *Political Participation.* 2nd ed. Chicago: Rand McNally, 1977.

Miller, Arthur H. "Partisanship Reinstated? A Comparison of the 1972 and 1976 United States Presidential Elections." *British Journal of Political Sciences* (1978) 8:129-52.

———. "Normal Vote Analysis: Sensitivity to Change Over Time." *American Journal of Political Science* (1979) 23:406-25.

Miller, Arthur H., Patricia Gurin, and Gerald Gurin. "Electoral Implications of Group Identification and Consciousness: The Reintroduction of a Concept." Paper presented at the annual meeting of the American Political Science Association, New York, 1978.

Miller, Arthur H., and Warren E. Miller. "Ideology in the 1972 Election: Myth or Reality—A Rejoinder." *American Political Science Review* (1976) 70:832-49.

———. "Partisanship and Performance: 'Rational' Choice in the 1976 Presidential Election." Paper presented at the annual meeting of the American Political Science Association, Washington, D.C., 1977.

Miller, Arthur H., Warren E. Miller, Alden S. Raine, and Thad H. Brown. "A Majority Party in Disarray: Policy Polarization in the 1972 Election." Paper presented at the annual meeting of the American Political Science Association, New Orleans, 1973.

———. "A Majority Party in Disarray: Policy Polarization in the 1972 Election." *American Political Science Review* (1976) 70:753-78. Chap. 10 in first ed. of this volume.

Miller, Arthur H., and Martin P. Wattenberg. "Policy and Performance Voting in the 1980 Election." Paper presented at the annual meeting of the American Political Science Association, New York, 1981.

———. "Measuring Party Identification: Independent or No Partisan Preference?" *American Journal of Political Science* (1983) 27:106-21.

Miller, Warren E. "The Cross-National Use of Party Identification as a Stimulus to Political Inquiry." In *Party Identification and Beyond,* ed. Ian Budge, Ivor Crewe, and Dennis Farlie. London: Wiley, 1976.

Miller, Warren E., and Teresa E. Levitin. *Leadership and Change: Presidential Elections from 1952-1976.* Cambridge, Mass.: Winthrop, 1976.

Miller, Warren E., Arthur H. Miller, and Edward J. Schneider. *American National Election Studies Sourcebook, 1952-1978.* Cambridge: Harvard University Press, 1980.

Miller, Warren E., and Donald E. Stokes. "Constituency Influence in Congress." *American Political Science Review* (1963) 57:45-56.

Mitchell, Austin. *Politics and People in New Zealand.* Christchurch: Whitecombe and Tombs, 1969.

Monroe, Kristen. "Economic Influences on Presidential Popularity." *Public Opinion Quarterly* (1978) 42:360-69.

Mossuz, Janine. *Les Jeunes et la Gauche.* Paris: Presses de la Fondation Nationale de Sciences Politiques, 1979.

Mueller, John E.. "Presidential Popularity from Truman to Johnson." *American Political Science Review* (1970) 64:18-34.

Mueller, John H., Karl Schuessler, and Herbert Costner. *Statistical Reasoning in Sociology.* Boston: Houghton-Mifflin, 1970.

Muller, Edward N., Pertti Pesonen, and Thomas O. Jukam. "Support for the Freedom of Assembly in Western Democracies." *European Journal of Political Research* (1980) 8:265-88.

Munroe, Ronald. "The Member of Parliament as Representative: The View from the Constituency." *Political Studies* (1977) 25:577-87.

Nardi, Rafaella. "Sono le condizioni economiche a influenzare I valori? Un controllo dell'ipotesi di Inglehart." *Revista Italiana di Scienza Politica* (1980) 10:293-315.

Nelkin, Dorothy, and Michael Pollak. *The Atom Besieged: Extraparliamentary Dissent in France and Germany.* Cambridge: MIT Press, 1981.

Nelson, Candice J. "The Effect of Incumbency on Voting in Congressional Elections, 1964-1974." *Political Science Quarterly* (1978) 93:665-78.

Nelson, Forrest, and Lawrence Olson. "Specification and Estimation of a Simultaneous-Equation Model with Limited Dependent Variables." *International Economic Review* (1978) 19:695-709.

Nelson, Garrison. "Partisan Patterns of House Leadership Change, 1789-1977." *American Political Science Review* (1977) 71:918-39.

Nie, Norman H., with Kristi Andersen. "Mass Belief Systems Revisited: Political Change and Attitude Structure." *Journal of Politics* (1974) 36:541-91. Chapter 7 in first ed. of this volume.

Nie, Norman H., G. Bingham Powell, Jr., and Kenneth Prewitt. "Social Structure and Political Participation." *American Political Science Review* (1969) 62:361-78; 808-32.

Nie, Norman H., Sidney Verba, and John R. Petrocik. *The Changing American Voter.* Cambridge: Harvard University Press, 1976, 1979.

———. "Reply to Abramson and to Smith." *American Political Science Review* (1981) 75:149-52.

Niemi, Richard G. *How Family Members Perceive Each Other.* New Haven: Yale University Press, 1974.

Niemi, Richard G., Richard S. Katz, and David Newman. "Reconstructing Past Partisanship: The Failure of the Party Identification Recall Questions." *American Journal of Political Science* (1980) 24:633-51.

Niemi, Richard G., Harold Stanley, and Charles L. Evans, "Age and Turnout Among the Newly Enfranchised." *European Journal of Political Research,* (1984) 12:371-386.

Niemi, Richard G., and Herbert F. Weisberg. *Controversies in American Voting Behavior.* San Francisco: W. H. Freeman, 1976.

Niemi, Richard G., and Anders Westholm. "Issues, Parties, and Attitudinal Stability: A Comparative Study of Sweden and the United States." *Electoral Studies* (1984) 3:65-83.

Nisbett, Richard E., Eugene Borgida, Rick Crandall, and Harvey Reed. "Popular Induction Information Is Not Necessarily Informative." In *Cognition and Social Behavior,* ed. J. Caroll and J. Payne. Hillsdale, N.J.: Erlbaum, 1976.

Nisbett, Richard E., and Timothy D. Wilson. "Telling More Than We Know: Verbal Reports on Mental Processes." *Psychological Review* (1977) 84:231-59.

Nishihira, Sigeki. "Changed and Unchanged Characteristics of the Japanese." *Japan Echo* (1974) 1:22-32.

Norpoth, Helmut. "Kanzlerkandidaten." *Politische Vierteljahresschrift* (1977) 18:551-72.

———. "Party Identification in West Germany: Tracing an Elusive Concept." *Comparative Political Studies* (1978) 11:36-61.

———. "The Parties Come to Order! Dimensions of Preferential Choice in the West German Electorate, 1961-1976." *American Political Science Review* (1979) 73:724-36.

Norpoth, Helmut, and Jerrold G. Rusk. "Partisan Dealignment in the American Electorate." *American Political Science Review* (1982) 76:522-37.

Norpoth, Helmut, and Thom Yantek. "Macroeconomic Conditions and Fluctuations of Presidential Popularity: The Question of Lagged Effects." *American Journal of Political Science* (1983) 27:785-807.

Norton, Philip. "The Changing Face of the British House of Commons in the 1970s." *Legislative Studies Quarterly* (1980) 5:333-58.

Nye, Russell B. "The Storm Breaks, 1892-1900." In *The Sweep of American History.* Vol. 2, ed. Robert R. Jones and Gustav L. Seligman, Jr. New York: Wiley, 1970.

Page, Benjamin I. *Choices and Echoes in Presidential Elections: Rational Man and Electoral Democracy.* Chicago: University of Chicago Press, 1978.

Page, Benjamin I., and Richard A. Brody. "Policy Voting and the Electoral Process: The Vietnam War Issue." *American Political Science Review* (1972) 66:979-95.

Page, Benjamin I., and Calvin Jones. "Reciprocal Effects of Policy Preferences, Party Loyalties and the Vote." *American Political Science Review* (1979) 73:1071-89. Chap. 6 in this volume.

Paldam, Martin. "An Essay on the Rationality of Economic Policy: The Test Case of the Electional Cycle." *Public Choice* (1981) 37:287-305.

Pappi, F. U. "Sozialstruktur und Wahlentscheidung bei Bundestagswahlen aus kommunalpolitischer Sicht." In *Kommunales Wahlverhalten,* ed. A. Stiftung. Bonn: Eichholz, 1976.

Parker, Glenn R. "The Advantage of Incumbency in House Elections." *American Politics Quarterly* (1980a) 8:449-64.

——. "Sources of Change in Congressional District Attentiveness." *American Journal of Political Science* (1980b) 24:115-24.

——. "Interpreting Candidate Awareness in U.S. Congressional Elections." *Legislative Studies Quarterly* (1981) 6:219-34.

Paul, Arnold M. *Conservative Crisis and the Rule of Law.* Ithaca, N.Y.: Cornell University Press, 1960.

Pedersen, Mogens N. "The Dynamics of European Party Systems: Changing Patterns of Electoral Volatility." *European Journal of Political Research* (1979) 7:1-26.

Peirce, Neal R. *The Deep South States of America.* New York: Norton, 1974.

Percheron, Annick, et al. *Les 10-16 Ans et la Politique.* Paris: Presses de la Fondation Nationale des Sciences Politiques, 1978.

Pesonen, Pertti, and Risto Sankiaho. *Kansalaiset je kansanvalta: Soumalaitsten kasityksia poliittisesta toiminnasta.* Helsinki: Werner Soderstrom Osakeyhtio, 1979.

Petrocik, John R. "An Analysis of Intransitivities in the Index of Party Identification." *Political Methodology* (1974) 1:31-47.

——. *Party Coalitions.* Chicago: University of Chicago Press, 1981.

Phillips, Kevin P., and Paul H. Blackman. *Electoral Reform and Voter Participation.* Washington, D.C.: American Enterprise Institute, 1975.

Pierce, John C., and Douglas D. Rose. "Non-Attitudes and American Public Opinion." *American Political Science Review* (1974) 68:626-49.

Pierce, Roy. "Left-Right Perceptions, Partisan Preferences, Electoral Participation, and Partisan Choice in France." Institute for Social Research, University of Michigan, 1980.

Pierce, Roy, and Philip E. Converse. "Candidate Visibility in France and the United States." *Legislative Studies Quarterly* (1981) 6:339-71.

Podhoretz, Norman. "The Adversary Culture and the New Class." In *The New Class,* ed. B. Bruce-Briggs. New Brunswick, N.J.: Transaction Books, 1979.

Polsby, Nelson W. "The Institutionalization of the House of Representatives." *American Political Science Review* (1968) 62:144-68.

——. "Presidential Cabinet Making: Lessons for the Political System." *Political Science Quarterly* (1978) 93:15-25.

Polsby, Nelson W., and Aaron Wildavsky. *Presidential Elections.* 4th ed. New York: Scribner, 1976.

Pomper, Gerald M. "Classification of Presidential Elections." *Journal of Politics* (1967) 29:535-66.

——. "From Confusion to Clarity: Issues and American Voters, 1956-1968." *American Political Science Review* (1972) 66:415-28.

——. *Voters' Choice.* New York: Dodd, Mead, 1975.

Popkin, Samuel, John W. Gorman, Charles Phillips, and Jeffrey A. Smith. "Comment: What Have You Done for Me Lately? Toward an Investment Theory of Voting." *American Political Science Review* (1976) 70:779-805.

Porter, Richard D. "On the Use of Survey Sample Weights in the Linear Model." *Annals of Economic and Social Measurement* (1973) 2:141-58.

Powell, G. Bingham, Jr. "Political Cleavage Structure, Cross-Pressure Processes and Partisanship." *American Journal of Political Science* (1976) 20:1-23.

Powell, Lynda W. "Constituency Service and Electoral Margin in the Congress." Paper presented at the annual meeting of the American Political Science Association, Denver, 1982.

Prewitt, Kenneth, and Norman H. Nie. "Election Studies of the Survey Research Center." *British Journal of Political Science* (1971) 1:479-502.

Prothro, James W., and Patricia E. Chapperio. "Public Opinion and the Movement of Chilean Government to the Left." *Journal of Politics* (1974) 36:2-43.

Prothro, James W., and Charles M. Grigg. "Fundamental Principles of Democracy: Bases of Agreement and Disagreement." *Journal of Politics* (1960) 22:276-94.

Przeworski, Adam. "Institutionalization of Voting Patterns." *American Political Science Review* (1975) 69:49-67.

Radtke, G. "Gibt es in der Bundesrepublic eine Parteienidentifikation?" *Verfassung und Verfassungswirklichkeit* (1972) 6:68-91.

Rae, Douglas. *The Political Consequences of Electoral Laws.* New Haven: Yale University Press, 1967, 1974.

Ragsdale, Lyn. "The Fiction of Congressional Elections as Presidential Events." *American Politics Quarterly* (1980) 8:375-98.

Ranney, Austin. "Parties in State Politics." In *Politics in the American States.* 2nd ed., ed. Herbert Jacob and Kenneth N. Vines. Boston: Little, Brown, 1972.

——. *Curing the Mischiefs of Faction.* Berkeley: University of California Press, 1975.

Reitman, Alan, and Robert B. Davidson. *The Election Process: Voting Laws and Procedures.* Dobbs Ferry, N.Y.: Oceana Publications, 1972.

RePass, David E. "Issue Salience and Party Choice." *American Political Science Review* (1971) 65:389-400.

——. "Comment: Political Methodologies in Disarray: Some Alternative Interpretations of the 1972 Election." *American Political Science Review* (1976) 70:814-31.

Research Committee on the Study of the Japanese National Character. *A Study of the Japanese National Character: The Sixth Nation-Wide Survey.* Tokyo: Institute of Statistical Mathematics, 1979.

Rhodebeck, Laurie. "Group Based Politics." Ph.D. diss., Yale University, 1980.

Richards, P. G. *The Backbencher.* London: Faber, 1972.

Richardson, Bradley M. *The Political Culture of Japan.* Berkeley: University of California Press, 1974.

Riker, William, and Peter Ordeshook. "A Theory of the Calculus of Voting." *American Political Science Review* (1968) 62:25-42.

——. *An Introduction to Positive Theory.* Englewood Cliffs, N.J.: Prentice-Hall, 1973.

Robeck, Bruce W. "Legislative Partisanship, Constituency, and Malapportionment: The Case of California." *American Political Science Review* (1972) 66:1246-55.

Robinson, John P., and Philip E. Converse. "Social Change in the Use of Time." In *The Human Meaning of Social Change,* ed. Angus Campbell and Philip E. Converse. New York: Russell Sage, 1972.

Robinson, John P., and John Holm. "Ideological Voting is Alive and Well." *Public Opinion* (1980) 3:52-58.

Robinson, Michael. "The Three Faces of Congressional Media." In *The New Congress,* ed. Thomas E. Mann and Norman J. Ornstein. Washington, D.C.: American Enterprise Institute, 1980.

Robinson, W. S. "Ecological Correlations and the Behavior of Individuals." *American Sociological Review* (1950) 15:351-57.

Roper, Elmo. "How to Lose Your Vote." *Saturday Review* (1961) 18:14-15.

Rosa, J. J., and D. Amson, "Conditions Économiques et Elections." *Review Française de Science Politique* (1976) 26:1101-24.

Rose, Richard, ed. *Electoral Behavior: A Comparative Handbook.* New York: Free Press, 1974.

——. *Citizen Participation in the Electoral Process.* Strathclyde: Center for the Study of Public Policy, 1978.

Rose, Richard, and Derek Urwin. "Social Cohesion, Political Parties and Strains in Regimes." *Comparative Political Studies* (1969) 2:7-67.

Rosenstone, Steven J. "Economic Adversity and Voter Turnout." *American Journal of Political Science* (1982) 26:25-46.

Rosenstone, Steven J., and Raymond E. Wolfinger. "The Effect of Registration Laws on Voting Turnout." *American Political Science Review* (1978) 72:22-45. Chap. 4 in this volume.

Rosenstone, Stephen J., Raymond E. Wolfinger, and Richard A. McIntosh. "Voter Turnout in Midterm Elections." Paper presented at the annual meeting of the American Political Science Association, New York, 1978.

Rosenthal, Howard, and Subrata Sen. "Electoral Participation in the French Fifth Republic." *American Political Science Review* (1973) 67:29-54.

——. "Spatial Voting Models for the French Fifth Republic." *American Political Science Review* (1977) 71:1447-66.

Rusk, Jerrold G. "The Effect of the Australian Ballot Reform on Split Ticket Voting: 1876-1908." *American Political Science Review* (1970) 64:1220-38. Chap. 29 in first ed. of this volume.

——. "Comment: The American Electoral Universe: Speculation and Evidence." *American Political Science Review* (1974) 68:1028-49.

Rusk, Jerrold G., and John J. Stucker. "The Effect of the Southern System of Election Laws on Voting Participation: A Reply to V. O. Key, Jr." In *The History of American Electoral Behavior,* ed. Joel H. Silbey, Allan G. Bogue, and William H. Flanigan. Princeton: Princeton University Press, 1978.

Russett, Bruce M., Hayward R. Alker, Karl W. Deutsch, and Harold Lasswell. *World Handbook of Political and Social Indicators.* New Haven: Yale Univerity Press, 1964.

Ryder, Norman. "The Cohort as a Concept in the Study of Social Change." *American Sociological Review* (1965) 30:843-61.

Sale, Kirkpatrick. *Human Scale.* New York: Coward McCann Geoghegan, 1980.

Sani, Giacomo. "A Test of the Least Distance Model of Voting Choice: Italy, 1972." *Comparative Political Studies* (1974) 7:193-208.

——. "Political Traditions as Contextual Variables: Partisanship in Italy." *American Journal of Political Science* (1976) 20:375-405.

——. "The Italian Electorate in the Mid-1970s." In *Italy at the Polls: 1976,* ed. Howard Penniman. Washington, D.C.: American Enterprise Institute, 1977.

Särlvik, Bo, and Ivor Crewe, *Decade of Dealignment: The Conservative Victory of 1979 and Electoral Trends in the 1970s.* Cambridge: Cambridge University Press, 1983.

Sartori, Giovanni. *Parties and Party Systems.* Cambridge: Cambridge University Press, 1976.

Scammon, Richard M., and Ben J. Wattenberg. *The Real Majority.* New York: Coward, McCann and Geoghegan, 1970.

Schattschneider, E. E. *The Semi-Sovereign People.* New York: Holt, Rinehart, and Winston, 1960.

Schleth, Uwe, and Erich Weede. "Casual Models on West German Voting Behavior." In *Sozialwiss.* Vol. 2, ed. R. Wildenmann. Munich: Olzof Verlag, 1971.

Schlozman, Kay L., and Sidney Verba. *Injury to Insult.* Cambridge: Harvard University Press, 1979.

Schulman, Mark A., and Gerald M. Pomper. "Variability in Electoral Behavior: Longitudinal Perspectives from Causal Modeling." *American Journal of Political Science* (1975) 19:1-18. Chap. 11 in first ed. of this volume.

Schumacher, E. F. *Small Is Beautiful.* New York: Harper, 1973.

Schwartz, John E. "Exploring a New Role in Policy Making: The British House of Commons in the 1970s." *American Political Science Review* (1980) 1:23-37.

Searing, Donald D., Joel J. Schwartz, and Alden E. Lind. "The Structuring Principle: Political Socialization and Belief Systems." *American Political Science Review* (1973) 67:415-32.

Sears, David O. "Political Behavior." In *The Handbook of Social Psychology,* ed. Gardner Lindzey and Elliot Aronson. Vol. 5, 2nd ed. Reading, Mass.: Addison-Wesley, 1969.

Sears, David O., Carl P. Hensler, and Leslie K. Speer. "Whites' Opposition to 'Busing': Self-Interest or Symbolic Politics?" *American Political Science Review* (1979) 73:369-84.

Sears, David O., and Donald R. Kinder. "Racial Tension and Voting in Los Angeles." In *Los Angeles: Viability and Prospects for Metropolitan Leadership,* ed. W. Z. Hirsch. New York: Praeger, 1971.

Sears, David O., Richard Lau, Tom R. Tylor, and Harris M. Allen, Jr. "Self Interest Versus Symbolic Politics in Policy Attitudes and Presidential Voting." *American Political Science Review* (1980) 74:139-51.

Sears, David O., Tom R. Tyler, Jack C. Citrin, and Donald R. Kinder. "Political System Support and Public Responses to the Energy Crisis." *American Journal of Political Science* (1978) 22:56-82.

Sellers, Charles. "The Equilibrium Cycle in Two-Party Politics." *Public Opinion Quarterly* (1965) 30:16-38.

Shapiro, Michael J. "Rational Political Man: A Synthesis of Economic and Social-Psychological Perspectives." *American Political Science Review* (1969) 63:1106-19.

Sheth, D. L. "Social Bases of Party Support." In *Citizens and Parties: Aspects of Campaign Politics in India,* ed. D. L. Sheth. New Delhi: Allied Publications, 1975.

Shively, W. Phillips. "A Reinterpretation of the New Deal Realignment." *Public Opinion Quarterly* (1971) 35:621-24.

———. "Voting Stability and the Nature of Party Attachments in the Weimar Republic." *American Political Science Review* (1972) 66:1203-25.

———. "Information Costs and the Partisan Life Cycle." Paper presented at the annual meeting of the American Political Science Association, Washington, D.C., 1977.

———. "The Development of Party Identification among Adults." *American Political Science Review* (1979) 73:1039-54.

Shover, John L. "The Emergency of a Two-Party System in Republican Philadelphia, 1924-1934." *Journal of American History* (1974) 60:985-1002.

Siegfried, André. *Geographie Electorale de l'Ardeche sous la IIème République.* Paris: A. Colin, 1949.

Sinclair, Barbara Deckard. "Party Realignment and the Transformation of the Political Agenda: "The House of Representatives, 1925-1938." *American Political Science Review* (1977) 71:940-53.

Smidt, Corwin E. "Negative Political Party Identification in the United States: 1964-1972." Paper presented at the annual meeting of the Southern Political Science Association, Nashville, 1975a.

—. *The Changing Patterns of Political Party Identification in the United States: 1964-1972.* Ph.D. diss., University of Iowa, 1975b.

—. "The Dynamics of Partisan Change in the United States: An Analysis of the Relationship between Change in Partisan Affections and Partisan Self-Images." Paper presented at the annual meeting of the Midwest Political Science Association, Cincinnati, 1981.

Smith, Eric R. A. N. "The Levels of Conceptualization: False Measures of Ideological Sophistication." *American Political Science Review* (1980) 74:685-96.

Sniderman, Paul M., and Richard A. Brody. "Coping: The Ethic of Self-Reliance." *American Journal of Political Science* (1977) 21:501-22.

Spackman, Ann. "Electoral Law and Administration in Jamaica." *Social and Economics Studies* (1969) 18:1-53.

Steeper, Frederick T., and Robert M. Teeter. "Comment on 'A Majority Party in Disarray.'" *American Political Science Review* (1976) 70:806-13.

Steiner, Jurg. *Amicable Agreement Versus Majority Rule: Conflict Resolution in Switzerland.* Chapel Hill: University of North Carolina Press, 1974.

Steinfels, Peter. *The Neo-Conservatives.* New York: Simon and Schuster, 1979.

Stigler, George J. "General Economic Conditions and National Elections." *American Economic Review* (1973) 63:160-67.

Stimson, James A. "Public Support for American Presidents: A Cyclical Model." *Public Opinion Quarterly* (1976) 40:1-21.

Stimson, James A., and Edward G. Carmines. "The Continuing Issue in American Politics." Paper presented at the annual meeting of the Southern Political Science Association, New Orleans, 1977.

Stokes, Donald E. "Some Dynamic Elements in Contests for the Presidency." *American Political Science Review* (1966) 60:19-28.

—. "Parties and the Nationalization of Electoral Forces." In *The American Party Systems,* ed. William Nisbet Chambers and Walter Dean Burnham. New York: Oxford University Press, 1967, 1975. Chap. 11 in first ed. of this volume.

Stokes, Donald E., Angus Campbell, and Warren E. Miller. "Components of Electoral Decision." *American Political Science Review* (1958) 52:367-87.

Stokes, Donald E., and Warren E. Miller. "Party Government and the Saliency of Congress." In *Elections and the Political Order,* Angus Campbell, Philip E. Converse, Warren E. Miller, and Donald E. Stokes. New York: Wiley, 1966.

Stone, Carl. *Class, Race and Political Behavior in Urban Jamaica.* Jamaica: University of West Indies, 1973.

Stouffer, Samuel A., et al. *The American Soldier.* Princeton: Princeton University Press, 1949.

Sullivan, John L., James E. Piereson, and George E. Marcus. "Ideological Constraint in the Mass Public: A Methodological Critique and Some New Findings." *American Journal of Political Science* (1978) 22:223-49.

Sundquist, James. *Dynamics of the Party System: Alignment and Realignment of Political Parties in the United States.* Washington, D.C.: Brookings, 1973.

Tanter, Raymond. "Toward a Theory of Political Development." *Midwest Journal of Political Science* (1967) 11:145-72.

Tarrance, V. Lance. "The Vanishing Voter: A Look at Non-Voting as a Purposive Act." In *Voters, Primaries and Parties,* ed. Jonathan Moore and Albert C. Pierce. Cambridge: Harvard University Institute of Politics, 1976.

Tedin, Kent L. "The Influence of Parents on the Political Attitudes of Adolescents." *American Political Science Review* (1974) 68:1579-92.

Theil, Henri. *Principles of Econometrics.* New York: Wiley, 1971.

Thomas, Alastair H. *Parliamentary Parties in Denmark 1945-1972.* Glascow: Survey Research Centre, University of Srathclyde, 1973.

Thomassen, Jacques. "Party Identification as a Cross-National Concept: Its Meaning in the Netherlands." In *Party Identification and Beyond,* ed. Ian Budge, Ivor Crewe, and Dennis Farlie. London: Wiley, 1976.

Thompson, Fred. "Closeness Counts in Horseshoes and Dancing ... and Elections." *Public Choice* (1982) 38:305-16.

Thompson, William R., and Gary Zuk. "American Elections and the International Electoral-Economic Cycle: A Test of the Tufte Hypothesis." *American Journal of Political Science* (1983) 27:464-84.

Tilly, Charles. *The Vendée.* Cambridge: Harvard University Press, 1964.

Tingsten, Herbert. *Political Behavior.* Totowa, N.J.: Bedminster, 1937.

Trilling, Richard J. "Party Image and Partisan Change." In *The Future of Political Parties*, ed. Louis Maisel and Paul M. Sacks. Beverly Hills: Sage, 1975.

——. *Party Image and Electoral Behavior.* New York: Wiley, 1976.

Tufte, Edward R. "The Relationship between Seats and Votes in Two-Party Systems." *American Political Science Review* (1973) 62:540-54.

——. "Determinants of the Outcomes of Midterm Congressional Elections." *American Political Science Review* (1975) 69:812-26. Chap. 15 in first ed. of this volume.

——. "Political Statistics for the United States: Observations on Some Major Data Sources." *American Political Science Review* (1977) 71:305-14.

——. *Political Control of the Economy.* Princeton: Princeton University Press, 1978.

Tullock, Gordon. *Toward a Mathematics of Politics.* Ann Arbor: University of Michigan Press, 1967.

Turner, Julius, and Edward V. Schneier, Jr. *Party and Constituency.* Baltimore: The Johns Hopkins Press, 1970.

Turrett, J. Stephen. "The Vulnerability of American Governors, 1900-1969." *Midwest Journal of Political Science* (1971) 15:108-32.

United Nations. Secretary General's Report. *Constitutions, Electoral Laws and Other Legal Instruments Relating to the Political Rights of Women.* New York, 1968.

U.S. Department of Labor. Bureau of Labor Statistics. *International Comparisons of Unemployment.* Bel Bulletin, 1979.

Valentine, David C., and John R. Van Wingen. "Partisanship, Independence, and the Partisan Identification." *American Politics Quarterly* (1980) 8:165-86.

van der Eijk, C., and B. Niemöller. *Electoral Change in the Netherlands*. Amstersdam: CT Press, 1983.

Van Wingen, John R., and David C. Valentine. "Biases in the Partisan Identification Index as a Measure of Partisanship." Paper presented at the annual meeting of the Midwest Political Science Association, Chicago, 1979.

Verba, Sidney, and Richard A. Brody. "Participation, Policy Preferences, and the War in Vietnam." *Public Opinion Quarterly* (1970) 34:325-32.

Verba, Sidney, Norman H. Nie, and Jae-on Kim. *The Modes of Democratic Participation*. Beverly Hills: Sage, 1971.

——. *Participation and Political Equality*. Cambridge: Cambridge University Press, 1978.

Wainer, Howard. "Estimating Coefficients in Linear Models: It Don't Make No Nevermind." *Psychological Bulletin* (1976) 83:312-17.

Warr, Peter B., H. M. Schroder, and S. Blackman. "The Structure of Political Judgment." *British Journal of Social and Clinical Psychology* (1969) 8:32-43.

Watanuki, Joji. "Patterns of Politics in Present Day Japan." In *Party Systems and Voter Alignments*, ed. Seymour Martin Lipset and Stein Rokkan. New York: Free Press, 1967.

——. "Japanese Politics: Changes, Continuities and Unknowns." In *Japanese Politics*, Joji Watanuki. Tokyo: Tokyo University Press, 1979.

Wattenberg, Martin P. "The Decline of Political Partisanship in the United States: Negativity or Neutrality?" *American Political Science Review* (1981) 75:941-50.

——. "Party Identification and Party Images." *Comparative Politics* (1982) 15:23-40.

Weatherford, M. Stephen. "Economic Conditions and Electoral Outcomes: Class Differences in the Political Response to Recession." *American Journal of Political Science* (1978) 22:917-38.

Weisberg, Herbert F. "A Multidimensional Conceptualization of Party Identification." *Political Behavior* (1980) 2:33-60. Chap. 25 in this volume.

——. "Party Evaluations: A Theory of Separate Effects." Paper presented at the annual meeting of the Midwest Political Science Association, Milwaukee, 1982.

——. "A New Scale of Partisanship." *Political Behavior* (1983) 5:363-76.

Weisberg, Herbert F., and Bernard Grofman. "Candidate Evaluations and Turnout." *American Politics Quarterly* (1981) 9:197-219.

Weisberg, Herbert F., and Jerrold G. Rusk. "Dimensions of Candidate Evaluation." *American Political Science Review* (1970) 64:1167-85.

Weissberg, Robert, and Richard Joslyn. "Methodological Appropriateness in Political Socialization Research." In *Handbook of Political Socialization*, ed. Stanley A. Renshon. New York: Free Press, 1977.

Whiteley, Paul. *Models of Political Economy*. London: Sage, 1980a.

——. "Politics-Econometric Estimation in Britain: An Alternative Interpretation." In *Models of Political Economy*, ed. Paul Whiteley. London: Sage, 1980b.

Wides, Jeffrey W. "Self-Perceived Economic Change and Political Orientations: A Preliminary Exploration." *American Politics Quarterly* (1976) 4:395-412.

Wiggins, Lee M. *Panel Analysis: Latent Probability Models for Attitude and Behavior Processes*. Amsterdam: Elsevier, 1973.

Wildavsky, Aaron. *The Politics of the Budgetary Process*. Boston: Little, Brown, 1964.

Wiley, David E., and James A. Wiley. "The Estimation of Measurement Error in Panel Data." *American Sociological Review* (1970) 35:112-17.

Williams, Oliver P., and Charles R. Adrian. "The Insulation of Local Politics under the Nonpartisan Ballot." *American Political Science Review* (1959) 53:1052-63.

Williams, P. M. "The M.P.'s Personal Vote." *Parliamentary Affairs* (1966-67): 24-30, WSW.

Wolfinger, Raymond E., and Steven J. Rosenstone. *Who Votes?* New Haven: Yale University Press, 1980.

Wolfinger, Raymond E., Steven J. Rosenstone, and Richard A. McIntosh. "Presidential and Congressional Voters Compared." *American Politics Quarterly* (1981) 9:245-56.

Woodward, C. A. *The Growth of a Party System in Ceylon.* Providence: Brown University Press, 1969.

Wright, Gerald C. "Linear Models for Evaluating Conditional Relationships." *American Journal of Political Science* (1976) 20:349-73.

Yalch, Richard F. "Pre-Election Interview Effects on Voter Turnout." *Public Opinion Quarterly* (1976) 40:331-36.

Yankelovitch, Skelly, and White, Inc. "The General Mills American Family Report: A Study of the American Family and Money." Minneapolis: General Mills, Inc., 1975.

Yantek, Thom. "Public Support for Presidential Performance: A Study of Macroeconomic Effects." *Polity* (1982) 15:268-78.

Yiannakis, Diana E. "The Grateful Electorate: Casework and Congressional Elections." *American Journal of Political Science* (1981) 25:568-80.

Zariski, Raphael. *Italy: The Politics of Uneven Development.* Hinsdale: Dryden Press, 1972.

Zeckman, Martin. "Dynamic Models of the Voter's Decision Calculus." *Public Choice* (1979) 34:297-315.

Zetterberg, Hans. *Arbete, Livsstil och Motivation.* Stockholm: Svenska Arbetsgivareforeningen, 1977.

Zohlnhofer, W. "Parteienidentifizierung in der Bundesrepublik und den Vereinigten Staaten." In *Zur Soziologie der Wahl,* ed. E. K. Scheuch and R. Wildenmann. Koln: Westdeutscher Verlag, 1965.

NAME INDEX

SUBJECT INDEX